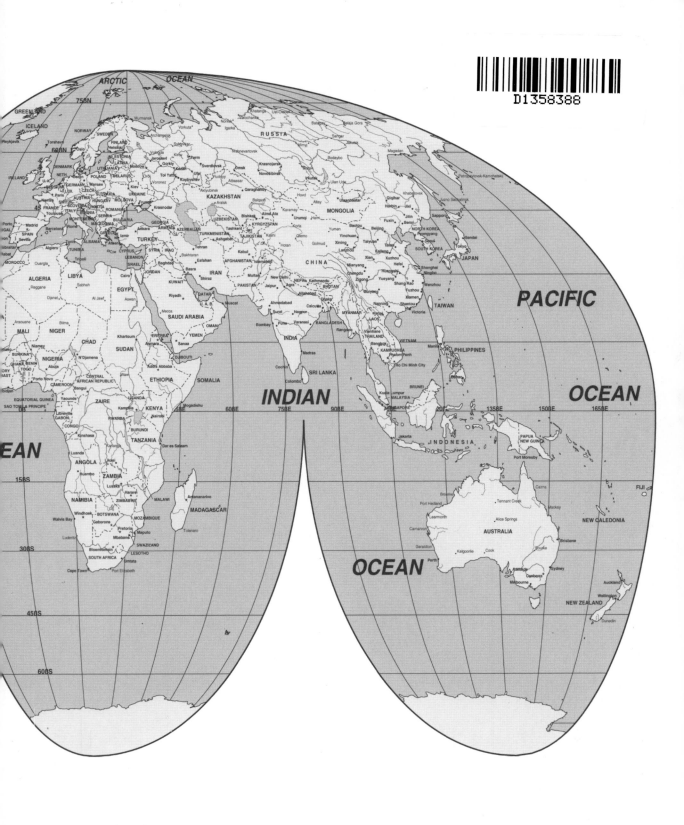

2ND EDITION

A NEW VIEW OF

Comparative Economics

DAVID KENNETT
Vassar College

THOMSON

SOUTH-WESTERN

Australia · Canada · Mexico · Singapore · Spain · United Kingdom · United States

THOMSON

SOUTH-WESTERN

A New View of Comparative Economic Systems, 2e
David Kennett

**Vice President/
Editorial Director:**
Jack Calhoun

Vice President/Editor-in-Chief:
Michael P. Roche

Publisher of Economics:
Michael B. Mercier

Acquisitions Editor:
Michael W. Worls

Sr. Developmental Editor:
Trish Taylor

Sr. Production Editor:
Elizabeth A. Shipp

Sr. Marketing Manager:
Janet Hennies

Media Developmental Editor:
Peggy Buskey

Media Production Editor:
Pam Wallace

Manufacturing Coordinator:
Sandee Milewski

Design Project Manager:
Rik Moore

Internal Designer:
Albonetti Design

Cover Designer:
Rik Moore

Cover Images:
© PhotoDisc, Inc.

Production House:
Trejo Production

Printer:
Phoenix Color/
Book Technology Park

To Lily and Michael

The first edition of this book was prompted by the changes that swept the socialist world at the end of the 1980s. The system of centralized command planning that had served since the 1920s as the polar alternative to market capitalism faltered, attempted to reform itself, and ultimately collapsed. Not only did these events transform the way that we viewed comparative economics; it focused attention on the various types of market capitalism and the necessary institutional arrangements that foster their growth. The study of economies in transition over the last decade provides numerous insights into the fundamental causes of economic change and growth.

Since the publication of the first edition of this book, several developments require some reassessment. The most significant is the East Asian model of development prompted by the Asian financial crisis and the continuing recession in the Japanese economy. The promise of state-led capitalist growth, for the moment at least, must face a reality of financial instability and low investment. Another important change comes from the continuing fusion of the economies of the European Union, highlighted by the launch of the single currency, the euro, in January 2002. Of equal significance is the eastern march of the EU with the number of members growing to 25 within a few years. Broadening and deepening requires thorough-going institutional reform. Finally, the stabilization of the Russian economy in the last couple of years gives hope for the process of transition. The stagnation of the 1980s and the free fall of 1990s created a deep hole to climb out of, but it now seems possible that young Russians can look forward to a brighter future.

Other developments are bound to affect our shared economic futures, the ultimate impact of which we can only speculate on. The events of September 11, 2001, brought home to the United States the realization that to some the prospect of an economic and military *Pax Americana* was not a pleasing vision and that great lengths might be gone to resist it. The long-run economic impact of that day and the responses in Afghanistan and Iraq are by no means clear today. The continued and inevitable march to universal market economies seen by some is obviously alarming to others. The economic crisis caused by the AIDS pandemic will soon be upon us. Though its economic impact in the rich countries of Western Europe and North America so far is slight, already its immense impact on Africa and sharply rising infection rates in China and Russia make clear the inevitability of substantial economic fallout. The pressures of economic growth and population increase are creating an environmental crisis in much of the world, while in Europe and Japan falling birth rates are raising dependency ratios to alarming levels.

It is by no means clear to me that our institutions are well-placed to resolve such issues. The currently fashionable economic and political ideologies tend to stress the primacy of the individual over the collective, and harp on the failure of both government and multi-national organizations. However, the problems we face— the global environment, public health on a world scale, and the sharply worsening distribution of income—would seem to require attention at the supranational level. So, I face the future with only guarded optimism.

Objectives

The objectives of this second edition remain largely those of the first. It tries to systematically introduce the student to the systems of capitalism seen in Europe and Asia, before launching into a fuller discussion of centralized planning, its downfall, and the problems of transition. It also tries to demonstrate the relevance of issues important in contemporary economic thought: in particular, law and legality, corruption, principal-agent problems, market contestability, the problem of regulation, and the consequences of government failure.

Structure

The book is designed to be taught in a 13-week semester at a rate of roughly two chapters per week. Although it can "stand alone," an advanced course can benefit from supplementary readings such as those suggested at the end of each chapter. Moreover, both students and faculty are welcome to visit my Web site at **http://irving.Vassar.edu/ComparativeEconomics/index.html**, which provides access to some material electronically as well as guidance toward useful resources of data and information.

Part One gives a basic introduction to the study of Comparative Economics in Chapter 1, and Chapter 2 provides a perspective on how and why economic institutions change over time. **Part Two** deals with the broad outline of how a market economy functions, the principal sources of market failure and the potential benefits and costs of government intervention. Chapter 3 describes how a competitive market works; it is necessarily somewhat stylized and serves only to highlight the more important issues. Chapter 4 looks at the issues of market failure and also covers a more recent and still growing literature on the issue of government failure. Chapter 5 reviews the important aspects of the institutional structure of a modern market economy. Even though it is possible to read this section with little or no formal economic training, introductory courses in microeconomics and macroeconomics will give students a broader treatment of competitive economies than I am able to provide in this space.

The organization of the remainder of this book is, to a large extent, along geographic lines. This structure is not merely convenience; these economies share ideology and considerable similarities in the relationship of government to business, as well as being spatial neighbors. **Part Three** focuses on capitalism in Europe. It discusses the French, Swedish, British, and German economies, before a comprehensive review of the evolution of the European Union, certainly one of the most important economic and political events of our times. The four countries studied are each chosen for a particular purpose. The focus of Chapter 6, *France: From Indicative Planning to European Integration,* is on one source of possible market failure, an absence of information, and its attempted amelioration through the use of indicative planning. The way in which the complexities of increasing globalization and integration in the EU render national planning increasingly problematic are discussed. An unacceptable distribution of income is not one of the four theoretical failures of markets, but it is generally regarded as one of the problems of a capitalist economy. Chapter 7, *Sweden and Social Democracy,* studies that nation's aggressive attempts to establish an egalitarian distribution of income while leaving the ownership of production in private hands, and its effect on economic growth.

One of the first widespread and rapid programs of privatization was in Margaret Thatcher's Britain of the 1980s. Chapter 8, *Britain: Privatization and Its Aftermath,* introduces the ideological and economic rationale behind the program, the meanings of privatization and the techniques available. Our examination of British experience is important for two reasons. First, it highlights the effects of diminished incentives on performance in a mixed market system. Extensive public ownership of industries made the soft-budget constraint a pervasive phenomenon. Moreover, an aggressive "tax and transfer" system eroded incentives at both ends of the income spectrum. High-earners in the 1970s saw as much as 80 percent of marginal income going into tax coffers while the consequence of joblessness for low-income individuals was minimal thanks to an extensive "safety net" of transfer payments and in-kind provision of services. "Thatcherism" involved, among other things, a vigorous program of privatization and tax reform. Its history provides us with a source of important analysis about the techniques and consequences of the large-scale sale of governmental assets. The depth and breadth of Britain's financial markets allowed for a greater reliance on initial public offerings than might be seen further east, but the process of privatization and its consequences are what make a study of the "Thatcherite" legacy important. Today, the economic performance in Britain is better than at any time during the last 90 years, but the profound reduction in the scope of government sets Britain in contrast to its partners in the European Union.

Further background on the transition process is provided in Chapter 9, *Germany: The Lessons of Reunification.* In 1989, the time of unification, most observers thought that the process would be quite painless as West German technology and managerial expertise could be combined with East Germany's underpaid but well-educated workers. The results were disappointing, and the failure of the two economies to exploit potential synergies helped economists to understand the need for specific institutional change in the other economies of the former Soviet Bloc as they moved toward market-based systems.

The final two chapters of this part are devoted to a discussion of the European Union. This continuing integration is perhaps the most important development in the world economy in the recent years, as against the opinion of skeptics, the various nations of Europe move toward an ever-closer, and ever-larger, economic union. Euroland (the somewhat clumsy name for the area made up of the 12 nations of the EU that share a common currency) is the largest economy in the world (measured in terms of output) using a single currency. Its impressive development in less than half a century enhances its prospects as we go further into the twenty-first century. Its evolution also calls into question the viability of the nation-state as both an economic and political unit. The evolution of European institutions, including the preparation for the new member states, is handled in Chapter 10, *The European Union: History and Institutions*, while the economic consequences of the EU are more thoroughly discussed in Chapter 11, *European Union: The Economic Consequences.*

Part Four is devoted to the Asian economies, starting with the first of the "late industrializers," *Japan: Financial Problems and the Corporate Economy* (Chapter 12). The reasons for Japan's ability to make the leap from the ranks of less developed nations are discussed, but attention is also paid to reasons for its current economic problems. State-led development proved a success but apparently carried with it the problems of a financial sector deprived of its disinterested status for several generations. Now mired in a depression for more than 10 years, though still the second economy of the world, Japan may find the reasons for its current failures lie in its former successes. Chapter 13 deals with *Korea: A Lesson in Late Industrialization,* whose rise was in many ways even more stellar than Japan's, but which faces, in turn, an even greater legacy of financial instability and corruption. Taken together these chapters provide much of the grist for a reassessment of the record of state-led development. The possibilities and costs of Korean reunification are discussed in a comparison with the problems of Germany. In Chapter 14, some of the smaller Asian economies are discussed. The island of Taiwan enjoyed considerable success in emerging as a leader in the technology sector and is now finally following through on a privatization and reform program that will relax the grip of the government on economic affairs. Its future, however, is clouded by the volatile issue of "cross-straits" economic relations with mainland China. The section on Singapore traces that city-state's evolution from its depressed condition in the 1960s—largely abandoned by the British and bereft of its hinterland—to becoming a vibrant economy with per-head income as great as its former colonial masters. It provides an interesting experiment in both forced saving and aggressive minimum wage legislation. It also provides an opportunity to question the issues of individual versus community values, and the intrusive role of a one-party government. The final country studied in Chapter 14 is Indonesia, once prized by Washington institutions as an example of successful market innovation but now a case-study in the corrosive impact of corruption on economic growth. Chapter 15 is an evaluation of the dual phenomena, *The Asian Miracle and the Asian Crisis*, assessing in what sense the performance of these economies was "out of this world," to what extent the performance is explicable in more prosaic terms such as the more extensive use of factors of production, and finally searching for the causes of the Asian Crisis within the context of the Asian Miracle.

Part Five is a largely systematic retrospective look at Soviet Planning with a particular eye to the system of incentives that led to its failure. Chapter 16, *The Com-*

mand Economy, introduces the reader to the principles of central planning and also reviews Russian economic history, a section that may be omitted by students with a good background. Chapter 17, *The Operation of the Soviet Planned Economy*, critically assesses the technique, the performance. and problems of centralized command planning as practiced in the Soviet Union. Special attention is paid to issues of agency problems and incentives that played a large part in the economic failure of the Soviet Union. To some, studying the economic history of the now-defunct Yugoslav state seems strange. However, it is still the only broadly based attempt to introduce a socialized market economy. Chapter 18, *The Participatory Economy: The Case of Yugoslavia*, assesses this attempt both in theoretical terms and in tracing the practices, success, and failures of the now-vanished Yugoslav state. Chapter 19, *The Possibilities of a Third Way*, examines the persistently tantalizing vision of an economy that accommodates socialism and the market. The "third way" received a lot of press recently, but despite its charm most people find its institutions difficult to envision in concrete terms. This chapter discusses some of the potentialities.

Part Six addresses the issues of transition that dominated much of economic thought in the last two decades. General issues of transition are introduced in Chapter 20, *The Process of Transition to a Market Economy*, which examines the starting points of the economies of the Soviet Union and its satellites at the start of the transition process. In Chapter 21, *Reform and Performance of the Russian Economy*, we look at the change in the former Super Power from the entry of Mikhail Gorbachev to the stabilizing policies of Vladimir Putin. It is a fascinating story of initial promise, crisis, apparent failure, and the eventual emergence of modest success. The process of privatization is central to the tale, and the mass theft, alarming shifts in the distribution of income, and financial failure are inevitable components. Compared to Russia, the two smaller East European economies dealt with in Chapter 22, *The Progress of Reform in Poland and the Czech Republic*, enjoyed a quieter ride. However, the difficulty in realizing the initial promise of both countries shows a leftward drift in popular sentiment as the benefits of the market proved difficult to grasp. In all three countries the radical nature of early Western advice that sought to produce a market form more pure than that encountered in the mixed market and welfare state economies of the West must be questioned.

Finally we turn in Chapter 23 to the world's most populous economy and perhaps most successful reformer, The People's Republic of China. In the first edition, China appeared in the section on Asian economies, but some readers of the book thought it would better to examine China in the light of the discussion of socialism. It was placed in the draft phase in Part Five, as a socialist economy befitting the largest economy still under Communist Party rule. However, a visit to China in early 2003 convinced me that if any nation deserved the label of "transition," it was China. I was deeply impressed by the sheer energy, imagination, and entrepreneurship that transformed the prospects of 1.3 billion people in only 25 years. As the chapter reveals, I am concerned about issues of income distribution, environmental pollution, financial instability, and the secretive nature of a political process that sought to conceal two health crises (AIDS and SARS). But certainly a transition is afoot. Taken together the experience of these four economies will enable the reader to ask questions about which policies proved most effective in bringing about a transition from socialism to market economy in terms of elevating the productivity and well-being of its people.

Apologies and Appreciation

I should offer some explanation of what is not here. In this print edition I give no space at all to Africa, Latin America, or South Asia, not because I consider the economies of these areas to be uninteresting but rather because I am short of space in this volume. Certainly, reviewers urge me to include something on these regions; their case is a good one, and chapters from Africa and Latin America will be available on the text's Web site by November 2003. I tried to be as up-to-date as possible, but the target is perpetually moving. Russian banking, Chinese output, Japanese finance, and Indonesian politics are among the things that change with dizzying speed.

Finally, I want to acknowledge some intellectual and personal debts, with the usual thanks, while assuming all responsibility myself. I took my first classes in Comparative Economics from Herb Levine, and had my initial exposure to Soviet Planning from Aron Katsenelinboigen, who I will always remember for his graphic depictions of struggle in that outwardly placid process. Fate and my first job put me next to Igor Birman, who tried to teach me about the Soviet system while I occasionally helped him to interpret Samuelson's *Economics*. My wife Susan first took me to Russia, and my children suffered from my distraction. To them the book is dedicated. Various reviewers looked at the manuscript. Francis Lees, Ed Stuart, and B. Abegaz dealt with my first drafts with necessary good humor and patience; they made many good suggestions, some of which are reflected in the final text, and others probably should have been. The same attention was given by Gérard Roland, Elliott Parker, Veree Etheridge, Katherine Huger, Kenneth Smith, Ranjeeta Ghita, E. Wayne Nafziger, Roger Frantz, and James R. Stanfield. Thanks to people at South-Western/Thomson Learning: Mike Roche, VP/editorial director for Economics; Mike Mercier, publisher of Economics; Mike Worls, acquisitions editor for Economics; and Janet Hennies, senior marketing manager for Economics. Trish Taylor should be acknowledged for her wisdom and practicality, but mostly for her forbearance and patience. Libby Shipp did a superb job in handling the production of the second edition, and Rik Moore managed the design process to create a lovely design that reinforces the book's global subject matter. Finally Cristina Carp served as typist, research assistant, and proofreader for the first edition. Nathaniel Bruhn and Steven Pavlov provided research assistantship and help with the second edition amendments.

Textbook Support Web Site: (http://kennett.swlearning.com)

Visit the support Web site for this textbook (**http://kennett.swlearning.com**) to find all of the instructor and student resources available at no charge to customers. The updated Web sites listed in the end-of-chapter materials in the book are included as study tools at the site.

Economic Applications (http://econapps.swlearning.com)

This site includes South-Western's dynamic Web features: EconNews, EconDebate, and EconData Online. Organized by pertinent economic topics, and searchable by topic or feature, these features are easy to integrate into the classroom. EconNews, EconDebate, and EconData all deepen your understanding of theoretical concepts through hands-on exploration and analysis for the latest economic news stories, policy debates, and data. These features are updated on a regular basis. The Economic Applications Web site is complimentary to every new book buyer via an access card packaged with the book. Used book buyers can purchase access to the site at **http://econapps.swlearning.com**.

InfoTrac

InfoTrac College Edition is packaged with every copy of the textbook. It is a fully searchable online university library containing complete articles and their images. Its database allows access to hundreds of scholarly and popular publications—all reliable sources, including magazines, journals, encyclopedias, and newsletters.

Turner Learning/CNN Economics Video with Integration Guide ISBN: 0-324-14778-3

Professors can bring the real world into the classroom by using the Turner Learning/CNN Economics Video. This VHS video provides current stories of economic interest. The accompanying integration guide provides a summary and discussion questions for each clip. The video is produced in cooperation with Turner Learning, Inc. Contact your South-Western/Thomson Learning sales representative for ordering information.

BRIEF CONTENTS

CONTENTS

Part Four Asian Economies

Chapter 12
Japan: Financial Problems and the Corporate Economy 282

A NEW VIEW OF

Comparative Economics

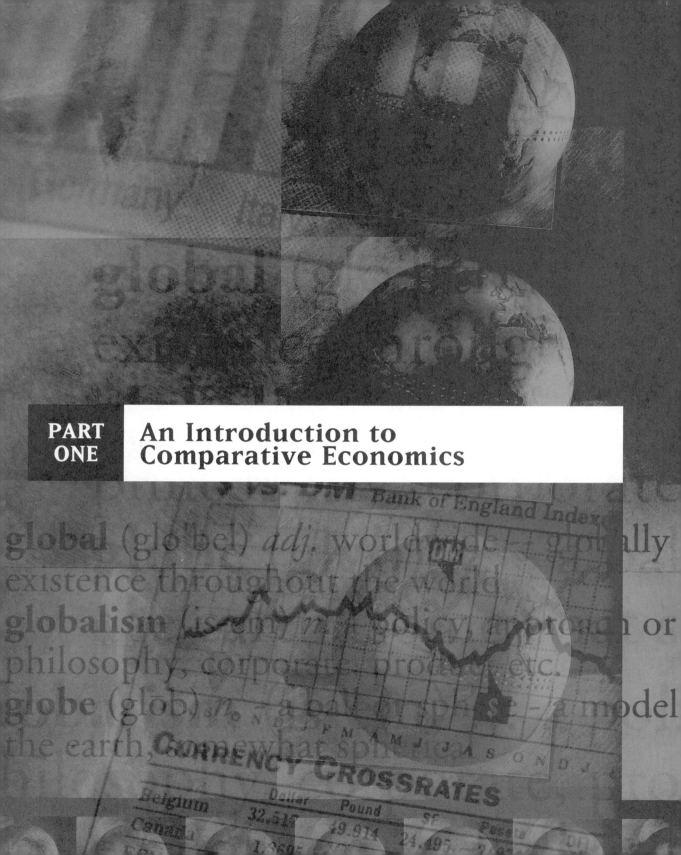

PART ONE

An Introduction to Comparative Economics

1

TYPES OF ECONOMIC SYSTEMS

INTRODUCTION

About 15 years ago the study of comparative economics underwent a series of dramatic changes. The principal reason was the collapse of the Soviet **centrally planned economic system** in the late 1980s. Soviet central planning served for many years as the clear polar alternative to the variety of capitalist systems that exist in the West. At the same time that reform swept the Soviet Union, the various offsprings of the Soviet system also experienced large-scale reform from within or change brought about by external forces. In China, economic restructuring and liberalization, although largely without the political counterpart so visible in the Russian experience, transformed its economy into one of the fastest changing and most rapidly growing on earth. Yugoslavia, the most frequently studied model of collectively owned, **worker-managed socialism**, broke apart and much of its economy still lies in ruins. Even Cuba, the bastion of socialism in the Western Hemisphere, deprived of support and subsidy from the Soviet Union, ruefully contemplates change.

In one sense market capitalism emerged the victor in this war of competing economic ideologies that was waged for much of the twentieth century. Whether this shift will be a permanent state of the world, an irreversible and linear evolution in economic and political arrangements, or merely a short-lived development is too soon to judge. A drift of popular sentiment back toward the former Communists played a feature role in recent elections in Eastern Europe and the former Soviet bloc, suggesting that it may be premature to assume that central planning is buried forever. Moreover, at the same time that economies based on centralized planning were faltering and forced toward reform, new variants of the capitalist model were emerging, especially in East Asia, as alternatives to the western model. Japan long ago joined the ranks of the "developed nations," and its success in terms of growth and world trade sparked great interest in its institutions, its economic culture, and its policies. These features of the Japanese economy are significantly different from the capitalist economies of Europe and North America.

Interest in **Pacific-Rim capitalism** found reinforcement in the emergence of the new **Asian Tigers**. Nations that only a decade before were universally regarded as "developing" made a leap into late industrial development. The economies of South Korea, Taiwan, Singapore, and Thailand seemed to exemplify a vision of rapid and sustained growth, at least until the Asian financial crisis of 1997. Western nations looked to learn lessons from their success. Scrutiny of their systems of economic organization increased accordingly, and investigation of the root causes of their present difficulties will doubtless provide further insights into the operation of alternative systems.

Even the core of Western Europe experienced substantial change. Sweden, for example, was for the entirety of the postwar period the nation whose economic system best exemplified the concept of **social democracy** and the **welfare state**. However, faced with slow growth and a deteriorating trade position, the Swedish system underwent considerable change in recent years, moving away from the extreme of egalitarian social democracy toward a less interventionist form of capitalism. At the same time, the evolution of the original six-member European Common Market into the 15-member **European Union** is a development of the greatest importance. The melding together of the various economies of Western Europe, which were until recently quite disparate institutions and traditions, is in itself a bold step. The replacement in 2002 of the national currencies of 12 of the member countries of the European Union with the "Euro," and the necessary constraints on national fiscal and monetary freedom, required substantial institutional change. Moreover, the proposed expansion of the European Union to include current economies in transition, which 15 years ago were fully centrally planned, is a major challenge. The strong interventionist spirit of the European Union, itself a product of the traditionally active role of government in the continental member states, will reinforce the contrast between the American (or Anglo-Saxon) concept of the relationship of government and business and the continental European concept, sometimes called the **Rhine model**.

These changes, far from making the study of comparative economics redundant, provide us with a new and incisive way of looking at how economies are organized and how they function. The process of transition in Eastern Europe, to take one example, forced us to compare the institutions of capitalism and socialism in a new and fundamental way. The dramatic and almost uniformly experienced collapse of output in the economies of the former Soviet bloc and the unexpectedly slow pace of recovery necessitate a careful evaluation of the differences in institutions, culture, history, and policy that made this transition more painful than predicted. These issues are the substance of comparative economics.

WHAT IS AN ECONOMIC SYSTEM?

In every society, whatever its structure, size, wealth, or level of development, certain economic decisions must be made. The most important of these decisions may be reduced to three types:

> First, it must be decided *what* goods and services are to be produced and in what quantities. This determination is generally referred to as the **production decision**, often represented in stylized form as the familiar "guns versus butter" choice. Such a two-dimensional representation simplifies society's choices and obscures the fact that decisions must be made among a huge array of goods. Nevertheless, the choice of the mix of goods that are to be produced must be faced and made in some way.

Second, a decision must be made about *how* these goods will be produced. The combination of factors of production (generally speaking labor, land, and capital—though all of these are not homogenous) that will be used and the organizations through which production will be achieved are the elements in the **choice of technique** decision.

The third set of choices relates to *who* will receive the benefit of this production, called the **distributional decision**. In all three of these broad types of decision is a temporal dimension. If we can, through saving and investment and through the choice of how rapidly we deplete or exhaust our scarce resources, alter the time pattern of consumption, then we make the choice of whether to consume now or later, and implicitly whether to benefit the current population or their descendants.

The mechanism by which these decisions are made within any economy is referred to as the economic system. The study of how such systems differ between economies and how differences in systems determine economic outcomes, comprises the field of study of comparative economic systems.

The concept of a **system** comes, albeit rather loosely, from the physical sciences. In those disciplines, a system is thought of as a collection of objects essentially closed to outside forces, within which the behavior of the objects is subject to physical laws. An economic system consists of analogies to the same essential ingredients. On the one hand are the objects (in this case economic institutions) and on the other hand are the "laws" (which in economic analysis include not only formal laws but also rules, procedures, and customs) that govern the interaction of these institutions.

Although they are broadly analogous, important differences separate the physical sciences from what we observe in economies. First, the institutions within an economic system do not always merely respond passively to the forces acting on them. Many institutions, which are organizations of human beings, are not merely inert, but seek to further specific objectives. In addition, these objectives may change over time. Second, while the laws that govern physical behavior are immutable, the "laws" that govern interactions within economies are by and large observed regularities and subject to change as culture and customs evolve.

ECONOMIC INSTITUTIONS

The kinds of institutions that characterize a modern industrial economy, whether that of the United States or any other developed market economy, will be familiar to most students from their courses in introductory economics, but some review is useful to set the stage. All economies do not, of course, possess identical sets of institutions. Different histories, cultures, ideologies, and priorities lead to different institutional forms and to differences in the way these institutions interact.

Households

The most fundamental components of almost any economic system are **households**. On the one hand, households are the suppliers of labor, and on the other, they are the ultimate consumers of the bulk of the goods and services produced in the economy. In most systems (the exceptions being primarily socialist economies), households are also responsible for the supply of capital and land to the productive sector. The household in some form is common to practically all economies, developed, less developed, and socialist, though the size, composition, makeup, and decision-making responsibilities differ substantially, even within industrial economies.

Households must be regarded as having objectives or goals, even if only in the loosest sense. Mainstream economists generally consider that the household is a "utility maximizing" institution, and they make assumptions about what factors enter into its utility function. We should note that utility maximization cannot be equated with a desire to maximize income or even material well-being, although today we seem to share a general belief that more material output is better than less. Other objectives, such as a desire for prestige, gaining satisfaction from leisure, patriotism, or a preference for an equitable distribution of income, may form important arguments in a household's utility function. Moreover, the nature of the utility function will vary from society to society, bearing the stamp of history, culture, and ideology.

Government

Common to all economies, except the most primitive ones (or theoretical conceptions of anarchy), is some form of government. In a modern industrialized economy, the government is complex and its authority far-reaching. All contemporary governments are, to some extent, involved in the establishment and protection of economic and individual rights, the regulation of business and industry, the provision of goods and services, and the redistribution of income. Because the government embodies a powerful set of agencies, and because it can make and change the rules by which the economy operates through legislation, it ranks, even in quite conservative societies, as one of the important institutions for answering the fundamental economic questions—*what, how,* and *for whom?*—that were introduced earlier. Clearly, the means by which a government derives its power, and the degree of control that it exercises over the behavior of its citizens and the other institutions that constitute the economy, varies greatly from country to country.

The goals, or objectives, that governments choose to pursue may also vary a great deal. When we speak of goals we are generally talking of something quite broad. For example, goals may be such vague objectives as "an accelerated rate of growth of output," "a more even distribution of income," "an increase in expected longevity," and so forth. A shift in these goals or in the strategy of their pursuit can take two forms: either a thorough-going reform of the system itself (as we are witnessing in Eastern Europe and the former Soviet Union), or the application of different **policies** operating within an existing system. The boundary between systemic reform and a radical policy initiative is necessarily a gray area. For example, many countries embark on extensive privatization by selling large parts of publicly owned (or "nationalized") industry to the private sector. Clearly when such an event takes place on the scale of the mass privatization that occurred in Russia, it constitutes systemic change. The sale of some public corporations within the context of the French economy is a different matter, however. Even the most radical "western" privatization as that of Margaret Thatcher in Britain in the period of (roughly) 1981 to 1989 is generally regarded more as a shift of policy within the mixed capitalist system than as a systemic change.

Policies may be defined as the actions that a government takes within an existing system in pursuit of its objectives. Examples of policies are the establishment of a fiscal deficit in an attempt to stimulate growth in national income, the use of taxes and expenditures to redistribute economic well-being from one group to another, the commitment of government to provide investment funds for industry, the creation of a national health service, and so forth. Such policies are facilitated by the use of **instruments** like the income tax, the money supply, government expenditure, or the structure of tariffs. Changes in these instruments are usually called **measures**. Thus a government of a mixed capitalist economy (system) might decide to reduce (measure) the income tax (instrument) to create a fiscal deficit (policy) to reduce unemployment (objective).

In the real world, things are necessarily more complex than depicted here, and more incisive analysis can help us understand how a system operates. For example, it is generally an oversimplification to view the government as a monolithic entity with a single objective. All governments consist of different ministries and agencies, each with different powers and functions. In all likelihood the agencies of government also have different objectives, because agencies cater to different constituencies. They are likely to be "captured" by those interests and serve them rather than some larger conception of the public good. For example, one arm of government might be responsible for furthering industrial growth, while another might have responsibility for the environment. Occasions likely arise in which the interests of these agencies are in conflict, and the outcome itself is a matter of political interaction.

Enterprises

The third broad group of institutions is composed of economic enterprises that produce goods and services. These enterprises may be owned privately, cooperatively (by a small group, usually consisting of the workforce), or socially (by society as a whole, through the agency of some level of government). Even within a market economy, enterprises may take on a wide range of institutional forms that affect their nature and performance. For example, they may be "incorporated," a form that carries with it the important characteristic of limited liability and particular tax treatment. In turn, privately owned corporations fall into two groups. They may be "public" in that their shares are traded freely, generally on a stock exchange, or "privately held," whereby ownership is limited to a small group of individuals and shares are not available for purchase or sale beyond that group. Other forms of enterprise in a market economy are partnerships or wholly owned proprietorships.

Economic enterprises, like households, pursue objectives. Economists commonly assume that in a free enterprise economy, privately owned firms are profit maximizers, at least in the long run. However, a growing body of research on the actual behavior of firms and managers within firms suggests that this view may be too simplistic. Conflicting goals, such as maximizing market share, rapid sales growth, employment maximization, or management's well-being, may all play a role, at least in the short term.

Moreover, even if profit maximization is the clear and overt objective, all firms that are more complex than a single proprietorship with no employees are beset with **principal/agent problems**. These problems arise because of the difficulty of getting workers, or management for that matter (the *agents*), to act in the way that best serves the interests of the owners (the *principals*). Thus, although the ultimate owner of the firm (the *shareholders*) might favor profit maximization, the management and the workers pursue their own goals (leisure, prestige, income, etc.), which might well be in conflict with shareholder objectives.

Labor Organizations

A fourth important set of institutions is composed of labor organizations, which may exert substantial influence on employment, workplace technique, and compensation. By uniting and solidifying the interests of individual workers and asserting a degree of monopoly power in labor negotiations, labor unions can affect decision making in the economy. Moreover, across economies unionization takes on different forms, and these distinctions result in various methods of political expression. One clear distinction is between **company unions** (common in Japan) and the **craft** or **occupational unions** (the norm in several European economies). In most of continental Europe it is generally accepted that organized labor plays an important role at the governmental level. In some countries (e.g., Sweden), the labor unions are actors in national negotiations to determine wages. In others (i.e., France) the unions have an official status in setting the objectives and priorities of governmental policy and were prominent actors in formulating the "National Plans" that were the centerpieces of French policy making for 50 years.

In the socialist, centrally planned economies, labor unions were largely powerless. The ideology of socialism asserted that, because the means of production were owned by the people, workers did not need to organize to protect their interests. Free labor organizations were therefore frequently repressed and only unions licensed by the state or party were allowed. Almost paradoxically the collapse of the "Workers' State" in Poland was brought about largely by the growth of Solidarity, the "alternative" labor union that opposed the state.

Nongovernmental Organizations

Recognition by economists and political scientists of the importance of a fifth set of institutions that play important roles in modern economies continues to grow. These **nongovernmental organizations (NGOs)** attracted considerable attention in recent years. The NGO sector is composed of organizations that are not only nongovernmental, but also operate on a not-for-profit basis, distinguishing them from firms in a capitalist economy. Broadly speaking, NGOs fall into three groups: organizations that exist to provide services to particular groups (e.g., the United Way in the United States or various developmental and health agencies that operate in the developing world), organizations that serve as centers of common interest (hobby groups and church organizations), and lobbying groups organized to influence government behavior (e.g., the AARP).[1]

Service-providing NGOs may fulfill some of the functions that are also performed by government, particularly in the fields of education, poverty relief, and health care. Given the determination to reduce the size of the governmental sector, which seems to be common to all developed market economies, the role of NGOs may be expected to expand in the years ahead. Most people would regard this increase in voluntarism to be beneficial to welfare; an NGO can replace some of the functions of government without needing to raise taxes or encountering the excess burdens that accompany taxing and spending. However, NGOs are organized to serve mainly the interests of particular groups and cannot be relied on to preserve the interests and well-being of those not in the group, and they frequently do burden the public purse because of the tax-exempt privileges extended to donors.

Markets

A final set of institutions that are significant in almost any economy is made up of the markets within which these institutions interact. In broad terms, these include goods markets, labor markets, financial markets, stock markets, and commodity markets. However, any "market" economy is characterized by many thousands of markets. Markets are organized in different ways in different economies, and the study of how they differ is one important feature of comparative economics. The depth, complexity, and richness of markets are important factors in determining economic outcomes. So too is the reliability, transparency, and probity of the markets. Market structure can only work well when participants are well-informed. Corruption, confusion, and fraud obviously have a deleterious impact on market performance, and can drive away investment and therefore growth and performance.

RULES

The preceding list is far from an exhaustive inventory of the institutions found in a modern economy. It does, however, provide us with an idea of their range and variety. These institutions interact with each other in addressing the production, distribution, and choice of technique decisions. Let us now turn to the rules that govern these interactions. It is important to note from the outset that the rules that govern any society are complex and hybrid. They consist of both *formal rules*, which are embodied and codified as **laws** and **regulations**, and *informal customs*, or **practices** and **beliefs** that influence behavior. At first glance it might seem that laws should be the more important, but the force of custom and tradition is decisive in

---

[1]AARP, formerly known as the American Association of Retired Persons, is a powerful organization that lobbies on behalf of senior citizens in the United States.

many issues. Moreover, custom, culture, and tradition determine not only the nature of the rules by which institutions interact; they also shape the nature of the institutions themselves.

The Legal Framework

All institutions within a society must operate under the rule of law. Laws are, by definition, those rules made by some level of government[2] and rely on the power of the government, which we may think of as having a monopoly on force in most societies, to ensure that they are obeyed. In a modern economy, the scope of the legal system is broad. As well as constituting a criminal code, laws also determine a variety of factors that are vital for the functioning of the economy. They include such things as the establishment and enforcement of contracts, the nature of property and property rights, the obligations of firms and individuals under the tax system, environmental regulations, health codes, the minimum age of workers, (in some societies) the minimum wage that must be paid to workers, what firms must disclose to their stockholders and potential owners, and how firms and individuals may enter bankruptcy.

Such laws help to determine both the character and the behavior of economic institutions. For example, the structure of the U.S. financial system was shaped by a series of federal and state regulations that limit the activities of commercial banks, investment banks, brokerage houses, and other institutions. These regulations mean that the organization and functioning of U.S. banking will be different from that in, for example, Germany, where different laws apply. Germany has never had an equivalent to the **Glass-Steagall Act**, which mandated the formal separation of the activities of investment and commercial banks.[3] Consequently, in Germany **universal banks** (sometimes referred to as U-banks), which perform a wide range of functions, are the norm, and the relationship between the financial and productive sectors is quite different from the one in the United States. Laws concerning the incorporation of firms and the liabilities of partnerships dictate the type of enterprises that may exist and the extent of their activity.

Laws mean little unless they are enforced. We can be quite deceived about the nature of a society or an economy if we only look at the laws as they are on the books and not at how they are actually administered. Later in this book we will discuss the nature of **legality** within society. Legality requires not only a comprehensive set of mutually consistent laws, but also the expectation that those laws will be generally and impartially enforced.

---

[2]Some clarification of the idea of making laws might be in order here. Laws are often made by active legislative initiative, but in many societies they evolve through precedent and may be codified after the fact or remain in force without any real form of codification. The most familiar example to most readers is the evolution of English Common Law.

[3]The Gramm-Leach-Bliley Financial Services Modernization Act of 1999 relaxes some of the Glass-Steagall separation of function and allows banks and securities firms to affiliate through a holding company structure.

Rules Within Organizations

The behavior of economic institutions is not determined by the laws and their enforcement alone. Indeed, institutions must operate within an externally imposed legal framework, but they also follow self-imposed rules that limit their behavior. These internal rules are present in government departments, stock markets, corporations, charities, or labor unions. Organizational rules are generally written and codified and must be subsidiary to the laws of society, at least as far as those laws are enforced. They pervasively influence the organization of economic activity.

Procedures

On a less formal level than that of rules, the day-to-day running of all organizations tends to be governed through procedures, which present less formal force than laws or the regulations by which organizations define themselves. It is tempting to presume that because they are less formal than laws or regulations, such procedures might be more easily changed; in reality they are perhaps more enduring. Some examples may be employment practices, systems of promotion, or the way that price or quality information is sought in purchasing.

Custom, Culture, and Tradition

The force of custom also determines the nature of economic outcomes and the behavior of economic actors within an economic system. Different societies do things in different ways and demonstrate particular beliefs and prejudices, which may be just as powerful in their effect as formal regulations or even procedures. These customs can influence a wide range of economic variables. For example, in some societies custom discourages girls from receiving anything above the most rudimentary education, a fact that greatly changes the supply of labor, productivity, and, in turn, per-head incomes. Some societies are, by custom, high consuming, while others show deep-seated tendencies toward saving and accumulation.

Such factors are frequently neglected but they can decisively influence the direction and performance of an economy. In a recent book, Francis Fukuyama made the case for the vital role of social institutions and cultural values in determining economic outcomes.[4] He argued that a distinction can be drawn between "high-trust" societies (among them Japan, Germany, and the United States), which developed the flexible civic institutions that a modern economy demands in greater abundance, and "low-trust" (or "familistic") nations such as China, France, and Italy. The presence of these institutions reduces the costs of economic interchange, which greatly facilitates commerce and leads to more rapid growth. It is, on the face of it, an interesting argument, although Fukuyama's premises may be questioned. For example, why is the United States (the most lawyer-ridden and

[4]Francis Fukuyama, *Trust: The Social Virtues and the Creation of Prosperity* (New York: Free Press, 1995). See also the review in *The Economist*, September 2, 1995.

litigious society in the world) classed with Japan (which is the developed economy with the fewest lawyers) as "trusting societies"?

ECONOMIC RESOURCES

Economies differ not only in their institutions and the rules that govern the inter-action of those institutions but also in the endowments of wealth that they possess. Each economy possesses at any point in time a stock of capital and resources, which is in part the result of the geography, geology, and climate of the country and in part the consequence of the cumulative impact of actions taken by individuals, productive enterprises, and governments in the past. These actions consist of the myriad savings, consumption, and investment decisions that determine the stock of human and physical, human-made capital inherited from previous generations. Although this wealth exists in many forms, it is convenient and useful for our cur-rent purpose to group it into three broad types.

Natural Assets

The most fundamental part of the wealth base consists of the **natural resources** of the economy, consisting primarily of minerals (coal, oil, natural gas, ores) located within the ground of a nation's economy, and the naturally occurring vegetation, like forests, found on it. Also included in an inventory of natural resources should be water resources and certain topographical features that facilitate commu-nication (harbors, navigable rivers, and the like). In addition, we can consider the weather and such naturally occurring features that might, for example, attract tourism.

Closely linked to the wealth that comes from natural resources is the stock of productive agricultural land. The value of this asset to the economy is determined by both the generosity of nature and the incidence of human-made improvements on it that create or enhance productivity. These improvements include infrastruc-tural developments (like irrigation in the American West or the terracing of rice paddies in Asia). Agricultural land is in fact a combination of nature and human-made resources, although some of the improvements (clearing forests, canalizing rivers) are so ancient as to defy any normal scheme of asset valuation that would dissociate the improvement from the value of the natural resource itself.

Produced Assets

Economists, in their analyses, tend to focus a lot of attention on an economy's stock of produced assets, the extant accretion of human-made capital created in previous periods.[5] The most easily envisaged examples of this stock are the machines, the factories, and the inventories of finished goods and goods-in-process

---

[5]Marx in fact referred to capital as "dead labor."

in **industrial capital**. That form of capital, however, is only part of the picture. We must also take notice of the social capital embodied in roads, bridges, dams, schools, universities and the like.

Human Capital

On a global level, the most important wealth resource is embodied as **human capital** in the skills and education of individuals. A recent World Bank Study found that almost two-thirds of the value of accumulated wealth in the world lies in human capital. The importance of human capital is most obvious in the highly developed industrial nations. Japan's land and natural resources are of trivial consequence compared to the value of its human capital, which is overwhelmingly the reason it ranks third in the world in resource wealth on a per-head basis. The same is true of Germany. Similarly, Singapore, an island state with few natural resources (though its location gives the land value), is wealthy because of a highly educated and enterprising population.

HOW WEALTH VARIES AMONG NATIONS

Several recent attempts to quantify the international distribution of these resources looked at the stock of wealth available to an economy, and compared the relative endowments of different economies, as well as the changes over time. The World Bank's Environmentally Sustainable Development Project embarked on the bold step of quantifying the wealth in each of 192 nations.[6]

The explicit recognition that a country's wealth is the combination of various forms of capital—produced, natural, and human resources—led to new thinking about what constitutes wealth and how it might be measured. The figures that the World Bank came up with were necessarily somewhat rough, and debate is inevitable as to the accuracy and appropriateness of some of the estimation procedures. However, the results are fascinating and instructive.

In the World Bank analysis, produced assets (fixed capital and infrastructure) were estimated using a perpetual inventory method, using flow data on depreciation and investment to estimate the current stock of capital. The value of natural resources was estimated by classifying the land into cropland, grassland, forests, and other uses, valuing each as a multiple of per-head income in the country where it is located. (This method means that an acre of cropland in Latin America represents less "wealth" than an acre in, say, the Netherlands purely because of location.) Adjustments were made for subsoil assets and standing timber.

In this analysis, human resources were valued as the residual, after allowing for the effect of natural resources and produced capital. Such a measure therefore

---

[6]See *Expanding the Measure of Wealth: Indicators of Environmentally Sustainable Development* (Washington, DC: World Bank, 1997); and *Monitoring Environmental Progress: A Report on Work in Progress* (Washington, DC: World Bank, 1995).

includes not only the human capital embodied in individuals by virtue of the education, experience, and training, but also the economic value of the social institutions. Also included in this residual effect would be any cultural factors that might make that society more productive than another. Significantly for the issue at hand, the measure of human capital is conflated with the efficiency of the economic system. Notwithstanding these problems, the results of the study give considerable food for thought. Figures for some selected nations are provided in Table 1.1.

1. As a global average, almost two-thirds, 64 percent, of total wealth is embodied in human resources composed of individual human capital and social institutions.

2. The wealthiest nation on a per-head basis is Australia, which possesses large natural wealth distributed among a small, but highly educated population.

3. Most of the top 25 nations in terms of aggregate wealth have natural assets comprising less than 10 percent (and most of these less than 5 percent) of total wealth, further suggesting that accrued human capital rather than initial resource endowment is the key to prosperity.

4. The variation in per-head wealth between nations is even more pronounced than the variation in per-head income. Australia, at the top, is rated as having about 500 times the wealth of Ethiopia, the bottom country.

■ TABLE 1.1

Estimates of the Wealth of Nations, Dollars per Head: Selected Nations, 1995

Rank for Total Wealth	Country	Total Wealth	Human Capital	Produced Capital	Natural Resources
1	Australia	835,000	175,350	58,450	592,850
11	United States	421,000	248,390	67,360	105,250
21	United Kingdom	324,000	268,920	45,360	9,720
22	Singapore	306,000	260,100	45,900	0
31	Saudi Arabia	184,000	51,520	33,120	101,200
39	Greece	142,000	106,500	19,880	15,620
54	Russia	98,000	14,700	14,700	68,600
61	Mexico	74,000	54,020	8,140	11,840
71	Estonia	55,000	39,050	7,700	7,700
87	Iran	38,000	12,920	14,060	11,020
96	Turkey	34,000	24,480	5,100	4,420
117	Romania	17,000	11,900	2,890	2,210
161	China	6,600	5,082	990	528
175	Kenya	3,800	2,128	1,216	456
181	Rwanda	2,900	2,030	638	261
192	Ethiopia	1,400	560	294	546
	World Average	86,000	55,040	13,760	17,200

SOURCE: World Bank, *Sustainability and the Wealth of Nations*, 1995.

THE DETERMINATION OF ECONOMIC OUTCOMES

By economic outcomes we mean measurable consequences such as per-head income, the distribution of income, employment, inflation, and even demographic factors such as life expectancy. These outcomes are the result of the interaction between the available resources, the institutions, and the rules that govern the system. These relationships might be easy to envisage in terms of a functional statement, rather like a production function.

$$O_i = F_i(NR_i, PA_i, HC_i)$$

where O represents the economic outcomes, NR the natural resources, PA the stock of produced assets, and HC human capital and the subscripts represent each country. Although in structure it is like a production function,[7] what differs is that the economic systems of all of the observations under review (the economies) are different. Thus, the F_i are different for all economies and depend upon the institutions and even the goals of the systems. In part, comparative economics is concerned with how the goals of different economies vary, and how the systems of different economies contrast, such that wealth endowments result in different outcomes. Our problem, in fact, is why some societies use their factors of production more efficiently. The economist Mancur Olsen once wrote that we would like to know why some economies are wasteful in converting inputs to outputs, in his words inefficiently "leave five dollar bills on the sidewalk," while other systems are much more adept at picking up such windfalls and using their resources productively.

SOME FUNDAMENTALS OF ECONOMIC SYSTEMS

Even a cursory glance at the world shows us that economic systems are complex and hybrid, embodying a range of features. However, we may use some fundamental approaches to distinguish between different systems. Economic systems differ from each other along three important dimensions: the extent of individual rights (particularly as they pertain to property), the means of coordination of economic activity, and the incentive systems that influence the response of individuals.

The Nature and Extent of Individual Rights

All systems of government put some constraints on the rights of individuals in economic matters, although the range and force of restraint differ dramatically. The extent of the rights that the government allows, either actively or passively, to remain with the individual, coupled with the degree to which the state effectively protects and guarantees those rights against the incursions of other individuals

---

[7]Indeed, some economists in the World Bank look forward to the arrival of a general production function that will be able to tell us the relationship between inputs and outputs.

(and possible incursions by the state itself), is of great importance in determining the shape and functioning of the economic system.

Property Ownership and Property Rights The character of a society is determined largely by the extent of rights and freedoms that are allowed to individuals within it. From the point of view of studying the functioning of an economic system, one of the most significant of these rights is the right to own property. In practical terms almost every society, even the most collectively or socialistically organized, allows individuals the right to own some personal property, possibly limited only to food for consumption, clothing, and furniture. From an economic perspective, the most important issue is whether individuals (or groups of individuals) are allowed to own "the means of production"—the enterprises, organizations, tools, and inventories used to make goods and services.

The existence of private ownership of the means of production has been the basis for distinguishing between the two great "isms" that dominated the study of comparative economic systems in the last century. **Socialism** is a system in which the means of production are owned collectively, generally by the state. **Capitalism**, often taken as synonymous with "free enterprise," is predicated on the means of production being owned by individuals or freely associated groups of individuals.

However, on closer inspection *ownership* is not the simple matter that it might initially seem to be. What is commonly called ownership actually involves a series of potentially separable qualities or **property rights**. Of these, three are particularly important. The first is the right *to use* a good or resource in the way that the "owner" of the property sees fit. In some discussions, especially those pertaining to the debate on the efficacy of privatization, also known as the **control right**.[8] The second is the right *to receive income* or other benefits generated by the use of the property, also known as the **cash-flow right**. The last is the right *to exchange or sell* property at a price deemed appropriate by the seller—the **disposal right**. If these rights are together vested in individuals, they constitute the "right to engage in economic activity," because they confer the right to establish or acquire businesses, the right to manufacture goods, and the right to buy and sell goods.[9]

However, it is important to note that even in societies regarded as "free enterprise" or "capitalist" these rights are seldom unrestricted. For example, zoning restrictions and environmental regulations frequently constrain the nominal owner's use of property. Such regulations take away some of the property rights of the owner and confer them upon others. An individual's right to use her property as she sees fit might be balanced by the property rights of others, who have rights to clean air, light, or unpolluted water. Licensing prevents the entry into some

---

[8]See, for example, Maxim Boycko, Andrei Shleifer, and Robert Vishny, *Privatizing Russia* (Cambridge, MA: MIT Press, 1995).

[9]This right to engage in economic activity was one of the fundamental rights demanded by Gregory Yavlinsky and Stanislav Shatalin, in the somewhat overly optimistic "five hundred day plan," and defined in many ways the emergence of Russia from a socialist to a market economy.

industries, while other industries may be restricted as a governmental or private monopoly. Most economies include systems of taxation that tax away some part of both corporate and personal income, an infringement of an individual's un-restricted right to income from property.

With respect to disposal rights, many societies with market-oriented economies choose at times to prevent owners from selling property, goods, or services to whomever and at prices that they see fit. Such restrictions might be short term and quite limited. In the United States, for example, laws can be used to control prices in order to prevent "profiteering" after a natural disaster. However, some controls may be of longer duration. Recent history produced examples of both general restrictions on price changes with a view to fighting inflation, which occurred under the Nixon administration, and on specific goods (e.g., gasoline, during the oil crises of the 1970s). Rent control is a familiar feature in many western economies, and all market economies regulate the pricing behavior of privately owned utility companies to counterbalance monopoly power.

Across societies there is a spectrum of such restrictions on individual economic freedom. At one polar extreme are countries (fewer since the demise of the Soviet Union) that adopted socialist economic systems and in which the economic rights of individuals are reduced to a minimum. For example, in the Soviet Union before its dissolution and the subsequent economic liberalization in the successor states, virtually all of the means of production were owned by the state. As late as the 1980s it was estimated that 97 percent of total economic output in the Soviet Union, as well as East Germany and Czechoslovakia, was in the control of the state. This was not the result of the state outcompeting private enterprise, but rather the con-sequence of the denial of the right of individuals to own productive resources and to establish enterprises. At the other extreme are the highly laissez-faire states, for example Hong Kong (before 1997 while it was under British rule), in which gov-ernmental restrictions on enterprise and the labor force were minimal.

Despite the fact that under such socialist systems practically all property rights were formally vested in the state, a *de facto* complex of property rights of individ-uals was established by practice and custom. Even in the most completely centrally planned systems, the managers of enterprises and the political leadership, in prac-tical terms, exercised a kind of ownership in the fruits of the enterprise. They held both some control rights (although most were held by the planners) and some cash-flow rights, because they could skim some income from the enterprises. It was well established that the *apparatchiks* in the Soviet Union had access to goods and privi-leges by virtue of their positions in the enterprises[10] and this access resulted in important consequences when the process of denationalizing, or privatizing, these economies occurred.

---

[10]The property rights of the bureaucrats and enterprise managers constituted a recurrent barrier to the reform of centrally planned systems. As we will see when we look at the issues of transition, the suc-cess of any liberalization agenda is contingent on the ability to ensure the participation of key players in the bureaucracy and enterprise management. They must be induced to give up the property rights and income that they held in the *status quo ante*. See, for example, Jan Winiecki, "Why Economic Reforms Fail in Soviet Type Systems: A Property Rights Approach," *Economic Inquiry* 28, no. 2 (April 1990), p. 195.

Freedom of Mobility and Employment Although property rights constitute an important dimension of the economic system, they are not the only set of rights that play a decisive role. Another set of rights relates to an individual's freedom to work and his or her choice of occupation and location. The ability to enter a profession or establish a business is an important right, the denial of which can crucially shape the nature of enterprise and economic activity.

Extent of Government Ownership A crude measure of economic freedom can be provided by the extent of government ownership of industry, services, and infrastructure. This measure varies greatly from country to country. Even within "free market" economies, governments control varying amounts of industry. Figure 1.1 shows the value added produced in the government sector in selected economies for the time period 1985–1990. It shows a considerable range. In the United States only 1.1 percent of total value occurred in the public productive sector, which is limited to a modest share of transportation (Amtrak), the U.S. Postal Service, and some utilities. Europe follows a stronger tradition of government production. In Britain, at that time undergoing the "Thatcher reforms," the share was 6.7 percent. Across the channel the French public sector, expanded by the Socialist Mitterand government, nationalized several major corporations in the early 1980s and stood at 11.2 percent. In general, less-developed countries are likely to have a larger government sector because the government promotes industry in an attempt to accelerate development. In oil-rich Venezuela, government-owned enterprise produces almost a quarter of total output, and in Zambia the comparable figure is almost one-third. It is important to recall that in centrally planned

■ **FIGURE 1.1**

Share of Total Value Added Produced in State-Owned Enterprise, 1985—1990, in Selected Countries

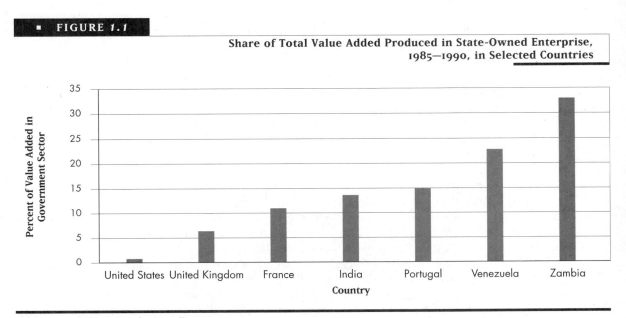

SOURCE: World Bank Development Report.

economies this figure would been close to 100 percent. These differences between countries apply not only to government production. The range of services that public authorities provide varies substantially. In some countries the government is a major supplier of health care, transportation, and financial services that are in other countries the province of private operation.

A better index of the role of government would be a measure the degree of government interference in the economy, because government regulation of private industry can be a substitute for public ownership. Privatization, the transference of assets from the government to the private sector, is often accompanied by an increase in regulation. Consequently countries with a high degree of private economic activity may be among the most heavily regulated. However, though such an index would be informative, the extent of government interference is hard to quantify.

Command Versus the Market

Another dimension by which we may compare the structure of economic systems is the degree of reliance on planning, on the one hand, or the market, on the other, as means of coordinating economic activity. Under planning, the government determines, or at least seeks to influence, the answers to those important economic questions of *what, how,* and *for whom* discussed earlier. Under a market system, in contrast, the action of individuals, acting through the institutions that they comprise, each pursuing their own objectives, leads to the set of outcomes. This process was called **the invisible hand** by **Adam Smith**, the great Scottish philosopher and economist, in his seminal book *An Inquiry into the Nature and Causes of the Wealth of Nations.*

Command Planning Planning can, of course, vary considerably in its scope and comprehensiveness. At one extreme we see the kind of economic organization established in the former Soviet Union, in which the government controlled almost all economic activity, and nearly all production occurred within enterprises owned and controlled by the government. In that system, detailed plans guided the flow of all resources, materials, and finished goods. Moreover, when those plans were finalized they were endowed with the force of law, and the economic actors on the production side were required to follow the procedures laid down, and achieve the targets prescribed, under threat of legal sanction. For obvious reasons this compulsive, top-down planning is called command planning. However, gentler variants occur as well.

Indicative Planning A different form of planning was pursued in several Western European nations (particularly France) and in Japan. In those countries the government relied primarily on the voluntary and uncoerced response of the private sector to a set of guidelines produced as a result of discussions between government, industry, and in some cases labor or other groups. The objective of the planning exercise was largely to establish a common information base and a consensus on the broad direction of the economy. The expertise of the government in marshaling statistics and producing forecasts was important, and it was the government that provided the forum and formalized the outcome. On the whole, this form of planning sought to coordinate, unify, and identify "bottlenecks" and to initiate remedial action. The powers of the government may be used to favor particular outcomes, but the scope of direct intervention was circumscribed (frequently limited to some intervention in credit markets) and scant scope for coercion was allowed. Because the main purpose of this planning was to lay out the likely course of the economy, this form is called **indicative planning**, and it was designed to function in parallel with, rather than to the exclusion of, the market. Indicative planning was quite widely used in the 1950s and 1960s but subsequently declined. In part this decline is the result of increased globalization, which makes predicting and coordinating performance within one country a more difficult task. This trend is unlikely to be reversed. Another reason for decline, however, is the widely held belief in the superiority of the market, which may well be called into question in the future.

Choice and the Market System One of the most important aspects of the market system lies in the limitation of coercion. The overall outcome of the economy must be determined primarily by the voluntary actions of individuals, and therefore the absence of bureaucratic constraints and the consequent maximization of the role of choice are essential features. As we will see in later chapters, the market cannot always be relied on to lead the economy to an optimal use of resources, nor are the distributional aspects of a market system always universally approved of. In particular, the market may lead to a pattern of income and access to basic consumer goods that might be considered unacceptable by some societies. The final distribution of income in a market and welfare are contingent on the initial distribution of wealth, position, and ability. In a variety of well-known instances of market failure, government intervention may plausibly lead to higher levels of social satisfaction. These issues will be more fully discussed in Chapter 4.

Centralization Versus Decentralization

Another way to classify economies is by looking at the centralization of the decision-making system. Again, we may take the example of Soviet-style planning, in which a single plan governing the use of all resources and the production of output was prepared, codified, and formalized as law. At the opposite pole we can conceive of nearly pure market systems in which all of the important decisions are taken by individuals or private institutions and the function of government is largely to provide a framework and stability within which markets can operate. Between these two poles is a continuum of decentralization of power; where a particular economy lies on this continuum is a useful way to gain insight into how its system operates.

Later when the difficulties of centralized planning are more fully examined, we will see that one of the major problems in the implementation and maintenance of a centralized planning system is the quantity of information that must be gathered and accurately reported to the center. Only when the planners are well informed does the plan stand a chance of using resources efficiently. This is more than a mechanical problem and involves important issues of incentives. Well-documented examples describe situations in which incentives may motivate the actors at the periphery (plant managers, etc.) to gain advantage by systematically misreporting information to the center. A simple example is to overestimate the need for capital or raw materials to ensure plenty on hand to meet the output quotas that the planners assign.

Incentives: Moral, Material, and Coercive

These issues lead us into a more general discussion of incentives. In all economic systems above the level of a totally individualistic economy we encounter what economists call principal/agent problems. As the name implies, this set of problems is concerned with the difficulties of creating a structure of incentives that encourages someone appointed as the "agent" to act for a "principal" to indeed pursue the principal's interest rather than his or her own. At the simplest level, an agency problem may be represented as: "If I hire a worker, how can I ensure that he works as hard and as well for me as I would for myself?"

This problem is pertinent from a "**Robinson Crusoe" economy** to the largest corporation, and to the most complex centrally planned economy. Why should Friday work hard when Crusoe is out of sight? Why should the management of IBM act in the interest of shareholders, who are ultimately the owners, rather than in their own interests? Why should workers or management in a factory pursue the targets that the architects of a central economic plan lay down, rather than act to maximize their own welfare?

The agency problem can be addressed in three general ways. One is to use **moral persuasion** to exhort actors to maximum performance. In such a scheme the management or government (principals) expect people (the agents) to behave appropriately because it is the "right thing to do," and perhaps find some way of granting prestige to those who conspicuously do well. This kind of incentive has frequently been found to be quite effective in the short run. In crises (wars, disasters, changes of regime), people are capable of making immense and seemingly irrational sacrifices when exhorted to do so. Encouragements such as "for the fatherland," "for the glory of God," or even John F. Kennedy's "ask not what your country can do for you; ask rather what you can do for your country" all proved effective to some degree. Communist regimes, especially during their early stages, asked for and often received large sacrifices from significant sections of the population who worked "for the revolution" or "for the Party." Moral suasion can even be effective within enterprises and corporations. A high degree of identification with the company is often cited as one of the causes of Japan's success. Governments can berate firms and achieve a modification of behavior, and sometimes rhetoric will even seem effective against other countries. However, in the longer run, moral incentives tend to be relatively ineffective unless they are backed up by the prospect of material improvement or, on the other hand, by the likelihood of **coercion**.

Material incentives apply when people work and adjust the level and intensity of their work because of the rewards, including advancement and promotion, that are proffered. On the whole we tend to think of market economies relying almost exclusively on material incentives, and the consequent absence of coercion is commonly regarded as one of that system's strengths. Each actor in a pure market system enters only into economic exchanges or contracts willingly, whether it is as a consumer or a supplier of factors of production. Work represents leisure sacrificed and will be performed only when the material compensations of work outweigh the loss of utility resultant from reduced leisure. Were it generally a reality, this aspect of choice ensures that welfare is maximized under a capitalist system. In fact, not all capitalist systems are as market reliant as may be initially assumed. First, as we noted, the initial endowments of factors are crucial in determining incomes, and the need to survive acts as an element of coercion. The "whip of hunger" does serve as a coercive element in many "market" societies. Second, within the workplace, capitalism frequently resorts to coercion, through timeclocks, piece rates, supervision, and so forth. This reality may be less draconian in the developed market economies than it once was, but overt workplace coercion is common in the developing world.

We often consider planned economies to be more reliant on coercion than market systems, which is true to some extent. Obviously under a command system of central planning, entry into many economic activities is limited because in general citizens cannot establish firms or form independent professional practices. Buying articles for resale, which in market economies would be regarded as healthy and necessary arbitrage or speculation is illegal. In some command economies the government maintain a tight grip on the labor market and allows the individual little choice in occupation, location, hours worked, or many other significant aspects of employment.

However, this scenario may not always be the case. Highly structured materials balance planning can be associated with a fair degree of liberalism in labor markets. For example, in the former Soviet Union it was illegal to be unemployed, and indeed no source of support was available for those who were able-bodied and of working age if they did not work. However, the planners assumed a reciprocal responsibility to provide a job for everyone, no matter how inept the worker. Restrictions on movement and the central determination of wages made the market for labor clumsy and unresponsive, but on the whole workers responded to material incentives just as in the developed market economies. Workers performed because of piece rates, bonuses, or the prospect of advancement as well as supervision, the same as in the West. Management operated largely in its own best interest and indulged in what economists refer to as "rent-seeking behavior." Truly coercive systems of labor allocation and job performance are those that rely on slavery, serfdom, indenturement, or peonage.

Experience suggests then that the best system of labor incentives is an eclectic one. Evidence indicates that higher productivity results when workers feel less alienated from their job, the organization that employs them, and the products that they produce. This heightened sense of identification stems in part from security of job tenure if minimum performance requirements are met. It is difficult to identify with a firm if it is about to fire you. In addition, it is useful to give workers a material stake in the enterprise, either through stock ownership or bonus systems, which encourage them to be personally interested in the firm's success. Such an approach combines the moral and the material, but it also includes a coercive element: the pressure of interested coworkers is frequently an excellent source of peer supervision.

MEASURING THE DIFFERENCES IN ECONOMIC SYSTEMS

The changes that swept through Eastern Europe and other planned economies in recent years eroded the clear contrast between the centrally planned and free market economies. These developments reinforced the recognition that the degree of economic freedom in various economies must be viewed as a continuum rather than as polar extremes. In turn, this change motivated attempts to measure the economic restrictions imposed in various economic systems and to compound the many dimensions of these restrictions into a single index. Such attempts must always be open to the criticisms that the methodology adopted, the grading methods, and the means of aggregation into an index are all highly subjective and therefore prone to manipulation.

Nevertheless, the results can be interesting and revealing if viewed with caution. Here, we consider two aggregate indices, both of which really seek to measure the degree of economic freedom and the extent to which economic and political institutions support economic growth and integration into the global economic system.

Economic Freedom

Table 1.2 shows the indices of **economic freedom** for 2002 prepared by the Heritage Foundation, a conservative U.S.–based organization. The index is computed by assessing the performance of the economy on each of 10 dimensions scoring on a 5-point scale, with 1 being "free" and 5 being "restricted." The 10 dimensions are as follows:

1. Trade policy
2. Taxation policy
3. Government consumption of output
4. Monetary policy
5. Capital flows and foreign investment
6. Banking policy
7. Wage and price controls
8. Property rights
9. Regulation policy
10. Presence of a black market

The relevance of most of these variables is self-evident. Low levels of tariffs and taxes, limited government consumption, an absence of price controls, a few restrictions on incoming foreign investment, and limited regulation in both banking and goods markets are all generally considered indicative of high degrees of economic freedom. A restrictive monetary policy is considered favorable in terms of economic freedom because money growth may produce inflation, which by acting as a hidden tax lets the government grab resources through the back door. Well-defined and well-enforced property rights are seen as essential to free enterprise, while the absence of a black market—which prospers when socially beneficial activity is prohibited—is another indicator of freedom to pursue market activity.

Most people would agree that the majority of these factors are correlated with economic freedom, but some of the particulars leave room for dispute. For example, the regulation of business might reduce the freedom of the capitalist, but it might enhance the freedom of the consumer if it is directed at limiting market failure resulting from limited information and externalities. A capitalist's freedom

■ TABLE 1.2

Heritage Foundation Indices of Economic Freedom

Rank	Country	Score	Rank	Country	Score	Rank	Country	Score	Rank	Country	Score
1	Hong Kong	1.35	38	Latvia	2.5	79	Algeria	3.1	118	Azerbaijan	3.5
2	Singapore	1.55	41	Uruguay	2.55	79	Brazil	3.1	118	Malawi	3.5
3	New Zealand	1.7	42	Cambodia	2.6	79	Djibouti	3.1	118	Niger	3.5
4	Estonia	1.8	43	Costa Rica	2.65	79	Gambia	3.1	121	China	3.55
4	Ireland	1.8	43	Israel	2.65	79	Madagascar	3.1	121	Egypt	3.55
4	Luxembourg	1.8	45	Armenia	2.7	79	Malaysia	3.1	121	Ethiopia	3.55
4	Netherlands	1.8	45	Belize	2.7	79	Paraguay	3.1	121	India	3.55
4	United States	1.8	45	Bolivia	2.7	79	Slovenia	3.1	125	Chad	3.6
9	Australia	1.85	45	France	2.7	79	Swaziland	3.1	125	Kazakhstan	3.6
9	Chile	1.85	45	Jordan	2.7	88	Benin	3.15	125	Kyrgyz Republic	3.6
9	United Kingdom	1.85	45	Malta	2.7	88	Cape Verde	3.15	125	Nigeria	3.6
12	Denmark	1.9	45	Panama	2.7	88	Honduras	3.15	125	Togo	3.6
12	Switzerland	1.9	45	Poland	2.7	88	Lebanon	3.15	130	Venezuela	3.65
14	Finland	1.95	53	Kuwait	2.75	88	Nicaragua	3.15	131	Bangladesh	3.7
15	Bahrain	2	53	Peru	2.75	93	Burkina Faso	3.2	131	Romania	3.7
15	Canada	2	55	Greece	2.8	93	Guyana	3.2	131	Russia	3.7
17	Bahamas	2.05	55	Guatemala	2.8	93	Kenya	3.2	134	Congo	3.75
17	El Salvador	2.05	55	Sri Lanka	2.8	93	Senegal	3.2	134	Yemen	3.75
17	Sweden	2.05	58	Colombia	2.85	97	Cameroon	3.25	136	Haiti	3.8
20	Austria	2.1	58	Tunisia	2.85	97	Gabon	3.25	137	Tajikistan	3.85
20	Belgium	2.1	60	Botswana	2.9	97	Macedonia	3.25	137	Ukraine	3.85
20	Germany	2.1	60	Ivory Coast	2.9	97	Zambia	3.25	137	Vietnam	3.85
23	Cyprus	2.15	60	Jamaica	2.9	101	Albania	3.3	140	Bosnia and Herzegovina	3.9
23	Iceland	2.15	60	Mali	2.9	101	Guinea	3.3	140	Equatorial Guinea	3.9
23	United Arab Em.	2.15	60	Mexico	2.9	101	Mauritania	3.3	142	Guinea-Bissau	3.95
26	Barbados	2.3	60	Mongolia	2.9	101	Pakistan	3.3	142	Suriname	3.95
26	Portugal	2.3	60	Namibia	2.9	105	Indonesia	3.35	144	Yugoslavia	4.05
26	Spain	2.3	60	Oman	2.9	105	Moldova	3.35	145	Myanmar (Burma)	4.1
29	Italy	2.35	60	Slovak Republic	2.9	105	Turkey	3.35	145	Syria	4.1
29	Lithuania	2.35	60	South Africa	2.9	108	Bulgaria	3.4	147	Zimbabwe	4.3
29	Taiwan	2.35	70	Philippines	2.95	108	Croatia	3.4	148	Belarus	4.35
32	Czech Republic	2.4	70	Qatar	2.95	108	Fiji	3.4	148	Uzbekistan	4.35
32	Hungary	2.4	72	Dominican Republic	3	108	Georgia	3.4	150	Turkmenistan	4.4
32	Thailand	2.4	72	Mauritius	3	108	Ghana	3.4	151	Iran	4.55
35	Japan	2.45	72	Saudi Arabia	3	108	Lesotho	3.4	151	Laos	4.55
35	Norway	2.45	72	Uganda	3	108	Nepal	3.4	153	Cuba	4.75
35	Trinidad and Tobago	2.45	76	Central African Rep.	3.05	108	Rwanda	3.4	153	Libya	4.75
38	Argentina	2.5	76	Morocco	3.05	108	Tanzania	3.4	155	Iraq	5
38	South Korea	2.5	76	Mozambique	3.05	117	Ecuador	3.45	155	North Korea	5

SOURCE: The Heritage Foundation: Index of Economic Freedom 2002, http://www.heritage.org/research/features/index.

to pollute might at some point collide with a citizen's freedom to breathe, and the issue of whose rights and freedoms are paramount becomes central. In addition, simply averaging the scores on these many dimensions to arrive at the "final score" is a questionable practice. It is possible to argue that, for example, a highly government-controlled banking structure is a bigger curb on domestic enterprise than high levels of import tariffs.

Bearing this important reservation in mind, some of the implications of the table prove quite interesting. The six "freest" nations are all small, with an average population of less than 4 million. Hong Kong is a particular puzzle. It became a special administrative region (SAR) of the People's Republic of China (PRC) on July 1, 1997. Four years later, the Heritage Foundation finds that it remains the world's freest economy, although the PRC that now embraces it ranks 122 out of 125. On the whole, it is difficult to draw lessons for the design and conduct of an economic system from the experience of such small states, no matter how rapid their recent growth experience. It is simply not realistic to assume that Russia or India will undergo sustained growth by adopting the same policies as Hong Kong or Singapore.

Economic Competitiveness

Even more ambitious than the attempt to measure economic freedom are the efforts to quantify the **economic competitiveness** of the world's economies. At least two international organizations produce such indices on an annual basis: the World Economic Forum (WEF) and the Institute for International Management Development (IMD) in Lausanne.[11] Table 1.3 is the WEF ranking of nations in terms of a growth competitiveness index (GCI), which aims to measure "the capacity of the national economy to achieve growth over the medium term, controlling for the current level of development."[12]

The GCI evolved from relatively simple beginnings in 1997 and has been refined by Jeffrey Sachs and John W. McArthur.[13] Its objective now is to provide a good predictor of economic growth and competitiveness in the medium term after allowing for the "catchup" potential of less-developed economies—ones that lie somewhat behind the growth frontier. The GCI is a composite of three subindices. The first attempts to quantify an economy's capacity to innovate and to absorb technology transfer. It is the product of 19 pieces of information, some of it hard statistical information and some survey data. The second subindex concerns the quality of public institutions, focusing on the legal environment and corruption. The final component is concerned with the macroeconomic environment.

---

[11]The IMD ranking for its *2002 World Competitiveness Yearbook* is available at http://www02.imd.ch/wcy/ranking/. The United States places first, followed by Finland, Luxembourg, and the Netherlands.
[12]Peter Cornelius, Jennifer Blank, and Fiona Paul, "The Growth Competitiveness Index: Recent Economic Developments and the Prospects for a Sustained Recovery," Chapter 1.1 of *Global Competitiveness Report 2002–2003* (New York: Oxford University Press, 2002), p. 8, available at http://www.weforum.org.
[13]See J. W. McArthur, and J. D. Sachs, "The Growth Competitiveness Index: Measuring Technological Advancement and the Stages of Development," in *The Global Competitiveness Report 2001–2002* (New York: Oxford University Press, 2002).

■ **TABLE 1.3**

WEF 2002 Growth Competitiveness Index Rankings and 2001 Comparisons

2002 GCI Rank	Country	2002 GCI Score	2001 GCI Rank	2002 GCI Rank	Country	2002 GCI Score	2001 GCI Rank
1	United States	5.93	2	41	Botswana	4.22	*
2	Finland	5.74	1	42	Uruguay	4.19	46
3	Taiwan	5.5	7	43	Costa Rica	4.19	35
4	Singapore	5.42	4	44	Latvia	4.14	47
5	Sweden	5.4	9	45	Mexico	4.11	42
6	Switzerland	5.36	15	46	Brazil	4.09	44
7	Australia	5.36	5	47	Jordan	4.07	45
8	Canada	5.27	3	48	India	4.03	57
9	Norway	5.24	6	49	Slovakia	4.02	40
10	Denmark	5.23	14	50	Panama	4	53
11	United Kingdom	5.17	12	51	Poland	3.98	41
12	Iceland	5.16	16	52	Dominican Republic	3.96	50
13	Japan	5.08	21	53	Namibia	3.93	*
14	Germany	5.06	17	54	Peru	3.87	55
15	Netherlands	5.03	8	55	Morocco	3.86	*
16	New Zealand	5.03	10	56	Colombia	3.86	65
17	Hong Kong	4.93	13	57	El Salvador	3.85	58
18	Austria	4.93	18	58	Croatia	3.8	*
19	Israel	4.93	24	59	Sri Lanka	3.8	61
20	Chile	4.89	27	60	Jamaica	3.76	52
21	Korea	4.89	23	61	Philippines	3.7	48
22	Spain	4.88	22	62	Bulgaria	3.68	59
23	Portugal	4.87	25	63	Argentina	3.66	49
24	Ireland	4.86	11	64	Russia	3.64	63
25	Belgium	4.81	19	65	Vietnam	3.63	60
26	Estonia	4.73	29	66	Romania	3.59	56
27	Malaysia	4.7	30	67	Indonesia	3.36	64
28	Slovenia	4.64	31	68	Venezuela	3.35	62
29	Hungary	4.63	28	69	Turkey	3.31	54
30	France	4.62	20	70	Guatemala	3.2	66
31	Thailand	4.52	33	71	Nigeria	3.17	74
32	South Africa	4.47	34	72	Paraguay	3.14	72
33	China	4.37	39	73	Ecuador	3.13	68
34	Tunisia	4.35	*	74	Bangladesh	3.12	71
35	Mauritius	4.34	32	75	Nicaragua	2.99	73
36	Lithuania	4.33	43	76	Honduras	2.98	70
37	Trinidad	4.32	38	77	Ukraine	0.97	69
38	Greece	4.32	36	78	Bolivia	2.96	67
39	Italy	4.31	26	79	Zimbabwe	2.8	75
40	Czech Republic	4.26	37	80	Haiti	2.47	*

* Not ranked in 2001.
SOURCE: World Economic Forum, *Global Competitiveness Report 2002–2003*.

The WEF continues to revise the methodology and content of the GCI in the attempt to make it a more accurate predictor. It now places more emphasis on the "fundamental drivers of growth"—technology and innovation—while keeping an eye on the quality of public institutions and the macroeconomic environment.

Top honors go to the United States, largely on its technological and innovative muscle. The U.S. institutional framework, however, is not thought of as strong.[14] A close overall second is Finland (the 2001 leader), although it places only twelfth in the Heritage Foundation list. As a group the Nordic countries fare well. The other three (Sweden, Norway, and Denmark) all place in the top 10. A close correlation is also evident between the WEF rankings and membership in the OECD, the association of 30 developed countries sometimes called "the rich nation club." Eight of the top 10, and 23 out of the top 30 on the GCI rankings are OECD members. (Luxembourg, an OECD member, is not ranked by the WEF but certainly would merit a high rank.) These rankings could represent a cultural bias in the assessment of institutional strength, but the OECD group of countries enjoys powerful economic advantages in technology and finance that position them well for future growth. EU countries are strongly placed too; of its 15 current members, only Italy and Greece are out of the top 30.

The WEF views Latin America as still in urgent need of reform. Only Chile figures in the top 20, with Mexico (45), Brazil (46), and Argentina (63), still facing daunting economic challenges. Nor does the WEF provide an optimistic prognosis for the transition economies. The best-placed ex-Soviet country is Estonia (26), but Russia is well down the list at 64 and the Ukraine comes in a disturbing fourth from last. The medium-term outlook for China (33) is judged to be rather mediocre despite its recent impressive growth record, and the prospects for Indonesia—another growth star of the early and mid-1990s—are poor. These economies are "competitive" at the moment only in their ability to exploit relatively cheap labor; they have not established an institutional basis—an economic and political system—that will lead to sustained growth. Further reform and institutional change are indicated.

The Extent of Corruption

One important determinant of the actual character of economic systems was neglected in the economic literature until recently. **Corruption** can mean that actors in the economy experience a real system that differs from the nominally defined system. "Whenever it is pervasive, corruption can deter investment, impede economic development, and undermine political legitimacy."[15] The presence of corruption in an economy can deter economic growth in two ways. First, it acts like a tax, increasing the cost of doing business and transferring income from "legitimate" participants to illegitimate ones. This might not always be the case. For example, tax officials might agree to turn a blind eye to a tax liability in return for a "cut" of the tax savings. Thus the costs for the individual firm might be reduced, because the effective rate of tax is lower than the nominal rate. However, this "selective oversight" in

---

[14]The United States is ranked 17, behind all of northwest Europe on the quality of its public institutions.
[15]Kimberly Ann Elliot, *Corruption and the Global Economy* (Washington DC: Institute for International Economics, 1997), p. vii.

turn is bound to lead to further inefficiency because the tax rate becomes discriminatory, favoring corrupt firms and channeling resources into the corrupt sector.

Second, corruption increases the level of uncertainty for investors because it puts the firm in a situation in which substantial consequences might result were the letter and spirit of the law to be enforced. Furthermore, the existence and tolerance of corruption opens the door for what economists now term "rent-seeking behavior." This situation occurs when resources are expended in the creation of regulations the sole point of which is to invite the payment of bribes.

Table 1.4 shows the consolidated results of several surveys, largely of foreign businesspeople experienced in dealing with national bureaucracies. Thus, the data describe perceptions of corruption in various nations, rather than actual corrup-

■ TABLE 1.4

Perceptions of Corruption Index, Selected Countries, 2001

Rank	Country	Score	Standard Deviation	Rank	Country	Score	Standard Deviation
1	Finland	9.9	0.6	28	Estonia	5.6	0.3
2	Denmark	9.5	0.7	29	Italy	5.5	1
3	New Zealand	9.4	0.6	30	Hungary	5.3	0.8
4	Iceland	9.2	1.1	31	Slovenia	5.2	1
5	Singapore	9.2	0.5	32	Uruguay	5.1	0.7
6	Sweden	9	0.5	33	Malaysia	5	0.7
7	Canada	8.9	0.5	34	Jordan	4.9	0.8
8	Netherlands	8.8	0.3	35	Lithuania	4.8	1.5
9	Luxembourg	8.7	0.5	36	South Africa	4.8	0.7
10	Norway	8.6	0.8	37	Costa Rica	4.5	0.7
11	Australia	8.5	0.9	38	Mauritius	4.5	0.7
12	Switzerland	8.4	0.5	39	Greece	4.2	0.6
13	United Kingdom	8.3	0.5	40	South Korea	4.2	0.7
14	Hong Kong	7.9	0.5	41	Peru	4.1	1.1
15	Austria	7.8	0.5	42	Poland	4.1	0.9
16	Israel	7.6	0.3	43	Brazil	4	0.3
17	United States	7.6	0.7	44	Bulgaria	3.9	0.6
18	Chile	7.5	0.6	45	Colombia	3.8	0.6
19	Ireland	7.5	0.3	46	Mexico	3.7	0.6
20	Germany	7.4	0.8	47	Slovak Republic	3.7	0.9
21	Japan	7.1	0.9	48	El Salvador	3.6	0.9
22	Spain	7	0.7	49	Turkey	3.6	0.8
23	France	6.7	0.8	50	Argentina	3.5	0.6
24	Belgium	6.6	0.7	51	China	3.5	0.4
25	Portugal	6.3	0.8	52	Zimbabwe	2.9	1.1
26	Botswana	6	0.5	53	India	2.7	0.5
27	Taiwan	5.9	1	54	Bolivia	2	0.6

NOTE: Only countries for which four or more surveys were extant are included.
SOURCE: Transparency International, Corruption Perceptions Index 2001, available from http://www.transparency.org/cpi/2001/cpi2001.html.

tion, and therefore considerable cultural bias is likely. The scores are standardized. A score of 10 indicates "totally clean" implying an incorruptible bureaucracy and enforcement of the letter of the law. A zero, on the other hand, indicates a totally corrupt country, with bribes to officials at all levels as the normal way of doing business. Because the data are responses to questions about perceptions, a high degree of variability results from each respondent's experience. The column labeled "Standard Deviation" indicates the statistical variance of the results, and is, therefore, an index on the level of agreement among the various sources.

Incorruptibility on this basis seems to be favored by cold climates. Finland appears at the top of the list, again, with its Baltic partners close behind. Singapore is the only non-European nation to appear in the top 10. In general this index shows a fairly close compliance to the WEF measures of competitiveness in Table 1.3. Generally speaking, Western European countries score well, which tends to confirm the existence of a certain amount of cultural bias. Note that among these nations the standard deviation is low, implying that the various surveys generally agreed on the status of these countries. Some exceptions occur among the European Union (EU) countries. The most obvious is Italy, which ranks at 29 with a score of only 5.5. Also interesting is the position of the group of countries that the World Bank calls the high-performing Asian economies (HPAEs). Although many studies stress the importance of an "insulated bureaucracy," able to respond without undue influence of business, this study finds a high perception of corruption in these countries. The best performer, after Singapore, is Japan, with a rank of 21.

OTHER MEANS OF CLASSIFICATION

As well as being classified by their structure, or some measure of competitiveness or freedom, economies may also be classified by the outcomes that the confluence of their history, endowments, and economic systems produces. We frequently speak of economies as being rich or poor, of having egalitarian or discriminatory income patterns, of achieving levels of human capital development, or of being environmentally sound with sustainable economies rather than tending to deplete resources. This approach is in some ways less analytically sound than examining the system, because it neglects the level of development and focuses on the immediate and obvious rather than the structural, but these comparisons are commonly made.

Levels of Income

One of the most obvious and frequently made comparisons of different nations is made by looking at income levels. Table 1.5 shows the division of most of the world's economies by level of recorded gross national product adjusted to dollars using 1993 exchange rates. An immediately apparent feature is that the global distribution of income is highly skewed. A few countries, representing less than 15 percent of the world's population, show high income levels and account for about 77 percent of the total of the world's gross product. At the other end of the scale, 56 percent of the global population lives in relative poverty and accounts for less than 5 percent of the world's gross product.

■ **TABLE** *1.5*

Distribution of World Economies by Income per Head, 2000

Income Level of Economy	Population (Millions)	Per-Head PPP GNI (2000)	Percent of Total Population	Percent of Total GNI
Low	2,459	$1,990	40.62	10.99
Lower Middle	2,046	$4,580	33.80	21.06
Upper Middle	647	$9,170	10.69	13.32
High	903	$27,450	14.92	55.68
Total	6,054	$7,350	100.0	100.0

SOURCE: The World Bank Development Report 2001/2002.

The group of the 27 countries that are richest in terms of national income per head is by and large the same as the group usually identified as "developed market economies."[16] Only two oil-rich Gulf nations fail to meet that criterion. The membership of this group is also close to rankings of the Organization for Economic Cooperation and Development (OECD), the association composed of 30 of the world's most developed economies. Only six OECD members fail to qualify for the World Bank's higher-income economy classification.[17]

Recent Economic Performance

Another way in which we commonly classify economies is by their recent economic performance. Some possible comparisons, though by no means all, are shown in Table 1.6. Ranking economies by the rate of growth of GDP is quite common. On this basis, of the countries shown, South Korea was the star performer in the 1990s, though as we shall see, it ran into serious problems at the end of the century. Russia, which saw an annual average contraction of 7 percent as it undertook the early stages of transition, was the loser. Similarly, we can look at economies in terms of their negative features—high rates of unemployment or high rates of inflation. Russia also fared badly when we look at the inflation rate. In terms of the rate of unemployment, Japan did best, despite its relatively low rate of GDP growth.

It is common to think of those economies that export more than they import as being successful, although such a "neomercantilist" view of the world is open to

---

[16]The richest countries in terms of income converted to dollars at international exchange rates, in ascending order, are Slovenia, Greece, Spain, New Zealand, Israel, United Arab Emirates, Ireland, Canada, Italy, Australia, United Kingdom, Hong Kong, Finland, Netherlands, France, Belgium, Sweden, Germany, Austria, Iceland, United States, Singapore, Japan, Denmark, Norway, Switzerland, and Luxembourg. Even within this group considerable variance occurs. Swiss per-head GNP at more than $40,000 is four times greater than that of Slovenia.

[17]The six are the Czech Republic, Hungary, South Korea, Mexico, Poland, and Turkey.

question.[18] A positive balance on current account produces a similarly sized deficit on capital account and means that such an economy is building up its portfolio of assets abroad. However, another way of looking at this situation is that investment opportunities abroad seem more attractive than those at home. Japan managed to run a substantial current account surplus and is a heavy investor in other economies around the world. The United States and, as Table 1.6 shows, the Czech Republic run deficits on current account and are therefore net capital importers. Even though the negative current account balance looks to be a weakness of the U.S. economy it can be seen as a feature of the confidence that the rest of the world places in it, and their willingness to invest there. A good case can be made for the relative strength of the U.S. economy in the 1990s compared with the Japanese despite the latter's positive current account and trade balance.

The Structure of Output

We can also distinguish between economies by looking at the ways in which value is added in the economy. Some economies are relatively heavily agricultural in nature, while in others, manufacturing activity predominates. In other economies (generally but not exclusively highly developed market economies), the service sector provides the greatest amount of employment and value added. Although we can note some clear exceptions, we generally observe a transition that occurs in

■ TABLE 1.6

Economic Indicators for Selected Economies

	United States	Japan	France	Sweden	Czech Republic	Russia	South Korea
Growth of GDP, 1990–98	2.2	1.3	1.5	1.2	–0.2	–7.0	6.2
Inflation, annual rate, 1990–98	2.2	0.4	1.7	2.3	17.1	235.3	5.1
Unemployment, 1990–98	5.4	3.3	10.4	4.8	6.2	12.0	3.3
Current account balance (as % of GDP, 2001)	–4.4	2.5	1.9	2.5	–4.8	1.8	2.4

SOURCE: *World Development Report* 2001, *International Financial Statistics*, September 2002; OECD Economic Outlook, June 2001.

[18]Mercantilism was a economic doctrine favored in the sixteenth century, which held that a positive balance of trade was a policy objective to be pursued, in part because it led to an inflow of precious metals. Neomercantilism is the pursuit of a positive balance of trade and a corresponding accretion of net overseas assets.

parallel with the general level of development, with the least developed societies being more agriculturally based.

Table 1.7 shows, for example, India's high proportion of agricultural output and relatively small manufacturing sector. As per-head incomes rise and the level of development increases, we see first a movement toward manufacturing and industry, and ultimately toward services. This general association of development with falling agriculture and rising services is true both in cross-sectional and historical analyses. An oddity here is that the distinction of having the greatest share of GDP in the agricultural sector actually falls to a European nation, Albania, in which 63 percent of its GDP originates. Although significantly underdeveloped by European standards, Albania is in fact quite highly developed relative to Africa and much of Asia. Its showing here is due to the total collapse of its industrial sector during the 1980s and 1990s, following the downfall of its hard-line socialist regime. Taking a seemingly huge step backwards in terms of development, the share of industry in GDP fell from 45 percent in 1980 to just 18 percent in 1998.

The Distribution of Income

Another way of comparing the economic systems of societies is by looking at how they answer the distributive question, "for whom?" Table 1.8 gives some summary data on the distribution of income in selected countries. The countries are ranked in ascending order of incomes, and the share of income for each quintile of the population is given. In general a discernible tendency for a more even distribution of income can be noted as income rises. Thus it is in the highly developed and rich market economies that we see the most even distribution of income, and within

■ **TABLE 1.7**

The Structure of Output in Selected Economies, 2001
(% of GDP originating in each sector)

	Agriculture	Extractive Industry	Manufacturing	Services	Income Per Head (in $, current exchange rates)
Albania	63	18	na	19	810
Benin	39	6	8	47	380
India	28	9	16	46	430
China	17	26	24	33	750
Brazil	9	6	23	62	4,570
Korea	5	12	32	51	7,970
United Kingdom	2	10	21	67	21,400
France	2	7	19	72	24,940
Japan	2	13	24	61	32,380

SOURCE: The World Bank.

■ TABLE *1.8*

Distribution of Economic Well-Being (% of GDP per quintile)

| Country | Quintile | | | | | PPP* |
	First	Second	Third	Fourth	Fifth	GNP/Head
India	8.1	11.6	15	19.3	46.1	$1,700
China	5.9	10.2	15.1	22.2	46.6	$3,220
Guatemala	2.1	5.8	10.5	18.6	63	$4,070
Russia	4.4	8.6	13.3	20.1	53.7	$3,950
Brazil	2.5	5.5	10	18.3	63.8	$6,160
Korea	7.5	12.9	17.4	22.9	39.3	$12,270
United Kingdom	6.6	11.5	16.3	22.7	43	$20,640
Netherlands	7.3	12.7	17.2	22.8	40.1	$21,620
Germany	8.2	13.2	17.5	22.7	38.5	$20,810
Sweden	9.6	14.5	18.1	23.2	34.5	$19,480
United States	5.2	10.5	15.6	22.4	46.4	$29,340
Japan	10.6	14.2	17.6	22	35.7	$23,180
Switzerland	6.9	12.7	17.3	22.9	40.3	$26,620

*PPP = Purchasing Power Parity
SOURCE: 2000 World Development Indicators, Table 2.8. Available at World Bank: Washington, DC, 2000.

that group in the welfare state societies of Western Europe—Sweden, the Netherlands, and Germany. Japan's fairly even distribution comes as a result of low unemployment rates.

The most inegalitarian nation shown in Table 1.8 is Brazil, where the richest 20 percent of society account for 63.8 percent of the income, while the poorest 20 percent only receive 2.1 percent of the product. Thus the average "rich individual" in the top 20 percent of society is more than 30 times better off than the average "poor" person. The situation is similar in Guatemala, although per-head incomes are only at 50 percent of Brazil's level. The People's Republic of China, despite its communist heritage, shows a distribution similar to India. The distribution in Russia, after 50 years of socialism, is less egalitarian than "capitalist" South Korea, and every sign concerning the impact of transition and privatization in the Russian economy indicates that the distribution is becoming more skewed. The countries of Western Europe are quite egalitarian in terms of income, and their comprehensive health and education systems, which are not reflected in these income data, tend to reinforce social equality.

The United Kingdom once saw a more uniform income distribution, but it experienced a sharp move away from the all-embracing welfare state, an ideological shift that we now refer to as "Thatcherism." A series of economic changes privatized most of state-owned industry, reduced the progressivity of the tax system, and reduced the coverage of the social safety net. The income profile of the United

Kingdom now more closely resembles that of the United States than the European social democracies. One of the more surprising features of these figures is that Hong Kong now has both a higher income per head and a more even distribution of income than the United Kingdom. However, summary figures of income distribution are incomplete descriptors of economic systems. The figures for Russia and the United Kingdom, for example, are (with the exception of income per head) quite similar.

Economists often use either diagrams or summary statistics to represent the important aspects of the distribution of income. The most frequently used graphical device is the **Lorenz Curve**, illustrated in Figure 1.2. The curve consists of a graph of the cumulative amount of wealth or income enjoyed by some cumulative breakdown of the population. Complete equality would be represented by a straight line across the diagonal of the box, and increasing degrees of inequality are expressed by the amount that the actual curve "bows away" from the diagonal. Hence the relatively egalitarian Swedish income distribution is represented by being closer to the diagonal than the more uneven distribution of income in Brazil.

■ **FIGURE 1.2**

Lorenz Curve for Brazil and Sweden

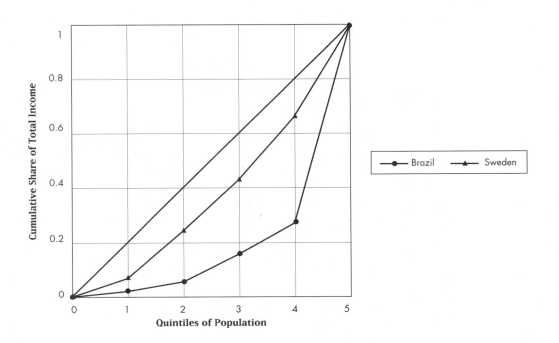

SOURCE: Data from Table 1.8.

Another way of summarizing the income distribution is by the **Gini coefficient**, which is defined by the ratio of the area between the diagonal and the Lorenz curve and the total area under the diagonal. Perfect equality would lead to the Lorenz curve and the diagonal being coincident, and hence the Gini coefficient would be zero. Complete inequality (one individual having all of the income) would lead to a Gini coefficient of 1.

ENVIRONMENTAL SUSTAINABILITY

The indices discussed to this point make no allowance for the long-term sustainability of the system, despite the fact that interest in the **environmental sustainability** of different economic systems continues to increase. The OECD, for example, recently devoted a section of its annual study reports to environmental issues and policies of its member nations. Table 1.9 shows an attempt by Yale Center for Environmental Law and Policy and Columbia University's Center for International Earth Science to establish a commonly based "environmental sustainability index" to indicate how each economic system is coping with environmental issues. The index is derived from some 67 primary variables that include the incidence of acid rain, population density, number of vehicles in a country, and the level of energy use per head. Somewhat surprisingly, Finland sits at the top of the table, again proving that economic competitiveness and respect for the environment need not be competing objectives.[19] Not all European nations perform well; the United Kingdom comes in a dismal 91. The United States, at 46, performs poorly on many indicators but is helped by a low population density, which enables it to weather the effect of environmental degradation due to overpopulation.

ARE SOME SYSTEMS BETTER THAN OTHERS?

In comparative economics it is tempting, and perhaps sometimes appropriate, to look at economies in terms of success and failure. Tables 1.2 to 1.9 provided views of different dimensions of the economic outcomes of particular systems, and show a wide variety of ways to adjudicate success. In comparing economies we must exercise the greatest care. As discussed earlier, an economy is not reducible to simple "production function" terms. The ultimate objective of human endeavor is to achieve well-being, which involves characteristics that transcend the economic. Economists tend to focus their attention on measurable concepts—like material income per head—leaving indicators of the social fabric to sociologists. Today we are increasingly aware of the costs that economic growth can impose on society and on our global environment. It does not mean an inevitable conflict between growth and social welfare, or growth and the environment. It merely emphasizes that we must look at a wide range of outcomes when we attempt to evaluate success and failure.

---

[19]Finland seems to be in the happy position of coming first in almost every index, including a recently released index of the freedom of the press.

■ TABLE *1.9*

The Environmental Sustainability Index

Rank	Country	ESI Score	Rank	Country	ESI Score	Rank	Country	ESI Score
1	Finland	73.9	49	Belarus	52.8	96	Vietnam	45.7
2	Norway	73.0	50	Germany	52.5	97	Cambodia	45.6
3	Sweden	72.6	51	Nicaragua	51.8	98	Guinea	45.3
4	Canada	70.6	52	Papua New Guinea	51.8	99	Nepal	45.2
5	Switzerland	66.5	53	Jordan	51.7	100	Indonesia	45.1
6	Uruguay	66.0	54	Thailand	51.6	101	Burkina Faso	45.0
7	Austria	64.2	55	Sri Lanka	51.3	102	Sudan	44.7
8	Iceland	63.9	56	Kyrgyzstan	51.3	103	Gambia	44.7
9	Costa Rica	63.2	57	Bosnia & Herzegovina	51.3	104	Iran	44.5
10	Latvia	63.0	58	Cuba	51.2	105	Togo	44.3
11	Hungary	62.7	59	Mozambique	51.1	106	Lebanon	43.8
12	Croatia	62.5	60	Greece	50.9	107	Syria	43.6
13	Botswana	61.8	61	Tunisia	50.8	108	Ivory Coast	43.4
14	Slovakia	61.6	62	Turkey	50.8	109	Zaire	43.3
15	Argentina	61.5	63	Israel	50.4	110	Tajikistan	42.4
16	Australia	60.3	64	Ghana	50.2	111	Angola	42.4
17	Panama	60.0	65	Czech Republic	50.2	112	Pakistan	42.1
18	Estonia	60.0	66	Romania	50.0	113	Azerbaijan	41.8
19	New Zealand	59.9	67	Guatemala	49.6	114	Ethiopia	41.8
20	Brazil	59.6	68	Zambia	49.5	115	India	41.6
21	Bolivia	59.4	69	Malaysia	49.5	116	Burundi	41.6
22	Colombia	59.1	70	Algeria	49.4	117	Philippines	41.6
23	Slovenia	58.8	71	Bulgaria	49.3	118	Uzbekistan	41.3
24	Albania	57.9	72	Russia	49.1	119	Rwanda	40.6
25	Paraguay	57.8	73	Morocco	49.1	120	Oman	40.2
26	Namibia	57.4	74	Egypt	48.8	121	Jamaica	40.1
27	Lithuania	57.2	75	South Africa	48.7	122	Trinidad & Tobago	40.1
28	Portugal	57.1	76	El Salvador	48.7	123	Niger	39.4
29	Peru	56.5	77	Uganda	48.7	124	Libya	39.3
30	Bhutan	56.3	78	Japan	48.6	125	Belgium	39.1
31	Laos	56.2	79	Dominican Republic	48.4	126	Mauritania	38.9
32	Denmark	56.2	80	Tanzania	48.1	127	Madagascar	38.8
33	France	55.5	81	Senegal	47.6	128	Guinea-Bissau	38.8
34	Netherlands	55.4	82	Malawi	47.3	129	China	38.5
35	Chile	55.1	83	Italy	47.2	130	Liberia	37.7
36	Gabon	54.9	84	Macedonia	47.2	131	Turkmenistan	37.3
37	Armenia	54.8	85	Mali	47.1	132	Somalia	37.1
38	Ireland	54.8	86	Bangladesh	46.9	133	Nigeria	36.7
39	Moldova	54.5	87	Poland	46.7	134	Sierra Leone	36.5
40	Congo	54.3	88	Kazakhstan	46.5	135	South Korea	35.9
41	Ecuador	54.3	89	Kenya	46.3	136	Ukraine	35.0
42	Mongolia	54.2	90	Myanmar (Burma)	46.2	137	Haiti	34.8
43	Spain	54.1	91	United Kingdom	46.1	138	Saudi Arabia	34.2
44	Central African Rep.	54.1	92	Mexico	45.9	139	Iraq	33.2
45	Zimbabwe	53.2	93	Cameroon	45.9	140	North Korea	32.3
46	United States	53.2	94	Chad	45.7	141	United Arab Em.	25.7
47	Honduras	53.1	95	Benin	45.7	142	Kuwait	23.9
48	Venezuela	53.0						

SOURCE: 2002 Environmental Sustainability Index, Yale Center for Environmental Law and Policy and the Center for International Earth Science Information Network, Columbia University, February, 2002. Available at http://www.ciesin.columbia.edu/indicators/ESI/.

KEY TERMS AND CONCEPTS

Asian Tigers

beliefs

capitalism

cash-flow right

centrally planned economic system

choice of technique

coercion

company unions

control right

corruption

craft or occupational unions

disposal right

distributional decision

economic competitiveness

economic freedom

environmental sustainability

European Union

Gini coefficient

Glass-Steagall Act

households

human capital

indicative planning

industrial capital

instruments

the invisible hand

laws

legality

Lorenz Curve

material incentives

measures

moral persuasion

natural resources

nongovernmental organizations, NGOs

Pacific-Rim capitalism

policies

practices

principal/agent problems

production decision

property rights

regulations

Rhine model

"Robinson Crusoe" economy

Smith, Adam

social democracy

socialism

system

universal banks

welfare state

worker-managed socialism

QUESTIONS FOR DISCUSSION

1. Discuss the nature of national wealth. Where do you believe the greatest source of long-term increase in wealth will lie?

2. Why might a high measure of economic freedom lead to a high growth of GNP?

3. Corruption is often compared to a tax. Why?

4. Why is a more even distribution of income considered an advantage for a society? Can you think of negative aspects of an even distribution of income?

5. Why are NGOs increasing their scope of activity?

6. Why is the contemporary fixation of achieving a favorable balance of trade sometimes called *neomercantilism*?

RESOURCES

The most useful resources to accompany this chapter are those that will give the reader access to comparative data on a range of characteristics for the economies of the world.

Web Sites

Some of the most valuable resources to a researcher, because they are current, easily accessible, and by and large free, are the Web pages of the major international organizations. The most useful single link is perhaps the page of links for the United Nations system, which can be found at http://www.unsystem.org/. It provides links to the Web pages of all of the organizations of the United Nations system. These links are useful in researching the economic structure and system of a country, but the most relevant for the economist, and likely to be among the most durable links, are the major multinational organizations.

Multilateral Agencies

The International Monetary Fund (IMF) ....http://www.imf.org/
Particularly valuable at this useful site are the downloadable full-text versions of the working paper and country reports series. This site is a necessary first stop for any research project whether topical or country based. Current data and some interesting studies are available through the access to a free downloadable version of *World Economic Outlook.*

The World Bank (IBRD) ....http://www.worldbank.org/
At this useful site for research on developed and developing economies, clicking on "publications" will connect the reader with the Digital Library, an online library of full-text publications and summaries of major World Bank publications, feature articles, and abstracts from World Bank journals.

The World Trade Organization (WTO) ....http://www.wto.org/
Although not as valuable a resource as the other United Nations organizations for the study of comparative economics, it offers a good place to check on issues such as the environment, intellectual property disputes, and regional trade issues. A first-rate document dissemination facility (DDF).

The United Nations Development Programme (UNDP)...................http://www.undp.org/
This excellent Web page provides access to both the Human Development Report (HDR) and to a large number of national Human Development Reports. The HDR gives access to the Human Development Index, which is an important supplement to GDP statistics and indices of competitiveness in evaluating economic success. The nations reports are useful because they generally include background pieces and descriptions of economic structure and recent economic history. Coverage is, however, patchy—very good for Europe East and West but poor for Asia and the Pacific.

Organisation for Economic Co-Operation and Development...........http://www.oecd.org/
Unlike the preceding sites, the OECD is not a part of the United Nations system but it is probably the best site available for information on developed countries. The statistical

series are comprehensive and standardized, and the OECD Surveys include a wealth of information on economic systems, institutions, policies, and prospects.

Regional Commissions of the UN

The Regional Economic Commissions of the United Nations are responsible for monitoring and analyzing economic developments by region. They provide useful country data and analysis, much of which can be obtained from their Web sites.

Economic Commission for Africa (ECA) .... http://www.uneca.org/
This site, a good starting point for work on liberalization and reform in Africa, allows free access to the ECA's annual report, a useful library, and good links.

Economic Commission for Europe (ECE) .... http://www.unece.org/
This site is excellent for research on recent developments in both the transition economies of Eastern Europe and the member nation of the European Union. Much of the annual survey of the ECE, which covers both western and eastern Europe, is accessible from this site as well as important selected charts and tables.

Economic Commission for Latin America and the Caribbean (ECLAC).................................
....http://www.eclac.cl/
For a good jumping off point for research on Latin America, *The Annual Survey* is available here and is a thoughtful document, with useful statistical appendices and tables.

Economic and Social Commission for Asia and the Pacific (ESCAP)......................................
....http://www.unescap.org/
The Annual Survey provides a good overview of the region, and the downloadable publications are an excellent source for country-by-country analysis of financial sector reform in the wake of the Asian financial crisis.

For studies on particular aspects of comparative economics the following Web sites of specific UN agencies with functional rather than general responsibilities are valuable:

Food and Agriculture Organization of the United Nations (FAO)..... http://www.fao.org/

International Labour Organization (ILO) ....http://www.ilo.org/

Multilateral Investment Guarantee Agency (MIGA) .... http://www.miga.org/

UN Conference on Trade and Development (UNCTAD) .... http://www.unctad.org/

UN Development Fund for Women (UNIFEM) .... http://www.unifem.org/

UN Educational, Scientific and Cultural Organization (UNESCO) ....
....http://www.unesco.org/

UN Environment Programme (UNEP).. http://www.unep.org/

UN Foundation .... http://www.unfoundation.org/

UN Industrial Development Organization (UNIDO)...................... http://www.unido.org/

UN Research Institute for Social Development (UNRISD)........... http://www.unrisd.org/

UN Human Settlements Programme ....http://www.unhabitat.org/

World Intellectual Property Organization (WIPO) .... http://www.wipo.int/

Other Web Sites

Columbia International Affairs Online (CIAO) .... http://www.ciaonet.org/

European Bank for Reconstruction and Development (EBRD)...... http://www.ebrd.com/

Heritage Foundation .... http://www.heritage.org/

Transparency International .... http://www.transparency.de/

World Economic Forum .... http://www.weforum.org/

Center for International Earth Science Information Network ....
....http//www.ciesin.columbia.edu/indicators/esi

Books and Articles

Brademas, J., and F. Heimann. "Tackling International Corruption." *Foreign Affairs,* September 1998, 17–23. Assessment of the consequence of corruption and the possibilities of reform to tackle it.

Elliot, Kimberley Ann. *Corruption and the Global Economy.* Washington, DC: Institute for International Economics, 1997. Collection of good readings concerning corruption. Particularly good is Paulo Mauro's "Cross Country Analysis," chapter 4. Comprehensive references and data sources.

Fukuyama, Francis. *Trust: The Social Virtues and the Creation of Prosperity.* New York: Free Press, 1995. Argues that social capital is vital for rapid economic development.

O'Driscoll, Gerald P. Jr., Kim R. Holmes, and Mary Anastasia O'Grady. *The 2002 Index of Economic Freedom.* Washington, DC: Heritage Foundation, 2002. The source of the Index of Economic Freedom.

Pearce, David W., and Jeremy J. Warford. *World without End: Economics, Environment and Sustainable Development: A Summary.* Washington, DC: World Bank, 1998.

Stapenhurst, Rick, and Sahr J. Kpundeh (eds.). *Curbing Corruption: Toward a Model for Building National Integrity.* Washington, DC: World Bank Institute Development Studies, 1999.

Tanzi, Vito. "Corruption Around the World Causes, Consequences, Scope, and Cures." Downloadable from the IMF site at http://www.imf.org/external/pubs/CAT/longres.cfm?sk52583.0.

United Nations Development Programme. *Human Development Report.* New York: Oxford University Press, 2002. A wealth of comparative data, excellent references, and each year tackles a different theme; 2002 dealt with deepening democracy. The WDR Web site can be accessed at http://www.undp.org.

World Bank. *Helping Countries Combat Corruption: The Role of the World Bank.* A downloadable synopsis is available from the World Bank site at http://www.worldbank.org/html/extdr/corruptn/coridx.htm.

World Bank. *World Development Indicators.* Washington, DC: World Bank, 1999. Useful compendium of data for developing countries.

World Bank. *World Development Report.* New York: Oxford University Press, 2002. Excellent source for all sorts of data. Excellent bibliography and each year a different theme; 2002 was concerned with the sustainable development.

Worldwatch Institute. *State of the World,* 2003. New York: W. W. Norton and Company, 2003. An annual assessment of environmental developments from an environmentalist viewpoint. Some good country data.

2

THE ROOTS OF ECONOMIC SYSTEMS

WHY AND HOW ECONOMIC INSTITUTIONS CHANGE

Economic systems are not static. A glance at history, even the history of merely the past decade, shows us that systemic change is relatively frequent. New institutions may be created and old ones terminated, and the rights of the various constituent groups and individuals of society with respect to property, economic activity, or mobility may be altered. The extent of government ownership in the productive sphere is by no means constant and varies with "privatization" (the current trend) and its converse "nationalization." Governments can change, sometimes in dramatic fashion, and new governments may bring with them an entirely new philosophical approach to the objectives of the system or the new ways of addressing those objectives. Consequently, they set about altering the web of laws and regulations that govern economic activity. Industries are taken into public ownership, or "privatized." Controls over output and prices may be tightened or relaxed.

Two questions are of great and enduring interest to students of comparative economics:

Why do economic systems change?

How do they change?

The answer to the first question is often considered to lie within two dynamics: **technological change** and **population growth**. However, neither of these is truly exogenous to the economic system and therefore cannot be regarded wholly as an external agent of change. In fact, we can see that often both the direction and pace of technology and population dynamics are influenced to a considerable degree by the nature of the economic system. For example, it can be argued that *laissez faire* capitalism rewards the kind of technical change that favors small enterprise, and therefore, as a system, it tends to foster relatively small-scale technology. Socialism, on the other hand, faces criticism both for being inimical to economic change and, where change occurred, biased to large-scale technology.

On the population side, we know that relatively less-developed societies with little provision for a social safety net tend to be characterized by high birthrates, because parents need some surviving offspring to provide care in their old age. Therefore the introduction of even modest public health measures leads to rapid population growth, at least in the short run, before societies adjust their behavior and lower the birthrate in response to changed circumstances. In subsequent sections we look at how changing technology and population are historically linked with substantial shifts in the economic system.

Evolutionary and Revolutionary Change ⭐

Studying development and change in economic systems in historical context prompts the observation that at certain points in time and space, change seems to be rapid. At other points it is much slower and even, more in line with our understanding of evolution in natural history. From this study, two schools of thought about economic change emerged. Adherents of the **evolutionary school** stress the gradual nature of change. They see shifts in an economic system as a process of gradual accommodation to the movements in technology, the resource base, and population through small continuous innovations in the institutions of the system and in the laws that govern their interaction. Problems are resolved by incremental adjustments. Societal progress is slow and, as once observed about evolution in nature, tends to "make no leaps."

In contrast to the gradualism of the evolutionist, the nineteenth-century philosopher and economist Karl Marx offered a theory of the revolutionary **laws of motion**. Marx's vision of social dynamics, like that of evolutionists, was linear. Each form of social organization gave way to a successor, in a progressive and irreversible way, but in Marx's view change tended to occur discontinuously, with periods of rapid change punctuating periods of relative constancy.

Marx's conception of the causality of social change lay in material factors. As populations grew and technology advanced, the growth of material output became constrained by the existing system of economic and social organization. These changes led to a growing tension between the societal groups that dominated the established economic system and those who would benefit from a new set of arrangements. The tension then produced antagonism, struggle, and eventually (generally after a series of crises and false starts) rapid revolutionary change. The old social order was overthrown and replaced by one better suited to maximize social output in the changed situation.

As a result of this revolution originating in material factors, the whole **superstructure** of society changed. This shift included not only political relations (who held the power and who governed) but also law, culture, custom, and even religion. The development of the social system grew out of the economic change. We can see in the thought of both the evolutionists and Marxists parallels to the theories of biological evolution propounded by Darwin. As conditions alter, the existing economic system becomes ill adapted to the maximization of output. The consequence is growing social stress. In both cases change results. In the evolutionary view it is creeping and may be tenuous, reversible, and experimental. In the other, the Marxian view, it is sweeping and total. Of course, the significant departure from biological Darwinism is that economic systems are human-made and involve therefore some human design and thought. Although natural selection occurs as the result of unplanned changes that favor the species that happen to be better suited, the change of economic system can be conscious, thoughtful, and imitative of changes that occurred elsewhere.

ECONOMIC SYSTEMS IN HISTORICAL PERSPECTIVE[1]

As a precursor to the study of the economies that exist today, it is useful to review, if only in bare outline, the procession and variety of economic systems that existed through history. In each instance we will try to outline briefly the structure of each system and to ask the following questions: What forces led these systems to change? How did that change occur? How did the change resolve the problems?

Hunter-Gatherer Societies

We begin with a look at the most primitive economic organization: the hunter-gatherer society. Our knowledge of the precise social organization of this prehistoric world is imperfect, but we can make some generalizations. We know that it was in this form of social organization that humankind existed for most of its time on earth. All successive forms of social and economic organization are crowded into the last 9,000 years or so. In fact, a few isolated hunter-gatherer societies survived until the present age.

At the heart of a hunter-gatherer system must lie the sustainability of the environment in which it exists. If the natural vegetative resources of the land are over-picked, or if the animal stocks are overhunted, then the equilibrium of such a system is threatened. Overexploitation of renewable resources arises from two roots. One lies in advancing technology; superior hunting techniques and more advanced tools and weapons take a greater toll of animal stocks and may perhaps encourage waste. The other cause lies in the growth of population. Greater numbers will place greater demands on resources. Of course, these two trends are closely related. The higher productivity associated with superior technology allows the population to enjoy living standards above subsistence, and consequently it expands. However, when overexploitation is encountered the greater difficulty of gathering food and hunting in a depleted environment causes productivity to fall. When average social productivity falls below subsistence level, the population will shrink, which in turn allows resources to replenish, generating a new cycle of potentially increased productivity. This cycle of growth and contraction of human and animal populations was the rule for many thousands of years.

Pastoral and Agrarian Societies

About 9,000 years ago, we know that some hunters began to switch to settled farming. This shift probably took the form of scratching a cultivable garden within the forest and tending edible plants. It also involved the primitive domestication of animals. Initially such enterprise provided a living only barely above subsistence, but it did enable survival in the face of increased demands on natural resources. Over time, learning from experience led to improved technique, and the develop-

---

[1]This section is concerned with the evolution of societies in historical perspective and can be omitted without damaging the overall flow of the text. It is recommended that any reader rejoin the discussion with "Contemporary Economic Systems" on page 57.

ment of better seed and livestock resulted in rising productivity. In turn, the growth in agricultural communities accelerated.

At this point in history, a series of social innovations could occur. First, the population engaged in agriculture generated a surplus that enabled a greater division of labor. The excess produce of the farmers could support artisans, priests, soldiers, lawyers, and doctors. In addition, the economic system and the legal framework within which it operated necessarily became more complex. A settled agricultural society requires a different set of institutions and more comprehensive laws than those needed to govern the hunter-gatherer societies. Whereas in the earlier society property was largely communal and resources open to all, in a farming society property rights become much more important. Some permanence in the tenure on the land is essential, if only between the planting season and harvest. Much longer tenure is desirable if land improvement is to be effected. Some authority competent to enforce property rights and adjudicate disputes is vital. The arrival of settled agriculture also allowed the creation of a greater social surplus than what was feasible in hunter-gatherer societies. This surplus, in turn, allowed the creation of a nobility, professional, and artisan classes that provided consumer goods and services, a religious establishment, and a permanent military.

"Oriental Despotism"

As the population of agrarian societies grew, pressure on resources increased. One of those resources, water, was essential to maintain the highly productive agriculture necessary to support the population. The social order and high productivity in agriculture depended on the preservation of the water supply for irrigation, making clear definition and enforcement of water rights imperative. In the view of Marx and others, this dependence on irrigation was the explanation of the durable, wealthy but inequitable states of Asia.[2]

In the nations of South and Eastern Asia, the organization and management of the water supply was especially important. Successful irrigation meant the difference between a highly populous and productive community and a sparsely inhabited and precarious subsistence economy. Irrigation projects were characterized by large economies of scale and required considerable, though well-rewarded, social investment. Consequently, a large public works bureaucracy emerged, with the resources and expertise to develop and maintain this water. It was precisely the great social return of these projects that accounted for what Karl Marx called **Oriental despotism** in Eastern **"hydraulic" societies**. The ruler and the associated bureaucracy were able to expropriate the greater part of the produce of society because that produce was dependent on the success of the irrigation project. The populace, aware of the importance of hydraulic organization and the great benefits provided, was powerless in the face of a bureaucracy that held a monopoly on organization and expertise as well as military power. It was forced to acquiesce to confiscatory rates of taxation.

---

[2]See especially Karl August Wittfogel, *Oriental Despotism: A Comparative Study of Total Power* (New Haven: Yale University Press, 1957), which embodies his seminal views on the relevance of water to political structure.

Classical Slave Economies

In Europe the great classical societies of Greece and Rome were less dependent on irrigation for agriculture. They relied to a much larger degree on the institution of slavery. Although the Greek city-states are frequently touted as the cradles of democracy, participation in political decision making was in fact highly circumscribed. Most residents of Greek cities had no say in their policy or destiny. The ratio of slaves to free citizen in Athens was perhaps as high as 18 to 1 at the height of its prosperity. In Rome, which was a highly centralized empire that supported a large urban population, production in agriculture was dominated by the *latifundia*. These large farms operated on a slave-labor plantation system. Slaves also formed the basic labor supply in mining, construction, and manufacturing, as well as supplying services within the household.

Although now we regard the institution as morally deplorable and therefore nonviable under any circumstances, the efficiency of slavery as an economic system depends on certain specific conditions. The objective of a slave system is to obtain labor at rates below those that would pertain under a market system of free labor. Where markets are competitive and labor is mobile, each worker is paid a wage approximate to his or her marginal productivity. Where labor is plentiful relative to land and capital, the marginal product of labor will be low and the wage will tend in the long run to move toward subsistence, the wage that ensures the survival and replication of the labor stock and no more. In such a situation slavery will not be viable because "free labor" may be had for an amount roughly equal to the subsistence wage. In contrast, slavery is likely to flourish in circumstances where labor is in short supply relative to capital and land, because then the marginal product of labor is high. Under such circumstances the potential savings in labor costs are likely to be the greatest.

However, slavery does involve costs that the employment of free labor does not, principally the cost of purchase and the cost of supervision. Purchase can be regarded as a form of capital investment. Supervisory costs consist of two components. The first involves protecting the investment from flight, theft, and illness. The second can be looked on as a form of the "agency problem" that was briefly discussed in Chapter 1. All users of labor face agency problems in getting workers to perform, to work as if they could appropriate all of the income from increased productivity. Overseers, time-clocks, and the practice of piecework all function to solve the agency problem in a free market. Under slavery these problems are more acute.

The centrality of supervision costs means that slavery is likely to be most enduring within a system characterized by a strong centralized authority, no refuge for slaves within or close to the slave society, and racial or ethnic distinction between the "free" population and slaves. When the Roman Empire was well ordered, the power of the state minimized the private costs of supervision. However, as centralized authority in Rome began to collapse under the weight of incursions by wandering tribes from the Eurasian heartland, the private costs of supervision and enforcement rose and the slave problem contributed considerably to Rome's difficulties and ultimate fall.

The Feudal System

In the aftermath of the collapse of the Western Roman Empire, Western European society became highly disordered. The institution of slavery was replaced by that of serfdom within the context of the feudal system. **Feudalism** was the dominant system of political and economic organization in Western Europe for a period of roughly 1,000 years. Although the duration of feudalism differed in different territories or regions, in broad terms we can think of it as persisting from the fall of Rome and the onset of the so-called Dark Ages of western Europe (in the fifth century) until the establishment of nation-states in about the sixteenth century. Feudalism therefore thrived in a situation where centralized control was absent, along with most of the restraints on individual behavior.

The basis of feudalism was one of hierarchical personal obligation, which, although largely determined by power, was to some extent reciprocal. In return for the provision of protection, which was necessary in such a chaotic society, individuals occupying the lower ranks of the social pyramid were required to pay rent in goods and service to those higher up. The rapaciousness of the higher-ups was curbed only by the possibility of revolt by the lower orders and the necessity of at least preserving the population and social capital for replication in the next time period. An additional constraint in some circumstances was the moderating doctrines of religion.

In feudal theory, all land was ultimately at the disposition of the monarch, but the effective title of estates was parceled out to the nobility as a reward for past services rendered and to ensure future loyalty. The upper echelons of the nobility enjoyed relatively autonomous control of their locality and its microeconomy. They in turn delegated property rights and political jurisdiction to a lower level of aristocracy, as a reward for tribute, loyalty, and service.

The nobility was to a great extent a self-appointed class that relied on power and coercion to secure its position. Herman Schwartz somewhat flippantly described them as

> [A] kind of dispersed biker gang: armor, horses, and their propensity to resort to violence elevated them above most of the rest of the population in the same way as leather and Harleys elevate movie bikers where state authority is absent.[3]

At the bottom of the social pyramid was the peasantry. In "typical" European society this class comprised about 90 percent of the rural population. Substantial variation was due to the differential productivity of the land and the peasants. Broadly speaking, higher productivity meant more superstructure (nobles, warriors, priests, etc.) could be supported. The peasantry itself was not a monolithic class; within it lay distinct gradations. The serfs (also called villeins), who constituted the most numerous group, could claim only limited property and personal rights. Serfdom as an institution differed from slavery (as, for example, in the United States) in that the serfs were regarded as part of the property of the *demesne*, or manor, and therefore could not be alienated from it by being sold in the market. Consequently the family under serfdom was a rather more stable institution than under slavery, but the lives and very existence of serfs depended on the frequently capricious and arbitrary rule of the lord. Above them in the social pyramid lay a stratum of free or

---

[3]See Herman Schwartz, *States Versus Markets: History, Geography, and the Development of International Political Economy* (New York: St. Martin's Press, 1994).

landed peasants, who held rights to a small plot of land, but who also owed service to the aristocrat and were just as dependent on his rule and protection.

The feudal economy was a command economy in most of its attributes, but with both centralized and decentralized aspects. At the state level, the monarch was responsible for a limited but important set of decisions, particularly over external trade, which was almost always under direct state control and usually organized as a licensed or sanctioned monopoly of the monarchs. In addition, the monarch also frequently designated the monopoly producer of certain important productive activities, or issued monopoly licenses for others to engage in them. These arrangements usually covered industries such as shipyards, ceramic factories, and armories. Resources flowed to the crown via monetary taxation, in-kind tribute of goods, and the conscription of labor for military and other service. The high frictional cost of transportation meant that most economic activity was local. Both economic hinterlands and political jurisdictions tended to be restricted to the feasible limit of a day's travel on foot or by wagon, a radius of roughly 10 miles in all directions around a central point. The manor and the village were relatively self-sufficient units in which economic activity fell largely under the direction of the lord of the manor or in many cases church authority (where the religious establishment was a major landowner).

The business of the manor and the village was largely agricultural. The basic organization of the northwest European manorial system will be familiar to most readers. The arable land of the village was commonly divided into three fields, one of which lay fallow each year. The land within the fields was divided into strips, which were allocated among the landed peasantry. Livestock was grazed on common land.

The landlords extracted their income in two ways: (1) by appropriating goods in kind, as rent, and in return for services, especially milling grain, and (2) by labor service provided as work on the aristocrat's lands. Market activity was limited, but landed peasants were able to sell the surplus produced in excess of the demands of the lord, the church, and their own subsistence, and could through purchase or barter acquire those goods (clothing, tools, etc.) that they were unable to produce themselves.

In summary, the important economic decisions were made by the commands of the monarchy and nobility: they controlled what was produced, how it was produced, and who then gleaned the benefit. In terms of incentives, the dominant mode was coercion, although elements of both moral and material incentives may be found. Some form of sharecropping was frequently practiced, giving the peasantry an incentive to maximize output in order to retain the most they could for consumption and sale in the market. Such a system did embody a material incentive, though the heavy "tax rate" tended to dull it. Great emphasis was placed by society, and especially by the church, on social order, adding an element of moral incentive. However, when all was said and done, the peasant worked for, and gave goods to, the lord of the manor because no alternative existed. The nobility's monopoly on force that could be used to coerce the peasant was also necessary to protect that same peasant from the predations of others.

Feudalism as a static economic and social system evolved following the wreck of the Roman Empire and the collapse of imperial order. Little within the system was oriented to, or supportive of, economic growth or development. The nobility were consumers rather than investors, and any economic surplus generated found its way into castles, churches, and military adventurism rather than into capital improvements to increase economic output in the long run. The uncertain status of the peasant and the absence of long-term tenure of any given piece of land under the strip system made land improvement by the peasant pointless. The authority of the monarch was limited by the power of the nobility and little impetus could come from the center.

Commercial activity as we know it today was largely incompatible with feudalism. The greatest European commercial center in the early Middle Ages was Venice, because of steps it took to separate itself from the feudal states of Western Europe, including its insular location and the maintenance of a deliberately and strategically vague allegiance to Byzantium. Within Venice, commercial activity, markets, and banking all began to thrive and to throw out seeds that eventually provided the impetus for a broader commercial revolution.

Mercantilism

Although it proved to be a durable system, lasting for about 1,000 years in parts of Western Europe, feudalism's basic economic weaknesses put it under attack from two directions. On the one hand, monarchs sought to consolidate their own power and to increase their own wealth by controlling more fully the territories nominally under their rule. On the other, the growth of market economies challenged the established system of labor servitude.

The extension of the control, and therefore the wealth, of the monarch could only be achieved by breaking the grip of the nobility on the microeconomies that existed within the state. In this respect the monarchy was assisted by change in military technology. The power of the feudal nobility to resist a centralized state derived from two sources: the fighting potential of the armored, mounted knight, and the defensive strength of the castle. The one enabled the wealthy aristocrat to be the physical superior of the unmounted fighter; the other gave the aristocrat the ability to withstand sieges and therefore to flaunt the authority of the monarchy. The arrival of gunpowder devalued both of these advantages. An aggressive monarch with a professional army and an artillery siege train was in a position to reduce any disruptive and defiant magnate. This capability cleared the way for the creation of nation-states, which established common currencies, standardized weights and measures, and uniform laws. Such states also experienced fewer internal obstacles to trade. Costly transportation still posed a problem, but much more effective division of labor was possible under a unified state. Similarly, the use of firearms became the great equalizer, because the knight became easy prey for the foot soldier.[4]

Feudalism was also under attack from within. As trade slowly revived, the potential to create wealth by arbitrage and exchange was realized and grasped by

---

[4]In Japan, feudalism lasted longer in part because firearms were prohibited, extending the *samurai* as a social class until the late nineteenth century.

a growing merchant class. Feudalism—static, consumption-oriented, and organized in geographically limited microeconomies—was antithetical to this growth of trade. Commercialism defied the existing social order by putting this wealth in the hands of commoners. When the barony attempted to confiscate the growing wealth of the merchants, those merchants turned directly to the monarch for protection. As a result, commercial activity became increasingly located in towns whose royal charters set them apart from the power of the nobility.

The growth of towns brought with it a surge in the demand for labor, and plunged the stake into the heart of feudalism—the servile system. The marginal productivity of urban employment was certainly greater than that of the serf on the manor. Town-based employers were inclined, and had an incentive, to pay workers more than laborers could receive from the rural aristocrats. Before the growth and independence of towns, a serf had no alternative to remaining on the manor, depending on a meager income and the protection of the lord. With the emergence of urban centers, flight to towns brought the prospect of freedom, independence, and a higher real standard of living. Furthermore, the *bourgeoisie*[5] were reluctant to return the serf to the manor for punishment and defied the feudal magnates. In Germany the change was expressed by the phrase *Stadtluft macht frei*—"the air of the cities makes one free." These growing towns afforded new opportunities to the peasant classes.

Competition between town and country, between capitalism and feudalism, intensified as a result of the epidemics of the "Black Death" in the fourteenth century. In many districts of Europe half of the population was lost, producing an acute shortage of labor. The surviving serfs were the beneficiaries of the competing needs of the countryside and the town. Land was so plentiful relative to labor that much of it fell out of production. The dramatic lack of rural labor caused the solidarity of the system to break down. Runaway serfs were welcomed on the land of other aristocrats and were seldom returned to their own manors. In the towns, even harder hit than the countryside by the pestilence, labor shortages pushed up wages and increased the lure to former serfs. Serfdom declined and was replaced by a much more freely operating labor market in much of Europe.[6] The simultaneous movement toward the establishment of markets and the blending of the micro-economies into a larger economic space produced the collapse of feudalism.

Mercantilism Defined The confluence of the state-building activities of the monarchy and the growing power and influence of the trading classes characterizes the system that we call "mercantile." The term **mercantilism** can be interpreted as meaning "the doctrine of merchants," which is perhaps its most literal rendering. It eventually came to mean something more complex, although loose application of the term resulted in a rather confused discussion.

Some of this confusion is due to the lack of any systematic statement of mercantilist theory by its adherents. Important arguments were laid out by pamphleteers

---

[5]Literally, *bourgeoisie* means "the townspeople," although it later came to have class connotations.
[6]Further east in Europe less change was seen in the institution of serfdom. In Russia the serfs were not freed until the 1860s.

usually working on behalf of a merchant lobby,[7] but they are incomplete and often conflicting. Our own understanding of mercantilism stems from the straw man created by Adam Smith in the *Wealth of Nations*, a rather coarse caricature intended to be easily demolished. In this work Smith advocated a new system better suited to the needs of an increasingly industrialized society. As a result of Smith's work, many people consider "mercantilists" as rather foolish people who failed to distinguish between real national wealth and a heap of precious metal.

What then do we mean by the term *mercantilism*? First, it involves an internal project, the creation of an integrated economic space greater than the size of the microeconomies that characterized the feudal system. In this sense the problems were quite similar to those faced in the construction of the European Union today, in that mercantilism involved the removal of fiscal and physical barriers to trade, the acceptance of a common legal code, a movement toward a common currency, and the use of a common language. Second, mercantilism is usually thought of as supporting state involvement in the development of the national economy. Thus it fell to the state to establish industries where they were lacking, especially where import substitution was possible, as well as to grant subsidies and monopolies to key industries.

Third, a positive balance of trade was desirable. In the eyes of the monarch the purpose of overseas trade was to increase national wealth, which could be directed to exert strategic influence. Even though today it might be said that the object of trade in such a system is to raise living standards by bringing plentiful cheap goods into the country and to effect a more efficient global division of labor, such a purpose was not the case under the mercantilist system. Thus a prime element was the achievement of a "favorable" **balance of trade**, or an inflow of precious metals into the country. The difference in the value between exports and imports would be settled by this inflow of precious metals, which was considered important because it could be taxed, borrowed, or otherwise acquired by the state and used to finance statecraft, conspicuous consumption, or military expenditure. This situation is the origin of the famous phrase that mercantile policy "put power [of the State] before plenty [for the individual]."

The preoccupation with the trade balance was one of the features of mercantile thought that attracted Adam Smith's derision in the *Wealth of Nations*, in which he accused mercantilists of confusing money with national wealth. Smith was at pains to explain in his seminal work that the wealth of nations lay in productive capacity, not in fallow stocks of precious metal. As a doctrine, trade fetishism was also taken to extreme by two branch "schools" of the mercantilist tree. "Bullionists" genuinely thought that the real source of a nation's wealth was the stock of precious metal within the country, rather than the productive capacity. "Cameralists" focused their attention on the fiscal position of the state, judging well-being to be measured essentially by the ability to tax and the accumulated stock of fiscal surpluses.

---

[7]*England's Treasure by Foreign Trade,* by Thomas Mun, a merchant, is one of the best known of these tracts. Although mainly directed at attacking legislation suggested to curb bullion export, it lays out a clear picture of the benefit of trade in national development. Available at http://socserv2.socsci. mcmaster.ca/econ/ugcm/3ll3/mun/treasure.txt.

Merchants, however, were generally not adherents of either of these extremes, and in England they lobbied against legislation advanced by bullionists that would outlaw the export of precious metals. Rather, merchants favored the positive trade balance because it acted to expand and therefore, in modern terms, "loosen" the money supply. A growing money supply led both to low interest rates and a higher rate of inflation than otherwise would prevail. Both of these factors were advantageous to mercantile interests, because traders were generally debt-financed and held a substantial inventory of goods.

The policy of promoting a positive balance of payments led in part to the aggressive acquisition of overseas possessions and colonies, which characterized the mercantile system. Incorporating into the home country, or "metropolis," territories that could produce raw materials not available at home (e.g., tropical produce) reduced the need for costly imports and for financing them with bullion. The preoccupation with trade balance also led to the widespread use of subsidies (or "bounties") for production and export. Goods that cost more to produce domestically than the prevailing price in the outside world became profitable for local producers; this practice saved bullion from foreign exchange while requiring taxation to raise the necessary subsidies.

A fourth premise of mercantilism was the establishment of a positive **balance of employment**. In simple terms, it prescribed that the labor content of exports should be greater than that of imports. Correspondingly, the most advantageous form of trade was to exchange domestically produced manufactured goods for foreign-produced raw materials, which in contemporary terms we can see as a desire to maximize value added and skilled employment in the metropolis. Such a policy would lead to a maximization of both the domestic population and the skill level embodied in that population. It led therefore to a policy of restricting, or in some cases reversing, the economic development of colonial possessions. To take an example from the British Empire, extensive legislation (the Iron Act, the Woolen Act, and the Hat Act) sought to curb development of the manufacturing industry in the American colonies in order to retain them as export markets for goods made in Britain itself. In another example, parallel policies actually led to the "undevelopment" of the possessions in India, by the destruction of textile production and the conversion of India into a producer of raw material alone.

Central to this strategy of maximizing growth within mercantilist practice were the measures that sought to control the direction of trade and the means by which trade was to be conducted. In England these measures took the form of a series of "navigation acts," but parallels are to be found in Spain, Portugal, and France. The earliest navigation acts in England determined that all trade to and from the nation should be carried in vessels of English registry; this legislation had the effect of strengthening demand for, and therefore the size and profitability of, the merchant marine. Subsequent acts ensured that all colonial imports and exports (often including those with other colonies) should be conducted through the metropolis.

It was also thought economically sensible to discourage economic development in the colonies, keeping them as suppliers of raw materials alone and not as competitors in the production of finished products. To this end, laws often prohibited the development of manufacturing industry and even certain kinds of agriculture in the colonies.[8]

Even though Adam Smith was able to attack the mercantile system to good effect, at least as far as England was concerned, many nations continue to pursue the basic ideas of mercantilism, among them late industrializing nations that successfully crossed the divide from "less developed" to "developed" status.[9] The essential ingredients introduced here (economic unification, state promotion of industry, favoring exports, discouraging imports, and an attempt to foster high value-added manufacturing) are all policies espoused by one country or another today. Indeed mercantilism seems to be a successful policy for the second best. The preeminent power of the seventeenth century was the Netherlands, which had little use for the close management of trade or state promotion of industry that lay at the heart of the mercantile system as practiced by the Spanish and the English.

The policy of establishing the Low Countries as an entrepôt of free trade was highly successful and the most competitive prices for many commodities were those on the Amsterdam market. Consumers in countries wrapped in mercantile regulations usually paid more for products and were taxed more for subsidies than where market rates pertained. However, the costs of the mercantile system fell hardest on colonial possessions that were treated as providers of raw materials and markets for the metropolis. Active policy to discourage development was the norm, but proved most injurious to the long-run economic health of colonies.

The routing of all trade with any of the colonies through the metropolis was also burdensome because it raised both the costs of exporting and the prices of imports. As a counterbalance, however, the colonies benefited from a protected market in the metropolis and from subsidies designed to encourage the production of many goods. Of the numerous attempts to estimate the economic cost of these trade acts with respect to British North America, the maximum figure arrived at was about 3 percent of annual colonial gross domestic product (GDP), a figure thought by most to be scarcely significant.

The Institutions of Commercial Capitalism

Although we can regard mercantilism as an overarching but general belief system espoused by the classes that effectively controlled society and the economy, the day-to-day economic system that prevailed between the end of feudalism and the advent of the industrial system is more descriptively called **commercial capitalism**. The title is appropriate because the dominant wealth-creating activity, at least as far as Western Europe was concerned, was commerce, and it was conducted by entrepreneurs who controlled capital and were interested in its accumulation.

---

[8]In English legislation these included the Hat Act, the Iron Act, and the Woolen Act. Spain prohibited the growth of olives and the production of wine in its American possessions.
[9]The most notable were Japan and Korea, which used regulation to good advantage while pursuing a "market friendly" approach.

This period was important in terms of institutional change because it saw the development of two innovations critical to subsequent capitalist development: the practice of incorporation of businesses and the emergence of banks as true financial intermediaries. Incorporation involves the creation of a legal entity with two essential features. First, corporations are an efficient means of commingling the funds of individuals, thereby gathering together the means for large investments. Second, the liabilities of corporations are limited by the extent of their assets. Consequently incorporation encourages risk taking, because the downside is limited, while the upside is not. Banks facilitate the pooling of saving and the lending of funds to individuals with ideas and enterprise but limited start-up capital.

Industrial Capitalism

Just as changing technology and a widening world first threatened and then destroyed the feudal order, supplanting it with mercantilism, by the end of the eighteenth century the commercial capitalist system was itself under threat. The proximate cause, in this case, was the growth of mass production and the rise of industrialized manufacturing, which was brought about by what has in the past been called the Industrial Revolution. Recent scholarship tends to dispute the idea of a short explosive burst of innovation, however, and tends to settle on a more extended and evolutionary series of innovations and institutional changes.[10] However, we can characterize the shift in productive technique as embodying four broad sorts of changes that were effected in the process of industrialization:

1. The replacement of muscle power (whether animal or human) by machine power, first water power and then steam
2. The replacement of skill and craftsmanship by the artificial and repetitive precision of the machine
3. The replacement of organic sources of raw materials by inorganic ones
4. The replacement of natural "time" by the clock (This last development was especially important for the creation of workforce discipline in the factory system.)

These developments made possible a factory system much as we know it today. In Britain, which was the first country to undergo substantial industrial urbanization, the system that developed was by and large highly competitive. Especially in the textile trades, which were the lead sector of technological change and were located largely in Northern England, the industrial structure approximated the model of competitive capitalism now embodied in textbook treatments of the theory of competitive firms. The product was close to totally homogeneous, the market included many buyers and many producers, and labor was largely undifferentiated.

[10]The debate on this issue continues to be lively, and an interested reader might want to look at Peter Temin's "Two Views of the British Industrial Revolution," *Journal of Economic History* 57, no. 1 (March 1997), pp. 63–82.

Decisions were made primarily by an entrepreneur who both managed the firm and put a substantial part of personal capital at risk. Government policy at that time was best described as "laissez faire, laissez passer."

The largest shifts in the economic regulation happened because mercantile restrictions adversely affected the long-term competitive prospects of manufacturing. At the beginning of the industrialization process, political power remained in the hands of the landholding and commercial classes, who favored comprehensive trade regulations. However, the increasing economic power of the manufacturers led, in England in 1832, to their enfranchisement, and within 15 years this growing political power resulted in sharp changes in the economic system.

The most visible of these changes was the outcome of the popular and parliamentary debate over the reform of the corn laws. The **corn laws** created tariffs that restricted the import of cereal grains into Britain leading to both higher food prices and increased returns to the owners of agricultural land. The manufacturers' interests, however, lay in minimizing costs, and higher food prices forced them to raise wages, ultimately hurting the competitiveness of British goods on international markets. After considerable pressure, the corn laws were repealed and Britain was able to freely import food and other materials. It represented in some ways recognition for the economic doctrines of David Ricardo, who rejected the idea of mercantile restrictions and presented a cogent case for the rise of the free trade movement.

The onset of British industrialization saw further changes in the role of government. Urbanization produced a plethora of problems associated with growth and the government was called on to deal with the issues of public health and pollution control (albeit in a rudimentary form). Unacceptable workplace dangers and the widespread use of child labor occasioned laws that regulated factory practices. The government also became involved in the development of human capital, in the form of education for the less privileged classes; this education increased labor productivity.

Industrialization also enabled labor to organize to an extent not previously possible. Unions began to spring up and were at first resolutely opposed by manufacturers and the government. The first union organizers were prosecuted under "combination acts" and imprisoned or deported. However, over time the legality of labor organization was confirmed and the stage was set for the emergence of mass unions representing the working class. In Britain these unions were modeled on the old craft guilds and were structured around occupations rather than around specific employers, which led to long-term consequences for the nature of collective bargaining in the British context.

The Industrial System in Continental Europe

Industrial development in continental Europe differed from that in Britain because of two factors. First, the role of government was generally greater due to different and less liberal political traditions. Second, European nations were playing catchup. Consequently, they could adopt technologies already pioneered and tested elsewhere, especially after Britain abandoned all attempts to control the export of machines and machine tools in the late 1840s. Continental industrial structures were from the start less competitive than those in Britain. Their industries, and often specific favored firms, enjoyed both more overt government support and closer relations with the banking sector than was true in Britain. It was the genesis of a political/economic system that involved much closer management of industry by government than was seen in Britain, at least prior to World War II. This close relation of government and business is in one respect a holdover from earlier mercantile practices. As one observer, Charles Tilly, put it, mercantilism appeals to the second best, or at least the latecomers, who require government support, direction, and protection against competition. This model of late industrialization that pertained to continental Europe in the late nineteenth century echoes in the policies and practices of the East Asian late industrializers in the late twentieth century.

The different role of banks on the continent was also significant. Banking had played only a small role in the creation of credit in the British Industrial Revolution. A surprisingly large amount of capital was generated through retained earnings and the granting of interfirm trade credits. Banking proved especially useful in overseas trade, and the financial sector developed in a differentiated pattern with a variety of specialized banks. On the continent, banking was much more central, largely because the average enterprise at inception was much larger than in Britain. Large firms did not grow from small start-ups but were created from whole cloth in order to take advantage of the scope of latest technology and to grasp the economies of scale required to compete with existing suppliers. Banks played a great role in providing start-up capital, and because of the size of their stake, the banks became closely associated with the management of the venture. Continental banks were not specialized but were "universal" in nature, providing loans, owning capital, granting trade credits, and being responsible for brokerage services.

Finance Capitalism and Imperialism

The close relationship between the banks and business in Europe, which was evolving in Britain and in the United States,[11] led neo-Marxian observers to see a new stage in the evolution of economic systems. Following Rudolf Hilferding, an Austrian, this system became labeled as **finance capitalism** and differed from early **industrial capitalism** in the role played by financial capital. In Hilferding's conception, which was significant to Lenin, a small coterie of bankers were capable of dominating the system. This resort to monopolization was a defensive technique employed to delay the inevitable decline in the rate of profit.

In Marxian analysis this same close group of financier/industrialists was potentially also influential on government policy. This aspect became especially important, because Marx believed that the capitalist system would face repeated crises.

---

[11]In the United States the most obvious example of this closeness was the takeover of the U.S. steel industry by J. P. Morgan.

The root cause of these crises was the basic tendency toward accumulation, the replacement of labor by ever-deepening capital. Capitalist societies would ultimately always be faced with problems of declining profits and insufficient demand in this system. Monopolization of production and the elimination of competition was one strategy that afforded some relief from these pressures. The other was to look abroad, outside the capitalist system. Colonies could provide both fields to invest capital at higher rates than applied at home and a source of demand for finished products. It was another way in which the fatal crisis might be postponed.

CONTEMPORARY ECONOMIC SYSTEMS

Socialism and Communism

Marx believed that capitalism would face repeated crises caused by the long-run decline in the rate of profit and ever-increasing problems of excess supply as demand failed to keep pace with production. These economic problems would be played out against a backdrop of growing worker alienation. The confluence of these forces would present the crucial limitation on capitalist production and the means by which the system would change. Like other systems before it, it would be swept away. The system that would replace it in his conception of history would be socialism, a transitional stage on the way to communism.

The word **socialism** first appeared in writings in France and Britain in the early nineteenth century. Today, this rather imprecise term covers a wide range of positions from total public ownership at one extreme to social democracy at the other. Most socialists, however, share the belief that the community as a whole should own and control the means of production, distribution, and exchange to ensure a more equitable division of a nation's wealth, either in the form of state ownership of industry or in the form of ownership by the workers themselves. In Marxian terms, the advent of socialism is characterized by a dictatorship of the proletariat and the continued existence of scarcity (which would be not be a characteristic of communism), but other conceptions also exist. Utopian socialists in Britain, for example, saw a much more limited shift in society. The economic organization they envisaged held much in common with worker-owned cooperatives.

Marx saw socialism as another stage to be passed through on the way to communism. Prior to Marx, this social and political ideology advocated that authority and property be vested in the community, each member working for the common benefit according to capacity and receiving according to needs. Numerous thinkers embraced the ideal of communism, including Plato, the early Christians, and the sixteenth-century humanist Thomas More, who saw it as expressing man's social nature to the highest degree. **Communism** was to be the final culmination of Marx's successive revolutions. In such a society, class would vanish and the state as such would largely be unnecessary. Each would contribute according to his or her ability, and each would take according to need.

Under Lenin and his successors, Soviet communism contained two main elements. The first was the leading role of the Communist Party, seen as representing the true interests of the working class. The party was to control the organs of the state, and was itself to be organized according to the principles of "democratic centralism" in which a narrow group of individuals controlled all aspects of political, economic, social, and cultural life. Thus, in effect communism became one variant of totalitarianism, with a narrow elite enjoying control. The second major element in communist doctrine was the social ownership of property and central planning of the economy.

The achievements of Soviet communism inspired revolutionary movements in many other countries, and in some developing countries, such as China, Vietnam, North Korea, and Cuba, communist parties came to power and established regimes based more or less closely on the Soviet model. In Eastern Europe, communist governments were installed under Soviet influence at the end of World War II.

However, the ideal communist state never materialized and support for communist regimes in the West fell, even among left-thinking intellectuals, as the inefficiency of the system and its lack of a democratic base became more apparent. We will study the history of the Communist experiments in Russia and in China in Chapters 21 and 23.

The Growth of the Welfare State

Although Marx was confident that the successive crises of capitalism would lead to socialist revolution in the most advanced capitalist societies, these expectations failed to materialize. Britain, the United States, and Germany, with large manufacturing workforces at the end of the nineteenth century, appeared to be the prime candidates for revolution. However, all escaped Marxist revolution. Rather than a violent shift to total public ownership and the dictatorship of the proletariat, these states instead evolved into societies that generally carry the label of **welfare state**.[12] In these nations the government assumed a much greater range of responsibilities, including responsibility for the management of the economy and the creation of what is called the social safety net. Labor got to share to a much greater degree in the increase in productivity that followed technical change, and consequently the revolutionary potential of working class discontent was diffused.

These shifts were gradual; the original impetus in Britain started before World War I, accelerated between the world wars, and culminated with a far-reaching social program immediately following World War II. This program included the creation of comprehensive social security, nationalized health care, and the assumption of public ownership of a large swath of industry. In the United States the key dates are the creation of the New Deal by the Roosevelt administration after 1933 and the Great Society program of Lyndon Johnson in the late 1960s. In this book we look at several of the welfare states and pay particular attention to

---

[12]*Evolution* is perhaps too mild a word for the metamorphosis in Germany, which throughout the 1920s teetered on the brink of revolution before falling to the fascists in the 1930s. After World War II, the occupying powers were highly influential in restructuring the economic system by decree. Only after this point can the German development of the welfare state be regarded as gradual evolution.

Sweden, which was especially aggressive in its pursuit of income equality since the 1930s. We also look at Britain, which was notable for its retreat from socialism in the early 1980s, in some detail.

Corporatism and Fascism

Later in this book we refer to certain economic systems as "corporatist" in nature. A corporatist society can be defined as one where interest groups, bound together by duty and obligation, triumph over the individual. The logic of **corporatism** dictates that such groups are not in conflict with each other, but seek non-confrontational relationships. In practical terms it generally means that the various institutions of both labor and capital are licensed by, and operate under, the close supervision and coordination of the state. Thus, corporatism combines the market institutions of private property and ownership of the means of production with the idea that the government is responsible for shaping and steering the actions of both labor and capital for the social good.

Corporatism has also been closely associated with the political system of **fascism**, which represented the state as being dominant in all aspects of life. The essence of fascism is that government should be the master not the servant of the people. The economic embodiment of fascism was the model of the corporate state pioneered by the Mussolini regime in interwar Italy.[13] In this system, all industries in the country were organized under state aegis into 12 "corporations," controlled by boards on which representatives of labor, business, and the Fascist Party served. In reality, they were government-sponsored trade associations, or cartels, with the responsibility for allocating output among members, fixing prices, and regulating wages. Although the objective was to promote state control of industry and rapid growth, in fact the monopolistic organization resulted in corruption and a loss of efficiency. In Germany a less-structured system gave the government a high degree of control of business and replaced free unions with the National Labor Front. Businesspeople were coerced into cooperation by the prospect of relief from the labor strife characteristic of the previous decade. In both cases the objective of the system was the triumph of collective interest over the individual, both at the level of the corporation and at the level of the state. It is, consequently, inimical to liberal capitalism because of the required trampling of individual rights and to socialists because of the nominal prevalence of private property.

Although usually associated with past dictators such as Mussolini, Peron (in Argentina), and Salazar (in Portugal), *corporatism* is a word also used to describe Sweden, where the government brings together labor unions and employers' federations to determine national wage settlements. Others used it to characterize Japan, where a triumvirate of politicians, bureaucrats, and industrialists jointly forge a national industrial policy. In its most extreme form it takes on the rather pejorative label of "Japan Inc."

---

[13]See Rondo Cameron, *A Concise Economic History of the World*, 2d ed. (Oxford: Oxford University Press, 1993), p. 363.

A recent confusion between corporatism as defined here, and the kind of political and economic system dominated by corporations in the current American sense of the word is unfortunate. A company such as General Motors is not at all the same institution as the Italian corporations organized by Mussolini. Mussolini famously remarked that "Fascism should be more correctly referred to as Corporatism," in an attempt to represent his politics as promoting the collective good and the general rights of the individual through requiring incorporation in government.[14] It is too frequently used in suggesting no distinction lies between today's corporate world and its links to government, and the political system of fascism with all its evils. Clearly many flaws can be associated with contemporary capitalism, but eliding the distinction between today's corporations and Mussolini's corporatism blocks sincere efforts to critically address them.

Economics and Islam

The apparently growing conflict between a section of the global Islamic community and the capitalist West is increasing interest in, among other things, Islamic economics. Timur Kuran tried to clarify the issues surrounding Islamic economics:

> The declared purpose of **Islamic economics** is to identify and establish an economic order that conforms to Islamic scripture and traditions. Its core positions took shape in the 1940s, and three decades later efforts to implement them were under way in dozens of countries. In Pakistan, Malaysia, and elsewhere, governments are now running centralized Islamic redistribution systems known as *zakat*. More than sixty countries have Islamic banks that claim to offer an interest-free alternative to conventional banking. Invoking religious principles, several countries, among them Pakistan and Iran, have gone so far as to outlaw every form of interest; they are forcing all banks, including foreign subsidiaries, to adopt, at least formally, ostensibly Islamic methods of deposit taking and loan making. Attempts are also under way to disseminate religious norms of price setting, bargaining, and wage determination. And for every such initiative, others are on the drawing board.[15]

Kuran is skeptical about the role that Islamic economics might play. He goes on to point out that "of all economists of the Muslim faith, only a small minority . . . identify with some variant of this new doctrine. Yet the doctrine is socially significant, if only because it advances the sprawling and headline-grabbing movement known as 'political Islam,' 'Islamic fundamentalism,' or simply 'Islamism.' "

However, its proponents argue that the practice of Islamic economics could unite the strengths of both capitalism and socialism. It is based on three fundamental precepts: (1) an opposition to the use of interest, based on an interpretation of the Qur'an; (2) the adoption of the *zakat,* a form of voluntary redistribution; and (3) the

---

[14]"The Fascist conception of life," Mussolini wrote, "stresses the importance of the State and accepts the individual only in so far as his interests coincide with the State. It is opposed to classical liberalism [which] denied the State in the name of the individual; Fascism reasserts the rights of the State as expressing the real essence of the individual."

[15]Timur Kuran, "The Genesis of Islamic Economics: A Chapter in the Politics of Muslim Identity, *Social Research* 64, no. 2 (Summer 1997).

ECONOMICS AND 9/11

It is tempting to see the events of September 11, 2001, as the result of ideological conflict between Islam and capitalism. However, it is not really a conflict of two exclusionary creeds, as was perhaps the case in the cold war rivalry between capitalism and Soviet-style communism that preoccupied the world for more than 40 years. The resentment that led to September 11 arose from clear, deep historical and religious, as well as economic, roots. Some of it can be traced to the relative decline of Islam in the last 500 years. Islamic civilization was dominant in much of the world in the sixteenth century. At that time, Moslems held power from mid-Europe to Zanzibar and from Morocco to the East Indies. The European "voyages of discovery" were actually an incursion into a vast civilization that was learned, skilled, sophisticated, and urban. The following five centuries saw progressive decline in Islamic global influence, with the twentieth century particularly catastrophic. The defeat and division of the Ottoman Empire, the extension of western political interests to ensure the reliability of the oil supply and the establishment of the state of Israel all dealt severe blows and incited anti-Western feeling.

Today the countries of the world that either have Islam as their official religion or are inhabited in the majority by Moslems are generally much worse off in terms of income per head than are the inhabitants of the developed western nations. According to the World Bank Development Report 2000/2001, average income per head in the United States is about $30,600. The average income in terms of purchasing power parity for the 28 richest countries is $23,430 per year. In contrast the average for the 291 million people living in North Africa and the Middle East is only $4,600 per year, about one-fifth of the level. Some Moslem countries are even poorer. Indonesia, Pakistan, and Bangladesh, which are the most populous of the Islamic nations, have together a population of 370 million people. Average per-head incomes are $2,439, $1,757, and $1,475, respectively. On this rough basis we can see that the average Moslem is likely to have an income of about $3,000 a year, 10 percent of the average in the U.S. income.

Moreover, poverty is reflected in other measures. Fifteen percent of children in the Middle East and North Africa are affected by malnutrition, 136 children out of every 1,000 die before the age of 5, compared with 15 in 1,000 in the high-income nations, and life expectancy is 67 years compared to 78 years in the developed West. Such relative poverty might well be a cause of anger, and might be a contributory cause of anti-American terrorism but cannot be said to be the sole cause. Other nations' relative standing in terms of income and health is even lower.

Americans and other Westerners tend to see their affluence as flowing from their own hard work and the productivity of their institutions. They tend to believe that the key to prosperity abroad lies in adopting similar ethics and structures. Nonwesterners, especially Moslems today, are much more likely to see the affluence of the West and the poverty of their own societies in terms of a zero-sum game, and consider the prosperity of the West to be the result of conquest, tribute, or unequal exchange. This argument is particularly cogent with respect to the Moslem Middle East and East Indies, so well-endowed with natural resource wealth but lacking the living standards that should follow.

filtering of all economic decisions through Islamic moral norms. The most important of these ideas in practice is the prohibition on interest. Other societies attempted to do without the use of interest but none very successfully.[16]

---

[16]Similar restrictions on "usury" were placed by the Roman Catholic church, which is thought to have been one of the factors that impeded economic growth in the predominantly Catholic countries of the Mediterranean. See, for example, R. H. Tawney's *Religion and the Rise of Capitalism: A Historical Study* (New York: Harcourt Brace, 1926).

The Islamic economists' solution is to rely on the sharing of risk through equity rather than a secure lender advancing investment funds to a borrower. One Islamic economist has articulated the essential principles of Islamic finance:

[N]either the principal nor a rate of profit (tied up with the principal) can be guaranteed. The subscribers must enter into the fund with a clear understanding that the return on their subscription is tied up with the actual profit earned or loss suffered by the Fund. If the Fund earns huge profits, the return in their subscription will increase to that proportion; however, in case the Fund suffers loss, they will have to share it also, unless the loss is caused by the negligence or mismanagement, in which case the management, and not the Fund, will be liable to compensate it.[17]

. . . [T]he amounts so pooled together must be invested in a business acceptable to Shariah. It means that not only the channels of investment, but also the terms agreed with them must conform to the Islamic principles.[18]

Kuran argues that the prohibition of interest, so key to the theory of Islamic economics, is due to a misinterpretation of the Qur'an, which sought only to outlaw a particularly grievous practice, whereby the principle was doubled in the event of a default.[19] However, fundamentalists insist on the notion that it is immoral to earn income from capital without assuming risk. Instead of the use of loans, therefore,

PAKISTAN AND INTEREST FREE ECONOMICS

Although the use of interest is generally thought of as being against fundamentalist Islamic belief, it is generally tolerated in most countries. Recently Pakistan looked as if it were going to make a serious move toward eliminating the use of interest payments. The Federal Shariat Court (FSC) is an unusual institution charged under the Pakistani constitution with determining whether "any law or provision of law is repugnant to the injunctions of Islam." In 1999, the FSC determined that the laws and commercial code necessary to support the use of interest rates in banking were repugnant to Islam and ordered all such laws to be removed from the statute books. The government appealed to the Supreme Court of Pakistan, which upheld the decision of the FSC. The supreme court ordered that all such legislation supporting the use of interest should cease as of June 30, 2001. Fearing that this move would seriously affect the economy, the government questioned the competence of the FSC in this area and did little to facilitate removing the "obnoxious" legislation. In the aftermath of the invasion of Afghanistan the government seemed more resolved to resist the Islamic fundamentalists and nothing further occurred. We now must wait to assess the practicality of a major economy operating without the use of interest.

---

[17]This statement was written by Muft Taqi Usmani, an expert in the fields of Islamic law and economics and Hadith. For the past 35 years, he taught at the Darul-Uloom in Karachi, established by his father Mufti Muhammad Shafi, the late Grand Mufti of Pakistan.

[18]Islamic law.

[19]Timur Kuran, "Islamic Economics and the Islamic Sub-Economy," *Journal of Economic Perspectives* 9, no. 4 (Fall 1995), pp. 155–173.

business finance must be placed exclusively on a basis of shares or "equity" participation. Thus, the Islamic Development Bank, founded in 1974 by the Organization of the Islamic Conference to promote Qur'anic principles in the economies of member states, makes no loans but finances development projects only in return for a share of the profits, or for a "commission rate." This practice is not unknown, of course, in Western economies. Indeed, the entire venture capital industry, which financed much of the high-tech small company growth in the United States, relies on equity participation rather than loans.

However, as we will see later in this book, modern economics tends to stress the role of interest as "the price of capital," considered necessary for the efficient operation of an economy, especially in the intertemporal context. In some ways the problem for Islamic systems is parallel to that experienced by centrally planned economies, which, too, eschewed interest rates on principle. Without a market for finance, both the savings/investment decision and the choice of technique decision become more complex and prone to an inefficient outcome.

KEY TERMS AND CONCEPTS

balance of employment

balance of trade

commercial capitalism

communism

corn laws

corporatism

evolutionary school

fascism

feudalism

finance capitalism

"hydraulic" societies

industrial capitalism

Islamic economics

laws of motion

mercantilism

Oriental despotism

population growth

socialism

superstructure

technological change

welfare state

QUESTIONS FOR DISCUSSION

1. Why does technological change frequently cause changes in the economic system? Can different economic systems be compatible with a single technology?

2. Why did the system of irrigated agriculture practiced in much of South and East Asia allow the surplus to be appropriated by the state?

3. How did the revival of trade and the advent of the Black Death undermine the feudal system?

4. What economic rationale might be given for a merchant class to favor a balance of payments surplus?

5. In what ways did the repeal of the corn laws in Britain represent a victory for the manufacturing classes over the landowners?

6. In what ways did economic development on Continental Europe differ from development in Britain?

7. Distinguish between socialism and communism as economic systems. What defines a corporatist state?

8. "Fascism should be more correctly called corporatism." Should this statement be a criticism of contemporary corporate America?

9. What alternatives do Islamic economies use to handle the restriction on the use of interest rates?

RESOURCES

Web Sites

This chapter is largely concerned with economic history and the history of economic thought. A good starting point for any research into the history of economic thought is the "History of Economic Thought" Web site, which can now be found at the New School University Web site at http://cepa.newschool.edu/het/. It provides links to Web information on all major economists (living and dead), access to biographies, critiques, and economists' work that is downloadable from the Web. Two particularly useful sites in the context of this course are the following:

1. A searchable and downloadable copy of Adam Smith's *An Inquiry into the Nature and Causes of the Wealth of Nations*, available at http://www.econlib.org/library/Smith/smwn.html.

2. The Marx/Engels Internet Archive contains links to all of the Web-accessible work of Karl Marx and Friedrich Engels and other Marxists. It is available at http://www.marxists.org.

A growing number of sites provide information about Islamic economics from the point of view of its proponents. One with useful links can be found at http://www.islamic-economics.com/.

Books and Articles

Cameron, Rondo. *A Concise Economic History of the World,* 2d ed. (p. 363). Oxford: Oxford University Press, 1993.

Coleman, D. C. *Revisions in Mercantilism.* London: Methuen, 1969.

Farouqui, Mahmood (ed.). *Islamic Banking and Investment: Challenge and Opportunity.* New York: Kegan Paul, 1998.

Fei, John C. H., with Gustav Ranis (contributor). *Growth and Development from an Evolutionary Perspective.* London: Blackwell, 1997.

Hansen, Ejvind Damsgard. *European Economic History: From Mercantilism to Maastricht.* Copenhagen: Copenhagen Business School Press, 2001. Available at http://www. amazon.com/exec/obidos/tg/detail/-/8716134966/qid=1035745143/sr=1-1/ ref=sr_1_1/103-0666588-0560602?v=glance.

Hodgson, Geoffrey M. *Evolution and Institutions: On Evolutionary Economics and the Evolution of Economics.* White Plains, NY: Edward Elgar, 1999.

Kuran, Timur. "Islamic Economics and the Islamic Sub-Economy." *Journal of Economic Perspectives* 9, no. 4 (Fall 1995), 155–173.

Kuran, Timur. "The Genesis of Islamic Economics: A Chapter in the Politics of Muslim Identity." *Social Research* 64, no. 2 (Summer 1997).

Nelson, Richard. *Evolutionary Theory of Economic Change.* Cambridge: Harvard University Press, 1985.

Presley, John, and John Sessions. "Islamic Economics: The Emergence of a New Paradigm." *Economic Journal* 104 (May 1994), 584–596.

Schwartz, Herman. *States Versus Markets: History, Geography, and the Development of the International Political Economy.* New York: St. Martin's Press, 1994.

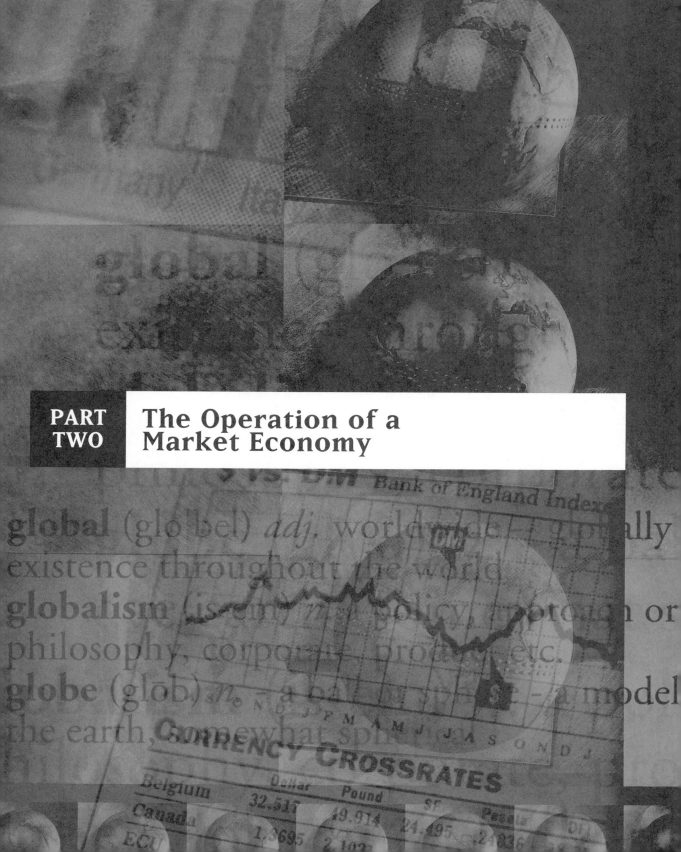

PART TWO

The Operation of a Market Economy

3

HOW A MARKET SYSTEM WORKS

ADAM SMITH AND THE INVISIBLE HAND

Adam Smith's description of the operation of a private property market system in his seminal work *An Inquiry into the Nature and Causes of the Wealth of Nations*, inspires an awe of the functioning of markets, rooted in the apparent paradox of his "invisible hand" theorem.[1] In Smith's conception, individuals act only to benefit themselves, yet, given certain preconditions, such behavior results in a social optimum. Selfish individuals collectively generate a level of efficiency and economic well-being that more "rational" systems of central planning are unable to match. In this chapter, we take a closer look at the operation of market capitalism. How, exactly, does a market system work? What are its essential features? Why does it perform so well in some areas—growth, allocative efficiency, and technological innovation—and what are its shortcomings?

Much of what we know about the market system today was well understood by Smith in 1776, although the tools that we use to analyze it differ. Smith argued that the ability to exchange and barter was both fundamental and universal to humankind. It was also unique, one of the things that set humans apart from the animals. In *The Wealth of Nations* he wrote:

> [T]he propensity to truck, barter, and exchange one thing for another . . . is common to all men, and is to be found in no other race of animals, which seem to know neither this nor any other species of contracts. Nobody ever saw a dog make a fair and deliberate exchange of one bone for another with another dog. Nobody ever saw one animal by its gestures and natural cries signify to another, this is mine, that yours; I am willing to give this for that.[2]

Another of Smith's important insights dealt with the need for specialization and **division of labor** in order to maximize the social product. Rather than meet all of their own needs, individuals are better served by concentrating on what they do

---

[1]Smith (1723–1790) was an eighteenth-century Scottish political economist and philosopher who laid the foundations of our understanding of the workings of competitive economies in his 1776 book *An Inquiry into the Nature and Causes of the Wealth of Nations*.

[2]Because the versions of *The Wealth of Nations* are so numerous, citing the page number of a particular edition might not be helpful to the reader. It is probably clearer to cite the book, chapter, and rough line number. This quote is from book I, chapter 2, line 4 and following. Links to useful hypertext version are given at the end of this chapter.

best and relying on exchange in the marketplace to meet their needs and to improve their welfare. In Smith's own language, it was

> the certainty of being able to exchange all that surplus part of the produce of his own labour, which is over and above his own consumption, for such parts of the produce of other men's labour as he may have occasion for, encourages every man to apply himself to a particular occupation, and to cultivate and bring to perfection whatever talent or genius he may possess for that particular species of business. The difference of natural talents in different men is, in reality, much less than we are aware of; and the very different genius which appears to distinguish men of different professions, when grown up to maturity, is not upon many occasions so much the cause, as the effect of the division of labour.[3]

The ability to specialize and exchange, coupled with the single-minded pursuit of their own interests, leads individuals to serve the public good in a much more effective way than if they altruistically sought to benefit others. This concept is the essence of Smith's **invisible hand**, one of the most compelling and important metaphors in modern social thought. It can be seen as both paradoxical and beautiful, in that individual self-interest leads to a social optimum much more effectively than when people try to promote the general well-being. In fact, as the last two sentences of this quotation reveal, Smith harbored a deep cynicism of the motives of people who claimed to act in the public good:

> [An individual] intends only his own gain, and he is in this, as in many other cases, led by an invisible hand to promote an end which was no part of his intention. Nor is it always the worse for the society that it was no part of it. By pursuing his own interest, he frequently promotes that of the society more effectually that when he really intends to promote it. I have never known much good done by those who affected to trade for the public good. It is an affectation, indeed, not very common among merchants, and very few words need be employed in dissuading them from it.[4]

MARKETS IN A MODERN ECONOMY

Smith's insights into the operation of markets remain in many respects as valid today as in the eighteenth century when he first made them. However, in the increasing complexity of modern economies, every economy based on exchange consists of many thousands of individual markets, for example, financial markets, labor markets (which exist for many different kinds of labor), agricultural markets, markets for intermediate goods, and so on. These markets do not function in isolation but are linked so that each one interacts in some way with the others. Changes in the taste for a single good require adjustment not only in its own market but also in all other markets; the present and future prices of labor, intermediate goods price, and factors of production will all change, perhaps only to some infinitesimally small degree. Because the consequences for other markets are in many cases

---

[3]Book I, chapter 2, line 30 and following.
[4]Book IV, chapter 2, line 40 and following.

small, economists often look at the impact of a disturbance on a single market alone. This approach is called **partial equilibrium**. However, we must always be aware of the impacts felt in all other markets, on all goods and factors, in all places and times. The full effect leads to an adjustment to a new **general equilibrium**.

Acting together, these markets determine a price for all goods, factors, and services, and they also determine the quantities of each that will be supplied. It is instructive to consider the alternative to reliance on the market to make these decisions. If a planning authority made all these decisions, the amount of information required at the center of the economy would be huge. Planners would need to estimate the demand for products and gear the entire production process toward its satisfaction. The ability of a market system to coordinate itself in the absence of a central coordinating authority provides one of its most appealing features.

Goods Markets

To illustrate this market function, let us begin by looking at a single market for a good, depicted in Figure 3.1. The tools we will need are familiar to most students from their work in introductory and intermediate economic theory, and a thorough review of that material would be beneficial. Here we look only at some important features of competitive markets, focusing on issues of supply and demand. Dr. Johnson, Adam Smith's contemporary, acerbically observed that he could teach a parrot all that was essential about economics if he could get it to say the two words *supply* and *demand.* Although this generalization oversimplifies the issue, the important features of competitive markets can be illustrated using these concepts.

On one side of the analysis we find a **market demand curve, D**. It consists of an array of pairs of prices and quantities that reflect how much of a good the individuals who compose the market would be willing to purchase at given prices. This market demand curve is an aggregation of the demands of individuals, households, firms, and government. It is in a sense an abstraction, and valid only instantaneously, based on the assumption that the prices of all other goods, as well as

■ **FIGURE 3.1**

A Simple Market Model

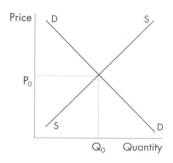

incomes and tastes, are constant. We expect and assume the demand curve to be downward sloping, which reflects the generally held principle that for all consumers the more of a good that they possess the less they will value the last, or marginal, unit of that good.

On the other hand we note the **market supply curve, S**. Like the demand curve, it indicates the collection of pairs of prices and quantities. This curve reflects how much the market participants would be prepared to sell at various prices. In the case of a good that can be newly produced (let us say agricultural products or manufactured goods), the supply curve appears as upward sloping because marginal costs of production are assumed to rise (in the medium term at least) as production increases. The intersection of the supply curve and the demand curve gives us the equilibrium price—that price at which the consumers will be able to buy all that they wish to and the sellers will be able to part with exactly what they want to sell. For a market to be competitive, many sellers and many buyers are necessary, and no one seller or buyer is important enough to affect the sale price. The price therefore moves to equilibrate the demand and the supply sides of the market, without any one individual or firm decisively influencing the outcome.

Two things should be noted here. First, neither demand nor supply curves are readily observable. The point defined by the equilibrium price and quantity pair is the only one that we actually observe on either curve.[5] Second, because of the interaction of the many thousands of markets, equilibrium in any product market is likely to be a fleeting affair. Conditions in other markets will change, creating changes in all markets as the interactive system searches, constantly, for a general equilibrium.

An important feature of markets is that, under competitive assumptions, the market price of a good will be equal to its marginal cost of production. This result follows because the equilibrium price lies on the supply curve, and the supply curve is the aggregation of the marginal cost curves of suppliers. Because the equilibrium price also lies on the demand curve, we can be sure that it will also be equal to the valuation that the marginal consumer puts on his or her last unit of purchase. Thus a competitive market ensures that goods will be produced up to, and not beyond, the point where the marginal cost of production is equal to the value that the marginal consumer places on it. If all markets were competitive, then all prices would be equal to their marginal costs. Economic theory further tells us that this outcome would be efficient in the sense that no other allocation of resources could produce more of any one good without reducing the output of another. It also appeals to some people as being equitable. Those who consume goods must pay the marginal costs of production of those goods.

A Shift in Demand What happens if the demand for a good changes as a result of some exogenous event? As a first example, consider a shift in consumer tastes favoring the good, which is represented in Figure 3.1. The higher demand is represented by a shift in the demand curve to the right—more is demanded at every

---

[5]Using econometric techniques we are able, under certain conditions, to estimate both curves.

price of the good. The adjustment to this disturbance can be looked at in three phases. In the short run, the supply of the good is fixed, and the supply curve S_{Short} will be perfectly inelastic, or vertical. The full response to the change in demand will be reflected by price change. The price of the good will increase sharply from P_0 to P_S reflecting the short-term scarcity. Those fortunate enough to be holding stocks of the good will be able to reap **windfall profits**. This scenario appears in Figure 3.2, where the shaded area reflects those windfall profits.

In the medium term, shown in Figure 3.3, the higher prices will encourage existing producers to increase their output, probably by hiring additional labor. Capital, which is normally regarded as invariate in the medium term, cannot be increased within this time frame. Only variable inputs (usually labor) can be changed. Therefore the supply curve S_{Medium} is upward sloping and moderately elastic (responsive to price). The additional output $(Q_M - Q_0)$ is produced at higher marginal cost than the original output, because on average each worker is working with less capital than previously. The "law of diminishing returns" suggests that as variable inputs (labor) are increased against a fixed input (capital) the marginal product of labor will fall. However, the rate of return on capital will rise, because capital is now relatively scarce in this industry. The higher than average rate represents "economic profit" and will attract new capital to the industry, lowering marginal costs and establishing a new long-term equilibrium.

Economic profits, defined as returns on capital above the normal rate, are vital for the efficient functioning of a market system in responding to changes. Such profits, or their equally important counterpart, economic losses, are generated in the short term and medium term when shifts occur in supply or demand. Profits and losses, therefore, are signaling devices in a market system. The existence in some industries or product lines of rates of return on capital that are above the economy-wide average, or normal, rate of return will cause capital to flow to those sectors. This capital will, in turn, lead to increased output, moderated prices, and the eventual complete erosion of the super-normal profits. Most important, capital will flow into those industries where its productivity is greatest, leading to a more

■ **FIGURE 3.2**

Adjustment to Demand Shift in the Short Run

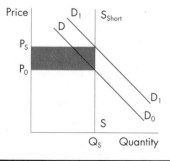

■ FIGURE 3.3

Adjustment to Demand Shift in the Medium Term

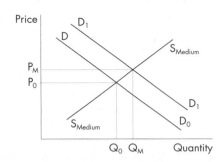

efficient allocation of resources. Figure 3.4 illustrates the consequences of this capital inflow. The long-run supply curve S_{Long} is likely to be more elastic (flatter) than its short and medium counterparts. The increase in consumer demand results in increased output and only moderately increased prices, which reflect the marginal cost of the production of the good after new investment enters the industry.

Innovation Let us consider now a second form of market disturbance. A single supplier makes an innovation in the production process that results in a lower marginal cost of production. Initially the single supplier who is the only producer to make this innovation will earn excess profits in the form of "economic rent." **Economic rent** is a return over and above the average rate of profit. This rent accrues to the supplier because of ownership of a specific factor of production; in this case the productive innovation. The rent will be earned as long as the innovator holds the monopoly of this knowledge and in all likelihood market share will

■ FIGURE 3.4

Adjustment to Demand Shift in the Long Run

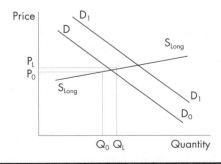

increase. In the long term, other producers must either match the cost savings that result from the innovation or go out of business.

The market encourages innovation by providing unusually high rates of return to those producers that successfully introduce a cost-saving improvement. The same process in effect requires that all producers match the innovation or improve on it, or they will lose their market share to more efficient competitors.

Other Disturbances We could show in a similar diagrammatic fashion how the market deals with other kinds of disturbances. A sudden exogenous reduction in supply (represented by a shift of the supply curve to left) will again, under conditions of constant demand, yield windfall profits to the remaining producers and provide incentives to channel new investment into the industry. A sharp exogenous increase in supply (a rightward shift in the supply curve) will result in the reverse effect. It will lower the market price and cut the rate of return in the industry below the level of the economy at large. New investment will be diverted from the industry to other uses, and when the historically committed capital is depleted by depreciation it will not be replaced until average rates of return rise to the economy-wide level.

Requirements for Market Efficiency

Perfect markets require such an exacting set of preconditions that we can, by and large, dismiss their existence in the real world. For example, perfection would require that all participants in the market know all prices for all goods and factors, both current and future. A more realistic concern centers on whether markets are reasonably allocatively efficient and handle the task of answering the essential economic questions in the fashion most prone to increase consumer welfare. Even this lesser standard requires a number of preconditions, some of which may not be met, resulting in "market failures." We mentioned some of these in passing. For example, efficient markets are characterized by many suppliers and many buyers so that there is no accretion of market power to be exploited. Efficiency also requires good information. Buyers must be aware of the prices of all substitute goods and need to know about the future movement of prices. Producers must be similarly well-informed about the prices of other potential products, as well as raw materials and factors of production.

The Role of the Entrepreneur The existence of the **entrepreneur** is vitally important for the efficient functioning of markets. The establishment of a super-normal rate of profit as a signal proves effective only insofar as someone recognizes, appreciates, and acts upon the signal. In the eighteenth-century world of Adam Smith, as well as in the nineteenth-century milieu of Alfred Marshall,[6] the

---

[6]Alfred Marshall (1842–1924), an Englishman, is regarded by many as the father of modern economics. Marshall's work pioneered the marginalist or neoclassical model of the functioning economy. A useful Web site for investigating the life of Marshall and for accessing many of his works is http://cepa. newschool.edu/het/profiles/marshall.htm.

ownership of capital and the management of business were by and large embodied in the same people. These entrepreneurs represented restless, potentially footloose capital, which was mobile enough to flow into industries in which profits were unusually high. One question that hangs over the analysis of contemporary markets is whether institutional change, particularly the separation of ownership from management, leads to the weakening of entrepreneurial activity, and a consequent reduction in market efficiency.

Factor Markets

So far we have discussed the functioning of markets for goods, but an efficient system also requires the market mechanisms to determine the allocation of factors of production (capital, land, and labor) between competing uses. Similar basic principles apply here as in the goods markets. In a free enterprise system individuals can offer their labor to any employer. Generally they will choose that occupation and employer who offers the highest wages or compensation package, although nonpecuniary factors like job satisfaction, working conditions, hours of work, and security of job tenure will also play a part in a worker's rational choice.

The employer in turn is free to hire as much labor as he or she chooses and will be indifferent between workers as long as they all contribute the same amount to output. It is a normal assumption of economics that, at least after a certain point, the marginal product of workers declines, the result of an important observed generality termed the *law of diminishing marginal returns*.[7] Employers will hire labor up to the point where the contribution that the marginal worker makes to revenues (termed the **marginal revenue product**) equals the wage that must be paid. If hiring proceeds beyond this point, under diminishing returns, additional workers will reduce profit. If all workers are indistinguishable in terms of their contribution, and therefore interchangeable, then the wage will be the same for all and will be equal to the revenue product of the marginal worker.

This situation embodies again both efficiency and a form of fairness. The worker is paid the contribution that he or she makes to the revenue of the enterprise. If this marginal revenue product were greater in other employment, the worker would, everything else being equal, change jobs and earn the higher wage. This migration to other employers would happen because the owner or manager of the firm in which the worker's marginal revenue product were greater would offer the worker a higher wage to leave his or her current occupation. No employer would offer more than its marginal product, but each would be prepared to pay up to that amount. The employer to whom the worker is most valuable would win out. This competitive process ensures that workers are employed in their socially highest value use, which would, in its turn, produce an efficient outcome for the economy as a whole. It can also be argued that this process is in a sense equitable, because each worker is paid the amount by which he or she increases the social product. Even though this feature of market systems appeals to some, to others it reveals a

---

[7]Like all economic laws, the law of diminishing marginal returns is a generalized assumption based on both reasoning and observation.

more problematic proposition and one that merits further examination in Chapter 4 when we consider whether the distribution of well-being that results in a market economy may appropriately be considered as a failure of the system.

Capital Markets

In a modern market economy the **capital market** plays a particularly central role. In the eighteenth or nineteenth century, it was often true that a single entrepreneur was both the manager of the enterprise and the owner of the capital. Today, enterprises are larger and much more use is made of financial intermediaries to provide the funds for investment. Small savers place their money in banks for which they receive interest payments, and these resources are commingled and loaned by the banks to firms. Alternatively, a firm can turn to venture capitalists for a loan (usually pledging some share of future profits) or issue instruments of debt, corporate bonds, in order to gather investment funds. A further avenue is provided by the sale of stocks or shares in the future profit stream of the enterprise.

The function of financial markets is to assess the combination of expected returns and potential risks and to allocate the capital to those ventures that offer the best combination of risk and return. In the case of a bank-financed start-up, the entrepreneur must present a business plan and collateral and the loan officer of the bank must decide whether the potential borrower is creditworthy. The bank wants to loan its limited resources to those borrowers with the highest probability of repayment. Alternatively, if the entrepreneur seeks finance by issuing stock, she or he will try to sell the shares into the stock market at an appropriate price. In this way the financial markets are the midwives for new ventures. Acting together, the individual actors will allocate society's scarce capital resources among potential users. It is important for the efficiency of the system that they act impartially, focusing solely on the hard financial facts, and remain unswayed by personal or political factors.

As well as providing means for the birth and growth of firms, the financial markets also act as undertakers, even executioners, by ensuring that existing firms whose prospects do not merit continued investment are culled from the system. By refusing to issue new loans, or by the protracted fall in the value of companies' shares, the financial markets signal to the management and ownerships of firms a judgment concerning the prospects and performance of the firm. In the short term this signal can just be a warning to mend its ways; in the longer term it is a death sentence. Michael Keren expressed this idea well:

> The capital market as well as providing for the birth of firms, also provides for their death, and for changes in their course in midlife. It plays a Darwinian role of selection. As in Darwinian natural evolution, here too the role of chance is great and the dependence on time is paramount. What succeeds today may be what failed yesterday, because yesterday was not ripe for the idea, or because it was not properly packaged.[8]

Most important, the judgment of the capital market is an impartial one. It is not the opinion of an individual, a politician, or even a "National Board of Investment"

---

[8]From "On the (Im)possibility of Market Socialism," *Eastern Economic Review* 19, no. 3 (1993), p. 333.

that motivates the decision in a free market economy, but the result of the interplay of many groups. The verdict is a weighted one that takes into account the informed views of a range of people. Bankers, loan officers, fund managers, and individual investors must all make the best informed decisions that they can, otherwise the capital that they own or manage will be lost. A loan officer who shows protracted and systematic bias puts at risk both job and future of the bank. A fund manager who favors pet theories that run counter to logic will see performance suffer and have less capital to manage. The dispassionate function of capital markets is one of the strengths of the market system.

As we shall see in subsequent chapters of this book, one of the drawbacks of centralized socialist planning is the pervasive influence of what is known as a **soft-budget constraint**. This phenomenon was observed long ago. In the 1930s the Austrian economist Ludwig von Mises[9] attacked the theory of socialism on the grounds that rational calculation was impossible without a clearly defined "bottom line."[10] However, the seminal work on the soft-budget constraint, and the coining of the term itself, was by an "insider," the Hungarian economist Janos Kornai[11] who observed firsthand, under central planning, the operation of an economy without capital markets. He noted that in the absence of impartiality in credit and investment funds, and with the lack of a mechanism to gauge and act on performance, an enterprise manager will feel little incentive to perform in a socially efficient way. Rather the manager can make more efficient use of time influencing those politicians and planners who determine access to credit. Instead of being confronted by a "hard" budget constraint, where the amount that they could spend or borrow relates to performance, managers operating under a soft-budget constraint have their fate determined in large part by the degree to which they are favored by their political masters.

Arbitrage and Speculation

Profits are important in a market system because they attract the attention of entrepreneurs and channel new capital into an industry. However, the quest for profit is also vital in keeping the markets themselves "orderly"—that is to say, consistent across space and time. The differential in the price of a good between any two geographical points should be no greater than the cost of transportation between those points. Orderly markets require the action of **arbitrageurs** who engage in a simultaneous transaction of buying where the price is high and selling where the price is low, earning a profit at least enough to cover the transaction and transportation costs.

The orderly nature of markets is furthered by the activity of **speculators**. Unlike arbitrageurs, speculators take a position based on the direction they anticipate

---

[9]Von Mises (1881–1973) was considered by Milton Friedman to have done more to spread the fundamental ideas of free markets than any other individual. The curious can start their search at http://cepa.newschool.edu/het/profiles/mises.htm.

[10]See Ludwig von Mises, *Socialism: An Economic and Sociological Analysis,* 2d ed. (New Haven: Yale University Press, 1951).

[11]See "The Soft Budget Constraint," *Kyklos* 39 (1986).

prices will move. Investing in shares traded on a stock exchange or the commodities traded on a mercantile exchange is classic speculative activity. It is a popular misconception that speculators increase the volatility of markets. Pure speculation will be profitable only if the speculator "buys low and sells high." A speculator, therefore, increases the demand for the good at the bottom of a price cycle and increases the supply when the price it at the highest. Thus speculation actually reduces the amplitude of market swings and assists in the efficient operation of markets. The exception occurs when the speculator is successful in gaining significant market power and in the extreme can become a monopolist by cornering the market.

CHARACTERISTICS OF THE MARKET SYSTEM

A competitive market system is characterized by a number of advantageous features worth briefly reviewing here:

Under a Market System Disequilibria Are Self-Correcting

Self-correction is certainly one of the most important features of a market system. Because of the flexible prices, disequilibria created by supply shocks or demand shifts invoke a coordinated and automatic response. Any disturbance in the system will set in motion a series of reactions that will adjust the entire system to take account of the changed circumstances, resulting in **self-correcting disequilibria**. Consider a rise in demand. As a first-order effect, the price of the good itself will rise, as will the factors of production and materials that go into making it. The prices of substitutes will rise too, those of complements will fall. Thousands of prices will change in thousands of markets without any central authority directing it. Under central planning the whole menu of prices would require adjustment, relying on ad hoc decisions or models to arrive at a new equilibrium.

An example of this process of adjustment was provided by the market response to the oil shocks of the 1970s. As an example it is complicated by the fact that some "free market" governments (including the United States) acted to impose price controls that prevented the market mechanism from adjusting swiftly and fully to the shock. However, what we did see was a restriction of supply, creating short-run profits and precipitating a series of further adjustments. Higher prices encouraged reduced consumption of oil and oil products. Homes became better insulated, thermostat sales increased, car engines became smaller. Industry sought new, less energy-intensive techniques. The prices of energy substitutes rose, and returns to capital and labor in those industries increased. New sources of supply were brought on line; new capital was invested in oil exploration, production, and oil field rehabilitation. Some believed it to be a potentially catastrophic blow to the global economy. By the early 1980s, however, market action absorbed and corrected those events. Government policy, whether price controls or promotion of alternative fuels, had little impact on the resolution of the crisis. In the Soviet bloc coun-

tries, energy prices did not change substantially despite the shift in world prices. Those countries continued with cheap energy, energy-intensive production techniques, and waste until the end of the 1980s, with damaging consequences for their competitiveness when they ultimately emerged into the world economy.

Markets Minimize the Need for Information Flows

For a planning agency to engineer the complex adjustment to prices, quantities, and production techniques across the board that the response to the oil shock produced, and to get the response right, it would have to be both extremely well informed and rather lucky. The market system relies on no such centralization of information. The individual actors in the system need only to know the information required for each unit to maximize its own welfare. No one individual or agency needs access to all price and cost information, and no one needs a full understanding how the whole system works. Thomas Schelling put it this way:

> The dairy farmer doesn't need to know how many people eat butter and how far away they are, how many other people raise cows, how many babies drink milk, or whether more money is spent on beer or milk. What he needs to know is the prices of different feeds, the characteristics of different cows, the different prices [for milk], the relative cost of hired labor and electrical machinery, and what his net earnings might be if he sold his cows and raised pigs instead.[12]

This economy of information is valuable. It saves the expense of collection and relay of data, and the resource cost of the bureaucracy to process it, issue directives, and monitor the fulfillment of the objectives. Perhaps most important, the market offers few opportunities to gain advantage by falsifying data or misrepresenting a situation. As we shall see when we discuss the economic consequences of the centrally planned economy in more detail in Chapter 17, the information gathered by central planners is frequently flawed because the enterprise managers in planned systems encounter incentives to provide inaccurate information to the center. In some cases they might deliberately understate their potential output, enabling them to limit their production quotas. In other cases they might overstate their need for material inputs. Gathering data is expensive, and checking the accuracy of data may be prohibitive. A system that minimizes information demands and decentralizes decision making avoids the problems of a whole system orientating itself on data that are themselves faulty.

A Market System Provides Stimulus to Innovation

Under a market system **innovators** who pioneer new, lower-cost processes or new products that appeal to consumers are rewarded in the short run by **super-normal profits**, or economic rent. It costs resources to develop new processes or goods, and

---

[12]Cited in Richard Lipsey, Peter Steiner, Douglas Purvis, and Paul Courant, *Economics,* 9th ed. (New York: Harper and Row, 1990), p. 423.

in a market system this investment is made in the expectation of gain through profit. Many innovative ventures fail, and the would-be innovator loses the investment, but some that greatly affect our well-being prove successful.

A planned system, on the other hand, leaves the development of new products largely to the research agencies of the state. An enterprise manager has little incentive to research new techniques or goods other than those that he or she is charged to adopt or produce by the planners. Attempts at innovation could only prove a distraction, taking the manager's attention and budgeted resources away from the prime task of meeting physical production targets.

Under a Market System Relative Prices Reflect Relative Costs

Under a competitive system, the tendency is for the price of a good to be driven toward the marginal cost of its production. At the margin of his or her consumption, therefore, the consumer must be prepared to pay the costs of the inputs and factors used in the production of the marginal unit of the good. The relative prices of goods thus reflect the relative costs of the production. This relationship is sometimes expressed in microeconomic terms as: The marginal rate of substitution in consumption is equal to the marginal rate of transformation in production. This outcome is allocatively efficient. Society directs its scarce resources toward the production of goods that demonstrate the highest values in the eyes of the consumer, maximizing social welfare. An increase in the cost of a resource will raise the cost of the good in whose production it is used. When governments intervene and determine either the quantities of goods to be produced or the prices that shall be charged for them, it is more than likely that relative prices and relative costs of production will diverge. This problem is not seen exclusively in centrally planned economies either. Western governments frequently use price controls to depress the costs of goods or services that politicians, in the name of equity, think should be cheap, generally with unfortunate results for both long-term supply and allocative efficiency.

A Market System Opposes the Concentration of Power

As we shall see when we look at the behavior of planned economies, their function requires combining political and economic power. The political masters not only control the lives of the citizenry through the legal system, but they also control their real incomes through the availability of goods and the prices charged for them. A highly competitive market structure discourages the concentration of economic power. Again, we note that the kind of capitalist market systems we actually confront allows for considerable accretion of economic power. The leaders of industry and trade unions do hold considerable power, both in the marketplace itself and through lobbying in the halls of government. In the late nineteenth century, economic power in the United States became so concentrated that it motivated the intervention of government to break up the mammoth trusts that emerged. The 1950s and 1960s saw considerable alarm over the possibility that the economic and political systems of the developed market economies were evolving into a form of corporatism, but one in which the state was subsidiary to the needs of the corporations rather than vice versa.[13] The sovereignty of the consumer is constantly under threat, but compared to the concentration of power that occurred in the Soviet Union under communism or that is still observed in China today, the consequences were modest.

Even if the leaders of an authoritarian state are well-intentioned and seek nothing but the general good of the population, the task of organization and necessary coercion are so onerous that relying on the enterprise of individuals is more likely to render a happier conclusion. This belief too was held by Adam Smith, and we conclude this chapter with another quote from his most insightful work:

> All systems either of preference or of restraint, therefore, being thus completely taken away, the obvious and simple system of natural liberty establishes itself of its own accord. Every man, as long as he does not violate the laws of justice, is left perfectly free to pursue his own interest in his own way and to bring both his industry and capital into competition with those of any other man or order of men. The sovereign is completely discharged from a duty, in the attempting to perform which he must always be exposed to innumerable delusions and for the proper performance of which no human wisdom or knowledge could ever be sufficient—the duty of superintending the industry of private people and of directing it toward the employments most suitable to the interest of the society. . . . [T]he sovereign has only three duties to attend to; three duties of great importance, indeed, but plain and intelligible to common understandings: first, the duty of protecting the society from the violence and invasion of other independent societies; secondly, the duty of protecting, as far as possible, every member of the society from the injustice or oppression of every other member of it, or the duty of establishing an exact administration of justice; and thirdly, the duty of erecting and maintaining certain public works and certain public institutions.[14]

KEY TERMS AND CONCEPTS

arbitrageurs	market demand curve
capital market	market supply curve
division of labor	partial equilibrium
economic rent	self-correcting disequilibria
entrepreneur	soft-budget constraint
general equilibrium	speculators
innovators	super-normal profits
invisible hand	windfall profits
marginal revenue product	

---

[13]These ideas about the concentration of economic and political power in the United States were addressed in John Kenneth Galbraith's *The New Industrial State.*
[14]Adam Smith, *An Inquiry into the Nature and Causes of the Wealth of Nations,* book IV, chapter IX.

QUESTIONS FOR DISCUSSION

1. Describe the role of profit and the role of the entrepreneur in correcting disequilibria.

2. Why are arbitrage and speculation important for the orderly operation of markets?

3. Why are market systems economical in the need for centralizing data?

4. Why is it important for relative prices to reflect relative costs of production in general?

5. What economic functions does Smith conceive of as being the preserve of the sovereign?

6. Why is the capital market both "midwife" and "undertaker"?

7. How does a competitive market system oppose the concentration of power?

8. Is the tendency of wages to reflect the marginal revenue product under competition a recipe for "fairness"?

RESOURCES

Web Sites

The History of Economic Thought ....http://cepa.newschool.edu/het/
More about Smith, Marshall, and von Mises can be found at this site.

The von Mises Institute ....http://www.mises.org/
The von Mises Institute is a libertarian think tank and lobby group.

The Cato Institute ....http://www.cato.org/
A great deal of other libertarian information and ideas can be found at this site.

The Adam Smith Institute ....http://www.adamsmith.org/
Devoted to the study of the founder of the modern Anglo-American approach to economics.

Books and Articles

Fry, Michael (ed.). *Adam Smith's Legacy: His Place in the Development of Modern Economics.* New York: Routledge, 1992.

Galbraith, John Kenneth. *The New Industrial State.* Boston: Houghton Mifflin, 1971.

Keren, Michael. "On the (Im)possibility of Market Socialism." *Eastern Economic Review* 19, no. 3 (1993), 333–344.

Kornai, Janos. *The Socialist System: The Political Economy of Communism.* Princeton: Princeton University Press, 1992.

Kornai, Janos. "The Soft Budget Constraint." *Kyklos* 39, no. 1 (1986), 3–30.

Smith, Adam. *The Wealth of Nations*, D. D. Raphael (ed.). London: Everyman's Library Series, 1991.

von Mises, Ludwig. *Economic Calculation in the Socialist Commonwealth*. Auburn, AL: Ludwig von Mises Institute, 1990.

4

MARKET FAILURE AND GOVERNMENT FAILURE

At the close of Chapter 3, we saw that Adam Smith envisaged the task of government as highly limited and beneficent only in three areas: national defense, the administration of justice, and in certain large-scale infrastructural investments that private industry would not, or could not, assume. However, a glance at any modern market economy reveals that government activity is not confined to these areas but extends into production, regulation, and redistribution. In the wealthy countries of the Organization for Economic Cooperation and Development (OECD) governments take in and spend an average of about 40 percent of gross domestic product (GDP).[1] Despite the common political rhetoric of the 1980s and 1990s on the need to downsize government, the trend, measured in terms of governments' share of GDP, seems to be inexorably upward.[2] How is such widespread interference in the market economy explained? The two main answers include (1) the correction of several well-known instances of "market failure" and (2) the redistribution of the social product toward disadvantaged, primarily economically inactive, groups.

MARKET FAILURE

One general justification for government intervention in the operation of free enterprise economy is **market failure**. Although many modern economies are characterized by highly competitive markets for some products and factors of production, the conditions necessary to establish perfect competition in all markets are seldom encountered. We briefly list the four phenomena considered to lead to serious inefficiencies here:

1. **Market power.** The possession of substantial market power by a single or small group of market participants creates conditions under which prices deviate from marginal costs, an allocatively inefficient outcome. Similarly we might encounter market power in the supply of labor through unionization,

---

[1] Average general government receipts comprised 38.2 percent of GDP in the OECD nations in 1996. Disbursements averaged 41 percent, creating an average general government deficit of 2.8 percent of GDP.
[2] This apparently universal and irresistible trend is labeled *Wagner's law,* after the work of the nineteenth-century German political economist Adolph Wagner.

implying that the price of labor will differ from the value of its marginal product.

2. **Lack of information.** Any inability of relevant market participants to access relevant information at reasonable cost prevents them from acting in an economically rational fashion.

3. **Public goods.** Goods that are nonrival in consumption and for which the marginal cost of supply is zero will not be produced in efficient quantities by a private market.

4. **Externalities.** Outcomes based on private costs and private benefits are inefficient when social costs and social benefits are economically significant.

Government intervention is frequently viewed as a corrective to these problems, but in recent years action by the government is criticized as more harmful than the market imperfections that occasioned it. In this chapter we first examine the rationale for such intervention and then assess to what degree government action is likely to benefit, rather than harm, the general welfare.

Sources of Market Failure: Market Power

Markets function efficiently only when no participant holds substantial market power. Such power may be found on either side of the market. However, it is power on the supply side, monopoly (a single seller) and oligopoly (a few sellers) are considered as most injurious to economic welfare and the frequent target of governmental legislative, judicial, and regulatory activity. Market power on the buying side (monopsony) is considered less harmful to public welfare and is rarely a target of regulatory activity.[3]

The Problem of Monopoly

In perfectly competitive markets, firms act as **price takers**, facing a horizontal, or infinitely elastic, demand curve. Any deviation of price from that dictated by the market will result either in a lower than normal profit rate, untenable in the long run, or a total loss of sales to lower-priced producers. Competitive pressures ensure that the market price is equal to the marginal cost of production. Whenever markets are not perfectly competitive, the demand curve that a firm faces is not horizontal but slopes downward; the firm becomes a **price setter** as it exercises some control over the prices that it charges.

Confronted by downward-sloping demand curves, profit-maximizing firms restrict production, raise prices, and, therefore, generate economic profits, returns above the "normal rate" for all industries. In the case of monopoly the existence of

---

[3]In fact monopsony is most likely to lie with the government, which is often the sole purchaser of defense output and which in the welfare states of many European countries is the sole purchaser of health-related goods. Little harm to the general welfare derives from this form of monopsony, which is frequently seen as a "countervailing power" to monopoly power.

barriers to entry prevents these super-normal profits from serving their important economic function, which should be to attract new entrants and capital into the industry that would, over time, return the profit rate to normal. Importantly, monopoly drives a wedge between the price that the buyer must pay and the marginal cost of production. Reduced consumption and lost consumers' surplus then create economic inefficiency as illustrated in Figure 4.1. The monopolist maximizes profit by setting output at the point where marginal cost is equal to marginal revenue. This results in a lower output than might be the case under competition Q_M as opposed to Q_C, and a higher price, P_M as opposed to P_C. The loss of welfare is denoted by the triangle labeled "Deadweight loss in consumption."

Monopoly also results in a transfer of welfare from consumers to the monopolist, as shown in Figure 4.1 by the area labeled monopoly profit. Such a transfer is not a loss to society in which both consumer and monopolist are members, but because it is often seen as inequitable and it can be at least as important as the deadweight loss in motivating government action. Correction of this form of market failure, in order to promote efficiency and protect consumers, is considered in many countries a reason for government action.

Natural Monopoly Economists traditionally distinguished between two forms of monopoly. One, usually termed **natural monopoly**, occurs because of high fixed costs and declining or constant marginal costs, which cause the long-run average cost curve to be falling across the relevant output quantities. Competition can be created only at the cost of the expensive and wasteful replication of facilities. In

■ **FIGURE 4.1**

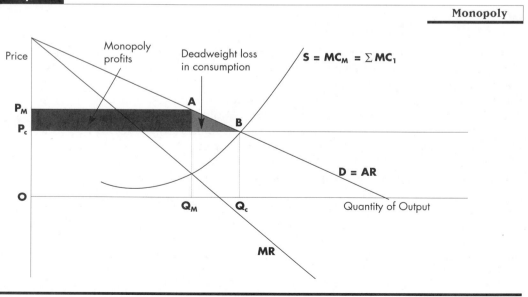

Monopoly

such cases monopoly is generally tolerated, but it is modified by government action, generally through the control of prices by a public agency.

Natural monopoly commonly can be found in industries in which high fixed costs result from extensive initial capital investment. Electricity supply, telephone networks, and TV cable distribution are frequently cited as typical examples of natural monopoly. The existence of natural monopoly in fact involves a dual problem. As shown in Figure 4.2, in the absence of price regulation, a profit-maximizing monopoly would fix output at Q_M and price at P_M, thus earning profits in excess of the normal rate of return and providing a rationale for government intervention to fix the price, usually through the activity of a public utility commission.

However, after the decision to regulate is made, the appropriate price remains a subject of contention. From an efficiency point of view, a case can be made for regulators to fix the price at marginal cost. In Figure 4.2, we can see that in declining average cost industries marginal cost lies below average cost for all relevant output levels. Marginal cost pricing would give a price of P_E, and would require an output of Q_E. However, at such a price, revenues would fail to cover the total costs of the enterprise. Such policy would require a subsidy (ideally in the form of a block grant) to the utility from the government to cover fixed costs. The political unattractiveness of subsidies of this kind often stimulate common "compromise" solutions in which regulatory commissions fix the price at average total cost, as shown in the diagram as P_R. This price, above the marginal cost, allows the utility to cover all fixed and variable costs including a "normal" rate of return on capital.

- **FIGURE 4.2**

Natural Monopoly

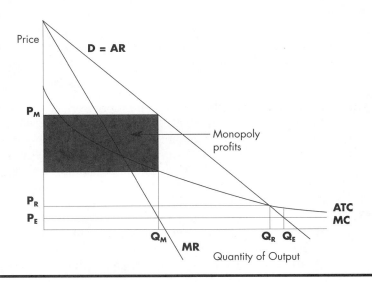

This solution avoids the "gouging" potentiality of an unregulated monopoly, but it does dilute incentives to strive for optimal efficiency. It also presents the possibility of capture of the regulatory agency by the regulatee, a topic we will return to as an example of "government failure."

Natural monopolies do not represent a fixed and unchanging set of industries but are a function of the state of technology. They are a much less significant phenomenon in the long run than in the short run, and economists now regard them as a less of an impediment to efficiently functioning markets than in the past. Changes in technology are capable of bringing about the emergence of competitors that may obviate the need for regulation, and sometimes regulation is a barrier to their emergence.

Consider, for example, long-distance telephone services. All phone traffic was once carried on fixed cables, and the construction of those networks meant great expense. It presented an opportunity to earn monopoly profits because the high cost of establishing the network made the entry of a second or third supplier unlikely. Furthermore, in most people's minds it would be socially wasteful to replicate the network. The emergence of satellite technology to replace cables profoundly affected competitive structure and eased entry, obviating the need for regulation. However, it took regulatory changes (in the United States it was the breaking up of AT&T, the telephone monopoly, and in much of Europe it meant the end of state-provided phone service) to allow the wind of competition to blow through the communications marketplace. In electricity supply, a similar change occurred, due to the realization that, although the grid of cables itself is a natural monopoly, vigorous competition is possible among the suppliers who serve users connected to the grid. Thus, rather than regulating the delivered price of electricity, most of the benefits of competition might be grasped through regulating the price of conveyance on the grid and allowing electricity suppliers to compete on a price basis.

In some cases, government's willingness to intervene in the market can lessen competition and act against the consumers' interest. For example, all transportation modes are gross substitutes and are to some degree in competition with each other. In a market context they can act as a limit on the price behavior of each other. Regulating transportation on a mode-by-mode basis, with mode-specific agencies, can tend to reduce competition in the broader industry and be counterproductive to consumer welfare.

Antitrust Policy The other form of monopoly, which can be termed *unnatural* or *artificial monopoly*, comes through the gathering of market share by a dominant enterprise that then erects barriers to entry to forestall competition. The United States counters this behavior through **antitrust policy**, regulatory and legal action designed to promote freedom of entry and to prohibit the merger (or collusion) of competitive firms that would result in harm to consumers.

All developed nations have a government agency nominally charged with the maintenance of competition, although in some countries it is more vigilant than in others. In the United States the relevant agency is the Federal Trade Commission, an arm of the Department of Justice, empowered to investigate and bring suit in defense of trade. In the United Kingdom it is the Competition Commission, formerly known as the Mergers and Monopoly Commission. Within the European Union competition policy is in the control of the Directorate General for Competition. Such agencies are charged with reviewing competitiveness on an industry basis, assessing the impact of mergers on competition, and, in cases where the evidence merits, taking legal action because of real or potential harm to the public interest.

In doing so, such agencies are looking for accretion of economic power and its impact on economic welfare. In the past much attention focused on the existence of power as measured by "concentration ratios," defined as the share of domestic market consumption represented by a given number of firms. The logic behind these ratios is that the greater the domination of the market by a small number of firms, the less likely is competition to be intense.[4] The most common index is the **four firm concentration ratio**—as calculated by the amount of total sales accounted for by the largest four firms. In the United States, using this basis, the most concentrated industries reported in the Census of Manufacturing were chewing gum and cigarettes (96 and 92, respectively). Another measure is the so-called **Herfindahl Hirschman index** (HHI, named for its originators, O. C. Herfindahl and A. O. Hirschman), which takes into account the market composition.[5]

However, recent developments led to a change of thought about how we should measure economic power or loss of welfare. First, there is skepticism of the view that either market share or concentration ratios are useful indices. Many economists today believe that what matters to keep a market functional, even if not perfect, is not how static market shares add up but the degree to which the market is **contestable**.[6] The threat of a competitor may be as effective as the existence of one in moderating excesses in pricing behavior. If few firms are in the market and **barriers to entry** are high, potential competition is certainly choked. However, even a total monopolist may be subject to restraint, and behave therefore more like a competitor, if entry into the market is easy. The issue therefore becomes not one of the size of market share at any moment in time but rather the height of the barriers to entry that determines the level of contestability.

Consider the position of Microsoft, Inc. In many areas of personal computer software, the company holds a near total monopoly. However, historically, entry into the industry has been relatively easy, and high product prices would serve to lure competitors into the industry. Consequently it is the threat, rather than the actuality, of competition that moderates Microsoft's pricing behavior. If, as was alleged

---

[4]A good discussion of these issues of entry can be found in W. Kip Viscusi, John Vernon, and Joseph Harrington, *Economics of Regulation*, 2d ed. (Cambridge: MIT Press, 1995).

[5]The HHI is calculated by summing the squares of the market share of all the firms in the market. Hence the highest value (perfect monopoly would be 100^2 or 10,000. Competition is reflected by a lower score. Ten firms each with 10 percent of the market would have an HHI of 1,000. A good discussion of these measures as well as issues of entry can be found in W. Kip Viscusi, John Vernon, and Joseph Harrington, *Economics of Regulation and Anti Trust*, 2d ed. (Cambridge: MIT Press, 1995).

[6]The original discussion on this topic can be read in William J. Baumol, John C. Panzar, and Robert Willig, *Contestable Markets and the Theory of Industry Structure* (New York: Harcourt Brace Jovanovich, 1982).

in the recent antitrust suit, Microsoft can use its market power to restrict entry, the market is no longer contestable and loss of welfare can result.

The growing integration of the world economy and generally falling barriers to international trade accelerated the decline in reliance on domestic concentration ratios as indices of market power.[7] In the past, domestic markets tended to be relatively closed to each other compared to the situation today. Tariff barriers were higher and frictional impediments to trade more significant because of high communications and transportation costs. **Trade to GDP ratios** were generally lower than they are today. Because of the comparatively closed nature of national economies, power in the domestic market represented a definite threat to the welfare of domestic consumers. Now in general the greater volume of trade, lower average tariff levels, and an increasing number of regional free trade blocs all make the structure of domestic concentration increasingly irrelevant. In such circumstances, domestic markets, although perhaps highly concentrated, may be highly contestable because of growing competition from abroad and relatively low barriers to entry to foreign firms. For example, the four firm concentration ratio for the U.S. automobile market in the late 1960s was high, with one firm, General Motors (GM), representing more than half of the market. Conventionally measured market power was high, but the surge of imports in the 1970s showed how easily contestable the market was. The Federal Trade Commission closed its ongoing investigation of GM in the mid-1970s.

In some cases the existence of this high degree of contestability of domestic markets due to potential entry of foreign firms led to the virtual abandonment of traditional antitrust policy. Many governments tolerate, encourage, or even help to create through merger **national champions** to monopolize the domestic market and control the resources to compete with foreign firms.[8] This policy is justified generally by the belief in substantial economies of scale in production or, more relevant recently, in research and development.

Labor Unions

So far we discussed only monopoly in the supply of goods and services. Labor organizations represent the attempt to monopolize a factor of production, generally with a view to restrict supply and raise its price. The consequences are usually higher wages and better benefits for workers, and a higher level of unemployment than would exist otherwise.

Governmental policy toward labor unions varies widely from country to country. It also changed a good deal over time. For example, in the first capitalist industrial society, nineteenth-century Britain, the government, elected by and

---

[7]On balance, trade barriers have been falling across the world due to unilateral tariff cutting and the action of the successive rounds of trade negotiations under the General Agreement on Tariffs and Trade (GATT) and now the World Trade Organization (WTO). One counter to this trend has been the increase in nontariff barriers to trade (NTBs) in recent years.

[8]French policy often leaned in this direction, especially in the 1970s and 1980s when a policy of creating publicly owned national champions in key industries was espoused.

largely beholden to property owners, took a dim view of the union movement because it sought to shift income from capital to labor. It was, therefore, criminalized through the Combination Acts,[9] and union organizers were arrested, imprisoned, and on occasion deported. After the extension of the electoral franchise to nonproperty owners in the 1880s, labor won the right to organize and formed its own political party to protect such gains. Other industrialized nations also saw violence and political upheaval in the birth of the movement.

Today most industrialized countries not only recognize unions, but also make organized labor part of the process of economic management. In Europe especially, organized labor plays a prominent role in both politics and economic management, as we will discuss more fully in the chapters on Sweden, France, and Germany. However, the decline of heavy industry and the growing surplus of labor in these economies, as indicated by historically high rates of unemployment, weakened the power of the union movement. Union power in the European economies remains greatest now in the public sector, where it shows resistance to market forces because of a clear link to electoral politics.

Late-industrializing countries are still passing through the stage of union establishment. The Japanese miracles of the 1960s through 1980s were assisted by the repression of the labor movement in the late 1950s. After decades of opposition by employers and government, Korean unions are now emerging. In countries more remote in development terms, such as Indonesia, independent unions are still banned.

LACK OF INFORMATION

Market systems work well only if consumers can access reliable information about the product that they are buying. In the case of simple commodities, reliance on the old maxim **caveat emptor** ("let the buyer beware") is probably adequate; in such cases information is relatively cheaply available and reputation is an important asset when repeat purchases are frequent. However, in the case of more complex goods or goods that are purchased infrequently, information might be difficult, or expensive to obtain.

Where information is expensive, governments frequently step in to "protect" the consumer. In some cases this is done by prescribing behavior for those who make and sell products to the public or by dictating particular product standards. Rules or laws specify what information a seller must offer to the buyer and what recourse is available to the buyer in the case of disappointment. In other industries or professions, the government may create barriers to entry by limiting access to the industry to those who demonstrate "appropriate qualifications," preventing the unqualified from offering such goods or services. Such licensing is common in a wide variety of professions from lawyers to morticians.

---

[9]The Combination Acts were legislated in 1800 and repealed in 1825; although unions were legal, leaders were still frequently prosecuted for specific job actions, such as strikes. See Rondo Cameron, *A Concise Economic History of the World* (New York: Oxford University Press, 1989), p. 218.

This type of regulation and licensing may provide an effective way of minimizing the consumers' need for expensive information. Consider, for example, a potential patient choosing a surgeon. In most countries only people who have attended medical school, served an internship, and passed examinations can hang up a shingle and offer surgical services. Performing surgery without such qualifications is forbidden. In contrast, fewer restrictions limit who can offer to shave people or cut hair. In more remote times, such licensing was not considered essential for surgeons, and indeed barbers performed surgery along with their shaving duties.

Why is government intervention merited in one case and not the other? The answer lies in the availability of information and the consequences of not being able to get it. When it comes to hairdressing, we feel we can rely on reputation to weed out poor performers. One bad haircut does not kill and serves in itself to tell others about performance. One poor surgery can kill, and licensing, while not eliminating the problem entirely, does, it is argued, reduce the risk to the public. The goal of protecting of the public has spawned a large regulatory industry. In the United States, the government hires inspectors to tell consumers what meat is "choice," requires product information on labels, looks for "misleading" advertising, requires approval of drugs, and so forth. Few people would argue that all of this regulation and inspection is necessary, especially in view of the fact that market remedies are available in many cases. Frequently such licensing is the result of rent-seeking behavior, a phenomenon that we will discuss in greater detail later in this chapter.

PUBLIC GOODS

The third major class of market failure is due to the existence of "public goods." The qualities of public goods may best be understood by looking first at those of private goods. Private goods and services, whose supply is left to individual rather than collective action, share two important qualities: excludability and diminishability. **Excludability** enables producers or sellers to charge a price for private goods and services because they can deny access to those who fail to pay the price. **Diminishability** implies that one person's consumption of a good or service reduces the supply available to others. It is really another way of saying that the marginal cost of consumption is greater than zero. Efficiency, therefore, requires that suppliers of private goods charge a price that is greater than zero as well. Excludability establishes a feasible mechanism by which to impose a charge.

In contrast, pure public goods are neither diminishable nor excludable. The marginal cost of additional unit of consumption is zero, and therefore economic efficiency requires a zero price. Anyway, the absence of excludability means no cost-effective way of charging for the service. The absence of excludability leads to the **free rider problem**, in which people are able to enjoy the service without payment and therefore may make no financial contribution to their "fair" share of costs. Consequently, private institutions will fail to supply, or will chronically undersupply, such goods, and only the government with its ability to coerce payment through taxation holds the potential to supply the goods at the optimal level.

Although pure public goods are theoretically important, in reality they represent a relatively small class. National defense, the system of administration of justice, and public health measures are salient examples. In none of these cases can an individual be excluded from benefit without fundamentally altering the nature of the good. In virtually all countries, these goods are provided by the government and are financed out of tax revenue. Moreover, such goods are probably essential for the existence of the modern state. It is difficult to imagine in these cases how a private substitute could be created.

The provision of lighthouses is a much-used example of public goods in the economic textbooks. Its frequency stems more from its tractability than its economic significance. Lighthouses are not as fundamental to an economy as defense or the law, but they obviously do provide economic benefits. Use of the services of lighthouses is susceptible to free ridership, and would therefore be undersupplied by private institutions,[10] which would have to rely on donations from shippers, sailors, and the general public to finance them. It requires a considerable step to assume that the government would get the level of provision right. To supply even pure public goods at an optimal level, the government must find a means of accurately estimating benefits or inducing consumers (in this case the shippers and sailors) to reveal their demand. It is quite conceivable that the government would err just as much as a private system based on subscription or contribution. In fact, the nature of politics and lobbying would probably lead to oversupply, for reasons discussed later in the chapter.

In general, socially provided goods are not "public" in the rigorous sense. In most cases they are excludable, as we can see by looking at the examples of education, health services, highways, recreation facilities, and so forth, all of which have counterparts in the private sector. In most countries, services that are clearly diminishable (for example, postal services or garbage disposal) are provided by the government as well as the private sector. To justify government supply of such potentially private goods and services, market failure is not sufficient. The actual motivations might include distributive concerns, a need to establish equitable standards, or a conviction that government is superior in efficiency terms to private enterprise in some tasks. In recent years economists focused considerable attention on public goods supply and frequently arrived at the conclusion that it is determined at least as much by the lobbying activity of interested parties as by a concern for correcting market failure.

EXTERNALITIES

The final class of market failure to be introduced here consists of imperfections created by the presence of *externalities*, external economies and diseconomies, sometimes called spillovers. These consequences to third parties (or bystanders) derive

---

[10]In fact, despite the clear public good qualities of lighthouses, in the nineteenth century they were provided largely by private charities or by placing a levy or surcharge on harbor fees.

from the economic activities of others. Such consequences may be either positive, contributing to the welfare of the third party, or negative. Because of the unrequited nature of externalities (we do not receive compensation for negative effects, nor do we pay for the positive ones), they do not enter into the decision process of the individuals initiating the activity. Both consumers and producers make decisions by considering private benefits and private costs. From a societal point of view, the appropriate considerations should be social benefit and social cost.

Figure 4.3 illustrates how the existence of a substantial externality (perhaps the ability of producers to emit smoke into the atmosphere without paying any pollution fee or compensation to those affected) causes a divergence between the **private marginal cost** and the **social marginal cost**. The consumer is confronted by prices based on the private, not the social marginal cost. Correspondingly, the market system with the imperfection of uncompensated externalities tends to overproduce the good, to the point Q_P in Figure 4.3, rather than the socially optimal position of Q_S.

One of the most obvious and pressing examples of externalities lies in the analysis of environmental issues. Consider a factory that emits air pollution as a by-product of manufacturing a good. In the absence of any control, the manufacturer considers only private benefit and treats the environment as a free resource, despoiling the air and reducing the welfare of others in the process.

Government regulatory activity to counter pollution can be of several kinds:

1. It can ban the polluting process entirely.
2. It can establish minimum compliance standards for the manufacturer to meet.
3. It can offer subsidies to the manufacturer to reduce pollution.
4. It can charge the manufacturer a fee per unit of pollution emitted.

■ **FIGURE 4.3**

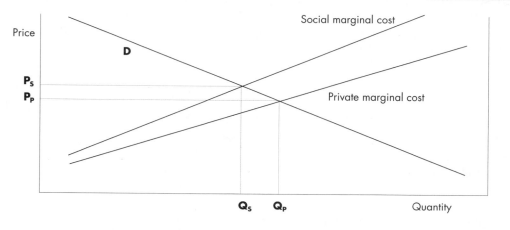

Private and Social Marginal Costs and Benefits

The first two remedies are generally held by economists to be allocatively inefficient. In the first case, banning the production totally will generally result in an undersupply of the polluting good; the loss of consumer welfare from the absolute nonavailability of the product may outweigh the gains of completely clean air or water. In the second case, establishing minimum standards for pollution leaves no incentive for manufacturers to press for a further reduction below the standard, even though an additional cut might be socially beneficial. The third and fourth courses of action can both lead to an economically efficient outcome. A subsidy to reduce pollution can produce the same effect as a pollution fee because either can be designed to reflect the marginal cost of the polluting activity. What is obviously different is the distributional impact of the two approaches. Policy 3 grants the right to pollute to manufacturers and bribes them to stop. Policy 4 gives the manufacturers no rights but forces them to purchase the ability to pollute from the state.

Some economists argue that the problem of externalities is solely the result of the inadequate specification of property rights. Private individuals who hold clear rights of ownership and live in countries where the legal system functions well, can pursue recourse against the despoliation of their property or loss of health through a civil suit. The threat of litigation results in negotiation and in many cases a contract that will result in a mutually acceptable, and therefore efficient, solution to "externality problems." Consider, for example, a case in which my neighbor was about to reduce my welfare by building a skyscraper that would block the sun. If my right to access to light were clear and legally guaranteed, then the neighbor could only proceed if we were able to arrive at a contract whereby my permission to build was granted on the basis of some form of compensation. Alternatively, if the neighbor clearly holds the right to use his site in any way he chooses, irrespective of third-party consequences, I might dissuade him from construction through a contract that appropriately compensated him for his lost opportunity and revenue. Either solution would be efficient although the distributional effects (who gained and who lost welfare) would be markedly different according to how the property rights were determined.

This approach to the problem of externalities is exemplified by the work of Ronald Coase.[11] His work suggests that the externality problem might be solved through the complete definition of property rights. Fully comprehensive and well-specified property rights would result in the "internalization" of externalities, and the optimal solution would be arrived at through negotiation and contract. This happy result of the Coase theorem is, however, subject to some limitations. "Internalization" leading to mutually agreeable contracts, and therefore efficiency, might be the outcome in cases where the number of participants is small, but as soon as we get to a case where either the affecting or the affected party is numerous the costs of negotiating the appropriate contract may become prohibitively high. In such cases government intervention may achieve close to equivalent results at the cost of fewer resources. Most of the discussion about externalities relates to negative effects, partly because issues as important as pollution, global warming, and

---

[11]Ronald Coase, "The Problem of Social Cost," *Journal of Law and Economics* 3 (October 1960), pp. 1–44.

traffic congestion play prominent roles in our lives. However, we should not discount the responsibility of governments to correct the market failure of the underprovision of positive externalities. Indeed, it can be argued that much of the benefit of public education lies in the production of external benefits stemming from educated and productive citizenry.

GOVERNMENT FAILURE

Each of the four phenomena discussed previously is real and each can cause markets to fail, leading to a less efficient outcome than would be the case if markets were perfect. Thus, there is an initial rationale to consider the use of government action to address market failure. However, it would be imprudent to conclude that government intervention in such cases will always increase welfare. Such a conclusion unwisely compares imperfect markets to a perfect government. In recent years, economists have taken a more skeptical view of the capabilities of government, recognizing that there are many sources of **government failure**, which can themselves be at least as damaging as the market failure they seek to correct.

We cannot assume that governments will always be, in Anne Krueger's phrase, "benevolent, costless social guardians."[12] It is problematic even to consider a homogenous "public" interest, because only rarely will all members of the public be affected in a symmetrical fashion; in any action, some will gain more than others. Government, even if it is motivated to increase aggregate welfare, will inevitably face the problems of determining the preferences of citizens in the absence of markets and meaningful prices. Furthermore, like the rest of us, bureaucrats and politicians are subject to complex incentives. They will, in most cases, pursue their own interest, as do employers, workers, and households. Of course, this dilemma is nothing new. It leads us back once more to Adam Smith, whose opinion of government was just as poor as his opinion of manufacturers. He wrote in *The Wealth of Nations*:

> Great nations are never impoverished by private, though they sometimes are by public, prodigality and misconduct. The whole, or almost the whole, public revenue is in most countries employed in maintaining unproductive hands. Such are the people who compose a numerous and splendid court, a great ecclesiastical establishment, great fleets and armies, who in time of peace produce nothing, and in time of war acquire nothing which can compensate the expense of maintaining them, even while the war lasts. Such people, as they themselves produce nothing, are all maintained by the produce of other men's labor.[13]

Sources of Government Failure

We turn now to look at some of the specific sources of government failure.

---

[12]Anne Krueger, "Economists' Changing Perceptions of Government," *Weltwirtschaftliches Archiv* 126, no. 3 (1990), p. 419.
[13]Adam Smith, *Wealth of Nations*, book II, chapter III.

Availability of Information One of the beauties of the market system lies in its economy of information: it operates in a decentralized way, with no participant needing to see "the whole picture." Government action, on the other hand, requires all relevant information to be centralized. Even if we make the contentious assumption that the objective of bureaucrats and politicians is to maximize public welfare, rational choices about what public goods to supply and in what quantity require an accurate picture of the total costs and benefits of that activity. Later in this book we discuss the experience of the socialist planned economies more fully and examine in some detail the problems and the resource costs of maintaining a reliable flow of information from periphery to center. However, the problem of gathering accurate information is not unique to centrally planned economies. In a mixed market economy, groups that benefit from the provision of a publicly supplied good find it in their interest to overstate their demand by strategically misleading behavior. Government will only outperform even an imperfect market if it has access to all appropriate information. This task, however, is at best expensive and at worst impossible when participants see an incentive to provide misleading information.

The Capture of Regulators The presence of monopoly power can reduce social welfare, and for this reason public policy to regulate monopolies often becomes a staple of government activity. The main device for the control of monopoly power generally lies with regulatory agencies established to supervise pricing and output. However, a large body of literature suggests that, over time, a regulated industry tends to "capture" the regulatory body set to oversee it. Regulators often identify more with those of the industry that they, in theory, control than with the public at large. In part this **capture of regulators** occurs because of a "revolving door" of personnel between the agency and the industry, as well as an understandable and human need to limit the frequency of adversarial behavior between the regulator and the regulated.

Regulation may also impair the long-term performance of an industry. A regulated industry generally enjoys guaranteed profit margins set by the agency. Given this guarantee, firms tend to grow cautious about innovation and often pay too little attention to cost control. The industry actually comes to enjoy the protection of the agency set to constrain it. A comfortable symbiosis develops, characterized by high costs, excess capacity, and a lack of enterprise. Prices to the consumer, often set by the regulatory agency to cover average costs, trend upward in accommodation of increasing inefficiency and waste. The actions of regulators establish a "soft-budget constraint," which alters the cost structure of the industry at the expense of consumers. Anne Krueger points out "that the real truth of the capture theory is frequently revealed when deregulation is proposed: it is more often than not, those in the regulated industry themselves who are the loudest in protest against deregulation!"

Collective Action In his important book *The Logic of Collective Action*, Mancur Olsen argues that small interest groups can organize much more easily and forcefully than large ones.[14] Small groups with intense preferences, through their **collective action**, will lobby hard for some types of expenditure, even if total costs well exceed benefits, precisely because the costs will be spread among large numbers, while the benefits are more compactly distributed. Members of beneficiary groups try to "free-ride" on the broader tax-paying population, and the consequence is that some public goods will be oversupplied. Moreover, in a process known as "log rolling," pressure groups band together to form coalitions and are thus able to receive the support of other small groups for their cause in return for reciprocal support of the other groups' schemes. The result of this process is a general over-supply of public goods.

The same lobbying phenomena carry implications elsewhere in the sphere of government action. Consider, for example, the issue of trade protection. An industry and its workers may maintain strong preferences concerning the imposi-tion of a protective tariff and may lobby hard for it. They will frequently prevail although the impact on overall consumer welfare might be strongly negative, purely because they are easily organized and highly focused, while the "losers" are dispersed and disorganized. A good example of this phenomenon can be seen in the U.S. automotive industry during the 1980s, which was adversely affected by foreign (primarily Japanese) competition and a surging import market share. Extensive lobbying in Washington produced government sympathy, which in turn led to pressure on the Japanese to impose "voluntary export restraints," which cur-tailed the number of vehicles shipped into the United States (though not their value). Estimates of the cost of this action include an increase of $960 in the price of each new automobile sold in the United States and an extra burden on consumers of $160,000 per job saved.[15] Automobile company profits rose sharply, and motor executives earned record salaries, not for their leadership in production but for their persuasive lobbying. In short, the total costs of government action certainly exceeded the benefits, but a compact lobbying group for control overwhelmed a dispersed opposition and earned monopoly rents.

Rent-Seeking Behavior This example from the U.S. automotive industry intro-duces us to **rent-seeking behavior**, defined as *the expenditure of real resources in the attempt to appropriate a surplus in the form of rent*. In the previous example, auto com-pany executives employed lobbyists (which represent real resources) to convince the government to restrict competition from abroad (the "voluntary" export restraints). Their efforts reduced supply and created monopoly rents, which accrue to management, capital, and labor in the motor industry.[16]

---

[14]See Mancur Olsen, *The Logic of Collective Action: Public Goods and the Theory of Groups* (Cambridge: Harvard University Press, 1971).

[15]Robert Crandall, "Import Quotas and the Automobile Industry: The Costs of Protection," *Brookings Review,* summer 1984, 8–16.

[16]Note that the Japanese motor industry shares in these rents that are extracted from the U.S. consumer. Also bear in mind that the government action produces a deadweight loss (due to reduced consump-tion) as well as the redistribution from consumers to the industry, which is due to increased prices.

A common form of government intervention, ostensibly motivated by a desire to protect the consumer, denies access to specific industries or professions to those not appropriately qualified. This regulation reduces the supply in such activities and enables the successful entrants to earn a monopoly rent. The possibility of this reward encourages rent-seeking behavior. The loss to society takes the form of use of real resources to secure monopoly rents as well as the dead weight loss of monopoly pricing policy. Rent seeking is frequently analyzed and discussed in the context of less-developed countries where it appears in many forms, from the ability of customs clerks to generate bribes to the allocation of large-scale import licenses. However, it is important to recognize that such behavior can be found in developed economies too.

Pork Barreling Politicians, whether democratically elected or not, are prone to use government expenditures to bolster their own position. James Buchanan was awarded the Nobel Prize in economics for work in political economy based on the premise that politicians in a democracy act to maximize the probability of their reelection.[17] Representatives of a particular district will lobby hard for specific expenditures that will benefit their own electorate. In this activity, known as **pork barreling**, projects may take the form of public expenditure on infrastructure or government facilities that benefit the locality but the cost of which is spread over the tax-paying population of the entire economy. We can also note that even though they show less sensitivity to the vagaries of public opinion, dictators or other authoritarian regimes also use the public exchequer to build coalitions of supporters.

We can find examples of politicians opportunistically using expenditures to enhance their future in many contexts. For example, in the runup to the Russian presidential elections in 1994, Boris Yeltsin acted to relax the relatively tight monetary policy of the central bank. This move ensured that joblessness and the failure of enterprises to pay wages to their workers would result in only minimal impact on electoral preference. U.S. presidential candidates may support higher levels of defense expenditure to capture votes in politically marginal areas where the local economy is highly defense dependent.

This "pork barrel" analysis presents three general implications for government activity. First, voters or groups of voters who care a great deal about a specific issue are likely to be rewarded for their concern, especially in the case of "single issue" voters. For example, in the United States it would be difficult to reduce health care expenditure for the elderly largely because this issue is so decisive for a large group of voters. Second, in countries where politicians rely on contributions to finance their election campaigns, the concerns of the check-writing rich are, *ceteris paribus*, likely to receive greater attention than those of the poor. Finally, because of log rolling, the creation of coalitions will result in a general oversupply of quasi-public goods.

---

[17]James M. Buchanan and Gordon Tullock, *The Calculus of Consent* (Ann Arbor: University of Michigan Press, 1989).

Agency Inertia Once created, bureaucracies tend to take on a life of their own, and they will seek to perpetuate their existence by finding work to do. In 1935 the Roosevelt administration founded the Rural Electrification Authority (REA) to facilitate the provision of electricity to rural farms and households. Practically all households now have power, and those who don't live a lifestyle so remote that they can be presumed to be avoiding it, its task is now finished. However, it managed to stay in business, albeit under the new name of the Rural Utilities Service, initially by providing subsidized funds to ski areas and golf courses. With the arrival of the Web, it found a new role ensuring that rural schools obtained high-speed Internet access. This **agency inertia** can occur when bureaucrats show little interest in cutting their own jobs and in some cases maintain a chokehold on the information about their own activities.

Deadweight Loss and Taxes The case for "correcting" market failure rests on imperfect markets causing a **deadweight loss**, a fall in economic welfare that accrues to no one. However, government action is not costless and must be financed in one of three ways—taxation, borrowing, or the printing of money—any of which inevitably produce an adverse effect on the operation of the market and therefore its own deadweight loss.

With the exception of lump-sum taxes, all taxes influence economic choices by changing relative prices.[18] They thereby impose an excess burden and reduce economic welfare. Taxes on income, for example, drive a "wedge" that distorts the household's choice between labor and leisure. Consumption, value-added, and excise taxes also change relative prices, distorting choice and creating deadweight losses.

Sometimes a particular tax results in a large excess burden while generating little revenue. In the late eighteenth century, for example, Britain imposed a revenue-raising tax on the improbable tax base of number of windows. The rationale behind this was that the number of windows in a dwelling provided a rough approximation of the wealth of the occupant. It also had the advantage of being a highly visible tax handle. However, in order to avoid the tax, many occupants simply bricked up windows, hence, reducing the tax base. Any change in behavior occasioned solely by the imposition of a tax is an example of deadweight loss.

Although less visible than taxes, the other means of finance for government also imply deadweight losses. An increase in government borrowing tends to raise interest rates, thereby distorting the choice between saving and consumption, and leading, to a crowding out of private-sector investment. Printing money prompts inflationary consequences that, even if anticipated, distort the choice between present and future consumption, and if unforeseen by some will cause profound distributional consequences. It is therefore important to recognize that any government expenditure must be financed by means that impose welfare losses. Any efficiency gains that can be anticipated by the establishment of regulatory agencies or the provision of public goods must be weighed against the efficiency losses that are occasioned by raising the revenue to finance them.

---

[18]Lump sum taxes are those levied on a base that is totally inelastic. An example is the **poll tax**, the base of which is population.

GOVERNMENT AND REDISTRIBUTION

Government action is not limited to regulation nor is government expenditure limited to the provision of goods and services. A large part of government spending, particularly in industrialized countries, consists of redistributive expenditures. This particular portion of the government budget grew most rapidly in recent years and will, for the reasons of interest group politics outlined earlier, be difficult to contain or curtail in the years ahead.

Redistributive expenditures can take two forms. They may be direct **transfer payments** of cash (such as old age pensions, unemployment compensation, and cash welfare benefits). Alternatively, redistribution may take an in-kind form such as the provision of subsidized housing, free education, free medicine, and so on. Although the market may provide these goods and services, those who are less well off will face limited access because they are constrained by limited budgets. These redistributional expenditures presently dominate the public finances in most of the developed market economies. In Western Europe and the United States, subsidized housing and social security payments taken together represent between 38 percent and 60 percent of total government expenditure. However, these and similar statistics tend to overstate the redistributive stance of most government policy toward lower income groups. Although many direct program expenditures are targeted toward the poor, they are by and large offset by **tax expenditures** that favor higher-income groups. Such tax expenditures take the form of tax relief for *inter alia* pension contributions, insurance premiums, mortgage payments, and property tax payments, all of which are expenditures that rise more than proportionally with income.

The justification for government's role in reshaping the distribution of income that results from market interaction must be different from that which legitimizes the "correction" of market imperfections that reduce allocative efficiency. Although the skewed income and wealth distributions that result from a market economy are frequently seen as one of its "failures," it is not apparent that efficiency suffers from this increased inequality. A somewhat tenuous case can been made that a more even income distribution can enhance social cohesion, and thus increase "social productivity," but it is by no means universally accepted.[19]

The claim for the "justness" of the distribution of income that results in a market system depends on the idea that material reward should be directly related to contribution.[20] Given the appropriate assumptions, each factor of production in a market economy may be thought of as being appropriately rewarded when it receives its marginal value product; that is, each factor is paid what it contributes at the margin. An individual or a family income is therefore the sum of the

---

[19]The "Swedish model," which we review in Chapter 7, emphasizes social cohesion and egalitarianism.

[20]For an interesting discussion of the justice of rewards in a market economy, see Arthur Okun, *Equity and Efficiency: The Big Trade-off* (Washington, DC: Brookings, 1975), pp. 40–50. Reprinted in part as "Rewards in a Market Economy," in Bornstein, *Comparative Economic Systems: Models and Cases*, 7th ed. (Burr Ridge, IL: Richard D. Irwin, 1994).

contributions of the factors of production that the unit owns or controls. These factors derive from six sources:

1. *Natural talent and ability.* Ability is not equally distributed at birth. Some people possess characteristics (intelligence, strength, stature) that allow them to be more productive and therefore more rewarded than others.

2. *Acquired skills.* The earning power of congenital characteristics is qualified by the skills and experience acquired during education and working life. Economists generally regard this process as the accumulation of human capital (investment in oneself) made by education and foregone earnings.

3. *Effort.* Inasmuch as effort is a determinant of productivity, it should affect earnings. Employers should hire the hard worker and pay him or her more than a time server. The ability to selectively compensate employees is conditioned on the ability of employers to pay different rates for the same job description, which is often organizationally difficult or in some cases legally prohibited.

4. *Inherited wealth.* In almost all of the countries for which good statistics are compiled, wealth is distributed less equally than income. Much of this inequity results from inheritance whereby blocs of wealth, represented by productive physical and financial assets, are passed from generation to generation. It is also important to note that human capital and inherited wealth are highly correlated. More affluent parents tend to invest more in the human capital of their offspring.

5. *Accumulated savings.* Not all physical and financial assets are inherited. One's stock of productive assets is also a function of savings and consumption decisions made over a lifetime. The more one foregoes in one time period, the greater will be the capital to be consumed in a later one.

6. *Related supply and demand considerations.* Finally, income depends a great deal on circumstances over which we can exercise little control. The value of a worker's marginal product, for example, is a function of the supply and demand, and therefore the price of the product that he or she makes. Consider a coal miner. His income would rise should the world oil supply be restricted, but it might fall were a technology for cheap solar energy devised.

Given these complex considerations (compounded by the many imperfections of both product and factor markets), it becomes difficult to sustain a belief in the unique justice of market-based distribution. Most people would accept the premise that the amount of effort (item) one puts into one's work, as well as the amount of saving and investment in one's own human capital (item), should be rewarded. These represent sacrifices that should be compensated, and should be seen to be compensated, because of favorable incentive effects.

On the other hand, strong disagreement on the ethics of inheritance still remains. In the immediate post–World War II period, especially in the European social democracies, egalitarian sentiment supported the enactment of almost confiscatory estate taxation designed to break up inherited wealth and "level the playing field" for a new generation. However, loopholes enabled those who availed themselves of forward-thinking estate planning to avoid the tax, and the incidence of estate taxation fell only on the unwary. Today, tax planners refer to the estate tax in the United States as "the voluntary tax." Republicans stigmatized it further by terming it the "death tax" and it looks as if it will disappear entirely in the United States in the next decade.

Governments not only affect the income distribution by tax and transfer, but they may also attempt to influence the structure of wages. One frequently used policy is the institution of a minimum wage. The original justification was that all jobs should pay at least "a living wage." Within the United States at least this goal clearly has not been achieved. Many critics claim that the imposition of a non-market-clearing wage resulted in high levels of unemployment, especially among young people.

Attempts are also made to address differences that may be related to income or gender. Currently in the United States and in some nations of Europe, governments face pressure to regulate the labor market through the imposition of a wage structure based on "comparable worth." In simple terms, this theory suggests that two jobs that require roughly similar effort, education, and qualifications should be paid similarly. It was used to justify setting public-sector pay scales in line with private ones as part of the Swedish system of wage settlement. It also plays a substantial role in an argument to raise the rates of pay in typically "female" occupations to eliminate the gap between male and female average wages.

Justifications for Redistributive Policy

The predominance of redistribution in government expenditures results in far-reaching effects on the economic system. It it is important to examine the rationale for government intervention to amend or correct the income distribution determined by the market. None of the following explanations is in itself dominating, but all were used in recent years to justify redistributive "tax and spend" policies.

Utilitarianism If we start from a generally held position in economics, that the more one has of a good the less it is valued at the margin, it can be argued that the intrinsic value of $1 is greater to a poor person than a rich one. Consequently, taking $1 from a rich person and giving it to a poor one would increase social well-being. **Utilitarianism** (or "the greatest happiness of the greatest number principle") makes a case for the maximization of social well-being through redistribution. It follows that an enlightened social guardian might pursue redistribution on these grounds, subject always to the caveat that the disincentive effects on total output are less than the welfare gain.[21] However, in reality such a picture of government is at variance with the views that we laid out earlier.

---

[21] Utilitarianism was a school of social philosophy founded by Jeremy Bentham (1748–1835). It provided much of the philosophical basis for nineteenth-century economic thought.

Altruism It is attractive to see the development of a wide system of social programs as the outgrowth of collective **altruism**. In such a view the welfare-promoting aspects are even greater than the utilitarian rationale. Under altruistic motivation, giving, like Portia's "quality of mercy" in Shakespeare's *Merchant of Venice*, would be twice blessed, enhancing the welfare of both givers and receivers. Again, however, this rationale falls short as an explanation for the growth of major social programs, although it might be important in private redistributive charities.

Social Contract A more contemporary view of redistribution sees it motivated by quasi-contractual relationships. In this concept of **social contract**, citizenship, or residence, endows everyone with rights to a minimum standard of living. Thus it is the right of the old, the young, the halt, the lame, and the unemployed or others who possess little to sell in the market system to be supported to some minimum level. A key question centers around where that minimum level should be located.

In early capitalist economies, the right was to subsistence alone, and no more. Support above that level was denied because it would reward indigence and, according to **vacuum theory of population**, attributed to Malthus, it would increase the number of paupers. Consequently, support for the poor whether "indoor" (that is in poorhouses) or "outdoor" using cash grants and in-kind support was minimal. The rise of the liberal welfare states and the extension of the voting franchise changed support levels. In contemporary European social democracies, the level of support is relatively high, and the income distribution that results is quite egalitarian. The income share of the richest 20 percent in Europe is generally around five times that of the poorest 20 percent, as opposed to about 8:1 in the United States. Such redistribution is criticized by supply-side economists because they feel it reduces the incentive to find work and contributes to the high level of unemployment. On the other side of the coin, financing redistributive policies require high rates of taxation, which lower the incentives to work and to save. Thus redistribution can be seen as a root cause of economic stagnation. When transfers are regarded as rights or entitlements, demographics play a powerful role in determining the structure of expenditures. Low birthrates and a sharp increase in life expectancy result in a pronounced aging of the population in industrial societies and require ever-higher levels of transfer.

The Increase of Social Productivity Redistribution is sometimes justified as contributing a positive impact on social productivity. This benefit might be achieved in two ways. By elevating social cohesion it might solidify institutions that are beneficial to growth. Moreover, redistribution can lower social problems, leading to savings on expenditures (like crime or remedial education). This line of thinking remains important in contemporary European political thought, and can be seen in the justification of redistribution in the European Union.

Social Control A fifth view sees redistribution in contemporary market economies as a tool in a struggle to maintain social peace and stability. Potentially disruptive elements of society are bought off by providing access to generous pensions and goods.

This strategy certainly relies on history. Imperial Rome secured the quiescence of the Roman unemployed through the provision of free "bread and circuses." In response to contemporary urban disturbances, industrialized countries frequently increase the number and funding of social programs oriented toward the disaffected group. Redistribution can be regarded as a substitute for expenditure on more conventional aspects of law enforcement. The level of distribution is not determined by concern for, or by rights of, groups disadvantaged by the market process but rather by the potential power of disaffected groups to create problems.

Shared Growth Economists are not unanimous about the relationship between income distribution and economic growth. Some consider egalitarianism to result in a lowering of incentives and a consequent slower growth path. Others are adamant that sharing of the proceeds of growth is essential to maintain a growth trajectory; growth that benefits only a few is likely to be unstable because it leads to a loss of social unity. Each opinion is based on some merit: both extreme egalitarianism and an extreme reliance on material incentives (which leads to an unequal distribution of income) are likely to present problems. Some commentators on the strong growth performance of East Asian economies in the 1990s note the sharing of growth as an important factor in sustaining economic expansion.

The Democratic Process In modern democracies the key to the increased share of redistributional expenditure is likely to be found in the ballot box. Earlier we discussed how politicians act so as to ensure their subsequent reelection, and providing access to redistribution is one way of influencing voter behavior. This explanation sounds especially potent when the potential group is unified and "single-issue oriented." This basic thought underlies much of the work of James Buchanan, Nobel laureate in economics.

Demand Stabilization Capitalist economies are subject to variations in the level of macroeconomic activity, and at times this variation can be ascribed to a systemic tendency toward underconsumption. Inasmuch as the less well off show a higher marginal propensity to consume than the better off, redistribution from rich to poor lowers the societal marginal propensity to save and reduces the chance of an "underconsumptionist trap." From the English liberal economist John Hobson[22] forward, and particularly in mainstream Keynesian schools of thought, some economists advocate domestic redistribution as an antidote to recession. While it is hard to see such a clear espousal of a particular macroeconomic theory by the politicians who ultimately determine redistributive policy, it is a fact that developed nations managed to steer clear of major recessions since the inception of mass redistribution programs.

---

[22]Hobson anticipated many of Keynes's views on the dangers of underconsumption, although his main agenda was to restrain overseas imperialism, which in its relentlessness to attach for foreign markets by force was an alternative remedy to redistribution for domestic stagnation.

CONCLUSION

Where does this discussion leave us in evaluating the role of government in correcting the inefficient or unacceptable features of market logic? In the light of these observations, few would assert that each and every market imperfection is a case for government intervention. The particular failures of the market must be evaluated against the cost and potential failures of government intervention before any action is initiated.

Even in those cases where market failure is so pronounced that some government intervention is merited, economists would be best employed in considering solutions that are designed to reduce the risk of government failure, rather than assuming that regulation by a government body was necessarily beneficial. The new view of government suggests that policies that provide individuals with incentives and freedom to correct market failure might be best. Experience to date offers us few examples of these kinds of policies, which might be described as **incentive-compatible** or **market augmenting policies**. Promising approaches seem to lie in the use of **quasi-markets** to assist in the provision of services currently supplied largely by the government. This approach would allow the simultaneous addressing of the equity and the efficiency issue. Such a device would be the use of vouchers provided gratis by the government to eligible families with children, but which could then be used to pay for educational services. Market-augmenting approaches used in Asian countries attempt to determine which firms should receive government support, and these efforts will be looked at again when the economies of Japan and Korea are presented in Chapters 12 and 13 of this book.

It is sufficient at this point to suggest that the direction of future research should be to identify the areas of comparative advantage for government and to examine how the logic of the market and appropriately designed incentives may be used to better the performance of government.

KEY TERMS AND CONCEPTS

agency inertia	externalities
altruism	four firm concentration ratio
antitrust policy	free rider problem
barriers to entry	government failure
capture of regulators	Herfindahl-Hirschman Index
caveat emptor	incentive-compatible policy
collective action	lack of information
contestable markets	market-augmenting policy
deadweight loss	market failure
diminishability	market power
excludability	national champions

natural monopoly

poll tax

pork barreling

price setter

price takers

private marginal cost

public goods

quasi-markets

rent-seeking behavior

social contract

social marginal cost

tax expenditures

trade to GDP ratio

transfer payments

utilitarianism

vacuum theory of population

QUESTIONS FOR DISCUSSION

1. Evaluate the arguments for and against the use of government power to curb monopolies.

2. How has the need to regulate "natural monopolies" changed in recent years?

3. Why are concentration ratios not thought of as good indices of the level of industry-wide competition? What may be a better approach?

4. How does lack of information impede the operation of a market system? How can a government act to correct this impediment?

5. Define *public goods*. Are pure public goods an important category? Give some examples. Is information a pure public good?

6. Why may government action be required to correct externality problems such as pollution? Which type of system, planned or market, would you expect to lead to most pollution?

7. Why is the government not a "benevolent, costless social guardian"?

8. Give some reasons why redistribution via both cash and in-kind payments is the fastest growing governmental activity.

RESOURCES

Web Sites

U.S. Federal Trade Commission.. http://www.ftc.gov/
This site provides useful information and downloadable papers on specific industries.

U.K. Office of Fair Trading.. http://www.oft.gov.uk/
This site gives the background, philosophy, and structure of U.K. policy against monopoly.

Books and Articles

Baumol, William J., John C. Panzar, and Robert Willig. *Contestable Markets and the Theory of Industry Structure.* New York: Harcourt Brace Jovanovich, 1982.

Brock, Gerald W. *Telecommunication Policy for the Information Age: From Monopoly to Competition.* Cambridge: Harvard University Press, 1998.

Buchanan, James M., and Richard A. Musgrave. *Public Finance and Public Choice: Two Contrasting Visions of the State.* Cambridge: MIT Press, 1999.

Buchanan, James M., and Gordon Tullock. *The Calculus of Consent.* Ann Arbor: University of Michigan Press, 1962.

Coase, Ronald. "The Problem of Social Cost." *Journal of Law and Economics* 3 (October 1960), 1–44.

Crandall, Robert. "Import Quotas and the Automobile Industry." *Brookings Review,* Summer 1984, 8–16.

Krueger, Anne. "Economists' Changing Perceptions of Government." *Weltwirtschaftliches Archiv* 126, no. 3 (1990), 419.

Musgrave, Richard A. *Public Finance in a Democratic Society: The Foundations of Taxation and Expenditure.* White Plains, NY: Edward Elgar, 2000.

Okun, Arthur. *Equity and Efficiency: The Big Trade-Off.* Washington, DC: Brookings Institution, 1975.

Olsen, Mancur. *The Logic of Collective Action: Public Goods and the Theory of Groups.* Cambridge: Harvard University Press, 1971.

Train, Kenneth E. *Optimal Regulation: The Economic Theory of Natural Monopoly.* Cambridge: MIT Press, 1991.

Viscusi, W. Kip, John Vernon, and Joseph Harrington. *Economics of Regulation and Antitrust,* 2d ed. Cambridge: MIT Press, 1995.

THE INSTITUTIONS OF A MODERN MARKET ECONOMY

In Chapter 1 we discussed in broad outline the types of institution that comprise any economy, and in Chapter 4 we visited the important issue of market failure and looked at some of the ways government acts to attempt to remedy market failures. In this chapter we will look in more detail at the framework of a "developed market economy," and how the established institutions operate to shape and steer the functions of the economy. We start with a discussion of the various objectives of government policy and how they fit together, and sometimes conflict, in an overall picture of government activity.

THE OBJECTIVES OF GOVERNMENT POLICY

It seems almost too obvious to state, but in a mixed market economy (like the United States, Japan, and Germany) the government is one of the most important institutions. Even in those countries that are popularly regarded as the bastions of free enterprise and capitalism, a large part of the gross domestic product (GDP) passes through the government sector, with public employment representing a considerable share of the total. The revenues of industrial giants such as General Motors, Exxon, or Microsoft are quite small compared to the receipts and expenditures of governments in developed industrial economies. The debts of banks, corporations, and households similarly pale when compared to government debt. Government regulations, civil, criminal, and administrative law control or shape almost every aspect of our lives. One way of viewing government activity is to see government as being divisible into three functions: allocation, categorization, and stabilization.[1] This functional characterization enables us to view the operation of government systematically. However, we must always bear in mind that policies implemented to achieve goals related to one function inevitably lead to "spillovers" that affect the others.

The Allocation Function

The existence of market failures, as discussed in Chapter 4, suggests the need for government intervention because the market alone either failed to supply some

---

[1]For a full discussion of this view of the responsibilities of government, see Richard and Peggy Musgrave, *Public Finance in Theory and Practice* (New York: McGraw-Hill, 1984).

goods altogether or supplied certain goods at allocatively inefficient quantities and prices. We also discussed the problem of government failure, which occurs when the costs of government intervention are greater than any potential social gain, or when the action of the governmental/political process frustrates the possibility of socially advantageous intervention. Nevertheless, governments of all mixed capitalist societies are involved in the production of goods and the regulation of business, with overt justification of improving the allocative efficiency of the economy. This activity is what we term the **allocation function** of government.

Government Production of Pure, Public, Quasi-Public, and Merit Goods

We established in Chapter 4 that although pure public goods are theoretically important, operationally they form a rather limited class of goods. The market could also provide most of the goods that are provided governments. A list of what is actually produced, at least in part, by some level of the government in the United States, includes national defense, passenger rail transportation, urban mass transit, law enforcement, electricity supply, education, health services, information, public health measures, research and development, water supply, postal services, and housing. We would obtain a similar list if we looked at most of the developed market economies in Europe or in Japan. As a general but not universal rule, the lower the overall level of development, the greater is the likelihood that the government assumes more extensive production responsibilities. Economic development tends to place greater reliance on private production, especially since the "transition" of the formerly planned economies. What is striking, however, is that almost all of the goods produced by governments are either also produced at the same time in the private sector or have close substitutes that are.

Some of the goods or services on the list of government production can be justified by the fact that the market would supply the goods only in suboptimal quantities and at prices that are too high. These goods generate substantial positive externalities or **spillovers** that are socially beneficial and not captured in the private market. Production by the public sector causes these goods to be supplied at a level closer to the optimum and priced more efficiently through the operation of a public subsidy, or at least priced at less than the profit-maximizing rate. Goods of this type might include information, education, electricity supply, public transportation, and water supply.[2] Finally, the government provides some goods as a form of income transfer; housing, health care, and to some degree education, fit this category.

Table 5.1 shows the structure of current government expenditure in 19 nations using standardized are Organization for Economic Cooperation and Development (OECD) classifications. The categories have been divided into "public goods" and "merit goods."[3] What characterizes the public goods is that they are supplied to the economy as a whole and there is no possibility of excluding any individuals. Merit

---

[2]One element that often becomes a factor in these industries is the possibility of cross-subsidization. High-cost users are charged the same rate as low-cost users, facilitating a single pricing scheme and coverage.

[3]"Merit goods" are supplied by the public sector at a level above that that would be demanded on a "fee for service basis," and involve, therefore, some interference with individual preferences.

■ **TABLE 5.1**

The Structure of Government Outlays by Function as a Percent of GDP

Total Expenditure		Public Goods				Merit Goods			
		Total	Defense	General Public Services	Other Functions	Total	Education	Health	Other Social Services
Australia	37.7	8.2	1.9	3.0	3.3	10.5	4.5	5.5	0.5
Austria	52.2	4.5	0.9	3.6	0.0	11.9	5.3	5.7	0.8
Canada	46.3	2.9	1.4	1.5	0.0	12.3	5.8	6.5	0.0
Czech Republic	40.8	3.9	1.6	2.3	0.0	11.1	4.4	6.1	0.5
Denmark	59.9	6.0	1.7	4.3	0.0	16.5	6.5	5.1	4.9
Finland	54.3	3.3	1.6	1.6	0.1	15.2	6.6	5.6	3.0
France	55.4	9.2	2.9	4.5	1.8	14.1	5.9	7.1	1.1
Germany	49.7	5.2	1.4	3.9	0.0	13.9	4.5	8.0	1.3
Italy	52.2	6.5	1.7	4.5	0.3	10.2	4.5	5.3	0.3
Japan	36.5	4.5	0.9	3.6	0.0	10.1	3.8	5.6	0.6
Korea	19.2	5.7	2.9	2.0	0.8	5.6	3.6	1.8	0.2
Netherlands	52.2	11.6	1.8	9.8	..	12.0	4.6	6.5	1.0
New Zealand	38.9	5.3	1.1	4.2	0.0	10.6	5.2	5.3	0.1
Norway	52.0	6.3	2.6	3.1	0.6	18.4	6.8	6.6	5.1
Portugal	49.9	8.3	2.2	2.0	4.1	10.6	5.4	4.7	, 0.5
Spain	45.2	9.9	1.4	1.8	6.7	10.6	4.8	5.5	0.3
Sweden	64.5	5.4	2.3	3.0	0.1	17.2	6.6	5.7	4.9
United Kingdom	43.6	5.4	3.2	1.9	0.2	11.5	4.6	5.7	1.2
United States	34.3	9.2	5.2	2.9	1.0	11.9	5.0	6.5	0.4

SOURCE: OECD 2001; Economic Survey of Czech Republic, 2001.

goods such as health and education could be provided by the private sector, but the government chooses to supply them as a redistributive or egalitarian measure. The first thing that strikes us about the data in Table 5.1 is the wide variation in the scope of government as a percentage of GDP; Korea is the lowest followed by the United States and Japan. In general, the continental European nations engage in the highest levels of government activity, reaching a peak in the Scandinavian states of Denmark and Sweden. Less variation appears between nations in terms of current expenditures, though the features of individual economies can be quite important. Some nations show especially high levels of particular social expenditures, for example health care in Germany or educational expenditures in Norway. The United States far outpaces the other OECD members in terms of defense spending.

Information as a Public Good The provision of information performs an important function of a modern government. Without good information on a wide range of topics (from the weather to the unemployment rate), the economic actors cannot make informed and therefore rational decisions. Information is not, however, a pure public good. Even though the marginal cost of providing information to additional users is low (especially in the age of television and the Web), it is quite possible to charge for information and exclude nonpayers from receiving it. A whole industry of consultants relies on the charging of a fee for "proprietary" information, at prices that reflect a monopoly rent rather than the cost of dissemination. Information may, therefore, be thought of as a *quasi-public good.*

Nevertheless, information gathering is costly, and social resources can be saved if needless duplication can be avoided. Thus a government's role in the collation and dissemination of information may be justifiable on efficiency grounds. Improved information flows allow better decisions to be made and enhance the overall efficiency of the market system.

Regulation of Products A large part of government activity is concerned with product regulation of one form or another. In the United States, for example, regulatory agencies set standards for the safety, quality, and efficacy of many products. The economic basis for regulation, in terms of improving the allocative efficiency of the economy, lies in the fact that it economizes information costs for consumers.

Regulation of Industry Moreover as we discussed in Chapter 4, governments have extensive powers to regulate prices and outputs in industry most frequently to address market failure due to monopoly.

The Distribution Function

Income Support The **distribution function** of government actually entails redistributing income. Although this activity is not new (even ancient Egypt and Rome instituted income support policies) it has grown enormously in importance in recent decades. A large part of government expenditure moves toward some form of amelioration of income distribution. In previous centuries, governments oriented their assistance toward poverty relief and intended only to raise the indigent to the subsistence level.

In the twentieth century the government assumed increased responsibility for stabilizing the economy. It also came to be held increasingly responsible for the individual as well as the aggregate consequences of joblessness. "Social security" became a common feature (and a burgeoning bureaucracy) in all developed economies during the twentieth century. Support was provided not only for the unemployed but also for the elderly, single parents, and the disabled. As a result, transfer payments required a larger share of government expenditure.

The economic consequences of this steady progress toward guaranteed income are much debated. Today the prevailing orthodox view is that redistributive payments have sharply reduced the flexibility of labor markets. Providing support for people without jobs reduces the urgency of job search, lowers incentives to find work, and encourages higher wage demands. These factors in turn lead to higher levels of unemployment. In the countries of Western Europe, where the reduction in take-home income on losing a job can be as little as 10 percent, the cost of being unemployed is correspondingly low and unemployment rates are high.

Concern over the disincentive consequences of income transfer schemes continues to grow. Measures to reduce unemployment benefits and tighten accessibility rules have been made in some developed market economies. Some evidence indicates that sharp falls in unemployment often accompany such steps. Britain provides a case in point, which following a trimming of the welfare state now experiences its lowest unemployment rate in decades. On the other hand, countries that maintain high benefit rates continue to see unemployment grow (e.g., France). Although these examples suggest a link, evidence that transfers payments actually *cause* unemployment is slight. Some income support for the jobless can be justified in terms of raising the allocative efficiency of the economy because it allows a more rational process of job search and a better resultant fit.

Redistribution In-Kind Economic theory tells us that an individual's welfare is raised by increasing his or her ability to choose. Consequently, welfare-maximizing redistribution, at least from the recipient's viewpoint, should consist of unrestricted cash grants. However, much **redistributive in-kind** activity actually takes the form of public provision of goods that might well be supplied privately, including health care, education, housing, and food. The adoption of such a system can be justified in two ways. First, it is claimed that these goods generate social externalities. Consequently, the loss of an individual recipient's welfare through constraining choice is compensated by a rise in the welfare of third parties. Second, some may argue that the recipients may be ill-informed or irrational and act against their own long-run welfare. If given free control over resources they would dispose of them in a fashion that would favor short-term gratification over long-term well-being. Hence an element of paternalism is used to justify the public provision of such goods, rather than providing cash to purchase the appropriate amount in private markets. This interference with individual preferences creates a class of goods that are referred to in the literature as **merit goods**, and they are widespread in most economies.

In recent years the state-owned industries and bureaucracies created by the public provision of these goods have come under attack because of their alleged inefficiency and inflexibility relative to the private sector. In the United States criticism focused on publicly provided education. In Britain the National Health Service fell under siege. One possible avenue of reform involves the use of **voucher systems**, which have attracted much support in recent years. Although they may result in interference with personal preferences, because of their (unlike cash) service-specific nature, they introduce consumer choice between suppliers and therefore foster competition, ideally leading to greater efficiency.

The Stabilization Function

The idea that governments should be responsible for the level of macroeconomic activity—the level of unemployment, the rate of inflation, and the rate of growth— is a relatively recent one. The argument for government's **stabilization function** comes from two sources. One was political reform that broadened the franchise and gave a louder voice to those most affected by unemployment. The second lay in the developments in macroeconomic theory and statistical collation that occurred in the twentieth century, especially in the Depression-troubled 1930s, which made government management of the economy more feasible. Emphasis on government responsibility for the macroeconomy reached its height in the 1960s when it was widely held that the principles underlying economic activity were so well-understood that the economic task of government was merely to fine-tune the economy. However, faith in the ability of government to deliver low inflation and high employment faltered in the economically turbulent 1970s. Stabilization policy apparently failed and came to have negative connotations. Confidence in the effectiveness of fiscal policy waned, and government activity came to be seen by a growing number of economists as the cause of instability rather than its antidote.

During the 1960s much of stabilization policy was framed in terms of the judicious trade-off between inflation and unemployment. Then, a new orthodoxy emerged in the 1970s suggesting that unemployment. Then, at least below a threshold "natural" level, was, after all, not something that the government could do much about. Attempts to raise employment accelerated the rate of inflation, without showing any long-term results. Slow growth became associated with government interference in demand management as public expenditure crowded out private investment. Today we find ourselves back in the middle of the road. Confidence in our ability to guarantee stability may occasionally be shaken, but postwar recessions proved to be relatively mild and most economists believe that economic policy can be effective in shaping economic outcomes for the better.

The Instruments of Stabilization In most mixed market economies governments have at their disposal two distinct sets of policy measures: fiscal (those that involve the changing of tax rates and government expenditure) and monetary (those that involve the manipulation of the money stock in the hands of the public).

Fiscal Policy To be effective, **fiscal policy** requires a well-developed and defined tax system in which tax rules are both visible and enforced. This system, in turn, presupposes a government supported by an established and competent bureaucracy. In less-developed economies, and also in the transition economies of Eastern Europe, the lack of the essential infrastructure for tax gathering limits the effectiveness of fiscal policy. Fiscal policy concerns itself not only with the changing of taxes and tax rates, but also with the role of government expenditures on macroeconomic activity. Stabilization can be effected by shifts in government expenditures (for example, by the initiation of public expenditure projects or the curtailment of unemployment insurance payments). Government expenditures, like taxes, tend to have an automatic stabilizer effect, because even in the absence of policy shifts they rise as the economy contracts.

In modern mixed market economies, tax capabilities are by and large similar. Some countries have more efficient tax systems and greater degrees of tax compliance than others, which affects economic performance. However, the larger differences lie in the kind of tax structure adopted. The United States, for example, relies heavily on income taxes, social security taxes, and corporate income taxes at the federal level.[4] State finance is predominantly based on sales taxes, supplemented by individual and business income taxes. Other economies depend more on indirect taxes at the national level. In Europe, for example, much greater reliance is on indirect taxation, largely through value-added taxes.

Monetary Policy The other broad technique of macroeconomic stabilization is the use of **monetary policy** to influence the rate of interest, the rate of inflation, and therefore the price level. Responsibility for the implementation (and in many economies the determination) of monetary policy resides with the central bank whose functioning we later discuss more fully in the context of the financial system.

THE TAX SYSTEM

What really sets the government apart from other institutions is that it holds a monopoly on the power to tax. No other institution can demand that resources be transferred to it with no specific *quid pro quo* under the threat of sanctions that include imprisonment. This unique feature makes the activity of government of prime importance and the design and functioning of the tax system a decisive feature for the operation of the economic system. Taxes are generally divided into two types: those imposed on people or firms (direct taxation) and those levied on goods (indirect taxation). The most important direct tax—measured in terms of the share of total revenue that it raises—is the personal income tax in most economies. Direct taxation also includes social security taxes, corporate taxes, expenditure taxes,[5] and some forms of wealth and estate taxation.

The degree of progressivity of direct taxation differs sharply between economies. Under a **progressive tax** the average tax rate rises as the individual's or household's base of the tax (income, expenditure, or wealth) increases. Progressivity was at one time almost universally considered a desirable characteristic in a tax system. Some people justified it on moral or ethical grounds arguing that equal sacrifice of welfare across the population required an increasing average rate of income tax because the marginal utility of money declines as income increases. To others it offered the more pragmatic virtue of constituting an "automatic stabilizer," which would limit or dampen the cyclical behavior of the macroeconomy. As the economy expanded, under a progressive tax system, tax revenues would increase at a faster rate than national income. Thus the size of the government fiscal deficit would shrink (or the size of the surplus increase), hence slowing economic growth. The reverse would hold in cyclical downturns.

---

[4]In 2000, 42.6 percent of federal revenue came from the individual income tax, 36 percent from social security taxes, and 12 percent from corporate income taxes, with the remaining 8 percent from other sources, chiefly excise taxes, as reported in the *Economic Report of the President.*

[5]Expenditure taxes are levied on an individual's or household's total aggregate consumption expenditure and should not be confused with sales taxes, which are indirect taxes imposed at the point of purchase.

In more recent years, however, the consensus favoring progressivity weakened, largely because the negative supply-side effects of high personal taxation attracted more concern. Equity and equal sacrifice are now thought of more in terms of proportionality (i.e., constant average and marginal rate taxation) rather than requiring progressivity. Consequently, the number of tax brackets declined and lower tax rates applied more generally. This change pertained especially to the taxation of capital. In many economies, so-called unearned income (interest, dividends, properties, rents, etc.) was once taxed at higher rates. Sometimes these rates were close to confiscatory—70 percent and higher. Today differential rates for earned and unearned income are largely a thing of the past. In fact, in some countries, the pendulum has swung toward the other extreme and income from capital is actually taxed at lower rates than that from labor. In the United States, changes in the treatment of capital gains resulted in some forms of capital income being taxed at a lower rate than wage or salary income. Lower marginal tax rates also provide the beneficial effect of lowering the incidence of both tax evasion and tax avoidance.[6]

Taxes can be levied on objects rather than on individuals, and this constitutes indirect taxation. Imposing taxes on things (commodities, imports, exports, houses, land, etc.) tends to be administratively easier than all but the simplest direct taxes on individuals. A glance at history tells us that states once generally relied on commodity or land taxation for public finance. In modern mixed capitalist societies, commodity taxation is still widely practiced (see Table 5.2). In the United States, local government is largely financed by taxes on real property, while some form of sales taxation predominates at the state level.

Countries in a lower state of economic development often rely on a relatively simple form of indirect taxation with highly visible "tax handles" that do not require a sophisticated enforcement mechanism (although evasion through an under-the-counter cash market is frequent). In history, several nations relied on "salt taxes," which, because the taxes fell on a good with a low price elasticity, were relatively efficient with minimal deadweight loss. However, such single commodity taxation cannot raise the volume of revenue required by a modern state. Consequently, a broader base is often sought. Unfortunately, simple turnover and gross receipts taxes, which are the easiest to administer, bring with them the drawbacks of being inefficient and distortionary, and nondistortionary indirect taxes like the value-added tax (VAT) are preferable where possible.

We have distinguished to this point between direct taxes, which are levied on the characteristics of individuals or families, and indirect taxes that fall upon objects or activities. Taxes levied on the profits of businesses, organized corporations, or public limited liability companies, are usually classed as direct, as if they fell upon an individual. Such taxes make up a significant element of the overall public finance system of developed economies, and the tax base is the profit stream of incorporated business.

---

[6]Tax evasion is the illegal concealment of tax liabilities from the authorities. Tax avoidance is the alteration of behavior to limit tax exposure; it involves a deadweight loss to society.

■ **TABLE 5.2**

**The Structure of the Tax System in Selected Countries
(tax structures as a percentage of total tax receipts)**

	Total Tax Receipts (percentage of GDP)	Personal Income Tax	Social Security Contributions		Total Taxes on Income	Corporate Income Tax	Taxes on Goods and Services	Other Taxes
			Employees	Employers				
Australia	29.9	43.3	0	0	43.3	15.2	25.5	16
Belgium	45.9	30.7	9.7	19.2	59.6	8.5	24.9	7
Canada	37.4	37.8	5.3	8.1	51.2	10.5	24.7	13.6
Czech Republic	38.3	13.6	10.1	28.8	52.5	9.7	31	6.8
Denmark	49.8	51.6	2.4	0.7	54.7	5.6	33.2	6.5
France	45.2	17.4	8.7	25.2	51.3	5.9	26.6	16.2
Italy	42.7	25	6.3	20.5	51.8	7	27.4	13.8
Japan	28.4	18.8	15	19.6	53.4	13.3	18.8	14.5
Korea	21.1	20.1	3.3	7.7	31.1	12.2	40.5	16.2
Poland	37.9	22	0	32.3	54.3	7.5	34.4	3.8
Sweden	52	35	5.8	22.5	63.3	5.7	21.6	9.4
Turkey	28.7	27	5.7	7.3	40	5.8	35.7	18.5
United Kingdom	37.2	27.5	7.3	9.4	44.2	11	32.6	12.2
United States	28.9	40.5	10.2	12.2	62.9	9	16.2	11.9
EU Average	41.3	25.6	8.2	15.9	49.7	8.7	30.2	11.4
OECD Average	37	27	7	14.9	48.9	8.9	31.3	10.8

SOURCE: *OECD in Figures,* 2001, p. 38.

At the federal level, the United States depends almost exclusively on direct taxation. The individual income tax constitutes 45 percent of total revenue, and the social security payroll taxes contribute 38 percent. Thus taxes on personal income comprise 83 percent of total revenues. Corporate income taxes constitute about 11 percent of total revenues, and the balance of about 6 percent is made up of excise taxes, gift and estate taxes, and custom duties. At the state level there is a much greater reliance on sales taxes and property taxes, indirect taxes which amount to more than half of the revenue. The tax systems of other nations differ in terms of the balance of reliance on direct versus indirect taxation. In Europe, for example, the value-added tax, an indirect tax, contributes an important part of central government revenue.

It is clear that both the design of the tax system and the overall tax burden have important effects on economic growth and performance. Taxes are not only generally distortionary, but also are frequently structured to favor particular groups or activities. However, just as important as the overt or nominal tax structure are the efficiency and the even-handedness of tax administration. Healthy economies require honest and efficient tax administrations. Without them it is hard for a nation to prosper.

THE LEGAL SYSTEM

Any modern market economy depends on a clear and enforceable system of property rights, and the clarification and enforcement of such rights are the most important economic roles of the legal system. A complex and resource-expensive system has grown up in market economies to control these functions. Some would argue that the role and scope of the law have become too broad and the cost of the legal system too high. Nowhere does the law and the role of lawyers figure so prominently as in the United States. In most market economies the percentage of national income accounted for by the legal system remains small compared to the United States, but is generally growing.

Ownership and Property Rights

In Chapter 1 we discussed the concept of property ownership, and we saw that it is a rather more complex matter than might seem at first glance, embracing the issue of property rights, which extend beyond merely physical property. It is concerned with rights as varied as the right to clean air, the right to quiet, the right to access to sunlight, the right to earn income from an invention, and the right to broadcast over the airwaves. In the West, property rights developed incrementally and subsequently adapted and extended to take account of new complexities, both by legislation and by precedent in law. New technologies and new external circumstances continue to require that new rights be defined. For example, the issues of environmental property rights, intellectual property rights, and the right of access to radio frequencies recently leaped to prominence.

Although even the limited right of ownership and transfer of physical property will ensure the development of some forms of market relations, it does not go far in stimulating economic efficiency. Alone it will lead, in the words of Evgenii Yasin, a Russian reform economist, to a "bazaar" rather than a "market." A market system requires much more. As one of its functions, the complex legal system of western nations promotes efficiency in the use of scarce resources. Of course, this is not the sole function of the law. It must also protect individual and group rights against a variety of incursions. Moreover, although many laws and regulations have evolved to contribute to the efficient operation of a market economy, a good deal of legislation serves the interest of quite narrow groups and does little either for economic efficiency or human rights.

Freedom to Engage in Economic Activity

In order for prices of goods to even approximate resource costs, markets must be relatively competitive, and this requiring that individuals, and groups of individuals or firms, have the right to engage in whatever economic activity they perceive as offering the greatest return. In simple terms, people must have the right to choose their own professions (among them being a self-employed entrepreneur) and choose the physical locations where they pursue these professions. This is much the same as granting individuals the right to enter any business or industry that they choose and to live wherever they want. Without a guarantee of free market entry, private monopolies, with their attendant inefficiencies, would arise. Under such conditions prices would not reflect the resource costs of production and monopoly rents[7] would be appropriated, harming efficiency. A major target of Adam Smith's *Wealth of Nations* was the system of royal licensing and monopoly that restricted the action of the individual. If the state can prevent the entry of individuals into a trade or profession, then the consumer, indeed society as a whole, is the loser while the monopolist or the official that grants it monopoly powers is the winner.

Even today free entry into all economic activities is not guaranteed in overtly market systems. Many professions and trades require licenses or permits; this practice is usually defended as being efficient because customers cannot always gather all the information they need. Certifying lawyers, stockbrokers, or auto mechanics provides cheap information designed to protect the consumer, though clearly certification is no guarantee of competence or honesty. Although market radicals, such as Milton Friedman, denounce such regulation as monopolistic and therefore inefficient, such barriers are an integral part of economic life in most market systems.

The Enforcement of Contracts and Compensation

Ownership and entry will create an infrastructure in which rudimentary exchange can take place, but such a market could operate only with a short time horizon. Longer-term economic relationships are made viable by the use of contracts that bind parties to specific performance standards. Contracts are an integral part of moving from the "bazaar," where already-produced goods are exchanged, into a longer-term system of stable interrelations enabling planning and foresight. A contract specifies what both parties must do, whatever the change in external circumstance, and provides for enforcement or compensation for nonperformance.

Some long-term relationships can be established even in the absence of enforceable contracts, because the market can produce its own remedies often through reputation effects. A supplier, for example, who persistently failed to deliver, would encounter a great deal of difficulty finding future customers as knowledge of his persistent failures to perform became widespread. However, contract law removes part of the costs of gathering information from the contracting parties by providing general remedies and compensation for failure to perform and to deliver. This feature obviates the need for a socially expensive search, although it introduces costs of making and enforcing contracts. To promote economic efficiency, contract enforcement need not always require strict performance to the letter of the contract, but it may instead give the injured party compensation for the losses incurred as a result of nonperformance. Strict enforcement would be burdensome and inefficient in some cases where expected circumstances have changed and fulfilling the contract in its literal terms becomes impossible. However, the law must provide both the means for the injured party to be compensated and an appropriate system of adjudicating damages resulting from nonperformance.

---

[7]Monopoly rent is the margin above normal profit that results from the exercise of monopoly power.

Bankruptcy Law

Frequently overlooked in the discussions of infrastructure is the role of bankruptcy legislation. Capitalism is, in Schumpeter's words, a "gale of creative destruction." Company failure and the dissolution of corporations must be regarded as a normal facet of the system. The efficient operation of that system, however, is highly dependent on the predictable disposition of the assets of the firm in the event of failure. A necessary condition for orderly capital markets is a full and enforceable set of defined property rights, and bankruptcy law is one component of these rights.[8] The risks that lenders and materials suppliers assume in supplying a firm can only be assessed when there is full knowledge of the pecking order in which debtors will be arrayed should the firm go into bankruptcy. As developments in the energy giant Enron and communications titan WorldCom recently showed us, lenders are well advised to look into their claims of repayment in the event of bankruptcy even when lending to firms that look large and prosperous.

Accounting and Financial Disclosure

The law plays a vital role by requiring that firms report their financial results in a specified standard accounting system and that this information be made publicly available. The efficiency aspects of this requirement become obvious if we consider the alternative: without required and standardized disclosure, the costs of information to an individual or other firms, whether potential shareholders, suppliers, or customers, would be very high. Thus required disclosure has clear social efficiency in reducing information costs. This is of great importance in the operation of equity markets, where buying shares without access to accurate information on the financial state of the company would be undesirably risky and share prices would not reflect underlying values. It is also of great relevance to those who supply the company with raw materials and inputs and those who provide credit to firms in more direct ways. The results of inadequate standards in financial disclosure can be seen in the scandals that plagued the U.S. economy in 2002.

A Clear Definition of Governmental Responsibility

Just as a lack of clarity and stability in tax regimes is a disincentive to business activity and investment, so is any imprecision or opaqueness in the role of government. Confusion about government restriction or subsidies, or which level of government has jurisdiction, can constitute an impediment to the growth of economic activity. As the size and scope of governmental activity has grown, the codification of governmental responsibility and its limits has become more vital. For example, a worker's rational behavior in the labor market is contingent on a clear understanding of his or her rights in the social security system. These rights must therefore be clearly and comprehensively stated to avoid their arbitrary implementation. Firms need to know government's responsibilities in providing services, enforcing

---

[8]See J. Mitchell, "Managerial Discipline, Productivity and Bankruptcy in Capitalist and Socialist Economies," *Comparative Economic Studies* 22, no. 3 (Fall 1990).

THE CRASH OF 2002

The consequences of failure to provide clear and reliable financial disclosure became abundantly clear in the United States during the stock market downturn of 2000–2002. After the boom of the late 1990s several important companies resorted to creative accounting techniques to boost the public's perception of their revenue and profits. The accounting firms proved too complacent and were often compromised by acting both as consultants to companies as well as auditor of their books. Investors became alarmed by their inability to determine a company's true financial position. Suppliers and buyers also felt reluctant to enter into contractual relationships with firms who might be closer to bankruptcy than their published accounts seemed to show. Among the major casualties were the energy trader, Enron, and the telecommunications firms, Global Crossing and WorldCom. Drastic consequences also befell Arthur Andersen, one of the world's largest accounting firms, which seemed to be a willing tool of the companies rather than an independent arbiter of a firm's financial condition.

The U.S. government's response focused on changing the regulating framework. In the short term, chief executive officers are to be required to certify, under penalty of law, the correctness of the accounting statements. More reform is probable, including a prohibition on ac-counting firms acting both as consultant and auditor.

The real consequences of the crisis for the U.S. economy remain at the present difficult to fathom. The flight of investors from the market may greatly affect the way that companies raise money, and may affect investment and the growth of the U.S. economy. The reaction of foreign investors might also be particularly severe. Far from being the safe haven of capitalism, the United States began to look riskier than many other markets, especially Europe where the heavier hand of government generally practiced high accounting standards.

standards, and regulating labor before they can optimize their behavior. In developed market economies, therefore, a large body of administrative law evolved to define governmental responsibility.

One area of the world where we can see a pressing need for a clear definition of governmental responsibility is in the economies now in transition where once the state was both all-powerful and all-responsible. With no distinction between where the activities of government ended and the activities of enterprises began, the state was both the producer of almost all goods and the provider of social services. In such a situation the productive enterprises, as wholly owned agents of the state, understandably assumed a much greater responsibility toward the social welfare of their employees. Now the smooth functioning of industry and the labor market requires a clear and comprehensive definition of a government-provided social safety net.

A System of Civil Compensation

A functioning civil code provides an aid to business. Just as incorporation[9] removes the shareholders from exposure to unlimited financial loss due to failure or the infliction of harm to third parties, so a **civil compensation** code removes businesspeople

---

[9]A fuller discussion of the corporate form and its advantages is provided later in this chapter.

from the threat of criminal proceedings in all but the most blatantly negligent incidents. It might be argued that chief executive officers would be even more careful about the behavior of their corporations and underlings if they were liable to a jail term rather than merely dipping into the shareholders' profits to settle a suit. However, a system of criminal redress would lead to two consequences. First, it would affect the behavior of potential victims by encouraging untoward caution because they know that no monetary compensation will be available. Second, it would discourage quite legitimate business activity because of fear of criminal punishment.

We can better understand the significance of a civil code by considering what would happen in the absence of civil compensation, a circumstance that existed in socialist economies where the law of liability was likened to military law. Blame, when it could be assigned, was a criminal matter and would be redressed by the punishment of the offender rather than by the compensation of the victim. **Tort law**, which deals with the redressing of private or civil wrongs through suit, did not exist in the centrally planned economies. Some may think that the United States suffers from a plague of lawyers, many of whom make their living through civil suits, and the prospect of a tort-free society might seem attractive. However, the threat of suit can clearly have positive influences; a firm found guilty of injury will ameliorate its behavior in the future, the more so if forced to pay punitive damages. Consider a Western business engaged in for example an extractive industry, wishing to start operations in, for example, Russia. The technique is not without risk either to the business's own workers or other nearby individuals. In the West, the businessperson would know that he or she is subject to civil suit in the case of accidents, but to criminal liability only in the case of gross negligence. In Eastern Europe and the former Soviet Union, it is quite possible that the redress would occur only through criminal proceedings. What is true for the Western investor is also true for the domestic Russian businessperson. Removing the greatest problems to investment while retaining some censure over dangerous behavior, and ensuring the ability of the victim to be compensated, requires the development of a civil liability code.

THE FINANCIAL SYSTEM

The role of a financial system in a mixed capitalist economy is paramount. It can be argued that, since it does not "produce" any final good, the financial superstructure of an economy is to some extent "unproductive," but the evidence of recent years seems to be that those countries with the least regulated and most competitive financial systems have been the ones that have prospered. This situation contrasts sharply with that of the 1970s and 1980s, when the economies with highly controlled (Japan and Korea) or noncompetitive (Germany) financial systems seemed to perform best in terms of economic aggregates.

The Central Bank

At the heart of the financial system is the central bank. The linchpin of monetary policy, the central bank has several important functions to discharge. Generally speaking, these include the following:

1. To act as a clearing bank for other banks
2. To act as the promulgator and enforcer of financial regulation, designed to enhance the stability and efficiency of the financial system
3. To act as a lender of last resort
4. To control the overall stock of money in the economy, and hence the interest rate
5. To monitor the foreign exchange value of the currency

The central bank has at its disposal several tools with which to influence the stock of money in the system:

1. Open-market operations, by which the central bank buys or sells government bonds to and from the public
2. Reserve requirements, which constitute controls on the minimum amount of liquid reserves that a bank must hold against the liabilities that it owes its depositors
3. The discount rate, which is the interest rate at which the central bank lends money to banks to provide the reserve base against which banks can lend to borrowers

In addition to these tools of the central bank, the money supply can also be changed by the obvious device of printing more money, although that is usually the activity of the treasury or finance ministry rather than the central bank.

The Independence of the Central Bank A key issue in comparing economic structures lies in the relative degree of **central bank independence**. In the United States and, for example, Germany, the central banks have constitutions and hold powers that insulate them to a high degree from the government and the political system. In other countries, autonomy is not the case. The Bank of Japan and the Bank of France are highly controlled by the government. The Bank of England, which was for most of the postwar period an obedient arm of the British government, has now been granted practically total independence.

A seven-member board of governors determines monetary policy in the United States. Each governor is appointed by the president of the United States and confirmed by the Senate. Vacancies occur on average about every two years, and during a maximum of two terms in office a president is likely to appoint at most four governors. Thus a president can structure the board of governors to his ideological liking only at the point at which his second term ends.

The argument for independence largely rests on the fact that central bankers have a tough job to do. Their expertise allows them to make impartial decisions and "do the right thing" if politicians are prevented from influencing them. After all, the prime job of the central bank is to preserve the value of the currency and it should therefore frequently take a restrictive and conservative line on credit creation. If politicians were given control over the central bank, monetary policy would tend to be too relaxed. The hard job of squeezing credit and watching enterprises fail, while unemployment mounted, would be avoided.

The opposing view argues is that a totally independent central bank answers to no one. In a market economy it is an institution of great power,[10] and it is odd that in a representative democracy the people have no say in this vital dimension of policy making. In this view the central bank responds largely to the narrow financial community from which members of the board of governors are likely to spring. As such, an independent central bank might be unduly austere, placing burdens on the less well off, and hence jeopardizing political stability by pursuing its own brand of financial rectitude.

This debate ultimately fails to produce a right or wrong answer. Politicians are adept at judging the public will, and when they control the central bank we could say that a form of representative democracy prevails. On the other hand, politicians do tend to have a short-term outlook and are prone to shallow compromise, where the financial experts insulated from pressure might effect the correct long-term policies.

Depository Institutions

The important tasks of the financial system are the pooling of savings, the assessment of borrowers, and the lending of funds at appropriate interest rates. The gathering of the savings of small savers is largely a task of the **depository institutions**: commercial banks, savings and loans (also known as thrifts, building societies, etc.), credit unions, and (in many countries) the postal savings system.

Commercial Banks Commercial banks are characterized mainly by the fact that they accept deposits from individuals and firms, they allow the transfer of funds by check from account to account, and they lend out money to individuals and businesses. Within these broad parameters they can take a variety of institutional forms. In most market economies they are privately owned (rather than nationalized) institutions, they are organized as limited liability corporations, and they are profit seeking. However, a quick glance at the commercial banking structure of various countries reveals wide differences. The United States is characterized by a large number of commercial banks, and this is a product of regulation. Banking is governed by state law, and interstate branching of banks was for a long time prohibited. Consequently, while other countries witnessed their banking system consolidated by mergers and takeovers, in the United States a large number of independent commercial banks survive to this day. There are some 12,000 commercial banks in the United States, a clear contrast to the much more concentrated systems in, for example, England or Canada, where only a handful of institutions dominate commercial banking.

Depositors use commercial banks largely as a matter of convenience and security. Demand deposits usually carry no, or a low, interest rate, but this rate is offset by accessibility and the safety provided by the banks' diversified portfolio of assets. Borrowers use commercial banks as a source of funds because transaction costs are likely to be lower than having direct access to the stock or bond markets.

---

[10]If confirmation of its power were required, we would only need to take note of the army of "Fed watchers" in the United States, who are concerned with predicting the Fed's behavior.

In most industrialized countries commercial banks are the dominant form of corporation finance for small and middle-sized companies. Stability and probity are essential in the commercial banking system. For those reasons, most commercial banking systems are heavily regulated, to avoid the prospect of bank failure, and the deposits of customers are often insured by the government to guard against runs on a bank.

Savings and Loan Banks   Savings institutions (otherwise known as thrifts or, in some countries, building societies) evolved largely as a means to finance home construction and ownership. They accept interest-paying deposits from savers and lend money to home buyers as mortgages. These activities can lead to a serious mismatch in the term structure of their assets and liabilities. Interest rates on mortgages are long-term and represent illiquid assets.[11] Deposits, the thrift's liabilities, on the other hand, are liquid. In the United States in the late 1970s and 1980s deposits flowed from the thrifts to the rapidly growing money market mutual funds, creating a shortage of liquidity that was popularly known as the "savings and loan" crisis.

Credit Unions   A growing alternative institution for savings and lending in the United States has been the credit union. One of the problems of lending to individuals is the difficulty of gathering information on the characteristics of the borrower and hence assessing the appropriate level of risk to assign. Credit unions tackle this problem by lending only to people who share some characteristics (generally occupation or employer). This familiarity reduces risk and makes the problem more tractable.

Postal Savings Banks   Although they are not found in every country, many economies make use of an extensive postal savings bank as a vehicle for mass banking. Such a system uses the wide distribution of post offices to create a highly accessible banking network, which provides a highly liquid form of savings but pays low interest. Post office banks do not make loans, but the accumulated and pooled saving is generally passed upward to the government. It is, therefore, either a way of subsidizing the general government deficit or a source of pooled savings to be used on some investment project. In Japan, for example, such saving is received from the post office and channeled by the Ministry of Finance to fund, via the major banks, chosen industrial projects.

Nondepository Institutions

Investment Banks   Investment banks are not depository institutions. Their principal function is to assist larger businesses in acquiring new capital by issuing and underwriting new stock or bond issues into the primary financial markets. In this underwriting function, **investment banks** guarantee a price to the issuer and try to

---

[11]In the United Kingdom, building society mortgages almost universally use a variable rate, and U.K. building societies were not placed in the squeeze that their counterparts in the United States experienced.

profit by selling the stock at a level above the guaranteed price. The difference between the guaranteed price and the sale price is known as the *spread*.

Investment banks increase the efficiency of the financial system by reducing information costs. A buyer of securities can rely on the name and reputation of the investment bank as a proxy for expensive research about the reliability of the issuer. Investment banks offer advice and help in the restructuring of firms and merger acquisitions. They also engage in merchant banking by lending their own capital to firms in the process of reorganization.

Mutual Funds Mutual funds are financial intermediaries that allow individual investors to take advantage of the returns and security offered by investing in diversified portfolios of stocks, bonds, or other instruments, such as short-term corporate debt. The mutual fund industry experienced enormous growth in recent years, especially in the United States, as smaller savers use it to gain access to stocks with the security of diversification. This growth meant negative implications for other parts of the financial system. Thrift institutions (i.e., savings and loans in the United States) found themselves fighting harder for deposits and raising interest payments to compete with mutual funds.

Venture Capital Funds In recent years venture capitalism made a strong comeback and can be credited with providing much of the finance for the small and medium-sized firms that powered the great expansion of the United States economy in the 1990s. Venture capital companies generally raise risk capital from private sources and grant it to start-up firms in return for a portion of the share capital. In general, venture capital companies prove more flexible and innovative than commercial or investment banks.

Insurance Companies Although one function of insurance is to protect individuals and companies from risk, the accretion of the premiums paid by policyholders puts a great deal of capital in the hands of the insurance companies and makes them important players in financial markets. As Table 5.3 shows, in the United States, insurance companies hold about 4 percent of all common stock. In other countries, Japan and the United Kingdom especially, the share is much greater.

The Market for Financial Assets

The financial sector concerns itself primarily with the transfer of the various forms of financial assets: stocks (or shares), which indicate ownership of corporations, or bonds or other forms of debit instruments that may be issued either by corporations or by any level of government. The action of the financial markets by and large determines which companies should grow and which should contract or become defunct by regulating access to investment capital.

The Ownership of Stock Financial structures vary between countries. One aspect of this variation can be found in how dispersed share ownership is within the population. Table 5.3 gives data on the major capitalist economies. One immediately

■ TABLE 5.3

Ownership of Common Stock: An International Comparison (percentage at year-end)

	United States	Japan	Germany	France	United Kingdom	Italy	Sweden
	1994	FY 1994	1993	1993	1993	1993	1993
Financial Sector	**45**	**44**	**29**	**8**	**62**	**19**	**24**
Banks	3	26	14	3	1	10	1
Insurance companies	4	16	7	1	17	2	8
Investment funds	0	0	0	0	0	0	8
Pension funds	26	0	0	0	34	0	0
Mutual funds	12	0	8	2	7	6	6
Other financial institutions	4	2	0	2	3	1	0
Nonfinancial Sector	**55**	**56**	**71**	**92**	**38**	**81**	**76**
Nonfinancial enterprises	0	24	39	59	2	32	34
Public authorities	0	1	4	4	1	28	7
Individuals	48	24	17	19	18	17	16
Foreign	6	7	12	11	16	5	9
Other	1	0	0	0	2	0	10
Total	**100**	**100**	**100**	**100**	**100**	**100**	**100**

NOTE: Due to rounding, the figures may not add up to the total. Pension funds in Japan are managed by trust banks and insurance companies. The assets in these funds are included under banks and insurance companies. No data are available on the extent to which mutual funds own shares. Security houses do manage such funds; these companies are included under other financial institutions.
SOURCE: Board of the Federal Reserve System. Round Table of National Stock Exchanges, "Survey of Stock Ownership Distribution," *Flow of Funds*, August 1995; Deutsche Bundesbank, Banque de France, CSO, Consob, Banca d'Italia, Statistika Centralbyran, Sweden. Quoted in OECD (1995b); Annual Security Statistics (1995); OECD Economic Surveys, 1995–1996, Japan, p. 152.

apparent feature is the wide distribution of stock in the United States relative to other countries. Individuals hold almost half (48%) of the total market capitalization, and a further 12 percent lies in mutual funds, generally as a proxy for individuals. Financial institutions, such as insurance companies, banks, and pension funds, own only one-third of total shares. This "popular capitalism" is an important feature of the U.S. system. It ensures broad support for the capitalist system (implying, for example, a resistance to high rates of capital and capital gains taxation). It also means that stock market movements directly affect the income and wealth of individuals, providing a much more direct link between financial performance and, say, consumer expenditure than in other countries. It also probably contributes to the stability of the system because a fall in the value of shares does not immediately endanger the financial well-being of other financial and nonfinancial corporations. The wide ownership of shares does, however increase the macroeconomic significance of stock market fluctuations via the "wealth effect." Families that watched the value of their portfolio shrink are likely to raise their savings rate to rebuild their assets, implying a recessionary fall in real demand following a stock market fall. The reverse is also true. Surging stock prices can fuel demand for real goods and services.

In Europe the level of stock ownership by individuals is much lower; the household sector holds roughly 18 percent of stock. In Germany, banks hold control of a sizable part of total shares, while in the United Kingdom pension funds and insurance companies predominate. In Japan the corporate sector is largely owned by banks and other corporations through cross-share holding within the large industrial groups, or *keiretsu*. In recent years this arrangement proved to be a source of great instability for the Japanese financial system. A fall in the price of shares puts pressure on the balance sheets of banks and raises the risk of cumulative collapse, which was nearly the case in the crisis of 1997.

How Financial Markets Provide Corporate Governance In most Western nations the exchange of both shares and bonds is handled by brokerage houses that are members of exchanges. Traditionally brokerages performed not only the functions of buying and selling for a customer, but provided extensive research departments, as do mutual funds companies and pension funds. In addition, specialist institutions also sell data useful to market participants. Of particular importance are the bond-rating services, which are influential in determining the interest costs faced by corporations and government. These institutions focus on the performance of firms, agencies, and municipalities, and draw attention to missteps of management, which provides a constant check on management performance, and is a force for good **corporate governance**.

The Market for Corporate Control Firms that perform badly in the eyes of financial analysts face two problems. First, they face an inability to raise loans, either directly from banks or in the debt markets. This obstacle places a serious and hard budget constraint on the firm and may curb expansion, force it to improve the efficiency of its operation, or possibly drive it to bankruptcy if it cannot ensure the credit it needs to survive. The other consequence comes when the value of a firm's shares falls on stock markets, making it vulnerable to an outside takeover bid. In such a case, the assets would fall under new management that would better realize the potential. This active **market for corporate control** is an important feature of capitalism in the United States and Britain.

THE ORGANIZATION OF BUSINESS

The Corporate Form

One of the most important innovations of Western economies is the ability to create corporations, legal entities that can, through the sale of stock, raise capital from a large number of individuals, each of whom shares in the profits of the firm. The corporation provides a second important feature; each investor is liable only for the amount of money that he or she invested. Thus, the overall liabilities of the firm are limited to the net worth of the firm, rather than its total debts and obligations. Consequently, the downside in a corporate venture is less than that in an equivalent partnership or proprietorship, where the owners would be liable for the full value of the obligations.

STOCKS, OPTIONS, AND CORPORATE GOVERNANCE

The rise of global stock markets in the 1990s had a strong impact both on stock ownership and on corporate governance. Several trends were at work. First the rise of the markets tended to attract first-time owners of shares. Second the wider use of vested stock ownership plans to replace traditional pension schemes broadened share ownership further. Perhaps most startling was the acceleration in the use of stock options as a means of compensating both management and worker. Two implications arose. One was that the ownership of the corporations was progressively transferred from the preexisting group of shareholders toward the management and workers. Although this shift might in some respects be a solution to the principal/agent problem by making management more closely identified with the profitability of the firm, it did represent a transfer of wealth from shareholders to management. There is now public pressure to ensure that the issuance of options be more carefully documented and reflected as an expense in the reporting of financial results. A serious problem was revealed when it became clear that too frequently the reward of management with options encouraged a short-term view of the future. It became in management's interest to manipulate the stock price higher, cash out options, and leave the firm. What appeared to be a positive device to reward management for a firm's success, by putting too much emphasis on the short run (and perhaps by allowing the reward to be great enough to facilitate premature retirement), actually encouraged the pillaging of the corporation. Having survived the challenge of the Marxists, people began to wonder whether capitalism was strong enough to survive the capitalists.

The development of the corporate form in Western economies was crucial in providing a means to raise large sums of capital and limiting the risk of each investor, particularly when the number of investors is large and no one investor can be responsible for oversight of the firm's operations. Without access to the corporate form it is difficult to gather the finances necessary to undertake large-scale operations. Corporations may be either privately held, in which the shares are not traded on stock markets, or publicly held, in which ownership is liquid and traded on stock markets. To be successful, economies in development or transition must establish stock markets and overcome the considerable barriers to their rapid expansion. It should be noted that although the corporation is efficient in encouraging large and risky ventures, its presence does limit the effectiveness of contract law. A corporation's liability is limited to the extent of its assets, and situations may result in which its liability under a contract exceeds those assets.

The Behavior of Firms

The corporation is undoubtedly the dominant form of enterprise in the major market economies. It accounts for most of output, most employment, and most research and development. In the United States, for example, some 3 million corporations make up almost 90 percent of total sales. Within that group, large publicly held corporations constitute the majority of employment and output.

However, the very existence of the modern corporation presents the theory of the market economy with some serious problems. The first is that large corporations necessarily require a separation between the ownership of the firm and its management. This separation causes a principal/agent problem. How can the owners of the firm—the shareholders or principals—be sure that management (the agents of the shareholder-owners) in fact pursues the shareholders' interests rather than its own? (This issue, of course, is in addition to a more general principal/agent issue—how do managers get workers to maximize their effort?)

This problem raises a further question. The whole paradigm of free enterprise and the market system relies for its efficiency on the idea of pursuit of profit maximization. If the corporate sector fails to ruthlessly pursue profit and settles instead for other objectives, then how efficient can the market system be? One clear way of resolving the issue is to make managers' interests more closely coincident with those of the owners. In large part, this attempt to merge interests accounts for the rapidly growing popularity of stock options as a form of remuneration, because rising share prices earn money for the managers and hence ensure that they will tend to pursue policies that will maximize share values.

The other constraint on the behavior of management comes from a contested market for corporate control. In theory, shareholders can band together to get rid of management that is underperforming, but in reality such "revolutions" are rare. It is more likely that a corporation that is underperforming will find itself the target of takeover interest from other companies or entrepreneurs who feel that the assets are underused. Because top management is likely to be ejected as a result of hostile takeover, this possibility provides a constraint on management behavior.

THE LABOR MARKET

An important set of institutions in most developed market economies emerges from the labor market. On one side are the workers, who can join together to form unions; on the other side are employers, who frequently unite to form a collective bargaining agency. A third agent, the government, can regulate the labor market by controlling the age of workers, the length of workweeks, and the minimum wages. It can also maintain institutions that improve the efficiency of labor markets through job exchanges and retraining policies. Government income support policies are also relevant. They affect the reservation wage of workers and so can tend to increase the unemployment rate.

Types of Labor Unions

In all industrial democracies, union power grew with the rise of large-scale industrial enterprise. A lag often occurs in this process, because in many countries unionization was opposed by employers and was initially illegal. Subsequently, unions were granted legal status, and in some countries they became important institutions in overall economic decision making. In the United States, the 1930s were decisive in union growth. The Wagner Act gave unions rights to organize, and the Congress of Industrial Organization (CIO) provided a powerful umbrella organization embracing all workers, skilled and unskilled. Union membership in U.S.

nonagricultural employment rose sharply in the 1930s and 1950s, reaching a high in 1955 when about one-third of the workforce was unionized.

American unions tend to be organized along industry lines. Thus, for example, almost all unionized workers in the automobile industry are members of the United Automobile Workers (UAW). Wage negotiation functions on a firm-by-firm basis, rather than being determined for the entire industry. In other countries unionization took a different path. Although the picture has changed somewhat in recent years, unions in Britain are organized along occupational rather than industrial lines. Thus all electricians belong to an electricians' union, irrespective of the industry in which they are actually employed. This structure makes labor negotiation more difficult and labor peace more fragile because each employer must negotiate with several unions within an individual factory or work site. In Germany, as in the United States, unions are organized on an industry basis, but labor negotiations occur between a union and a confederation of employers. Thus wages and conditions are broadly the same across industries. In Sweden a similar system now exists, although until recently unions, through the national labor federation, were an important part of national wage determination procedures. In Finland and Portugal this kind of system is still in place. In Japan unions are organized along company lines and represent both white- and blue-collar workers. As an established part of the enterprise they are characterized by considerable docility.

Relative Rates of Unionization

The Scandinavian countries are the most highly unionized societies in the world, with some sources giving unionization rates in Sweden at over 90 percent. The United States in contrast has the lowest rates, with an aggregate economy-wide rate of 19 percent. Although Japan's overall rate hovers at about 28 percent, as noted earlier, its unions tend to be rather nonmilitant because they are company unions. Most other industrialized countries' union rates for full-time workers fall between 33 percent and 50 percent (Table 5.4).

In industrial countries the rate of unionization in the private sector fell sharply in recent years. In part this decline stems from the contraction of large-scale "rustbelt" industries—steel, textiles, rubber, ceramics—and the growth of the service sector, which proved historically more difficult to unionize. Federal, state, and local government remain an exception. Unionization among governmental employees increased sharply with important ramifications for overall political economy. One reason that explains the difficulty in restricting the growth of government sector unionization lies in the high level of organization among government workers and their opposition to initiatives designed to reduce public-sector employment.

Income Support

The extent and generosity of the "social safety net" varies considerably from country to country. In the United States, although comprehensive and relatively generous in supporting retired workers, the level of support for the unemployed (especially long-term unemployed) and single parent families tended to decline,

■ TABLE 5.4

Union Membership, Selected Countries, 1987–1989 (membership as a percentage of total employment)

Country	Nonagricultural Employment	Full-Time Employment	Full-Time Manual Workers
Sweden	96	n.a.	n.a.
Austria	61	52	57
Australia	56	70	69
Ireland	51	48	49
United Kingdom	50	47	53
Italy	45	33	37
Germany	43	34	39
Canada	36	n.a.	n.a.
Netherlands	35	42	47
Switzerland	33	37	37
France	28	n.a.	n.a.
Japan	28	n.a.	n.a.
United States	17	19	27

SOURCE: David G. Blanchflower and Richard B. Freeman, "Unionism in the United States and Other O.E.C.D. Countries," *Industrial Relations* 31 (Winter 1992), pp. 56–79; Richard B. Freeman, "American Exceptionalism in the Labor Market: Union-Nonunion Differentials in the United States and Other Countries," in *Labor Economics and Industrial Relations: Markets and Institutions,* ed. Clark Kerr and Paul D. Staudohar (Cambridge, MA: Harvard University Press, 1994), p. 279.

while in Europe the level of support for the unemployed remains high. In the European Union take-home pay after losing a job can frequently be as much as 80 percent of the working rate. Consequently, there tends to be little downward flexibility in wages, and the consequence is high unemployment. Japan's income support systems are not generous, but whether they are the cause or the effect of low levels of unemployment is debatable. What is clear is that the difficulties currently encountered by large corporations in maintaining the system of "nenko" or lifetime employment are particularly important, given the low level of income support.

INDUSTRIAL POLICY

Industrial policy is a general term that encompasses the involvement of the government in the promotion of economic growth. As such, it involves both macroeconomic and microeconomic aspects. In its macro form, industrial policy involves the successful pursuit of economic stabilization, the determination of exchange rates and interest rates calculated to support economic growth and due attention to infrastructure and human capital development. Normally, however, when we speak of industrial policy we mean particular policies that aim to affect the prospects of specific sectors of the economy or even individual firms within these sectors. This microeconomic form of industrial policy is widely practiced in many countries, although considerable debate continues over its effectiveness. Industrial policy can either promote the growth of an industry, seek to stabilize against (for example) inroads of foreign competition, or assist in the orderly decline of an industry, mitigated by the consequences for unemployment or the waste of social infrastructure and human capital.

Government may pursue a variety of measures in forming its microindustrial policy. These measures include direct subsidy payments to firms, government funding of research and development, discriminatory tax relief, government-subsidized or government-directed finance, and the use of tariffs or quotas to protect domestic products. The most aggressive example of industrial policy in recent years can be found in the late industrializing countries of East Asia. Slightly earlier, comprehensive industrial policy was practiced in Germany and France. These examples point out immediately a relevant fact: The most successful industrial policy is practiced by those economies that are well behind the frontier of best practice and advanced technology and have ground to make up.

Consequently, Japan was able to use industrial policy successfully in its transformation after the Meiji restoration in the 1860s as well as in the post–World War II "miracle" period. Similarly, German industrialization relied a great deal on state intervention and direction in both the late nineteenth century and during the 1950s and 1960s. The success of Germany and France in the 1950s, Japan in the 1960s, and Korea in the 1970s attracted favorable attention to the concept of industrial policy, and some advocated the institution of more extensive industrial policy in the United States. However, the rationale behind any government intervention in the economy must be based on the existence of some form of market imperfection, and it is difficult, in the context of the United States today, to imagine the bureaucracy performing better than the market.

Thus while macroindustrial policy might be used to address, for example, the incompleteness of capital markets or failures of coordination due to poor information, justifying microindustrial policy is more difficult. When an economy is behind cutting-edge technology and the government can see the "state of the art" and is knowledgeable about its structure of comparative advantage, it might be able to outperform the market because of this superior information. However, the closer an economy gets to the "frontier," the more difficult the task of "picking winners" becomes. Moreover, intervention in credit markets, frequently a facet of industrial policy, carries with it the loss of the independent impartiality and of the financial system. Industrial policy might be valuable in encouraging growth of specific geographical regions where the preservation of infrastructure might carry externalities that the market fails to reflect.

TRADE POLICY

The postwar years saw a concerted and sustained effort toward liberalization in trade. These efforts led to the burgeoning of international commerce, and practically all economies opening up more than they used to be. Consequently, the implications of trade for growth and employment loom greater, and despite lower tariff levels, trade policy now plays an active part in economic diplomacy.

Trade policy has two clear dimensions: assisting exports and protecting the home market. In some countries, economic agencies act aggressively in export promotion. In Japan, for example, the Ministry of International Trade and Industry (MITI) took an active and strong role in coordinating Japanese exports abroad. The other side of trade policy centers on the protection of the home market and employment. This kind of policy has its roots in the mercantile doctrines of the sixteenth and seventeenth centuries that sought protection for domestic industries against colonial and other competition. Economists generally believe that restraints on trade not only lower global welfare but also reduce the welfare of the countries that impose them. They are therefore explicable largely in terms of politically motivated redistribution.

DEVELOPING HUMAN RESOURCES

We saw in Chapter 1 that the greatest source of the wealth of nations lies in the stock of human capital embodied in its population. We should also give thought to the role of the institutions responsible for the development and maintenance of human capital—the educational system and the health care system.

TRADE AND PROTECTIONISM

The United States traditionally views itself as a strong advocate of free trade and it has been largely responsible for pushing international trade liberalization agreements since World War II. Most economists believe that free trade enhances both world welfare and the aggregate welfare of countries that engage in it. However, within a country international trade results in costs to particular groups. In general we may say that the broad consuming public benefits from liberalization because it provides access to lower-cost imports. However, the labor and capital engaged in the industries at home with which the imports compete are likely to bear the costs. As a rule the broad benefits to the consuming public are greater than the narrower losses to specific labor and capital. However, trade policy is almost always a political issue, which was demonstrated clearly in March of 2002 when President George W. Bush announced tariffs on steel of up to 30 percent. Bush generally sided with the antitax, antitariff wing of the Republican Party, which was disconcerted by the measures. Moreover, the shift put the president at odds with many of his steel-producing allies. Generally speaking economists accept few arguments in favor of tariffs— the chief being the protection of infant industries and the preservation of strategic assets. Protection of steel might be seen as strategic consideration but it is more likely that protectionism was promoted by domestic political considerations than by long-run strategic concerns. The point is that protectionism always exacts a cost, and in this case will raise the costs in every industry that uses steel as an input. As such it will negatively affect the United States' competitive position in industries such as automobiles and machinery. It will raise the costs of U.S. construction and have knock-on effects in every corner of the economy. It might succeed in saving some jobs in steel but the downside clearly shows a likelihood that those jobs saved will be offset by the increase in prices and the effect on competitiveness in other industries.

The Educational System

In most developed market economies, the government makes much of the educational investment. As we noted earlier, education is not a pure public good because it is both excludable and diminishable. Its public provision can probably best be justified on grounds of externalities. An educated individual provides **spillovers** that increase the productivity of those around him or her (and often other measures of welfare, too). A high degree of variance exists even among the wealthier nations in the delivery of education: who pays, who sets standards, who evaluates, and who receives the greatest level of service. In most European nations education represents a social expense, and the school and university systems are almost entirely public. Access is frequently determined by national examination and purports to be largely meritocratic—though clearly class, background, and wealth play a role. In "Anglo-Saxon" nations a greater role is played by the private sector, especially in the United States, implying that education is more a personal rather than social investment.

The scope, efficiency, and finance of educational systems are vital because education is a major determinant of economic outcomes. The performance of the educational system is crucial in understanding the functioning of the larger economic system. A particular puzzle is the performance of socialist countries, where universal literacy and high participation in tertiary education was the rule, but economic performance lagged. Today we must ask what implications the large stock of well-educated workers has for successful transition to a market economy?

The Health Care System

The health care system shares many characteristics with education. It is not a pure public good, but it is frequently supplied by the government, particularly in Europe, where national health services are the norm, and less so in the United States. The importance of health care is likely to increase in the next decades. In most developed economies, including Western Europe, Japan, the United States, and Eastern Europe, the populations are aging rapidly. The burden of health care is likely to grow and may represent a potentially suffocating load for the economies of these countries.

A debate also focuses sharply on the advantages and disadvantages of market provision versus public supply. Europe continues to follow a public model that proved itself both more effective in containing costs of medical services and pharmaceuticals and in providing a more equitable distribution of medical care. Cost containment results mainly from the government's considerable monopsony power that it exerts against physicians, nurses, and pharmaceutical companies. The equitable access to health care in turn reveals that basic indicators of health fail to correlate highly with income. The early years of the Clinton administration saw an attempt to introduce aspects of publicly provided national health care into the United States. It was soundly rejected by the configuration of political forces, though medical costs ballooned in the aftermath.

KEY TERMS AND CONCEPTS

allocation function

central bank independence

civil compensation

corporate governance

depository institutions

distribution function

fiscal policy

industrial policy

investment banks

market for corporate control

merit goods

monetary policy

progressive tax

quasi-public goods

redistribution in-kind

spillovers

stabilization function

tort law

voucher systems

QUESTIONS FOR DISCUSSION

1. Tax systems become less progressive in many societies even as transfers continue to rise. Can you account for these apparently contradictory trends?
2. Why is contract enforcement necessary for the functioning of a modern market system?
3. Why should central banks be independent of the political process?
4. Excessive management compensation and "perks" are the inevitable result of the separation of ownership from management. Discuss.
5. Does the widespread holding of shares in the United States influence the effectiveness of corporate governance? Why?
6. The corporate form enables businesspeople to escape the full consequences of their actions. Discuss.
7. Do you think that the abuse and fraud revealed in the U.S. economy provide a full justification for a return to much heavier regulation?
8. The low level of unionization in the United States is a key reason for the low rates of unemployment relative to Europe. Discuss.
9. Why does domestic political agenda make it difficult for any regime, no matter how committed to the market, to stick to a policy of free trade?

RESOURCES

Web Sites

Mark Bernkopf's Central Banking Resource Center...
....http://patriot.net/~bernkopf/

This site offers a comprehensive series of links to almost every central bank and ministry of finance in the world, as well as ministries of finance, research departments, and an excellent page on the history of central banking. The site is a first step for any research on comparative central banking.

The Cato Institute ....http://www.cato.org/
The home page of this conservative think tank and lobby organization contains a great deal of information and papers on the introduction of markets into public service provision (health and education), welfare reform, and the privatization of social security. All the work conforms to the institute's agenda but it is comprehensive and useful, and much can be downloaded free of charge.

The Milken Institute ....http://www.milkeninstitute.org/
This site also contains some useful books and position papers.

Books and Articles

Alstenstetter, Christine (ed.). *Health Policy Reform: National Variations and Globalization.* London: St. Martin's Press, 1997.

Blanchflower, David G., and Richard B. Freeman. "Unionism in the United States and Other O.E.C.D. Countries." *Industrial Relations* 31 (Winter 1992), 56–79.

Crumper, George. *Evaluation of National Health Systems.* Oxford: Oxford University Press, 1991.

Freeman, Richard B. "American Exceptionalism in the Labor Market: Union-Nonunion Differentials in the United States and Other Countries." In *Labor Economics and Industrial Relations: Markets and Institutions,* Clark Kerr and Paul D. Staudohar (eds.). Cambridge, MA: Harvard University Press, 1994.

Friedman, Milton, with Rose Friedman. *Free to Choose.* Fort Worth, TX: Harcourt Brace, 1990.

Goodhart, Charles. *The Central Bank and the Financial System.* Cambridge, MA: MIT Press, 1995.

Kwoka John E., and Lawrence J. White (eds.). *The Antitrust Revolution: Economics, Competition, and Policy,* 4th ed. New York: Oxford University Press, 1997.

Lippo, Francesco. *Central Bank Independence: Political and Economic Aspects of Delegating Arrangements for Monetary Policy.* White Plains, NY: Edward Elgar Press, 1999.

McGroarty, David, and William J. Bennett. *Break These Chains: The Battle for School Choice.* Rocklin, CA: Prima Publishing, 1996.

Musgrave, Richard, and Peggy Musgrave. *Public Finance in Theory and Practice.* New York: McGraw-Hill, 1984.

Nester, William R. *American Industrial Policy: Free or Managed Markets?* New York: St. Martin's Press, 1997.

Okimoto, Daniel I. *Between MITI and the Market: Japanese Industrial Policy for High Technology.* Stanford, CA: Stanford University Press, 1990.

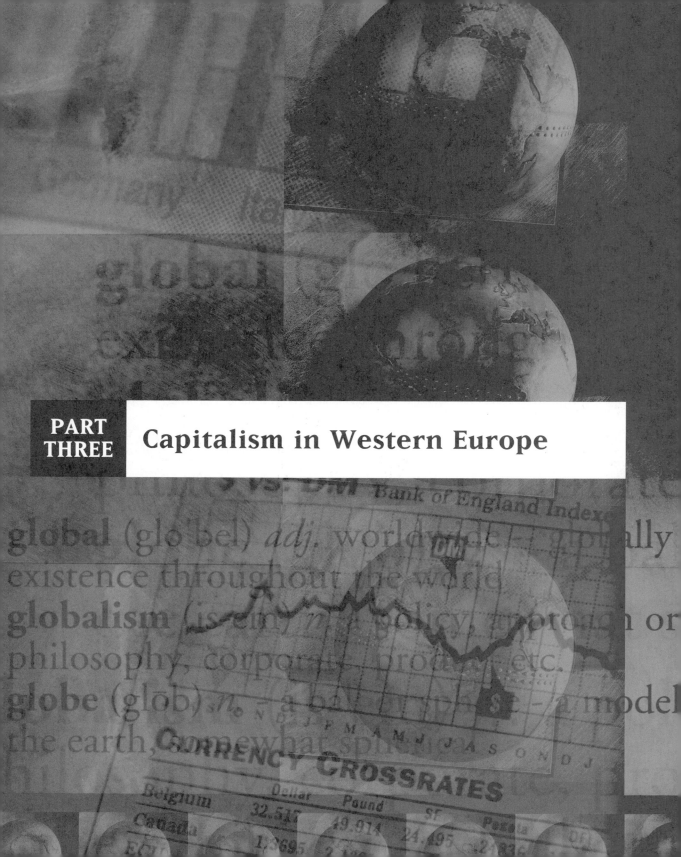

PART THREE

Capitalism in Western Europe

6

FRANCE: FROM INDICATIVE PLANNING
TO EUROPEAN INTEGRATION

FRANCE	
Area (thousand sq. km.)	552
Currency	euro
Exchange Rate (August 2002)	1.0234 = US$1
Population 2000 (millions)	59.00
Population Growth Rate	0.4%
GNI per Capita, 2000	$23,673
GNI per Capita, PPP	$24,470
GDP Growth 1990–2000	1.7%
Value Added as % of GDP 2000 Agriculture	3%
Industry	23%
Services	74%
% of GDP Government Expenditure	50%
Exports	29%

France is one of the four "big" members of the European Union with a population of some 60 million people. Its political system is based on proportional representation, which has tended to weaken the tendency toward a two-party democracy, a characteristic of many western democracies. The country has moved sharply to the right in recent years, first reflected in the demise of the powerful Communist party and subsequently with the relative decline of the Socialists. After several years of "cohabitation" between a Gaullist (conservative) president, Jacques Chirac, and a Socialist Prime Minister, Lionel Jospin, the political system shifted once more to the right, with the formation of a center-right administration in the spring of 2002.

The government of France always involved itself in the economy of the nation, never more so than in the strong recovery of the French economy after the Second World War, fondly remembered as the "trente gloirieures." During this period, 1945–1975, the government developed a system of indicative planning, which can be conceived as an attempt by the government to overcome the market failure of inadequate or costly information. Although the agency responsible for planning (the Commissariat General du Plan, or CGP) still survives, France has now abandoned the formal system of five-year plans. The history of the French experience provides valuable insights, particularly into the profound difficulties of planning for one nation in the face of rising integration (into the EU) and globalization.

THE THEORY OF INDICATIVE PLANNING

One of the failures of a market economy, which we considered in Chapter 4, resulted from the inability of participants to have access to reliable information. The discussion at that point focused on the difficulty and expense of consumers acquiring full information about products, but market failure can also result from enterprise managers knowing too little about the future economic environment to make optimal investment decisions. Informed investment choices require knowledge about a wide range of macroeconomic variables, among them the future prices and availability of inputs, the rate of growth of the economy, movements in the value of the currency, and the inflation rate. In a pure market environment, firms must either estimate such movements based on their experience or purchase information from some proprietary source, such as consultancies. Even though the marginal cost of disseminating such information is very close to zero, it will tend to be undersupplied and incomplete under market arrangements.

Indicative planning is one attempt to bridge this information gap. The government's capacity to marshal information and its ability to draw the actors in the economy into a dialogue about their needs and intentions put it in a strong position to compile a comprehensive and consistent set of forecasts about the future direction of the economy. If leaders of industry accept these projections, investment decisions will be consistent and based on a common set of assumptions and the forecasts stand a better chance of being realized. In the words of one authority on French planning:

> The aim of pure indicative planning is to improve the performance of the economy by the provision of better economic information: forecasts or targets are published but compliance with them is voluntary. The underlying logic is that the plan, via collective action, can supply economically valuable information which, as a public good, the market mechanism does not disseminate efficiently.[1]

An economy with complete and efficient forward markets would not need indicative planning or any shared set of assumptions because enterprises could use

[1]Peter Holmes, "Indicative Planning" in *New Palgrave Dictionary of Economics*, John Eatwell and Murray Milgate, eds. (New York: Stockton Press, 1987), p. 781.

such markets to hedge the risks attendant on their investment decisions. Pierre Massé, the powerful planning commissioner from 1959 to 1965, justified French indicative planning in terms of its capability to informally correct the absence of such forward markets. The economic forecasts embodied in an indicative plan give both buyers and sellers confidence that the general levels of demand for products and supply of materials would be forthcoming. By identifying early the existence of oversupply or bottlenecks, investment behavior can be modified in a timely fashion and the incidence of market disequilibria reduced. Thus, both business and consumers benefit from an exercise in collective and consistent market research freely distributed to all the relevant actors in the economy.

Not everyone accepts this view of the value of indicative planning. Strong believers in the efficiency of market mechanisms insist that firms are better forecasters of the variables that affect their business than governments, precisely because of their pecuniary interest in getting those forecasts right. Those most efficient at producing reliable estimates put themselves in a position to earn super-normal profits, which provides an incentive for private firms that the government does not experience.

Such fundamental objections aside, the effectiveness of indicative planning depends to a large degree on the reliability of the estimates. The government may indeed be better able to see the overall economic landscape than individual participants, but as we shall see in the case of central planning, the government largely depends on information provided by the firms, who might have an incentive to mislead the government. Consider an example used by Peter Holmes to illustrate this problem. The users of, say, electrical components might have an incentive to overstate their demand for such components. If embodied in the plan such overstated demand might produce overinvestment by component suppliers, a corresponding artificial glut of components, and an opportunity for the users to take advantage of the cheap prices. Such strategic behavior can apply to a wide range of goods and factors of production including the supply of qualified labor. An overestimation of the demand for computer engineers, for example, might induce both public and private (human capital) investment in training to the advantage of employers but the disadvantage of newly qualified workers and society as a whole.

Even if successful in its objective of reconciling potential endogenous disequilibria, indicative planning may run into serious problems because of shocks to the external environment in which the economy functions. In theory it might be possible to bring endogenous supply and demand into closer equilibrium by the judicious use of indicative planning, but unless the economy is totally closed the projections can be made irrelevant by exogenous changes over which neither the government nor the internal actors can exercise any control. For example, the explosion in oil and energy prices that occurred during the 1970s would have confounded even the best of indicative plans. The increase in the real price of oil by 1978 made any investment projections based on the oil prices of 1971 nonviable.

The more open the economy, and the greater the uncertainty concerning exogenous variables, the more difficult and the more hazardous becomes the indicative planning exercise. This risk can be dealt with to some degree by producing multiple projections based on different "scenarios." The problem is that there are so many factors in the external environment, and the number of scenarios increases literally exponentially with the addition of each relevant factor. Even if the exogenous state variables number as few as three, and each of which could assume two values (high and low), then eight different sets of estimates would be required for each year. Consider then the case of 10 state variables, each of which could assume any one of three values in any given year, then the total number of scenarios to be investigated in a five-year planning period would be a staggering 24 million.

Proponents of indicative planning pragmatically overlook these theoretical problems. They believe, even within relatively open economies operating in an uncertain world, that advantages come from sharing, in Commissioner Massé's words, "a common view of the future." However, there remains a temptation to make the plan embody as rosy a view of the future as possible in the hopes that it will induce the actors to operate in an expansionary fashion. Setting a growth forecast of 5 percent per year, for example, might cause the aggregate level of investment to rise by appealing to optimism and the "animal spirits" of entrepreneurs. Using plans as self-fulfilling prophecies provides an attractive option to governments interested in accelerating the rate of growth. Sir Roy Harrod, the pioneer of modern growth theory, suggested that an appropriate policy would be for the government to forecast growth at the **warranted growth rate**, which would tend to reduce the discrepancy between the actual and the warranted rates.[2] This position has a sound theoretical underpinning, but it presents the possibility of using the plan as undisciplined boosterism: forecasting a high rate of growth to induce a high rate of private investment. Such a practice might be successful in the short term, but it will only last as long as no great divergence occurs between the outcome and the forecast. A highly visible shortfall might erode the credibility of the plan, and a plan perceived as being systematically misleading and overly optimistic might well be worse than no plan at all!

Even if the indicative plan proves highly successful in forecasting key macroeconomic variables and the levels of demand in various sectors, this outcome does not directly imply that an investment decision by a particular firm is legitimated. Only substantial collusion between the constituent firms of an industry, which systematically divided the total investment between them, could guarantee it. This behavior might be tolerated or actively encouraged by the government, but it shows the potential anticompetitive dangers of indicative planning. Say, for example, four firms operate within a particular industry forecasted to experience a 20 percent increase in demand. A government may be tempted to encourage each of the firms to increase its investment and output at the same percentage rate as industry growth and to tolerate some form of price fixing. This approach ensures the actualization of the investment required to meet the plan target. The potential dangers include an erosion of competition, the sanctioning of a government-sponsored cartel, and the rewarding of less-efficient firms. This behavior perhaps becomes more prevalent in downturns, when the government might see fit to allocate shares of a shrinking pie equally among competitors.

---

[2]The warranted growth rate is the rate of expansion of GDP that equates planned saving with planned investment. It can be shown, under simple assumptions, to be equal to the ratio of the marginal propensity to save to capital output.

Despite these problems, the practice of indicative planning carries a pragmatic appeal for many people. At the very least, the process of planning requires the systematic collation and reconciliation of a large amount of data useful to government and business alike. Moreover, the preparation of the plan involves the exchange of information among the principal economic actors. Technocratic planners engage in a dialogue with labor unions, business associations, and the representatives of other branches of government, as well as any other groups that may be included. This process, known to the French as *concertation*, plays an important part in the exercise itself. In the words of the First French Plan (1947–1952), it represents "a permanent exchange of ideas between the government and the public." In addition to this rather vertical arrangement, it also facilitates horizontal exchange between, say, business and labor leaders and, often neglected but equally important, the various government agencies.

An important question is which parties should be included in the dialogue. If the participants are narrowly defined, the result is a corporatist state where only those institutions sanctioned by the state take part in formulating policy. In Japan, for example, the debate is largely limited to business leaders and bureaucrats, with the third side of the "iron triangle," the politicians, holding a watching brief. It excludes labor and community groups for the most part, although the well-known concerns of certain powerful lobby groups (e.g., the farmers) may receive attention. Initially, France established a different, but equally corporatist composition. The First Plan sought input only from unions, the civil service, employers' federations, and farmers' alliances. However over time, considerable "dialogue broadening" brought in new participants representing women's groups, senior citizens, young people, and environmentalists. This broadening did not always appeal to the original core participants, who saw the newcomers as somewhat "soft," tending to distract attention from the "hard" issue of defining the relationship of labor, capital, and government.

No simple way can be used to decide whether indicative planning constitutes a worthwhile exercise. Perhaps the best test requires a careful look at the experience of the nations that practiced it. Much of indicative planning's appeal to would-be imitators certainly lay in the conspicuous economic success of its two most prominent practitioners—France and Japan. In the 1960s, an envious glance at their growth records persuaded Britain to initiate a planning system similar to the French, producing a so-called National Plan. In the British case, however, one important lesson emerged: plan targets cannot be set in isolation of macroeconomic constraints. In Britain the plan attempted to promulgate a growth rate of 4 percent, but one of many balance of payments crises derailed this goal, forcing the ignominious abandonment of the targets.

INDICATIVE PLANNING IN FRANCE

Background

France demonstrates a long history of state involvement in economic development that sets it at variance to the "Anglo-Saxon" tradition of **laissez faire**. Jean-Baptiste Colbert, the finance minister under Louis XIV, pursued aggressive and comprehensive governmental policies. **Colbertism** became a byword for interventionist state activity and provides a prime example of "mercantilism," state manipulation of industry and trade to maximize its power. Similarly in the nineteenth century, France, as a "late industrializer" relative to the rapid start of Britain, directed its policy toward nurturing and protecting industry.

Because of this interventionist history, no sharp cultural or political discontinuity developed when, in the aftermath of World War II, France initiated a system of planning. French procedures contrasted sharply in philosophy and method to the highly formal centralized command planning adopted in the Soviet Union in the 1920s and 1930s. France never held an assumption that all of the means of production should be nationalized, nor that the power of coordination should rest exclusively at the center. Rather, the government viewed the market as the principal tool of coordination in a mixed economy where private production would dominate. As its role, the government supplied information, oversaw a dialogue between the various actors, provided guidance and, where necessary, provided the infrastructure required to meet the targets of the plan. The essential principles of such a model, which involves a large element of industrial policy, were expressed in the First Plan:

> In our economy, made up of nationalized industries and as well as an extensive free-market sector, the Plan should provide guidance as well as directives. Its means of implementation, while laying down disciplines, should at the same time promote creative initiatives in all sectors and maintain within businesses both justifiable profits and risk-taking, which provide the necessary impetus and sanctions.[3]

Nor did the planning apparatus imply that French industry should be isolated from the world economy, but it stressed the centrality of trade and international competitiveness for success in a market economy. In fact, the first plan emphasized the restoration of France to a position of international competitiveness after the war.

The Organization of Planning

One of the most obvious features of planning in France was the small number of people permanently employed in plan production. The agency responsible for the plan, the General Planning Commissariat for Equipment and Productivity (CGP), never employed more than 50 professional staff. It enjoyed power disproportionate to its size, however, because of its direct attachment to the office of the prime minister. Its function continues to be largely one of coordination, and it draws personnel to prepare the plans from other ministries—primarily from the Ministry of the Economy and Finance (MEF), especially from the forecasting directorate (DP) and the National Institute of Statistics (Insée). These agencies held the responsibility for the initial collation of basic economic data forecasts. The production of the final plan consisted of three distinct stages—information gathering, concentration, and consistency—and although the nature and objectives of the planning system show change over time, these features remained permanent.

---

[3]From the *First Plan* cited by Bernard Cazes, "Indicative Planning in France," in *Comparative Economic Systems: Issues and Cases*, Morris Bornstein, ed. (Burr Ridge, IL: Irwin, 1993), p. 161.

Information Gathering An essential step in any planning exercise entails gathering basic data on the economy for use in forecasting. This step also benefits from the assembling of research, both retrospective and forward looking, on the policy options and likely movement of exogenous factors that influence the functioning of the economy. The forward-looking elements in this exercise can be characterized as "throwing a light on the future." They involve raising such questions as: What major developments occurred in technology and industry? How will these developments affect employment and industrial structure? What potential developments in the international economy will significantly affect the French economy?

As the plan "softened" and more social considerations became part of the process, more "futurism" finds its way into this phase. For example, in preparing the Tenth Plan (1989–1992), a group led by the historian E. Le Roy Ladurie engaged in long-range speculation on possible futures for society, technology, and the economy beyond the year 2000. Plan preparation also involved model building in order to forecast the movement of the economy across several time periods from the short term (one year) to the long term (five years) to point out potential difficulties.

Concertration (or Dialogue) Much activity in French planning centered around a process known in French as *concertation*, usually translated into English as "dialogue," though it involves rather more than that. The French still regard their economy as one that resolves problems through a constant exchange of ideas between the government and the public. Thus rather than a guided economy *(economie dirigée)*, they see a concerted economy *(economie concertée)*, where through exchange of opinion and debate the participants arrive at a common conception of the future.

During this phase all parties with a role in plan preparation participated with civil servants in a series of about 30 "modernization commissions." Some of these commissions used vertical structures and deal with specific productive sectors of the economy. The Sixth Plan, for example, used nine vertical commissions: energy, agriculture, food, transport, industry, communications, commerce, tourism, and handicrafts. Other commissions took a broader interest in national issues: finance, employment, social benefits, research, economic information, regional development, and the overseas departments. Another set of commissions dealt with social issues.

In the early plans only the employers' groups, trade unions, and representatives of agriculture contributed a substantial voice in the *concertation* process. As noted earlier, this limited participation tended to give a corporatist aspect to French planning; only those institutions that were solicited and licensed by the state could participate. Over time, however, the government enlarged the number of participants, and less formal groups (representing young people, women's groups, consumers' groups, and so forth) came to play roles in the planning process. As the process became more inclusive, the nature of the plans necessarily changed and involved the development of various models of French growth in which quality of life and equity became important elements of the debate.

Consistency After the modernization commissions completed their discussions, and emerged with the broad outline of the plan, planners then provided consistency to the plan. This consistency occurred along two dimensions: longitudinal (i.e., across time) and cross-sectional (i.e., between the various sectors of the economy).

Committing to the Plan

Indicative planning does not involve compulsion or direction, and one immediate question about its effectiveness concerns whether the existence of the successive French plans changes anything. In what sense did the participants of the plan "commit" to it, and what concrete result came from their commitment?

Commitment Through Participation One possible answer sees involvement in the production of the plan in the *concertation* stage as binding the participants to the common vision of the plan. Early plans involved only a narrow constituency in their preparation (labor, business, and agriculture), in which the exchange of views between these groups could be described as intensive, or "deep." The participants, while not bound in any contractual sense to conform to the norms, felt strong moral pressure to do so because of their full and active involvement in their establishment. These plans, produced from a narrow, corporatist constituency, might be called the State's Plan *(Plan de l'État)*.

In later plans the constituency involved in *concertation* broadened, and though more participants provided input in *concertation*, the exchange was less deep, possibly implying less commitment. To some the ideal would be to create a dialogue, both broad and deep, that would produce a Nation's Plan *(Plan de la Nation)*, to which, because everyone participated in its development, the entire nation would be committed. This is a utopian—and questionable—conception of the world. Extending participation to a broader constituency does not necessarily mean full acceptance of the fundamental assumptions and goals of the plan. In fact, the more groups represented in the discussion, the greater grows the likelihood of conflict and failure to arrive at a consensus.

Commitment to Expertise Another view of the plan sees it as a comprehensive "market research" document that throws a revealing light on the future. People accept the plan, and commit to its findings, because it provides in some sense the best available vision of the future, one produced by pooled intelligence and hard work. Precisely because it offers a well-produced document, authored by experts, individual players may rationally accept this common vision. Any other behavior would be suboptimal.

Commitment by Contract The two types of commitment discussed up to this point are voluntaristic and therefore binding in only the loosest way. A third category of commitment to the targets of the plan involves the signing of contracts that specify performance, particularly in terms of commitment to specific investments or infrastructural improvements. In theory such contracts could be undertaken by any of the principal actors, whether private or public. In reality, however, the public sector—state-owned enterprises, agencies of central government, or regional authorities—shows the greatest likelihood of making the commitment. Private firms might be induced to commit to specific actions in return for grants, loans, or concessionary tax treatment. In the 1980s the French introduced planning contracts *(contrats de plan)* as part of a revamping of the indicative planning process.

The Changing Nature of the Plans over Time

The First Plan Since the inception of planning in 1947, the French used a five-year planning horizon. The First Plan—generally known as the Monnet Plan after its chief architect, **Jean Monnet**, who moved on to play a vital and formative role in the development of the European Union—consisted largely of a recovery plan quite different in character from its successors. It focused on the reconstruction and modernization of industry after the war time occupation, during which the Germans expropriated a great deal of heavy capital equipment, and investment and maintenance was inadequate. This plan emphasized long-run growth and development, rather than short-run stability, and focused on investment in basic industry: coal, electricity, steel, cement, railways, and agricultural inputs. The task of planning was made easier because at this time most of the firms in all of these industries were under public ownership and in many cases were sectoral monopolies. Thus, planning was by and large a matter of rendering consistency to the investment plans of the nationalized firms.

The period of the First Plan coincided with substantial inflow of capital under the Marshall Plan, the major American postwar reconstruction initiative in Europe. The central planning commissariat provided the principal interface between the Marshall Plan administration and the French government. More than one-third of total capital investment covered by the plan originated from Marshall Aid.

1952—1965: The "Harmonizing Plans" The next three plans[4] attempted to bring to the other sectors of industry the systematic investment and modernization fostered in the basic sectors by the First Plan. The environment presented greater difficulty because Marshall assistance had been terminated. Moreover, the planners' emphasis on the longer term brought them into frequent conflict with the Ministry of Economics and Finance (MEF), which tried to refocus policy on short-term stabilization. An attempt to resolve this conflict led to the planning commissariat being detached from the office of the prime minister and located with the MEF in 1954. The government restored its "independence" in 1962, but the problems of linking short-term stabilization policy to the medium- and long-term plan objectives of maximizing investment and growth remained. In terms of the continued development of the basic sector, the plan enjoyed success until the 1960s. Outcomes for basic industries (steel, gas, coal, etc.) usually fell within 10 percent of the target (see Table 6.1). However, the performance of the private industrial and service sector generally veered widely off target, either over- or underperforming, depending on the sector, as can be seen from the performance of motor vehicles

[4]Note that although this range of years covers three planning periods, the elapsed time is only 13 years. France aborted the Third Plan after two years.

and machine tools in Table 6.1. Despite these problems, overall growth of national income came close to target, and investment generally exceeded it, reflecting perhaps the confidence that the planning framework gave to industrialists.

1965—1975: Social Concerns and Rising Complexities In the late 1960s, two distinctly new features of the planning process evolved. First, social objectives (including regional policy) began to take a much more prominent role. These objectives crept into the process during the previous planning periods but their consideration became more explicit in the Fifth Plan. The range of representation on the modernization commissions increased, pushing issues such as income policy to the fore.

The second change involved an increase in the complexity and technical detail of the planning process itself. Complex macroeconomic models, featured for the first time in the Fifth Plan (1965–1970), represented an attempt to resolve the conflict of the short-term stabilization aspects and long-term growth aspects of government policy. This trend toward increasing complexity escalated in the Sixth Plan—implemented between 1971 and 1975, but actually in preparation from 1966. In this plan the technical modeling exercises became even more ambitious. In particular a physical and financial resources model (wittily and universally known as FIFI) took the center stage. As its main purposes, it revealed the medium-term macro-development problem in the economy, promoted to study over time the results of

▪ TABLE 6.1

	Percentage Achievement of Plan in France		
France	Plan II 1954—1957	Plan III 1958—1961	Plan IV 1962—1965
National income	103	98	100
Investment	110	100	1051
Private consumption	106	97	01
Industrial production	115	105	n.a.
Agricultural production	93	97	n.a.
Steel	99	102	86
Coal	97	89	84
Oil	93	101	127
Electricity	104	101	93
Gas	95	n.a.	92
Machine tools	75	91	88
Motor vehicles	147	91	93
Textiles	117	88	95
Meat	104	95	94
Milk	100	104	94

SOURCE: Vera Lutz, *Central Planning for the Market Economy: An Analysis of the French Theory and Experience, Institute of Economic Affairs* (Harlow, England: Longmans, 1969).

different policy options, and took a long-term view of the problems of France as "a competitioned economy" (i.e., highly open to world trade and therefore conditioned by international developments in costs). In this sense the plan shifted from a **normative planning** model, with clear targets to be achieved, to what Holmes terms (with some understatement) "a modest forecasting exercise." Nevertheless, the idea of the plan as an attempt to articulate some kind of common consensual vision of the future remained.

The Late 1970s: The Decline of Planning and the Rise of Laissez Faire

The 1970s proved to be a decade of turbulence for the global economy and, as we noted in earlier sections in this chapter, even endogenously consistent plans can be made irrelevant by sudden exogenous shocks. Sharp increases in oil prices, surging global inflation, and the collapse and restructuring of the system of international payments all occurred in the first four years of the decade and rendered the forecasting estimates of the Sixth Plan all but useless.

Moreover, French politics took a rather sharp lurch to the right with the advent of the conservative administration of Giscard d'Estaing. His administration placed a much greater faith than previous governments in the unfettered operation of the market. For these ideological reasons, the importance of planning receded. The plan continued to exist, and the formal mechanisms went largely unchanged, but it served only in a forecasting function.

The 1980s: The Socialist Reforms

In May of 1981 the Socialist François Mitterrand won the presidency and in the subsequent general election his party captured 285 of the assembly's 491 seats while the Socialists' Communist allies won another 44. This victory gave the left a powerful mandate and the parliamentary majority. The most obvious manifestation of this radical turn was the nationalization of a large part of French industry. Already public enterprises accounted for a substantial part of productive activity. Nationalized firms held a virtual monopoly of electricity supply, coal, gas, public transport, and air transport, accounting for about 5 percent of gross domestic product (GDP). In addition, several industrial enterprises (including Renault, the automaker, and SEITA, a tobacco company) competed with private industry.

Mitterand added 12 major industrial firms to the public sector, among them seven of France's largest enterprises (employing together more than 800,000 people). In addition, a large part of the private financial sector joined the banks already under public ownership. As a result, 25 percent of industrial output, all of the major utilities, and almost the entire financial sector lay in public hands. This step took the French economy in the opposite direction from the broad trends apparent in most other parts of the world, and it stood in particular contrast to the events on the other side of the English Channel, where two years earlier Margaret Thatcher embarked on the denationalization of all publicly held enterprises in the competitive sector and a large part of public utilities as well.

The increase in the scope of the state in France provided an opportunity to revive planning and to give it a purpose above the primarily forecasting function to which it was relegated during the 1970s. To further this end, the government created a new Ministry of the Plan and Regional Planning to replace the old planning commissariat, and convened a national commission to investigate how the planning procedure might be improved. This commission recommended two reforms, both of which were embodied in the Planning Reform Law of 1982. The first, an organizational reform, aimed at promoting a more democratic planning process by increasing the role of parliament and broadening the *concertation* under the coordination of a new National Planning Commission. The phasing out of the planning ministry reestablished the old system of a commissariat reporting directly to the prime minister. A further feature of this reform, perhaps the one with the most enduring consequences, was the devolution of a substantial amount of power from the national level to the regional and provincial levels.

The second dimension of the reforms sought to increase the level of formal commitment to the plan through the introduction of **planning contracts**—between the central government and both regional governments and the nationalized industries. These contracts committed both parties to specific actions and levels of expenditure for certain priority projects defined in the national plan and the subsidiary regional plans. This step answered, at least in part, the perennial question of who is committed to what in the framework of the plan. Of course, these contracts excluded private industry, and the significance of the nationalized industries faced a likely decline with more aggressive pursuit of reprivatization. However, the issue of government's commitment to the plan was largely resolved.

The 1990s The return of a conservative coalition government in 1986 reversed the fortunes of planning once more. Ideologically, the new administration saw the prime determinant of the vitality of the economy as lying in the competence and ambition of individual entrepreneurs rather than in the planning activity of the government sector. The government immediately halted the increase in the scope of the nationalized sector and initiated a privatization program with particular emphasis on the liberalization of the financial sector. Industrial firms were to be sold off at the fastest pace that France's relatively shallow stock market would allow.

The conservative administration toyed with the idea of getting rid of the CGP, transforming it into the "office of strategy." Planning activity went into a hiatus during 1986 and 1987 but emerged with the Tenth Plan in 1988 to cover the four-year period 1988–1992 and make the plan period coincident with the completion of the internal market of the European Community (EC) in 1992. With its high commitment to the plan, the central government pledged some FF52 billion to completing regional planned projects.

The planning process now included coordination with European objectives. In the production of the Tenth Plan, *concertation* extended to private and public leaders in the other members of the European Union (EU), as well as to representatives of "young people" (aged 18–25) within France.

After some administrative reshuffling the planning commissariat was once more attached to the office of the prime minister, at that time a Socialist, Lionel Jospin, who took on the difficult job of "cohabitating" with the conservative president Jacques Chirac. The conflicting philosophies within the government and the growing integration of the European Union, making independent economic policy increasingly difficult, necessitated a change in planning's role. The planning commissariat, although no longer charged with producing a clear blueprint for economic action and change, remained important in initiating debate and in the development of consensus. The commissioner for planning, Jean-Michel Charpin, recently redefined the role of planning in France:

> The government deems it necessary to have a long-term vision of economic and social development to allow better coherence of action between institutions and economic actors.[5]

Lionel Jospin, who served as prime minister until March of 2002, recalled that the CGP fulfilled a special function in arriving at government decisions. It is, he wrote in his mission letter to the commissioner, "the animator of strategic and forward-looking analysis, a privileged place for debate and inter-ministerial cooperation, and the evaluation of public policy."[6]

Today, the mission of the CGP covers three aspects:

1. The development of the French economy in the context of globalization and European integration
2. The reinforcement of social cohesion, including the social safety net and the problems of young and old
3. The modernization of the institutions of government, including regulation of industry and the environment

Was French Indicative Planning Successful?

For 30 years or so after the inception of planning in 1946–1947, the French economy was one of the fastest-growing market economies in the world. The growth of GDP was both high in the average and also quite consistent and steady over time. It would be tempting to ascribe this "miracle" of the 30 glorious years (*les trentes gloreuses*, as the French fondly remember them) to the planning effort. In truth, little separates the performance of the "French miracle" from the miracles in Germany, Italy, or the Netherlands where planning was much less a part of the apparatus. No irrefutable cross-section or time series evidence supports indicative planning's efficacy.

In its initial manifestation, say for the first 20 years, the plan set out a vision of the future. This plan extended beyond a cold prediction of what was likely to occur, but it represented rather the consensus view of what should occur. It therefore functioned as a normative exercise, not merely a positive one. This important observation affects what approach we can take in evaluating the failure or success of indicative planning. Pierre Massé put it this way:

> [T]he Plan is in principle normative, the projection [on which the Plan is based] is partly normative and partly predictional. Plan and projection not being identical, the invalidation of the projection does not mean failure for the plan. This is why the question to what extent are French Plans implemented is ambiguous. This ambiguity cannot be removed

---

[5]*La Lettre du Commissariat du Plan*, P.I. no. 1 (November 1998).
[6]Letter of Mission from Jospin to the CGP (January 9, 1998).

simply by comparing projection with reality. Falling short of the projection is not in itself significant. In measuring success or failure of the Plan, one must assess, to a certain extent subjectively, the underlying significance of falling short in any particular way.[7]

In some ways this normative exhortation for the leaders of industry to accept and conform to the targets of the plan presents the most important aspect of planning. This common vision and shared market research might produce salutary effects on investment planning and growth. As Charles Kindleberger observed:

> Knowledge of income and industry projections and faith in the inevitability of expansion are communicated to firms at intra- and inter-industry meetings. This is perhaps the most powerful effect [of French planning] and one which has a faint resemblance to a revivalist prayer meeting.[8]

Of course, the danger of such an evangelical approach to planning comes when any failure causes a crisis of faith. This danger became apparent during the 1970s when planners somewhat cynically manipulated the plan projections for political ends, and in this process destroyed overall confidence in planning as a disinterested and technical exercise. Following that, planning held a more detached forecasting function, until its "revival" by the socialist administration of the early 1980s. In this new form planning does pack more of a punch, because the existence of the planning contracts guarantees the performance of some of the major players. Thus private enterprise can see exactly the commitments of the government and can make its plans appropriately.

Indicative planning operated in France for more than 50 years. Its durability throughout different governments and economic regimes suggests that the participants in the planning process thought that they gained something by their involvement in the exercise. If the exercise offered nothing, then the various participants would likely show reluctance to become involved, but in contrast, the list of groups seeking inclusion tended to grow.

During the 1970s planning experienced a sharp decline. The integration of France into the European Communities and the external shocks that ripped through the international economy with many domestic consequences made the planning exercise seem obsolete. How could planning be effective when vital variables such as energy prices remained far beyond domestic control? However, the advent of the socialist government in 1981 brought with it a rebirth in the confidence in planning, an increase in the extent of nationalized industry (and therefore state control of the economy), and a restructuring of the institutional mechanism of planning. The return of the conservatives, the relaxation of controls, and the reprivatization process undercut some of that momentum. It remains to be seen whether the return of a socialist administration will put another breath of life into the process. In some sense, the likelihood seems remote. Today the French involvement

[7]Pierre Massé, "The French Plan and Economic Theory," *Econometrica* (April 1965), p. 267. Cited in Charles Kindleberger, "French Planning" in *National Economic Planning*, Max Millikan, ed. (New York: Columbia University Press, 1967), p. 301.

[8]Charles P. Kindleberger, "The Postwar Resurgence of the French Economy," in *In Search of France*, ed. Stanley Hoffman, C. P. Kindlebeger, J. R. Pitts, and L. Wylie, J. B. Duroselle, and F. Goguel, eds. (Cambridge, MA: MIT Press, 1963), p. 15.

in the European Union, and the necessity of conforming to the broader structure and rules of the European Union, reduces the importance of the plan.

For most of the period of indicative planning the French economy stayed buoyant. In the past decade, however, economic performance lagged significantly behind the average for industrial nations. Growth has slowed and unemployment has ballooned, particularly among young people. A debate centers on whether current conditions arose because of too much planning or too little. Proponents of planning can point to greater success when a more directed process involved fewer participants and produced specific targets rather than loose scenarios. They claim that a return to a more aggressive planning would pay dividends. In contrast, free marketeers feel that French performance suffers because of the rigidities of French life and a reluctance to let the market pick winners. They see high levels of controls, an extensive public sector, a rigid labor market, and misguided industrial policy as well as the attempts at planning as the causes of the malaise.

PROSPECTS FOR THE FRENCH ECONOMY

The Shift Toward Laissez Faire

This chapter focused on the role of the plan in the historic development of the French economy. Today we see a clear shift away from traditional *dirigisme*, the control, or literally "steering," of the economy by the state, and a sharp reduction in the degree of government intervention. In the past the state held the dominant role but now markets, firms, and other institutions not part of the "establishment" play a key part.

Table 6.2 compares French performance with the performance in both its neighbor Germany and the G7 nations as a whole since 1970. Until 1996–1997, it shows a record of declining growth accompanied by rising unemployment and increasing government deficits, for which the increasing burden of social expenditure must take much of the responsibility. After 1997, however, the reforms instituted in the French economy during the mid-1990s begin to bear fruit. France's relative performance improved considerably. The growth rate moved up relative to the other members of G7, and the output gap (the difference between the national product at full capacity and that actually realized) began to shrink, however, bringing considerable improvement in the relative position. This improvement can be largely credited to three factors—privatization, labor market reform, and consolidation of the budget—that made the French economy more flexible than in the past.

Since 1996, much of state-owned enterprise, which historically embraced not only manufacturing industry (major firms such as Renault, Thomson, Péchiney), but also utilities (France Télécom), insurance (Assurances Générale de France), banking (Crédit Lyonais and Credit Foncier), and the defense sector (Aérospatiale) was sold in whole or in part to private owners. This represents an asset sale as great as the sell-off in the United Kingdom under the Thatcher administration and is remarkable in that the Socialists, while in office, pursued privatization with greater enthusiasm than did the Conservative administration that preceded them.

- **TABLE 6.2**

Recent French Economic Performance: Average Annual Growth Rates Compared to Germany and the Group of Seven

	1971–1980	1981–1990	1994	1995	1996	1997	1998	1999	2000	2001
Real GDP										
France	3.3	2.4	1.8	1.9	1.0	1.9	3.3	3.2	3.2	2.6
Germany	2.7	2.3	2.3	1.7	0.8	1.4	2.1	1.6	3.0	1.9
G7	3.3	2.9	3.1	2.3	2.7	3.3	2.8	3.0	3.8	1.6
Inflation										
France	9.7	6.4	1.7	1.8	2.1	1.3	0.7	0.6	1.8	1.8
Germany	5.1	2.6	2.7	1.7	1.2	1.5	0.6	0.7	2.1	2.4
G7	8.7	4.8	2.1	2.3	2.1	1.9	1.3	1.3	2.0	1.9
Employment										
France	0.5	0.3	–0.1	1.1	0.0	0.8	1.3	3.0	2.7	1.6
Germany	0.2	0.5	–0.7	–0.4	–1.3	–1.4	0.7	1.7	0.5	0.0
G7	1.3	1.2	1.0	0.8	0.7	1.3	1.0	1.3	1.1	0.1
Unemployment										
France	4.2	9.3	12.3	11.7	12.4	12.3	11.8	11.2	9.5	8.7
Germany	2.7	7.3	9.6	9.4	10.4	11.5	11.2	10.8	7.5	7.4
G7	4.5	6.9	7.2	6.8	6.9	6.7	7.9	7.6	6.9	6.8
General Government—Overall Balance										
France	–0.5	–2.3	–5.5	–5.5	–4.1	–3.0	–2.7	–1.8	–1.4	–1.4
Germany	–2.0	–2.0	–2.4	–3.3	–3.4	–2.7	–2.2	–1.6	1.2	–2.7
G7	–2.1	–2.9	–5.3	–5.0	–4.1	–2.1	–1.8	–1.3	0.0	–1.6

SOURCE: World Economic Outlook Database April 2002, available at http://www.imf.org/external/pubs/ft/weo/2002/01/data/index.htm#1 (accessed May 2001).

Considerable doubt remains, however, about whether the improvement in the economy will prove a durable phenomenon, and future success seems to be contingent upon the further pursuit of reform. Although it is almost universally accepted in France that the first waves of deregulation and privatization reform produced a salutary effect in terms of increasing output, improving quality, and lowering prices, a rather puzzling lack of momentum now characterizes the efforts for further change. In Britain, in contrast, privatization became an unstoppable force that swept into all areas of the economy, including some unlikely candidates such as the London Underground. In France the distinct dearth of enthusiasm may be credited to the perception of overindulgence across the channel. Several other reasons explain this absence of enthusiasm for further reform.

1. Many fear that the mission of public service might be jeopardized. In France the spread of liberalization brought forward concerns that the essential role of the "network industries" (telecommunications, transport, and energy supply) in the life of the nation might be jeopardized. In France, unlike the United States, people hold no general assumption that "private is better" and there remains a continuing perception that the problems of externalities and public goods continue to require a strong state role in certain areas.

2. The special nature of the publicly owned network industries attracted a well-paid and highly regarded workforce of quasi-civil servants. Working for the government in the United States is generally regarded as something of an affliction or the last refuge of scoundrels, but in France such service carries prestige. The employees of these industries require reassurance that their careers will be safe from downsizing or a loss of pay or social status.

3. The publicly owned industries provided strong technological leadership, an important aspect of the innovative dynamic in the economy and society as a whole. Critics feel that the demise of the public sector will lead to the loss of this important vector for change.

4. Finally many feel the commonplace and reasonable fear that replacing a public sector monopoly with a private sector monopoly (or at least oligopoly) can lead to severe market failure to the detriment of consumers and will necessitate the remedy of strict regulation.

Changes in Taxation France traditionally imposed higher levels of tax pressure than most of its partners in Europe, and, especially the non-European members of the OECD. Increased factor mobility, a facet of both the continued integration of the EU and the more general trend to globalization, makes this taxation a liability for growth, as capital tends to flee high-tax environments.

The OECD states that

> The top marginal rate of personal income tax is higher than in most OECD countries, because this tax is steeply progressive. Summing up all the various obligatory charges and taxes on personal earned income, the average rate of tax of an unmarried employee can be as high as 58% of his earnings. In an environment of pronounced tax competition, the high level of direct taxes and welfare contributions may place French producers at a disadvantage, encourage human capital to move abroad and cause heavy flows of out-ward direct investment.[9]

These high rates of tax tend to produce "inactivity traps." A person who received basic income support (known in France as RMI) frequently faced an implicit marginal tax rate of more than 100 percent (i.e., his/her income and benefits actually fell at the return to work). The French authorities, long aware of these problems, instituted a series of measures designed to improve the employability of the less-skilled workers, as well as to retain high-skilled labor and productive capital. The reforms planned for 2000–2003 include income tax reform, reduction of the corporation tax,

[9]OECD, *Country Sources*, France, 2001.

and cutting VAT. The bottom rate of personal income tax will be cut from 10.5 percent to 7 percent, in an attempt to remove one inactivity trap, while the top rate will fall from 54 percent to 52.5 percent, making a small concession to another. For small and medium-sized enterprises the corporate income tax rate will be lowered from 36.7 percent to 15 percent over a three-year period. For large firms the rate will fall to 33 percent from 36.7 percent. The value added tax (VAT or, in France, TVA) fell by about 1 percent, while the rate on home improvements was sharply cut from 20.6 percent to 5.5 percent. This reduction should lead to a boom in home reconstruction, and also eliminate a sizable part of the black market activity.

The Unemployment Problem

A particular problem for France today, though one it shares with other members of the EU, continues to be the unemployment rate. Though now down once more to single digits from the 12 to 13 percent experienced from 1994–1997, it remains high. Based on standardized definitions, France holds the second highest unemployment rate in the G7 (behind Italy alone). Moreover, estimates of NAIRU, which is the lowest rate of unemployment that does not tend to stimulate accelerating inflation, placed it at just over 9 percent. In other words, the institutional makeup of the French labor market means that any attempt to drive unemployment below 9 percent (by, for example, aggressive fiscal or monetary policy) will lead to acceleration in price increase.

It can be argued that this characteristic of the French labor market owes much to a historic official policy of discouraging the supply of labor through accelerating retirement and reducing the workweek. French workers, when in work, put in fewer hours per year than those in other countries (about 1,532 per year before absenteeism is factored in) due to short workweeks, long vacations, and a plethora of public holidays. Participation rates are low at both ends of the population pyramid. In the 55 to 64 age group, only 40 percent of men have jobs, and only 33 percent of women. Among young people (16 to 24) only 33 percent of men are working, and only 25 percent of women. The high level of income support and high tax rates discourage effort, while taxes on employees tend to discourage firms from hiring. All these factors add up to an acute problem in France. Recruitment difficulties for firms coexist with high rates of unemployment. Only further institutional reform can lessen the impact of this apparent paradox, and the emphasis must shift to providing incentives to work.

However, present policy seems to some observers to be making matters worse. The government cut the standard workweek to 39 hours from 40 in 1982, and more recent reforms require that all firms conform to a statutory workweek of 35 hours by January 2002. The impact of such a change remains unclear. One consequence may take the form of an increase in employer costs, both due to necessary reorganization and higher unit labor costs, which in turn, by reducing French competitiveness, will lead to a loss of jobs. More sanguine commentators see a sharp fall in unemployment through the creation of 700,000 "new" jobs, a result of requiring more workers to provide the same inputs of labor-hours. Reducing the workweek will further reduce the supply of labor, and likely do little to solve the paradox of high unemployment coexisting with vacancies.

Successive administrations also responded to the threat of unemployment by reducing the normal retirement age. Promoting and subsidizing early retirement in France subjects it to one of the highest **dependency ratios** (the proportion of the economically inactive to those in work) in the developed world. In addition, the average French worker puts in fewer hours of work over a lifetime than anywhere else in the world. These statistics appear in Table 6.3.

Shortening the workweek and accelerating retirement exacerbates the dependency problem created by an aging population. "Graying," a condition common to all European nations, results from falling birthrates and increased longevity, but it is particularly acute in France. It inevitably causes a further increase in the dependency ratio as shown in Table 6.4. Despite France's natural prosperity it is hard to see how a nation can both increase the ratio of nonworkers to workers and reduce the work time of those employed while still maintaining average income levels commensurate with the most affluent nations.

CONCLUSION

Many skeptics still wonder whether France can develop sufficient faith in market institutions and supportive social organizations to thrive as a "new economy" in which state direction plays a much smaller role. The pervasive presence of the French state in all aspects of life has a long history and was much criticized by Alexis de Tocqueville in the eighteenth century. More recently Francis Fukuyama characterized French society as "low trust" and lacking the capacity for informal association that he believes the current economy requires. He wrote:

■ TABLE 6.3

	Average Effective Duration of Work per Employee	Effective Duration of Work for Selected Countries	
		Average Effective Duration of Work Men Aged 15–60	Average Lifetime Hours Worked of Men 14–70
United States	1,976	1,458	61,343
Japan	1,990	1,408	71,123
New Zealand	1,838	1,307	—
Spain	1,745	856	62,257
United Kingdom	1,731	1,223	73,904
Canada	1,721	1,182	—
Italy	1,682	861	61,825
Switzerland	1,643	—	—
France	1,539	973	60,635
Germany	1,519	1,014	64,578
Netherlands	1,397	896	61,622

SOURCE: OECD, *Employment Outlook,* 1998, p. 207; and Commission d'Enquête du Senat sur les 35 Heures, 1998.

■ **TABLE 6.4**

	1995	2000	2010	2020	2030	2050
				France: Demographic Transition		
Population (thousands)	58,048	59,425	60,993	62,121	62,661	62,120
Elderly dependency ratio	22.1	23.6	24.6	32.3	39.1	43.5
Total dependency ratio	52.2	52.8	51.2	59.6	67.9	73.6

SOURCE: International Monetary Fund.

French *dirigisme*, or the active involvement of the state in economic life, was thus both the cause and the effect of the weakness of the French private sector and of its inability to create competitive large-scale enterprises of its own. That is, in the distant historical past, the centralized French state deliberately undermined the independence of the private sector through taxes and privileges in order to bring it under political control, which had the effect of weakening the entrepreneurial and organizational habits of businesses. But in later years, that very weakness of entrepreneurial spirit became a motive for the renewed intervention of the state, which sought to reenergize a cautious and unimaginative private sector. The willingness of the state to step in then perpetuated the dependence of the private sector. The issue became complicated in the twentieth century by socialist governments, which wanted to nationalize private businesses for ideological reasons, even when they would have been viable on their own, and later by conservative governments, which wanted to privatize out of similarly ideological convictions.[10]

Although the government reduced its role, uncertainty continues to surround the issue of how quickly and how vigorously private enterprise can emerge from two centuries of subservience to the state and provide an enduring engine of growth.

KEY TERMS AND CONCEPTS

Colbertism

concertation

dependency ratio

dirigisme

economie concertée

economie dirigée

inactivity trap

indicative planning

Jean Monnet

laissez faire

normative planning

Plan de l'État

Plan de la Nation

planning contracts

warranted growth rate

---

[10]Francis Fukuyuma, *Trust: The Social Virtues and the Creation of Prosperity* (New York: The Free Press, 1995).

QUESTIONS FOR DISCUSSION

1. What "market failure" was indicative planning designed to address?
2. Do you think that French planning was normative (prescribing what should be) rather than positive (describing what is)?
3. Why does Charles Kindleberger compare the process of French planning to a revivalist meeting?
4. What are the ways by which the actors in the French economy might be induced to commit to the targets of the plan?
5. What is *dirigisme*?
6. Why does France's membership in the European Union make the process of planning more difficult?
7. Why does "broadening" the dialogue make the practice of planning less precise?

RESOURCES

Web Sites

Commissariat Général du Plan..http://www.plan.gouv.fr/
At this Web site of the Planning Commission, you can find information about the CGP's current mission and projects.

Ministry of the Environment (In French).......................http://www.environnement.gouv.fr/

Ministry of the Economy, Finance, and Industry (In French) ....
....http://www.finances.gouv.fr/
From the homepage of the economics super-ministry, one can get to the Ministry of Economics, Finance, and Industry, the Ministry of Trade, the Ministry of Industry and Communications, and even the Mint.

Ministry of Foreign Affairs (In French).............................http://www.france.diplomatie.fr/

Ministry of Social Affairs, Labour and Solidarity (In French)...
....http://www.travail.gouv.fr/
This ministry handles employment, social security, and health. A major segment addresses the reduction of the workweek.

National Institute of Statistics and Economic Studies ....http://www.insee.fr/
A good source for economic statistics, now in English.

Le Monde ....http://www.lemonde.fr/
A national newspaper in French.

La Liberation...http://www.liberation.fr/
A national newspaper in French.

France.Com ....http://www.france.com/index.html

Books and Articles

Adams, William J. *Restructuring the French Economy: Government and the Rise of Market Competition Since World War II.* Washington, DC: Brookings Institution, 1989.

Adams, William J., and Christian Stoffaës, eds. *French Industrial Policy.* Washington, DC: Brookings Institution, 1986.

Estrin, Saul, and Peter Holmes. *French Planning in Theory and Practice.* London: George Allen & Unwin, 1983.

Hayward, Jack. *The State and the Market Economy: Industrial Patriotism and Economic Intervention in France.* New York: New York University Press, 1991.

IMF. *France: Selected Issues.* IMF Staff Country Report No. 02/249.

Javetski, Bill. "France Wants Out of Business; Balladur's Sell-off of State-Owned Companies Ends the Dirigiste Era," *Business Week*, June 7, 1993, 46–48.

Levy, Jonah D. *Tocqueville's Revenge: State, Society, and Economy in Contemporary France.* Cambridge, MA: Harvard University Press, 1999.

Liggins, David. *National Economic Planning in France.* Lexington, MA: Lexington Books, D.C. Heath & Co., 1975.

Lutz, Vera C. *Central Planning for the Market Economy: An Analysis of the French Theory and Experience.* Harlow, England: Longmans [for] the Institute of Economic Affairs, 1969.

Mayer, Colin, and Tim Jenkinson. "The Privatisation Process in France and the U.K." *European Economic Review*, March 1988, 482–491.

McCarthy, Patrick. *The French Socialists in Power, 1981–1986.* Westport, CT: Greenwood Publishing Group, 1987.

Muet, Pierre-Alain, Alain Fonteneau, and Malcolm Slater. *Reflation and Austerity: Economic Policy under Mitterrand.* New York: Berg Publishing, 1991.

OECD, *Economic Survey of France*, November 29, 2001.

"A Survey of France: A Divided Self." *The Economist*, November 14, 2002.

7

SWEDEN AND SOCIAL DEMOCRACY

SWEDEN	
Area (thousand sq. km.)	450
Currency	krona
Exchange Rate	SEK 9.16 = US$1
Population 2000 (millions)	9.00
Population Growth Rate	0.4%
GNI per Capita, 2000	$26,780
GNI per Capita, PPP	$23,770
GDP Growth 1990–2000	1.8%
Value Added as % of GDP 2000 Agriculture	2%
Industry	29%
Services	69%
% of GDP Government Expenditure	53%
Exports	38%

FUNDAMENTAL FEATURES OF THE SWEDISH MODEL

In Chapter 4 we discussed the operation of a market economy and some of the failures that might result. The problems of externalities and public goods differed in type from concern that income distribution resulting from the operation of a market economy might not be equitable or "fair." In a pure market system, an individual's income depends on his or her ownership of factors of production. The pattern of economic well-being generated might be considered unsatisfactory from a variety of points of view, which may provide a motivation for government action. In fact, one of the principal activities of governments in modern market economies involves modifying the income distribution. This involves the use of transfer payments, the public provision of goods that might otherwise be supplied privately and the finance of both these expenditures out of taxation. We generally refer to this activity as the operation of a "welfare state."

Sweden is generally regarded as the quintessence of the welfare state; the state guarantees everyone who is prepared to work a high standard of living, and provides the entire population with access to a wide range of services. These services include free education at all levels (with stipends for students above the high school level), free health care, and a comprehensive retirement scheme. Such policies ensure a high profile for the government in many aspects of economic life. Total government expenditures in Sweden are more than half of total gross domestic product. Payroll taxes amount to more than one-third of the total payroll, and most blue-collar workers pay a marginal income tax rate greater than 40 percent.

As a further feature of the "Swedish model," government maintains a high level of activity in the labor market. This has two aspects. In macroeconomic terms, the government aggressively uses monetary, fiscal, and exchange rate measures to maintain a high level of employment. On the microeconomic side, the government offers a comprehensive system of assisted job search and retraining programs to keep the level of frictional unemployment low.[1] These policies ensured that the rate of unemployment in Sweden until recently remained consistently below that of most other market economies.

By maintaining low unemployment and high levels of social goods and social insurance, Sweden has avoided the sharp contrasts between the affluent and the poor that can characterize pure market capitalism. The Swedish model also went a step further by its use of highly centralized collective bargaining practices. Negotiations between representatives of labor and employers on the national level largely determine wages. These negotiations, undertaken under the stewardship of the government, involve the various parties in the most heavily unionized society in the world. In Sweden, where some form of collective bargaining agreement covers 85 percent of workers, such central bargaining determines to a great extent the distribution of the social product.

One objective of this collective bargaining system has been the elimination of social waste by arriving at settlements without resort to socially and economically damaging strikes and labor disputes. Another objective has been the promotion of "wage solidarity," which involves an overt attempt to keep the earnings of all workers more closely grouped than is the case in less socially conscious societies. This aspect of policy aims to produce a higher degree of social cohesion within the population, and the consequent elimination, or at least minimization, of class conflict.

Although government strongly shapes the distribution of income and goods in kind in Sweden, ownership of the means of production falls almost entirely within

---

[1]Frictional unemployment results when a worker engages in some form of job search while out of work and represents behavior compatible with a high level of demand in the labor market.

the private sector. Thus, many authors describe Sweden as being representative of a "middle way"—socialist in terms of its distribution policy but capitalist (relying on markets and competition) in production. Because of its approach, and the apparent elimination of the "market failure" of highly skewed distribution of well-being, the Swedish model appears, at first sight, highly attractive. However, critics point to the high level of taxes required to finance redistribution policies, and the consequent erosion of incentives, as the flaw that ultimately hobbled the Swedish system. Moreover, although Swedish firms are capitalist in terms of ownership, the strength of unions, powerful labor laws, and other government restrictions place constraints on Swedish managers' ability to operate. In the long term, these constraints may adversely affect international competitiveness. This chapter looks at the key features of the Swedish model and asks whether other countries—developed, developing, or in transition from some form of socialism—might profitably learn from the Swedish experience.

Characteristics of Swedish Society

First, one tends to note Sweden is a small country. Its population of only 9 million is remarkably homogenous, both politically and ethnically. Without any great racial or class conflict, the political debate remains rather localized in terms of the ideological spectrum. Most Swedes accept the essential propositions of Swedish society, a commitment to wage solidarity and social cohesion.

Whether this consensus comes as a product of the Swedish economic model or is a cause of it represents an open question. The Social Democratic Party has been in power for 61 of the last 70 years. It won its third successive general election in September 2002. Although the Social Democrats received only 40 percent of the popular vote, they enjoy a stable majority in Parliament because of the support of the Greens and several left-wing former communists. No matter which party held power, the political system remained highly corporatist. Decision making is collective, but only through institutions sanctioned by the state and granted access to the process. Groups outside of those formally recognized by the government (and therefore policy making) have only a small voice. Although individuals enjoy a relatively high level of liberty, they also live within an expectation of conformity to the basic objectives of society.

Sweden is also a prosperous society. Only Switzerland, the United States, and Japan score significantly above Sweden in terms of income measured by purchasing per head. The Swedish economy distributes income quite equitably. The ratio of the income share of the most affluent quintile to the least affluent is only 3.5 to 1, thus Sweden may be thought of as about twice as "equitable" as the United States. This equality owes much to the strong role of the government; general government total outlays were 52.7 percent of GDP in the year 2000, the highest in the world.[2] Although down from a peak near 67 percent in 1993, this percentage is well above the average for the European Union (EU), which sat at only 44.2 percent, and

---

[2]See OECD *Economic Outlook*, June 2001.

almost twice the relevant U.S. figure of 29.6 percent. Social security transfer payments alone account for 19 percent of GDP, against an average of 10 percent for the industrialized world as a whole and only 7 percent for the United States. However, although the Swedish government experienced a considerable deficit in the early 1990s, as much as 8 percent of GDP, fiscal prudence, falling unemployment and a growing economy restored the balance.

Contrary to popular wisdom, Sweden does not attract a plethora of social problems, and statistics show it does well on most measures. It records one of the highest life expectancies in the world (second only to Japan) and one of the lowest infant mortality rates. Fewer people populate Sweden's prisons than the average in the industrial world; in fact, its incarceration rate equals only about 11 percent of that of the United States. Suicides rank at about the mean for developed nations. In terms of overall "human development,"[3] as defined by the United Nations Development Programme (UNDP), Sweden ranked fourth in the world in 2001. The divorce rate is about the same as that of the United States, though births outside of matrimony are higher. Alcohol consumption is low, and injuries due to traffic accidents (perhaps not coincidentally) occur at one-fifth of the U.S. level. Sweden's population continues to age—now one of the oldest populations in the world—with 18 percent of the population above the age of 65. This growing share of elderly gives Sweden one of the highest dependency ratios in industrialized countries, and the necessity of providing for an increasing proportion of retired further strains the public finances.

Although it is a member of the European Union, Sweden has so far declined to be a part of the common currency system. It has traditionally guarded its sovereignty and continues to regard the exchange rate as a means of promoting the high levels of employment essential to its system. However, sentiment is shifting in favor of the Euro. Sweden, a small and highly open economy, would gain a great deal from the common currency. Prime Minister Persson will probably try to prod the country in the direction of monetary accession during 2003.

SOCIAL DEMOCRACY

Even after the reforms of the early 1990s, which curtailed some aspects of public spending, Sweden remains the best example of **social democracy.** Henry Milner defines a social democratic system in terms of six basic principles governing the interaction of government and citizens.[4] These principles can be summarized as follows:

1. *A fair distribution of economic well-being.* The fruits of economic prosperity are to be distributed fairly, but in such a way as not to undermine that prosperity. In other words, taxes and transfer payments must be used but care should be

---

[3]The World Bank's Human Development Index uses a weighted average of life expectancy, literacy, higher education, and income per head.

[4]This section on the underlying principles of social democracy is taken and modified from Henry Millner's *Sweden: Social Democracy in Practice* (New York: Oxford University Press, 1989), pp. 4–5.

taken lest high tax rates or overgenerous transfers create substantial disincentives to effort.

2. *Work for all as the primary means of eliminating deprivation.* Because human beings seek to live productively, fair distribution is to be effected through decently remunerated employment rather than simply cash or services.

3. *A high degree of social solidarity to bind individuals to a common purpose.* Individuals are members of communities through ties of culture and history. Members enjoy reciprocal rights and obligations over and above the right of all human beings to be treated with tolerance and compassion without distinction as to race, sex, disability, and so on.

4. *Rules to be made by a democratic process.* A society of justice must follow rules, without which it degenerates into a jungle in which the "fittest" prosper. Democracy entails that the rules to be obeyed—by leaders and followers alike—result from decisions made by the people themselves through free elections that fully safeguard fundamental political freedoms.

5. *Participation must extend beyond electoral democracy.* Especially in modern societies with complex systems of economic coordination, democracy entails active decentralized decision making and employee participation in management.

6. *Access to information for all citizens.* Democratic participation requires open and informed discussion—that is, a free and responsible press; an informed, well-educated citizenry; full public access to information based on data reliably gathered and presented; and publicly accountable independent boards of inquiry into matters of controversy.[5]

Although Sweden provides perhaps the best real-world example of a social democracy, it falls short of these defining characteristics in key ways. In particular, the first principle's drive for egalitarianism clashes with economic efficiency, hampering the operation of the labor market, reducing saving, and leading to high rates of absenteeism. This conflict has led to rising unemployment and a falling sense of solidarity. Although democratic in terms of its electoral policies, real power in Sweden is held by a small group of individuals within a limited set of institutions. This chapter asks, among other things, whether egalitarian labor market policies and a high degree of redistribution through transfer payments are compatible with relatively high rates of economic growth in the long run.

THE TAX AND TRANSFER SYSTEM

Sweden's comprehensive system of social insurance and redistribution forms the cornerstone of its social solidarity, which ensures that a worker who is willing to work will not be unduly harmed by involuntary job loss, injury, sickness, or even family responsibilities. The Organization of Economic Cooperation and Develop-

---

[5]A final principle could be added: respect for the environment. Through creative decentralized planning, social democracy ideally protects and enhances the natural environment as vital to human existence.

ment (OECD) calls it "[a] universal and generous system of social protection [that] has combined with progressive income taxes to achieve a high degree of poverty alleviation and equalization of incomes." Sweden outperforms most other countries in terms of relative income levels for key groups such as families with children and old-age pensioners.[6] A full 35 percent of all household income in Sweden results from transfer payments, up from only 15 percent in the mid-1960s. Table 7.1 shows that today Swedish workers lose little of their take-home pay for most unwelcome circumstances, and on the whole fare much better than the other countries illustrated, all of whom can be called something of a welfare state.

Although government financed, unemployment insurance funds are administered by the powerful and omnipresent labor unions. Membership is voluntary and open to all members of the labor force. Members may claim benefits after 12 months of membership with a replacement rate of 80 percent of gross earnings. Younger workers exhaust benefits after 300 days. If the worker remains out of work for a year, the last 65 days carry no unemployment benefit. Hence the **replacement wage** for a full year's unemployment is only 71 percent, as seen in Table 7.1, though workers over 55 can receive benefits for a total of 450 days. The same table also shows Sweden's generous sickness, injury, maternity, and retirement schemes.

Households unable to reach a reasonable living standard can claim social assistance benefits, administered by local authorities, although access is subject to strict

■ TABLE 7.1

International Comparison of Social Insurance Scheme (percentage change in annual disposable income for the average production worker in moving from employment to social insurance, 1996)

Benefit	Sweden, 1997[a]	Denmark	Finland	Germany	United Kingdom	Netherlands	Canada
12 months unemployment, insured	−29	−35	−38	−42	−79	−27	−44
Sickness, 1 week[b]	−0.8	0	0	0	−0.4	0	−1.5
Work injury, total incapacity	0	+26	−8	+15	−57	−27	−10
Maternity leave, common duration	−2	−3	−2	0	−3	0	−4
Old-age pension,[c] full work record	−36	−44	−33	−25	−47	−53	−45

[a]Based on a general replacement rate of 75 percent in social insurance, the increase to 80 percent in unemployment insurance in the fourth quarter is taken into account.
[b]Includes occupational pensions.
[c]Maximum (and not average) benefit in public schemes but without additions from occupational schemes.
SOURCE: OECD *Economic Survey of Sweden*, 1999, p. 125.

---

[6] OECD *Economic Survey of Sweden*, 1999, p. 16.

means testing, requiring recipients to sell capital assets. Housing benefits are means tested too and availability depends on the number of children, the income of the household, and the level of housing costs. Weekly cash payments are issued for each child in the family, with a higher rate effective from the third child on. Family benefits compensate parents for staying at home to take care of their children during the period immediate after their birth. The replacement rate amounts to about 80 percent (as elsewhere in the social insurance system) for the first 12 months. Day care for children is provided at prices below cost and dependent on parental income. Transfers are taxed on a par with labor income when they substitute for a short- or long-term earnings loss to avoid tax considerations playing into the take-up of benefits. Social insurance benefits are thus generally provided gross of taxes, the exception being social assistance. Child and housing benefits are consequently provided net of taxes.

This comprehensive welfare system does not come cheaply, making Sweden notorious for its high level of personal taxation. However, concerns about the disincentive effects of high taxation brought about a comprehensive reform in the tax system. The top rates of tax on unearned income remain high because reforms only cut the effective tax rate[7] from about 63 percent in 1989 to 60 percent today, still almost twice the U.S. rate of 35 percent. Table 7.2 shows that capital taxation in

■ TABLE 7.2

				Dimensions of Capital Income Taxation		
	Highest Tax Rate on Interest Income	Corporate Tax Rate	Total Dividend Taxation	Taxation of Capital Gains	Rate	Threshold
Sweden	30	28	50	30	1.5	0.9
Austria	25	34	50	0	0	
Belgium	15	40	49	0	0	
Denmark	59	34	60	0–40	0	
Finland	28	28	28	28	0.9	1.65
France	25	33	66	26	0.5–1.5	6.25
Germany	56	58	49	0	0	
Ireland	48	32	55	40	0	
Netherlands	60	35	74	0	0.7	0.77
Norway	28	28	28	28	0.7–1.1	0.13
United Kingdom	40	31	48	0–40	0	
United States	47	35	68	0–20	0	

NOTES: Tax rates are in percentages and thresholds are in SKr million.
SOURCE: OECD *Economic Survey of Sweden*, 1999, p. 133.

[7]Defined as employees' social security contributions plus personal income taxes as a percentage of gross labor costs.

Sweden compares favorably with the United States, although Sweden does impose a wealth tax of 1½ percent per annum in principle levied on all personal wealth greater than about $110,000 (however, loopholes abound and evasion is common).

CORPORATISM

Though ideally social democracy gives everyone a role in the decision-making process, in reality Sweden is a highly corporatist state with much of the power, especially in economic matters, being located in the government (with power held by the Social Democrats for most of the postwar period), the employers' federations, and the labor unions. The discussion of **corporatism** in Chapter 5 showed Sweden as the most highly unionized society in the world with the vast majority of workers represented by unions. However, this concentration of power by labor is matched by a similar centralization in capital. A disproportionately large number of major companies calls Sweden home. Table 7.3 shows it has the highest density of large companies of any European nation. Moreover, because of a limited domestic market, those companies must be globally competitive and reach markets beyond Sweden's seven million consumers. These export-oriented industries are vital for Sweden's well-being and play a key role in wage negotiations. Government's close relationship with the few business leaders who dominate Swedish industry is one reason why rates of taxation on capital are relatively modest compared to those falling on labor income—28 percent for corporate taxes as opposed to more than 60 percent for wage income under the personal income tax.

Not only is Swedish industry dominated by large firms, the corporatist structure of the country is more pronounced because of the dominance of a single holding company, Investor AB, which holds controlling interests in many of the big companies. Firms either controlled by Investor or in which it maintains a dominant interest make up about 40 percent of the Stockholm stock market's capitalization. In addition, 40 percent of Investor AB is owned by members of, or trusts controlled by, the Wallenberg family. Economic power in Sweden, more centralized than in any other

▪ TABLE 7.3

	Large Companies per Million Inhabitants, 1998: Number of Companies Among Europe's 500 Largest Companies		
Country	**Number of Companies**	**Country**	**Number of Companies**
Sweden	3.6	Ireland	1.7
Switzerland	3.5	Denmark	1.3
United Kingdom	2.7	Portugal	1.1
Belgium/Luxembourg	2.3	France	1.1
Netherlands	2.1	Norway	0.9

SOURCE: *Financial Times*, 1999.

SWEDEN'S MISSING ENTREPRENEURS

Sweden's deserved reputation as welfare state with an industrial sector dominated by a few large firms may be a problem for its long-term growth prospects. Despite Sweden's excellent education system and the high level of human capital embodied in its workforce it may lack one specific factor of production that has been found to be important in furthering growth—entrepreneurship. In 2000 two economists at the Stockholm School of Economics undertook a study of the determinants of the start-ups and high-growth firms. With the Internet and communications revolution being led by the small growth firms of Silicon Valley and the success of other small companies and services and retailing, it was thought to be on the keys to economic growth. They tried to measure entrepreneurship, and also the economic and cultural environment, by establishing by survey the number of people who actually tried to start their own company. They found that Sweden was the lowest of any of the European countries that they studied; only 2.2 percent of Swedish adults indicated experience as entrepreneurs against 3.1 percent in the United Kingdom and 3.8 percent in Norway. Europe as a whole, however, fared poorly against the United States where 8.4 percent of adults had, at one time or another, tried to start a business. Whether this contrast is due to "national character," the tax regime or other aspects of government policy is not clear. It can be used to support a general thesis that provision of job security does deplete initiative.

SOURCE: Magnus Henrekson and Per Davidsson, "Determinants of the Prevalence of Start-ups and High-Growth Firms," *Small Business Economics* 19, no. 2, 2002.

major capitalist country, facilitates the operation of the troika of employers, unions, and the Social Democratic Party that has controlled Sweden for decades.

THE SYSTEM OF LABOR RELATIONS

The Basic System

One of the most distinctive features of the Swedish economy, and the one we wish to focus on here, is its system of collective bargaining and industrial relations. This system originated in the late 1930s in discussions motivated by the need to reduce the then high degree of industrial unrest that Sweden experienced in the 1930s. In 1938, the employers' federation (the SAF) and the Swedish Trade Union Confederation (the LO) signed the basic agreement in the resort town of Saltsjöbaden, near Stockholm. The **Saltsjöbaden agreement** is the cornerstone of the system, providing a mechanism of collective bargaining to determine the rate of wage increase across industry and placing limits on the nature of industrial action by the unions.

As we noted, Sweden is one of the most heavily unionized societies in the world. Some 85 percent of workers claim membership of some union.[8] The LO represents

---

[8]United Nations Development Programme, *Human Development Report*, 1995, p. 201.

only blue-collar workers and now has about 2.2 million members. White-collar workers, a growing percentage of the workforce, are represented by their own confederations, the largest of which is the Swedish Confederation of Professional Associations (TCO). The SAF now represents some 42,000 firms of all sizes including all of the major employers. Government-sector employees are represented by their own agency.

Throughout the entire postwar era, until the end of the 1980s, national-level negotiations between the SAF and the LO provided the framework for changes in wage costs. Both sides saw benefit in this arrangement. The employers viewed the agreements as being able to deliver lower increases in labor costs, and lower prospects of strike activity, than might result from disaggregated bargaining. The unions supported the policy because it offered an avenue toward their overall political goal of **wage solidarity** (discussed later). Negotiations conducted at the national level hammered out a framework agreement that determined the overall increase in the wage bill. This framework was subsequently supplemented by industry agreements, which translated the total settlement with norms for the various sectors of the economy.

The EFO Model

A primary constraint on the system of wage settlement came from the need to maintain international competitiveness. Sweden, a small and relatively open economy, exports roughly one-quarter of its GDP, and wage cost inflation could not be allowed to jeopardize international competitiveness. The system of negotiation therefore explicitly differentiated between a competitive ("exposed") sector (comprised of firms such as Volvo, Saab-Scania, and Electrolux) which operated in world markets, the price structure of which lay beyond the control of anyone within Sweden, and a domestic ("protected") sector in which prices might be endogenously determined.[9] The rate of wage increase in the competitive sector was determined first on the proposition that the rate of growth of unit labor costs (basically wage cost increases less any anticipated productivity gains) should not outpace the rate of growth of prices for Swedish exports, as determined in world markets. This implies that:

$$\dot{W}_x = \dot{P}_x + (\dot{Q}_x - \dot{L}_x)$$

where $\dot{W}$ is the rate of change of wages; $\dot{P}$ is the rate of change of prices; $\dot{Q}$ is the rate of change of output; and $\dot{L}$ is the change in the use of labor. $\dot{Q}_x - \dot{L}_x$ therefore indicates the change in productivity; subscript x denotes the **exposed sector**. Any wage increase above this rate harms international competitiveness, resulting in a fall in exports, balance of payments problems, depreciation of the currency, and

---

[9]This procedure is known as the EFO model after the Gösta Edgren, Karl-Olaf Faxen, and Clas-Eric Odhner, who were the chief economists for the SAF, LO, and TCO, and who literally wrote the book on Swedish collective bargaining, *Wage Formation and the Economy*.

serious inflation in an open economy like Sweden's. An arithmetic example of the process is useful. If world prices for Swedish exports are expected to advance by 4 percent and productivity gains in Swedish industry are predicted to lower costs by 2 percent, the maximum increase in unit wages compatible with sustained export competitiveness is 6 percent. This calculation determined the wage settlement in the exposed sector. Subsequently, the rate of wage increases in the protected (i.e., nonexport) sector would be fixed at a rate comparable to that determined for the exposed sector. Such agreements were truly national and employees in the non-tradable service and government sector enjoyed a rate of increase of wages predicated on the rate of price increases and productivity gain in the most competitive sector.

Wage Solidarity

This model enabled the trade union movement to pursue one of its most cherished objectives—wage solidarity—with the underlying idea that the wage rate for all jobs requiring comparable effort and comparable skills should be the same across all industries. To put it another way, the unions committed to equal pay for equal work and to the notion that one's wage should not depend on the profitability of the industry in which one works. This proposition conflicts with the market logic that links wages to the marginal value product. Critics predicted that adherence to wage solidarity would lead to a variety of problems. Growing firms would find it hard to attract labor. Work incentives would be lowered, and the workforce would be inefficiently allocated between occupations and industries. Nevertheless, the unions experienced considerable success in eroding wage differentials between industries. In 1959 the spread between average wages in the highest and the lowest paid industries stood at 39 percent. By 1964 it had fallen to 26 percent and by 1981 was only 12 percent. A similar narrowing occurred in terms of wage differentials by sex. An average female worker in Sweden earns 90 percent of the male level, considerably above the "60 cents on the dollar" experienced in the United States.

The sustained growth of the government's role in the Swedish economy and the extensive provision of social goods made the public sector Sweden's largest employer. The Municipal Employees' Union is now the largest union in Sweden. The workforce actually engaged in the exposed sector shrank as a share of total employment as the services and government sectors grew. Furthermore, because any increase in pay for government-sector workers must be financed from taxes, a system where public-sector wages shadowed those of the most competitive sector embodied a serious problem. Simply, whenever productivity or prices rose in the export, or exposed, sector, wages for the workers in that sector would increase. The system of national wage negotiation meant that a wage increase in the service and government sectors would inevitably follow. This wage increase implied domestic inflation, as well as tax increases to pay the increased wages in the government sector, both of which resulted in ultimately injurious consequences for competitiveness in export markets.

The Breakdown of National Agreements

Although praiseworthy in terms of equity, attempts to ensure that equal work meant equal pay dulled the efficiency of the labor market. Wages in a market system, like other prices, act as signaling devices that indicate shortages; rising wages set in motion shifts that act to eliminate shortages. Because Swedish policy explicitly tried to eliminate wage differentials, the labor market could not adjust to rectify shortages in particular industries or sectors. With high demand for Swedish products in world markets, employers in the exposed sector found themselves short of labor and unable to increase wages to attract new workers. Expansionary macroeconomic policies ensured that the aggregate level of employment stayed high, and because of the national agreements, wages in **protected sectors** roughly equaled those in the exposed sector, making workers reluctant to change jobs.

Initially, employers in firms short of labor attempted to attract new workers while nominally living within the wages determined by the national agreement. Because nominal wage rates could not be raised at a rate above the agreed level, employers introduced special "perks" and fringe benefits as inducements to retain the workforce and attract new recruits. These incentives included productivity-related bonuses, premiums for shift work, shorter hours, and longer vacations. This phenomenon of raising the effective wage per unit labor while leaving the nominal hourly wage unchanged is known as **wage drift**. During the 1980s, an estimated 50 percent of effective wage increase could be attributed to wage drift. Wage drift is still present but has fallen to a smaller share of overall wage increase; in 1998 it represented less than 25 percent of the total changes. (See Table 7.4.)

Nonetheless, the employers in firms facing high product demand still felt shackled and in 1983 the Engineering Employers' Association (VF), a member unit of the SAF, decided to go alone and concluded its own set of wage agreements with the Metal Workers Union signaling the end of effective national wage determination. Since 1983, no national agreement on wage increases has been reached, although in some years the LO and the SAF recommended a nonbinding norm to their membership. The role of the union confederation now involves one of coordination and oversight rather than that of lead negotiator.

■ TABLE 7.4

		Aggregate Wage Growth (percent)			
	1994	1995	1996	1997	1998
Aggregate wage growth	2.4	3.3	6.0	4.5	3.6
Contribution from					
Central bargaining	1.5	2.1	4.4	3.8	2.8
Wage drift	1.0	1.2	1.7	0.7	0.8

SOURCE: Statistics Sweden; National Institute of Economic Research; Ministry of Finance, in OECD *Economic Survey of Sweden*, 1999, p. 68.

Other Aspects of Labor Market Policy

Although centralized wage negotiation formed the centerpiece of the labor market policies, it did not tell the whole of the story. Sweden's highly **active labor market policy** remains in place despite the demise of centralized wage bargaining and the consequent slippage of wage solidarity. This policy embraces relocation grants, training, and retraining schemes, private-sector employment subsidies, and where necessary, public-sector job schemes.

Active labor market policy supplied the necessary complement to centralized wage bargaining. In a free labor market, wage differentials between industries and occupations provide the incentives for workers to change jobs and so resolve shortages. This interaction ensures the flow of labor between occupations and a consequent microeconomic equilibrium, while real wage flexibility maintains full employment. Because the Swedish system for many years actively discouraged the development of wage differentials, the government resorted to active labor market schemes to solve the problem.

"Labor exchanges," government offices that assist in matching displaced workers with vacancies are the first point of intervention. In Europe, active labor market policy plays a more important role than in the United States, but in most countries labor exchanges operate with high levels of caseloads per staff worker. In Britain, for example, the ratio is 375 cases per employee; in Germany it is 370, and in the Netherlands 160. In Sweden, in contrast, it varies between 15 and 30, depending on the region and as a result offers high individual attention to each job seeker. The law requires that employers must report all vacancies to the authorities, and the labor exchange professionals know all essential information concerning all job openings in the country. Consequently they can work actively with the human resource departments of firms to find the best match between job seekers and vacancies. To further decrease rigidities and frictional cost to the unemployed, the government makes available funds for site visits and, should a job seeker accept a distant vacancy, for relocation expenses. If no suitable openings can be found for a job seeker, then the job seeker can participate in retraining funded by the government. Furthermore, in order to cope with potentially large crises, the authorities require that they be told well in advance about plant closings and downsizing, allowing forward thinking on strategies to address the problem and the institution of retraining schemes even before plant closings occur.

Generous unemployment benefits in Sweden result in only small reduction of take-home income consequent to a job loss. However, benefits are contingent on active job search and subject to strict time limits. Should an individual's benefits run out, the government acts as an "employer of last resort" and will provide a job for at least six months. As a result of this combination of policies, unemployment rates in Sweden remained low until recently, generally between 1 and 1.5 percent, but rose to more than 8 percent by the mid-1990s.

In August 2001 the government introduced a system of "activity guarantee." This plan requires that any person registered with the public employment to receive unemployment or social benefits must enroll in some education program if his or her unemployment lasts for more than six months. The nominal objective of this policy is to augment human capital, but the effectiveness of the policy is under question; it might merely serve to reduce the recorded rate of unemployment.

Attempts to Socialize Capital

The policy of wage solidarity resulted in the repression of wages in the profitable, exposed sectors of industry, and although this policy contributed to managers' problems by lessening their ability to recruit qualified labor, it positively affected profits by keeping wage costs low. Workers in these industries felt that they should share in the excess profits generated by their restraint. In 1976 the Congress of the LO adopted a resolution proposed by Rudolf Meidner, their chief economist, to establish **wage earner funds**. The ambitious original plan prescribed that each year all firms that employed more than 500 workers would hand over 20 percent of their pretax profits to a union-controlled fund specific to that industry. Under the plan these monies would be used by the union to purchase (at book value) shares of the firm in which the "excess" profits were made. Consequently, the share capital of the large, profitable elements of Swedish industry (which were concentrated in the exposed, export sector) would be increasingly accumulated by the unions. In the limit the unions might control all industrial capital, with the most profitable firms passing most quickly to union control. When the union share holdings represented a majority, they would be in a position to appoint management and assume strategic control of the firm. Had the **Meidner plan** been followed the Swedish system would eventually resemble the Yugoslav system of worker management, except for two important differences:

1. Union workers, rather than society as a whole, would be owners of capital.
2. Control of the firm would pass to industry-wide unions, rather than to the workers in the specific enterprise.

The Swedish parliament balked at enacting the Meidner plan into law, despite aggressive union lobbying. Such a radical idea would transform the Swedish model by progressively eliminating private capital, leading to union control of both sides of the labor process. It proved too ambitious, even for the ruling Social Democrats, and Sweden's tight group of capitalists staunchly opposed it. As a compromise Parliament went for a watered-down version, establishing five regional funds financed by a 20 percent tax on "excess profits," which were empowered to buy shares not at book value but at the much higher market value. This legislation also restricts accumulation to no more than 8 percent of the capital of any one firm, and total ownership by all of the funds together must not exceed 49 percent, thus denying the possibility of union control of business.

Recent Labor Market Developments

A startling development in Sweden in the early 1990s was a sharp rise in unemployment, shocking in an economy predicated on the idea of a universal right to work. Unemployment peaked at about 8 percent between 1994 and 1997, and has fallen back considerably since, at least in measured terms.

Table 7.5 shows recent developments in the labor market. The unemployment rate fell from its highs of greater than 8 percent in 1996 to about 5.5 percent in the year 2000. However, the government achieved this reduction by providing occupations to the potentially unemployed rather than by increasing the number of people in jobs actually created without overt government intervention. Thus the percentage of the workforce that is actually covered by unemployment, make-work, and special education programs together remained almost constant at 14.3 percent. Because more people enroll in education programs (especially in the adult education initiative introduced in 1997), fewer actually remain idle or in a make-work program. In theory this approach should lead to a better-trained and more productive workforce, though there is too little evidence to judge the effectiveness of job retraining schemes. The OECD reports that:

> The authorities have launched an extensive adult education programme. This is aimed at those with inadequate qualifications and has now been running, in line with the quantified objectives set, for two years. Insofar as educational qualifications are closely linked to unemployment risk, an emphasis on human capital enhancement is a key ingredient in the long-term improvement of labour-market outcomes.[10]

In February 2001 government, unions, and employers readied a guideline agreement to cover the entire labor sector for three years. The agreement specified hourly wage increases of 2.8 percent per annum, and a reduction in working hours added roughly another 0.5 percent to labor costs. Most analysts expect the pace of unit labor cost increases to be somewhat more rapid over the previous three years. Although still coordinated at the national level, Swedish labor negotiations show movement toward decentralization with more agreed upon at the plant or office level. This trend means greater difficulty in distinguishing between the agreed "official settlement" and "wage drift" as more deviations from the national agreements

■ **TABLE 7.5**

	Labor Market Developments, 1996–2000				
	1996	1997	1998	1999	2000
Labor force, 1,000 persons	4,310	4,264	4,255	4,308	4,364
Unemployment rate	8.1	8	6.5	6.4	5.6
Unemployed and covered by government programs (%)	14.3	14.8	13.8	16.3	14.3
Covered by make-work programs	4.5	4.3	3.9	3.3	2.8
Covered by education programs	1.7	2.4	3.4	6.6	5.9
Of Which: Adult Education Initiative	n.a.	2.7	3.3	3.3	3.1

SOURCE: OECD, *Economic Survey of Sweden*, 2001.

[10]OECD, *Economic Survey of Sweden*, 1999, pp. 13–14.

become codified into a local arrangement. The successful conclusion of this round of collective agreements represented in many ways "the ultimate test of the wage formation system in Sweden to deliver appropriate outcomes.[11]

Generally speaking, the agreement "passed" this test. The size of the increase, however, might pose a certain amount of difficulty for Swedish industry. The pace of labor cost increases during the period 1995–2001 led, in a competitive pricing environment, to a fall in the profit share of value added. As indicated in Table 7.6, labor gained considerably at capital's expense, averaging 4 percent of value added per annum over a six-year period. In manufacturing industry ("the exposed sector"), a healthy pace of productivity increase (4.7% per annum) did minimize the rate of labor cost increase, but the slow rate of price increases for manufactured goods in international markets still squeezed profits.

LESSONS OF THE SWEDISH MODEL

During the period from the establishment of the system of centralized wage bargaining in the late 1930s to the early 1980s, Sweden compiled an enviable record of labor peace and economic growth. However, during the 1980s recurrent economic problems called the success of the corporatist Swedish model into question.

Swedish experience in the labor market exemplifies the problems that confront a society's attempts to suspend the role of wages in furthering an efficient allocation of labor. Even though the convergence of wages toward equality might be regarded as a laudable social goal, without differential wages to encourage worker mobility the labor market cannot function smoothly. The conflict between the drive for equity in society at large and the needs of export-oriented industry caused the

■ TABLE 7.6

**Costs, Prices, and Profitability in the Business Sector
(average annual increase in percent, 1995–2001)**

	Total	Manufacturing	Construction	Nonfinancial Services
Unit labor costs	2.5	0.2	4.2	3.3
Hourly compensation	5.0	4.9	4.0	5.4
Labor productivity	2.5	4.7	−0.2	2.1
Output price	1.3	0.8	2.9	2.2
Profit share in value added (% change)	−4.0	−4.4	−3.5	−1.4

SOURCE: National Institute of Economic Research.

[11]OECD, *Economic Survey of Sweden*, June 2002, p. 26.

ABSENTEEISM, TAXES, AND HEALTH

Sweden's population can be considered healthy by most measures. Swedes smoke less, drink less, and weigh less than the European average. It is curious then, that the Swedish workforce leads the world in staying home sick. In the European Union as a whole, only 1.9 percent of workers stay out sick for an entire week in any given year; in Sweden the figure is 4.5 percent. On any working weekday almost 10 percent of the workforce is out sick, and the figure doubled in the last ten years. The question is why. One possible answer is that the Swedish workforce, which is older than most other nations with high participation rates for workers over 60, actually is more illness prone. Another is that the Swedish work ethic has collapsed as workers become more alienated from the large firms and governmental organizations in which they work. Another is fiscal; the supportive welfare state almost completely protects workers' income from the consequence of being off work. For most factory and office workers the worker loses all pay for the first day but subsequently receives 80 percent of wages up to $2,600 per month. After two weeks the employer is relieved of most burden and the state pays the bulk of support which can be up to 90 percent of the work wage. Some workers actually see their take-home pay increase as a result of tax changes and the elimination of commutation expenses. The policy response largely depends on the diagnosis of the problem. The government has now created a ministerial post charged with reducing absenteeism, which costs the government more than $12 billion annually in lost taxes and support payments, to one half the current level by 2008. That level will put the incidence back where it was in 1996, when unemployment was at a post-war high.

SOURCE: *The Economist,* October 26, 2002, p. 49.

breakdown in the national system of wage bargaining. The question remains: Can it be put back together, or is it permanently consigned to history? Both parties to the labor agreement seem to be optimistic:

> Whether the social partners will be able to act in concert in order to get the economy moving again is something we cannot yet tell. . . . We can only express the hope that out of the present labor pains a new Swedish model will be born, resembling its forerunner. There are, in fact, good chances of this. Despite the adverse trends . . . there are many sound elements of the Swedish economy and industrial relations system that have survived and can be built on. . . . In their hearts the Swedes share a deep community of values. The representatives of labor and management can still mix with each other centrally and locally in a spirit of trust and are capable of working together on matters of common interest. Promising signs are the agreements that have been concluded in recent years on such collaboration and, above all, the fact that the debate on wage policy is now being conducted in the broader context of the nation's economic health.[12]

A similar guarded optimism came from the union side:

> Many people in Sweden see . . . the frequent breaches of labor peace as linked to the departure from the centralized bargaining system. At the same time there is widespread agreement that prosperity must be safeguarded and equitably shared. This is why I

[12]Both this and the following quote were from the *International Labour Review,* 1986, cited in Milner, pp. 225–226. The employer's view is from L. G. Albåge, and the union position from Harry Fjällström.

believe that the pressures favoring the return to coordinated central negotiations will prevail, even if slight changes may be expected in the unions' distribution policy. The bargaining system that has come to be known as the Swedish model of industrial relations has stood the test of time and I am confident that given the opportunity it will continue to serve both sides of industry well for many years yet.

Whatever the future of national labor negotiations, most analysts seem to agree that the umbrella nature of the Swedish social welfare system hurt macroeconomic performance. The high rates of taxation required to finance the welfare state probably cast a disincentive effect over both worker effort and savings, retarding growth to a rate that was in the 1970s half the OECD average. It represents perhaps the most important issue to be addressed in a comprehensive welfare state. Milner noted it in the 1980s:

> The most important and difficult question raised by critics of the welfare state concern the system of rewards resulting from the combination of wages, taxes, transfers, and other sources of income on individuals and, ultimately, its effect on the workings of the economy. They are perhaps most fully explored in the work of the distinguished and increasingly critical Swedish economist Assar Lindbeck. In Lindbeck's recent work is found perhaps the most sophisticated expression of the often-made argument that somewhere in the 1970s the excessive redistributiveness of Swedish welfare policy began to actually decrease the aggregate quantity of socially useful work by significantly increasing leisure through shorter work years and absenteeism and pushing activity into the "unofficial economy" in the form of barter, do-it-yourself work, and other forms of tax avoidance.[13]

Disincentive effects of high benefits and taxes manifest themselves in a variety of ways. A 1986 report by the engineering employers' association found that blue-collar Swedish workers were on the job less—putting in only 1,546 hours a year compared to 1,654 in West Germany and 1,930 in the United States—in part due to increased absenteeism and "sick outs." High tax rates forced activity into the black economy. One study found that between 12 and 25 percent of income in Sweden was unrecorded.[14]

An OECD report a decade later addressed the issue of incentive and came to the following conclusion:

> A universal and generous system of social protection has combined with progressive income taxes to achieve a high degree of poverty alleviation and equalisation of incomes. Sweden outperforms most other countries in terms of relative income levels for key target groups such as families with children and old-age pensioners. This redistribution has been accompanied by a continuous extension of transfers, from 15 per cent of household incomes in the mid-1960s to 35 per cent in the late 1990s, with the result that as much as two-thirds of transfers reflect redistribution over the life-cycle of individuals and only one-third interpersonal ("pure") redistribution.

---

[13]Henry Milner, *Sweden: Social Democracy in Practice* (New York: Oxford University Press, 1989). The best example of Lindbeck's views may be found in Assar Lindbeck, *Swedish Economic Policy* (Berkeley: University of California Press, 1974).

[14]Edward Feige, "Sweden's Underground Economy," in *The Economics of Institutions and Markets*, Gunnar Eliason, ed. (Stockholm: UIU, 1986), p. 127.

High tax rates and generous replacement rates, with a *de facto* indefinite duration of unemployment and sickness benefits, have worked to this effect. Income taxes and social security contributions combine with means-tested housing and day-care benefits to reduce substantially the return from taking a better-paid job or increasing hours worked. The added effect of the internationally high 80 per cent replacement rate in benefits actually produces a substantial penalty for many on moving from unemployment to employment. Close to 40 per cent of unemployed would see no or insignificant increases in disposable incomes from moving back into work.[15]

Troubling problems arise from the high levels of distribution as well as from the high level of taxation that such redistribution requires. Material incentives, thought by many to be crucial to the prosperity of any economic system, are undeniably dulled. However, Sweden's relative economic success over many years demands that we take the "Swedish model" seriously. Despite the dip in the middle and late-1990s, Sweden reemerged as one of the most prosperous economies in the world. An active debate currently centers on the measurement and evaluation of Sweden's performance.[16] A few years ago the picture turned somewhat grim as Sweden fell in most cross-country comparisons of well-being, but in recent years it experienced higher growth and lower inflation than in most of the developed world. To what extent this performance results from the durability of the Swedish model and to what extent the revival may be attributed to promarket reform is still open to question.

KEY TERMS AND CONCEPTS

active labor market policy

corporatism

EFO model

exposed sector

labor exchanges

means testing

Meidner plan

protected sector

replacement wage

Saltsjöbaden agreement

social democracy

wage drift

wage earner funds

wage solidarity

QUESTIONS FOR DISCUSSION

1. Why is the concept of wage solidarity central to Swedish society?

2. How does an attempt to limit the distribution of wages lessen the effectiveness of the labor market?

3. Why is an active labor market policy a possible remedy for the absence of wage signaling?

[15]OECD, *Economic Survey of Sweden*, 1999, pp. 16–18.
[16]See Magnus Henrekson, "Swedish Economic Growth. A Favorable View of Reform," *Challenge* 44, no. 4 (July–August 2001).

4. In what ways does Sweden as a society differ from an "ideal" social democracy?

5. Is it appropriate to describe Sweden as corporatist? Why?

6. What pressures from the exposed sector led to the breakdown of national agreements?

7. What sort of socialism would the extensive use of wage funds lead to?

RESOURCES

Web Sites

Central Bank ....http://www.riksbank.com/

Swedish Municipal Workers Union..http://www.kommunal.se/

Investor AB ....http://www.investorab.se/

Stockholm School of Economics..http://www.hhs.se/

Swedish Confederation of Professional Employees................................http://www.tco.se/

Swedish Employers Federation (SAF) ....http://www.saf.se/

The Swedish Trade Union Confederation, LO ....http://www.lo.se/

Swedish Government Web site ....http://www.sweden.gov.se/

Books and Articles

Bosworth, Barry P., and Alice M. Rivlin (eds.). *The Swedish Economy.* Washington, DC: Brookings, 1987.

Davies, Steven, and Magnus Henreksen. "Wage-Setting Institutions as Industrial Policy." NBER Working Paper No. 7502 and SSE/EFI Working Paper No. 352, January 2000.

Davidsson, Per, and Magnus Henrekson. "Determinants of the Prevalence of Start-Ups and High-Growth Firms." *Small Business Economics*, 19, no. 2 (2002).

Calmfors, Lars (ed.). *Wage Formation and Macroeconomic Policy in the Nordic Countries.* Oxford: Oxford University Press, 1990.

Canova, Timothy A. "The Swedish Model Betrayed." *Challenge,* May–June 1994, 36–40.

Cohen, Peter. "Sweden: The Model That Never Was." *Monthly Review,* July–August 1994, 41–59.

European Parliament. *Social and Labour Markets Policy in Sweden.* Directorate-General for Research, Working Papers, Social Affairs Series, July 1997.

Henrekson, Magnus. "Swedish Economic Growth. A Favorable View of Reform." *Challenge,* 44, no. 4 (July–August 2001).

Lindbeck, Assar, Per Molander, Torsten Persson, Olof Peterson, Agnar Sandmo, Birgitta Swedenborg, and Niels Thygesen. "Options for Economic and Political Reform in Sweden." *Economic Policy,* October 1993, 219–263.

Maccoby, Michael (ed.). *Sweden at the Edge: Lessons for American and Swedish Managers.* Philadelphia: University of Pennsylvania Press, 1991.

Milner, Henry. *Sweden: Social Democracy in Practice.* New York: Oxford University Press, 1989.

Palme, Marten O., and Robert E. Wright. "Gender Discrimination and Compensating Differentials in Sweden." *Applied Economics* 24 (1992), 751–759.

Persson, Inga (ed.). *Generating Equality in the Welfare State: The Swedish Experience.* Oslo: Norwegian University Press, 1990.

Ramaswamy, Ramana. "Wage Bargaining Institutions, Adaptability, and Structural Change: The Swedish Experience." *Journal of Economic Issues* 26, no. 4 (December 1992), 1041–1061.

"A Survey of the Nordic Countries: Happy Family?" *The Economist,* January 23, 1999, 50.

"A Survey of Women and Work." *The Economist,* July 18, 1998, 48.

"The Entrepreneur and the Swedish Model." In M. Henrekson, M. Larsson and H. Sjögren, eds., *Entrepreneurship in Business and Research. Essays in Honour of Håkan Lindgren.* Stockholm: Probus Förlag and Institute for Research in Economic History, 2001.

BRITAIN: PRIVATIZATION AND ITS AFTERMATH

UNITED KINGDOM	
Area (thousand sq. km.)	245
Currency	British pound
Exchange Rate	£0.64 = US$1
Population 2000 (millions)	60
Population Growth Rate	0.4%
GNI per Capita, 2000	$24,500
GNI per Capita, PPP	$23,550
GDP Growth 1990–2000	2.5%
Value Added as % of GDP 2000 Agriculture	1%
Industry	25%
Services	74%
% of GDP Government Expenditure	37.0%
Exports	28.1%

THATCHERISM: A CHANGE IN DIRECTION

We focus in this chapter on the short- and long-term effects of a sharp turn in the British government's relationship to the economy, in some ways a shift so fast that whether it constitutes a change in policy or a change in system continues to be debated. The shift involved the privatization of almost the entire public sector, which accounted for more than 12 percent of GDP, and a turn away from a "welfare state" toward a more market dominated economy. This change offers lessons that can be applied to other nations making an even more radical shift from state to market orientation.

Margaret Thatcher took office as prime minister of a Conservative government in 1979, at the end of a dispiriting decade. The 1970s had proved difficult for most of the world economy but in Britain **stagflation**, the combination of high inflation, low growth, and rising unemployment, took a particularly severe toll and marked the culmination of a century of decline relative to the rest of the developed world. After a fast start as the world's first industrial power, most economic historians pick the period between 1870 and 1913 as the time when the United States and Germany challenged and ultimately overthrew Britain's industrial supremacy.

Between 1913 and 1945, two world wars (1914–1918 and 1939–1945) and the Great Depression, which lasted from the end of 1929 until roughly 1938, obscured the underlying trends in the global economy. In Britain the decades between the wars saw social friction and labor unrest, while each of the conflicts cost it dearly in terms of domestic investment foregone and foreign assets liquidated. However, Britain emerged from World War II with an aggressive plan to socialize industry and construct a welfare state. The postwar Labour government nationalized much of industry, including steel; coal; road, rail, and air transportation; and electricity and gas supply. The financial sector remained in private hands, though subject to considerable regulation. Extensive planning controls inherited from the war period, including the rationing of consumer goods, extended into land-use planning by the 1948 Town and Country Planning Act.

On the social side, the government moved to construct a comprehensive welfare state, with free socialized medicine, increased publicly provided higher education, and extensive income support for the old, the unemployed, the young, and the sick.[1] While government's share of the economy failed to shrink from wartime levels, highly progressive taxation fell heavily on so-called unearned income originating from capital and land.

Viewed in retrospect, the two decades after World War II present a conundrum. On one hand, they can be remembered as a golden age of strong and consistent growth, low inflation, and low levels of unemployment, almost living up to their billing as the "new Elizabethan era." As Table 8.1 shows, between 1950 and 1973 Britain enjoyed real growth of 3.0 percent per annum, with the output doubling in 23 years. Per-head income rose by 2.5 percent per annum, more than 76 percent over the period, while unemployment was both low and stable by historic standards, particularly when compared to the disastrous 1930s. In terms of overall macroeconomic performance, the period 1950–1973 probably can be rated about as good as Britain ever got, even when compared to the middle decades of the nineteenth century, which laid the foundation of British prosperity. Were it not for the performance of continental Europe and Japan, the 1950s and 1960s might remembered for economic growth and expansion. However, though strong, Britain's growth fell dismally short of that of Germany, France, and Japan. Per-head income in Germany, defeated and humiliated in two world wars, passed that of Britain in

---

[1]The income support policy was modeled on the recommendations of a 1942 report authored by Sir William Beveridge, which outlined a blueprint for universal social insurance.

■ TABLE 8.1

Average Annual Percentage Growth Rates of GDP in Five Economies

	United Kingdom	France	Germany	Japan	United States
GDP					
1870–1913	1.9	1.5	2.8	2.3	3.9
1913–1950	1.3	1.1	1.3	2.2	2.8
1950–1973	3	5	5.9	9.3	3.6
GDP per Capita					
1870–1913	1	1.3	1.6	1.4	1.8
1913–1950	0.8	1.1	0.7	0.9	1.6
1950–1973	2.5	4	4.9	8	2.2
GDP per Hour Worked					
1870–1913	1.2	1.6	1.9	1.9	1.9
1913–1950	1.6	1.9	1	1.8	2.4
1950–1973	3.2	5	5.9	7.6	2.5

SOURCE: Angus Maddison, *Dynamic Forces in Capitalist Development* (Oxford: Oxford University Press, 1991).

1961, and France followed in 1969. Of most concern, British labor productivity only increased at two-thirds the pace of the average of the 12 most-developed nations. Although growing in absolute terms, Britain found itself drifting to the back of the pack.

Although the whole world experienced a worsening macroeconomic environment in the 1970s, Britain's performance became even more noticeably below par, managing barely half the average growth rate of the rest of the developed world. Both unemployment and inflation exceeded those in the average industrialized country, and as labor unrest worsened, Britain became generally regarded as the "sick man" of Europe and indeed of the whole of the Organization for Economic Cooperation and Development (OECD).

This perceived failure provoked a determined inquiry into the roots of Britain's economic performance. Some observers saw a cultural malaise characterized by over satisfaction and laziness, but several economic candidates possibly warranted a share of the blame:

1. The high and steeply progressive rates of income taxation reduced the incentive to work, particularly among the more productive members of society, by lowering the take-home wage. Heavy taxes on capital income deterred saving and investment and led to the outflow of capital from Britain to offshore havens and to a consequent underinvestment in domestic industry.

2. The comprehensive social safety net provided by the postwar welfare state reduced work incentive at the lower end of the income scale, reducing the cost of job loss to workers. High taxes and income guarantees together wrought a suffocating effect on effort at both ends of the income distribution.

3. Workplace relations remained poor as conservative management confronted a highly unionized and militant workforce. To make matters worse, British union organization followed craft or occupation lines, rather than by place of work. Each employer was, as a result, forced to negotiate with many unions, with the potential to disrupt output by using its power to maximize the short-term income of its membership. The introduction of new work practices to raise productivity consequently proved extremely difficult, and attempts to rationalize the use of labor often led to "demarcation disputes" between different unions. An undemocratic command structure within many unions neither held regular elections for leadership nor relied on ballots of the membership to ratify strike decisions. Individual union leaders often held unchecked power and personally saw little to lose in industrial disputes. As a result, strikes became common, driving away foreign investment and leading British capital to look for more profitable locations overseas.

4. Many perceived the large public sector to be wasting a substantial part of potential investment by pouring resources into declining industries without raising productivity. A study by Richard Pryke published in 1972 found that on the whole the performance of the public sector was comparable to that of private industry during the 1950s and 1960s.[2] However, a later study by the same author found that the performance of the nationalized industries had deteriorated during the 1970s and that the overall record of the nationalized industry qualified as "third rate" in comparison to the record of the private sector.[3]

As economic conditions worsened in the 1970s, the popularity of the Labour government waned. Surprisingly, Britain elected a Conservative government under Margaret Thatcher in 1979, initiating the policies that bore her name and earning her an immortality shared by few.[4] The main elements of the set of policies that make up **Thatcherism** consisted of curtailing public services, reducing both the level and the progressivity of taxation (on both income and real estate), coupled with a comprehensive program of "privatization." In 1979 some 12 percent of British value added originated in the government sector; by 1997 when the electorate voted the Tories from power the figure was only 2 percent. *Privatization*, not a precise term, is used to describe a variety of actions, ranging from the sale of state assets to the increased reliance on private suppliers for activity that traditionally occurred within the government sector.[5]

---

[2]Richard Pryke, *Public Enterprise in Practice* (London: MacGibbon and Kee, 1971).
[3]Richard Pryke, *Nationalized Industries: Policy and Performance Since 1968* (Oxford: Robert Martin, 1981).
[4]Marx, Keynes, Colbert, and Ricardo are members of the same elite club who have economic doctrines named for them.
[5]Theo Thiemeyer actually identified some 12 different meanings of the word. See Theo Thiemeyer, "Privatization: On the Many Senses in Which This Word Is Used in an International Discussion of Economic Theory," *Annals of Public and Cooperative Economy* 57, no. 2 (April–June 1986), pp. 147–152.

KINDS OF PRIVATIZATION

There are four main dimensions of privatization that affect the process of economic transition.

A Transfer of Ownership

Privatization's most common meaning concerns the transfer of ownership from the public to the private sector, the opposite of nationalization. Such a transfer can be achieved in several ways: shares can be given away—to workers, management, or the general public—or they can be sold by several means. In Britain almost all of the assets were sold, although some were disposed of at less than the fair market value of the assets employed. The choice of technique for share transfer has proved particularly important in the transformation of the former socialist systems in Central and Eastern Europe. We discuss these institutional arrangements more fully later.

The Process of Deregulation

The term *privatization* may also denote the process of deregulation, the paring back of government intervention in determination of industrial structure and prices. This process involves no formal change in the nominal ownership of assets, but it entails a shift in property rights—generally the right to determine prices or the right to enter an industry.

Franchising

Franchising "involves conferring rights in the supply or distribution of goods or services to a sole producer or operator for a specific period."[6] By allowing operators to compete for the franchise, some element of market discipline can be introduced into an area that might be regarded as a natural monopoly. The grantor of the franchise, in this case the government, must follow some device to determine who receives it. The first method—of the two main candidates—grants the right to the potential supplier who offers to charge the lowest price. Under competitive bidding, this so-called **Chadwick-Demsetz auction** would result in "normal" expected profits (i.e., the monopoly rent would be bid away and would accrue to the government).[7] A second possibility looks more like a standard auction, where the contestants offer an up-front sum for the right to the monopoly. This scheme again provides revenue for the government, but unlike the Chadwick-Demsetz auction, it allows monopoly pricing and therefore harms allocative efficiency.

---

[6]Simon Domberger and John Piggott, "Privatization Policies and Public Enterprise: A Survey," in *Privatization and Economic Performance,* Matthew Bishop, John Kay, and Colin Mayer, eds. (Oxford: Oxford University Press, 1994), p. 51.

[7]These ideas, first put forward by the British economist Edwin Chadwick in 1859, were subsequently promoted as an alternative to regulation by Harold Demsetz in 1968.

Replacement of Public Production by Private Production

The final relevant meaning of privatization is the replacement of the public pro-duction of goods by private industry under contract to the government. The most common forms of this kind of privatization involves the use of private firms to col-lect refuse, supply health services, or even, in some cases, to operate prisons.

BRITAIN'S PUBLIC SECTOR:
STRUCTURE AND PERFORMANCE

In 1979 Britain's large public sector was not out of line with most European coun-tries. Public ownership in Britain embraced the whole of the public utility sector—electricity and gas supply, telephones, water supply, rail transportation—and also included a considerable part of manufacturing. Some industries had been taken into public ownership as part of the Labour Party's policies of controlling key eco-nomic sectors, but others had been acquired for other reasons: Often the govern-ment had been the buyer of last resort, and nationalization provided a politically attractive alternative to bankruptcy and the consequent loss of output and employ-ment. As a result, the British taxpayer was also the nominal owner of the coal industry, the steel industry, much of the automobile manufacturing industry, ship-building, and a great deal of aerospace and defense-related production, a collection of lame ducks saved from the extinction dictated by the market.

The industries that were still under public ownership in 1981 appear in Table 8.2. A few firms, sold previously, were anomalies. These companies, for which no real rationale could be given for public ownership, "accidentally" ended up in the state sector; they included Amersham International, Cable and Wireless, and Thomas Cook (the tour operator). Even those remaining comprised a mixed bag. Some rep-resented obvious "natural monopolies," defined by falling long-run average costs and homogeneous product, for which economists generally accept the case for nationalization, or at least regulation: the post office, British Gas, British Telecom, British Rail, and electricity supply. Some others could not be defined in strict terms as natural monopolies, but were taken into public ownership after World War II as part of the Labour Party's policy to occupy, in Lenin's phrase, the "commanding heights" of the economy. The most important of these included the National Coal Board and British Steel. The political necessity of maintaining employment in the depressed regions where mining dominated prevented successive Conservative governments from even attempting to denationalize coal at any time. Steel, on the other hand, passed in and out of the public sector but was renationalized in the 1960s when the largest firms began to fail. The remaining firms in the publicly owned sector were lame ducks, which had little reason to be either socially owned or regulated; bad management or market logic, however, had brought them to the brink of bankruptcy, at which time the government acted as buyer of last resort to save employment or preserve a strategic industry. Among them were British Ley-land (automobiles), British Shipbuilders, and Rolls-Royce, the airplane engine maker.

■ **TABLE 8.2**

British Nationalized Industries, 1981

	Turnover (£ millions)	Capital Employed (£ millions)	Employment (in thousands)	Percentage Change in Employment Since 1979
Electricity Industry	8,057	32,605	147	28
British Telecom	5,708	16,099	246	2
British Gas	5,235	10,955	105	0
National Coal Board	4,727	5,891	279	25
British Steel	3,443	2,502	104	238
British Leyland	3,072	1,521	83	231
British Rail	2,899	2,746	277	27
Post Office	2,636	1,347	183	0
British Airways	2,241	1,338	43	224
Rolls-Royce	1,493	992	45	223
British Shipbuilders	1,026	655	67	218
S. Scotland Electricity	716	2,817	13	25
National Bus Company	618	508	53	216
British Airports Authority	277	852	7	27
N. Scotland Hydro-Electric	270	1,981	4	23
Civil Aviation Authority	206	162	7	22
Scottish Transport Group	152	157	11	217
British Waterways Board	16	50	3	22
Total	42,792	83,178	1,627	

SOURCE: Matthew Bishop, John Kay, and Colin Mayer, eds., *Privatization and Economic Performance* (Oxford: Oxford University Perss, 1994), p. 23.

THE RATIONALES FOR PRIVATIZATION

In its pursuit of privatization, the conservative government sought to satisfy simultaneously a series of objectives.

A Boost for Productivity

The first, and most discussed, goal of the privatization program centered on raising the level of performance and productivity in those industries held in public hands. Some evidence did suggest that the efficiency of nationalized industry could not match that of the private sector, but this claim was by no means unambiguous. In retrospect we now know that public enterprise began to show a sharp improvement in performance from 1978, well before the start of privatization. Moreover, as the publicly owned firms in the manufacturing sector encountered financial difficulties, acquisition of them as "lame ducks" saved them from bankruptcy. Therefore a straight comparison between the public and private sectors cannot be deemed fair.

In general, we can say that we expect productivity gains as a result of clearer corporate governance and defining profits as the unequivocal measure of performance. Put in theoretical terms, management can be a better agent for a clearly defined group of shareholders/owners than it can be for the nation as a whole, which is composed of individuals with different demands and expectations.

Creating Popular Capitalism

The second objective focused on broadening the base of capitalism in the United Kingdom, a move that political pundits almost unanimously thought would strengthen the Conservative Party's hold on power. A historically narrow share ownership in Britain, at least compared to the United States, meant that, in 1979, only 3 million Britons (5 percent of the population) owned shares either directly or through mutual funds. Selling shares in nationalized industry offered an opportunity to create what was euphemistically called **popular capitalism**, by targeting sales to middle- and low-income households and offering shares at discount prices. The 1980s saw a dramatic change in share ownership. By 1991 an additional 8 million Britons owned shares, some induced by preferential prices in the privatization and some by the advantages of tax-sheltered personal equity plans (PEPs), similar to individual retirement accounts (IRAs) and 401(k)s in the United States. In terms of currying support for the Conservative Party this strategy apparently backfired. High levels of share ownership coincided with the reemergence of a Labour government with a commanding majority in Parliament.

Reducing the Public-Sector Borrowing Requirement

The third objective was to raise revenue for the public exchequer. Proceeds from privatization did remove the budget constraint from the government for a decade. Asset sales also provided the resources for a thoroughgoing overhaul of the tax system, sharply reducing marginal income tax rates, especially on "unearned" income for upper income groups. Supply-side proponents claimed this move provided incentives for savings, investment, and the work effort of the most productive members of society. Critics saw the tax reforms as regressive and targeted to the wealthier, traditional supporters of the Conservative Party. Moreover, selling of the nationalized industries left the assets no longer available to the nation in the future, which led Harold MacMillan, a Tory Prime Minister of the 1960s, to accuse Thatcher of "selling the family silver."[8]

Reducing the Problems of Public-Sector Pay Determination

Understanding the last objective of the privatization program requires more familiarity with British politics. Setting wage rates in the public sector presented a persistent problem for successive governments. In the private sector, wage negotiations

---

[8]The rather gloomy conclusion of *The Economist* at the end of process was that privatization in Europe was "more about raising money than promoting enterprise." *The Economist*, June 27, 2002.

might be contentious, but ultimately the existence of a "hard-budget constraint" forced compromise. Management could not allow a settlement that would drive the company into bankruptcy, a fact that curtailed union militancy through the knowledge that excessive demands might lead to closure and job loss. The public sector lacks these kinds of constraints. Subsidies from tax revenues can be used to pay increased wages, and this "soft-budget constraint" makes each round of wage negotiation a test of political will. Even if the public industries were constrained to break even, monopoly power often meant that prices could be adjusted to provide the extra revenue. Attempts to base pay settlements on "comparability" with the private sector proved problematic, just as in the Swedish case.[9] Privatization offered a chance for government to get out of this politically treacherous and potentially inflationary business.

THE TECHNIQUES OF PRIVATIZATION

The sharp change brought about by Thatcherism marked 1979 as the high water of Britain as a social market economy. The pace of asset sale, however, proceeded slowly. The publicly owned sector represented a limited share of productive capacity (at least compared to the former planned economies), and the volume of assets disposed of in any given year consisted of only a small percentage of the total. Moreover, because of the sophistication and depth of British financial markets, a variety of privatization techniques could be used without overburdening, and depressing, the markets. Such a wide range of techniques was not available to the former centrally planned economies nor to many of today's developing countries that wish to change course.

Initial Public Offerings

The most widely used technique was the **initial public offering (IPO)**. Underwriters with access to financial statements determine the value of the enterprise. They then offer shares at a price calculated to ensure complete disposal. The communications giant British Telecom was sold off in this way and, as in several of the other major privatizations, the government introduced special incentives allowing small buyers access to shares at preferential rates. This policy was intended to raise public participation in the ownership of industry and to make any reversal more difficult. For example, any future Labour government could not easily renationalize British Telecom because among its owners were Labour voters who benefited from share ownership.[10] Most Britons who bought shares at the offer price made money as the average price rose by 40 percent on the day of issue, leading to criticism that the nation's assets were sold too cheaply.

---

[9] See Chapter 7 and the discussion of Sweden for more about the problems that can result from a comparability wage policy.

[10] In almost all cases, the initial prices of shares of privatized firms were low, and a rapid appreciation of share prices followed privatization. In most cases, the price rose by 40 percent on the day of issue.

IPOs with Golden Shares As a variation of an initial public offering, governments sell only part of the share capital, keeping a substantial portion either in public hands or placing it with a single private buyer in return for certain undertakings. This device, known as a **golden share**, retains some control over management and prevents it from exercising full freedom in the disposition of the assets. The golden share can be used to prevent management from stripping out the assets and liquidating the firm, as well as to prevent foreign buyers from purchasing "national champions."

Negotiated Sale

Some firms were sold in one piece to a single buyer at a negotiated price, such as the disposal of the remnant of the British car industry—British Rover, which was sold to British Aerospace. The wide criticism of such sales stemmed mainly from their discretionary nature and their ability to favor friends or supporters who acquire the assets at low prices.[11]

Employee or Management Buyout

In a few cases, the nationalized enterprises were sold off to insiders—the management and employees—usually the insiders paid extremely cheap prices because the financial resources of the potential purchasers were small. The most celebrated case in the British context was National Freight Corporation (NFC), a publicly owned road transportation company, in existence since 1947, which for the most part recorded only significant losses. The assets of the company showed a book value of £93 million, and the government sold it to employees for £53 million, of which £46 million was earmarked to fund the pensions owed to employees themselves. Consequently, the sale netted the government only £7 million.

The subsequent history of the NFC is a case study beloved by advocates of privatization and offers powerful evidence of the role of incentives. Productivity soared, profits mounted, and the value of the company increased. After only seven years under private management, profits grew to £90 million. In 1989 the company went public at a market capitalization of £890 million. The average employee stake of £600 had risen a hundredfold to £60,000, certainly strong anecdotal evidence that efficiency, productivity, and incentives can all grow under private ownership.

THE EFFECTS OF PRIVATIZATION ON EFFICIENCY

Such anecdotes aside, showing that privatization's strong effect on productivity in Britain or elsewhere remains a dubious task. Certainly most of the industries showed much stronger productivity growth in the 1980s than in the 1970s, but many concerns showed a rapid improvement *before* they actually passed into the

---

[11]This criticism was frequently heard in Germany over the negotiated sale policy of the post-unification privatization agency, the Treuhandanstalt. See Chapter 9 for more on this subject.

PRIVATIZATION AND THE RAILWAYS

The Conservative government started the privatization of Britain's extensive railroad system in 1993 when the running and maintenance of the track were separated from the provision of passenger service. At the time the plan was implemented many observers thought that the solution to railway privatization was both imaginative and made good economic sense. By separating the natural monopoly aspects of the system from the potentially competitive providers of train service many hoped that the benefits of privatization could be grasped in an industry characterized by long-term declining average cost.

Initially the track remained in public ownership while 25 different companies competed on it to ferry the passengers. As a last act in power the Conservatives privatized the track company, Railtrack. Among other things this released a large amount of valuable real estate into the private sector at below market prices. In the old style, the government set a regulatory body, the Office of the Rail Regulator, to watch for abuse of monopoly privilege.

Railway privatization cannot be deemed an unambiguous success, despite the fact that rail ridership reversed a 50-year downswing, rising 26 percent in a three-year period. This surge paid social dividends by helping to alleviate the pressure of passenger traffic on Britain's congested roads. Also, new services were instituted and it seemed that the presumed benefits of competition in service provision could be realized. However, it also became clear that not only was inadequate investment being made in the track for future growth, the condition of the track was actually deteriorating due to inadequate maintenance. In order to plan better for the future the government instituted a Strategic Rail Authority, which was ultimately merged with the Office of the Rail Regulator.

The real crisis occurred when Railtrack went bankrupt in October 2001. In the old days this event would have triggered the government takeover of the assets, but these days the word *nationalization* is taboo, even with a Labour government in power. A new private but nonprofit company called Network Rail emerged, burdened with all of the assets and debts of the forlorn Railtrack: $13 billion in debt and needing another $15 billion to tackle track maintenance and improvement. All this money will come from the taxpayer, making most people wonder whether privatizing the track was a good idea in the first place. The moral may well be that certain natural monopolies, and rail tracks certainly qualify, are best in public hands if the safety is to be preserved and monopoly exploitation avoided. The most puzzling point arises as Labour presses on with plans to privatize London's Underground with private companies owning the track and public entities running the trains. Many think that economic sense and experience would check such policy.

---

private sector. Steel, for example, which experienced falling productivity in the 1970s, showed a rapid surge immediately prior to privatization. In large part, this shift resulted from the closure of smaller and more obsolete steel mills as part of the process of preparing for privatization. Because the plants with low labor productivity closed, the average inevitably rose.

A strong upward trend in labor productivity occurred in the British utilities while still in public hands during the 1970s.[12] The movement started well before their privatization, possibly as early as 1978, predating Thatcher's surprise electoral victory.

---

[12]"Utilities" strictly covers nine enterprises: British Airways, British Airports Authority, British Gas, British Telecom, British Steel, and Electricity Supply, all of which were privatized, and British Coal, British Rail, and the post office, which were still in public hands at the time of this study.

Consequently, Bishop and Thompson argue that any increase in productivity could be attributed to a change in **corporate culture**, rather than a change of ownership. A greater clarity of objectives, substantial management reorganization, an incentive pay structure, as well as an increase in investment capital and a shift in the external environment (all of which are in principle compatible with public ownership) contributed to increased efficiency.

POST-PRIVATIZATION REFORM AND REGULATION

One immediate effect of British asset sales meant that privately owned monopolies took the place of publicly owned ones. Although some increase in productivity might result from better incentives and managerial organization, the presence of private monopolies constitutes a threat to the allocative efficiency of the economy, because monopoly prices generally fail to reflect resource cost. In this respect, the privatization presented a potentially worse situation than government-run utilities, because private monopolists with clear profit-maximizing goals might be more damaging to consumer welfare than a publicly owned monopoly with less aggressive policies and a vague mandate to contribute to general welfare.

Consumers would clearly be better served by competition, but because many of the enterprises created "natural" monopolies, introducing a competitive element required creative attention to industrial structure.[13] Reorganization in some industries allowed greater competition. In the case of the railways, separating the management and ownership of the track from the operating companies allowed different firms to ply the same route competing on the basis of price and service (see the featured article, "Privatization and the Railways."). Similarly, an alienation of the ownership of the electricity supply grid from the producers of power furthered competition.

Without an effective way to introduce competition into a monopolized sector of the economy, regulation becomes necessary to protect public interest. In the United States, regulated utilities are generally subject to a cap on the rate of return on capital. In the United Kingdom, regulation now frequently takes the form known as **RPI-X**. This regime allows a regulated utility to increase its prices by the rate of increase in the retail price index (RPI),[14] less the amount of increase in productivity due to technological change that the regulators deem to be expected on average within the industry. For example, if retail prices were rising at 3 percent and regulators anticipated that unit costs in the industry should be falling at 2 percent, then the allowable annual pace of price increase would be 3 percent minus 2 percent, or 1 percent. RPI-X regulation can be superior to the rate of return regulation because it provides greater incentives. If a firm can cut costs faster than the regulators anticipate, profit margins will increase and managers and shareholders will receive the advantage of greater efficiency by being free to increase prices.

---

[13]New technologies allow competition in traditional natural monopolies. The best example is telephones, where satellite technology did away with need for expensive fixed lines for long-distance traffic, and now cell phones are making inroads into local phone monopolies.
[14]The retail price index is similar to the U.S. consumer price index.

PRIVATIZATION AND THE LABOR MARKET

In a large public sector, politics rather than the market determine the wages of a considerable part of the workforce. Public corporations generally exist on a soft-budget rather than a hard-budget constraint, which means that deficits can be endured because the government tends to intervene with subsidies. Unions, therefore, can push for higher wages, secure in the knowledge that if the enterprise goes into the red, they can use political pressure to increase the size of the public subsidy. Historically, the same principles affected the ability of management in the nationalized sector to reduce the size of the workforce or introduce productivity-augmenting work practices against union opposition. As these enterprises entered the track to privatization, the budget constraint hardened and management's strength increased, reducing the unions' power.

Table 8.3 shows how steeply employment fell in almost all the nationalized firms between 1980 and 1988. The exceptions to this downward shift, the ever-expanding British Airports Authority and the post office, remained in public ownership. The table also shows wage increases in each industry for the same period. Consumer prices in the United Kingdom rose by about 65 percent between 1980 and 1988,[15] so in most cases real wage gains were modest and in some cases, negative. The largest increase in wages occurred in the steel industry, possibly driven by a sharp increase in labor productivity.

■ **TABLE 8.3**

Changes in Wages and Employment: Nationalized Sector, 1980—1988 (percentage)

Company	Employment	Wages
British Airports Authority	15.9	68.6
British Airways	−4.5	79
British Coal	−61.7	82.1
British Gas	−23.2	62.3
British Rail	−27.8	85.4
British Steel	−62.4	120.1
British Telecom	−0.9	114.4
Electricity Supply Industry	−16.1	89.5
North of Scotland Hydro-Electric Board	−6.3	71
South of Scotland Hydro-Electric Board	−14	87.2
London Regional Transport	−31.2	101.6
Post Office	10.7	42.9
Regional Water Authority	−23.6	81
Scottish Transport Group	−16.9	64.8
Totals	−25.6	81.5

SOURCE: Jonathan Haskel and Stefan Szymanski, "Privatization and the Labor Market," in *Privatization and Economic Performance* Bishop, Kay, and Mayer, eds. (Oxford: Oxford University Press, 1994), p. 347.

[15]*International Financial Statistics* (Washington, DC: International Monetary Fund, 1989).

Although workers did not fare especially well in the period after privatization, management treated itself more kindly. Table 8.4 illustrates another aspect of the privatization program—the sharp increase in executive remuneration that occurred during the 1980s. The causes remain open to debate. One reason might be that the heads of nationalized enterprises were underpaid because of the political difficulty of paying high salaries to corporations requiring public subsidies to stay afloat. Another problem came from the idea of paying the chiefs of public enterprise much more than their political bosses. In this light, the increases merely brought management into line with the private market. The more skeptical explanation that once free of restraint enterprise managers chose to reward themselves at the expense of consumers can be countered by the fact that even after increases, the average executive pay in these industries remained below the average for all private industry.

OTHER ASPECTS OF THATCHERISM

Shrinking the Welfare State

Although the Thatcher administration followed through on its plans to privatize industry, it managed little progress on another agenda item, slashing expenditure

■ TABLE 8.4

Top Executive Remuneration Privatized and Public Sector (1988 prices)			
	1979 (pounds)	1988 (pounds)	Percentage Change
Privatized			
Amersham	31,000	90,000	190.3
BAA	37,000	151,000	308.1
British Airways	45,000	253,000	462.2
British Gas	49,000	184,000	257.5
Cable and Wireless	31,000	208,000	571.0
National Freight Consortium	44,000	143,000	225.0
Rolls-Royce	95,000	130,000	36.8
Average	47,400	164,300	246.6
Public Sector (1979)			
British Coal	49,000	145,000	196.0
British Rail	54,000	90,000	66.7
British Steel	58,000	134,000	131.0
Electricity Supply	45,000	82,000	82.2
Post Office	48,000	84,000	75.0
Average	50,800	107,000	110.6
Average private sector*	115,000	213,000	85.2

*Private-sector average is based on a sample of leading industrial companies, equivalent to those in the 1979 public sector.
SOURCE: Matthew Bishop, John Kay, and Colin Mayer, *Privatization and Economic Performance* (Oxford: Oxford University Press, 1994), p. 349, Table 17.2.

on the **welfare state**. In 1979, the start of Thatcher's government, welfare spending[16] stood at £122 billion (at 1995 prices), or about 23 percent of GDP. It fell marginally during the 1980s, but by 1995 it rose to just over 25 percent of GNP, to £183 billion. Although spending remained high, attempts to raise quality included the introduction of **quasi-markets** into both education and the health service. The 1988 Educational Reform Act established a national curriculum, allowed for open school enrollment, and enabled public schools[17] to compete with each other for students. In the same year a review board examined the operation of the National Health Service. Again, while not questioning the basic principle of free provision, the board allowed both hospitals and doctors more control over their budgets and the opportunity to compete for patients. In theory such competition should lead to cost saving, but the evidence remains scanty so far. A 1994 Audit Commission investigating the consequences of reorganization in the delivery of doctors' services found that costs increased by £232 million, while efficiency savings amounted to only £206 million.

Reform of the social services encountered considerable skepticism among the British population. Although free provision was not challenged, many feared that the introduction of quasi-markets marked a first step toward a pay-for-service market system. The sentiment that the values of the marketplace were corrosive to the traditional view of the welfare state hardened, and the public remains lukewarm at best on the issue of further reform, which essentially halted following the election of a Labour government in 1997.

Tax Reform

In the area of tax reform, Thatcherism contributed a much more decisive effect. During the Iron Lady's years in office the top rates of income taxation fell sharply, while those at the bottom of the scale remained largely unchanged and at times increased. Table 8.5 shows the change in tax rates on earned income over an 18-year period. Earned income means income from labor activities. This table does not show the rates levied on unearned income, which consists of dividends, interest, and capital gains. Before Thatcher came to power, rates rose progressively to a top rate on earned income of 83 percent, with the rate on unearned income as high as 98 percent. By 1989, only two applicable rates remained—25 percent and 40 percent—with the distinction between earned and unearned income eliminated. Subsequently in 1992 a new lower rate of 20 percent was introduced. The shortfall in revenue caused by lower rates was bridged by the revenue from the sale of nationalized corporations. The Labour government of Tony Blair continued the program of lowering tax rates and cut the lower rate to just 10 percent while chipping away at the middle rate, cutting it to 22 percent.

---

[16]"Welfare spending" includes the sum of spending on housing, social security, health, education, and personal social services (counseling, home help, etc.).
[17]"Public school" is used here in the American sense and should not be confused with the elite British "Public Schools," which are exclusive private establishments.

	1979	1980	1981–1986	1987	1988	1989	1990	1991	1992	1993–1996	1997	1998	1999	2000	2001	2002
Lower rate	25	25	—	—	—	—	—	20	—	20	20	20	20	10	10	10
Basic rate	33	30	30	29	27	25	25	25	25	25	24	23	23	23	22	22
Top rate	83	60	60	60	60	40	40	40	40	40	40	40	40	40	40	40

Income Tax Rates on Earned Income, 1979–2002

SOURCE: Institute for Fiscal Studies: *A Survey of the UK Tax System,* available at http://www.ifs.org.uk.

Thatcher made equally sweeping attempts to reform local government finance. Local government revenues in Britain originated largely from the "rates," taxes on real property, which were moderately progressive because wealthier families owned larger and more valuable homes. Thatcher substituted a more regressive tax system, officially called the "community charge," but universally referred to as the "poll tax," the base of which was the number of adults resident within a dwelling. In the eyes of the Conservative government, this assessment reflected the pattern of expenditures by local government and changed the foundation of the system from one of redistribution to one of payment for benefit. Strong resistance to the poll tax resulted in its abandonment in 1993 in favor of the less regressive "council tax."

Reform of Trade Unions

Until 1979 trade unions acted as a major force in the labor markets and British politics. As many as 13.2 million workers belonged to unions, the primary bargaining agents for two-thirds of all employees. Moreover, the unions maintained close links to the Labour Party, which held power for 10 of the previous 15 years. The turbulence of the 1970s included a great deal of strike activity. Thatcher's philosophy deviated from normal European consensus politics because she did not consider the trade unions to be **social partners** on the model of Sweden or Germany, to be cooperated with and given a legitimate voice in economic policy. Rather she regarded unions as an enemy to be confronted and, where possible, smashed. She enjoyed considerable success in this crusade and fundamentally changed the nature of British labor markets.

A series of laws on industrial relations progressively encroached on union power. The new laws curbed the right of unions to automatic recognition by employers. They outlawed secondary picketing (demonstrations by workers not directly involved in a dispute). They required secret ballots before strike action could be taken, and limited union leadership to finite lengths of service. In 1984 the government emerged victorious in a confrontation over pay and mine closures with the once-powerful National Union of Mineworkers, a decisive victory that shaped future British workplace relations.

Not all of the decline in union power could be directly traced to Conservative legislation, however. Britain experienced the same economic changes that eroded the power of unions elsewhere, and traditional bastions of union power declined because of falling demand and competition from abroad. The power of the mineworkers' union once came from coal's near monopoly on energy supply in the United Kingdom. Growing use of oil and gas, much of it from the North Sea fields, cut into coal's traditional role. Road travel overtook rail and diminished the power of the railway workers. The British auto industry faced serious competition from Europe and Japan, and once militant autoworkers feared for their jobs. Furthermore, the growing smaller high-tech enterprises were less unionized than the older factory environment, and service trades provided less fertile breeding grounds for union organization than the old factories. Only in the civil service did unionization continue to rise.

THE RHINE MODEL AND THE ANGLO-AMERICAN MODEL

It is common today to broadly classify the kinds of capitalism into the type found in those countries that follow the **Rhine Model** and those that adhere to an **Anglo-Saxon** or Anglo-American **Model**. In the former group are Germany and France (the countries that lie either side of the Rhine) and frequently Japan. The economic and political system in these countries are said to favor consensus, group action, and long-term consequences. In the Anglo-Saxon model of Britain and the United States the system favors the individual and the entrepreneur. Among other things this implies a closer coordination of the economic actors in the Rhine model and willingness on the part of firms and financial intermediaries to follow guidance from the government. On the other hand the Anglo-American model favors action by firms that will favor the shareholders rather than other "stakeholders" in a more short-run time frame.

While this is a convenient division, the picture is in many ways more complex than that. For example, Britain in the 1970s could hardly be said to favor entrepre-

neurs. The tax system was heavily weighted against the accumulation of wealth, while government production and regulation were as extensive as anywhere in Western Europe. The Trade Unions certainly had a strong role in the determination of economic policy. Thus pre-1979, at least, Britain was more closely comparable to Germany and France than the United States. The Labour Administration in the 1960s had even taken steps to introduce a National Plan, an imitation of the indicative plan found in France and Japan.

Somewhat surprisingly Britain's entry into the then EC coincided with a move away from the European model of social market capitalism. Thatcherism and its aftermath have left Britain with a smaller public sector and a reformed tax code that is certainly more sympathetic to the self-made capitalist. The unions have been knocked from their position of power and now have less influence than in Germany and France, and the Social Chapter of the Maastricht Treaty was long delayed in ratification in the United Kingdom because of the

formal recognition of worker rights in company management. In recent years the Blair administration has made steps back toward the European model; he has embraced the Social Chapter and pays a great deal of lip service to the idea of the corporation as a social institution, indebted to many types of "stakeholder" beyond merely share ownership.

There are also clear differences in economic structure between the members of the Rhine club. An important one is in the independence of the central bank. While both the Bank of France and the Bank of Japan were tightly held by the government, the German Central bank, the Bundesbank, enjoyed a great deal of independence in common with the U.S. Federal Reserve system and the newly reformed bank of England. (However, the French will now have to live with a largely independent European Central bank to determine monetary policy.) Thus the terms Rhine Model and Anglo-Saxon Model seem to imply a greater uniformity than can be seen on the ground and should be used with some care.

Under Margaret Thatcher's government, this collection of factors led to a more placid climate in British industrial relations. Table 8.6 shows a high level of British strike activity relative to other economies in the 1970s and early 1980s. By the beginning of the 1990s, the British record more closely resembles that of its West European partners, considerably better than that of the United States. A recent upsurge of militancy in the union movement in Britain comes as leftwing union leaders attempt to use industrial stoppages to political effect. Despite Labour's roots in the union movement, the government continues to resist militancy in the public sector, refusing to roll back any substantial element of Thatcher's union reforms.

THE LESSONS OF THATCHERISM

In 1979 some 12 percent of British value added originated in the government sector; by 1997 when the electorate voted the Tories from power the figure was only 2 percent. In terms of overall economic performance, the 1980s certainly represented a sea change in the performance of the British economy. From being the perennial underperformer among G7 nations, Britain now comes close to the top of the tree in terms of economic growth (see Table 8.7). The same improvement may be seen in the change of other measures. Labor productivity in manufacturing, for example, showed the sharpest growth. Britain went from the bottom of the league in the 1970s to the top in the 1980s and 1990s. So it is fair to say that "something" happened. In the words of *The Economist*:

> [The] figures accord with the voluminous, albeit unsystematic, testimony of factory floor anecdote. Almost anybody who works in one will say that Britain's factories and offices are very much better run and very much more productive than they were in the late 1970s—and many will say that the change since then has been revolutionary rather than evolutionary.[18]

■ TABLE 8.6

Days Lost per 1,000 Employees: Selected Industrial Nations, 1970–1993				
	1970–1979	1980–1984	1985–1989	1989–1993
United Kingdom	570	480	180	70
United States	n.a.	160	90	200
France	210	90	60	90
Germany	40	50	n.a.	30
Italy	1,310	950	300	360

NOTE: N.a. means less than five days per 1,000 employees.
SOURCE: *Employment Gazette*, December 1990, 1994.

---

[18]"Britain's New Politics," *The Economist*, September 21, 1996, p. 7.

To some extent the rapid increase in manufacturing productivity is a statistical arti-fact. Many factories closed in the 1980s, in general those with a poor productivity record. Their closure necessarily raised the average among the remainder. How-ever, Britain subsequently grew to take up some of the slack. The unemployment rate is now among the lowest in Europe, implying that displaced low-productivity workers managed to find new jobs. Even the broadest economic aggregate, the rate of growth of real gross domestic product (Table 8.7), shows a distinct shift between the 1970s and the 1980s. In the 1970s, Britain experienced the lowest growth among the G7 countries, barely 58 percent of the average. Throughout the 1980s and 1990s, the country managed almost 90 percent of the average, although much of this com-parative percentage results from slower growth among the other industrial coun-tries rather than accelerated growth in Britain.

A rising inequality accompanied accelerating growth in Britain. Figure 8.1 plots the relationship of growth of GDP and the change in the Gini coefficient for house-hold income between 1980 and 1991 and shows that inequality in Britain increased much more than in comparable countries. In fact, within the OECD only New Zealand—also involved in a shift away from a highly socialized economy—showed a similar increase in the growth of inequality. The rise in inequality in Britain exceeded that in the United States, even though the growth rates of the two economies were roughly the same and the Reagan years are usually thought of as a time when income distribution became more polarized in the United States.

The question remains whether the British experience of privatization offers important lessons for economies in transition, both those reforming a European-style social democracy and those attempting to move from a command planning system to a market-based economy.

1. The British experience suggests that managerial culture, rather than the issue of ownership, actually determines productivity, and gains can be achieved without privatization. A counterargument suggests that industries that remain in public hands will inevitably be burdened with nonmarket objectives and nurtured on public subsidy—and the soft-budget constraint would ultimately

■ TABLE 8.7

			Real GDP Growth
	Average 1970—1980	Average 1980—1990	Average 1990—2000
United States	3.1	2.9	3.12
Japan	4.4	4	1.78
Germany	2.7	2.24	2.25
France	3.3	2.36	1.89
United Kingdom	1.9	2.67	2.16
G7 Average	3.3	2.93	2.2
OECD Average	3.6	3.02	2.7

SOURCE: OECD, *Economic Outlook-Statistical Annex,* June 2002, p. 207.

Au: add the 7th?

■ FIGURE 8.1

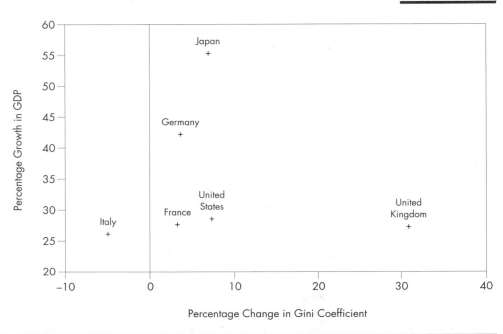

Growth in GDP and Change in Gini Coefficient, G6 Economies 1980–1991

SOURCE: OECD.

resurface. Consider this measurable aspect of the Thatcher program: prior to privatization an average citizen of the United Kingdom paid some £300 to subsidize state-owned industry; today the net taxes paid by the recently privatized firms amount to £100 per person.

2. Legislation curbing the power of the labor unions, coupled with sectoral shifts and changes in technology, resulted in a much more flexible labor market. One consequence is lower unemployment, but another is rising inequality in the distribution of income.

3. When privatized industries form natural monopolies, regulation will be required to protect the public interest. Therefore some of the benefits of increased productive efficiency that could result from privatization might be countervailed by a decrease in allocative efficiency and by the administrative costs of regulation.

4. In the British case, privatization resulted in substantial short-term gains to public revenues that facilitated tax reform. Nevertheless, revenues from sales in most of the former centrally planned economies were small.

Recent Developments in the British Economy

After 11 years in government Margaret Thatcher somewhat unceremoniously found herself removed from power in 1990, not by the British electorate but by powerful elements in the Conservative party. The exact reasons for her removal will be debated for many years but it widely held to be the result of her profoundly anti-European policy, which alarmed the British financial establishment. Although the largest financial center within the EU, London could scarcely continue to be so if its government indulged in anti-European polemics. John Major, her one-time protégé, replaced Margaret Thatcher and held on to power into the mid-1990s. After 18 years in government, the Tories, looking a little tired, suffered a series of personal and financial scandals among its leadership that weakened the electoral base.

However, in the early 1990s the Labour Party was wedded to the policies that created popular frustration and caused its loss of power in the late 1970s. "Clause Four," the commitment to the renationalization of state industry, was still part of its official manifesto. The trades unions still held much power within the party and looked to a restored Labour government to reinstate the privileges that Margaret Thatcher and the Conservatives took away during the years of reform.

The Labour Party's new leader, Tony Blair, recognized the unelectable aspects of his own party, as well as the boredom and discontent with Tory policies. In 1995 he campaigned successful to radically change the platform and commit, by and large, to leave in place the recent privatizations and union reform while promising to implement a more supportive agenda in terms of social medicine, education, and income redistribution. He renamed the party New Labour in an attempt to make its socialist past less prominent. In 1997 he won election by a landslide with more than 10 percent of the electorate switching sides. With a huge majority in Parliament, a growing economy, a government budget surplus, and low levels of unemployment, Blair enjoyed, therefore, an essentially free hand to pursue what policies he wished in the five-year life of his first term in office.

In fact Blair pursued a middle-of-the-road policy. One feature of this policy focuses on his determination to maintain the strategic alliance with the United States. In domestic policy, he seized the middle ground from the conservatives and determined not to relinquish it. He gave no hint of renationalizing anything privatized under the Tories. In fact, Labour continued to privatize many assets remaining in state hands. The idea of **public-private partnerships (PPPs)** attracted a good deal of attention, with **private finance initiatives (PFIs)** seen as a way of drawing private cash into needed infrastructure projects. As many as 400 deals involving private money in transport, health, education, and public safety occurred since 1966.

The National Health Service, which came under siege during the Thatcher administration, remains secure as an important symbol of social security for many British citizens. It suffers however from chronic underfunding, with health workers in the United Kingdom being paid a fraction of what their counterparts in the United States would earn. Consequently pay determination rounds are always fractious.[19] Because the root cause of the problems is underfunding, only a greater flow of resources will help to solve the problem.

Under Blair, Britain plays the role of the reluctant European with more subtlety. It declined to be a part of the group of nations that adopted the euro, citing the need

---

[19]This fractiousness is true elsewhere in the public sector. In November 2002 Fire Service Workers went on strike for higher pay, and the army functioned as a firefighting service.

to maintain an independent exchange rate, fiscal, and monetary policy as tools of macroeconomic management. Even though technical grounds can be cited for Britain's stance, and Blair's Chancellor of the Exchequer,[20] Gordon Brown strongly opposes joining the euro area, the reason is largely political. Skepticism at both ends of the political spectrum question the wisdom of deeper integration into Europe, and both major parties fear the loss of electoral support if the pace picks up. Many foresee the adoption of the euro in Britain as inevitable as the currency infiltrates deeper into the British economy—a phenomenon known at *The Economist* as "eurocreep." How long Britain can afford to be in opposition to the main policy dynamic in the European Union is an open question.

The forthcoming expansion provides ammunition to both sides of the debate. As eager East Europeans line up to join the EU, Britain becomes more politically exposed in its opposition to monetary union. However, the downside of expansion is that the redistributed budget of the EU must grow and Britons will be taxed to promote the development of the former Soviet satellite states. Left to his own devices, Blair would lead Britain deeper into EU commitments, but even his own party is skeptical.

KEY TERMS AND CONCEPTS

Anglo-Saxon Model	public-private partnerships (PPPs)
Chadwick-Demsetz auction	quasi-markets
corporate culture	Rhine Model
franchising	RPI-X
golden share	social partners
initial public offering (IPO)	stagflation
popular capitalism	Thatcherism
private finance initiatives (PFIs)	welfare state

QUESTIONS FOR DISCUSSION

1. What were the possible economic causes of Britain's malaise in the 1970s?
2. What were the objectives of the privatization drive of Margaret Thatcher's government?
3. Did privatization have a demonstrable effect on efficiency? What was the role of corporate culture?
4. What was the impact of privatization on workers' and executive pay?
5. How was the trade union movement reformed under Thatcher?
6. Was perceptible progress made in either reducing government expenditure or changing the tax code?

---

[20]This office is equivalent to the U.S. Secretary of the Treasury.

RESOURCES

Web Sites

All British Government Sites Homepage (searchable)................http://www.open.gov.uk/

Bank of England ....http://www.bankofengland.co.uk/

Competition Commission.............................http://www.competition-commission.org.uk/

Department of Trade and Industry..http://www.dti.gov.uk/

Her Majesty's Treasury ....http://www.hm-treasury.gov.uk/

The Stationery Office...http://www.tso-online.co.uk/

Office of Telecommunications ....http://www.oftel.gov.uk/

Office of the Rail Regulator..http://www.rail-reg.gov.uk/

Office of Gas and Electricity Markets ....http://www.ofgem.gov.uk/

Books and Articles

Ball, James. *The British Economy at the Crossroads.* London: Financial Times–Pitman Publishing, 1998.

Bishop, Matthew, John Kay, and Colin Mayer (eds.). *Privatization and Economic Performance.* Oxford: Oxford University Press, 1994.

Bos, Dieter. *Privatization: A Theoretical Treatment.* Oxford: Oxford University Press, 1991. Reviewed in *Journal of Comparative Economics,* October 1994, 281.

Buxton, Tony, Paul Chapman, and Paul Temple (eds.). *Britain's Economic Performance,* 2nd ed. New York: Routledge, 1998.

Cairncross, Alec. *The British Economy Since 1945: Economic Policy and Performance, 1945–1995 (Making Contemporary Britain Series).* Cambridge, MA: Blackwell, 1995.

Collier, Irwin, Herwig Roggemann, Oliver Scholz, and Horst Tomann. *Welfare States in Transition: East and West (Studies in Economic Transition).* New York: St. Martin's Press, 1999.

Cook, Paul (ed.), and Colin Kirkpatrick. *Privatisation Policy and Performance: International Perspectives.* London: Harvester Wheatsheaf, 1996.

Crafts, N. F. R., and Nicholas Woodward (eds.). *The British Economy Since 1945.* New York: Oxford University Press, 1991.

Foster, Christopher D. *Privatization, Public Ownership and the Regulation of Natural Monopoly.* Oxford: Blackwell, 1992.

Hetzner, Candace. *The Unfinished Business of Thatcherism: The Values of the Enterprise Culture.* Vol. 46, *American University Studies X: Political Science.* Bern, Switzerland: Peter Lang, 1999.

"How to Privatize: What the Rest of the World Can Learn from the Unpopularity of Privatisation in Britain." *The Economist,* March 11, 1995, 16–17.

Kiekeri, Sunita, John Nellis, and Mary Shirley. "Privatization: Lessons from Market Economies." *The World Bank Research Observer,* July 1994, 241–272.

Kramnick, Isaac (ed.). *Is Britain Dying? Perspectives on the Current Crisis.* Ithaca, NY: Cornell University Press, 1979.

Marsh, David. *The New Politics of British Trade Unionism: Union Power and the Thatcher Legacy.* Ithaca, NY: ILR Press, 1992.

Martin, Stephen, and David Parker. *The Impact of Privatisation: Ownership and Corporate Performance in the UK (Industrial Economic Strategies for Europe).* London: Routledge, 1997.

Mayer, Colin, and Tim Jenkinson. "The Privatisation Process in France and the U.K." *European Economic Review,* March 1988, 382–391.

"The Mother of Privatisation: Sell-off of Britain's State Industries" (editorial). *The Economist,* September 16, 1989, 15–16.

Pryke, Richard. *Nationalized Industries: Policy and Performance Since 1968.* Oxford: Robert Martin, 1981.

Pryke, Richard. *Public Enterprise in Practice.* London: MacGibbon and Kee, 1971.

Pulkingham, Jane. "From Public Provisions to Privatisation: The Crisis in Welfare Reassessed." *Sociology,* August 1989, 387–407.

Swann, Dennis. *The Retreat of the State: Deregulation and Privatization in the UK and US.* Ann Arbor: University of Michigan Press, 1988.

Turner, Royce Logan (ed.). *The British Economy in Transition: From the Old to the New?* New York: Routledge, 1995.

Vickers, John, and George Yarrow. *Privatization: An Economic Analysis.* Cambridge, MA: MIT Press, 1988.

9

GERMANY: THE LESSONS OF REUNIFICATION

GERMANY	
Area (thousand sq. km.)	357
Currency	euro
Exchange Rate	€1.1 = US$1
Population 2000 (millions)	82
Population Growth Rate	0.3%
GNI per Capita, 2000	$25,050
GNI per Capita, PPP	$25,010
GDP Growth 1990–2000	1.5%
Value Added as % of GDP 2000 Agriculture	1%
Industry	28%
Services	71%
% of GDP Government Expenditure	44.4%
Exports	29.3%

THE GERMAN TRANSFORMATION

Although it is the third largest economy in the world and therefore deserves discussion in its own right, we direct our focus on Germany in this book toward understanding the process of reunification of the German state and economy that occurred following the fall of the Berlin wall in 1989. At that point East Germany's

40 years of command planning contrasted sharply with West Germany's development of a vibrant and successful form of capitalism. In a single move, these two entities merged. By looking at the German experience and assessing its advantages, flaws, success, and failures, we can better understand the process of transition faced by all other countries as they emerged from the experience of social ownership and central planning. Those readers not fully familiar with recent German history might find the brief historical background to be useful.

Historical Background

Germany, a late industrializer, remained fragmented both politically and economically until the end of the nineteenth century. Only after the unification of Germany under the Prussian monarchy and Chancellor Otto von Bismarck did the economy really take off. With strong state support the industrial sector grew rapidly. By the outbreak of the First World War, Germany had overhauled Britain to become the second greatest industrial power in the world. The defeat in the Great War and the terms of the Treaty of Versailles crippled the German economy. The 1920s were difficult times with high unemployment and growing poverty, which fueled the rise of the National Socialist party (Nazis) who came to power in 1933. Despite the use of the term *socialism* in their title, the Nazis were not committed to extensive public ownership of industry and Hitler enjoyed the support of many of the industrial barons and financiers.

Dr. Hjalmar Schacht took over the direction of economic policy in 1933 and put into practice the kind of bootstrap reflation that John Maynard Keynes recommended in his *General Theory of Employment, Interest and Prices,* published three years later. Schacht's policies focused on the restriction of imports, low interest rates, lower taxes, and an extensive system of public works and government sponsored employed. Even though ideologically committed to the Nazi party, Schacht quarreled with Hitler over the pace of rearmament and found himself shunted to one side while the direction of economic policy passed to Hermann Goering. Goering maintained Schacht's basic approach of reflation and job creation behind high tariff walls while instituting rapid rearmament that required the creation of an even greater deficit. Under these policies, almost alone among western nations, Germany grew rapidly 1930s. Britain and France only began to grow as rapidly when they initiated their own rearmament programs. Despite Roosevelt's policy of the New Deal, the United States slipped into recession again in 1938.

After the hostilities the German economy lay in ruins. The war's heavy bombing destroyed many of the cities and industrial regions, public finance was in tatters, and inflation raged. In the East, the Soviet Union removed piece-by-piece much of the industrial equipment. The boundaries of Germany were redrawn with Russia annexing not only Konigsberg but also a large slice of Poland, which in turn was compensated by receiving a piece of prewar Germany. The Allied powers carved up the country into four zones, a process replicated within the capital of Berlin, though it lay entirely within the Soviet zone. Stalinist-style central planning was imposed in the East, which became the German Democratic Republic (GDR). In the

West, the Allies rejected a proposal to comprehensively deindustrialize Germany.[1] After a short period of neglect the United States recognized its own long-term interests in encouraging an economically sound West Germany to counter balance Soviet expansionism. Aid and technical assistance began to flow in. Industrialists who were jailed immediately after the war for their behavior during it were released and given access to their corporations once more.

The German Miracle

The 1950s saw the start of the German miracle, a period of sustained double digit growth that restored Germany as the leading industrial power in Europe. Out of the ruins of the war, the rebuilding of the industrial powerhouse strongly emphasized engineering. The German economic system defines itself as a "social market system," relying for the most part on private capital and market coordination, but using the power of the state to weave a comprehensive social safety net.

Germany's constitution explicitly lays out the economic and social goals that any government of the republic is required to pursue. Although a bit unusual and to a degree symbolic, this aspect makes clear the shared values embodied in the constitution and contributes to the low degree of partisanship in the determination of domestic social and economic policies because all major parties are required to accept the basic goals. In the economic realm these goals include price stability, a stable currency, full employment, and steady growth. On the social side, the goals of social equity, social security, and social progress represent vague principles but express a common purpose.

The German model in a sense provides an extreme case but it shares features with other nations of the European Union. The economy is organized on market principles, but it is subject to extensive social regulation. The purpose of social regulation "is intended to ensure that the impersonal workings of markets do not interfere with or undermine basic needs ranging from adequate income and health care to organized representation in the workplace."[2] In other words, the regulation relies on the impersonality or disinterested quality of the marketplace, but recognizes that this reliance might involve intolerable distributional consequences or implications for individuals.

Codetermination Between Workers and Management At the heart of Germany's social market economy lies the idea that society's various groups are partners rather than competitors or rivals. In the workplace this idea manifests itself as a system of *Mitbestimmung*, or **codetermination**, which gives workers a guaranteed say in the operation of companies and full access to most data on their operation.

---

[1]This proposal was made by Henry Morgenthau, U.S. Secretary of the Treasury. See *The Conquerors: Roosevelt, Truman and the Destruction of Hitler's Germany, 1941–45* (New York: Simon and Schuster, 2002).
[2]Lowell Turner, *Negotiating the New Germany: Can Social Partnership Survive?* (Ithaca, NY: ILR Press, 1997), p. 3.

By law, workers must occupy at least half of the seats on the **supervisory boards** of companies, which hold the responsibility for the broad direction of the enterprise and for hiring and firing of senior management.[3] The German system also guarantees a role for a works council *(Betriebsrat)* for all except the smallest firms. General ballot determines representation on the works councils, and a strong union presence is normal but not guaranteed. The works councils have specific rights, including the right to veto management decisions in matters of employment classification, overtime, and to some degree recruitment and dismissal.

Codetermination extends beyond the workplace and embraces the wage determination process that consists of collective bargaining between the unions and the employer organizations on an industry-wide basis under government supervision. Generally speaking, the process proceeds in a cooperative manner and results in an annual wage settlement common across the industry, although it can erupt into conflict.

Wage determination in Germany occurs at the state level through agreements (generally of two-year duration) between the state level branches of the major unions and the major employers; a high degree of conformity can be found between state agreements. The system allows for some variation for those regions with particular labor market problems, but the level of aggregation reduces labor flexibility and can be seen as being a drag on productivity growth. Currently, some 73 percent of workers in former West Germany are covered by collective bargaining agreements. In the East the unionization rate is somewhat lower with 57 percent of employed persons covered. The key union in setting the pace of wage increases is IG Metall, the giant union that represents some 3.4 million workers throughout the engineering industries, including Germany's prominent and successful automobile exporters. It is usually the first of the unions to conclude agreements and determines the tone for settlements throughout industry. Though it is not a formally involved party to the negotiations the government takes a keen interest in the negotiations and does its best to broker a settlement that will not be unduly inflationary.

BANKING IN GERMANY

The banking system in Germany can be credited with playing a key role in Germany's postwar miracle, but it came under some fire for its recent lack of flexibility. It differs in important ways from that found in the United States, or even in the United Kingdom. The financial system is not divided into investment banks, commercial banks, and stockbrokers. Its banks perform all of these functions and are therefore known as **universal banks**, or occasionally U-banks for short. This system can involve some advantages. The relationships between the bank and the firm are close and multifaceted U-bank can act as a direct lender to a firm, sell and

---

[3]This provision was the result of the Code Termination Act of 1976. In the event of a tie, the chair, always a representative of capital, casts the deciding vote.

hold bonds that it issues, hold and trade its stocks, give it financial advice as well as handle its day to day transaction banking. Because banks can vote not only the shares that they own but also the shares that they hold on deposit for their customers, they therefore gain a powerful influence in the governance of the firm. This closeness perhaps provides the advantages that paid dividends in Germany's economic growth:

- It can lower the transactions costs of borrowing to the firms.
- It limits adverse selection, the danger that bad borrowers will seek loans from banks in disproportionate numbers.
- It limits the risk of moral hazard problem, the tendency of debtors to divert borrowed money to riskier investments.
- It improves the quality of guidance that the bank can offer to the firm.

Compensating difficulties arise, of course. One, the presence of these few and powerful banks, limits the degree of competition and innovation in the financial sector. Perhaps a more important difficulty comes from the banks' conflicting roles. The policies that maximize the probability of a repayment of loan capital may not always coincide with those that maximize shareholder value. The banks can use the voting power that results from being able to vote deposited shares to implement policies that may be against shareholders' interests. Finally, smaller firms may experience difficulty obtaining finance in the German system. The attention of the banks focuses on their large industrial customers and may not view the financing of potential insurgent competitors as a priority. On the whole, the German system favors stability and long-term relations, but it does not facilitate innovation and change. The German miracle may owe much to the steadiness of banking arrangements, which may in turn short-change the the future.

The Role of Bundesbank and the European Central Bank

Central banking in Germany is also worthy of note. The Bundesbank was one of the most independent and conservative central banks in the world. The Constitution of the Republic carefully insulated it from the political system, and specifically charges it with the maintenance of price stability—a gesture to the devastating hyperinflations that followed both World Wars. Germany's membership in the "Euroland" means that the determination of monetary policy passed to the European Central Bank (ECB). Though a German does not lead it (the current President is Wim Duisenberg from the Netherlands), the ECB is based in Germany with the general presumption that it will pursue conservative policies like the Bundesbank.

GERMAN REUNIFICATION

The last years of the 1980s saw the collapse of Soviet-style planning throughout Eastern Europe and movement toward a market economy. From the outset, most socialist economies clearly faced considerable difficulty in moving to a market system and integrating into the world economy.[4] Among those economies, the GDR was seen by most as having the best chance of a smooth transition. However, more than a decade after the fall of the Berlin Wall, the economy of eastern Germany remains in the doldrums. In the fall of 2002, unemployment in the "New Federal States," the official term for the territory of the former GDR, reached 1,297,000. Emigration from east to west pulled the population down from 17 million to about 13.8 million. A further 291,000 people were working on federally financed job creation schemes and 147,000 were in sponsored job retraining. The total "underemployment" percentage was 22.6 percent. Another 350,000 commuted daily to work in the former Federal Republic of Germany (FRG). Conventional measures of unemployment put the eastern German rate at about 16.8 percent, well above twice the rate of western Germany. Adjustment for the make-work programs make the rate closer to 22.8 percent.

Many anticipated a **catching-up**, or **convergence**, process at the fall of the Wall. The economy there showed some evidence of this process for the first five years after reunification, when output in the East rose and unemployment actually fell from the level it had risen to immediately after reunification. In 1995, however, the process began to stall, and by 1998 a working party of the German Economic Research Institutes concluded that

> The "catching up" process in East Germany rapidly ground to a halt [after 1995]. In 1996 the rate of growth of the new federal states was, at just under 2 percent, still marginally higher than in West Germany; already by 1997 it was lagging behind the West German result at just 1.6 percent, and no fundamental change can be expected either in the current or the coming year. In per capita terms, nominal value added in East Germany remains at less than 57 percent of the West German level. Productivity has so far risen to only 60 percent of the West German level. Labor costs per employee in the current year represent just under 75 percent of the average figure paid in West Germany.[5]

Given the high hopes for the East German economy at the outset of reunification, these developments raise fundamental issues about the process of economic transformation and lessons learned from the German experience that might be applied to other nations further to the east.

EAST GERMAN PERFORMANCE UNDER COMMUNISM

In the context of the Soviet bloc, the GDR enjoyed a very successful economy. Living standards remained above any other centrally planned state, and productivity in industry and agriculture was believed to be the highest in the Soviet bloc. Estimates of income per head are generally unreliable for centrally planned economies, but, as shown by Table 9.1, in 1989 the United Nations put real pur-

---

[4]However, in many quarters there was a great deal of optimism about the speed and completeness of transition. For example, in Russia a well-known report by academician S. Shatalin was titled "500 Days to a Market Economy."

[5]German Economic Research Institute, "The German Economy in the Spring of 1998," available at http://www.diw.de.

■ **TABLE 9.1**

	GNP per Head for Selected Socialist Countries, 1987 ($PPP)
GDR	8,000
Czech Republic	7,750
Soviet Union	6,000
Yugoslavia	5,000
Bulgaria	4,750
Hungary	4,500
Poland	4,000

SOURCE: *Human Development Report,* United Nations Development Programme (New York: Oxford University Press, 1990).

chasing power parity income per head in the GDR at about $8,000 per annum. This figure stood some 25 percent above that of the Soviet Union, roughly comparable to Ireland and Spain, and higher than either Portugal or Greece, though considerably below the $14,730 recorded for West Germany. The GDR also stood up well on many other measures, particularly basic indicators of social well-being. In educational attainment, life expectancy, and infant mortality, East Germany performed as well as many of the Western industrialized economies. In addition, its distribution of income was considerably more uniform than that in the West, usually considered a positive feature of an economic system.[6]

These achievements are especially impressive in the light of East Germany's late start on postwar recovery relative to the West. As early as 1948 the Marshall Plan led to a sharp injection of funds into the Federal Republic, with a salutary impact on growth, but at the same time in the East the Soviet Union hindered recovery in the GDR by removing plant and equipment as part of a scheme of war reparation. The strong performance in the face of handicaps led supporters of central planning to see the East German experience as a positive model of the potential of socialism, but the persistently unfavorable comparison of material standards between East and West Germany could not be discounted. The problems created by the physical division of Berlin by the Wall (built to prevent population escape to the West) and the obviously greater prosperity of the FRG persisted. Moreover, the accessibility of information from the West contributed to discontent in the East.

Political and Economic Unification

After the fall of the Wall, the reunification of Germany took place in two steps. On July 1, 1990, a **monetary, economic, and social union** took effect, followed on October 3 by a political union. The decisive features of the economic and social union included the following:

---

[6]Andrew Zimbalist, Howard Sherman, and Stuart Brown, *Comparing Economic Systems: A Political Economic Approach* (Orlando, FL: Academic Press, 1984), p. 469.

- The adoption of a 1:1 exchange rate between the East German mark (the Ost-mark) and the Deutschmark for all wages, prices, pensions, and so on
- The conversion of most monetary assets at a rate of 2:1, except for a quota of personal savings, which was converted at 1:1
- The creation of a common legal and regulatory environment based on West German laws
- The introduction of the main features of the West German social market economy, including collective wage negotiation, extensive social insurance, and active worker involvement in company management

East Germany's Advantages

Hopes for a seamless and rapid transition were high and rested mainly on two factors. The first lay on the apparent strength of the East German economy, with its higher productivity and greater efficiency than any other centrally planned state. The second hinged on the belief that a "merger" with an existing, strong, developed economy would be easier than going it alone, which would be the case in Russia and the other former socialist states. In fact *The Economist* trumpeted reunification as "the largest leveraged buyout in history." That the East German transition progressed far from smoothly despite these advantages gives a perspective on the immense difficulties faced by other nations in transition.[7]

Legal Structure and Accounting Practice From the moment of the signing of the economic and monetary unification pact, eastern Germany fell under a legal and regulatory structure covering most aspects of business and commerce. The absence of enforceable contracts and a consistent code of bankruptcy law presented enormous problems for business development and deterred investment in other formerly planned states, but Germany provided a universal commercial code. In addition, the new federal states of Germany enjoyed the advantage of a regulatory system designed to tackle market failure due to monopoly and environmental degradation. A further advantage lay in the existence of an established accounting system; admittedly it would take time for the East German enterprises to adopt different accounting standards, but the model already in place provided a pool of skilled workers speaking the same language.

Finance Considerable advantages were also present in finance. Other transition countries needed to grow a modern banking sector from the bottom up, but in Germany the sophisticated system of the federal republic simply expanded eastward as banks opened branches in the new federal states. Moreover, newly privatized or start-up companies in the East gained access to the financial institutions and the savings of the West.

---

[7]Total and immediate integration with the former West Germany did present some problems to East Germany as we will see. Other states were able to protect industries in transition with trade barriers and to use currency valuation changes to absorb external shocks.

Supply of Entrepreneurship In the transition from a socialized system to a market structure, entrepreneurship and management skills are often the factors in shortest supply. This constraint proved less binding on East Germany because an inflow of qualified personnel from the West could fill almost any gap, a process encouraged by the techniques chosen by the privatization agency, as we shall see later.

Access to Markets The fall of communism brought with it the end of the Soviet-sponsored international trade organization, the Council for Mutual Economic Assistance (CMEA), which resulted in the loss of traditional export markets as managed trade between the socialist nations collapsed. Other transitional economies forced a fight for access to markets in developed countries, but firms in East Germany gained immediate and unimpeded entry not only into the West German market of 80 million consumers, but also the larger European Union (EU) market of 350 million of the world's richest customers.

Infrastructure Not the least of East Germany's advantages was the willingness of the federal government to pour resources into eastern Germany's social and economic fabric. As in other planned economies, infrastructure suffered under socialism. Examples included underprovided and badly maintained roads, out-of-date communications technology, a badly abused environment, and a short supply of housing. Fortunately the federal German government worked to close the gap and provide the basis for sustained growth in eastern Germany. In addition, rising infrastructural investment created a strong and positive macroeconomic effect that partially compensated for the fall of demand caused by the dislocation of trade.

A Social Safety Net The provisions of the monetary and economic union extended West Germany's comprehensive **social safety net** to East Germany. The economies of all former socialist nations in the early stages of transition generally exhibited a collapse of output in the manufacturing and industrial sectors. Fear of the social unrest put pressure on governments to maintain employment in existing enterprises through subsidies and delayed industrial restructuring. East Germany found itself able to support high unemployment and early retirement, without real fear of either extreme poverty or social unrest.

The willingness and ability of the West German government to finance the social expenses associated with transition should not be underestimated. As Table 9.2 shows, net transfers to East Germany amounted, in 1993, to some 150.6 billion DM, roughly $100 billion at current values, or 5.4 percent of total German GDP.[8] This figure does not make allowance for the subsidized interest rates for investment in the new federal states. Total annual net transfers continued at roughly the same rate, $100 billion annually, or 4.5 percent of Germany's GDP. In just 10 years, the cumulative value of the transfers from West to East Germany amounted to more

---

[8]Reiner Flassbeck and Gustav Horn put the figure at DM 170 billion. See *German Unification: An Example for Korea?* (Brookfield, VT: Dartmouth, 1996), p. 192.

Transfers from West to East Germany, 1993–1999 (DM billions)

	1993	1995	1997	1999
Federal government	115.7	136.7	129.6	140.0
State governments	10.3	11.2	11.6	11.6
German unity funds	15	0	0.0	0
Social security system	23	33.3	34.7	36
EU	5	7	7	7
Treuhandanstalt	23.8	0	0	0
Revenues	40.2	48.2	47.8	50.6
Net transfers	150.6	137.7	135.1	144
As a % of Western GDP	5.4	4.7	4.4	4.4

SOURCE: OECD *Economic Survey of Germany*, May 2001.

than $1 trillion. Compared to this total, the amounts loaned or granted by the multilateral funding agencies to other nations looks tiny, and no other economy in transition received anything approaching the level of fiscal support received by East Germany.

THE CURRENCY ISSUE

Choice of Exchange Rates

One of the most heated controversies within the union of East and West Germany concerned the choice of exchange rate, a decision that involved both economic and political considerations. Clearly the West German deutschemark was much stronger than the East German ostmark, but by precisely how much was difficult to determine because of the ostmark's controlled convertibility. One index derived from the price of the d-mark on the black market, about 12 ostmarks per d-mark. Another measure used the rate implicit in the pricing of East German goods on world markets. The rate implied by the price structure of GDR exports to West Germany averaged 4.4 ostmarks per d-mark. This evidence indicated an appropriate policy might value the ostmark well below the d-mark, perhaps 4 or 5 ostmarks per d-mark. However, political pressures favored parity, largely because of lower wages in the East than the West, even when expressed in terms of their respective currencies. The onset of economic reunification would immediately lead to West German prices being common to both economies, and if the ostmark were valued at a fraction of the d-mark, living standards in the East would fall at a stroke—not an auspicious start for a political union.

Ultimately a compromise converted all current payments at a 1:1 rate, with a higher rate for capital accounts. For example, if a pensioner received a monthly pension of 1,000 ostmarks, then she or he would receive in the future 1,000 d-marks. The same held true for wages, stipends, and rental agreements. However, financial assets converted at the more realistic rate of 2:1, with the exception of a limited amount of savings per individual, allowed as a concession at a 1:1 rate. The overall average for the consolidated balance sheet of financial institutions converted at roughly 1.8:1.

The Consequences of Parity

Even though political considerations mandated the 1:1 current rate, the economic consequences of its adoption came close to catastrophic. As we can see from Table 9.3, the 1:1 rate made labor in East Germany more expensive. In 1991 wages in East German industry ran about 49 percent of those in western Germany, while productivity came to only about 44 percent of the West German level. Hence unit labor costs were about 20 percent higher than in the West.[9] As an immediate consequence, goods made in the East cost too much to find a market, either in Western Europe, or in eastern Germany itself. Although wages rose sharply, significant productivity gains resulted largely with the closing of the worst of the productive facilities. Unit labor costs fell in the East but stalled out in 1995–1996 at about 13 percent above the West German level, and since then some slippage occurred.

Prior to the collapse of the planned Soviet-bloc trading system, the highly export-oriented economy of the GDR sent relatively sophisticated goods throughout Eastern Europe. These markets evaporated with the dissolution of planned trade, while the

■ TABLE 9.3

	Labor Productivity and Wage Cost: East German Figures as a Percentage of West German Figures		
	Wages/Salary per Employee	Labor Productivity	Unit Labor Costs
1991	49.3	41.4	118.9
1992	63.2	53.2	118.9
1993	70.4	60.9	115.5
1994	73.2	64.8	113.0
1995	74.3	65.8	112.9
1996	75.2	67.5	111.4
1997	75.8	68.2	111.1
1998	76.0	67.9	112.0
1999	77.7	68.8	112.9

NOTE: Berlin not included.
SOURCE: Deutsches Institut für Wirtschaftsforschung, "The German Economy in the Autumn of 2000."

---

[9]Unit labor costs are computed by dividing wages by productivity.

high unit cost of East German labor made the capture of markets in the West an impossibility. Meanwhile, West German goods flooded into the East, and the domestic demand for goods produced in eastern Germany itself collapsed. A second effect of the exchange-rate compromise manifested itself on the balance sheets of enterprises and banks, with financial institutions being hardest hit. A substantial part of their assets converted at the 2:1 rate, while the bulk of liabilities converted at 1:1, meaning that, expressed in d-marks, liabilities exceeded assets. The choice of the 1:1 exchange rate for current transactions bore much of the blame for the initial output collapse in eastern Germany. No doubt a lower rate for the East German mark might have maintained the competitiveness of some of eastern Germany's production, in the short term at least; however, much of the problem stemmed from a failure to appreciate at the time of unification the size of the productivity differential between East and West. The estimates anticipated some 70 percent of eastern German companies would experience losses as a result of the 1:1 exchange rate, with 30 percent actually in acute danger of going bankrupt. In reality, bankruptcy threatened some 90 percent of all of eastern Germany's enterprises.[10]

THE TREUHANDANSTALT

The Structure of Industry in the GDR

In common with their colleagues in other planned economies, the planners and technocrats of the GDR placed a lot of faith in economies of scale. Large East German enterprises resulted. About two-thirds of the workforce were employed in firms of more than 1,000 workers, a much higher proportion than in western industrial economies. Furthermore, more than 50 percent worked in firms with more than 2,500 employees. In addition, East German firms organized into groups known as combines (**Kombinate**), which integrated and controlled their activities. Immediately before reunification, East German industry comprised a total of 221 combines, which together accounted for almost all output. The combines focused on coordinating production and avoiding duplication, but in time many came to resemble diversified holding companies. They held considerable monopoly power and, although subject to some planning control, tended to impose high prices and pay inadequate attention to efficiency and quality.

In June 1990, immediately prior to the economic and social union, all of East Germany's industrial assets were put into the hands of a 'trust agency,' the **Treuhandanstalt (THA)**. The THA oversaw the disposition of some 8,500 state enterprises, a broad swath of retail activity, as well as extensive holdings of agricultural land and forest. Though based in Berlin, the THA staff consisted predominantly of West Germans and included 15 regional offices in eastern Germany empowered to dispose of enterprises of fewer than 1,500 persons.

---

[10]Martin Myant, et al., *Successful Transformations? The Creation of Market Economies in Eastern Germany and the Czech Republic* (Brookfield, VT: Edward Elgar, 1996), p. 50.

The mandate given to the THA involved reducing the commercial activity of the state, restructuring state-owned industrial enterprises, and passing those enterprises into the private sector. The main issues for the THA centered around how fast to dispose of its massive portfolio of assets and how much reorganization to attempt before sale. One possible model looked at a comprehensive restructuring of the entire economy prior to privatization and to rationalize enterprises to conform to that structure while holding them in public ownership. However, the THA considered that such a policy lay beyond its powers, resources, and expertise. A second, more modest approach would keep the firms under THA ownership long enough to achieve substantial restructuring on a firm-by-firm basis. Again, that task required a great deal of management time and considerable investment, not to mention the subsequent accusations from firms in the West of unfair competition from East German enterprises operating under state subsidy.

Ultimately the THA chose to go with a strategy of speedy privatization. It adopted a slogan best translated as "rapid privatization, resolute restructuring, and cautious closure" but gave primacy to speedy divestment. It based its choice largely on a greater confidence in the market's power than its own expertise to restructure enterprises. Although the expenses of maintaining an enterprise while held within the portfolio of the THA were regarded as a necessary evil, the THA kept investment in firms during its stewardship to a minimum.

The policy precluding substantial investment in new plant or equipment became particularly important as evidence showed the physically rundown state of the existing capital stock in East Germany. The Federal Statistical Office estimated that in 1991 roughly 55 percent of fixed assets in manufacturing inherited from the GDR (and 75 percent of the plant and equipment) were no longer useful. Because of its condition and because much equipment produced goods for Eastern Europe that were not in demand in the West, the assets of the firms to be privatized proved to be worth much less than originally thought. Each firm held by the THA faced strategic choices for the future, pared back its operations, and positioned itself for restructuring. However, the THA's hands-off policy in terms of management meant it would only make limited investor-neutral investments. As Martin Myant put it:

> In other words decisions on basic changes in production profiles and technology were to be left to the future owners. Thus, for a long time these companies were not allowed to invest in technological changes, even though reorientation in the market demanded just this. This was a particularly severe handicap when set in the context of the collapse of exports to the east, the shrinking domestic sales and the rapidly rising wage levels.[11]

The Strategy of Privatization

The THA decided that "the best way of achieving urgently needed rehabilitation in most companies [was] by gaining a new, business-oriented owner, able to bring

---

[11]Martin Myant, et al., *Successful Transformations?* (Brookfield, VT: Edward Elgar, 1996), p. 55.

management skills, technology, markets, and new product."[12] This decision ruled out voucher privatization, which though it would involve a change of ownership, would not result in a change in management or inflow of capital. Initial public offerings (IPOs) used as the primary vehicle in the United Kingdom were not possible either; they provide no injection of cash for the firm (the revenues go to the government) and management is initially unchanged. Before IPOs are presented, potential buyers need time to appropriately evaluate the firm, which would slow the process. Moreover, the sale of all or even a substantial part of the East German capital stock would put a great deal of pressure on Germany's capital markets. After eliminating voucher auctions and IPOs, the remaining potential strategies reduced to auction sales for cash among competing bidders and negotiated sales to specific purchasers—the method eventually chosen. Generally speaking, the buyers were companies or investment groups from outside of eastern Germany, although in some cases a sale to management was possible if appropriate assurances about finance and technological capability were forthcoming.

Its reliance on negotiated sales gave the THA a high degree of discretion, which became a source of considerable criticism. Political interests came to play a large part in the disposition of assets, but because the economic well-being of whole regions often depended on the fate of single enterprises, political lobbying was inevitable and to some extent desirable. Greater concern came from accusations that West German competitors of East German firms influenced the disposal of assets and that THA employees and associates profited through corruption.

Despite the degree of latitude granted to the agency, privatization of large East German ventures proved difficult. In many cases the aging capital stock, poor product line, and low labor productivity demanded the immediate closure of the firm. Better quality and lower cost substitutes for East German products, freely available from West Germany shortly after the start of the reunification process, caused a precipitous drop in demand for East German goods. In some cases, the THA did grasp the nettle and make immediate closures, including Trabant, the leading automobile manufacturer. Analysis of the real costs of production indicated that each underpowered two-stroke vehicle cost roughly $11,000 to produce and at best might sell for $7,000 after extensive modifications to meet environmental standards. Consequently, the Trabant factory in Zwickau closed, though generous subsidies from the state government induced the establishment of a Volkswagen factory to employ many of the Trabant workforce.

Table 9.4 gives some statistics on the record of the THA. By September 1993, it processed some 13,241 firms and fully or partially privatized about 12,000 of them.[13] In revenue terms the privatization program caused a great disappointment; near the end of the program in 1993 it showed only some DM 44.7 billion raised through asset sales, about one-fourth of the annual transfer payments to East Germany. The experience completely discredits the idea of the union as a profitable leveraged buyout suggested by *The Economist*. Moreover, disappointingly few

---

[12]Ibid.

[13]The number of firms in its portfolio continued to grow throughout the period of privatization because it divided enterprises in order to dispense of them.

■ TABLE 9.4

Change of Status in Stock of Companies Held by the Treuhandanstalt, 1991—1993

	January 1991		December 1991		December 1992		September 1993	
	Absolute	%	Absolute	%	Absolute	%	Absolute	%
Total portfolio of								
TH companies	8,489	100	10,970	100	12,599	100	13,241	100
Dissolutions/liquidations	120	1.4	1,014	9.2	2,534	20.1	3,374	25.5
Fully/partially privatized	574	6.8	2,996	27.3	5,456	43.4	5,998	45.3
Revenue from sales in billion DM					40.1		44.7	
From foreigners							5.3	
Investment commitments								
(in billion DM)	44.5		114.2		169.5		182.4	
From foreigners					17.0		19.9	
Employment commitments								
(in units of 1,000)	255		930		1,401		1,493	
From foreigners					121		145	
Employees in units of 1,000								
In TH companies	2,937		1,372		408		213	
In ex-TH companies			285		1,047		964	
Total employees	2,937		1,657		1,455		1,177	

SOURCE: Reiner Flassbeck and Gustav Horn, *German Unification: An Example for Korea?* (Brookfield, VT: Dartmouth, 1996), p. 121.

purchases involved foreign buyers, with only DM 5.3 billion coming from purchasers outside of Germany.

Table 9.4 also shows the rapid fall of industrial employment in eastern Germany. At the outset of the privatization process, 2,937,000 employees worked in companies controlled by the Treuhandanstalt. By September 1993 this group of companies employed only 1,177,000 persons (40 percent of the original). More than one and three-quarter million workers lost their jobs in closures and restructuring orchestrated by the THA. As part of its negotiations the THA tried to get commitments from new management about investments to be made in the enterprises and the levels of employment to be achieved. Table 9.4 gives total commitments for employment of 1,493,000, but this figure proved too optimistic. The THA held little power to hold a purchaser to its pledges on either labor use or capital injection.

The recession that gripped Western Europe magnified the THA's problems. Spare capacity in the West, a reluctance of management to move east, and opposition from West German unions to the "export" of jobs to the new federal states limited interest in East German industry, and the THA strategy of finding western buyers to modernize East German industry stalled. Meanwhile, resistance to seek the views of existing management and the preference given to sales to western buyers over potential management "buyouts" led to resentment in the East. As time went on the THA's problems in disposing rapidly of its assets allowed potential buyers to become increasingly selective. Because of scarce interest, they felt they could improve the terms of purchase by delaying. The THA, anxious to complete its task and sensitive about criticism of growing unemployment, felt obliged to dispose of its assets on terms increasingly favorable to the buyers. Disappointing outside interest resulted in less than 10 percent of sales revenues or investment pledges coming from outside Germany.

THE IMPACT OF REUNIFICATION ON SOCIAL CONSENSUS WITHIN GERMANY

Despite the high expectations that greeted the fall of the Berlin Wall, by the mid-1990s both West and East Germans were disenchanted by the outcome. Westerners (Wessis) resented the increase in taxes and interest rates required to keep the East German economy afloat, while Easterners (Ossis) bemoaned the collapse of the indigenous economy, the reduction of benefits (e.g., free day care and subsidized vacation), and the movement into East Germany of West German officials and "carpet-bagging" businesspeople.

The catching-up process remains stalled. By 1995 productivity in the formerly socialist East rose to about 60 percent of the level in the West, an impressive achievement, but one due mostly to the collapse of the enterprises with lowest productivity. Removing those workers from the totals raised the average quite quickly, but at the cost of massive unemployment. To further raise productivity to western levels proved much more difficult from 1995 onward because it involved increasing the efficiency of workers already on the job. If West German labor productivity increases at an annual rate of 1.5 percent (quite modest by historical standards), productivity in East Germany must grow at more than 7 percent per annum in order to catch up even by 2010. One of the difficulties in transition states comes from the expectation that living standards can adjust to western levels in short periods of time. The dashing of these hopes inevitably cause increased social and political pressures.

The changes following the fall of the Wall irreversibly altered the East German economic system but also raised the possibility that the strains of unification could destroy the West German system too. Its citizens regard West Germany as a **social market economy**.[14] With most of the capital privately owned, coordination relies primarily on market principles. The "social" aspect, however, involves subjecting the market to regulation to ensure that the "impersonal working of the market does not interfere with or undermine basic social needs, ranging from adequate income and health care, to organized representation in the workplace, to comprehensive vocational training."[15]

---

[14]See Chapter 19.
[15]Lowell Turner, ed., *Negotiating the New Germany* (Ithaca, NY: ILR Press, 1997), p. 3.

The inclusion of eastern Germany put pressure on a German model already somewhat beleaguered by global competition, recession, and rising unemployment. Whereas convergence seemed a likely outcome in 1989, today many think in terms of a **mezzogiorno scenario**, a reference to the income and productivity differential between northern and southern Italy.[16] There wide regional differences persist despite relatively easy labor and capital mobility and persistent government policy aimed at closing the gap.

LESSONS FROM THE GERMAN UNIFICATION

Although Germany represents a special case, it offers lessons from its experience that might inform our evaluation of policy and events in other transition economies.

Currency Valuation

An overvalued currency resulting from political considerations that forced parity between the d-mark and the ostmark caused some of East Germany's problems. Other economies with greater latitude should balance carefully the role of a low currency value in assisting export- and import-substituting industries against the benefits of a highly valued currency in keeping inflation in check.

Privatization

One of the desirable features of any privatization scheme should be the establishment of a sense of equity. East Germans saw most of their capital stock given away or sold to West Germans at what seemed to be low prices. In return they got access to the federal social safety net that did not fully assuage the feeling of dispossession. A strengthened social solidarity might come with some greater involvement of the citizens in the share capital of the privatized enterprises.

Market Restructuring Versus Planned Restructuring

Germany relied on the market as the agent of change; therefore, neither the privatization agency nor the government developed a clear blueprint of industrial structure after liberalization. Moreover, it performed internal restructuring of firms only on the limited basis necessary to facilitate a sale. In the disorderly conditions of an economic and political transition, markets may not perform optimally and a more active governmental role in both macro and micro restructuring might ease the process.

---

[16]See Andrea Boltho and Wendy Carlin, "Will East Germany Become a New Mezzogiorno?" *Journal of Comparative Economics* 24, no. 3 (1997), p. 249.

The Time Frame

German unification represented the ultimate in an economic Big Bang that, almost in an instant, swept away the discretionary tools of economic policy. The exchange rate was determined by the value of the d-mark. The infeasibility of tariff or quota barriers and capital controls meant imports flooded in from the West, and prices assumed world market values. Although these factors might be desirable in the longer term, no authority in East Germany controlled the timing. Only the vast financial reserves of the West German state prevented the eruption of a social crisis.

RECENT DEVELOPMENTS IN THE GERMAN ECONOMY

The Progress of Transition in the East

Elections in the fall of 2002 returned Chancellor Gerhard Schroeder and his Social Democrats to power by a slim majority, preserved largely by a big win in the states of the former East Germany. The new government faces a series of big problems. The chief problem remains the integration of formerly "new federal states" into the whole of the Federal Republic. The presumed catchup in terms of productivity and income sits stalled, and slower growth in the East than in the West makes the problem worse. The slow rate of growth of the economy as a whole compounds the reluctance of investment to move to the East. Disastrous floods in the spring of 2002 destroyed a great deal of social capital in the East but strangely, this event might provide a substantial silver lining. Both public and private disaster aid poured into the eastern *lander,* which will receive the vast bulk of the $13.5 billion injection. These new transfers, on top of the $100 billion in "normal" aid, is expected to raise the growth rate in the east to about 2.3 percent in 2003, up from an average of just 1 percent per annum over the last six years. This transfer burden must be paid for and the government postponed tax reform and raised corporate taxes to close the deficit, doubtless slowing the growth of the western part of the country. Even though "wessis" doubtless felt sympathy for their "ossi" compatriots, these latest measures raised the percent of German GDP going to the East in aid to about 6 percent. This percentage creates an intolerable burden over the long haul, one likely to harm relationships between East and West once again. Clearly, the transition of East Germany is far from complete, a fact that continues to underline the problems further east.

Policies to Cut Unemployment

Although unemployment fell from its highs in 1997–1998, it still remains a serious problem. In Germany today the rate is about 9 percent, or 4 million persons, and finding work for them is the most pressing problem. Most economists feel that the culprit is Germany's high nonwage cost to employers, which discourages them from hiring more workers. They may be partly right, but the other side of the coin shows that as in many other European social democracies, the worker experiences only slight income reduction during periods of unemployment, eliminating the incentive to aggressively go out and find work. Despite the 4 million unemployed and the slow growth rate, some 1 million current unfilled job vacancies exist in Germany.

In the midst of this severe situation, evidence revealed that the Federal Labor Office grossly exaggerated its own success by claiming it found work for 60 percent of the jobless than crossed its thresholds. In truth, the effective rate scarcely topped 20 percent. The embarrassed government created a commission headed by Peter Hartz, the director for human resources at Volkswagen to find a way to halve the unemployment rate. Hartz still puts his faith in active labor market policies (ALMPs) and hopes to make Germany's 181 Federal Labor offices more effective by styling them as user-friendly "Job Centers," an insubstantial rebranding already tried in the United Kingdom. Although this move struck many critics as a woolly approach, other recommendations saw the reduction of unemployment benefits and the use of government loans to subsidize the employment of already jobless persons in the eastern *lander*. Those unemployed for more than six months would be given "make work" in the Swedish style, while long-term unemployed over the age of 55 would be excluded from the statistics. Altogether Hartz feels that his proposals would cut the jobless from 4 million to 2 million. What might really be required is a strong fiscal stimulus to promote growth across the economy, but the 2002 budget deficit already stood at a full 3% of GDP, the maximum allowed under the stringent rules that govern the member of the euro common currency group. In January 2003 the European Union declared Germany in violation of the so-called stability and growth rules and required fiscal stringency to rectify the balance or face fines.

THE PROBLEMS OF GERMAN EDUCATION

One of the problems confronting Germany today surprises both Germans and foreigners. Conventional wisdom assures us that German growth, even dating back to the nineteenth century, was sustained by the achievements of the German education system. Therefore, when a new OECD study of school pupils' performance ranked Germany a lackluster 21st out of the 31 countries in the study for the reading abilities of its 15-year-olds, 20th in mathematics, and 20th in science, it led to plenty of consternation all round. This shock only worsened with the realization that Germany ranked about last in the percentage of its young people who go on into tertiary education. At present, only 28 percent do so—compared with an OECD average of 45 percent—and only 16 percent emerge with a degree.

The revelations led to a serious search for answers because, in Germany, as elsewhere, long-run high wages must stem from high productivity, fueled by high educational attainment. Several candidates provide reasons for failure. One is the high proportion of students of foreign birth who are not native German speakers. However, Austria has a higher percentage and emerges with better results. Britain and France, both thought of as facing "immigrant problems," do much better in measured educational attainment. Although it is not easily amenable to policy change, this kind of analysis reinforces the case of those who see immigration as a cause of German downfall. Another explanation is the German fondness for rote learning though the same characteristic in Korea and Japan did not seem to hinder their attainment. The answer probably lies in few teachers per pupil than elsewhere (though they are better paid) and too short a school day. A commission will certainly be formed to address the issue, although the solution may be difficult to find.

KEY TERMS AND CONCEPTS

catching-up (convergence) process	social market economy
codetermination	social safety net
Kombinate	supervisory boards
mezzogiorno scenario	Treuhandanstalt (THA)
monetary, economic, and social union	universal banks

QUESTIONS FOR DISCUSSION

1. Describe East Germany's economic performance relative to the rest of the Eastern bloc prior to reunification.
2. What were East Germany's advantages over other potential transition states?
3. What was the strategy of privatization adopted by the Treuhandanstalt?
4. What issues surrounded the choice of the conversion rate for the ostmark to the d-mark?
5. How successful was the THA in attracting foreign capital? Why?

RESOURCES

Web Sites

Central Bank ....http://www.bundesbank.de/

Federal Ministry of Health and Social Security ....http://www.bma.de/

Ministry of Finance (In German) ....http://www.bundesfinanzministerium.de/

Federal Ministry of Economics and Labour...http://www.bmwi.de/

Federal Statistical Office ....http://www.statistik-bund.de/

German Institute for Economic Research ....http://www.diw.de/english/

The German Embassy and Information Center...................http://www.germany-info.org/

Handelsblatt—National Business Newspaper.....http://www.handelsblatt.de/englishsum/

Berliner Morgenpost International..http://morgenpost.berlin1.de/

Federal Commissioner for Foreign Investmen in Germany ....
....http://www.invest-in-germany.de/

Trabant..http://www.trabi.de/

Books and Articles

Boltho, Andrea, and Wendy Carlin. "Will East Germany Become a New Mezzogiorno?" *Journal of Comparative Economics* 24, no. 3 (1997), 241–264.

Bos, Dieter. "Privatization in East Germany." In *The Transition to Market,* Vito Tanzi, ed., 202–223. Washington, DC: International Monetary Fund, 1993.

Collier, Irwin L., Jr., and Horst Siebert. "The Economic Integration of Post-Wall Germany." *Economic Developments and Prospects* 81, no. 2 (May 1991).

Hall, John, and Udo Ludwig. "East Germany's Transitional Economy." *Challenge,* September–October 1994, 26–32.

Heilemann, Ullrich, and Reimut Jochimsen. *Christmas in July? The Political Economy of the German Unification Reconsidered.* Washington, DC: Brookings Occasional Papers, 1993.

Jones, Alun. *The New Germany: A Human Geography.* Chichester, West Sussex, England: John Wiley and Sons, 1994.

Myant, Martin, et al. *Successful Transformations? The Creation of Market Economies in Eastern Germany and the Czech Republic.* Brookfield, VT: Edward Elgar, 1996.

Owen, Robert F. "The Challenges of German Unification for EC Policymaking and Performance." *American Economic Association Papers and Proceedings* 81, no. 2 (May 1991).

OECD. *Economic Survey of Germany,* May 2001.

Siebert, Horst. "The Integration of Germany: Real Economic Adjustment." *European Economic Review* 35 (1991), 591–602.

Sinn, Hans-Werner. *International Implications of the German Unification.* Working Paper Series, Working Paper 5839. Cambridge, MA: National Bureau of Economic Research, 1996.

"Survey: Germany." *The Economist,* November 9, 1996, 1–22.

"Survey: Germany: The Berlin Republic." *The Economist,* February 6, 1999.

"Survey: Germany." *The Economist,* December 5, 2002.

The East German Economy in the Fall of 2002. Berlin: DIW. Available at http://www.diw.de/.

The Germany Economy in the Fall of 2002. Berlin: DIW. Available at http://www.diw.de/.

Turner, Lowell (ed.). *Negotiating the New Germany: Can Social Partnership Survive?* Ithaca, NY: ILR Press, 1997.

10

THE EUROPEAN UNION: HISTORY AND INSTITUTIONS

THE CREATION OF THE EUROPEAN UNION: A BRIEF CHRONOLOGY	
Date	Event
1947	Initiation of the Marshall Plan to promote the economic revival of a Europe devastated by war
1948	Benelux Treaty creating the common economic space of Belgium, the Netherlands, and Luxembourg enters into force
1948	Creation of the Organization for European Economic Cooperation (OEEC) to administer the Marshall Plan
1949	Creation of the Council of Europe located in Strasbourg
1950	Schuman Declaration
1951	The Treaty of Paris establishes the European Coal and Steel Community (ECSC)
1952–1954	Preparation, and failure, of plans for a European Defense Community (EDC)
1955	Renewed vitality for the idea of European unity provided by the Messina Conference
1957	Signing of the Treaties of Rome establishing the European Economic Community (EEC) and the European Atomic Energy Community (Euratom)
1967	Merger of the institutions of the three communities (ECSC, EEC, and Euratom)
1968	Completion of the customs union
1972	Treaties of Accession of Denmark, Ireland, Norway, and the United Kingdom
1973	Denmark, Ireland, and the United Kingdom join the European Community; Norway chooses to stay outside
1979	Signing of the Treaty of Accession of Greece
1979	First election of the European Parliament by direct universal suffrage
1981	Greece joins the Community
1985	Signing of the Treaties of Accession of Portugal and Spain
1986	Portugal and Spain join the European Community
1987	Signing of the treaty and entry into force of the Single European Act
1989	Signing of the Social Charter by all members except Britain
1990	Unification of Germany
1992	Signing of the Treaty on European Union (the Maastricht Treaty)
1993	Introduction of the single European market and the European Economic Area
1993	Maastricht Treaty becomes effective creating the European Union; Austria, Finland, and Sweden join the European Union
1997	Signing of the Amsterdam treaty
1999	Economic and Monetary Union established: Sweden, Britain, and Denmark opt out, and Greece is denied entry.

1999	The European Parliament comes of age. It calls for investigation of corruption and fraud at the Commission leading to the resignation of the Commission in March. A new Commission formed in August.
2000	Treaty of Nice is signed redefining voting rules in the EU.
2001	National currencies are phased out in "euro zone"; Greece joins as the twelfth member.
2002	Agreement that Poland, the Czech Republic, Hungary, Slovakia, Lithuania, Latvia, Slovenia, Estonia, Cyprus, and Malta could join in 2004. Bulgarian and Romanian accession in 2007 an "objective." Turkey snubbed again.

PRECURSORS TO THE EUROPEAN UNION

Many visionaries sought the peaceful unification of Europe, and a few dictators looked to do the job by force, but serious planning for economic and political unification in Europe did not occur until after World War II. The damage caused by nationalism and war in the three decades between 1914 and 1945 created a strong impetus for change. Even after the war, raised tensions contributed to the dispute between the conflicting and, to many eyes, largely bankrupt ideologies of nationalism, communism, and fascism. "Europeanism" offered an alternative, which could both influence domestic political agendas and provide a supranational goal to diffuse nationalist tensions. The potential economic rewards of a united Europe, although appreciated from the beginning, initially carried less importance than the prospect of political gain.

A further push toward unity came shortly after the war by the creation of the American-financed **Marshall Plan** and the institution created to administer it, the Paris-based **Organization for European Economic Cooperation (OEEC)**.[1] Today the Marshall Plan is almost universally remembered and revered as a rare example of enlightened altruism on the part of the United States. Rather than extracting revenge and reparations from the defeated powers in the manner of the Treaty of Versailles, which concluded the First World War, the Marshall Plan contributed to the reconstruction of Europe by helping both victor and vanquished. As well as administering project aid, the OEEC actively alleviated the dollar shortage, financed the bilateral currency imbalances, and helped to remove the trade barriers instituted in the prewar periods. After three years of slow growth across the continent, the OEEC efforts began to bear fruit. American exports to and investment in Europe soared and prosperity began to return to the continent. Some scholars view the Marshall Plan, even though often credited with the revival of Western Europe, as a decisive step in the division of postwar Europe. Stalin rejected the invitation to the Soviet bloc participation in the Marshall Plan because of its condition of

---

[1]This body with a larger membership is now known as the Organization for Economic Cooperation and Development, or OECD.

extensive information sharing. The exclusion of Eastern Europe helped draw the "iron curtain" that divided the nations of Europe until 1989.

In 1948, a conference attended by all the major Western European nations convened at The Hague. Originally called the Congress of Europe, this body became known as the Council of Europe and made its permanent home in Strasbourg in eastern France. It became a useful forum in which to debate and define the competing models of European integration. Britain's role became an important issue. Britain emerged from the war with a great deal of moral authority and might have taken the leadership role on European unity had it not favored European integration through intergovernmental cooperation rather than by creating supranational organization. In retrospect we can see that the British leadership failed to appreciate that major changes had occurred in the global political landscape. It viewed World War II as merely the latest in a series of continental conflicts requiring British intervention to restore the balance of power. At the end of the war, Britain turned to concentrate on world trade and the remnants of its empire to the neglect of its interests in Europe. The Scandinavians supported Britain's position of cooperation without political integration, and the Council of Europe remained unable to offer a clear path toward the federal solution preferred by the other West Europeans.

The real precursor of the contemporary European Union (EU) came in the form of the **European Coal and Steel Community (ECSC)**, first suggested by **Jean Monnet** and later advanced by another Frenchman, **Robert Schumann**. The fear that revival of the German economy might cause German military power to rise once more originally prompted its proposal. The ECSC created a "common market" in coal and steel, which would remove the basic ingredients of a war machine from national control and place oversight with a "high authority," independent of national governments. Initially the ECSC consisted only of France and Germany, but the Benelux countries and Italy joined to form "the Six," signing the Treaty of Paris in 1951. The ECSC not only succeeded in reducing tensions in Western Europe, but it also provided a compelling model of the value of pooling national markets.

Buoyed by the success of the ECSC, the Six tried to move toward political unity at an unrealistic pace. In 1952 representatives drafted a treaty establishing a European Defense Community (EDC), followed in 1953 by the draft of a treaty creating a European Political Community (EPC). Although five of the members of the ECSC happily went along with these proposals, in 1954 the French National Assembly failed to ratify the EDC, a move that proved fatal for the EPC as well. Persuading European governments to yield sovereignty in the defense and political arenas always presented a tougher task than harmonizing economic arrangements.

The Treaty of Rome

The failure of the EDC and EPC initiatives set back the European movement; Europeanists shifted their emphasis from rapid political unification toward consolidating economic integration. The foreign ministers of the Six met at Messina in 1955 and began a process that culminated in the **Treaty of Rome**. This agreement established two new bodies: the European Economic Community (the EEC, often called the European Common Market), and Euratom, the European Atomic Energy Community. Together with the ECSC, these bodies constituted the European Communities (EC).

The most important body was the EEC. The success of the ECSC demonstrated that economic gains could be made by increasing the size of the market, thereby allowing both greater competition (with a long-term impact on efficiency and dynamism) and a greater degree of specialization. Moreover, confidence in the power of economies of scale characterized the 1950s. National firms might be uncompetitive in global terms because of the limited size of the domestic market, but European firms could amass the size to compete internationally.

Although generally accepted that economic integration offers benefits to all participants, there are different degrees of economic integration. At the lowest level, a **free trade area** allows the movement of goods between countries without the hindrance of tariffs or quotas. A **customs union** not only provides for such movement but also requires that the members apply a **common external tariff (CET)** to their imports from third-party countries. A **common market** encompasses a customs union with the additional commitment to the free movement of factors of production within the member states. The member countries held as their ultimate goal a common market, but the first step toward this common market required completion of a customs unions and the establishment of a common external tariff.

The Community of Six

The Community of Six, established by the Treaty of Rome, gave itself a 12-year adjustment period to establish a customs union. During this time, members worked to progressively reduce internal tariffs between constituent nations were to be to zero and to harmonize the tariffs on goods originating outside the community. By 1968 the members had completed this customs union, although progress toward the liberalization of factor movements, required for a true common market, proceeded at a much slower pace and would, in fact, take another quarter of a century to complete.[2]

Outside the EC concern grew about the prospect of **fortress Europe**, a market shielded by high tariffs, which went against the prevailing trend of multilateral tariff liberalization. However, despite the threat to its economic interests, the United States supported the development of the EC because it offered the political reward of European stability. Fears on the economic front subsided when it became clear that the final external tariff structure of the EC would be more liberal than that of the original members. Trade relations between the EC and the United States sometimes can be described as less than harmonious, and fears of restricted access to the European market remain chronically recurrent. Nevertheless, the tariff reductions negotiated in both the Dillon and Kennedy rounds of General Agreement on Tariffs and Trade (GATT) translated into cuts in the common external tariff.

---

[2]The common market was finally completed in 1993 due to the Euro-92 program.

Although economic aspects of the Europeanism thrived, progress toward a politically united Europe lagged, with both defense policy and foreign policy remaining the domain of national governments. However, the stances of Germany and France, the two most powerful nations, became increasingly coordinated as German Chancellor Konrad Adenauer and French President Charles de Gaulle cooperated closely in "the Bonn-Paris axis," and their interaction frequently determined European policy. However, despite increased cooperation such policy making took place at the national and not the Community level.

Shortly after the Treaty of Rome, Britain rethought its position on EC membership. With the remnant of its empire, the British Commonwealth, largely dispersed and the treasured "special relationship"[3] with the United States dissipating, Britain took the lead in 1959 in the creation of the **European Free Trade Area (EFTA)**, otherwise known as the "outer seven," consisting of Britain, three Nordic nations (Sweden, Denmark, and Norway), Austria, Switzerland, and Portugal. It was designed to capture the benefits of a free trade area without any commitment to social expenditures or to political union. The British came to regret that each of its small partners gained much more in terms of market access than did Britain. Quickly recognizing the limitations of EFTA, Britain formally reversed its position on the EC, announcing in 1961 its interests in full European membership, but French President de Gaulle unilaterally terminated negotiations using the French veto to deny entry.

Expansions of the 1970s and 1980s

After de Gaulle resigned in 1969, British entry became a possibility once more. In December 1969 talks began to admit not only Britain, but also Ireland, Norway, and Denmark. Britain secured entry, but paid a price in terms of budget contribution that required a higher share of gross national product (GNP) than that of any other member. Ireland and Denmark also joined, but Norway, although admitted, rejected membership in a national referendum, influenced by the fear that its valuable fisheries would be opened to wider exploitation. The short-term consequences of membership proved unfavorable for Britain. Food prices soared as a result of the protectionist **common agricultural policy (CAP)** that ended cheap imports from Australia and New Zealand.[4] The lack of competitiveness in British industry resulted in lost market share at home without significant expansion of exports to continental Europe. In the early 1980s the Thatcher administration eventually negotiated a lower British budgetary contribution and even secured a modest refund, but the British population remained skeptical about the benefits of membership.

Greece joined the EC in 1981 and Spain and Portugal in 1986. These new members, noticeably poorer and less developed than the existing EC nations, increased the population of the community by one-fifth but its income by only one-tenth.

---

[3]The Suez crisis and the U.S. insistence that Britain withdraw from Egypt or face economic sanctions was, in some ways, the final straw in pursuit of the special relationship.
[4]See Chapter 11 for a discussion of the CAP.

They therefore acted as a net drain on EC finances. Membership for these nations involved a different calculus of gains and losses. Although the newcomers did contribute something in terms of increasing the accessible market for existing members, the main gains were political. Popular thinking believed entry into the EC created a centralizing impact on the domestic politics of member nations, and many hoped that membership would put these countries, all of them recently under fascist regimes, on the road to moderate politics.

EC-1992: Completing the Internal Market

Experience showed that deepening the political links of the EC to be a difficult operation because it involved the sacrifice of domestic sovereignty. Liberalizing the internal economy of Europe, on the other hand, felt less contentious. In 1985, with the absorption of Spain and Portugal almost complete, the European Commission issued a White Paper containing 300 proposals for the "completion of the internal market." In 1987 the passage of the **Single European Act** amended the Treaty of Rome. This most important proviso ended any individual country's power to veto economic legislation on the grounds of national interest. It cleared the way for the project known as **EC-1992**, the completion of the internal economic space to allow totally free movement of goods, persons, services, and capital.

Total liberalization of trade within the EC required the elimination of three types of trade impediment. The first were the physical barriers at national borders. Pre-existing arrangements resulted in excessive customs regulation and paperwork that wasted a good deal of resources and time at borders. EC-1992 sought to eliminate these barriers by harmonizing both product standards and value-added taxation. A second set of barriers related to the procurement patterns of national and local government, which tended to favor local firms with resultant anti-competitiveness and efficiency loss. The third group of barriers lay in the financial services industries and their slow integration, protecting inefficient national markets. The elimination of these barriers would bring substantial gains, but they would also produce so-called supply-side effects by fostering increased competition and facilitating economies of scale.

Table 10.1 summarizes the European Commission's official estimates of the gains of EC-1992. The Commission thought that the elimination of border controls would yield a once-and-for-all increase in gross domestic product (GDP) of 0.4 percent, cut consumer prices by 1 percent, and lead to the creation of an additional 200,000 jobs within the Community. Similar gains were seen to result from increased integration of financial services and a "level playing field" for public procurement. The estimated supply-side effects of the extended market—resulting from economies of scale formerly constrained by national market size and increased transnational competition—would raise GDP by 2.1 percent, cut consumer prices by 6.1 percent, and lead to the creation of 1.8 million jobs. The single market program also held the potential to cut the budget deficits of the member countries by 2.2 percent and improve external position of the EC vis-a-vis the world. In addition to these medium-term consequences, predicted second-order effects included a virtuous circle of high investment, stable prices, and rapid growth.

■ **TABLE *10.1***

Medium-Term Prospective Gains from the Completion of the Internal Market, EC-1992 (% of GDP)

	Border Controls	Public Procurement	Financial Services	Supply-Side Effects*	Total Average Value
GDP	0.4	0.5	1.5	2.1	4.5
Inflation	21.0	1.4	21.4	22.3	26.1
Budgetary balance	0.2	0.3	1.1	0.6	2.2
External balance	0.2	0.1	0.3	0.4	1
Employment (in thousands)	200	350	400	850	1800

*Due to economies of scale and increase in competition.
SOURCE: Paolo Cecchini, *The Cost of Non-Europe* (Brussels: European Commission 1988).

Despite slow progress, by 1993 most of the legislation to complete the internal market was finished. The Commission encountered its most serious problems in service industries where complex national rules, many ostensibly designed for consumer protection, required attention. Although public procurement was, in theory, liberalized, strong indications of national bias still persist. Integrating labor markets also proved difficult, but EU members no longer required passports within the EU for EU citizens.[5]

The growth and success of the EU overshadowed the modest achievements of EFTA, whose members saw that the free trade area could never offer a market of the size and depth of the EU. Consensus favored a closer alliance with the EC, and several EFTA members actually applied for full membership. In 1991 EFTA and the EC combined to establish a common free trade area, for manufactured but not agricultural goods, an institution that became known as the **European Economic Area (EEA)**.

Gauging the success of the internal market project is difficult. It has failed to deliver the promised economic gains, with only lackluster EU growth since the completion of the market. In the period 1993–2002, GDP growth in the EU averaged 2.3 percent per annum, faster than stagnant Japan but well below the pace of 3.5 percent set by the United States (see Table 10.2). European employment showed even slower growth during this period with job creation lagging behind the labor market entry rate; rising unemployment now stands as one of Europe's largest social problems. Whether the position would be even more dire without EC-1992 is impossible to tell.

-----

[5]The Maastricht Treaty was responsible for formally changing the European Communities to the European Union, hence the acronym from EC to EU.

■ **TABLE** *10.2*

Economic Growth in Europe, Japan, and the United States
(average annual percentage changes)

Real GDP Growth

	1974—1985	1983—1992	1993—2002
European Union	2.0	2.6	2.3
United States	2.3	3.4	3.5
Japan	3.4	3.9	1.2

Employment Growth

	1974—1985	1983—1992	1993—2002
European Union	0.0	0.6	0.8
United States	1.8	1.8	1.4
Japan	0.7	1.3	0.1

SOURCE: Eurostat, *IMF: World Economic Outlook,* May 2001.

The Social Charter

The heads of state or government of 11 member states of the European Community[6] adopted the **Social Charter** (officially the "Community Charter of Fundamental Social Rights of Workers") declaration at the meeting of the European Council in Strasbourg in December 1989. It set out broad principles shared by the signatories and constituted a first step in the harmonization and establishment of consistent labor law across the EU. The Conservative British government of that time, committed to the interests of business, felt that the clauses in the Social Charter designed to strengthen the power of labor in the workplace would both lessen the freedom of management and the mobility of labor.

The rights expressed in the Social Charter are quite general and involve shared commitment to a safe workplace and social protection. One clause asserts the right of all workers to a paying job, clearly a dead letter given the high rates of unemployment in the Community. Three specific sets of provisions were obnoxious to the British Conservatives. The first protects labor unions and guarantees their right to engage in collective bargaining. This provision might have been palatable, but the charter went beyond this point in providing that workers must be informed about the activities and plans of the management and that workers participate in

[6]The EU included 12 member states at that time, but the United Kingdom "opted out."

the running of the company through representation on the board. To the business-oriented Conservatives, it seemed to allow the unions to usurp management prerogatives and was styled by Margaret Thatcher as "backdoor socialism." A second set of provisions guarantees the absolute freedom of workers to move within the EC, and a third guarantees the equal treatment of men and women, including equal pay for comparative work. The Social Charter presents a statement of general commitment but does not impose any specific action on a member country.

The Maastricht Treaty

Following the relative success of EC-1992 in completing the economic space, the EC faced new challenges in both economic and political spheres. Progress toward an ever-closer political union was put on one side while leaders pursued the single market project. The economic sphere offered clear and sometimes quantifiable benefits. It involved less sacrifice of sovereignty than the political agenda and was supported even by "euroskeptics" like Margaret Thatcher. However, the next and more controversial step toward full economic integration involved the creation of a single currency, which, Europeanists argued, would tie the European economy closer together in the way that the common dollar ties together the elements of the United States.

In December of 1991 the European Council, consisting of the heads of state and of government of the member nations, met in the previously obscure Dutch town of Maastricht and drafted the **Treaty on European Union**, almost always referred to as the **Maastricht Treaty**. This document was the foundation of the next stage of the European project, even changing the name of the community to the **European Union (EU)**.

In a rather ponderous architectural metaphor, the treaty defined the Union as resting on three "pillars." Pillar One concerns economic matters and covers agriculture, transportation, the environment, energy, research and development, and regional policy. Pillar Two establishes a common foreign and security policy, a priority objective for some time, but achieving a halting sort of progress. Joint Community policy failed to emerge in either the conflict in the former Yugoslav territories or in the response to the first or second Gulf Wars. Pillar Three focuses on cooperation in the fields of justice and home affairs and aims to achieve the free movement of persons inside the Union and to promote measures of common interest in the fields of external border control, asylum policy, immigration policy, terrorism, drug trafficking, and other serious forms of international crime. Because Britain refused to sign the Social Charter, the Maastricht Treaty embodied those principles in a separate protocol entitled "The Agreement on Social Policy," usually referred to as "the Social Chapter."[7] In a sense, therefore, the "social chapter" provides a fourth pillar of the Union.

---

[7]The current Labour government led by Prime Minister Tony Blair finally committed Britain to the Social Charter and the agreement on social policy.

The Principle of Subsidiarity

One of the most difficult political issues facing the EU centers on how much sovereignty and power should be gathered in Brussels and how much should be allowed to remain with the governments of the member nations or some lower regional authority. Citizens of member nations frequently criticize the EU as being remote, dictatorial, and bureaucratic, laying down directives impinging on the local culture and economy without due regard to circumstance. The Maastricht Treaty sought to meet this criticism by establishing limits to EU action. Article 3b of Title II of the treaty requires that

> [i]n areas which do not fall within its exclusive competence, the Community shall take action, in accordance with the principle of subsidiarity, only if and in so far as the objectives of the proposed action cannot be sufficiently achieved by the Member.

In short, this **principle of subsidiarity** affirms that all issues must be handled at the lowest level that can effectively deal with them. Any organ of the EU (including the European Council, the European Parliament, and the Commission) can intervene only in areas of common concern when the individual states cannot act effectively on their own. Even then, impositions from above must respect the specific characteristics of the states and regions and highlight their diversity. Any item of EU legislation proposed in Brussels must therefore satisfy three key criteria: that the item acts at the all-union level, that the EU's action is not excessive, and that any legislation is clear and transparent.

The principle of subsidiarity is relevant in many areas, not all of them specifically economic. For example, one issue in the news concerns the protection of migratory birds, and in fact the EU itself used this matter as an example of how the principle might work. The Commission determined that it is not for the European Union to set the dates for the opening and closing of hunting seasons in specific EU regions. Hunting seasons should be decided on according to local hunting traditions, with agreement reached on how each of the EU's member states complies with the overall objectives of bird protection. However, classic "externality" problems remain. France allowed generous hunting rules, extending into breeding seasons, which threatened the continent-wide bird population. Other countries demanded action by Brussels as France resisted, citing the principle of subsidiarity. In more strictly economic matters, the principle emerges in other important ways. Two examples are worth mentioning here, though they will be dealt with in more detail in Chapter 11. The first deals with competition and merger policy, traditionally handled at the national level. The introduction of the single market requires, for some industries at least, Union-wide treatment. The other issue revolves around the expenditure of monies granted through the structural funds. The recipient nations feel that they know better how such monies should be spent, while the Commission as grantor feels it deserves a say in its use.

The Treaty of Amsterdam

The Treaty of Amsterdam, concluded in 1997, did not fundamentally change the nature of the union but rather highlighted some specific issues for action. It included four main objectives:

1. *To place employment and citizens' rights at the heart of the Union.* Although no specific policy measures accompanied the treaty, it committed the European Union to the achievement of full employment within the member states.

2. *To sweep away the last remaining obstacles to freedom of movement and to strengthen security.* A long-standing concern of member states in increasing elimination of barriers to movement within the EU centers around the issue of loosening the control of member states over criminal activity and illegal immigration. The treaty committed the Union to continue to remove barriers to the movement of people and at the same time strengthened the cooperation between police and security forces and promoted the growth of "Europol," the European police network.

3. *To give Europe a stronger voice in world affairs.* Committing the Union to the development of a unified foreign policy, one of the most serious stumbling blocks in the drive to unity, increases its power in influencing international policy.

4. *To make the Union's institutional structure more efficient with a view to enlarging the Union.*

The Treaty of Nice

The Treaty of Nice, concluded in 2000, makes the last objective of the Treaty of Amsterdam more concrete by modifying the structure of the EU to render policy making tractable as the Union expands from 15 members to 25 in the year 2004, and then, probably, to 27 in 2007. As the number of members increases, so does the difficulty of enacting legislation. Although the Maastricht Treaty stripped member countries of the power of veto in the economic sphere and substituted qualified majority voting (QMV), the Treaty of Nice changed the rules again.

Enlargement of the EU in 2004 and 2007

Over the last five years the EU defined its strategy for future enlargement to the east, which will give rise to many difficulties. Unlike the last expansion, which admitted three rich nations (Austria, Finland, and Sweden), all prosperous with a long market tradition, the next expansion allows relatively poor nations emerging from a 55-year history of socialism and central planning.[8] These potential members will create a drag on the budget as well as the concern that the cheap labor available in Eastern Europe will draw investment away from current members and aggravate the high levels of unemployment now endemic through continental Western Europe. However, expansion offers clear political gains by ensuring the stability and moderation of the countries to the east.

---

[8]Two of the entrants, Malta and Cyprus, do not fit this description, but have pronounced singularities of their own. Cyprus remains partitioned, and only the Greek Cypriot part is destined to enter, while Malta is a small island economy.

The European Union opened negotiations with six countries in October 1998 and broadened the field to 12 a year later. Enlargement raises a number of thorny issues, including how soon new members should join the euro, immigration, agricultural subsidies, and concern about border security in the East.

In 1997 the European Commission conducted a comprehensive evaluation of each candidate country's political and economic readiness for EU membership. Initially it seemed that only five Central European countries (Hungary, Poland, Estonia, the Czech Republic, and Slovenia) were favored for "fast-track" entry. They, in the words of the Commission's report, "came closest to satisfying the membership eligibility criteria of having secure democratic government, a well-functioning market economy and the ability to take on the obligations of EU membership."

However, in 2002, the Commission decided to go ahead and start the admission process for a total of 10 nations (the above group plus Latvia, Lithuania, Slovakia, Cyprus, and Malta) with entry in 2004. Two other countries—Bulgaria and Romania—were listed with a target entry in 2007. Turkey, the thirteenth candidate, is the last in the queue, ostensibly because of concerns about its human rights record, though there are other factors. The original Treaty of Rome defined the Communities as being made up of European nations, and the bulk of Turkey's land area lies geographically in Asia. Other factors include its population, its relative poverty, and its non-Christian culture. This last point was emphasized by the former French President Valery Giscard d'Estaing who currently chairs a constitutional commission on the future of the EU. Even though politicians moved quickly to dissociate themselves from his comments, it left little doubt that Turkey faces an uphill struggle. The election of an Islamist government in the fall of 2002 did not advance Turkey's case, although the United States, with a eye on the geopolitical situation in the Middle East, continues to push hard to anchor Turkey firmly in Europe.

THE INSTITUTIONS OF THE EUROPEAN UNION

The European Union can be a confusing political entity to an outsider.[9] Its powers consist of issuing directives and regulations that are binding on members to various degrees, managing a budget, and making a limited number of agreements in the international sphere. Common institutions residing in Brussels, Strasbourg, and Luxembourg, with complex structures unfamiliar to most non-Europeans and baffling to many Europeans as well, exercise EU powers. Therefore it is useful to outline the distribution of decision-making authority in some detail. This analysis looks at the relationships of the nation-states to the EU, the "democratic" structure of the EU, and the direction of further integration.

---

[9]Madeleine Albright, U.S. Secretary of State under Clinton, once remarked that to understand the EU one "had to be either a European or a genius."

The European Council

The overall agenda of the European Union is determined by the **European Council**, composed of the political leaders ("the heads of state and government") of the 15 member nations. It sets the key policy guidelines and provides the impetus on the most important subjects. It also arbitrates disputed questions in which agreement has not been reached within the European Union Council of Ministers. Each member country presides over the European Council in turn for a six-month period (e.g., Greece and Italy in 2003, Ireland and the Netherlands in 2004, and the United Kingdom and Luxembourg in 2005). During the six-month presidency, therefore, each country holds the power to determine the agenda of what is discussed and to some extent what is pushed forward.

The European Commission

The **European Commission** is the Brussels-based permanent bureaucracy of the EU, employing some 17,000 people. The Commission draws up common projects and, after the European Union Council of Ministers makes a decision, sees that it is properly implemented.

Twenty commissioners, led by a permanent president, now Romano Prodi of Italy who replaced Jacques Santer of Luxembourg, direct the work of the Commission. As one of its important principles, the Commission operates independently of the national governments. Each commissioner takes an oath of office by which he or she forswears consideration of national interest in favor of a European perspective. Despite this ideal, the commissioners are not selected from the member nations strictly according to ability. Each nation sends at least one commissioner, and the larger nations send two, and because commissioners are appointed by national governments, the job frequently goes as a reward for loyal political service. Despite the rhetoric, commissioners are likely to act to some extent in the interests of the government of their home nation.

Commissioners are politically appointed, but the bureaucracies of the various directorates general that compose the Commission are long-serving permanent officials, which provides them with considerable power. Their commissioners rely on them as the repository of experience and knowledge, which allows them to control information flows and to some degree the agenda. The function of the Commission is to implement the common policies of the Union: agriculture, fishing, research, energy, environment, and so on. Also, when it is mandated by the member countries, it negotiates international agreements on cooperation and trade.

The Commission, not merely a passive body, also holds the power to initiate reform. For that reason the principle of subsidiarity, which places power whenever appropriate on a lower level of government, carries great significance. On its own initiative or in response to a citizen's complaint, it may bring an action before the European Court of Justice should the Union's laws not be respected in member states. The Commission also manages the Union's annual budget (ECU 86 billion in 1996), which is dominated by farm spending allocated by the European Agricultural Guidance and Guarantee Fund and by the Structural Funds, designed to even out the economic disparities between the richer and poorer areas.

The European Parliament

The EU's directly elected parliament consists of 626 members who serve five-year terms to sit in Strasbourg. The powers of the **European Parliament** are limited and, although its responsibilities have grown, it remains largely a symbolic and consultative group rather than an embodiment of representative democracy.

All of Europe's major political currents are represented in the Parliament, ranging from far left to far right. Members of the European Parliament (MEPs) come from nearly 100 political parties and are organized in a limited number of groups (presently eight) along ideological, not national, lines. Parliament conducts much of its effective work in its 20 committees that cover all areas of the European Union's activities, ranging from agriculture to common foreign and security policy, from legal affairs and citizens' rights to overseas cooperation and development. Parliament maintains friendly relations with elected assemblies all over the world and MEPs meet regularly with representatives from the parliaments of member states in interparliamentary committees and delegations.

The Powers of the Parliament The European parliament's powers fall into three areas:

1. *Legislation.* The original Treaty of Rome gave the European Parliament only a consultative role, providing at best a "talking shop" on legislative matters. However, subsequent amendments (through to the Maastricht Treaty) extended its authority, and now the Parliament holds the power of codecision (with the European Council) over policy areas, such as the free movement of workers, consumer protection, education, culture, health, and trans-European networks. Many legislative proposals now require an opinion from Parliament before they can be resolved by the Council. In the event of a conflict, a conciliation committee made up of equal numbers of MEPs and Council members is formed to seek a compromise. In the case of insoluble conflict, Parliament can pass a motion of censure on the Commission and force it to resign.

2. *The Budget.* The Parliament approves the EU's budget each year and can propose modifications or amendments to the Commission's initial proposals. The Council has the last word on agricultural spending and costs arising from international agreements, but the Parliament decides on other expenditures in, for example, education, social programs, regional funds, and environmental and cultural projects. In exceptional circumstances, the European Parliament can vote to reject the budget if it feels that its wishes were not adequately respected.

3. *Supervision of the Executive.* The Parliament exercises overall political supervision over the conduct of the European Union's policies. Executive power in the EU is shared between the Commission and the Council of Ministers, and their representatives appear regularly before Parliament. Parliament is also responsible for selecting a new president of the Commission every five years.

For many years the Parliament carried the reputation of a toothless body within the EU; but in 1999, it tackled the Commission with some effectiveness. It questioned the budget and required an independent committee to examine the behavior of the Commission, singling out two commissioners for special scrutiny. The committee's finding suggested fraud, nepotism, and corruption in the Commission's behavior. In March of 1999, the entire Commission of 20 members resigned. In August of 1999, Parliament approved a newly reformed Commission.

The European Union Council of Ministers

Most of the day-to-day decision-making power within the European Union lies in the **Council of Ministers** and in its permanent bureaucratic counterpart *Coreper* (the French acronym for the Council of Permanent Representatives). Each member state sends a national delegation to Brussels headed by permanent representatives, normally senior diplomats. Though nominally only an administrative adjunct of the Council of Ministers, Coreper exercises a great deal of power in day-to-day matters, leaving only the most sensitive matters to be handled by the Council of Ministers.

Actions of the Council take several forms:

- *Regulations* are binding and directly applicable to all citizens.
- *Directives,* a level of compulsion below the regulations, are binding on all, but they are indirect. They must be first "transposed" into the law of each country in a way that satisfies the intent of the directive.
- *Decisions* are binding and directly applicable but only to the institutions, bodies, businesses, or citizens specifically named.
- *Recommendations, advisory opinions,* and *resolutions* offer consultative or guidance texts addressed to the states.

Other European Bodies

The Economic and Social Committee and the Committee of the Regions are major consultative committees that relay the advice of professional groups and local bodies to the Commission, the Council, and the Parliament. All the guidance documents (known as White Papers and Green Papers) and all the proposed European laws are submitted for consultation to these two committees. The Economic and Social Committee consists of representatives of the workers, large and small businesses, farmers, families, and consumers of each country. The Committee of the Regions represents the voice of the municipalities, departments, and regions of the European Union.

The European Court of Justice is responsible for the proper implementation of the treaties and community legislation. It consists of judges and independent advocates general. Citizens may appeal to it through the European Commission (complaint) or a national court. The European Court of Auditors examines the legality and regularity of EU revenues and expenditures.

The **Ombudsman** is a peculiar European institution, the name and function of which are Scandinavian in origin. As its purpose, the office provides a clear avenue for any European citizen or resident of the EU with a complaint against a policy or institution of the EU. The Ombudsman hears grievances and holds authority to investigate and if necessary take action on them. In the United States, the function would be achieved by bringing suit against the federal government or its agency, but the Ombudsman is less formal and less expensive. The European Parliament names the Ombudsman after each Parliamentary election for the duration of that legislature.

MAKING DECISIONS IN THE EUROPEAN UNION

One of the most important features of the Maastricht Treaty was to reduce the power of any single member state to frustrate change within the Union. For matters within Pillar One, action generally starts with a proposal from the Commission, which, after consultation with Parliament and the Economic, Social, and Regional Committees, the Council of Ministers can adopt, amend, or ignore. In most cases (including issues that involve agriculture, fisheries, internal market, environment, and transport), the Council decides on the basis of a "qualified majority vote," with member states exercising voting power as shown in Table 10.3. Under the current pre-expansion arrangements a proposal needs the support of 62 votes (71.26 percent of the total of 87), which must be cast by at least 10 different member states. In practice the Council tries to reach the widest possible consensus at the committee stage before taking a vote, and historically only 14 percent of the legislation adopted by the Council was the subject of any negative votes or abstentions. Other policy areas within Pillar One (including taxation, industry, culture) remain subject to unanimity. In Pillars Two and Three unanimity (and therefore the veto) remains the rule.

The enlargements proposed will inevitably change this situation, and the **Treaty of Nice** determined the new allocation of voting among the members of the expanded EU. This structure is illustrated in Table 10.3. In the future, the sum of the votes in the European Council will rise to 345 and the number of votes needed for the acceptance of a measure will be 258. The Big Four (Germany, France, Italy, and the United Kingdom) will continue to have the same number of votes, but their share of the total will fall from the current 11.49 percent each to 8.41, which reduces their power. Formerly, if the four agreed, they already held nearly 46 percent of the vote and needed only to attract six other countries to assure passage of legislation. Now they start with less than 34 percent of the vote, and a winning coalition must include at least 14 countries. Consequently, passing legislation becomes more difficult.[10] The number of MEPs also increases with enlargement, from 626 to 732.

Table 10.3 also illustrates an important aspect of governance and democracy within the EU that did not change a great deal with the Treaty of Nice. Citizens of small states hold a disproportionately large say in the workings of the Union. For example, Germany with 17 percent of the population of the expanded union holds only 8.4 percent of the council votes and 13.5 percent of the representation in Parliament. Finland, with 1.1 percent of the population, holds 3.45 percent of the council votes and 2.56 percent of the representation in Parliament. Luxembourg has an even more privileged position.

---

[10]Other simpler procedures were rejected, including the so-called double majority consisting of a majority of nations and at least 50 percent of the council votes.

■ **TABLE 10.3**

Voting in the European Union Council and Parliament Before and After Expansion

	Population (2000)		In the Council				In Parliament			
	Share in EU 15	Share in EU 27	Current Votes Number	Share	Votes in EU 27 Number	Share	Current Votes Number	Share	Votes in EU 27 Number	Share
Germany	21.8	17	10	11.49	29	8.41	99	15.81	99	13.52
United Kingdom	15.8	12.4	10	11.49	29	8.41	87	13.90	72	9.84
France	15.7	12.3	10	11.49	29	8.41	87	13.90	72	9.84
Italy	15.3	12	10	11.49	29	8.41	87	13.90	72	9.84
Spain	10.5	8.2	8	9.20	27	7.83	64	10.22	50	6.83
Poland		8			27	7.83			50	6.83
Romania		4.7			14	4.06			33	4.51
Netherlands	4.2	3.3	5	5.75	13	3.77	31	4.95	25	3.42
Greece	2.8	2.2	5	5.75	12	3.48	25	3.99	22	3.01
Czech Republic		2.1			12	3.48			20	2.73
Belgium	2.7	2.1	5	5.75	12	3.48	25	3.99	22	3.01
Hungary		2.1			12	3.48			20	2.73
Portugal	2.7	2.1	5	5.75	12	3.48	25	3.99	22	3.01
Sweden	2.4	1.8	4	4.60	10	2.90	22	3.51	18	2.46
Bulgaria		1.7			10	2.90			17	2.32
Austria	2.2	1.7	4	4.60	10	2.90	21	3.35	17	2.32
Slovak Republic		1.1			7	2.03			13	1.78
Denmark	1.4	1.1	3	3.45	7	2.03	16	2.56	13	1.78
Finland	1.4	1.1	3	3.45	7	2.03	16	2.56	13	1.78
Ireland	1	0.8	3	3.45	7	2.03	15	2.40	12	1.64
Lithuania		0.8			7	2.03			12	1.64
Latvia		0.5			4	1.16			8	1.09
Slovenia		0.4			4	1.16			7	0.96
Estonia		0.3			4	1.16			6	0.82
Cyprus		0.1			4	1.16			6	0.82
Luxembourg	0.1	0.1	2	2.30	4	1.16	6	0.96	6	0.82
Malta		0.1			3	0.87			5	0.68
Total	100	100			345	100.00	626	100.00	732	100.00

Votes required for:

QMV			62	71.26	258	74.78				
Blocking Minority			26	29.89	91	26.38				

SOURCE: Draft Nice Treaty, Annex II (as published on December 12, 2000), Eurostat, OECD, in OECD Economic Surveys: Euro Area, 2001.

CONCLUSION

With this historical background to the development of the European Union and some analysis of how it functions, we now turn in the next chapter to the consequences of evolution in the EU, how it affected the economic systems of its member states, and what economic outcomes resulted.

KEY TERMS AND CONCEPTS

common agricultural policy (CAP)	fortress Europe
common external tariff (CET)	free trade area
common market	Maastricht Treaty
Coreper	Marshall Plan
Council of Ministers	Monnet, Jean
customs union	Ombudsman
EC-1992	Organization for European
European Coal and Steel	Economic Cooperation (OEEC)
Community (ECSC)	principle of subsidiarity
European Commission	Schumann, Robert
European Council	Single European Act
European Economic Area (EEA)	Social Charter
European Free Trade Area (EFTA)	Treaty of Nice
European Parliament	Treaty of Rome
European Union (EU)	Treaty on European Union

QUESTIONS FOR DISCUSSION

1. Why did Britain perceive it gained little from EFTA and needed the larger market afforded by the EU?

2. Why was the ending of the veto by the Maastricht Treaty important for the development of the EU?

3. What is the principle of subsidiarity and how might it lessen the popular fear of Brussels bureaucrats?

4. Why will admitting the poorer nations of Eastern Europe be a challenge to the EU?

5. What are the particular problems of Turkey's application to the EU?

6. In what sense is the EU a democracy?

7. How do the new voting rules in the Treaty of Nice reduce the power of the larger nations?

8. For what are the reasons do existing members of the EU favor the admission of new nations from the former Soviet Bloc?

RESOURCES

Web Sites

Europa ....http://europa.eu.int/
This site acts as front door to all of the official sites of the European Union. It gives access to Eurostat, the statistical agency, and the Web sites of the Commission, Parliament, the Court of Justice, the Court of Auditors, all of the secretariats, and the Economic and Social Committee.

European Central Bank..http://www.ecb.int/
This useful is for statistics, policy statements, and working papers will grow in importance in the years ahead.

Center for West European Studies, University of Pittsburgh..
....http://www.ucis.pitt.edu/cwes/CWES/cwes.html
This useful site for research provides many links.

The EU Information Society Web site ....http://www.europa.eu.int/ISPO/
This English-language site in Belgium addresses issues concerning the EU and the "information society."

The European Parliament ....http://www.europarl.eu.int/

European Union in the United States..http://www.eurunion.org/
The official site of the EU delegation in the United States offers good information and useful links.

European Parliament ....http://www.europarl.eu.int/

Policies and Legislation of the European Union..
....http://www.eurunion.org/legislat/index.htm

The Texts of Treaties....................................http://www.europa.eu.int/eur-lex/en/treaties/

Books and Articles

Britton, Andrew, and David Mayes. *Achieving Monetary Union in Europe.* London: Sage Publications, 1992.

Calleo, David, and Richard Leone. *Rethinking Europe's Future.* Princeton, NJ: Princeton University Press, 2001.

Cecchini, Paolo. *The Cost of Non-Europe.* Brussels: European Commission, 1988.

Devinney, Timothy M., and William C. Hightower. *European Markets after 1992.* Lexington, MA: D. C. Heath and Co., 1991.

Fossati, Amedeo, and Giorgio Panella (eds.). *Fiscal Federalism in the European Union.* Vol. 9 of *Routledge Studies in the European Economy.* New York: Routledge, 1999.

Giordano, Francesco, and Sharda Persaud. *The Political Economy of Monetary Union: Toward the Euro.* New York: Routledge, 1998.

Gros, D., and N. Thygesen. *European Monetary Integration*. New York: St. Martin's Press, 1992.

Kluth, Michael F. *The Political Economy of a Social Europe: Understanding Labour Market Integration in the European Union*. New York: St. Martin's Press, 1998.

Leonard, Dick. *Guide to the European Union*, 8th ed. London: Economist Books, 2002.

Milward, Alan S. *The Reconstruction of Western Europe: 1945–51*. London: Methuen & Co., 1984.

Nevin, Edward. *The Economics of Europe*. New York: St. Martin's Press, 1990.

Padoa-Schioppa, Tommaso. *Efficiency, Stability and Equity: A Strategy for the Evolution of the Economic System of the European Community*. Oxford: Oxford University Press, 1987.

Pinder, John. *European Community: The Building of a Union*. New York: Oxford University Press, 1991.

Pinder, John. *The European Union*. New York: Oxford University Press, 2001.

Pohl, Gerhard, and Piritta Sorsa. "Is European Integration Bad News for Developing Countries?: A Comment on Hughes Hallet." *World Bank Research Observer*, January 1994, 147–155.

Price, Victoria Curzon, Alice Landau, and Richard Whitman. *The Enlargement of the European Union: Issue and Strategies*. Vol. 7 of *Routledge Studies in the European Economy*. New York: Routledge, 1999.

Story, Jonathan, and Ingo Walter. *Political Economy of Financial Integration in Europe: The Battle of the Systems*. Cambridge, MA: MIT Press, 1997.

"A Survey of EMU: An Awfully Big Adventure." *The Economist*, April 11, 1998, 42.

"A Survey of the European Union: Europe's Mid-life Crisis," *The Economist*, May 31, 1997, 52.

"European Enlargement," *The Economist*, May 19, 2001.

United Nations. *Economic Commission for Europe Annual Reports*.

11

THE EUROPEAN UNION: ECONOMIC CONSEQUENCES

THE MAKEUP OF THE EU

Since its last expansion on January 1, 1995, the European Union (EU) includes 15 member states with a total population of 371 million persons. Its average gross national income (GNI) per head measured at current exchange rates is a prosperous $23,000 (Table 11.1). Calculations based on the purchasing power of domestic currencies places it slightly higher at $25,231. The total GNP of the EU (the sum of the national GNPs) is about $8.9 trillion at current exchange rates making it a larger economic entity than the United States and, therefore, a formidable global force. Although economic growth in Europe was strong during the early days of the European Economic Union (EEC), the pace slackened recently as the EU grew more slowly than North America, although it turned in a better performance than slumping Japan. Few Europeans regard the growth rate of income per head of 2.1 percent per annum, exhibited between 1980 and 1999, as creditable, especially as slow growth in output has led to an increasing unemployment. The causes of this poor performance are much debated, but most observers place some blame on inflexible labor markets and a lag in the pace of technological innovation relative to other nations.

THE WELFARE EFFECTS OF THE COMMON MARKET

The theory of the economic consequences of the creation of the EEC, and its successor the European Union, is well developed. The impact can be divided into static effects, which are examined formally next, and the longer-term dynamic effects, looked at in the following section.

Static Effects

The static effects of a common market, or customs union, are shown in Figure 11.1. Let us start with the assumption that the same good is produced in three countries: A (the domestic economy), B (its neighbor and ultimate partner in a customs union), and C (the lowest cost producer in the world). For simplicity we assume that Country C can supply effectively unlimited quantities of the good to Country A, which is relatively small, at a constant price of P_c. Under these conditions all of A's

■ **TABLE 11.1**

Selected Macroeconomic Indicators for EU Members

	Population (millions)	GNI per Capita, 2000	GNI per Capita PPP, 2000	GDP, 1999 (billions)	Real GDP Growth % per Annum 1990–1999	Inflation % per Annum 1991–2001
Germany	82	$25,050	$25,010	$2,112	1.00	2.0
United Kingdom	60	$24,500	$23,550	$1,442	2.10	3.4
France	59	$23,670	$24,470	$1,432	1.10	1.7
Italy	58	$20,010	$23,370	$1,171	1.20	4.1
Spain	39	$14,960	$19,180	$ 596	2.00	4.4
Netherlands	16	$25,140	$26,170	$ 394	2.10	2.4
Greece	11	$11,960	$19,640	$ 125	1.80	10.0
Belgium	10	$24,630	$27,500	$ 248	1.40	2.1
Portugal	10	$11,060	$16,880	$ 114	2.30	6.2
Sweden	9	$26,780	$23,770	$ 239	1.20	2.8
Austria	8	$25,220	$26,310	$ 208	1.40	2.1
Finland	5	$24,990	$24,610	$ 130	2.00	2.2
Denmark	5	$32,020	$27,120	$ 174	2.00	2.4
Ireland	4	$22,960	$25,470	$ 93	6.10	3.3
Luxembourg	0.438	$44,340	$45,410	$ 19	3.80	2.5
European Union	376.438	$23,819	$25,231	$8,497	2.10	3.0

SOURCE: World Development Report 2002; Human Development Report 2001.

imports of the good (an amount shown by gh in the diagram) originate in C, and the balance of consumption Q_1. B is by and large a lower cost producer than A, selling at P_b, but it cannot compete with C's price of P_c. Now let us consider the effect of a protective tariff of magnitude t. Because of the small country assumption, C's output remains at the same price on world markets, but within A is increased by the full amount of the tariff. Therefore the price within A's economy rises from P_c to P_t. The output of neighboring Country B is, in the presence of the tariff, priced at P_b + t, which is still above C's price of P_c + t or P_t. Imports, therefore, come exclusively from the lowest cost producer country C, but they are now restricted by the tariff to a level of ab. The balance of domestic consumption is supplied by A's own protected producers, who are able to expand production behind protective barriers. Revenue from the tariff is the rectangle abji—that is, the volume of imports, ab, multiplied by the tariff, t. The welfare consequences of this tariff are a fall in consumers' surplus of $P_c hbP_t$, and the protection raises producers' surplus by an amount $P_c gaP_t$. Total deadweight loss is given by the two triangles aig and bjh.

From this point we can consider the results if the neighboring countries A and B form a customs union. They agree to eliminate all tariff and quota restrictions between each other but maintain a common external tariff of size t with respect to the rest of the world. Now tariff-free goods from B are cheaper than the tariffed goods that originate in C. As a result, imports from the rest of world are eliminated,

The Static Effects of a Customs Union

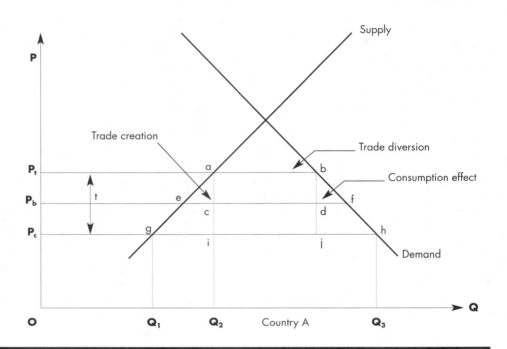

and instead they originate in B. The price of the good established in A is the production cost of B, (i.e., P_b). Total imports are of a magnitude ef. Part of this total, an amount cd (= ab), replaces the imports from C. This result is called the **trade diversion effect** of a customs union. However, total imports are greater than in the case of a general tariff. An amount ec replaces a part of domestic production and is termed the **trade creation effect**. The amount ef is an increase in consumption brought about by lower prices and is termed the **consumption effect**.

Compared to the situation in which A imposes a tariff on imports from all sources, the customs union does represent a welfare gain. Consumers in A gain access to goods at a lower price, P_b, than would be the case if tariff barriers were imposed on all imports. The gain in consumers' surplus is $P_b fbP_t$ and is clearly greater than the sum of the loss of producers' surplus $P_b aeP_t$ and the foregone tariff revenue abdc. However, these welfare gains are smaller than those that would result under free trade. The largest benefit from A's entry into the market in this example goes to the producers, and workers, of B who gain access to A's market; they see their production increase by an amount ef to meet the demand from A. Compared to free trade, A's consumers are losers, and the only gainers are the producers of B.

Consequently, viewed in a strictly static way, A would only join a customs union if it felt that in some industries it was in the position of lowest cost producer of the member nations. In reality this outcome does reflect the perceived benefits of joining the EU. The greater overall size of market allows greater specialization and division of labor. Economies become more open and trade flows increase. Some domestic industries are likely to decline as imports from other member countries cut into the market, while the output of other industries increases.

Dynamic Effects

Even though the static effects of a customs union are important, long-term dynamic considerations are probably more significant in providing a rationale for the creation of a common market than the static ones. Certainly from the inception of the EEC, one driving motivation was the beneficial effects of exposure of European firms to greater competition from its partners within the common market. A second was the ability to grasp economies of scale from the larger domestic market.

Table 11.2 indicates some of the changes in trade volumes that occurred following the formation of the EEC and its successor the EU between the 1960s and 1990s. In terms of the openness of the whole Community as a bloc of economies,

■ **TABLE 11.2**

Openness of EU Economies, 1960–1994
(average of imports and exports of goods as a percentage of GDP)

	1960–1967		1991–1994	
	World	Intra-EU	World	Intra-EU
Belgium and Luxembourg	37.5	64.8	53.3	70.0
Denmark	27.0	52.3	25.4	53.0
Germany	15.9	44.8	20.7	52.2
Greece	12.7	50.6	17.0	59.2
Spain	8.1	47.8	15.2	62.9
France	11.0	45.8	18.7	63.3
Ireland	33.6	72.2	50.3	68.8
Italy	11.7	42.9	15.9	56.4
Netherlands	37.7	62.7	43.9	65.9
Portugal	19.8	48.3	28.5	73.3
United Kingdom	16.0	26.7	20.2	52.1
EU-12	**8.8**	**45.0**	**8.9**	**58.6**
Austria	—	—	25.6	66.1
Finland	—	—	22.4	46.7
Sweden	—	—	23.6	54.9

NOTE: For the member states, these figures include intra-Union trade; for EU-12, intra-Union trade has been excluded. Intra-EU trade is given as a percentage of total trade.
SOURCE: Eurostat; Loukas Tsoukalis, *The New European Economy Revisited*, p. 182.

little changed during this 30-year period. Between 1960 to 1967, about 8.8 percent of the GNP of the 12 nations, then part of the EEC, was traded. The comparable figure for the same group of countries between 1991 and 1994 was 8.9 percent. This stability is surprising, especially in light of the sharp increase in the openness of most of the economies in the world during this time, as the trade-to-GNP ratios rose rapidly on a global basis. Although trade with nations outside of the EU only kept pace with the growth of output, trade within the EU grew considerably more rapidly. On average the nations of the EU conducted 45 percent of their trade with other members in 1960; by 1991–1994 level this had risen to 58.6 percent. The evidence therefore points to substantial trade creation and trade diversion effects.

THE EXTERNAL TRADE POLICY OF THE EU

Developed Nations

After the end of World War II, the United States directed its energy into creating a nonpreferential system of world trade predicated on the most favored nation principle of the General Agreement on Tariffs and Trade (GATT). The creation of customs unions like the European Community (EC) was facilitated by a special clause in the GATT (Article XXIV), which allowed the establishment of formal free trade areas. The United States allowed and even encouraged this development because it felt a strong Europe was essential to contain an expansionist Soviet Union. Nevertheless, many Americans held on to a certain ambivalence because of a recurrent fear that Europe might choose to close itself behind high tariff or walls.

Fortunately, the trade policy of the EU remained in line with GATT policy. The fears of Fortress Europe have been soothed by successive reduction in the **common external tariff (CET)**. The EU also sought to extend the free trade area beyond its core membership. The first extension was the creation of a free trade area linking the EC and the European Free Trade Area (EFTA) called the **European Economic Area (EEA)**. Subsequently the central and east European economies in transition were afforded special status through the signing of economic agreements (EAs) committing the parties to move toward a zero-tariff status over a 10-year period. After U.S. pressure, and in partial compensation for the stalling over its full membership, Turkey was admitted into the customs union without participating in the other aspects of the EU.

Trade Wars

Despite overall conformity with the rules of the GATT, the EU often uses nontariff barriers to protect sensitive industry. These barriers have led to frequent disputes, especially between the EU and the United States. The biggest problem has been related to agricultural products, not surprising given that agriculture lay beyond the purview of the GATT and the highly protectionist postures of both Europe and the United States. One outburst in 1997 erupted over new European Union rules requiring that exporting countries comply with the EU's food hygiene standards.

The EU blocked the import of U.S.-raised chickens and turkeys, and the Clinton administration responded by promising to block $300 million worth of meat imports annually. Like other disputes before it, it was resolved; but an undercurrent of mutual suspicion endures.

Policy toward Developing Nations

The EU's relationships with the "developing" world are governed by the **Lomé agreements**; the latest of these (Lomé IV) was signed in 1989 and subsequently modified in 1995. The signatories of the Lomé pact include the 15 nations of the EU and some 70 Third World countries known as the African, Caribbean, and Pacific (ACP) nations, many of which have historic colonial ties to members of the EU. The agreements allow virtually tariff-free access into the EU for most exports of the ACP nations without any reciprocal obligation. Furthermore, the Lomé arrangements were backed by the stabilization of prices of agricultural exports (Stabex) and mineral exports (Sysmin). In addition, the European Development Fund disburses about 6 percent of European Union revenue in aid to the ACP nations.

However, despite their apparent generosity, the Lomé agreements have done little to assist either development in, or exports from, the ACP group. In fact, EU imports from the ACP countries fell sharply between 1970 and 1994, from more than 8 percent of total non-EU imports to about 3 percent. Even though the pure transfer element of the grants-in-aid and the stabilization schemes is still important, the trade concessions have become less valuable over time as the size of the common external tariff has fallen.

THE ECONOMICS OF A SINGLE CURRENCY

The biggest recent change in the European Union is the adoption of a single currency. The launch of the euro must surely be ranked one of the most important events of the late twentieth century, both for its ramifications for the global system of finance and for its impact on the policies of the member countries of the EU. The single currency remains, however, a controversial issue. On balance, most studies find economic gains from the creation of a single currency, but they also note substantial attendant costs that must be balanced against those gains.

Economic and Monetary Union

In March 1971, the member states of the EC expressed "their political will to establish an economic and monetary union." The first step toward this **Economic and Monetary Union (EMU)** was the adoption of the "currency snake" linking the European currencies through fixed exchange rates while the rest of the industrial world moved toward floating rates. The next step, in 1979, was the creation of the **European Monetary System (EMS)** and the **European currency unit (ECU)**. The EMS was a fixed exchange rate scheme in which most currencies were held in a narrow band against each other (2.25 percent either side of the central parity). Rates were not totally stable, and considerable realignment resulted from differential inflation rates. The ECU was used as a unit of valuation only.

In June 1989, the European Council adopted the proposal of Jacques Delors, then president of the Commission, to embark on a three-stage program leading to a single currency. The first step beginning in 1990 consisted of closer coordination in monetary policy under the supervision of the Committee of Governors of the EC Central Banks.

In late 1992, progress to monetary union was set back by the consequences of German reunification. The need for income support and reconstruction assistance required that the German government pour some DM100 billion per year into the territories of the former East Germany. This expenditure depleted federal finances and led to increased borrowing by the German government, which raised interest rates and pushed up the value of the mark, severely straining the fixed exchange rates of the EMS. The maintenance of existing parities within the EMS required other countries to increase their own interest rates. Both Britain and Italy were unwilling to surrender monetary policy to the EMS in this way and left the system. For the countries remaining, the bands around parity were widened to 15 percent, and their width meant that although the EMS survived, it could no longer be regarded as a truly fixed parity arrangement.

Despite the disruption to the system and the threat to the EMU, the leaders of the member nations resolved to initiate the second stage at the beginning of 1994. The most visible development was the establishment of the **European Monetary Institute (EMI)** in Frankfurt. This location was the subject of some contention because Britain felt that the EMI should be located near the European Union's largest financial market, London. However, the fact that the United Kingdom had removed itself from the EMS, and the political reality that the mark dominates the EMS, favored a German site.

Proponents of the EMU felt that the key to a successful common currency lay in the economic convergence; the so-called **Maastricht criteria** were adopted to ensure that the economies were on a similar path. No state was to be admitted into Stage 3 of monetary union unless it met the following criteria:

1. Its inflation rate did not exceed by more than 1.5 percent that of the average of the three member states with the lowest inflation.

2. Its long-term interest rate did not exceed by more than 2 percentage points that of the three best states in terms with the lowest inflation rates.

3. Its current public sector deficit was less than 3 percent of GDP.

4. Its public sector debt was less than 60 percent of GDP, or approaching 60 percent at a satisfactory pace.

5. Finally, a member state's exchange rate must have been stable over the two preceding years, showing no more than "normal variation."

As late as 1997 no EU nation (exception tiny, wealthy Luxembourg) met these criteria, and a desperate drive to conform (especially to items 3 and 4) initiated a period of fiscal austerity that slowed growth of the EU economies. In March 1998 the European Monetary Institute produced an assessment of each country's performance in meeting the criteria, which was to be the basis for accession to the EMU. When it came to the crunch, only Greece was found to have failed to meet the criteria, although Britain, Denmark, and Sweden were skeptical about monetary union and opted not to enter the system at its initiation in 1999. Only three nations met the strictest definition of condition 4, all the other nations were found to be reducing their ratio of public debt to GDP at a "satisfactory" pace. This interpretation was something of a stretch. Belgium (with a debt/GDP ratio of 122.2 percent) and Italy (121.6 percent) were on the face of it well beyond the limits, but political considerations led to their inclusion under the generous "fudge factor." Consequently, a group of 11 nations (styled Euro-11) were admitted to initiate the monetary union. Subsequently in 2001, Greece was accepted into Euroland as the twelfth member. It now seems only a matter of time before Sweden joins, leaving only the United Kingdom and Denmark on the outside.

The Benefits of a Single Currency

Currency union is expected to bring several benefits. The most obvious is the elimination of currency conversion, releasing substantial resources in the banking sector.[1] Another is the end of exchange rate uncertainty, which should encourage trade and allow more efficient allocation of resources within the EU, through specialization and economies of scale.

A third benefit is that participating nations can largely eliminate their holdings of international currency and bullion reserves. The combined reserves of the members of the EU in 1990 was about ECU 200 billion, while the United States with an economy similar in size had reserves of only about ECU 40 billion. Although the special position of the dollar as a reserve and intervention currency means that the United States can keep lower reserves than other economies, a substantial reduction in overall European reserves can be anticipated.[2] Finally, the creation of a common European currency unit will increase the importance of European currency in world markets. More of the world's reserves will be held in euros and the EU will be able to benefit from seigniorage (the process of creating money to be held by others) and lower interest rates than would otherwise be the case.

The Costs of a Single Currency

Adopting a single currency, however, involves costs, the chief of which is the elimination of exchange rate policy as a means of accommodating shocks and balancing the external accounts. To understand this loss, consider a country that experiences a sudden fall in the demand for its exports. If it has its own currency, it can devalue,

---

[1]The quantification of these benefits involves making some assumptions but the adoption of a single currency is estimated by the European Commission as providing cost savings equivalent to some ECU 15 billion per annum, capable of creating a boost to the GNP of the participant countries of about 0.4 percent if, of course, the unemployed resources are put to use.
[2]Most of these reserves are currently held in interest-bearing assets, which means the actual degree of saving might well be small.

or allow it to depreciate, and can regain international competitiveness at lower real incomes without causing a fall in nominal income or a rise in unemployment at home. If it is part of a currency union, it must absorb the shock in terms of lower income and higher short-term unemployment. The size and openness of the economy determines the seriousness of losing currency flexibility. Small countries have relatively large propensities to import and therefore are able to achieve external balance through proportionately small changes in GDP. Bigger countries, which are generally more closed, require a larger movement of output to rectify external imbalances. As a rule therefore small countries incur lower costs in joining a fixed-rate system and especially a monetary union.

A second factor is the exposure of a national economy to an asymmetric shock, one affecting it more severely than the rest of the monetary union. If all parts of the union are hit similarly by an economic shock, it can be accommodated by coordi-nated union-wide monetary, and possibly fiscal, policy. The relationship between the economic structure of each member country and the whole of currency union becomes key. The more a country resembles the union-wide average, the less harmful is the loss of an exchange rate flexibility. The greater the similarity between the structures of all the member countries, the more likely is it that it comprises "optimum currency area." Table 11.3 shows that even though considerable vari-ance characterizes the industrial structure of the members of the Europe Union, it

■ **TABLE 11.3**

European and American Industrial Structure:
Europe by Nation, United States by State

Sector	European Community		United States	
	Mean Percentage Share	Variance	Mean Percentage Share	Variance
Food, beverages, and tobacco	11.2	11.3	8.3	3.9
Textiles, clothing, and leather	8.1	25.9	4.8	15.9
Wood and wood products	3.8	1.4	4.3	3.1
Paper and paper products	7.4	5.9	8.8	8.6
Chemical and chemical products	17	5.8	17.1	33.9
Nonmetallic mineral products	4.8	1.4	2.7	0.3
Basic metals	6.2	2.4	4.1	3.7
Metal products	9.3	2.9	7.4	5
Nonelectrical machinery	10.1	12.9	19.8	27.2
Electrical machinery	10.5	8.6	10.3	9.6
Transport equipment	11.7	7.5	12.5	26.4
Totals	100.1	8.4	100.1	18.0

SOURCE: Bini Smaghi, L. Vori, and S. Vori, "Rating the EU as an Optimum Currency Area," *Banca D'Italia Temi do Discussione,* January 1982.

is actually less than that between the states of the United States, which share a common currency.

The degree of mobility factor also affects the desirability of a currency union. Highly mobile labor or capital helps adjustment to a negative shock by moving quickly from the impacted region to areas where they are in higher demand. Consider an example from the United States. The state of Maine had a high proportion of employment in footwear manufacture, much higher than the U.S. average. When cheap shoes from low labor-cost countries began to flow into the United States, unemployment mounted in Maine. If the state had its own currency, we would see a depreciation of the "Maine $" and a movement toward restoring external balance. However, the shock was absorbed by lower real wages in Maine, which prompted an outflow of labor to states where wages were higher, and some investment in new industry in Maine to take advantage of the cheap labor. Labor mobility between the EU nations is, however, much lower than interstate mobility in the United States. Language and cultural factors, as well as generous unemployment assistance, tends to keep people at home. Net regional migration in the EU represented only 0.2 percent of the total population in the five-year period from 1980 to 1985, only 25 percent of the level in the United States.

Who Gains and Who Loses from a Single Currency?

Because of the complexity of these considerations, it is difficult to establish whether a particular group of countries does indeed constitute an **optimum currency area**, or even which countries will benefit from membership. Nevertheless, using heroic assumptions it is possible to get a quantitative handle on the issue. Table 11.4 shows one attempt to forecast the gainers and losers for the EC-12.[3] The measure of benefits consists of the proportion of GDP that is traded within the community. The measure of cost is the degree to which the industrial structure of the member countries differs from the community average, a gauge of the degree of susceptibility to asymmetric shocks. In general, the smaller, more open economies show the greatest gains. However, these same countries also tend to have less diversified industrial structures, differing from the community average. However, net benefits seem to be enjoyed by all potential members except Greece.

Such a two-dimensional representation of the costs and benefits is potentially misleading. In reality, the economic implications of the EMU are still shadowy, and it is probable that political factors dominated economic in its formation. Some suggest that, like a bicycle rider, the EU needs forward momentum to maintain its stability. After the completion of the internal market, a new project was needed and it was found in monetary unification. Although it maintains the momentum of EU integration, the current two-tier structure creates a rift between the fast-track members of the monetary union (Euroland 12) and the more cautious or less integrated remainder (Denmark, Sweden, United Kingdom).

---

[3]D. Gros and N. Thygesen, *European Monetary Integration* (New York: Addison Wesley, 1998), p. 258.

■ **TABLE 11.4**

Estimates of Net Benefits of EMU Membership (EU of 12)

	Benefits	Costs	Net Benefits
Belgium/Luxembourg	44.5	−1.39	43.11
Denmark	13.65	−6.47	7.18
Germany	14.35	−1.81	12.54
Greece	13.25	−14.01	−0.76
Spain	8.95	−2.07	6.88
France	12.95	−0.71	12.24
Ireland	38.85	−8.48	30.37
Italy	9.7	−2.02	7.68
Netherlands	34.2	−5.14	29.06
Portugal	24.55	−10.31	14.24
United Kingdom	10.7	−8.4	2.3

BENEFITS: Intra-EC trade as a percentage of GDP.
COSTS: Difference between nation's economic structure and the EC average.
SOURCE: D. Gros and N. Thygesen, *European Monetary Integration* (New York: Addison Wesley, 1998), p. 258.

The Stability and Growth Pact

Although all the members of the EU, including ultimately Greece, "satisfied" the Maastricht criteria, much was owed to the generous use of the "fudge factor." However, the new monetary union needed a way to ensure that the convergence required for countries to enter the system is maintained into the future. Given the rigors that some countries underwent to meet the criteria, or at least to appear to be moving in that direction, and the high level of unemployment throughout the EU,[4] the temptation is now for countries to indulge in expansionary fiscal policy. All members of the EMU have committed themselves to a stability and growth pact requiring the continued enforcement of the Maastricht criteria. Germany, which traditionally had the strongest and most stable currency in Europe, was justifiably nervous about entering into a union with countries such as Italy, renowned for its mountainous government debts and consequent inflation. It therefore insisted on the **stability and growth pact**. The pact stipulates that all EU countries will run balanced budgets in normal times. If any of the 12 that adopted the euro ever lets its budget deficit exceed 3 percent of GDP, it will be forced back into line with the threat of substantial fines. However, recent tough times have cut central government tax revenues, and standard "Keynesian" economic theory insists that the correct way out of a recession is to increase the size of the deficit. Portugal became the

---

[4]The levels are high except, somewhat ironically, in Britain, which has the lowest EC joblessness rate and has chosen not to be a member.

first to break the deficit limit by notching up 4.1 percent for the 2001 tax year. Italy and France are coming dangerously near the trigger point, and Germany crossed the 3 percent threshold during 2002.

In the fall of 2002, the president of the Commission, Romano Prodi, an Italian former economics professor, publicly characterized the pact as "stupid." When the EU recovers from this iconoclasm it is probable that some form of flexibility will be built in to take account of the need for deficit-based reflation in tough times. Three main suggestions for reform are being considered. The first is that countries with low debt to GNP ratios (such as Germany) may be allowed to exceed the deficit limit. Another is to reclassify public outlays into "current" and "investment" expenditures, and allow some latitude for the latter. This approach would allow extensive public works projects to escape the guillotine. The final possibility is to recognize that 3 percent was too low and raise it to 5 percent while still insisting on balancing budgets over a longer-term (10-year) horizon. Because any shift would require the unanimous consent of participants, change is unlikely. It does not mean that the 3 percent limit will be adhered to, but rather that transgressors and the other members will likely deal leniently with their failures. The more who fail to keep the line, the lower will be the fines.

The Independence of the European Central Bank

In theory, the new **European Central Bank (ECB)** will be highly insulated from political pressure from member governments. If this theory proves to be the reality it will be an unusual European institution, because the European Council or the Council of Ministers, both of which are responsible to the national governments, decide most of the major issues. The rationale for independence is clear. Only in the absence of direct political pressure will the president of the ECB and the members of its executive board be able to make decisions based on expertise rather than on political exigency. Therefore, both the board and the president are appointed to eight-year nonrenewable terms. The Council of Ministers, the Commission, and the European Parliament can make their views known to the ECB through defined avenues, but the bank is under no obligation to respond. However, despite its theoretical independence, the status of the ECB was undermined at the outset by the French insistence on their own candidate, the governor of the Bank of France, as president of the ECB, and their refusal to accept the consensus candidate, Wim Duisenberg, the president of the ECB's precursor, the European Monetary Institute. A compromise was achieved by splitting the eight-year term into two four-year terms, but the prospects for independence are not good. Things were complicated in 2002 when the prime French candidate was accused of malfeasance in his dealings as a private banker.

THE UNION BUDGET

The European Union has a surprisingly modest budget, but it does not provide many services. In 2002 it amounted to €96 billion ($97 billion at the current exchange rates), little more than 1 percent of total GDP of the member states. Expenditures averaged 2.4 percent of total public expenditure of member states—€314 per head per year.

Finance comes from four sources, as shown in Figure 11.2. The first is the levies imposed on imported agricultural goods. These tariffs are an integral part of the common agricultural policy (CAP) and are designed to bring the price of imported food into line with European costs. It is a useful source of revenue, although one raised at considerable cost, with a high excess burden that falls on the European consumer. It represents only 1.48 percent of total EU revenue and will probably decline in the future as a result of the Uruguay accords of the World Trade Organization, which require the EU to bring agricultural prices into closer alignment with world prices. The second source of revenue consists of tariffs levied on industrial goods as they enter the EU. This source contributes about 15 percent of the budget. The third source of income is the proceeds of a 1.4 percent surcharge, levied as a part of the member countries' value-added tax (VAT), which brings in 38 percent of revenue. Finally, and now most importantly, an additional contribution is demanded of members to bring their budget contribution to 1.27 percent of their GDP, known as the "fourth resource."

The common agricultural policy is the largest element of expenditure in the EU. It currently represents 45 percent of the total budget expenditures, about €44 billion. The second largest component is broadly grouped as structural measures, consisting primarily of regional development and income transfer measures. They account for an additional 34 percent (€30 billion). Industry, research, the environ-

■ FIGURE 11.2

Sources of EU Revenue, Budget 2001

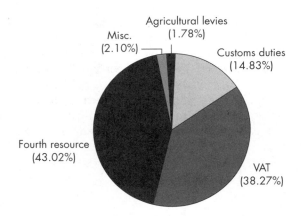

SOURCE: Eurostat.

ment, and transport share 6 percent of the budget. External activities (emergency aid and cooperation) correspond to 8 percent of the budget. Of this portion, about 3 percent is allocated as pre-accession to the countries of Eastern Europe. Other foreign activities account for 5%. Administrative expenses represent 5 percent of the budget. In all, 92 percent of the EU budget expenditures benefit the member countries themselves. The 1995 enlargement of the European Union from 12 to 15 members (after the accession of Austria, Sweden, and Finland) resulted in an increase of 6 percent in the budget, and expansions in 2004 and 2007 will increase it again. Whereas the last group of entrants were net contributors to the EU finances (the taxes and levies they contribute to the budget are greater than the direct expenditure received) that will not be true of the group of countries to join.

The financial management of the European Commission is overseen internally by financial auditors and externally by the European Court of Auditors and the European Parliament. Fraud is a persistent charge in EU institutions, and concern in the European Parliament and in member states forced the Commission to step up the fight against it.

THE COMMON AGRICULTURAL POLICY

As Figure 11.3 shows, about 45 percent of the budget goes to support agriculture. Although its share of total expenditure fell over recent years and will fall further in the near future, the dominance of the **common agricultural policy (CAP)** is still

- **FIGURE 11.3**

Expenditures of the EU, Budget 2002

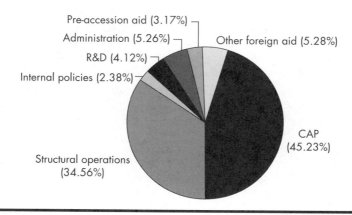

Pre-accession aid (3.17%)
Administration (5.26%)
R&D (4.12%)
Internal policies (2.38%)
Other foreign aid (5.28%)
CAP (45.23%)
Structural operations (34.56%)

SOURCE: Eurostat.

obvious. The system is complex and varies from commodity to commodity, but in essence it consists of manipulating prices within the EU to produce a desired level of farm income. This manipulation is achieved by both high intervention prices (at which the EU buys excess produce) and various output restriction schemes. Excess production is stored (in "butter mountains," "oil lakes," etc.) and exported to other countries, often at low prices.[5] To keep EU prices above world levels, agricultural goods entering the EU pay a variable import levy, which bridges the difference between world and EU prices. The main beneficiaries of CAP are the producers within the EU, and to some extent foreign consumers, while the losers are consumers within the EU and foreign producers. The system certainly imposes substantial deadweight losses.

At one level, CAP transfers income from country to country. A big agricultural sector leads to an inflow of funds, and because the CAP guarantees prices, nations with efficient agricultural sectors, relative to the European average, gain most. "Winners" fall into two groups. One consists of Greece, Ireland, and Spain, relatively poor countries with large, low productivity agricultural sectors. The other is made up of France and Denmark, rich countries with high productivity in agriculture. The rest of the countries are losers with the largest being Germany, Italy, and the United Kingdom. These transfers are no accident. Freeing trade in manufactured goods benefitted Germany's expanding industrial machine, and CAP was a political counterweight, ensuring membership benefits for France, which had a large agricultural sector. Support is more generous for meat, dairy, and cereals than for "Mediterranean produce," which in part explains why both Italy and Portugal with large agricultural sectors are net losers.

However, viewing redistribution as a national issue alone misses much of the picture. CAP involves subsidies that enable poorer farmers in Scotland, Ireland, Finland, and the "Club Med" countries to stay in business. These subsidies provide several benefits, including the maintenance of a basic level of prosperity in remote regions, contributing to one of the objectives of regional policy. However, the system also favors rich, efficient farmers, and the overall distributional effect of CAP is regressive, moving funds from relatively poor urban consumers (who spend a large proportion of their income on food) to the wealthier farmers of northern France, East Anglia, and Denmark. This pattern of transfers lowers social support or cohesion within the EU by taking from the poor and giving to the more affluent. Partly to rectify this undesirable consequence, but also to meet the objectives of the Uruguay agreement and the World Trade Organization, the EU will shift the emphasis of CAP from price support (which not only is a drain on the budget but also increases agricultural prices and the cost of living[6]) to targeted income maintenance for poor farmers. By eliminating the subsidies to the "rich"

---

[5]At one point in the late 1980s, the then-Soviet Union was able to buy European butter at 12 cents a pound. Stocks of beef were so high in 1986 that the Commission had to hire refrigerated ships lying in Rotterdam harbor to store the surplus. See Dennis Swann, *The Economics of the Common Market*, 6th ed. (London: Penguin, 1988), p. 219.
[6]The OECD reckons that the CAP adds 15 to 20 percent to the cost of food in the EU.

farmers of northern Europe, the cost of CAP will be reduced, European prices will be more in line with world prices, and the expensive and inefficient system of purchasing, inventory, and resale at a loss will be eliminated.

The German Commissioner for Agriculture, Franz Fischler, outlined his proposals for CAP reform in July 2002. His chief proposal was to delink the subsidies from production and direct them instead toward the income support of poor farmers and to investment in rural development. He was strongly backed by Britain, the Netherlands, and Germany, countries which, although they receive substantial CAP aid, are net losers to the scheme because of their high contributions to the EU budget. Predictably France and Spain, big net gainers, protested and French president Jacques Chirac was able to extract support from the Germans to maintain the current system in place until at least 2007. After that, when the accession of the Eastern European countries is complete, the aid to the new members will be limited to just 20 percent of the total. Given the poverty and heavy dependence on agriculture of the newcomers, this policy is far from what would appear to be fair.

The success of CAP as a policy is debatable, and the verdict depends largely on one's viewpoint. One objective was to stabilize prices with the Community, which was achieved. Less price volatility occurred in the Community than in world markets or even within the United States, which also maintains an extensive and expensive system of supports. However, the cost of stability is the most expensive food in the world, except perhaps in Japan. A second goal was certainty of supply. With the EU now self-sufficient, this target has been met. However, one might question the value of the objective itself. Food is easily available from a variety of producers, most of whom can reasonably be expected to remain politically friendly to Europe. Therefore it is hard to make a case for strategic self-sufficiency. (This state of affairs contrasts with, say, the energy sector, which has fewer supply points, many of which are beset with political problems.) Moreover, self-sufficiency has been more than achieved; overproduction and the disposal of excess now constitute a major preoccupation of the EU. A third objective was to raise agricultural productivity in Europe. The existence of CAP did coincide with a sharp improvement in agricultural productivity, though a cause-and-effect relationship is unclear. All developed countries have seen in the last 40 years an increase in both yield per acre and labor productivity. It can be argued that by guaranteeing the incomes of marginal farmers, CAP shielded producers from market discipline, an effect that will become stronger when CAP's emphasis shifts from price support to income guarantee.

Thus CAP's success lies in the eye of the beholder. Farmers like the policy, while consumers in general suffer, but in a surprisingly uncomplaining manner. The policy contributes to the cohesion of the EU, by winning the support of the poorer nations at the periphery. It is no coincidence that Ireland, a significant gainer from CAP, was the first country to enthusiastically embrace the Maastricht Treaty in a popular referendum. Moreover, CAP is instrumental in preserving an economic pulse in depressed regions. However, it may not provide such a cohesive effect if agricultural aid to the 12 countries due to join between 2004 and 2007 are subject to a different and less generous formula than that enjoyed by the current membership. It would instead be a recipe for resentment and disunity.

THE STRUCTURAL FUNDS

Composed of 15 nations, many of whom have wide regional differences within themselves, the EU is characterized and enriched by diversity. These differences include language, culture, and landscape between nations and between regions of nations. While Europe celebrates these differences, concern continues to grow that socioeconomic disparities may prove harmful to the unity of the EU. Now, policy makers regard economic and social cohesion as a prerequisite for both political stability and economic efficiency.

In the 1960s and 1970s most member countries of the EU developed aggressive "regional policies" designed to foster convergence in regional incomes and employment. Over time, these policies became discredited as expensive, achieving little of lasting consequence, and attempting to overrule the market as arbiter of efficiency. Far from producing national cohesion, regional policy often led to resentment in the territories that had been "net payers." Italy provides a significant example. Despite a battery of policies designed to encourage growth in the "Mezzogiorno," or South, regional disparities persisted and grew. The burden of the expense of redistributive transfers led to the emergence of a political party (the Northern League) devoted to promoting regional separatism.

However, the Single European Act brought regional policy to the fore. This act added a new title to the Treaty of Rome specifically stressing economic and social cohesion and providing specific instruments—the **structural funds**—to address it. Structural funds were not themselves new.[7] What changed was the willingness of the EU to finance regional development. In 1993, ECU 21 billion ($25 billion) was spent on the structural funds, and this amount rose to €34 billion ($33 billion) by 2001, including €3 billion in a specially established cohesion fund directed to the poorest members of the EU known as the "cohesion four": Greece, Ireland, Spain, and Portugal.

The structural funds have clear objectives:

1. To promote development and economic adjustment in regions whose GDP per head is less than 75 percent of the EU average[8]

2. To radically improve the economic base of regions most seriously affected by industrial decline

3. To combat long-term unemployment

4. To address the labor market problems of young people

---

[7]The European Social Fund (ESF) existed since the beginnings of the Europe of Six. The European Regional Development Fund was established in 1975, in the aftermath of the expansion of the early 1970s. The third structural fund was made up of the guidance component of the CAP. A fourth structural fund was added in 1993—for fisheries.

[8]This single objective absorbed three-quarters of total regional expenditure in 1999, and practically all goes to Portugal, Spain, Southern Italy, Eastern Germany, and the overseas departments of France.

5. To promote rural development and structural adjustment in agriculture and fisheries

6. To assist regions with an extremely low population density

Expenditure on the structural funds will necessarily rise with the accession of the poorer countries of eastern Europe. Although the Czech Republic and Slovenia are relatively prosperous, their per-head income is less than 50 percent of the EU average, even when measured in purchasing power terms. Other potential entrants have incomes as low as 20 percent of the average.

INDUSTRIAL POLICY

Although much smaller than the agricultural or the structural funds, the next largest item in the EU budget is expenditure on internal policies, embracing research and development, industrial subsidy, and transportation. Together these activities take almost 6 percent of the total budget.

General Trends in European Industrial Policy

European nations have traditionally taken an interventionist stance on economic development, a feature that distinguished a "continental school," more inclined to government intervention than the **laissez faire** Anglo-Saxon school more dominant in Great Britain and the United States. Furthermore, since the early 1970s Europeans have been concerned that the EU lags behind the United States (and Japan) in technology, in the ability to grasp scale economies, and in finance. Finally, many Europeans feared that U.S.-based multinational corporations had established an almost irresistibly dominant position.[9] These concerns nurtured a series of initiatives specifically directed to putting European industry on a more competitive footing.

National Industrial Policy and the Era of National Champions

As the single market in Europe emerged, member nations instituted industrial policy that favored the promotion of "national champions" with the size and resources to compete in the European arena. National antitrust policy was jettisoned in the face of growing competition from other European firms, and governments engaged in brokered mergers designed to grasp the largest share of the European market. This "new mercantilism" ran counter to the logic of division of resources and comparative advantage that underpinned the idea of the common

---

[9]This belief was articulated in a popular book authored by Jean Jacques Servan-Schreiber, *The American Challenge (Le Defi Americain)* (New York: Athenaum, 1968).

market. It was also a limited and expensive policy, and one doomed to failure if, as indeed seemed to be the case, the European high-tech and communications industry lost to rivals in North America and the Far East. The use of nontariff barriers and subsidies to promote national champions in each of the countries led to a fragmentation of the market, and the consequent reduction in competition within Europe was itself a key ingredient in the loss of global competitiveness and the failure to innovate.

The Industrial Policy of the EU

As barriers to trade and investment came down within the EC, it became apparent that a truly European stance on industrial policy was necessary. One possibility involved the Commission working to promote the development of "European Champions" able to compete against the giants of North America and Japan in the same way that national governments had acted in the 1960s and 1970s. This approach had several potential defects. First, it favored creating great market power within the Community, to the probable detriment of European consumers. It also failed to give European industry access to advanced technology from Japan and the United States while many companies looked to mergers and joint ventures with non-European firms as a more attractive avenue. Rather than risk these outcomes, the Commission assumed a facilitating, but not an active role, limiting its activities to the removal of fiscal and legal impediments to cross-border mergers.

EU industrial policy is based in the belief that public authorities can play a vital role in promoting successful competitive strategies and that comparative advantage can be created by policy initiative rather than being the result of factor endowment alone. However, in theory at least, EU industrial policy rejects outright protectionism and favors market orientation.

Its most important dimension is fostering collaborative research and development initiatives. These policies started in the early 1980s when the "technological gap" by which Europe lagged the United States and Japan was estimated at between one and two years. The Commission considered two broad strategies to catch up. One, strongly preferred by the French, was to erect protective barriers around the markets for sensitive products; behind these walls European firms would grow strong enough to meet potential international competition. This strategy was rejected by the majority of nations because it would have insulated Europe from the global competitive trends. Instead a policy of promoting Community-wide cooperation and collaboration in research and development was adopted. First the Commission would identify industries that were at risk of falling further behind, then a jointly funded international research effort involving all of Europe's leading firms in the industry would be established.

Information technology was seen as the greatest risk, and in 1982 the European commissioner for industrial affairs, Viscount Davignon, succeeded in getting the heads of the 12 largest European electronics firms around one table. As a result, the **European Strategic Programme for Research in Information Technology**

(ESPRIT) was born. The program's emphasis was on precompetitive basic research, and it operated on a multiyear planned basis. Its success is questionable. It initiated cross-border cooperation and established agreement on basic standards and protocols, but it has not succeeded in closing the technology gap, although it can be argued that the gap would have widened in its absence.

Despite the uncertain record, ESPRIT's promise was enough to encourage imitators, notable for the subtlety of their acronyms, if not for their results. A new program for **Basic Research in Industrial Technology (BRITE)** and another that sought to perform Research in Advance Communications for Europe (RACE) were two examples. Finally, collaborative research was sought even beyond the borders of the EC. The **European Research Coordinating Agency (EUREKA),** an agency to institute shared research throughout western Europe, was established in 1985.

In most industries, heavy-handed protectionist and national champion policies were abandoned in favor of greater market logic, augmented and rationalized by the use of collaborative research; the exceptions to this were the defense and aerospace industries. These industries, not subject to initiatives from the European Union itself, were organized and promoted by agreements between national governments and companies acting through consortia. The most prominent of these is the Airbus Industrie, which is a subsidized and aggressive attempt to maintain European production of civilian air transport and to seize part of the global market from Boeing, which as a result of growth and merger had a near global monopoly.

European industrial policy has been most evident not in the promotion of growth but in easing the death throes of industrial contraction. The ancestor of today's EU was the European Coal and Steel Community, largely concerned with managing a downturn in demand in those basic industries. In steel, for example, the Commission considered itself faced with a crisis. It has at times organized the cartelization of the industry, used quotas to divide output between national firms, and adopted both price guidelines and required minimum prices to avoid "excess" competition between producers and to coordinate an orderly reduction in overall output. The EU has also interceded with foreign suppliers to initiate voluntary export restraint. However, it also acted in both steel and textiles to prevent the subsidy of output by member governments. Any government grants to industry were only allowable if they were a part of a systematic industrial restructuring designed to reduce output in the medium term.

Competition Policy

In its early years the EC lacked a centralized competition policy. Each member country had its own approach, but only Britain, France, and Germany had effective antimerger legislation. The growing integration of the European market brought with it the need for a European policy, although member countries were reluctant to relinquish their authority to Brussels. As a compromise it was agreed that only large mergers would be an issue for the EU. If the combined annual turnover of the merging firms was in excess of ECU 5 billion, and at least ECU 250 million of that

THE GE-HONEYWELL MERGER

In 2001, the EU Competition Directorate headed by its Italian Commissioner Mario Monti, earned the distinction of squelching the world's largest ever industrial merger—the $42 billion offer of General Electric for Honeywell. These companies, both of which had considerable markets in aviation-related industry, were set to merge and already had secured the approval of U.S. authorities. However, the European authorities saw in the merger strong anti-competitive elements and produced a series of theories of how the merger might harm competition. One was that the merged entity would enjoy dominance in avionics; another was that the "bundling" of GE's financial might with Honeywell's expertise in instrumentation would force customers to buy packages of products rather than supporting independent suppliers.

The American attitude was that the competition agency's antagonism lay more in seeking to protect European producers than in protecting European consumers. GE offered to divest a substantial part of the avionics production of the merged firm, but balked at the amount demanded by the EU. In the end GE walked away from the deal to the dissatisfaction of Honeywell shareholders, giving ample proof of the effectiveness, though perhaps not the benefits, of EU competition policy.

---

turnover was in nations of the EU, Brussels could act; otherwise action would be guided by national regulations.

These rules give European regulators a reach well beyond Europe's borders. For example, when the world's largest aircraft manufacturer, Boeing, sought to merge with McDonnell Douglas in 1997, the joint turnover and European sales put the case within the EU purview, and the deal was saved only by an eleventh-hour compromise but the 2001 GE-Honeywell merger was prevented (see the boxed feature). One of Europe's merger problems stems from an asymmetry in the ease of hostile takeovers between countries. Takeovers are more feasible where an active **market for corporate control** is present. When most companies are publicly traded, rather than held by large institutional or family investors, the chance of rivalry for control increases, which can be an effective means of correcting managerial failure and ensuring that investors get full share value. Within the EU, the market for corporate control is most active in the United Kingdom, which has a high ratio of stock capitalization to GDP (112 percent in 1994) and an active stock market. As barriers to international mergers fall, takeovers and industrial restructuring are occurring in the United Kingdom at a rapid pace. In countries characterized by low market capitalization (34 percent of GDP in France and only 26 percent in Germany in 1994), the scope for mergers is much more limited.

In many countries, other factors augment the barriers to takeovers caused by low stock market activity. These factors included the predominance of family holdings in Italy, the important role of banks as shareholders in Germany, and legislation against hostile takeovers in France. Thus merger policy represents another example of the clash between an Anglo-Saxon market-reliant approach and a continental model (which we also see in Japan) that puts greater emphasis on long-term relations between investors, managers, and employees.[10] A certain irony arises as the lowered barriers to intra-European mergers make firms in the market-oriented United Kingdom easy takeover targets for German and French companies that subscribe to an approach that puts much less reliance on short-term value realization. The British in turn lobby for a level playing field that would make continental European firms easier to acquire. Although it is conceivable, and even likely, that specific legislation that impedes mergers will be removed, the takeover barriers imposed by low capitalization, or block holding, are not easy to legislate away.

As well as being able to deny or modify mergers, the Commission also holds the power to investigate any anticompetitive arrangement and levy fines for such issues as price fixing or supply constraint. For example, it charged that a cartel existed in the cement industry and imposed fines totaling ECU 248 million on 33 producers. The Commission also tried to deny the use of subsidies for national firms and acted several times especially against "flag" airlines—including Air France, Iberia, and Olympic.

Competition policy in the EU is currently under revision. The GE-Honeywell affair (see the boxed feature) ruffled some feathers and in the summer of 2002 the Commissioner was roundly attacked, and some decisions reversed, by the European Court for overstepping its authority. The most substantial criticism is the lack of a clear theoretical underpinning to competition policy that allows the individual case officers too much discretionary authority. Reform will seek to establish clearer guidelines as to what constitutes harm to the consumer and is likely to employ the more transatlantic concepts of dynamic markets and contestable markets. It will also probably see an increase in staffing for the agency, which currently reviews about 300 mergers annually with a professional staff of only 100.

SOCIAL POLICY

What should be apparent from much of this discussion is that the prevailing social philosophy of the European Union is concerned with the construction and maintenance of what is now referred to as **cohesion**, and this approach frequently has adverse consequences for competitiveness. In some ways the debate that occupied economists in the 1960s—the two "Es," equity versus efficiency—has become within the EU the conflict of two "Cs," cohesion versus competitiveness.

---

[10]The clash of cultures was vividly illustrated in November 1999 when Vodafone of the United Kingdom attempted the takeover of Mannesmann. It was not only the biggest ever hostile takeover, it was also the first attempted hostile acquisition of a German company. The takeover was even opposed by German Chancellor Gerhard Schroeder, who opined, "Hostile takeovers destroy the culture of the company . . . those who launch such ventures in Germany underestimate the virtues of our joint [union-management] codirection. . . . For these reasons I am warning those who want to jump into such an adventure to be careful." Following a considerable increase in the offer price, Vodafone was ultimately successful in acquiring the German company (*The Economist*, February 12, 2000, p. 68).

The Problem of Unemployment

The most serious problem undermining the cohesion of the European Union as a whole is unemployment. For the bulk of the postwar period, unemployment within the countries that now make up the EU was low, especially relative to the United States. Through the 1960s and until the middle of the 1970s the rate was between 2 percent and 2.5 percent of the active workforce. However, global stagnation of the late 1970s and early 1980s saw a sharp rise to almost double digits, and despite a decline in the activity rate, it failed to fall significantly since. By 1996, more than 17 million people were registered as unemployed (see Table 11.5). In comparative terms the situation may have been worse because activity rates (the number of people in work or seeking work) fell relative to the 1960s and were even lower relative to the United States and Japan. One study estimated that the "employment gap," the difference between the employment required to employ everyone who actually wanted a job (including "discouraged workers") and actual employment was as high as 26 million. Since 1996 the situation improved but remains high at 13.5 million workers within the labor force. Add to that discouraged workers, premature retirees, and those on make-work projects and the figure is probably close to 20 million.

Causes of Unemployment in Europe

Whatever measure is used, it is clear that Europe's employment performance gives cause for alarm. It represents a nexus of problems with no easy solutions, and threatens, because of its cost, the very nature of the welfare state in the EU. Europe (as a group of nations) and the European Union (as an institution) are committed to an idea of a high degree of social stability and social cohesion. These goals indicate a strong preference for maintaining a substantial degree of social protection, guaranteeing incomes and services for those out of work, and to maintaining a commitment to a principle of "equal pay for equal work," rather than relying on the unfettered operation of a labor market. Both of these objectives tend to lessen labor

■ TABLE *11.5*

Employment and Unemployment in the EU, 1985–2001 (millions)

	1985	1991	1996	2001
1 Labor Force	151.0	167.0	168.8	178.2
2 Employment	136.0	154.0	151.5	164.7
3 Unemployment	15.0	12.9	17.3	13.5
4 Unemployment rate (%)	9.9	7.5	10.3	7.6

SOURCE: OECD.

market flexibility, creating unemployment. The high degree of joblessness entails a high degree of expenditure on social protection.

> Public expenditure on social protection averages 22 percent of GDP in EU-15 on the basis of 1990 data, approaching 35 percent in some Northern European countries, as opposed to 15 percent in the U.S. and only 12 percent in Japan. The difference in the amount spent by governments is reflected in different popular expectations; a very large majority of Europeans seem to expect their governments to provide a basic income for all, including income support for the unemployed. . . . Solidarity has become a key word in the political culture of European societies; is it likely to change in the new economic environment characterized by high rates of unemployment and the growing financial pressures on the welfare states.[11]

The System of Collective Bargaining In Western Europe most workers are covered by national wage agreements negotiated at the industry-wide level, as opposed to being subject to more flexible plant or enterprise agreements more common in the U.S. context. Individual employers, therefore have remarkably little control over what they pay their workers, a source of labor market inflexibility contributing to joblessness. The rising unemployment rates in EU countries favor the trend toward decentralization, and national and industry-wide bargaining are now losing ground. Even in countries such as Germany, where industry-wide negotiations are still the norm, an increasing recourse to "opening clauses" allows works councils and employers to negotiate amendments to these agreements at the enterprise level.

Despite these trends, decentralization is still limited in most western European countries. An International Labour Organization (ILO) report found that

> In 1995, enterprise agreements covered only 8 percent of the private sector in the Netherlands (compared to 75 percent for industry-wide agreements), 14 percent in Spain (compared to about 70 percent for industry-wide agreements) and 25 percent in France (compared to over 80 percent for industry-wide agreements). In Sweden, while central wage agreements are no longer the order of the day, bargaining at industry level remains a current practice. Even in Germany, considered a bastion of the European model, employers in the chemical and metal industries continue to favor industry-wide bargaining. The major change that has occurred is that industry-wide bargaining now offers much more scope for enterprise negotiation on day-to-day productivity issues.[12]

Although most bargaining is at the industry—not the firm—level, works councils are increasingly relied on to encourage dialogue and cooperation within the enterprise. The goal of these councils is, in most cases, to restructure work assignments in line with technological changes and competitive pressures and to maintain employment. The ILO report concludes that "with very few exceptions,

---

[11]Tsoukalis, *The New European Economy Revisited* (Oxford: Oxford University Press, 1997), p. 115.
[12]International Labour Organization, *World Labour Report*, 1996–1997.

collective bargaining in Europe focuses primarily on the issue of working time (taken here in the broadest sense: reduction, organization, job sharing, retirement, etc.) and related means of saving jobs." The same report finds that both industry-wide and enterprise level agreements show similar preoccupations: "The most frequent job-related topics are wage moderation or even reduction, reduction in working time with a corresponding drop in wages, and payment of overtime at the base rate or in the form of compensatory leave." Measures to ease access to employment, including hiring at reduced rates and increasing the number of apprenticeship places, are often parts of the agreements.

High Reservation Wages The high degree of social protection in Europe means that the cost of losing a job is much less than elsewhere, which has an impact on productivity. Furthermore, the generous income support for the unemployed means that a job search tends to be less pressured than in, say, the United States; this degree of support leads to workers adopting a high **reservation wage**, defined as the lowest wage that will induce an unemployed person to accept a job. The "replacement" rate (the percentage of take-home pay that continues to be received after loss of employment) varies from country to country within the EU and according to family circumstance, as well as with the duration of unemployment. In France, for example, a married person with two children receives 88 percent of take-home pay when first unemployed. The Organization for Economic Cooperation and Development (OECD) average is a more modest 77 percent, largely because of low replacement levels in the United States. Even by the 60th month of unemployment, a French worker would still receive 83 percent of initial in-work take-home pay.[13] Recognizing these high levels of support as being in part responsible for unemployment, European governments struggle to contain the costs of social protection and to lower benefit levels. Until 1993, an unemployed worker in Sweden would receive more than 90 percent of in-work pay when first unemployed. Reforms in 1993 reduced that amount to 80 percent and in 1996 it was further reduced to 75 percent.[14]

A case can be made for the economic efficiency of more protracted periods of unemployment, because a longer period of search should ultimately ensure a better match between the requirements of the vacancy and the skills of the applicant. Moreover, European nations tend to pay close attention to active labor market policy, using government institutions to place the unemployed and using job training schemes and public employment as a means of changing the skills of the unemployed. However, while labor exchanges might speed up the process somewhat, the high level of income protection means a loss of urgency on the part of the job seeker and leads to higher rates of unemployment and a less flexible labor market.

---

[13]OECD, *Economic Survey of France*, 1996–1997, p. 81.
[14]European Parliament, Directorate General for Research, "Social and Labour Market Policy in Sweden," W-13, 39, July 1997.

Nonwage Costs Even though the maintenance of social solidarity is a priority in the EU, concern about its cost is growing. Transfers to the unemployed, the disabled, and the elderly are generally financed by heavy payroll taxes, nominally shared by employers and workers, although the real incidence drives up the cost of labor and acts as a deterrent to taking on more workers. The actual burden varies from nation to nation within the EU. France, for example, with its generous social protection scheme, has experienced one of the sharpest increases in the level of unemployment. This shift has instituted a vicious cycle: rising unemployment pushes up the total cost of social protection, causing in turn an increase in the payroll taxes. However, because payroll taxes are levied on a shrinking workforce and must support more dependents, the tax rates must rise, discouraging employment. By the mid-1990s the combined payroll tax on the lowest paid, and least skilled, workers was about 62 percent, with employers paying social security contributions of about 40 percent of gross wages and the employees contributing an additional 22 percent.[15] Thus, although increases in wages themselves were moderating, real costs for unskilled labor in France were about 40 percent higher than in the United States.

Table 11.6 shows the total taxes (payroll—both employers' and employees' shares—and income taxes) that fall on wage income of the members of the EU. The various components of the total tax bite vary by country,[16] but in every country a sizable "wedge" distorts the labor-leisure decision and raises costs to employers, creating a bias for off-shore production and capital intensity.

Fragmented Labor Markets Although the European Union constitutes a single economic space, its labor market is highly fragmented because regional, national, cultural, and linguistic differences cause pockets of high unemployment to coexist with areas of tight labor demand. This fragmentation occurs even within a single member country. For example, unemployment in northern Italy's Alto Adige region is only 3.4 percent, a figure that would be regarded as close to full employment by most economists, whereas in Campania and Calabria in the south (barely a day's drive), the rate is more than 25 percent. Within the EU as a whole even wider differences exist. Luxembourg has a jobless rate of 3.2 percent, while Andalucia, a poor region of southern Spain, experiences 32 percent unemployment, an unusually pronounced difference in the absence of legal barriers to the movement of labor. In fact labor flows among the nations of the EU actually decreased as the barriers to movement have been removed. "The internal market programme seems to have had very little effect on Intra-EU labour flows which remain very small. Thus, labour mobility should not be expected to play a significant role as a means of economic adjustment in the context of a . . . monetary union."[17]

---

[15]OECD, *Economic Survey of France* 1996–1997, p. 71.

[16]Denmark, for example, provides generous social protection, but finances it almost entirely out of general tax revenue and has only a small social insurance tax.

[17]Tsoukalis, *The New European Economy Revisited* (Oxford: Oxford University Press, 1997), p. 120.

■ **TABLE 11.6**

				Total Taxes on Labor in the EU	
	Income Tax	Employee	Employer	Total SSCs	Total
Belgium	21.4	10.5	24.7	35.2	56.6
Denmark	32.4	11.7	0.4	12	44.4
Germany	17.3	17	17	34	51.3
Greece	1.8	12.4	21.9	34.3	36.1
Spain	9.3	4.9	23.4	28.3	37.6
France	10.4	9.6	28.1	37.7	48.1
Ireland	13.6	4.6	10.7	15.2	28.8
Italy	14.2	6.9	25.3	32.2	46.4
Luxembourg	11.2	12.1	12	24	35.2
Netherlands	5.3	25.3	13.9	39.2	44.5
Austria	7.4	13.8	24	37.7	45.1
Portugal	5.4	8.9	19.2	28.1	33.5
Finland	21.4	5.6	20.6	26.2	47.5
Sweden	19.5	5.3	24.7	30	49.5
United Kingdom	14.5	7.2	8.5	15.8	30.3
EU15	14	11.4	19.6	31	45
United States	16.6	7.2	7.1	14.3	30.9
Japan	6.3	9.1	9.4	18.5	24.8

SOURCE: Eurostat.

The Antiemployment Bias of Growth Europe's performance was not strong during the 1990s, and certainly unemployment would be lower had the aggregate growth rate been higher. But as Table 11.7 shows, Europe's growth, at least through the mid-1990s, remained "antiemployment" in its character, both in the absolute and when compared to the United States and Japan. At 1.4 percent per year, European growth rate was slower than that of the United States, which averaged 2.3 percent per year over the same period. However, the residual growth of GDP that cannot be explained by increases in the employment of factors of production was more rapid than in the United States. Such growth, so-called total factor productivity growth (TFP), is generally ascribed to technical progress and innovation. TFP alone accounted for 1 percent of Europe's 1.4 percent average growth performance. In addition, the European economies substituted increased capital for labor, and this increase in capital accounted for a further 1.1 percent annual expansion. Labor employed actually fell. Although economists regard growth due to both technical change and capital deepening as a positive long-term development for an economy, the consequence for Europe in the medium term is growing unemployment.

In short, Europe's slow pace of growth is biased toward economizing on labor, which results in growing joblessness. The data of Table 11.7 are merely an accounting

■ TABLE 11.7

Output, Productivity, and Capital Labor Substitution (annual percentage rates)

	1961–1973	1974–1985	1986–1995	1986–1990	1991–1995
1. Technical Progress = TFP Growth					
European Union	2.8	1.0	1.2	1.5	1.0
United States	0.6	0.9	0.8	0.6	0.9
Japan	6.3	1.1	0.9	2.3	–0.5
2. Macroeconomic Capital-Labor Substitution = Labor Saving Growth (2 = 3 — 1)					
European Union	1.5	1.0	0.7	0.4	1.1
United States	0.3	0.1	0.1	0.0	0.2
Japan	1.8	1.6	1.1	1.2	1.1
3. Apparent Labor Productivity Growth (3 = 5 + 2)					
European Union	4.4	2.0	1.9	1.9	1.9
United States	1.9	0.5	0.8	0.6	1.1
Japan	8.2	2.7	2.0	3.6	0.6
4. Employment Creating Growth (4 + 5 = 3)					
European Union	0.3	0.0	0.4	1.3	–0.5
United States	1.9	1.8	1.7	2.1	1.2
Japan	1.3	0.7	0.9	1.0	0.7
5. Actual GDP Growth (5 = 1 + 2 + 4)					
European Union	4.7	2.0	2.3	3.3	1.4
United States	3.9	2.3	2.5	2.8	2.3
Japan	9.7	3.4	2.9	4.6	1.3

SOURCE: European Commission.

of this process; the causes include the system of collective bargaining, the high reservation wage brought about by generous social protection, high nonwage costs, and fragmented labor markets. To this list should probably be added another factor: the shift to more restrictive fiscal policy occasioned by the Maastricht criteria and the growth and stability pact.

The EU Program on Unemployment

The Commission and the European Council are aware that unemployment threatens social cohesion, despite the paradox that joblessness has been created by an attempt to promote social cohesion through highly redistributive policies. At the 1994 meeting of the European Council in Essen, an outline plan to address unemployment was presented, building on a 1990 White Paper on Employment and Growth. The plan envisaged five sets of policies to tackle the joblessness problem.[18]

Some of these are rather "old hat" and represent the repetition of long-held beliefs rather than a true change in policy. Among these policies is a faith in **vocational training** and **life-long education**, and aid for groups most hard hit by unemployment. It also establishes a commitment to "increase the **employment-intensiveness** of growth." However, among the more innovative ideas is a wage policy that encourages labor-intensive investment by moderating wage increases to a rate below the growth of productivity. Another is a series of initiatives, particularly at regional and local levels, that create jobs in the environmental and social services spheres. The European Council also attempted to come to grips with some of the root causes of unemployment—high nonwage labor costs and income support policies that are "detrimental to readiness to work."

REDISTRIBUTION AMONG NATIONS IN THE EU

The European Union is a redistributive organization. A variety of programs redistribute income among individuals and nations. Table 11.8 gives some estimates of the extent of that redistribution. Because of administrative operations costs and the provision of foreign aid, the costs of the EU outweigh the allocated benefits by about 5 percent. Some countries benefit from administrative operations more than others. Belgium has the benefit of the Commission being located in its capital, a considerable gain to the economy of the Brussels region. Luxembourg and France also gain from the Court of Justice and the Parliament, respectively. Given these limitations we can see five consistent gainers: Greece, Ireland, Portugal, Spain, and Denmark. The first four are the poorest nations in the Union at present. The gains of some of these countries are considerable, with 2 to 5 percent of national income coming from Brussels. Denmark is relatively well off but gains disproportionately because of its higher share of subsidized agriculture in its GDP. The five consistent payers then are Germany, Britain, France, Austria, and Luxembourg. The other five members drift between being receivers and givers.

The entry of the additional twelve countries in 2004 and 2007 will change this balance. All of the newcomers are relatively poor and most are highly agricultural. Although the deal on agricultural aid cut between Germany and France will limit agricultural aid to the new members, they will inevitably be net gainers, which means the countries in the middle will doubtless have to contribute more.

---

[18]"The Presidency Conclusions" of the European Council Meeting, Essen, Germany, December 1994, available at http://www.europarl.eu.int/summits/ess1_en.htm?redirected=1.

■ TABLE *11.8*

Net Transfers through the EU Budget, 1994—2000 (receipts minus contributions expressed in € millions and as a percentage of national GDP)

	1994 ECU (in millions)	Percentage of National GDP	1997 ECU (in millions)	Percentage of National GDP	2000 ECU (in millions)	Percentage of National GDP	Share of Total EU Receipts
Austria	–	–	–886.1	–0.49	–543.5	–0.27	2.5
Belgium	–138.6	–0.07	–505.5	–0.24	–327.3	0.13	4.0
Denmark	388.7	0.32	61.8	0.04	169.1	0.10	2.0
Finland	–	–	–12.4	–0.01	216.9	0.17	1.5
France	–1,900.9	–0.17	–1,486.7	–0.12	–1,415.3	–0.10	16.7
Germany	–11,302.2	–0.65	–8,962.7	–0.48	–9,273.2	–0.47	24.4
Greece	3,934.4	4.68	4,312.5	4.05	4,373.9	3.61	1.6
Ireland	1,938.8	4.65	2,788.0	4.40	1,674.6	1.83	1.4
Italy	–1,881.3	–0.23	–1,888.2	–0.18	713.4	0.06	13.0
Luxembourg	–64.5	–0.46	–62.8	–0.39	–65.1	–0.35	0.2
Netherlands	394.5	0.32	1150	0.6	–1,224	–0.38	6.5
Portugal	–	–	514.9	1.45	2,675.4	3.07	1.5
Spain	3,354.1	0.81	5,512.2	1.15	5,055.9	0.86	7.7
Sweden	–	–	–1,210.2	–0.60	–1,177.4	–0.50	2.7
United Kingdom	1,078.3	0.13	–3,547.7	–0.05	–3,506.8	–0.25	14.3
Total	–3,143.8	–0.05	–3,802.9	–0.05	–3,998.5	–0.05	100.0

NOTE: Approximately 5 percent of all expenditure is absorbed by administrative costs or is used for development aid. These outlays cannot be apportioned among the member states and consequently the aggregate of member states' contributions to the EU budget exceeds the total for receipts.
SOURCE: Court of Auditors.

KEY TERMS AND CONCEPTS

Basic Research in Industrial
    Technology (BRITE)
cohesion
common agricultural policy (CAP)
common external tariff (CET)
consumption effect
Economic and Monetary
    Union (EMU)
employment intensiveness
European Central Bank (ECB)

European currency unit (ECU)
European Economic Area (EEA)
European Monetary Institute (EMI)
European Monetary System (EMS)
European Research Coordinating
    Agency (EUREKA)
European Strategic Programme for
    Research in Information Technology
    (ESPRIT)
laissez faire

life-long education

Lomé agreements

Maastricht criteria

market for corporate control

optimum currency area

reservation wages

stability and growth pact

structural funds

trade creation effect

trade diversion effect

vocational training

QUESTIONS FOR DISCUSSION

1. Do you think that the creation of regional organizations like the EU will hasten or impede moves to freer global trade?

2. Why does the trade creation effect enhance welfare, while trade diversion lessens it?

3. Are you surprised that the openness of the EU with respect to the rest of the world has not changed since the 1960s? What accounts for this lack of change?

4. Why was it thought necessary to improve the Maastricht criteria on potential entrants of the EMU?

5. How is the convergence issue to be handled after the creation of the EMU?

6. Is Europe an optimum currency area?

7. Why is it important to have an independent central bank for Europe?

8. Has the common agricultural policy been a success? How would you reform it?

9. Why is cohesion now the most important issue in the EU? How will enlargement change it?

10. Discuss the evolution of competition policy in the EU. Why is the EU concerned at the merger of two U.S. firms like GE and Honeywell?

11. What are the root causes of growing unemployment in the EU? Are they the result of the economic system?

RESOURCES

See Chapter 10 for useful Web sites concerning the EU.

Books and Articles

Britton, Andrew, and David Mayes. *Achieving Monetary Union in Europe.* London: Sage Publications, 1992.

Buiter, Willem, Giancarlo Corsetti, and Nouriel Roubini. "Excessive Deficits: Sense and Nonsense in the Treaty of Maastricht." *Economic Policy*, April 1993, 58–100.

Devinney, Timothy M., and William C. Hightower. *European Markets after 1992.* Lexington, MA: D.C. Heath and Co., 1991, 52.

El-Agraa, Ali M. (ed.). *The Economics of the European Community.* 3rd ed. New York: St. Martin's Press, 1990.

Field, Graham, *Euroland: Integrating European Capital Markets*, London: Euromoney, 2000.

Fossati, Amedeo, and Giorgio Panella (eds.). *Fiscal Federalism in the European Union.* Vol. 9 of *Routledge Studies in the European Economy.* New York: Routledge, 1999.

Frieden, Jeffrey, Daniel Gros, and Erik Jones (eds.). *The New Political Economy of EMU.* London: Rowman and Littlefield, 1998.

Molle, Willem. *The Economics of European Integration (Theory, Practice, Policy).* Aldershot, England: Dartmouth Publishing, 1990.

Nevin, Edward. *The Economics of Europe.* New York: St. Martin's Press, 1990.

"A Survey of Business in Europe: Present Pupils." *The Economist,* November 23, 1996, 1–16.

Swann, Dennis. *The Economics of the Common Market,* 6th ed. London: Penguin Books, 1988.

Tsoukalis, Loukas. *The New European Economy Revisited.* Oxford: Oxford University Press, 1997.

United Nations. *Economic Commission for Europe Annual Reports.*

PART FOUR Asian Economies

JAPAN: FINANCIAL PROBLEMS AND THE CORPORATE ECONOMY

JAPAN	
Area (thousand sq. km.)	378
Currency	yen
Exchange Rate (August 2002)	¥120 = US$1
Population 2000 (millions)	127
Population Growth Rate	0.3%
GNI per Capita, 2000	$34,210
GNI per Capita, PPP	$26,460
GDP Growth 1990–2000	1.3%
Value Added as % of GDP 2000 Agriculture	2%
Industry	36%
Services	62%
% of GDP Public Revenue	28.9%
Exports	10.8%

INTRODUCTION

With a population of 127 million and a GDP of roughly well over $4 trillion,[1] still the second largest in the world, Japan undoubtedly remains a formidable economic power, though much diminished from a decade ago. In the late 1980s, many politicians and economists regarded the Japanese economic system as a juggernaut on

---

[1]This figure was determined by using the current official exchange rate.

an inexorable course to being the world's leading economy. Western commentators were prone to see in Japan's interventionist policies an advantage that would lead to the eclipse of U.S. business unless strong countermeasures were enacted or Japanese practices imitated.[2] The situation is now differs significantly. In recent years, growth of real gross domestic product (GDP) in Japan lagged behind that in the United States and much of Europe; between 1990 and 2000 it was a mere 1.3 percent per year. Japan's financial system, the core of its industrial policy, is under great pressure; most banks need refinancing, and many need closing. Perhaps most important, Japan has lost self-confidence, reflected in indecisive policy making while consumers and investors lack faith in the future. Admired, envied, and imitated a decade ago, the Japanese system is now openly questioned, and reform demanded at the most fundamental level. This chapter provides an overview of the development and operation of the Japanese system and examines its prospects for success and reform.

HISTORICAL BACKGROUND

Early Development

The modern development of Japan dates from the appearance of the so-called black ships of the American Commodore Matthew Perry in Tokyo Bay in 1853. This intrusion of the world into Japan's isolationism prompted rapid social and economic change, fostered and accelerated by the restoration of the Meiji dynasty in 1868. The feudal system, which had been preserved in Japan, was brushed aside, and the warrior **Samurai** class was integrated into the civil society. Most important, the government initiated a program of state-led industrialization and modernization, which not only transformed Japan's economic base but also imbued Japanese capitalism with many of the distinctive characteristics visible today. A strong governmental role in industrial development remains a characteristic of the Japanese model. Aggressive public investment provided the basic infrastructure for growth through spending on communication, railways, postal services, and education. The government also entered direct production in many industries including steel, engineering, and shipbuilding. The financial sector to this day is dominated by the publicly owned Bank of Japan, established in 1882.

Alongside the growth of the state-sponsored industries, social pressure was used to stimulate the growth of the private sector. The government assisted and guided development, encouraging the acquisition of foreign techniques and the imitation of western industrial and military technology. The members of the Samurai aristocracy, who were at best an anachronism in Japan and who constituted a potential deterrent to progress, were financed and encouraged to undertake industrial ventures. Although not all of the new industrial class had Samurai roots, the effect of government sponsorship of a

---

[2]See, for example, Clyde Prestowitz, *Trading Places: How We Are Giving Our Future to Japan and How to Reclaim It* (New York: Basic Books, 1993).

limited number of leading families was to be one of the important features of Japanese economic development for the succeeding century.

The favored family industrial groups grew into *zaibatsu*—closely held diversified industrial and financial combines that dominated economic activity. Each combine was composed of roughly 20 to 30 firms that generally spanned the gamut of economic activity—coal mines, steelworks, shipyards, banks, trading companies, insurance, and so forth. This system led to the substantial concentration of economic power in a relatively small number of diversified groups. Mitsui, the largest of the prewar *zaibatsu*, employed about 1.8 million workers; Mitsubishi, the second largest, employed more than 1 million.

Class links between the leaders of industry and the members of the government, and the great concentration of economic power, led the Japanese political system toward corporatism, a close alliance of government, finance, industry, and, importantly in the Japanese case, the military. Economic growth in Japan was rapid, shown in Figure 12.1, which depicts an index of real gross national product (GNP) from 1885 to 1930. The early part of this period might well be termed the first

■ FIGURE *12.1*

Japanese Economic Growth 1887–1930

SOURCE: Data from Boulding and Gleason, "War As Investment," in *Economic Imperialism* (Ann Arbor, MI: University of Michigan Press, 1972), pp. 242–243.

Japanese economic miracle, during which time Japan established itself as an industrial power. Real GNP rose by 60 percent between 1887 and 1897. Despite some setbacks between 1898 and 1904, GNP doubled once again between 1905 and 1917. Growth was spurred by the onset of World War I in 1914, which sharply raised global demand for heavy industrial goods. The Japanese metal, defense, and engineering industries all benefited, and the resultant surge in exports spilled over into all sectors of the economy. The collapse of demand after 1918 hurt output in the short run, but the economy recovered by the late 1920s.

In contrast to the rest of the world economy, Japan continued to expand throughout the global depression of the 1930s. Growth was led by the surge in military purchases required for the military occupation of Manchuria and China, and continued until the onset of more general warfare in 1939, when the military burden began to crowd out industrial investment. The destruction and economic dislocation caused by the conclusion of World War II led to the complete collapse of the Japanese economy. Figure 12.2 shows that by 1946 output was well below the levels of 1930.

■ **FIGURE 12.2**

Japanese Growth 1930—1960

SOURCE: Data from Boulding and Gleason, "War As Investment," in *Economic Imperialism* (Ann Arbor, MI: University of Michigan Press, 1972).

Postwar Reconstruction

After the war, the U.S. occupation authorities radically restructured the Japanese economy. The *zaibatsu* and the close relationship between industry and state were considered by the Americans at least partly responsible for Japanese military adventurism in China and the Pacific.[3] Therefore the occupation authorities decided that breaking up the *zaibatsu* was essential to curbing future expansionism.

Subsidiary enterprises of parent holding companies were converted into independent entities and their share capital sold off. For example, the Mitsui *zaibatsu* was split into 180 nominally independent firms whose shares were then sold into and traded on an open market. However, the destruction of the Japanese economy during the war left little wealth in the hands of individuals. Most of the demand for shares of the newly independent enterprises necessarily came from other corporations, often in the form of exchange for their own shares. In fact, much of the stock in many firms was acquired by companies that were themselves former members of the same *zaibatsu*. Such "sister" companies held historical allegiances, trading links, and a high degree of proprietary information that naturally gave them interest in each other. The dissolution of the *zaibatsu* was accompanied by antitrust regulation, which was modeled on U.S. policy, but in actuality was weakly enforced. The result was that the *zaibatsu* were not eliminated but rather were transformed into **keiretsu**—diversified industrial groups similar to the *zaibatsu* but held together by interlocking shareholding rather than being held by a single parent. (More on the structure of these *keiretsu* is presented later.)

The Emergence of the "Iron Triangle"

The late 1940s and 1950s saw rapid and sustained economic growth, mostly attributable to the reemployment of the labor and capital idled at the end of the war. Japan exploited its comparative advantage in labor-intensive goods, and by 1955 output once more reached the levels of the 1930s. By 1960 the "gap" created by the war and its aftermath was largely eliminated. (See Figure 12.2.) Although expansion was rapid in the 1950s, Japan was far from a harmonious society.

Labor/management relations were contentious and strikes, frequently quite violent, were common. The government threw its weight behind the employers and helped them break the more radical labor unions, especially in the coal-mining industry. This period saw the modern model of Japanese economic system evolve more clearly. Power rested on three supports: the politicians (principally those of the Liberal Party, which held a near monopoly of government throughout the postwar period), the leadership of industry (primarily the heads of the *keiretsu*), and the planning and financial technocracy, mainly in the **Ministry of International Trade and**

---

[3]In fact, later scholarship found that the link between the traditional *zaibatsu* and the expansionist policy of the 1930s was questionable. The highest involvement seems to have been with a collection of new firms with specific interests in Manchuria and China. See Boulding and Gleason, "War as Investment," in *Economic Imperialism*, K. Boulding and T. Mukherjee, eds. (Ann Arbor, MI: University of Michigan Press, 1972), p. 253.

Industry (MITI) and the **Ministry of Finance (MoF).** This constellation of power is usually called the "iron triangle." In Japan, in contrast to most West European countries, labor took a backseat. Docile company-organized unions emerged, and aggressive collective bargaining was abandoned in return for the paternalistic principle of "life time employment."

Success of the Japanese Economy

Throughout most of the postwar period, Japan must be regarded as an immensely successful economy. From the low point of 1945, Japan enjoyed rapid and sustained year-on-year economic expansion for more than 50 years. Growth slowed over time as the potentialities for expansive growth, using underemployed factors of production, and "catchup," facilitated by importing more advanced technology from abroad, became exhausted. From an average of 4.3 percent per year in the 1970s, growth of GDP slowed to 4.0 percent in the 1980s. The pace slackened further in the 1990s and turned negative by 1998. However, Japan is today still the second largest economy in the world and is also second in terms of gross national income per head, which in 2001 measured about $35,610 in current exchange terms.[4] Unemployment remains low by international standards, although it has risen recently to levels that are uncomfortable in the Japanese context. In 2002 it reached 5.6 percent, the highest since the 1950s. For the past three decades, Japan enjoyed a balance of payments surplus and is currently the world's largest overseas investor in terms of annual capital flows, with its net creditor position fast becoming the world's largest. The distribution of income in Japan is quite even in comparison to most developed market economies, close to the social democracies of northern Europe. The average income of the top 20 percent of households is only 4.3 times that of the lowest. Japan also performs well in social terms. Conventional measures of social dislocation (crime rates, incarceration rates, etc.) are all modest relative to other developed market economies.

No single cause explains Japan's growth, and many different policy lessons can be drawn from the country's experience. Success has been attributed to the system of labor management, the determining role of industrial policy, the system of directed credit, respect for social order, and the absence of large defense expenditures that perhaps allowed for high investment rates. Nevertheless, the current slow growth of the economy sparked a critical reassessment of the Japanese model, and a skeptical reappraisal of the lessons to be learned, particularly with regard to the financial sector.

SOCIAL CHARACTERISTICS

The Japanese economy and its performance must be viewed in the context of a broader society. Westerners, particularly those in the Anglo-Saxon tradition, value

---

[4]Data are from the *World Development Report*. Comparisons are less favorable in terms of purchasing power parity because of the high cost of living in Japan, particularly for food and accommodation. In this measure Japan ranks sixth with per-head GDP of $23,400. The comparable figure for the United States is $28,740.

a market system, in part at least, for its impersonal rationality. This view is not the case in Japan. A deep sense of interpersonal responsibility permeates both society and the economy. In some ways Japanese society still resembles the vertical and reciprocal personal obligations that characterized feudalism. Relations within the firm tend to be hierarchical and, by and large, respectful. This behavior also reflects Confucian thought, which stresses personal respect for authority and mutual obligation between members of society. Consequently, while bureaucrats tend to be mistrusted in the United States, in Japan they enjoy great respect because they are the immediate embodiment of authority. Strangely to western eyes, similar respect is also often afforded to politicians, despite the almost ceaseless corruption scandals that characterize recent political life in Japan.

In Japan a high degree of individual identification with a variety of collective institutions reinforces the system of reciprocal obligation. The family is of prime importance. Children, for example, are expected to care for their parents, and they do to a much higher degree than in the United States. In Japan more than half of all retired persons live with their offspring, although this tendency is declining with time. School and university affiliations tend to be long lasting. The workers of the major firms identify with their employers to a higher degree than would be found in the United States. When asked for their occupation, Japanese are prone to tell you whom they work for, rather than what they do. This close identification is a result of the "lifetime employment" obligation of the employers to some workers (discussed later), is a relationship has come under some pressure as Japanese firms respond to economic problems by downsizing. Within firms, workers are organized in groups, or cliques, that again are characterized by personal obligation and mutual assistance.

INDUSTRIAL GROUPS—THE *KEIRETSU*

Because the prewar *zaibatsu* were considered by the United States to bear some responsibility for the aggressive nationalism that led to World War II, the U.S. occupying authorities insisted on their dissolution and, to prevent their reemergence, a ban against holding companies was written into antimonopoly legislation. The *keiretsu* groups that emerged are looser in structure than the *zaibatsu* and are held together by a variety of devices including cross-holding of shares, the use of a single group bank, reliance on a group trading company for sales and project coordination, consultation between CEOs in a presidential council, and the foundation of joint subsidiaries.

Figure 12.3 shows the eight largest conglomerate *keiretsu* in Japan, of which six are traditionally considered to be major. Three are linear descendants of the prewar *zaibatsu*: Mitsubishi, Mitsui, and Sumitomo. Each is grouped around a *sogo sosha*, or major **trading company** (discussed later) that creates a center for the group. An example of the operation of the various companies within a single "conglomerate" *keiretsu*, the Mitsubishi Group, is given in Table 12.1. This table gives only figures for the largest members of the group, the ones that themselves showed up in the *Fortune* 500 listings in 2002. The group, or "Community of Companies," as Mit-

■ **FIGURE** *12.3*

Japan's Industrial Groups: The *Keiretsu*

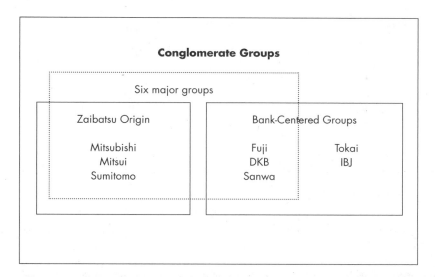

Conglomerate Groups

Six major groups

Zaibatsu Origin	Bank-Centered Groups	
Mitsubishi	Fuji	Tokai
Mitsui	DKB	IBJ
Sumitomo	Sanwa	

Vertical Groups

Total of 39 including
Nippon Steel
Hitachi
Nissan
Toyota
Matsushita
Toshiba
NEC
NTT
Seibu Saison
Nippon Oil

SOURCE: Nanto, "Japan's Industrial Groups," in *Comparative Economic Systems* (Burr Ridge, IL: Irwin, 1994), p. 238.

subishi likes to call itself, is much larger, embracing 40 major corporations in Japan and literally hundreds of overseas subsidiaries and joint ventures.

The principal way in which these groups are held together is by the cross-holding of equity capital, a practice that became prevalent immediately after the war, during the division and disposition of the *zaibatsu*. A further impetus to cross-holding of shares within a *keiretsu* was provided in the 1960s and 1970s when fears of hostile takeovers (possibly from foreign firms) arose and cross-holding presented an effective defense.

Table 12.2 shows the extent of cross-holding of shares in the major *keiretsu*, the conglomerates illustrated in Figure 12.3. These data show that 38.2 percent of the capital of all the constituent members of the Mitsubishi group is held by firms that are themselves a part of the group. It is the highest rate of cross-holding of shares of any of the major *keiretsu*. The comparable figure for the Sumitomo Group, for example, is 28.0 percent, and that for Mitsui is only 19 percent. For the **bank-centered** *keiretsu* groups (Fuji, Sanwa, and DKB), the percentage is uniformly lower. The same table also shows a greater than 55 percent probability that any one firm within a major *keiretsu* will hold shares of any other firm within the group. For the economy as a whole, Hugh Patrick, a well-known authority on the Japanese economy, estimates that the cross-holdings amount to as much as 22 percent of total paid-up capital.

■ TABLE 12.1

The Seven Largest Components of the Mitsubishi *Keiretsu*, 2001

	Revenue ($ millions)	Profits ($ millions)	Assets ($ millions)	Stockholder's Equity ($ millions)	Employment
Mitsubishi	10,5813.9	481.7	61,455.1	7,761.1	43,000
Mitsubishi Electric	2,9183.2	−623.6	30,613.5	4,087.3	116,192
Mitsubishi Tokyo Financial Group	2,6091.0	−1,218.2	750,713.5	25,083.3	22,261
Mitsubishi Motors	2,5598.0	90.0	21,839.7	2,042.2	64,000
Nippon Mitsubishi Oil	2,3520.6	192.0	25,990.9	6,972.7	14,368
Mitsubishi Heavy Industries	2,2905.0	211.5	29,541.1	9,678.3	62,753
Mitsubishi Chemical	1,4238.5	−361.9	16,947.4	2,593.6	38,617

SOURCE: *Fortune* 500, 2002.

This cross-holding not only leads to close relationships within the group, but also creates a mutuality of interest and a reason to look to group members as both suppliers and customers. On the downside, however, the impact of cross-holding is to insulate management from an impartial "market for corporate control." Shares held within the group are rarely sold, and consequently executives are largely safe from outside takeover bids. Hence a depressed share price, the failure to realize a firm's potential, does not trigger the hostile mergers and asset stripping that occur in more aggressive capitalist markets. Table 12.3 contrasts the structure of share-holding in the United States and Japan, showing why the market for corporate control is likely to be more active in the United States.

■ TABLE 12.2

Intragroup Shareholding of the Six Major *Keiretsu*

	Average Linkage to Other Members*	Average Stake Size	Ratio to Total Capitalization
Mitsubishi	75.3%	1.8%	38.2
Sumitomo	94.5	1.6	28
Mitsui	57.6	1.3	19.3
Average of the prewar *zaibatsu*	75.8	1.6	28.5
Fuji	46.8	1.3	16.9
Sanwa	27.5	1.4	16.7
DKB	29.4	1	14.2
Average of the bank-centered groups	34.6	1.2	15.9
Average of the six major groups	55.2	1.4	22.2

*Average linkage is the percentage probability that any member firm of the group holds shares in another firm within the group.
SOURCE: OECD, *Economic Surveys of Japan*, 1995–1996, p. 156.

■ **TABLE 12.3**

Shareholding of Public Companies: Japan and the United States Compared by Category

Category	U.S. Companies	Japanese Companies
Institutional investors	71.7	12.9
Financial institutions with business relationships	1.9	35.6
Nonfinancial institutions with business relationships	1.9	9.4
Parent companies or companies in same group (*keiretsu*)	1.9	30.7
Owner families	15.1	5.4
General investors	5.7	2.5
Other	1.9	3.5

SOURCE: OECD, *Economic Surveys of Japan*, 1995–1996, p. 153.

Cross-holding is not the only means by which *keiretsu* are held together. Cohesion within the group is enhanced by the operation of presidential councils, made up of the chief executive officers of the larger firms of the group. They generally convene once a month, and though they are not in theory policy-making bodies, they do discuss the current economic outlook, investment policies, market research, R&D, and other factors with a direct bearing on the efficient operation of the firms, as well as the potentialities of new business ventures. At a slightly lower level, *keiretsu* solidarity is further enhanced by the reciprocal representation of company officers on the boards of sister companies. Furthermore, startup companies to exploit new areas of business activity are often established as joint enterprises between group members, with equity capital put up by member companies, and a board including officers from the parent companies.

Conglomerate *keiretsu* groups (those with activities in a broad range of industries) are frequently grouped around a core company, which plays a leadership role in group management. Such a company may be a general integrated trading company or it may be a bank. Trading companies that specialize in sales and marketing, especially overseas, are, on this scale, institutions largely unique to Japan. Not only are the general trading companies themselves among the largest commercial operations in the world, but also each of the groups that are led by these companies has several major corporations that stand high in the *Fortune* 500 list. The *keiretsu* with origins in the prewar *zaibatsu* are also quite old, tracing their history back some hundreds of years. The boxed feature titled "The Mitsui Group" traces the history of that organization from its origins in 1568.

Other conglomerate groups are best described as bank centered. (Although the *keiretsu*, of *zaibatsu* origin, include a group bank, the lead company in these cases is the general trading company.) These groups are Fuyo (centered on Fuji Bank), DKB (Dai-Ichi Kangyo Bank),[5] and Sanwa (Sanwa Bank). These banks at the core of these

[5]These relationships became more complex in 1999 when Fuji Bank acquired both Dai-Ichi Kangyo Bank and the Industrial Bank of Japan. See Table 12.8 for details on this and other bank mergers.

THE MITSUI GROUP

The Mitsui Group is perhaps the largest business enterprise in the world. Its flagship company claims the world's oldest general trading concern, Mitsui & Co. Ltd. The group, or *keiretsu*, consists of 842 companies, of which 333 are located outside Japan. The group has major operations in construction, investment, finance, transportation, machinery, chemicals, nonferrous metals, and foodstuffs. Japan's largest liquid propane gas transport fleet is operated by a Mitsui company, and Mitsui & Co. dominates the Japanese import market for cigarettes and sports and hobby goods. The economic slowdown in Japan and the strong yen prompted Mitsui management to pursue a range of projects overseas, particularly around the Pacific Rim.

A Brief History

After they were defeated by the Japanese shogun Nobunaga, the Mitsui family fled Omi Province in 1568. Unemployed, the samurai Sokubei Mitsui opened a sake and soy sauce brewery at the urging of his wife, who eventually took over management of the business. She encouraged her sons to enter business and the youngest, Hachirobei, went to Edo (now Tokyo) and opened a dry goods store in 1673. Breaking with Japanese retailing tradition, the store offered merchandise at fixed prices on a cash-and-carry basis.

In 1683 Hachirobei started a currency exchange that ultimately evolved into Mitsui Bank. The business received a boost in 1691 when it became the Osaka government's official money changer. The bank introduced money orders to Japan and profited by securing up to a 90-day float on funds transfers between Osaka, Edo, and Kyoto. Before he died in 1694, Hachirobei wrote a nontraditional will, by which control of the business passed to all related family members, not just to the eldest son's family.

In the mid-1800s the Japanese government ordered Mitsui to help finance its war with rebels. The family hired an outsider with government links, who managed to protect Mitsui from increasing demands for cash. The company then made a timely switch of support to the victorious rebel side and Mitsui became the bank of the Meiji government at the time of the restoration. The new government encouraged, as part of its industrialization drive, and supported Mitsui's diversification into paper and textiles, and a machinery business that was an antecedent of Toshiba. Expansion in foreign trade and banking led to the creation of Mitsui Bussan (now the Mitsui & Co. trading company) in 1876. In the late 1800s the Mitsui *zaibatsu* profited from Japanese military activity, and also moved into shipping, challenging Mitsubishi's monopoly. The Mitsui family withdrew from management of the company in 1936, following a violent campaign by nationalist, expansionist fanatics against the more liberal members of the capitalist establishment.

Prior to World War II the group benefited from the Japanese military buildup. After the war, the U.S. occupation forces split the Mitsui *zaibatsu* into more than 180 separate entities. However, in 1950, 27 leaders of former Mitsui companies began meeting and the Mitsui group became established. The group has expanded rapidly in petrochemicals and metals. In 1990 Mitsui Bank and Taiyo Kobe Bank merged to form the world's second largest bank. Its recent emphasis has been on China.

keiretsu still remain, despite their present difficulties, among the most powerful financial institutions in the world. (See Table 12.8, presented later in the chapter.) Today both legislation and practice place limits on the role of the bank within the group. The law prohibits *keiretsu* banks from lending exclusively within the group and requires that nongroup borrowers receive equal access. Similarly, companies increasingly sought financing from outside the group. Both of these changes represent prudent risk diversification. Nevertheless, the role of the bank within the group continues to be important, and this aspect may be a source of inherent weakness in the Japanese system. The group bank is likely to be more compliant in granting loans to member companies and might as a result end up with a badly performing loan portfolio, reflecting a form of soft-budget constraint. Moreover, banks are unlikely to force group members into liquidation, although it may be rational for them to do so. On the other hand, proximity offers an opportunity for close monitoring of creditworthiness and loan performance.

Distinct from the conglomerate *keiretsu* are the groups that are vertically integrated and oriented around the production of a single product. Patrick identified 39 of these vertical *keiretsu*, the largest of which is the Toyota Group, focused on automobiles and parts, with involvement in distribution and finance. In 2002 Toyota was the tenth largest company in the world in terms of turnover, and its structure differs little from other automobile firms such as General Motors, which is ninth, Ford, which is fifth, or even Fiat, 49th. They are all complex groups involving all stages of manufacturing and distribution.

Despite the intent of U.S.-inspired legislation to break up the groups, tight-knit linkages reemerged in Japanese industry. Rather than a holding-company/subsidiary structure, the case in the *zaibatsu*, linkages within a *keiretsu* are subtler and more "around a circle." Successive Japanese governments took a lenient view toward the reemergence of highly concentrated power in the corporate sector. This tolerance is not surprising because the government, too, was part of the "triangle" of power and saw the existence of a relatively few groups as an easy way to facilitate policy making and implementation. Moreover, recent scandals showed that leading politicians, predominantly those of the dominant Liberal Democratic Party (LDP), received substantial bribes and illegal political contributions. However, the effect of the reemergence of the major groups on consumer welfare and economic growth is unclear. Even though the trend toward concentration did lessen competition as traditionally measured in some markets, as we will discuss in more detail later, Japanese industrial policy did foster effective competition albeit between a limited number of participants in a wide range of product markets.

The *keiretsu* system implies a closer relationship than exists between purchaser and supplier in most countries. The relationships are long term and largely nonmarket. Mutual reliance and trust replace detailed contracts (thus economizing on the services of lawyers), and an enduring sense of dependence and obligation is key. This form of relationship also extends to the many suppliers and subcontractors who are not group members but whose businesses are tightly dependent on the group. The Japanese economy contains many small and marginally profitable firms as well as global giants (a feature often termed **duality**). The impression of Japan from the outside is that most employment is within the large firms, but in fact most Japanese work in firms that employ fewer than 200 employees, which exist as suppliers to the big companies. Again, this proximity offers mixed blessings. Closeness enables stability, coordination, and such productivity-enhancing systems as **just-in-time (JIT) inventory control**. It also is conducive to tight quality control, as the ultimate user is closely involved with the supplier. Moreover, supply contracts in Japan often call for prices to fall over time based on the expectation that the amortization of capital and a leaning curve will enable costs to be cut over the long run.

On the other hand, the system entails certain costs that proponents of market coordination see as important. First, it is difficult for a new supplier to break into this tight circle. Even innovations to improved products, or lower costs, might be slow to be introduced into production. Second, the close relationships necessarily involve a high degree of interdependence and the potential for one firm's failure having repercussive effects is high. In the past the strength and dynamism of the Japanese economy made such contingencies unlikely; however, today the stability of the Japanese system is more open to question, and the risk is greater.

Distribution *Keiretsu*

A feature of the group structure in Japan is its extension into the retail market. Major manufacturers frequently establish a network of stores to handle their own products exclusively. This structure is unusual; in the United States, though a system of exclusive outlets dominates in automobile retailing, it would not be acceptable in most product lines. In some industries the groups are almost totally dominant. For example, in electronics, Matsushita owns 24,000 shops, Toshiba 11,000, Hitachi 9,000, Sanyo and Sharp, 5,000 each, and Sony 3,000. Clearly this structure can be regarded as anticompetitive, and it makes changing the existing balance of market share extremely difficult. New firms and foreign imports are at a particular disadvantage because of these substantial barriers to entry.

Trading Companies

A unique and significant feature of the Japanese economic system is the existence of the "general, integrated trading companies" or *sogo shoshas*. Although some companies operate with similar ranges of activities in western economies, they do not have the same centrality to the overall economic system as in Japan.

Among the eight major trading companies in Japan are the largest companies in the world.[6] Table 12.4 shows that in 2001 Japanese general trading companies made up 3 of the 20 largest companies in the world when measured in terms of revenues.[7] It is important to emphasize, however, that such revenue comparisons overstate the importance of these firms. In terms of assets or employment, the companies are by no means as significant. Mitsubishi, for example, ranks 12th in revenue, 103rd in assets, and 295th in terms of employment. However, purely because of its turnover, which represents enormous buying power and selling ability, the company carries great importance. Three of the largest general trading companies (Mitsui, Mitsubishi, and Sumitomo) form the core of three of the largest *keiretsu*. The trading

---

[6]The integrated Japanese trading companies are Mitsubishi, Mitsui, Itochu, Sumitomo, Marubeni, Nissho Iwai, Tomen, and Nichimen.
[7]The rankings have, in fact, been greatly altered by poor Japanese economic performance and by the "Asia crisis." In 1995 Japanese general trading companies made up five out of the six largest companies in the world measured by revenue, but by 1997 had fallen to six out of the top 20. Two other trading companies, Sumitomo and Marubeni, figure in the top 25 firms in the world.

■ **TABLE 12.4**

The 20 Largest Global Companies by Revenue, 2001

Rank Company		Revenue ($ billion)	Profits ($ billion)	Assets ($ billion)	Stockholders' Equity ($ billion)	Employees
1 Wal-Mart Stores	Retail	219,812	6,671	83,375	35,102	1,383,000
2 Exxon Mobil	Petroleum	191,581	15,320	143,174	73,161	97,900
3 General Motors	Autos	177,260	601	323,969	19,707	365,000
4 BP	Petroleum	174,218	8,010	141,158	74,367	110,150
5 Ford Motor	Autos	162,412	−5,453	276,543	7,786	352,748
6 Enron	Energy	138,718	—	—	—	15,388
7 Daimler Chrysler	Autos	136,897.3	−592.8	184,671.4	34,727.9	372,470
8 Royal Dutch/Shell Group	Petroleum	135,211	10,852	111,543	56,160	91,000
9 General Electric	Machinery	125,913	13,684	495,023	54,824	310,000
10 Toyota Motor	Autos	120,814.4	4,925.1	150,064	55,268.4	246,702
11 Citigroup	Banking	112,022	14,126	1,051,450	81,247	268,000
12 Mitsubishi	Trading	105,813.9	481.7	61,455.1	7,761.1	43,000
13 Mitsui	Trading	101,205.6	442.8	50,313.5	6,903.5	36,116
14 Chevron Texaco	Petroleum	99,699	3,288	77,572	33,958	67,569
15 Total Fina Elf	Petroleum	94,311.9	6,857.7	78,886.7	30,212	122,025
16 Nippon Telegraph &Telephone	Communications	93,424.8	−6,495.5	157,550.7	44,563.7	213,000
17 Itochu	Trading	91,176.6	241.5	35,856.7	3,000.4	36,529
18 Allianz	Insurance	85,929.2	1,453.4	839,551.1	28,192.6	179,946
19 International Business Machines	Technology	85,866	7,723	88,313	23,614	319,876
20 ING Group	Insurance	82,999.1	4,098.7	627,816	19,155.4	113,143

SOURCE: *Fortune* 500, 2002.

companies played a formative role in Japanese growth and development, and they constitute a formidable force for nonmarket-based economic coordination. First and foremost the trading companies are the eyes and ears of the *keiretsu* and the Japanese industrial base. They have been influential in identifying market demand as they scour the globe for sales opportunities, inputs, and raw materials. They also bring companies together to form joint ventures to produce new products. In short, they perform market research, provide a window on the world, take a stand on the future, and provide coordination within a group.

LABOR RELATIONS

Conventional wisdom sees the Japanese workplace as characterized by an absence of conflict revealed in a low rate of strikes, shared objectives for the firm, and a generally harmonious and consensual set of on-the-job relationships. Like many of our preconceptions about Japanese life, this picture is only partly true. Moreover, harmonious industrial relations in any real sense have only been a feature of the past 35 years. The 15 years immediately after the end of World War II were characterized by deep acrimony and even violence. However, since 1960 strike incidence was relatively low, certainly less than in the United Kingdom or the United States, but on a par with Germany.

Although the Japanese system of wage determination is in theory decentralized, it contains strong elements of national coordination. The International Labor Organization considers the state a major protagonist in industrial relations, intervening both through legislative action and the conduct of industrial policy. The most prominent form of national coordination is the *shunto*, organized annual wage bargaining, the outcome of which directly affects about 25 percent of Japanese workers and which sets a benchmark for wage increases in small and medium-sized enterprises where unionization levels are low.

Japanese industrial relations are often referred to as having three "treasures": **lifetime employment**, known in Japanese as *sushin koyo*, which protects many of the workers from being laid off; **seniority wages** *(nenko)*, which ensures that compensation increases in terms of an employee's age rather than one's responsibilities; and the widespread reliance on **company unions**. In fact, however, although these institutions are very important in some spheres of Japanese economic life, they are by no means universal. Moreover, as well as constituting advantages that have assisted Japan's remarkable growth, these so-called three treasures also entail limitations and may be detrimental to the long-term development of the economy.

Lifetime Employment Policies

Lifetime employment refers to the practice that, once employed, the firm has an obligation to retain a worker despite downturns in business activity. In return the worker recognizes his or her responsibility to work productively and to show loyalty to and identify with the company. Lifetime employment is an important feature for those who enjoy it, but it applies to only roughly 30 percent of the total workforce. It is another feature of the duality of Japanese industrial structure. Only 15 percent of all workers are employed in organizations of more than 1,000 persons, and only these larger firms offer guaranteed lifetime employment to most workers. Moreover, they exclude from coverage part-time employees and a growing force of "contract workers." The 40 percent of Japanese workers employed by firms of fewer than 30 workers never receive any explicit or implicit lifetime guarantee. A second caveat relates to the worker's age of retirement from primary lifetime employment. Lifetime employment is guaranteed only to the age of 55, but most workers need to work at least another decade. Thus even the most privileged of the workforce must find a new occupation for the last 10 years before retirement.

Table 12.5 shows that the Japanese labor market is considerably less fluid than that of other Organisation for Economic Cooperation and Development (OECD) countries. Approximately 63 percent of Japanese workers have been with their employer for more than five years compared with about 50 percent for the OECD average and less than 40 percent for the United States, which is the most labor mobile economy. The same trend is confirmed by Table 12.6, which shows that in 1995 more than 45 percent of Japanese workers aged 40 had only had one employer. Smaller Japanese

■ TABLE *12.5*

Average Employment Longevity in Selected OECD Countries (percentage of workforce)

	Less Than 1 year	1—5 years	5—10 years	10—20 years	More Than 20 years
Australia	21.4	39.2	16.2	15.2	8.1
Canada	23.5	31.9	15.2	19.4	10.0
Finland	11.9	37.3	16.7	21.4	12.8
France	15.7	26.3	16.2	25.6	15.8
Germany	12.8	28.2	17.8	24.5	16.7
Japan	9.8	27.6	19.7	23.7	19.3
Netherlands	24.0	38.4	11.4	15.2	11.0
Norway	14.9	29	19.7	24.1	12.3
Spain	23.9	22.5	14	21.3	18.4
Switzerland	17.6	32.3	16.8	18.8	13.8
United Kingdom	18.6	36.2	16.1	19.3	9.6
United States	28.8	32.9	11.7	17.8	8.8
Unweighted average	18.6	31.8	16	20.5	13

SOURCE: OECD, *Economic Surveys of Japan,* 1995–1996, p. 98.

firms, however, those that constitute the secondary sector, experience greater mobility, and the labor market is fluid, with flexible employment and wages.

Downsizing, a common phenomenon in the United States today, is much more difficult in Japan, because a sizable proportion of employees of large firms enjoy lifetime guarantees. But it is not the only cost of *sushin koyo.* Lifetime contracts are also an impediment in getting the "right people to the right job." They present a barrier to promotion based on ability and may stifle corporate innovation and progressiveness. Deadwood accumulates at the middle management level, and it is difficult to reward the productivity and initiative of younger workers. This

■ TABLE *12.6*

Percentage of Male Graduates in Japan with Only One Employer

	Age			
	40	45	50	55
1980	37.6	30.9	20.2	6.3
1985	45.4	34.4	24.8	12.5
1990	42.9	42.5	29.1	16.2
1995	45.3	40.4	35.3	21.7

SOURCE: OECD, *Economic Surveys of Japan,* 1995–1996, p. 100.

problem is in part resolved by the fact that the lifetime contract covers workers only into their early fifties, rather than their middle sixties, the normal retirement age in the United States. Workers are expected to move on at that time to another post if they have not risen appropriately in the company. Here another feature of the Japanese system comes into play—the close relationship between a firm and its suppliers. Many larger companies try to place their senior workers and middle management with their suppliers, who often cannot refuse for fear of upsetting an important business relationship and who sometimes see it as an advantage for deepening relations.

Seniority Wages

In some sectors of the Japanese economy, wages are more dependent on length of service than is the common practice in other developed economies. Managerial pay is less a function of perceived individual productivity than the number of years an employee already spent with the firm. Like guaranteed employment, the scope of this *nenko* system is limited and generally applies only to those privileged workers who have a lifetime commitment with the firm.

The combination of lifetime employment and seniority wages presents larger Japanese firms with serious problems. Because the natural management structure in most organizations is pyramidal, the upper echelons of Japanese management tend to become crowded as a cohort advances. Enough productive upper management positions are simply not available for those whose seniority with the company would qualify them. Moreover, a seniority wage demands that these employees be paid more than their younger colleagues, who because of their education, energy, and competence might logically be better paid and faster advancing. The net result is an overcrowded, and overpaid, management structure that is a drag on profits in good times and is dangerous to the livelihood of the company in recessions.

Company Unions

The third of Japan's "treasures" is the institution of company unions. More than 80 percent of unionized workers are organized in unions that are unique to the organization for which they work. In other countries, occupational unions organized across firms are more often the rule. From the perspective of collective bargaining, the system is not altogether unique, however. Where Japanese practice does differ is in the close consultation and information flow between the unionized workers and management that usually takes the form of a consultation meeting, held monthly, in which issues of management policy, production plans, and work practices are raised. This high degree of consultation means that unions, and their workers, operate closely in line with the company and tend to identify with it.

This system of company unions and consultation was introduced during the 1950s in an attempt to reduce militancy, lower the high degree of labor conflict, and combat the possibility of rising communist power. The government and employers confronted the unions in a series of important industrial actions in the steel and coal industries. In the aftermath of the 1970's oil shocks, many more large companies established worker-employer cooperation committees, which continue today and which many non-Japanese enterprises have sought to imitate. Unions are a major factor in facilitating the committees. In 1994, 56 percent of enterprises maintained such committees, but in enterprises where labor unions are present, the figure was 81 percent, versus 32 percent for nonunion enterprises.

The degree of unionization in large enterprises remains high in Japan, but it is balanced by low levels of union representation in small firms. In 1993, trade union membership in enterprises with more than 1,000 workers stood at an average of 58.2 percent, compared to only 1.8 percent in enterprises with fewer than 100 employees. Although the large company union is under no real threat, the pressure felt by the union movement worldwide is also apparent in Japan. The problem of getting a job amid mounting unemployment makes Japanese workers in second-tier labor markets increasingly individualistic. Nearly half of all small and medium-sized enterprises encourage alternative forms of representation for determining conditions of employment.

Active Labor Market Policy

One consequence of the high longevity of job occupancy and the low level of unemployment is that the scope of active labor market policy (those policies designed to retrain workers, match applicants and vacancies, and provide public-sector employment) in Japan is limited, as shown in Table 12.7. In a highly interventionist state, this aspect is surprising. Japan spends only one-tenth of 1 percent of its GDP on active labor market policy, about the same as the United States. Germany, in contrast, spends more than 1.3 percent of its GDP on active labor intervention, which is still low compared to the Nordic countries, especially Sweden. This difference is in part explained by the historically low unemployment rate, but Japan also displays a low intensity of expenditure. The share of GDP expended per unemployed worker is also very low—about one-half the OECD average.

■ **TABLE 12.7**

Expenditure on Active Labor Market Policy: Selected OECD Countries, 1995

	Expenditure (percentage of GDP)	Unemployment Rate (percentage of labor force)	Expenditure Intensity
United States	0.2	5.6	0.04
Japan	0.1	2.9	0.04
Germany	1.3	9.4	0.14
France	1.2	12.3	0.1
Italy	0.9	10.5	0.09
United Kingdom	0.5	8.2	0.06
Canada	0.6	9.5	0.06
Average (unweighted)	0.7	8.3	0.07

SOURCE: OECD, *Employment Outlook*. OECD, *Economic Surveys of Japan*, 1995–1996, p. 125.

FINANCIAL STRUCTURE

The Japanese financial system is characterized by four essential features. First, the central bank, the Bank of Japan, with only limited independence, functions largely as an arm of government policy rather than an independent balance to the administration. Second, the highly concentrated system of commercial banks operates closely with the government, which has strongly influenced their lending patterns while limiting competition between them. Third, a high degree of functional separation between the various forms of financial intermediaries is maintained. The government promised to deregulate the financial sector to lower these barriers (discussed later), but so far achieved little. Fourth, the high rate of household saving finds only a limited choice of investment instruments. Most household saving, and 20 percent of all saving in Japan, is gathered through the postal savings system, universal across Japan and the prime means of saving for the less affluent. The postal savings bank has more than $1 trillion in assets. Savings are accumulated by the postal savings system and then passed through the Bank of Japan, the central bank, to the city banks.

Unlike the European Central Bank or the U.S. Federal Reserve, the Bank of Japan (BoJ) has no pretensions to independence and generally acts in concert with the government. Its importance as a tool of macroeconomic policy is not especially surprising or unique. However, unlike most other central banks, the BoJ plays an important role in microeconomic industrial policy because it enables the system of directed credit to priority industries to function.

The Banks

The large commercial banks of Japan are known as the city banks. The late 1990s saw a period of aggressive consolidation, the largest instance of which was the merger of the Industrial Bank of Japan (IBJ) with Dai-Ichi Kangyo Bank (DKB) and Fuji Bank, which produced Mizuho Holdings, the largest financial corporation in the world as measured in assets.[8] The remaining six banking groups, and the recent mergers are shown in Table 12.8.

City banks play a key role in fostering and financing the projects that are favored by the Ministry of International Trade and Industry (known as MITI). The process of industrial policy in Japan is more fully discussed later, but the essential procedure is that a dialogue between MITI and industry determines the sectors and projects that are to receive priority treatment. MITI then determines exactly which companies are to have the central role, and the next step is to ensure that the required finance is available. At this point, MITI consults with the Bank of Japan and the Ministry of Finance, and the BoJ provides the necessary liquidity to the banks that will be responsible for providing the financing, under the general umbrella of the Fiscal Investment and Loan Program.

---

[8]At the time of the merger in 1999 assets were ¥141 trillion ($1,270 billion), and it had 645 branches, and 34,000 employees. Assets fell after the merger, the result of bad loans, but it is still the largest bank in the world in terms of assets with $1,419 billion.

■ TABLE 12.8

The Major Japanese Banks, 2001

	Previously	Revenues ($ million)	Profits ($ million)	Assets ($ million)	Stockholders' Equity ($ million)	Rate of Return on Assets 2001
Mizuho Holdings	Fuji Bank Dai-Ichi Kangyo Bank Industrial Bank of Japan	41,445.1	−7,806	1,141,667	35,699	−0.68%
Sumitomo Mitsui Banking	Sakura Bank Sumitomo Bank	30,228.6	−3710	814,908.5	21,976	−0.46%
Mitsubishi Tokyo Financial Group	—	26,091	−1,218.2	750,713.5	25,083.3	−0.16%
UFJ Holdings	Sanwa Bank Tokai Bank Tokyo Trust	25,299.9	−9,816.5	601,895.1	19,623.1	−1.63%
Norinchukin Bank	—	12,939.1	564.7	434,446.7	14,198	0.13%
Daiwa Bank Holdings	—	10,887.5	−7,425.8	339,171	9,726.1	−2.19%

SOURCE: *Fortune* 500, 2002.

A fundamental criticism of this system is that the banks in Japan are simply not allowed to act as rational and profit-maximizing entities, which is essential to market discipline, but are rather the tools of the bureaucracy. This limitation implies that they cannot fulfill the impartial role in assessing the viability of investment projects, which is essential for the capital market to do its job. It has now become clear that the MITI officials frequently erred in their assessment concerning which projects to support; as a result they induced banks to make loans to enterprises that failed to show the appropriate economic viability. This failure saddles the banks with nonperforming loans and jeopardizes their financial stability.

As Table 12.8 shows, Japanese banks are still large and powerful in terms, but their poor performance in recent years certainly reduced their stature as global players. A few years ago 8 of the world's 10 largest banks measured in terms of assets were Japanese. However, their assets shrank because of the high number of nonperforming loans in their portfolios. Five out of the six major banking groups actually incurred losses in 2001, and the rate of return on assets of the other was only 0.13 percent. Japan's banks are not particularly inefficient in their day-to-day operations, and the revenue from loans exceeds borrowing and other costs. However, the need to perpetually increase the bad loan provisions swamps operating profits and leads to overall losses. The OECD estimates that the Japanese commercial banking sector lost ¥70.5 trillion in bad loans in an seven-year period from 1994 to 2000.[9] This amount is roughly equivalent to 13 percent of Japan's current annual GDP. Most of these bad loans entered the bank's portfolio because of the system of directed credit of the government influence on the banks' lending decisions. In turn the problems of the banks contributes to financial instability in Japan and lay behind the larger Asian banking crisis. The Japanese government publicly estimates that non-performing loans in the asset sheets of banks stand at ¥37 trillion (about 7% of GDP). Many observers think that this figure is optimistic, and a consensus is closer to ¥80 trillion. *The Economist* reports that Goldman Sachs, the U.S. investment bank, put the likely total of bad debts as high as ¥170 trillion in 2000.[10] Conditions worsened since then, with both industrial companies and real estate loans turning bad.[11] If the higher figure is true, then bad debt amounts to almost one-third of Japan's GDP, in addition to the 13% of GDP that the banks have already conceded as lost.

Deregulating the Financial System

Japan still relies heavily on a system of **directed credit** that requires the banking sector to be responsive to and complicit in the government's investment plans, largely through the Fiscal Investment and Loan Program (FILP), probably the largest government-sponsored loan program in the world. As a result, the financial system in Japan was highly regulated by a plethora of rules designed to control the banks and to limit competition, especially from abroad. Critics inside Japan and overseas increasingly regarded this protectionism as a weakness of the Japanese system, and they intensified pressure for a comprehensive package of financial-market reforms. The government launched such a reform package in June 1997. It was known as the **big bang**, because it was similar on paper to the reforms known by the same name in the United States in the 1970s and in Britain in the 1980s. Measures phased in over a five-year period ending in 2002 were expected to transform the Japanese financial landscape. However, in reality the reforms were more cosmetic than substantive and a weak and over-regulated financial sector still lies at the heart of the troubled economy. When Prime Minister Koizumi assumed office in April 2001 he promised a renewed reform effort. However, entrenched opposition from within the LDP, the bureaucracy, and the banks delayed the onset of reform. Subsequently, Koizumi's prestige slipped while the required reform failed to occur. The creation of a modern efficient financial sector depends on reform in several areas.

Reducing Financial Repression An advantage enjoyed, and exploited, by Japanese firms is cheap capital, the result of **financial repression**. The government limits the opportunities for small savers and forces them to put their money in low-yielding deposit accounts, generally in the postal savings system (PSS). Deposit insurance in the private sector is much more limited than in the United States and for safety the majority of small savers turn to the PSS because of the security it offers, despite the extremely low interest rates. These savings are recycled through the

---

[9]See *OECD: Economic Survey of Japan*, November 2001, Table 11, p. 53.
[10]"Survey of Japan," *The Economist*, April 18, 2002.
[11]Average commercial real estate prices in Japan's 10 biggest cities fell by 84 percent between 1991 and 2001.

Bank of Japan and the city banks to become the source of low-interest investment funds for prioritized sectors through the FILP. The "big bang" legislation proposed the end of repression, allowing small savers access to higher interest instruments.

Critics were skeptical of the outcome, and their suspicion proved well-founded. For one thing, the end of repression would have created a mismatch in the term structure of bank balance sheets. The assets of banks are long term, consisting largely of industrial and housing loans). The withdrawal of savings in pursuit of higher interest would potentially exacerbat the crisis in the banking sector, just as parallel reforms in the United States crippled the savings and loan industry. Given the fragile state of banking in Japan at present, the reform can proceed without the commitment of extensive government subsidies to banks in the short to medium term. Moreover, the essence of the Japanese industrial policy lies in the use of directed credit. Opening opportunities for small savers would inevitably reduce the leverage of the bureaucrats and the LDP to favor prioritized projects. Although this option might enhance efficiency, it would also involve a reduction in bureaucratic power that the authorities might be unwilling to allow.

Cutting Financial Market Segmentation The Japanese system follows a "Glass-Steagall" style of regulation, creating legal barriers between commercial banking, investment banking, brokerage, and insurance. Everywhere in the world market forces are tending to erode these distinctions, and changes in technology are making them obsolete. In Japan, regulatory change must accommodate these shifts, but the fragile banks need continued protection from competition.

The Role of Foreign Financial Intermediaries The weakness of Japanese banking forced the government to recognize that foreign financial intermediaries perform better than their domestic counterparts. The big bang in theory allowed a more level playing field and should have let foreign banks, brokerages, and insurance companies into the Japanese market. One substantial problem is that the efficiency differential between "best worldwide practice" and average Japanese performance is huge. It may force Japanese companies to the wall or open them to acquisition by foreign firms. Given the traditional protectionist bent of Japanese policy, the government's move to preserve the essentially Japanese character of the banking sector remains somewhat slow.

INDUSTRIAL POLICY

The Japanese system embodies a high degree of "industrial policy," the active intervention of the government to promote or change the course of industrial development. Of course, Japan is not alone. Many countries actively institute policies to promote industrial growth, and many examples may be taken from history. However, in Japan industrial policy assumes a comprehensiveness that prompted some observers to use the rather biting sobriquet of "Japan Inc." It is useful to distinguish, however, between what Hugh Patrick has termed **macroeconomic industrial policy** and its microeconomic counterpart.

Macroeconomic Industrial Policy

This category embraces measures designed to increase the pace of overall industrial growth, while having only a limited impact on industrial structure. Such policies include measures to promote savings, to provide universal and accessible education, to protect industry from overseas competition, and to stimulate exports. All of these measures, as long as they provide a level playing field across industry and do not favor any particular sector or type of firm, are not particularly invasive. They have long been a part of the Japanese scene and led to a large share of the country's savings finding its way to the industrial groups, rather than to consumer spending or investment in social projects—like housing. On the whole, such macroeconomic industrial policy successfully accelerated the pace of industrial growth, albeit at the expense of the consumer.

Microeconomic Industrial Policy

When we talk of industrial policy, however, we generally envisage its microeconomic form. Indeed, one prominent economist, Richard Cooper, has defined industrial policy as action "whose intended purpose is to affect the structure of output." In this sense, industrial policy is designed as a substitute for the allocative function of the market and may be justified by the existence of some form of market failure. Again a broad range of policy instruments are available: access to investment funds, direct subsidies, differentially favorable tax treatments, tariff or quota protection, and so forth. The success of **microeconomic industrial policy** in Japan is open to question. Despite notable successes, in equally notable examples promotion of a specific industry or products led to failure and wasted investment. It is important to bear in mind that microindustrial policy has two faces. The more glamorous aspect is the promotion of industries selected as candidates for growth; however, equally important, especially as older "rust-belt" industries lose markets, is the rationalization of industries that are inevitably in decline.

Picking Winners If microeconomic industrial policy is to improve economic performance, it requires an economic justification as why bureaucrats are able to outperform the market. Industrial policy in Japan originated with the Ministry of International Trade and Industry (MITI), which gives several rationales for intervention.[12] First is a belief that the Japanese economy is characterized by substantial market failure, including the existence of significant economies of scale, the strong linkages between industries, public good effects, and capital market imperfections. In addition to these general justifications, MITI also took the view that the *keiretsu* system actually encourages unhealthy competition because each of the major groups feels that it must have a presence in practically every product line. This concern about the wasteful duplication of investment results in the belief that restraint on competition can be socially beneficial. Hence government intervention to shape market structure can lead to a more efficient use of capital. A further rationale for

---

[12]This bureaucracy has now been renamed the Ministry of Economy Trade and Industry, or METI but the rest of the chapter will use the acronym by which it became famous.

industrial policy is that markets are myopic and left to themselves, they fail to assume the long-run optimal level of risk. By anticipating the direction of change, industrial policy can actually speed up the operation of the market. MITI also took a long-term view on the industrial mix required to raise Japan to the level of a first-class economic power and keep it there.

The interventionism of MITI started in the early 1950s and initially relied on four measures—import restrictions, directed credit, tax incentives, and foreign exchange controls. The Export and Import Trading Act of 1953 legalized the formation of cartels and price fixing and limited imports. In these early years the system of directed credit consisted of funneling the savings gathered through the postal savings system and civil service pension surpluses into Japan Development Bank (JDB) and other trust funds created under the **Fiscal Investment and Loan Program (FILP)** that were functionally oriented toward industrial finance. Between 1952 and 1955, 28 percent of total finance to Japanese industry was through the FILP trust programs. A discretionary tax system enabled the adoption of discriminatory tax rates and depreciation codes. Finally, because foreign exchange control existed throughout the period, MITI was able to control the access to foreign technology and scarce imports, allocating the required permits only to favored firms whose projects received approval.

As well as using material incentives and restrictions, MITI also made use of propaganda and moral suasion. Such jawboning was not always successful. In 1955, MITI put forward a plan to create a single automobile company in Japan, believing economies of scale to be so strong as to prevent multiple Japanese firms from competing in the world market. It was forced to abandon the scheme in the face of protest from the various *keiretsu*. After this episode, vigorous competition between the various companies ensued, and ultimately four strong, exporting motor companies resulted.

In the late 1950s, MITI was forced to modify its policies. After Japan became a signatory of the General Agreement on Tariffs and Trade (1955) and joined the OECD (1964), Japanese economic policy was subject to international regulation. Trade was required to be liberalized and foreign exchange convertibility increased. It removed some weapons from MITI's arsenal, and greater reliance began to be placed on moral suasion and the establishment of consensus. The importance of the FILP trust funds began to recede, and more emphasis was placed on directing credit through the private banks.

The 1960s saw MITI make another misstep in promoting the development of an oil and petrochemical industry. This effort failed as world energy prices rose sharply following the OPEC oil crises. MITI then took a hard look at the future and decided to promote "knowledge-intensive industry," especially computers and communications. The Agency for Industrial Science and Technology (AIST) was created within MITI. Its purpose was to conduct and finance basic and applied research to assist in the development of the computer, communications, ceramics, and computer-aided manufacturing systems (robotics).

Planning the Decline of Losers Japan's success in the 1960s was to a large extent based on the development of industries that comparative advantage favored while Japan's labor costs were low—textiles, steel, rubber, shipbuilding. Now, as in the United States and Europe, these industries are in decline. An issue is whether the market should be allowed to be the arbiter of who survives and who sinks, or whether government can play a constructive role. Japan has taken the latter tack. Using legislation that dates back to the early 1950s, MITI frequently sponsored the cartelization of declining industries so as to see an orderly restructuring of output. The Japanese believe this approach proved more beneficial in terms of the preservation of industrial capital, social infrastructure, and healthy communities than merely allowing the market to choose the losers.

The Efficacy of Industrial Policy It is not easy to evaluate the success of Japanese industrial policy because of the difficulty in establishing a counterfactual, a consensus on what kind of path Japan would have followed in the absence of industrial policy. Japan indeed demonstrated impressive growth since the war, but what Hugh Patrick characterizes as "myths" are frequently wrongly credited for the success and in his opinion the biggest myth is that of industrial policy, which he finds to be the subject of facile and misleading generalizations. He considers that the macroeconomic elements of industrial policy that created a platform for growth without favoring any particular industry or initiative have been successful, while microeconomic industrial policy ("picking winners") resulted in a much more mixed record. Although the successes might be the ones that catch the eye, several conspicuous failures occurred as well. Patrick documents the ill-starred, energy-intensive industry drive in the 1950s and 1960s and MITI's aborted attempt to promote concentration in the automobile industry in the 1950s. A more recent case is the promotion of the analog system of high-definition television (HDTV), which lost out to a digital version, a misjudgment that perhaps cost as much as $10 billion. Moreover, many of Japan's most impressive achievements were brought about without MITI's help, and in some cases over MITI's objections. The performance of the Japanese economy in the 1990s and the fragility of the banking system (caused in large part by the system of microeconomic industrial policy and directed credit) have thrown the validity of the entire system into doubt. Now the winning strategies promoted by MITI seem to be fewer and the losers more conspicuous. Popular wisdom is moving toward favoring a less prominent role for the now renamed Ministry of Economy Trade and Industry (METI) and a greater reliance on market logic.

WHAT'S WRONG WITH THE JAPANESE SYSTEM?

The Japanese economy seemed only a decade ago to be the success story of the second half of the twentieth century. In the early 1990s, a debate, key to the election of Bill Clinton, centered on how the United States might compete in the long run with the Japanese. Now Japan seems to be almost universally regarded as the sick economy of the developed world. The close relationships between business, bureaucracy, and politics, once lauded as the key to stable and sustained long-term growth, are now decried as the basic cause of the longest recession among major developed economies in the last 50 years. The Japanese economy has been depressed for some

12 years and is not only failing to grow but it is failing to fully utilize its industrial capacity to the detriment of its population. Unless the corner is turned soon, it is likely that the situation will unravel further.

The situation is a compound of problems. First and foremost is the financial sector. It was once seen as a source of great power as, under government direction, cheap investment funds were funneled into industries identified by the bureaucrats of MITI as the source of future growth. Now, the banks wallow in a sorry state; because of bureaucratic intervention they are saddled with loans to corporations who simply cannot repay them, while the value of equities on their balance sheets plummeted. Despite mergers and consolidation, and the continued flow of savings, the banks are fundamentally insolvent.

Secondly, the labor system, particularly lifetime employment and seniority wages, an asset in a growing economy, cannot deal with contraction or even stability, and leaves many of the corporations top-heavy and unresponsive. The non-export sector, sheltered from foreign competition by the government shows little in productivity growth and is inefficient by world standards. The duality of the Japanese system has increased over time.

Third, the population as a whole is fearful of the future and yet conservative in outlook and unwilling to change. Consumer confidence is low and as a result consumer spending suffers. Saving, an individual virtue, is a collective problem as demand lags behind capacity. The conservatism also reflects itself in a fear of changing government. Despite the manifold economic problems, the Liberal Party still holds a virtual monopoly on power. The prime ministership changed hands with considerable regularity and speed, in 11 of the last 12 years, but structural reform remains halting and incomplete, largely because of the power and permanence of the bureaucracy that determines policy.

Fourth, policy options are limited. Inflation in Japan is currently nonexistent. Both producer prices and consumer prices are falling at a rate of just less than 1 percent. Short-term interest rates are zero in both short-term money markets and on two-year government bonds; 10-year government bonds pay only 1 percent interest, which is a real rate of only about 0.25 percent. The economy cannot be stimulated by lowering the nominal rates, and it is possible that highly aggressive government policy can be used to accelerate the rate of inflation and hence drive the real interest rate into negative territory.

Fiscal policy is similarly problematic. None of the 11 different fiscal stimulus packages in the last decade has worked, probably because each was too small to have a dramatic impact on consumer sentiment. However, the effect on government finance has been profound. The deficit grew inexorably and the national debt is more than 130 percent of GDP, more than twice the level imposed on European countries by the Maastricht treaty. However the economy remains stubbornly immobile.

Japan needs both fundamental restructuring, especially in the finance sector, and consumer sentiment must be turned around. Until Japanese feel more confident in the future and start to spend appropriately, the recession will drag on. Japan Inc., once so strong, could be stalled in a perpetual state of low growth, low confidence, and stagnation.

KEY TERMS AND CONCEPTS

bank-centered *keiretsu*

"big bang"

company unions

directed credit

duality

financial repression

Fiscal Investment and Loan Program
(FILP)

just-in-time (JIT) inventory control

keiretsu

lifetime employment

macroeconomic industrial policy

microeconomic industrial policy

Ministry of Finance (MoF)

Ministry of International Trade and
Industry (MITI)

nenko

Samurai

seniority wages

shunto

sogo sosha

sushin koyo

trading company

zaibatsu

QUESTIONS FOR DISCUSSION

1. What are the *keiretsu?* In what ways do they resemble and in what ways do they differ from the *zaibatsu?* How are *keiretsu* held together?

2. How general is the system of lifetime employment? In what ways does it help and in what way does it hurt productivity?

3. How are Japanese trade unions organized? Does this structure contribute to labor peace?

4. How does a system of "seniority wages" differ from the normal assumptions of microeconomic theory? Can you see any advantages?

5. How has Japan's system of directed credit harmed its financial sector?

6. What constitutes "macroeconomic" industrial policy in Japan? Has it been successful?

7. Is microeconomic industrial policy just about "picking winners"? What else is important?

RESOURCES

Web Sites

Ministry of Finance ....http://www.mof.go.jp/

Central Bank ....http://www.boj.or.jp/

Ministry of Economy, Trade and Industry ....http://www.meti.go.jp/

Statistics Bureau ....http://www.stat.go.jp/

National Tax Agency...http://www.nta.go.jp/

Tokyo Stock Exchange...http://www.tse.or.jp/

Development Bank of Japan ....http://www.dbj.go.jp/

Japan External Trade Organization ....http://www.jetro.go.jp/top/

Mitsubishi Companies...http://www.mitsubishi.or.jp/

Japan Times National Newspaper..http://www.japantimes.co.jp/

Embassy of Japan in the United States ....http://www.embjapan.org/

Books and Articles

Abe, Etsuo, and Robert Fitzgerald. "Japanese Economic Success: Timing, Culture, and Organizational Capability." *Business History,* April 1995, 1–31.

Alam, M. Shahid. *Governments and Markets in Economic Development Strategies: Lessons from Korea, Taiwan, and Japan.* New York: Praeger, 1989.

Aoki, Masahiko. "Toward an Economic Model of the Japanese Firm." *Journal of Economic Literature* 78, no.1 (March 1990), 1–27.

Boulding, Kenneth, and Alan Gleason, "War as Investment: The Strange Case of Japan." In *Economic Imperialism,* Kenneth Boulding and Tapan Mukherjee (eds.), 240–261. Ann Arbor, MI: University of Michigan Press, 1972.

Calder, Kent E. *Strategic Capitalism: Private Business and Public Purpose in Japan.* Princeton, NJ: Princeton University Press, 1993.

Callon, Scott. *Divided Sun: MITI and the Breakdown of Japanese High-Tech Industrial Policy, 1975–1993.* Stanford, CA: Stanford University Press, 1997.

Carlile, Lonny E., and Mark Tilton (eds.). *Is Japan Really Changing Its Ways?: Regulatory Reform and the Japanese Economy.* Washington, DC: The Brookings Institution, 1998.

Drucker, Peter F. "The End of Japan, Inc.?: An Economic Monolith Fractures." *Foreign Affairs,* Spring 1993, 10–15.

Fingleton, Eamonn. "Japan's Invisible Leviathan." *Foreign Affairs,* March/April 1995, 69–85.

Francks, Penelope. *Japanese Economic Development: Theory and Practice.* London: Routledge, 1992.

Gerlach, Michael L. *Alliance Capitalism: The Social Organization of Japanese Business.* Berkeley, CA: University of California Press, 1993.

Gibney, Frank. *Unlocking the Bureaucrat's Kingdom: Deregulation and the Japanese Economy.* Washington, DC: The Brookings Institution, 1998.

Grabowski, Richard. "The State and Economic Development." *Studies in Comparative International Development,* Spring 1994, 3–17.

Hart, Jeffrey A. *Rival Capitalists: International Competitiveness in the United States, Japan and Western Europe.* Ithaca, NY: Cornell University Press, 1992.

Hobday, Michael. *Innovation in East Asia: The Challenge to Japan.* Aldershot, England: Edward Elgar Publishing, 1995.

Hollerman, Leon. *Japan, Disincorporated: The Economic Liberalization Process.* Stanford, CA: Hoover Institution Press, 1988.

Ito, Takatoshi. *The Japanese Economy.* Cambridge, MA: MIT Press, 1992.

Japan Science Foundation. *U.S.–Japan Comparison in National Formation and Transformation of Technology Centering around Mass Production Systems, 1900–1990.* Tokyo: Japan Science Foundation, 1992.

Johnson, Chalmers. *MITI and the Japanese Miracle: The Growth of Industrial Policy, 1925–1975.* Stanford, CA: Stanford University Press, 1982.

Johnson, Chalmers, Laura D'Andrea Tyson, and John Zysman. *Politics and Productivity: The Real Story of Why Japan Works.* Cambridge, MA: Ballinger Publishing, 1989.

Katz, Richard. *Japan, The System That Soured: The Rise and Fall of the Japanese Economic Miracle.* Armonk, NY: M.E. Sharpe, 1998.

Kikkawa, Takeo. "Kigyo Shuda: The Formation and Function of Enterprise Groups." *Business History*, April 1995, 44–53.

Komiya, Ryutaro, Masahiro Okumo, and Kotaro Suzumara (eds.). *Industrial Policy of Japan.* Tokyo: Academic Press, 1988.

Kosai, Yutaka, and Yoshitaro Ogino. *The Contemporary Japanese Economy.* Armonk, NY: M.E. Sharpe, 1984.

Lee, Chung H., and Ippei Yamazawa (eds.). *The Economic Development of Japan and Korea: A Parallel with Lessons.* New York: Praeger, 1990.

Lincoln, Edward J. *Japan: Facing Economic Maturity.* Washington, DC: The Brookings Institution, 1988.

Lincoln, Edward J. *Japan's Unequal Trade.* Washington, DC: The Brookings Institution, 1990.

Morikawa, Hidemasa. *Zaibatsu: The Rise and Fall of Family Enterprise Groups in Japan.* Tokyo: University of Tokyo Press, 1992.

Morishima, Michio. *Why Has Japan "Succeeded"?: Western Technology and the Japanese Ethos.* Cambridge, MA: Cambridge University Press, 1982.

Mosk, Carl. *Competition and Cooperation in Japanese Labour Markets (Studies in the Modern Japanese Economy).* New York: St. Martin's Press, 1995.

Nanto, Dick K. "Japan's Industrial Groups: The *Keiretsu.*" In *Comparative Economic Systems: Models and Cases*, 7th ed., 236–251, Morris Bernstein (ed.). Burr Ridge, IL: Irwin, 1994.

Nester, William R. *The Foundation of Japanese Power: Continuities, Changes, Challenges.* Armonk, NY: M.E. Sharpe, 1990.

OECD. *Economic Survey of Japan*, November 2002.

Odagiri, Hiroyuki. *Growth Through Competition, Competition Through Growth: Strategic Management and the Economy in Japan.* Oxford: Oxford University Press, 1992.

Okazaki, Tetsuji. "The Evolution of the Financial System in Post-War Japan." *Business History*, April 1995, 89–106.

Oppenheim, Phillip. *Japan without Blinders: Coming to Terms with Japan's Economic Success.* Tokyo: Kodansha International, 1992.

Patrick, Hugh T., and Yung Chul Park. *The Financial Development of Japan, Korea and Taiwan: Growth, Repression and Liberalization.* Oxford: Oxford University Press, 1994.

Pempel, T. J. *Regime Shift: Comparative Dynamics of the Japanese Political Economy (Cornell Studies in Political Economy).* Ithaca, NY: Cornell University Press, 1998.

Sato, Kazuo. *The Transformation of the Japanese Economy.* Armonk, NY: M.E. Sharpe, 1999.

Shichihei, Yamamoto. *The Spirit of Japanese Capitalism and Selected Essays.* Lanham: Madison Books, 1992.

Shigeto, Tsuru. *Japan's Capitalism, Creative Defeat and Beyond.* Cambridge, England: University of Cambridge Press, 1993.

Shimotani, Masahiro. "The Formation of Distribution Keiretsu: The Case of Matsushita Electric." *Business History,* April 1995, 54–69.

"Survey: Japan." *The Economist,* April 18, 2002.

Tai, Hung-chao (ed.). *Confucianism and Economic Development: An Oriental Alternative?* Washington, DC: The Washington Institute Press, 1989.

Takenaka, Heizo. *Contemporary Japanese Economy and Economic Policy.* Ann Arbor, MI: University of Michigan Press, 1991.

Tatsuki, Mariko. "The Rise of the Mass Market and Modern Retailers in Japan." *Business History,* April 1995, 70–88.

Teranishi, Juro. "Economic Recovery, Growth and Policies: 'Gradualism' in the Japanese Context," *Economic Policy,* 19 supp. (December 1994), 137–154.

Udagawa, Masaru. "The Development of Production Management at the Toyota Motor Corporation." *Business History,* April 1995, 107–119.

Werner, Richard. *Princes of the Yen: Japan's Central Banks and the Transformation of the Economy.* Armonk, NY: M.E. Sharpe, 2003.

Whitehill, Arthur M. *Japanese Management: Tradition and Transition.* London: Routledge, 1991.

13

SOUTH KOREA: A LESSON IN LATE INDUSTRIALIZATION

SOUTH KOREA	
Area (thousand sq. km.)	99
Currency	won
Exchange Rate (August 2002)	1,200 won = US$1
Population 2000 (millions)	47
Population Growth Rate	1.0%
GNI per Capita, 2000	$8,910
GNI per Capita, PPP	$17,340
GDP Growth 1990–2000	5.7%
Value Added as % of GDP 2000 Agriculture	5%
Industry	44%
Services	51%
% of GDP Central Government Revenue	26.3%
Exports	37.8%

INTRODUCTION

The Republic of Korea, generally known as South Korea, shows one of the most impressive records of economic growth over the past 35 years. In 1961 the economy was largely agrarian (65 percent of the workforce was in agriculture), the state was weak, labor unrest was frequent, and industrial growth was slow. In that year, a group of army officers seized control of the country, initiating a series of events that resulted ultimately in the elevation of General Park Chung Hee to the presidency. Park ruled as an authoritarian dictator for the next 25 years, during which Korea was transformed from an agrarian state to a modern industrial society.

312

Korean development strongly parallels that of Japan, including the dominance of large diversified industrial groups (in Japan prewar *zaibatsu* and postwar *keiretsu*, in Korea **chaebol**, or **jaebul**), the powerful role of the bureaucracy, the rapid import and implementation of foreign technology, the low levels of direct foreign investment, and the export-orientation of growth. Nevertheless, it would be an oversimplification to consider Korea merely a new application of the "Japanese model." Korea offers lessons in its own right, not the least in how it will resolve the economic and political difficulties pressing on it in the early twenty-first century.

HISTORICAL BACKGROUND

The Colonial Legacy

For about 600 years (between the thirteenth and nineteenth centuries), Korea was ruled as a feudal state by the Yi dynasty. Power was held by an elite (the *yangban*) composed of the monarchy, the landowners, and the scholars. The conservative interests of these groups effectively blocked economic and political reform. The vast majority of the population were peasants living in subsistence conditions. Any agricultural surplus was used either to support the consumption of the elite groups, or went as tribute to Imperial China, which maintained a sleepy suzerainty over the peninsula.

In the late nineteenth century, this stability was disturbed by two forces. First, rapid population growth increased the demands on the fragile agricultural resources of the mountainous Korean peninsula, leading to peasant unrest. Second, following the Meiji reformation (see Chapter 12), Japan embarked on an outward-oriented policy, trying to augment its limited resource base by acquiring territory in China's waning sphere of influence. The Treaty of Khangwa in 1876 established Japanese commerce through Korean ports, and by 1910 Japan's military muscle allowed the establishment of formal colonial status. A lively debate surrounds the role of Japanese colonialism on Korean development. Some authorities see it as "modernizing," because it swept away the feudal barriers to economic progress; Japanese occupation destroyed the class system, abolished slavery, broke up the great estates, and paved the way for land reform. The colonial period led to increased education for the average Korean, the transfer of managerial skills in industry and commerce to Koreans, and the creation of an urban industrial workforce.

While admitting the elimination of barriers to change, another view emphasizes the distortionary nature of Japanese colonialism and the negative effects of subsuming Korean development to Japanese needs. Certainly the Japanese occupation did not result in Korean-controlled industrialization or create a large Korean business community. The vast majority of industrial investment in Korea was Japanese. By 1938 Koreans held only 12 percent of the total capital of Korean industry, and just six Japanese *zaibatsu* accounted for fully 70 percent of Korean industrial capital. During the 1920s, after a decade of intense discrimination against Koreans, the Japanese did allow the evolution of what economist Alice Amsden calls a "wafer-thin stratum" of indigenous capitalists. Among this group were some of the families that would in the postwar period develop the great Korean industrial groups, but who in the interwar years were allowed only to serve Japanese interests.[1] Korea produced food, raw materials, and semifinished goods for Japanese industry. As war approached, the Japanese created a Korean heavy industrial base using the peninsula's mineral wealth, which remained nevertheless completely under Japanese control. Table 13.1 shows some indices of Korean growth for the start of Japanese colonial rule until 1941.

The Postwar Period

By the end of World War II in 1945, Korea's economy had been shattered. The industrial base built in the interwar and early war years had been stripped toward the end of the war. Moreover, Korea's economy had been part of an integrated Japanese trading system involving close links with Japan, North Korea, and Manchukuo (the Japanese-controlled puppet state in Manchuria). As these links dissolved, the economy collapsed. Half of the manufacturing establishments operating under the Japanese closed during the immediate postwar period, and many others drastically reduced employment and production. In addition, the U.S. occupying forces dismantled and removed most of the Japanese facilities that had produced war material. Industrial output fell by 85 percent in less than two years.[2]

Agriculture was little better. Neglect during the war years, a shortage of inputs, and an inadequate distribution system put Korean agriculture in difficulty. The several years following the war saw a general shortage of food and some localized cases

■ TABLE 13.1

Indices of Output and Population, 1910—1941

Period	Agriculture	Forestry, Fishing, and Mining	Manufacturing	Total	Population
1910–1912	67.3	33.7	17.4	54.2	66
1914–1916	86.5	45.9	31.5	69.6	—
1919–1921	88.6	46.2	59.7	76.9	84.5
1924–1926	91.2	69	97.5	89.6	—
1929–1931	100	100	100	100	100
1934–1936	98.7	161.5	194.2	127.1	—
1939–1941	117.3	227.6	255.5	165.5	115.2

SOURCE: Hwang, *The Korean Economies* (Oxford: Clarendon, 1993), p. 17.

[1] For a full exposition of the thesis that the Korean miracle had its roots in the Japanese occupation, see Carter J. Eckert, *Offspring of Empire: The Koch'ang Kims and the Colonial Origins of Korean Capitalism* (Seattle: University of Washington Press, 1991).
[2] Vittorio Corbo and Sang-Mok Suh, eds. *Structural Adjustment in a Newly Industrialized Country: The Korean Experience* (Baltimore, MD: Johns Hopkins University Press, 1992), p. 7.

of famine. The food crisis was exacerbated by the repatriation to South Korea of about two million Koreans who had been working in Japan or who had fled to China to avoid Japanese occupation. On top of this factor, 2 to 3 million refugees fled from the communist north as the country was partitioned. Finally, the outbreak of the Korean War not only hampered economic reconstruction but also resulted in the destruction of 40 percent of industrial capacity and 20 percent of the housing stock.

Extensive U.S. aid got Korea through the 1950s. In 1960, exports amounted to only 3 percent of Korean gross domestic product (GDP), while imports amounted to about 13 percent. However, financial inflows from the United States, consisting of "development aid" (in excess of $200 million annually) and substantial expenditure by the U.S. military, represented 10 percent of GDP. Like Japanese rule, the U.S. presence in Korea had a modernizing function, but it was also highly distortionary. U.S. military needs warped industrial growth and led to bias toward the service sector. Simultaneously, the generous economic development aid enriched a new entrepreneurial class, whose prosperity depended on close political links to the government and military.

Corruption was pervasive during the First Republic (1948–1960) and great fortunes were amassed by a new capitalist class. The gravy train started with sales of formerly Japanese-owned property at below-market prices to friends of the government. Subsequently the favored firms were allocated the hard currency required to import scarce materials—especially grains and fertilizers—to be resold on the domestic market at monopoly prices. Some firms were also given access to loans at subsidized interest rates, granted tax exemptions, and awarded preferential contracts for large-scale government projects.[3] Despite their shady origins, these entrepreneurs enjoyed certain advantages in promoting economic development. First, they came without preconceptions; they were less conservative in style than Korea's older textile industry chiefs and were far more growth oriented. Second, although these businessmen came from a wide range of industries, they were not wedded to any particular sector, but were business generalists, specializing in making money by whatever means. Third, steering aid in their direction gave them substantial funds for investment and solved the problem of initial capital accumulation. Finally, their corrupt past gave the Park administration a hold over them that could be used as a lever to ensure complicit behavior. These men were the founders of many of the diversified business groups, or *chaebol* that remain so important in Korea today.

The Policies of Park Chung Hee

The First Republic ended in 1960 with the death of Syngman Rhee, and a brief experiment with democracy concluded when General Park Chung Hee led an army coup, which went unopposed by the United States. Two years later Park resigned from the army and was elected president of the Republic, though his close military links persisted through the 25 years of his presidency. Park was an ascetic

[3]Alice Amsden, *Asia's Next Giant* (New York: Oxford University Press, 1984), p. 39.

individual who expected and demanded that all Koreans make sacrifices to further his vision of the new Korea. His views were highly influenced by South Korea's security problems and the need to develop a strong industrial base to support the military establishment. In particular, it was clear that North Korea (Democratic People's Republic of Korea), by pursuing a program of Stalinist industrialization, was outgrowing South Korea and worsening the strategic position of the south. Park's pursuit of industrial growth was oriented to furthering the creation of military power rather than toward the economic well-being of the population. In that sense, Park's policies may be viewed as being purely mercantilist, "the pursuit of power over plenty."

Park was able to centralize power because of a lack of opposition. Japanese colonization, World War II, and the Korean War had transformed the class structure of Korean society, leveling landlord and scholar classes. The communist threat tended to solidify society, and also silenced U.S. criticism of the regime's excesses. Plentiful labor and high unemployment initially made the unions powerless. Park was also able to call on Korea's heritage of **Confucianism** to enrich his rhetoric on the relation of the individual to the state and, by extension, of the individual to his or her employer.[4]

In addition to these political advantages, Park could pull two important levers to control business: access to imports and access to finance. In the early 1960s Korea's international trade was governed by a complex system of licensing and tariffs. To receive a license, a firm had to show both the absence of a domestic substitute and the necessity of the imports for the production of goods that were either to be exported or vital to the domestic economy. In addition, protective tariffs averaged more than 40 percent in 1962 and a complex system of multiple exchange rates put further restraint on trade. By giving favored firms import licenses, hard currency at discounted rates, and tariff wavers, the government allowed the appropriation of economic rents by selected industrial leaders.

Park further tightened control of the economy by the nationalization of the commercial banks, which made about one-third of all loans in Korea and provided most industrial finance.[5] The four specialized banks, which together made about 12 percent of loans, were also taken under public control.[6] This move gave the government the ability to control credit and the power to discipline any firm that displeased it by blocking any refinancing of its debt.

---

[4]The role of Confucianism in economic development is a much-debated topic. Max Weber argued that Confucianism, with its emphasis on the moral over the material, was a major deterrent to the development of capitalism in China, analogous to the role of Catholicism and orthodoxy in Europe. Morishima in turn tried to distinguish between the Confucianism of Japan, which tended to support economic growth, from Chinese Confucianism, which did not. Nowadays, however, the Confucian ethic of obedience to superiors is seen as a major positive factor in the growth of Korea, Hong Kong, Taiwan, and Singapore. Lee Kuan Yew, the former prime minister of Singapore, is especially eloquent on the role of Confucian philosophy on economic growth.
[5]Commercial banks had been privatized in 1957, brought back under government management in 1961, and reprivatized in 1982, but until 1993 the government appointed all bank presidents.
[6]The Industrial Bank of Korea, the Citizen's National Bank, the Korea Housing Bank, and the National Agricultural Cooperative.

PHASES OF KOREAN GROWTH

Export Promotion, 1961—1973

The early years of the Park regime saw a heavy emphasis on exporting. Initially exports consisted mostly of textiles and light manufactured goods because Korea's cheap labor gave it comparative advantage in these industries. Policy changes in 1961, including a 50 percent devaluation of the Korean currency (the won) and the elimination of multiple exchange rates, did a lot to boost exports. The government also used more direct action. Successful exporters were assured import licenses, finance for expansion, tariff relief, and direct subsidies. The government also imposed a 1 percent surcharge on imports and used the proceeds to finance specialized institutions to promote exports.[7] Export targets were established for individual firms, and although no direct penalties were imposed for failing to achieve these goals, finance was more likely given to those who succeeded in such competition, an early example of the "market-augmenting" competitions used by Asian economies to allocate credit.

The results of the **export promotion** campaign were staggeringly successful. Between 1963 and 1973, exports grew at an annual rate of 44 percent, and increased from about 1 percent of gross national product (GNP) in 1963 to more than 25 percent in 1973. The commodity composition of exports also changed, from a heavy concentration in textiles in the early years, to more diversified light manufacturing in the later ones. Imports increased as well, although at a slightly lower rate. Imports also rose because of the need for raw materials and capital goods. Investment rose from 11.5 percent of GNP in 1964 to 27 percent in 1969 before moderating to 23 percent in 1973 as global economic conditions worsened.

The Heavy and Chemical Industries Drive, 1973—1979

Despite the economic success of the late 1960s, the Park government decided that the future of the Korean economy lay in heavy industry and in 1973 inaugurated the **Heavy and Chemical Industries Development Plan (HCI)**. This shift was motivated by three factors. First was the belief that military self-sufficiency, necessary in an era of a reduced U.S. presence, required the development of a heavy industrial base. Second, increased globalization of production and accelerating integration of Asian countries into the global economy was eroding Korea's comparative advantage in light industry, which was based on cheap labor. Wage costs in Indonesia, the Philippines, and Malaysia were much lower than in Korea, and higher Korean wages and living standards could only be sustained by higher labor productivity, which required more capital-intensive industry. Third, despite rapid export growth, the Korean balance of payments remained in deficit and a greater

---

[7]These specialized institutions were the Korean Trade Promotion Association, founded in 1964 to perform market research abroad, and the Korean Traders' Association, which was financed by a 1 percent levy on imports.

production of heavy industrial materials and chemicals would reduce import dependence. The HCI initiative was opposed by most of Korea's economic advisors, particularly the World Bank and the United States, on the grounds that it ran counter to the established pattern of comparative advantage.

Iron and steel, nonferrous metals, shipbuilding, machinery, and chemical industries were chosen as growth sectors. The HCI drive illustrates the financial leverage wielded by the Korean government. Large firms, selected on the basis of their past performance and connections, were "invited" to expand production into specific industries. They were guaranteed generous access to finance at favorable rates from the nationalized banking sector, priority access to imports, assistance with technology and frequently direct subsidies, tax holidays, accelerated depreciation, and investment tax credits. By the end of the 1970s, the effective marginal corporate tax rate on heavy industry was 30 percent less than the comparable rate on light industry. The level of import protection in these industries also rose during this time, reversing the global trend toward freer trade.

Directed credit, however, was the most powerful tool. At the outset of the HCI drive in 1973–1974, heavy industry accounted for just one-third of total bank loans to industry; just two years later in 1975–1976, heavy industry received over 60 percent of such loans. Increased government involvement in the credit allocation process occurred at the same time. The share of "policy loans" from the commercial banks (i.e., those loans made at the behest of the government) rose from less than 50 percent in 1970 to more than 60 percent in 1978.

Controversy about the effect of the HCI campaign still remains. It did succeed in sustaining expansion during a period of severe global stagnation; GNP growth in the 1970s averaged 9.6 percent per year, on a pace with the 1960s. Exports, too, continued their rapid expansion at a rate of 31 percent per year, slower than the 44 percent managed in the 1960s but still remarkable by most standards. The structure of output in Korean industry was certainly changed. In 1971 light industry represented 56 percent of the total, and heavy industry 44 percent, but by 1980 this proportion had reversed. However, the drive also represented a distortion of the economy, and even after allowing for all of the material incentives enjoyed by firms to induce them to enter heavy industry, considerable short-term economic sacrifice was still required. Amsden presents evidence that throughout the 1970s, profitability remained highest in labor-intensive industry; was greater in light, rather than heavy, industry; and was higher in the older established industries as opposed to the new ones.[8]

The HCI drive probably went against the short-term interests of Korean industrialists, who participated because of government pressure. That fact in itself does not mean it was misguided, because it is possible that dynamic and short-term efficiency are not coincident. One way to view the HCI drive is as a massive infant-industry protection scheme in which firms were induced to follow long-term national interests by both the carrot and the stick. The result was technological inflow, learning-by-doing, the grasping of economies of scale, and the establishment of an entirely new basis for the Korean economy. Adherence to strictly market logic,

[8]Amsden, *Asia's Next Giant* (New York: Oxford University Press, 1989), p. 85.

a **market-conforming approach**, would not promote the rapid development of a heavy industrial sector in Korea. The alternate **market-augmenting approach** forced industrialists to accept a lower rate of return on capital in the short run, but it may well have ensured the continuation of the "miracle" into the 1990s. That said, much evidence also suggests that the HCI drive was carried too far, and that the extirpation of criticism or open-thinking by the government was counterproductive.

Despite its success in sustaining the growth of both GDP and exports, by the late 1970s it was clear that the HCI was creating serious problems, particularly over-heating in some sectors. Unemployment fell to an all-time low of 3.2 percent in 1978; and the real income of workers in manufacturing rose by 110 percent between 1974 and 1979, well above the rate of productivity increase. Coupled with the rise in oil prices, the wage increases pushed inflation over 20 percent. International competitiveness suffered, the current account lurched into deficit, raising inter-national debt, which reached $20.3 billion in 1979, a five-fold increase over 1974. Imports surged, led by the growing need for imported energy, and the increased openness raised Korea's dependence on export markets. As a result, Korea became more vulnerable to shifts in international economic activity, and serious conse-quences for the Korean economy resulted from the global downturn in 1980.

The HCI also increased the fragility of the financial sector. The extensive use of directed credit to finance the expansion of the heavy industrial sector left the banks with a high proportion of badly performing loans, eroding the asset base of the banking sector.

Economic Liberalization

The years 1979 and 1980 were bleak for a country conditioned to success. In 1979 Park was assassinated by members of his own secret service. In 1980 the global recession and falling competitiveness caused exports, and output, to fall for the first time in a quarter of a century. The incoming government of General Chun Doo Hwan moved quickly to stabilize the economy through restrictive fiscal and mon-etary policies, which by 1984 had cooled inflation, at the cost of domestic recession.

The new government feared that the protectionism and isolation of the Korean economy were having a detrimental effect on long-term prospects, so it outlined an ambitious liberalization program. This plan included partial privatization of the financial sector, lower barriers to entry for nonbank financial intermediaries, reduced use of priority loans (directed credit), and liberalization of foreign trade and capital flows. However, the pace of liberalization was disappointing, and the changes initiated in the early 1980s represented more scaling back the system of state-directed development rather than the establishment of a genuinely free market economy.

PLANNING IN KOREA

Formal economic planning dates from the beginning of the Park regime in 1961 when the Economic Planning Board (EPB), staffed largely by U.S.-trained econo-mists, was established to prepare five-year plans. The First Plan covered the period

1962–1966. Korean planning has always been "top down," initiated by the politicians and technocracy, largely in isolation of the views of business or labor. This contrasts with the role of Ministry of Industry and Trade (MITI) in Japan, or the *concertation* of the indicative planning procedure in France, where consensus building is an important part of the process. Policy proposals are not in general open for discussion, although the process has become more transparent in recent years. This unilateralism was especially characteristic of the Second Plan, and the HCI initiative of the 1970s. The deliberate insulation of the EPB from Korean society had both good and bad points. Although it minimized corruption and the possibility of "capture" of the bureaucracy by business, it encouraged bureaucratic arrogance and kept fruitful discussion between government and industry to a minimum. One U.S. advisor to the EPB reported that insulation was so great that there was actually debate within the EPB as to whether policy proposals that originated from outside the board would even be considered.

The EPB used an input/output model, supplemented by industry studies and projections of economic conditions in a wider global context, arriving at a list of products and projects to be pursued by Korean business. Then, in conjunction with the **Ministry of Finance (MoF)**, the **Ministry of Trade and Industry (MTI)**, and other relevant ministries, these projects were allocated to particular firms and the necessary inputs, imports, and finances arranged.

Although it used input/output matrices, Korean planning did not establish firm production targets, as in the Soviet system. Consistent with the priority of exports in economic thinking, each firm was given an **export quota**. These quotas were not absolutely binding, but governmental support in future projects or continued access to finance was frequently contingent on success in meeting export targets. A survey of Korean firms in the 1970s found that about 37 percent of firms reported that these targets had a positive effect leading to increased production. Ten percent reported no effect, while 53 percent found some negative impact for the firm, including lower quality, lower productivity, and lower profitability.[9]

In a symbolic move signaling an attempt to shift away from government direction and toward a system of market coordination, the government announced it phased out the Economic Planning Board in 1994. Because this agency was created by Park to implement his own personal development strategy, it means a shift from the past, but it will not mean an end to interventionism. Most of EPB's powers still reside within the Ministry of Finance.

INDUSTRIAL STRUCTURE

The Dominance of the *Chaebol*

One of the most singular features of the Korean economy is the role played by its large, diversified industrial groups, the *chaebol*. Generally these groups developed out of the aid-rich, rent-dominated economy of the 1950s. However, they continued

---

[9]Amsden, *Asia's Next Giant* (New York: Oxford University Press, 1989), p. 69.

to grow largely as a result of state-sponsorship under the system of state-directed capitalism in which the government controlled entry into industry, access to raw materials and imports, and, most important, finance. The ascent to dominance by a small group of leading *chaebol* is documented in Table 13.2. In 1974, the combined sales of the top 10 *chaebol* accounted for only 15 percent of GNP, but only a decade later the comparable figure was 67.4 percent. The two largest *chaebol* (Hyundai and Samsung) each had sales equal to 12 percent of GNP.

In 1992, 78 groups were registered as *chaebol* under the Fair Trade Act.[10] These groups were composed of a total of 1,056 subsidiaries. The average number of subsidiaries was therefore 13. The *chaebol* ranged considerably in size. By the end of 1996 the two largest were Hyundai and Samsung. Both groups had assets of about $63 billion, and each was made up of about 50 subsidiaries. They were followed by Lucky Goldstar (now renamed the LG group), with assets of $48 billion, and Daewoo ($40 billion).

The dominance of these "big four" groups in the Korean economy during the mid-1990s was huge. Together they accounted in 1994 for 22 percent of total assets, 32 percent of total sales, 57 percent of total exports, but only 3 percent of total employment. The top 10 *chaebol* accounted for more than 70 percent of sales and roughly one-quarter of all the value added in the economy.

Chaebol and *Keiretsu* Compared

In frequent comparisons of *chaebol* with Japanese *keiretsu*, clear similarities emerge. However, important differences are also present:

■ TABLE *13.2*

Cumulative Combined Sales of Top 10 *Chaebol*, 1974–1984 (percentage of GNP)

Groups	1974	1976	1978	1980	1982	1984
1	4.9	4.7	6.9	8.3	10.4	12
2	7.2	8.1	12.9	16.3	19	24
3	9	11.3	16.9	23.9	27.4	35.8
4	10.3	12.9	20.7	30.1	35.6	44.3
5	11.6	14.5	22.9	35	42.2	52.4
6	12.7	16.1	24.7	38.2	46	56.2
7	13.5	17.5	26.4	41	49.2	59.4
8	14.3	18.4	27.7	43.6	52.2	62.1
9	14.7	19.3	28.9	46	55.1	64.8
10	15.1	19.8	30.1	48.1	57.6	67.4

SOURCE: Amsden, *Asia's Next Giant* (New York: Oxford University Press, 1989), p. 116.

[10]Under the old rules, all groups of companies with combined assets of more than $500 million were considered to be *chaebol*. New rules introduced in 1993 define only the largest 30 of these groups as *chaebol*.

1. The first, and perhaps most important difference is that the equity capital within a Korean *chaebol* is even more closely held than in a Japanese *keiretsu*. Many groups are still led by the original founders, who still hold the majority of the capital. Many of the subsidiaries within the groups are wholly owned and not publicly listed. Only 163 of the 623 subsidiaries of the largest *chaebol* are listed. High debt-to-equity ratios within the *chaebol* (Daewoo, for example, has a 9:1 ratio) allow relatively small amounts of equity capital to control large assets. In Japan the policy of the postwar occupation authorities to dissolve the close-held *zaibatsu* system led to a greater dispersion of equity holdings.

2. The family nature of *chaebol* ownership is reflected in the management structure. Many *chaebol* are still headed by their original founder and senior management is often recruited from within the family. In general, the major Japanese groups are led by professional management.[11]

3. The relationship between the groups and the government has been less cooperative in Korea than in Japan. President Park needed the *chaebol* to pursue heavy industrial growth, on which depended military security. Consequently he cajoled, bullied, and bribed them into compliance. Decision making was unilateral, flowing from government to industry. In Japan "the iron triangle" worked more cooperatively and ideas flowed in both directions. After Park's assassination business-government relations did change, but not in a healthy way. The power that Park had established over the *chaebol* became more open to manipulation, and Park's single-minded, somewhat ascetic approach became tempered by corruption. Recent court proceedings have revealed that President Roh Tae Woo received more than $650 million dollars in bribes from business during his eight-year career. Although scandals rocked the Japanese political establishment too, the stakes were not this high.

4. A feature of most of the Japanese *keiretsu* is the group bank, which provides credit to member companies. In Korea, the government nationalized the banking system, and groups had no access to internal finance, heightening the degree of government control over the groups.

5. *Chaebol* conduct an even wider range of activities than *keiretsu*. Many *keiretsu* are vertically oriented (like Toyota) and although the group consists of many firms, all are oriented around a core activity. Even the horizontal *keiretsu*, which are diversified, tend in general to be more closely grouped around core activities than the *chaebol*.

6. *Chaebol* are even more burdened by debt than Japanese companies. The use of soft loans rather than equity fostered rapid growth in Korea, but resulted in high debt-to-equity ratios, threatening both industry and finance. It also complicates reform. At this point in time, imposing a hard-budget constraint on enterprises nurtured on soft loans would produce bankruptcies, which would reduce bank assets and produce failure in the financial sector. The government would need to guarantee the debts of the firm, or else the consequences on the financial system would be serious.

---

[11]As always, exceptions occur on both sides. Sony, Honda, and Toyota are all headed by founders, while Daewoo is in the hands of professional managers.

The *Chaebol* and Economic Efficiency

The Korean government played a leading role in establishing the dominance of the major *chaebol*, particularly during the HCI drive and the subsequent business downturn. Table 13.2 shows that in 1974, at the start of the drive, the combined sales of the top 10 groups amounted to only 15 percent of GDP; no group had sales of more than 4.9 percent of GDP. However, government policy nurtured heavy industry by inviting the major *chaebol* to enter into new fields while providing the necessary loan capital and import licenses. Each success was rewarded by new invitations and new privileges. By 1984, the largest two groups (Hyundai and Samsung) each had sales of 12 percent of GDP, and the share of the top 10 had risen to 67.4 percent.

Most goods markets in Korea are characterized by concentration ratios that are high relative to western standards; an economy-wide analysis in 1981 showed an average three-firm concentration ratio of 62 percent, indicating even greater concentration than Japan or Taiwan. Though this ratio did not mean the total absence of competition—*chaebol* compete with each other aggressively over market share—and although competition is often nonprice in nature, it does put limits on the abuse of monopoly power and promotes efficiency.

However, the main force for efficiency comes from the need to compete in international markets. Since the early 1960s, when Park declared that exports were Korea's "economic lifeline," industry's success was evaluated in terms of export performance and larger enterprises had to face, and prevail against, international competition in foreign markets. However, by the late 1980s doubts about the ability of an industrial structure dominated by the *chaebol* to sustain growth became widespread.

REFORMING THE *CHAEBOL*

The *chaebol*, and the unwavering government guidance and support that they enjoyed, are usually credited with the rapid growth of the Korean economy, its development of a heavy industrial base, and its export performance. Although performance in export markets provided some check on competitiveness, until the Asian financial crisis of the late 1990s the government never allowed any of the groups, or even parts of groups, to fail. Sometimes operations were transferred from one group to another in search of better performance, but by and large a soft-budget constraint operated as universally as in any socialist country. Moreover, the high ratios of debt to equity in Korean business meant that any failure in manufacturing could result in dire consequences for the banking system. Consequently, the government acted to bail out almost any failing enterprise.

Korean economic performance actually began to falter in the late 1980s, raising doubts as to whether a *chaebol*-dominated structure was adequate to sustain the economy into the next century. In 1992 the incoming administration of Kim Young Sam made a serious commitment to systematic reform of the economy, including the *chaebol*, whose influence was seen as a barrier to further economic growth due to several factors:

1. They represented an unhealthy concentration of power in product markets. As noted earlier, the *chaebol* (especially the "big four") dominated many markets, exports, and investment.

2. The demands of the *chaebol* for investment funds tended to squeeze out nascent small enterprise and handicapped the growth of innovative companies.

3. The *chaebol* were integrally connected with the corruption of the Korean economy.

4. Diversification within the *chaebol* created substantial diseconomies of organization. Top management, often drawn from the founding family, lacked the expertise to operate in wide-ranging markets, yet these managers failed to delegate.

5. Finally, the government was concerned that the strategy of aggressive globalization pursued by the major *chaebol* involves too many risks. This fear owed much to the costly disaster of the 1980s when Korean overseas construction operations fell victim to recession, became bankrupt, and left the government to clean up the mess. The pace and scale of globalization in the mid-1990s was impressive. In 1994 Korean companies initiated almost 2,000 overseas investment projects with a total value of more than $3.5 billion; the figures for 1995 were comparable. Daewoo planned to establish 600 overseas companies by the year 2000. LG Group planned to invest $10 billion in mainland China alone between 1991 and 2008, a figure larger than Korea's total overseas investment in 1994.

In the late 1990s the Korean government began a policy of reining in the *chaebol* by intervention and regulation, rather than by allowing increased competition. Foreign economists questioned this move, arguing that a quicker way would be to liberalize financial markets and open the door for foreign firms to market and invest in Korea. That approach would force *chaebol* to retrench into their core areas where they held an advantage and to sell off less productive assets to owners who can put them to higher value uses. However, such retrenchment and downsizing brings with it loss of employment and increased foreign ownership, both of which in Korea at the time were politically unpopular. Fear of political reaction, and its own preconceptions, led the government to try to fashion reform rather than to liberalize, getting the *chaebol* to agree to reduce the number of subsidiaries and transfer assets to each other in return for continued protection and support. This tactic led to skepticism about both the government's commitment to a market solution and the overall outcome. Other elements were included in the reform agenda:

1. *Real name financial accounting.* Korean corruption was facilitated by a system that allowed bank accounts to be opened with dummy names, which made tracing bribes difficult. Now such accounts are now outlawed and only "real name" accounts will be legal.

2. *Restriction of founding family's investments.* Only subsidiaries in which the founding family's holding is less than 8 percent are now able to raise capital and pursue new businesses.

3. *Restrictions on **intragroup cross investment**.* No company in a *chaebol* can invest more than 40 percent of its capital in a company in the same group. This percent will decline with time, reducing the within-group financial linkages.

4. *Restricting outgoing foreign investment.* To curb overseas investment by Korean firms, new regulations require that all overseas investments greater than $100 million require at least 20 percent domestic capital.

Beyond these reforms, the government tried to take an active approach to restructuring the groups. It stipulated that the debt-to-equity ratio be reduced to 200 percent by the end of 1999, involving a considerable amount of debt-equity swapping, whereby the banks receive shares in payment for loans. (In mid-1997 the *average* debt-to-equity ratio for the top 10 *chaebol* was more than 800 percent.) An attempt was made, through the Financial Supervisory Commission (FSC) created in 1988, to rationalize the groups by swapping subsidiaries to reduce the horizontal spread of the groups and foster greater specialization, allowing concentration of management expertise. The commission has since been implicated in bribery scandals, throwing a question mark over its efficacy as a watchdog.

However, this program ran into predictable difficulty and the groups fought over who should control particular sectors of industry. To encourage the growth of small and medium-sized industry, the government created a special fund of $1.2 billion for development loans. The top five *chaebol* were banned from access to this fund altogether and the next 25 largest are limited to only 30 percent of the total capital available. Although the intent is good, the implementation is still interventionist and supplants the "level playing field" of the market with a new form of directed credit.[12]

In any event, this program of regulated reform was overtaken by the events of the 1997 financial crisis. Much of the blame for the eruption of the crisis lay with the *chaebol* system itself. The largest of the groups were overstretched in terms of their range of output, and were much too heavily levered in terms of debt versus equity. As their profitability suffered, they were unable to service their debt burden. The banks that uncritically loaned capital to the *chaebol* at the government's behest, accumulated nonperforming loans on their books, driving them to insolvency. Six of the leading commercial banks were acquired by the government to keep them out of bankruptcy.

The crisis brought home in short order the economic lessons that the *chaebol* and the government were beginning to learn. Many of the *chaebol* had already begun to evaluate their structure and to question whether, in the view of the problems created by size and complexity, it was necessary to offer such a breadth of products. Moreover, the dynastic nature of many *chaebol* is leading to division of power within the group. Just as Charlemagne's empire was split among his sons, so the need to accommodate a new generation is leading to the breakup of the tight autocratic structure that prevailed to this point. Each of the four brothers of Chung Ju Woon, the founder of Hyundai, runs a satellite *chaebol*; the largest, Halla, is the

---

[12]See "The Chaebol That Ate Korea," *The Economist*, November 14, 1998, p. 67.

sixteenth biggest in the country.[13] Samsung spun off two smaller groups in the last two years—one run by the founder's sister and one by his niece.

A major test of the government's resolve occurred in August 1999 when Daewoo, then the second largest *chaebol*, was unable to meet its obligations on its $50 billion of debt.[14] Its continued expansion as it picked up companies at cheap prices throughout the Asian financial crisis resulted in its debt becoming unmanageable. Although the government of Kim Dae Jung stated emphatically that it would not bail out the group, neither government nor the banks have moved to liquidate a single Daewoo company. Financial restructuring will give bondholders a title to 80 percent of the value of the debt they hold, but the group will continue to be under the direction of Kim Woo Chang, who founded the firm in 1967. Even though government policy is overtly directed to destroying the hold of the major *chaebol*, it is unwilling to let any die through bankruptcy.

Restructuring on an economy-wide basis will be difficult until a tightening of Korea's rather toothless bankruptcy law occurs. As *The Economist* has reported:

> To reform a country's economy, weak firms must be weeded out so that the strong have more room to grow. Yet South Korean bankruptcy does not work like that. In the United States, under Chapter 11, a court typically appoints new managers to restructure the firm or to liquidate it in an orderly fashion; in Korea, most bankrupt firms simply carry on as before. Managers stay at their desks and rarely shut down business. The most popular bankruptcy route, chosen by more than 80 percent of the firms that filed for court protection last year, leaves the existing management untouched. Called *Hwaeui*, it allows firms to defer their existing debts and interest payments, and even to take out new loans, without relinquishing day-to-day control.[15]

Perhaps even more worrisome is that government is allowing bankrupt firms a more lenient path if it considers their core business to be sound. Under this arrangement government sponsorship gives some firms preferential access to bank loans, once more setting the bureaucrats above the market. Credit to the big companies was eased when in 1998 the IMF stepped in with a generous package of supports ($60 billion in total) that were in principle tied to economic reform, especially imposing a hard-budget constraint on the *chaebol*. However, the cheap won stimulated the economy and exports boomed again. The revival began to persuade many Koreans that their economy was structurally fine after all. Growth perked up in 2000 and 2001 and the unemployment rate fell sharply. The IMF aid was used to refinance into the failing companies and in 2002 the debt-to-equity ratio of the leading *chaebol* fell to a more respectable 174%—down from 352% in 2001 and more than 800% in 1997.

Daewoo, the weakest of the big four *chaebol*, declared bankruptcy in 1999, but it teetered on for two more years, maintaining its core businesses, while the government looked around for possible buyers for some of its subsidiaries. This situation brought to the fore an important dilemma for Korea. The companies best placed to

---

[13]*The Economist*, May 18, 1996, p. 69.
[14]"The Death of Daewoo," *The Economist*, August 21, 1999, p. 55.
[15]"Death Where Is Thy Sting?" *The Economist*, July 17, 1999, p. 59.

buy the bankrupt entities were foreign, but the Korean government was reluctant to give foreigners control over economically strategic enterprises. In turn, overseas corporations, historically excluded from the Korean market, feared that they would be discriminated against in favor of Korean-held corporations. They were reluctant to pay much for the assets while the government feared the political repercussions of selling Korean industry to them. In the end, after much hesitation, it succeeded in selling off Daewoo motors to General Motor after a long-pursued deal with Ford fell through. Nevertheless, the government can hardly be said to have passed the test of truly liberalizing the Korean economy. The *chaebol* may be down but they are not out.

INVESTMENT AND SAVINGS

Korea maintained a high investment rate since the early 1960s. Fixed capital formation took at least a quarter of GDP in every time period since then. Following the outset of the HCI, private investment averaged more than 30 percent of GDP per year. However, the savings behavior of Koreans changed considerably.

Table 13.3 shows the rate of gross domestic capital formation as well as the means of finance. One of the most salient features of the table is the high degree of reliance on foreign saving as a source of funds for investment during the early years. In the 1960s and early 1970s, this category (comprised largely of foreign aid transfers and net borrowing from the rest of the world) made up at least 30 percent of total capital formation. It fell sharply in the early 1980s and in fact turned negative (repayments were greater than new borrowing) by the 1990s. This extensive overseas borrowing implied a growing external debt, which peaked at the end of 1985, at a level of $47 billion.

Private domestic saving rose considerably in recent years.[16] Studies of the Korean economy in the 1980s noted the relatively low level of personal saving in

■ TABLE *13.3*

	Savings and Investment Rates, 1961–1990 (as a percentage of GDP)			
	Private Saving	Government Saving	Foreign Saving	Investment
1961–1965	6.8	0	8.1	14.8
1966–1970	10.3	5.5	9.8	25.8
1971–1975	15.5	3.7	9.1	27.6
1976–1980	18	6.2	6.4	31.3
1981–1985	18.4	6.5	4.9	30.1
1986–1990	29.2	7.5	−4.5	31.6

SOURCE: Kuznets, *Korean Economic Development* (Westport, CT: Praeger, 1994), p. 43.

---

[16]Private saving is the saving of both businesses (through retained earnings and depreciation allowances) and private households.

Korea, relative to Taiwan and Japan.[17] Since then, however, personal saving in Korea increased to about one-quarter of disposal income, implying relatively high personal marginal savings rates. Korea now shows a higher gross savings rate (domestic savings/GDP) than any member of the Organization for Economic Cooperation and Development (OECD), including Japan.[18] The World Bank reported that at 35 percent of GDP in 1993, Korea posted the sixth highest gross savings rate in the world, an achievement bettered only by Thailand, Malaysia, Singapore, Gabon, and Jamaica.

THE FINANCIAL SYSTEM

Banking

The structure of the Korean financial system is relatively simple. At the top is the central bank, the **Bank of Korea (BoK)**. Since May 1962, when the military government made the central bank subject to its political will, the BoK has enjoyed little independence. Despite the retention of a board of governors, all important matters are decided by the minister of finance, and, in cases of deep disagreement between the minister and the board of governors, by the cabinet as a whole.

Korea has two types of deposit institutions are commercial banks and specialized banks. In operation are some 17 nationwide commercial banks (including six held by the government since 1997), and 10 regional ones.[19] The commercial banks are largely funded by retail deposits, augmented by borrowing from the central bank. The military regime nationalized the commercial banks in 1962, and they remained under government control until 1982. Although nominally private, the government controlled their actions and until 1993 vetted all important personnel changes. The commercial banks made about one-third of total loans in the 1990s. Six specialized deposit banks, all government controlled, represent about 12 percent of total loans made in Korea. The oldest of these is the Korean Development Bank, which finances major development projects. The Industrial Bank of Korea is oriented to small and medium-sized business, and the Citizens' National Bank operates in household finance. Three banking cooperatives include those for farmers, livestock producers, and fisheries.

Until recently, the conduct of banking in the formal sector was rarely based on market principles. Interest rates paid to depositors were controlled by the government and kept low. Loans to industry were directed by the government and frequently carried lower interest rates than the depositor received. Depending on inflation, it was not uncommon for depositors to receive, and for borrowers to pay, negative real interest rates, which led to several undesirable effects. The supply of

[17]For example, see Tibor Scitovsky, "Economic Development in Taiwan and South Korea, 1965–1981," in *Models of Development: A Comparative Study of Korea and Taiwan* Lawrence J. Lau, ed. (San Francisco: San Francisco, Institute of Contemporary Studies, 1986), 168–178.
[18]Actually Luxembourg's rate is greater due to small size and special circumstance.
[19]In addition, 55 foreign banks operate branches in Korea.

savings was consequently depressed, and businesses, especially those not in favor with the government, were denied access to funds.

Inevitably an unofficial street or **curb market** arose. Interest rates paid to lenders were substantially above those paid in the banks.[20] The size of this market was difficult to gauge, but estimates put it at between one-third and 40 percent of all business loans.[21] In 1972 the government attempted both to suppress the curb market and to meet industry demands for cheaper credit. Nominal bank deposit rates were cut (to 12%), loan rates to industry reduced, and the curb market penalized. However, with inflation hovering around 20 percent throughout the 1970s, real interest rates in the formal sector were negative, and the curb market paying positive real rates continued to prosper well into the 1980s. The cause of the curb market was **financial repression** in the formal market, but from the 1970s onward the government allowed and encouraged the growth of nonbank financial institutions. This segment, coupled with the higher rates paid by the commercial banks, greatly reduced the scope of the curb market.

Equity Markets

The privately incorporated **Korean Stock Exchange (KSE)** is the sole official stock exchange. It is overseen by a **Securities and Exchange Commission** responsible to the Ministry of Finance. Government policy toward the stock market has been interventionist and has, through tax and other measures, encouraged its growth. In the 1960s; for example, the government required large companies to issue attractively priced shares and use the proceeds to reduce bank debt. The number of traded stocks rose sharply, from 34 in 1968 to 688 in 1992. Market capitalization was $107 billion at the end of 1993; about one-third of GDP and the 14th largest market in the world. Further use of the equity market is desirable because it would reduce the debt-to-equity ratios of Korean industry, contributing to both business and financial-sector stability.

Some are concerned about the stability of the stock market itself. The government, as in many other areas, saw fit to intervene. It actively promoted the market, encouraging the activity of small and unsophisticated participants, making the market quite volatile. The government also manipulated stock prices ostensibly in the interest of stabilization, a policy fraught with danger because markets in which the government is known to intervene are more likely to be unstable. The market needs a more even-handed approach and more transparent supervision at this point.

Further Liberalization

The development of the Korean economy has been distorted by the fact that investment capital was available in different industries at widely different rates of interest.

---

[20]In 1970 the time deposit rate was 22.8 percent, where the curb rate for deposits was 50.8 percent.
[21]Song, *The Rise of the Korean Economy* (Oxford: Oxford University Press), p. 162; Cho and Yoon, *Economic Development of the Republic of Korea* (Honolulu: University of Hawaii Press, 1991), p. 130.

As late as 1992 the Bank of Korea reported that the average cost of funds in the electricity industry was 7.6 percent, but in textiles it was 12 percent and in food production 17 percent.[22] Even though this dispersion was considerably lower than observed a decade earlier, its biased investment in favor of heavy industry and against the consumer sector still precipitated injurious consequences for Korean economic welfare.

The five-year liberalization program for the financial sector, introduced in 1993, further reduced distortion by deregulating interest rates for both borrowing and lending, which lessened the implicit subsidy to heavy industry and the *chaebol*. The main beneficiary has been the household sector, which will receive higher interest rates on deposits (possibly causing the household saving rate to rise further) and a reduction in the cost of credit for consumption and home construction.

PUBLIC FINANCE

Size of the Government Sector

Despite its continued heavy intervention in many areas, the government sector in Korea is small relative to most developed countries. About 25 percent of GDP is gathered by the government in taxes, the lowest of any OECD member. This amounts to about two-thirds of the Japanese level and about half of the average level in the OECD. The main reason for this low percentage is the relatively rudimentary social security system, introduced only in 1988, and the consequent low level of transfer payments.

The Value-Added Tax

The revenue system places heavy reliance on the value-added tax (VAT). Its nominal single rate of 10 percent is supplemented by additional levies on certain goods, imposed both to discourage consumption and to raise revenue. Taken together, these indirect taxes on consumption provide 46 percent of general government revenue. Property taxes raise an additional 14 percent. Consumption taxes such as VAT are generally regressive, taking a larger share of the income of less well-off families. Studies indicated that this generalization is true in Korea, but the reliance on indirect taxation, and the regressivity of the system, may be helpful in meeting development objectives. The disincentive effects of progressive income tax rates are avoided while capital accumulation and savings by high-income groups are promoted.

The Personal Income Tax

Income taxation (i.e., the personal income tax plus corporate income taxes) accounts for about 35 percent of tax revenue. Both corporate and personal taxes

---

[22]The rates are lowest for heavy industry because the government usually acts to secure foreign finance at a level below Korean rates.

were recently reformed to move them away from a "schedular" system, in which the rates varied sharply between sources and industry. This system was an overt tool in selective industrial development. The new "global" system seeks to provide a more level playing field.

Most Koreans pay no income tax at all; only about 5 percent of the total population files a tax return, against about 45 percent in the United States. Even among those who file, most pay only an effective rate of 3.8 percent of income. Rates are progressive and rise to a maximum of 50 percent, but this amount is paid at the margin only by those whose income is more than 6.5 times the average. To encourage saving, and as a hangover of the schedular system, a ceiling tax rate on interest and dividend income is set at 20 percent.[23]

The Corporate Income Tax

Corporate taxes once varied between industry and between source. Profits from exports, for example, were once tax exempt. Now, however, the corporate tax is flat: 20 percent for small companies and 34 percent for large. Incentives are retained in the form of tax credits for exports (2 percent of total sales) and a 10 percent credit for investment in research and development.

LABOR MARKETS

The Role of Abundant Labor

Korea's success in penetrating export markets relied on plentiful cheap labor, which was the result of three factors:

1. The existence of a large subsistence agricultural sector, with low marginal productivity, from which labor could be drawn at low wages and with little impact on agricultural output.

2. The failure of an active and radical union movement to emerge during the first 25 years of rapid growth. Amsden considers this failure to be common among late industrializers and attributes it to the absence of a cadre of skilled workers, "a labor aristocracy," which provided the model for unionization in Europe and the United States.

3. The policy of the successive governments (especially Park and Chun) to repress worker activity and intervene with force in labor disputes. A general feature of regime changes in Korea has been a great deal of strike activity immediately after a change of president.[24] Strong government action usually restored a "law-and-order" antiunion policy.

---

[23]To encourage "going public," dividends of unlisted companies are taxed at a higher rate of 25 percent.
[24]Peaks of strike activity occurred in 1960–1961 after the death of Syngman Rhee, in 1979–1980 after the death of Park, and in 1987–1989 after the replacement of Chun with Roh Tae Woo. See Rodgers in Lawrence B. Krause and Fun-koo Park, *Social Issues in Korea: Korean and American Perspectives* (Seoul, Korea: Korean Development Institute, 1993), p. 78.

The Progress of Unionization

In the late 1980s, however, the situation changed permanently. Incoming President Roh was confronted by worker and student activism. Loathe to use force, lest world reaction lead to a cancellation of the 1988 Seoul Olympics, Roh changed legislation to allow more union activity. Union membership rose to more than 1.7 million members in 1996 with 14.3 percent of all Korean workers represented, but fell during the financial crisis of 1997–98. About two-thirds of unionized workers are nominally members of the moderate government-recognized and sponsored Korea Federation of Trade Unions (FKTU) and about one-third are affiliated with the much more active and radical Korean Confederation of Trade Unions (KCTU). Some member unions of the KCTU are actually illegal, and the KCTU is not officially recognized though it is allowed to have access to some aspects of policy making.

Union militancy rose rapidly. In the period 1990–1996 an average of almost 2 million worker days were lost. Considerable wage increases were won, averaging 17 percent annually between 1987 and 1996; real increases, after inflation, were considerably less, around 10 percent, but still substantial and greater than the gain in labor productivity, implying increasing labor costs. However, in the aftermath of the financial crisis, union membership and militancy both fell. The unionization rate fell from 14.35 in 1990–1996 to 11.8 percent in 1999. Days lost to strikes fell by 75 percent between 1996 and 1997, but are on the increase once more.

The Tripartite Commission

Wages in Korea historically were negotiated at the plant level, between the employers and the representative unions. However, the government sponsored national negotiation between the FKTU and its employers' counterpart, the Korean Employers Federation (KEF). In 1998 in an attempt to coordinate a national response to the crisis the government formed the Korea Tripartite Commission (KTC) with involvement of labor and the unions. Initially the radical KCTU rejected the commission and pursued a militant path, but constrained by its membership it eventually accepted representation in the KTC in 2001.

Managing Labor in the Workplace

Labor management in Korea has been criticized for its rigidity. Although generalizations are dangerous and exceptions may be found, emphasis in Korean factories seems to be placed on discipline rather than on worker initiative. Deference is paid to the conception of workplace efficiency, Taylorism, rather than to modern methods. This approach contrasts with the policies in Japan's large corporations. These repressive practices might become a greater problem as the economy develops because they stifle individual initiative.

Education and Human Capital

Korea has made a large social investment in the education of its young people. In 1990, 3.6 percent of GDP was devoted to expenditure on education, up from just 2 percent in 1960, which represented a huge increase in real terms because of the growth of the economy. Education ranks high in the government's priorities, evidenced by the 22.5 percent of total government outlays devoted to educational expenditures in 1990. Today, school attendance is on a par with almost all of the developed market economies, as indicated in Table 13.4. Particularly noteworthy is universal primary school attendance and the gains in middle and high school and tertiary education. Moreover, unlike many developing or recently developed countries, little bias exists in the education system between male and female children. Female enrollment ratios in primary school are 100 percent, which slips to 85 percent in high school, much the same as the overall figure. Female enrollment in tertiary education is slightly lower than male. However, statistics show substantial bias in the workplace against women. Women make up only 3 percent of the managerial and administrative workforce. This low rate might in part be a generational problem. Female educational attainment has increased rapidly, but if Korea follows the Japanese experience, women will still have a hard time reaching the upper echelons of management.

The gain in education can be seen not only been in terms of numbers attending school. The educational achievement of Korean children also ranks high. Standardized international tests (see Table 13.5) show Korean students with extraordinary attainment in math and science-related areas of the curriculum.

SOURCES OF GROWTH

Until the mid-1990s Korean growth was remarkable not only for its rapidity, but also for its consistency. Real GDP grew at 9 percent in 1963–1973, accelerated slightly during 1973–1979 (the period of HCI), and pulled back slightly to 8.2 percent between 1979 and 1990 (see Table 13.6). Later figures (not included in the table because they lack the accompanying breakdown on the sources of growth) indicate that the rate recovered to greater than 9 percent during 1990 and 1991, slipped to about 5 percent in 1992 and 1993, but was trending upward again in 1994 before falling during the Asian crisis of 1997–1998.

■ TABLE 13.4

		Education Attendance in Korea (percentage of relevant age group)							
		Pre-Primary		Primary		Secondary		Tertiary	
		Male	Female	Male	Female	Male	Female	Male	Female
1970		2.7	2.3	100	100	50.2	32.5	11	3.7
1980		8.3	7.3	100	100	82.1	73.8	21.3	7.5
1990		56.1	54.7	100	100	91.1	88.5	51.3	25.1
1997		86.9	89.1	100	100	93.8	94.8	82	52.4

SOURCE: Unesco Institute for Statistics, "World Education Statistics," available at http://www.uis.unesco.org/en/stats/stats0.htm.

■ TABLE *13.5*

Educational Performance: Attainment on Standardized Test, Age 13, 1997

	Math	Science
Korea	73.4	77.7
Switzerland	70.8	73.7
France	64.2	68.6
Italy	64.0	69.9
Canada	62.0	68.8
Scotland	60.6	67.9
England	60.6	68.7
Ireland	60.5	63.3
Spain	55.4	67.2
United States	55.3	67.0

SOURCE: OECD.

However, the bulk of that growth resulted from an increase in factor inputs, rather than an improvement in **total factor productivity (TFP)**.[25] In other words, most of Korean growth was attributable to the increase in the number of hours worked, an increase in the amount of capital per worker, and the movement of workers from the low productivity rural and self-employed sector into the industrialized urban sector. Only in the early period of growth did advances in knowledge produce a distinct effect on the increase in output. TFP grew at a rate of about 2.4 percent across the whole period, falling between the earlier and the later years. In the export-oriented period of 1963–1973, total growth of 9 percent could be decomposed into 5.6 percent due to factor inputs and 3.4 percent TFP. Labor inputs grew at 3.2 percent, largely due to an increased labor force participation rate. Capital inputs (residential and nonresidential) grew at 2.4 percent. In terms of increase in efficiency, the biggest free lunch was the movement of workers from the agricultural sector into higher productivity manufacturing and service sector jobs, and a substantial increase due to increased applied technology.

During the HCI period, both labor and capital inputs increased more rapidly; the movement of labor from the rural to the industrial sector increased its role, but advances in knowledge and other residual factors showed no positive impact on growth, confirming the suspicions that the distortions of the HCI drive led to a negative effect on overall efficiency. In the final period of the table, capital increased its role once more, and reallocation of labor had a smaller effect as the reserve of labor in agriculture was largely used up.

---

[25]Recall that TFP is defined as the increase in output per factor input, and is usually measured as a residual after controlling for the increase in inputs. It represents mostly the growth that results from an improvement in allocative efficiency, the grasping of scale economies, and the effect of increases in technical expertise.

■ **TABLE 13.6**

Growth of GDP and Its Sources (by subperiod, annual percent)

	1963—1973	1973—1979	1979—1990	1963—1990
GDP growth rate (annual average)	9.00%	9.26%	8.21%	8.74%
Contributions to Growth				
Factor inputs	5.64	7.01	6.66	6.36
Business labor input	3.18	3.49	2.66	3.04
Employment	2.28	2.13	1.64	1.99
Hours worked	0.5	0.52	20.07	0.27
Age-sex composition	20.06	0.3	0.14	0.1
Education	0.47	0.55	0.94	0.68
Nonresidential capital input	1.19	1.79	2.66	1.92
Residential capital input	1.24	1.67	1.26	1.35
Land	0.03	0.06	0.08	0.06
Output per unit of input (TFP)	3.37	2.25	1.55	2.38
Improved resource allocation	1.23	1.76	0.96	1.24
Effect of weather on farming	0.23	0.18	20.11	0.08
Economies of scale	0.26	0.34	0.21	0.26
Advances in knowledge	1.64	20.02	0.50	0.80

SOURCE: OECD. *Economic Survey: Korea* (Paris: OECD, 1996).

This profile led to a reexamination of the nature of the "Korean miracle." In an influential article published in *Foreign Affairs* in 1994, Paul Krugman drew attention to a large and growing literature that indicated that the "miracle" owed far more to increased participation rates, the movement of labor, and rapid accumulation of capital than it did to increases in efficiency per se. He compared the industrialization of South Korea with that of Stalin's Soviet Union: it was due much more to increase in factors of production (labor and capital) than to the more efficient use of those factors. We will return to this assessment in a fuller discussion of the Asian miracle.[26]

UNIFYING NORTH AND SOUTH KOREA?

In our discussion of Asian economies we concentrated on capitalist systems and said little about North Korea, which remains one of the most closed and isolationist states in the world. Although information is scarce, it seems that currently the economy is in crisis and faces possible collapse. In these circumstances the military standoff that has dominated Korean political life (and has had a sizable impact on

[26]See more on this issue in Chapter 15.

economic development) might soon be a thing of the past.[27] Moreover, it seems increasingly likely that we shall see the reunification of the two Korean states, as we witnessed in Vietnam in the 1970s and in Germany in the late 1980s. Therefore it is logical to inquire as to what the economic impact of such a reunification would be.

In the long run, the reunification might give South Korean industry access to substantial additional natural resources, but the economic benefit of this alone will be slight. Despite the optimistic prediction of many economists in 1989, the unification of Germany was a traumatic episode. We reviewed some of that history in Chapter 9. The main cause of the difficulties was the low level of productivity in East German industry coupled with the political necessity of unifying the currency system at a rate that would provide comparable standards of living. The impact of that unification is now well known. After unification, East German labor was highly paid relative to its productivity, and therefore the region could not compete with manufacturing industry in the European Community. The result was a massive loss of jobs, considerable out-migration, the commitment of 5 percent of West Germany's GDP to Eastern reconstruction, and considerable ill will. The task in the Korean peninsula would be even more formidable. The data provided in Table 13.7 give some indication of this challenge. Unification led to an increase of the West German population of about 23 percent. In Korea the addition would be almost 52 percent.

On average, East Germans were about 30 percent as well off as West Germans. GDP per head in North Korea is less than 10 percent of that in the South. Equal distribution of the joint GDP in Korea would involve a transfer of about one-third of the total product of the South. Even the much more modest goal of raising average

■ TABLE 13.7

The Koreas and the Germanys: Social and Economic Indicators

	(1) South Korea	(2) North Korea	(3) (2) as a Percent of (1)	(4) West Germany	(5) East Germany	(6) (5) as a Percent of (6)
Population	44.9	23.3	51.9	62.1	16.6	26.7
GDP per head, $ PPP	10,067	957	9.5	19,283	5,840	30.3
Exports, % of GDP	27.7	3.3	11.9	28.3	24.5	86.6
Imports, % of GDP	29.9	5.9	19.7	22.4	24.3	108.5
Infant mortality per 1,000 births	12.8	31.3	244.5	7.4	7.7	101.4
Farm population, % of total	13.1	37.6	287	3.7	10.8	291.9
Radios per 1,000 population	1,003	207	20.6	830	990	119.3

NOTE: Data for the Koreas is 1995 and that for Germany is 1989.
SOURCE: Dresdner Bank, reproduced in *The Economist,* May 10, 1997, p. 78.

[27]Despite its economic difficulties, North Korea continues to prioritize the military and add technologically advanced weaponry to its arsenal.

income in the North to 50 percent of that in the South would involve a transfer of about $60 billion annually, more than 13 percent of South Korean GDP. In Germany the level of transfers was close to 5 percent of West German GDP. Although significant savings would be realized in terms of military expenditure on the forces now ranged across the 50th parallel, the short-term consequences would be deflationary, and the "peace dividend" would be secured only after substantial changes in the structure of production. In short, as an economic proposition, reuniting the North with South Korea would be extremely costly to South Korea in the short run.

PROSPECTS FOR THE KOREAN ECONOMY

Korea is a strong economy with considerable prowess in both traditional engineering industries and a growing role in the information and communications technology businesses. It is also true that since the onset of the Asian financial crisis in 1997, the government attempted to restrict the power of the major groups, promote the growth of small and medium-sized industry, and allow some of the fundamentally unprofitable companies go to the wall. However, in Korea an attitude still exists that bankruptcies are to be avoided wherever possible, and to this end the Korean Development Bank (KDB), a public institution, has underwritten a substantial volume of corporate sector debt. In theory firms that are not economically viable are excluded from this scheme, but doubt remains as to whether the triage process has been conducted even-handedly. In October 2000, 563 firms were identified as unable to meet debt service for three successive years, yet of these only 29 were classified as being appropriate for receivership.[28] The others were authorized to have their bonds underwritten by the KDB. The previous evaluation occurred 30 months before, and the next is currently unscheduled. This process raises a serious question of moral hazard. Few firms are subject to a hard-budget constraint, and therefore genuine austerity moves are not required for survival, feeding the problems of the financial sector. Commercial banks failed to yield profits in two years, because of increasing need for bad loan provisions. Until substantial corporate restructuring is achieved, the Korean financial sector will continued to be weak.

However, the great *chaebol* are less dominant than they were prior to the crisis, most visibly in the area of start-ups, where independent small and medium-sized firms, rather than *chaebol* subsidiaries, are more common. However, it is also true that the big groups are beginning to expand once more, especially in the areas of high technology, and are lobbying hard to remove some of the restrictions on group investment.[29] A particular restriction is the rule that limits a firm's investment activity to 25 percent of its assets. The victory of Roh Moo Hyun in the presidential election of December 2002 is certain to keep some of the pressure on the groups. His opponent Lee Hoi Chang campaigned on a platform of unshackling the *chaebol* of

---

[28]OECD, *Economic Survey of Korea,* September 2001, p. 13.
[29]See "Return of the Behemoths," *Far Eastern Economic Review,* October 11, 2001.

the restrictions placed during the era of Kim Dae Jung. Lee also wanted to crack down on the power of the unofficial trade union movement, while Roh has a record of strong support for workers' rights. Consequently, the new regime can be anticipated to be on the side of small businesses and the workers. Whether this approach is compatible with accelerated and sustained growth remains to be seen.

KEY TERMS AND CONCEPTS

Bank of Korea (BoK)	intragroup cross investment
chaebol	*jaebul*
Confucianism	Korean Stock Exchange (KSE)
curb market	market-augmenting approach
export promotion	market-conforming approach
export quota	Ministry of Finance (MoF)
financial repression	Ministry of Trade and Industry (MTI)
Heavy and Chemical Industries	Securities and Exchange Commission
Development Plan (HCI)	total factor productivity (TFP)

QUESTIONS FOR DISCUSSION

1. In what ways may the Japanese colonial period be said to have assisted Korean development? How did it hurt it?
2. Why was the Korean economy "distorted" in the 1950s?
3. Did the export promotion drive follow comparative advantage?
4. In what ways was the chemical industries drive an exercise in creating comparative advantage?
5. What tools did Korean planners use to favor particular *chaebol?*
6. Why is the concentration of power in *chaebol* alarming? Does it hasten or retard growth?
7. What are the chief differences between the *keiretsu* and the *chaebol?*
8. What impact did the Asian financial crisis have on the *chaebol?*
9. How will increased union activity change the Korean economy?
10. Has Korean growth been extensive or intensive in nature?
11. Why would Korean unification be different from the reunification of Germany?
12. Why has the government attempted to control the investment activity of *chaebol* subsidiaries? Make a case for why these efforts harm economic growth.

RESOURCES

Web Sites

Central Bank ....http://www.bok.or.kr/

Ministry of Finance and Economy ....http://www.mofe.go.kr/

Ministry of Commerce, Industry, and Energy ....http://www.mocie.go.kr/

Korea Herald—National Newspaper ....http://www.koreaherald.co.kr/

Korea Net Information Site ....http://www.korea.net/

Embassy of Korea in the United States ....http://www.koreaembassyusa.org/

Books and Articles

Alam, M. Shahid. *Governments and Markets in Economic Development Strategies: Lessons from Korea, Taiwan, and Japan.* New York: Praeger, 1989.

Amsden, Alice H. *Asia's Next Giant: South Korea and Late Industrialization.* New York: Oxford University Press, 1989.

Bedeski, Robert E. *The Transformation of South Korea: Reform and Reconstruction in the Sixth Republic under Roh Tae Woo, 1987–1992.* New York: Routledge, 1994.

Chang, Ha-Joon. "The Political Economy of Industrial Policy in Korea." *Cambridge Journal of Economics* 17 (1993), 131–157.

Cho, Lee-Jay, and Yoon Hyung Kim (eds.). *Economic Development in the Republic of Korea: A Policy Perspective.* Honolulu: University of Hawaii Press, 1991.

Clifford, Mark L. *Troubled Tiger: Businessmen, Bureaucrats, and Generals in South Korea.* Armonk, NY: M.E. Sharpe, 1994 (rev. by William McGurn in The American Spectator, March 1995, 59–61).

Corbo, Vittorio, and Sang-Mok Suh (eds.). *Structural Adjustment in a Newly Industrialized Country: The Korean Experience.* Baltimore, MD: Johns Hopkins University Press, 1992.

Eckert, Carter J. *Offspring of Empire: The Koch'ang Kims and the Colonial Origins of Korean Capitalism, 1876–1945.* Seattle: University of Washington Press, 1991.

Hamilton, Clive. *Capitalist Industrialization in Korea.* Boulder, CO: Westview Press, 1986.

Hwang, Eui-Gak. *The Korean Economies: A Comparison of North and South.* Oxford: Clarendon Press, 1993.

Jacobs, Norman. *The Korean Road to Modernization and Development.* Urbana, IL: University of Chicago Press, 1985.

Kim, Eun Mee (ed.). *The Four Asian Tigers: Economic Development and the Global Political Economy.* London: Academic Press, 1998.

Kim, June Dong. "Incidence of Protection: The Case of Korea." *Economic Development and Cultural Change,* April 1994, 617–629.

Kuznets, Paul W. *Korean Economic Development: An Interpretive Model.* Westport, CT: Praeger, 1994.

Kwon, Jene K. (ed.). *Korean Economic Development.* New York: Greenwood Press, 1990.

Lee, Chung H., and Ippei Yamazawa (eds.). *The Economic Development of Japan and Korea: A Parallel with Lessons.* New York: Praeger, 1990.

Leightner, Jonathan Edward. "The Compatibility of Growth and Increased Equality: Korea." *The Journal of Development Studies,* October 1992, 49–71.

Lie, John. Han *Unbound: The Political Economy of South Korea.* Stanford, CA: Stanford University Press, 1998.

Mo, Jongryn, and Chung-In Moon (eds.). *Democracy and the Korean Economy.* Stanford, CA: Hoover Institution Press, 1998.

OECD. *Economic Survey: Korea,* February 2003.

Park, Hans S. *North Korea: Ideology, Politics, Economy.* Upper Saddle River, NJ: Prentice Hall, 1995.

Patrick, Hugh T., and Yung Chul Park. *The Financial Development of Japan, Korea and Taiwan: Growth, Repression and Liberalization.* Oxford: Oxford University Press, 1994.

Pettman, Ralph. "Labor, Gender and the Balance of Productivity: South Korea and Singapore." *Journal of Contemporary Asia,* no. 1 (1992), 45–56.

Song, Byung-Nak. *The Rise of the Korean Economy.* Oxford: Oxford University Press.

"A Survey of the Koreas: Yesterday's War, Tomorrow's Peace." *The Economist,* July 10, 1999, 52–56.

Wornoff, Jon. *Korea's Economy: Man-made Miracle.* Seoul: Si-sa-yong-o-sa, 1983.

14

TAIWAN, SINGAPORE, AND INDONESIA

FROM REFUGE TO SILICON ISLAND: TAIWAN

TAIWAN	
Area (thousand sq. km.)	36
Currency	Taiwan dollar
Exchange Rate	36 Taiwan $ = US$1
Population 2000 (millions)	22
GNI per Capita, PPP	$13,950
GDP Growth, 1990–2000	6.1%
Inflation Rate, 1996–2001	0.8%
Value Added as % of GDP 2000 Agriculture	8%
Industry	37%
Services	55%
% of GDP General Government Expenditure	18.2%
Exports	47.8%

HISTORICAL BACKGROUND

Understanding the development of the Taiwanese economy from the 1950s onward requires a little history. The island was a colonial possession of the Japanese for almost a half-century and its economy was well integrated into the Japanese imperial system. This colonial association was by and large economically positive. Taiwan's gross domestic product (GDP) grew at a rate of about 3.8 percent per year between 1911 to 1938, faster than that of Japan itself. At the start of World War II, the island had a productive agricultural sector and a growing industrial base.

At the end of World War II, Taiwan became part of China once more, but the nation was divided by civil war. After defeat by the Communists, the Nationalist **Kuomintang (KMT)** government, with the remnants of its army evacuated to the island, ostensibly pending the reestablishment of control over all of China. The indigenous Taiwanese population of about 6 million was confronted by the influx of almost 2 million soldiers, politicians, and their families. The incoming regime took up the reins of economic control left by the Japanese colonial administration, and assumed ownership of much of the property on the island, including agricultural land and manufacturing plants. Because of its claim to rule all of China, the KMT depended little on local approval; as the nominal government of 1 billion Chinese, it had little reason to cede influence to ethnic Taiwanese, who represented in theory only a single, small province of the whole. Today the population of Taiwan is about 21.5 million people, 84 percent of Taiwanese descent (they or their parents lived on the island prior to 1948) and 14 percent of mainland Chinese stock whose families immigrated after the communist revolution. They are among the most prosperous people in Asia, with a GDP per head of about $13,500 per year, quite equitably distributed across the population.

Agricultural Development and Land Reform

Embarrassed by the victory of the Communists in 1948, and dissatisfied with the quality of nationalist leadership, the United States initially tried to terminate its relationship with the KMT. However, the outbreak of the Korean War made the preservation of "free China" in Taiwan an important strategic objective. U.S. aid and advice flowed toward the island, playing an important role in the development of the economy.

The first priority for the Americans was land reform, and they persuaded the Nationalists to pursue this goal aggressively. In the early 1950s, ownership of 37 percent of the island's cultivable land passed from landlord to tenant, making agriculture a dynamic and export-oriented sector.[1] Output grew at 4.4 percent per year, and crop yields were the highest in Asia outside Japan, providing the surplus needed as preconditions for industrial growth. Restrictions on agricultural exports kept food cheap, to the benefit of the industrialists because it enabled wages to be kept down.

Industrial Growth

With a rapidly rising population and limited resources and land area, Taiwan's comparative advantage lay in a labor-intensive, relatively small-scale manufacturing industry; although a disproportionate volume of output was in large enterprise (see Table 14.1). Manufacturing output doubled between 1952 and 1958 (an annual rate of 12%). To market-oriented economists,[2] Taiwan was a clear example of the power of competitive capitalism and a lesson for other developing nations.

[1]Robert Wade, *Governing the Market* (Princeton, NJ: Princeton University Press, 1970), p. 10.
[2]See W. Galensen, *Economic Growth and Structural Change in Taiwan: The Postwar Experience of the Republic of China* (Ithaca, NY: Cornell University Press, 1979).

■ TABLE 14.1

The Structure of Manufacturing Enterprise in Taiwan, 1984
(number, employment, and production as a percentage of the total)

	Employment per Establishment				
	1—19	20—99	100—499	500—999	1,000+
Enterprises in Employment Category %	82.1	13.8	3.5	0.4	0.2
Share of Total Employment %	17.4	24.1	28.8	10.3	19.6
Share of Total Production %	8.9	17.6	26.0	10.6	36.8

SOURCE: Provisional Data from Sixth Census (February 1984), Wade, *Governing the Market*, (Princeton, NJ: Princeton University Press, 1970), p. 67.

However, more recently "revisionists"[3] stressed the central role of the government in the management of the development effort.

The Neoclassical Interpretation of Taiwanese Growth

Neoclassical economists[4] emphasized the lack of government intervention in the Taiwanese economy especially after trade liberalization in 1958, which established a single realistic exchange rate, low tariffs, and easy access for foreign capital. In addition, Taiwan enjoyed free and fluid labor markets, with an increasingly well-trained labor force. The industrial structure was highly competitive compared to other East Asian economies, with a relative absence of large companies and monopoly. Although Taiwan does have "business groups," they are less central to the economy than the *keiretsu* in Japan, the *chaebol* in Korea, or even the family holding companies that emerged in Indonesia. For example, even though Korea's Hyundai *chaebol* employs hundreds of thousands, Taiwan's largest group, the Formosa Plastics Group, employs only 30,000 people.

Perhaps one of the strongest indices of the laissez faire nature of Taiwanese capitalism is the rapid turnover of firms on the island. Research indicates that it is easy both to go bankrupt and to start a business in Taiwan.[5] Competition drives a lot of companies to the wall, and, more important, the government does not intervene with soft money to save them but rather lets them die. This Schumpeterian process of creative destruction requires efficiency for survival and might be one source of Taiwan's impressive growth of total factor productivity. In 1991, for example, 40 percent of Taiwan's chemical output came from firms that had not existed five years before; from another perspective, the firms that contributed 58 percent of the output in 1981 had gone out of the business by 1991. Competitive pressures ensure constant attention to efficiency and little evidence of a soft-budget constraint.

[3]*The East Asian Miracle: A World Bank Policy Research Report* (New York: Oxford University Press, 1993), p. 9.
[4]The most prominent economists with these views on Taiwan are Ian Little and Gustav Ranis.
[5]Bee An Aw, M. Roberts, and X. Chen, "Firm-Level Evidence of Productivity Differentials," *National Bureau for Economic Research,* working paper #6235, October 1997.

THE FINANCIAL SYSTEM

Critics often characterize the Taiwanese financial system as rigid, slow-footed, and antiquated. However, whatever its shortcomings, the system was remarkably effective in financing much of the sustained economic development that occurred from the 1950s through the 1980s and proved much more robust than other Asian banking systems when financial markets came under pressure in the mid-1990s. Consequently, some reevaluation of the Taiwanese system and its slow pace of change is in order.

Historically, the government dominated banking and owned virtually all banks until the mid-1990s.[6] Direction of credit was less overt than in Korea or Japan. Periodically the Council for Economic Planning and Development, with the cooperation of the Ministry of Finance and Economic Affairs, issued a list of "preferred industries." Inclusion on the list indicated a priority borrower to the bank and generally ensured access to credit. The system favored larger enterprises; smaller firms were often forced to a semilegal and unregulated **curb market** charging rates 50 to 100 percent higher than the banks. The curb system relied on the **postdated check**. On receiving the loan a borrower gave the lender a check for the value of the loan plus interest, dated for the day the loan is due. If the check bounced, the issuer was subject to criminal penalties.

At the commercial level, Taiwanese banking functions quite conservatively. Loan maturities tend to be short, with up to 75 percent of all bank loans having a maturity of one year or less. Additionally, Taiwanese bankers are almost obsessive about collateral and lend only against assets that are liquid and easily fungible. These two tendencies make the banking system unresponsive to industry's demands, but keep bank balance sheets solid and well-protected against financial crises. The stability of the commercial banks was not reflected in local **community financial institutions**, roughly equivalent to U.S. savings and loans (S&Ls), which were frequently under the control of local agricultural or fishermen's associations. Loans were often made to acquaintances or political connections, and are therefore "soft," leaving the institutions vulnerable. They suffered much more than the commercial banks in the recent Asian banking crisis. Out of roughly 300 institutions, 24 suffered from crippling runs in 1996, and many experienced bad loan ratios of more than 50 percent.

Liberalization of the banking sector began in the early 1980s when foreign banks were first allowed to establish branches on the island. Change accelerated in 1985 with a push to privatize state-controlled commercial banks, a move motivated in part by a desire to modernize banking and in part by the need to raise revenue to close a growing government budget deficit. Two large banks (Farmers' Bank and Chiao Tung Bank) are now fully privatized, and the big three commercial banks (Chang Hwo, First Commercial, and Hua Nan) were partially sold with the government retaining between 30 percent and 40 percent of capital in each case.

---

[6]In fact, one major bank was privatized in 1971, following the "derecognition" of Taiwan by the United Nations and many countries, in order to have a nongovernmental entity that could operate overseas.

INDUSTRIAL STRUCTURE

The economic philosophy of the Taiwanese government owes much to the doctrines of Sun Yat Sen, the founding Nationalist leader. He emphasized that the state not only had a strong role in economic affairs, but could also demand obedience from a population that should value the well-being of the whole nation above their own. In this respect, the Nationalist philosophy may be thought of as a type of **Confucianism**. In practical economic development terms, although private property was protected and entrepreneurship encouraged, the state was central. The government in Taiwan invested in and developed large-scale upstream facilities that provided raw material for downstream privately owned manufacturing establishments. Thus the government dominated such industries as petroleum, plastic feedstock, and steel, as well as more traditional areas of state activity such as utilities, finance, and communications.

Table 14.2 shows the Taiwanese industrial structure of the mid-1980s. At that time, there were 221 state-owned manufacturing enterprises. Although they represented only 3.5 percent of the workforce, the state-owned enterprises (SOEs) were highly productive and capital intensive, constituting almost 10 percent of the economy's value added and more than 20 percent of its fixed capital stock. The average state-owned firm was 10 times larger in employment terms than a private-sector corporation and employed about 8 times as much capital per employee. In addition to its medium-sized and large private corporations (of which there were about 60,000 in 1986), Taiwan has many family firms that employ on average about five persons. These highly labor-intensive firms (about 61,000 in 1986) accounted for about 11 percent of employment in 1986.

■ **TABLE 14.2**

Characteristics of Manufacturing Enterprises in Taiwan by Form of Ownership, 1986

	Private Corporations	Family Firms	State-Owned Enterprises	State-Owned Enterprise Share of Total (%)
Number of firms	57,477	61,224	221	0.19
Employment (thousands)	2,299	337	93	3.41
Fixed capital (millions NT$*)	1,013	101	294	20.88
Value added (millions NT$)	2,835	170	325	9.76
Employment per firm (thousands)	40	5.5	420	—
Capital per employee (thousands NT$)	440	300	3,161.2	—
Value-added per employee (thousands NT$)	1,233	504.4	3,161.3	—
Output-capital ratio	2.8	1.6	1.1	—

*New Taiwanese dollars.
SOURCE: *The Report on the 1986 Industrial and Commercial Census,* Taiwan-Fukien Area, Republic of China (1988), p. 178; Wing Thye Woo, Stephen Parker, and Jeffrey Sachs, eds., *Economies in Transition Comparing Asia and Europe* (Cambridge, MA: MIT Press, 1996), p. 211.

INDUSTRIAL POLICY

Ownership of upstream enterprise gave the government one of the keys to a comprehensive industrial policy. The other controls were over (1) credit direction via the banking system, (2) tax incentives and subsidies, and (3) tariff and nontariff barriers to influence trade. Taiwan instituted a formal system of planning in the early 1950s, producing four- or five-year development plans. These plans are prepared by the **Council for Economic Planning and Development (CEPD)**, an advisory body attached to the cabinet. The plans are not command, but are broadly indicative in nature and express the desired direction of the economy rather than specific targets.

The emphasis of these plans shifted over time. In the 1950s the focus was on agricultural development and strengthening the balance of payments via import substitution. In the 1960s the priority shifted to export-oriented growth concentrated on light manufacturing industry. The 1970s saw an emphasis on large-scale basic manufacturing, while in the 1980s high-technology exports were given prominence. The task in the 1990s was seen as reducing the role of government, streamlining regulation, and privatizing much of the state-owned sector. At the same time, a new emphasis on social welfare, quality of life, and sustainable development emerged in the plans. Government expenditure on social welfare and transfer programs increased rapidly, creating fiscal problems.

Implementation of the guidelines drawn up by the CEPD is the responsibility of the Ministry of Finance (MOF) and the Ministry of Economic Affairs (MOEA). Because a great deal of power resides directly in the central bank, the MOF is less influential than in other Asian economies. Most planning of industrial production is done by the Industrial Development Bureau (IDB), an agency within the MOEA, which turns the CEPD's broad plans into specific action. Because it has responsibility for foreign trade and foreign investment, as well as industrial development, IDB makes use of a wide range of policy levers, including the issuance of import licenses and control over fiscal incentives.

Taiwan always had a high savings rate, limiting the need for foreign borrowing. Table 14.3 shows that even in the 1950s, savings exceeded investment, creating a net capital outflow.[7] During the 1960s and 1970s all sources of savings increased sharply and financed an investment boom. As incomes rose, household savings grew particularly quickly, ballooning to more than 16 percent of GDP. However, in the mid-1980s investment in Taiwan fell, for two main reasons. One was a fall in confidence in the economy's growth prospects. The other, more positive, was the opening up of mainland China to foreign investment. In 1985 net capital outflows totaled 14.8 percent of GDP, a trend that rapidly established a large overseas investment position. Although net flows moderated in the 1990s, Taiwanese investment in mainland China now totals more than $60 billion, with at least an equal amount invested elsewhere in Southeast Asia.

---

[7]Because of the large inflow of U.S. aid in the 1950s, the export of capital by Taiwanese residents was much greater than the 1.2 percent of GDP shown in Table 14.3.

■ TABLE *14*.3

Taiwan: Saving by Sector and Investment as a Percentage of GNP

| | Gross Domestic Savings | | | | | | |
| | Private | | Government | | | Gross Domestic Investment | Net Foreign Flow |
Year	Households	Enterprises	General	Enterprises	Total		
1955	2.7	4.5	5.1	2.3	14.6	13.3	−1.2
1960	4.8	4.9	4.0	4.1	17.8	20.2	2.4
1965	8.2	6.2	2.6	3.7	20.7	22.7	2.0
1970	11.0	6.4	3.6	4.6	25.6	25.6	0.0
1975	11.0	4.6	7.1	4.0	26.7	30.5	3.8
1980	11.5	8.0	7.9	4.9	32.3	33.8	1.6
1985	16.3	6.5	5.2	5.5	33.5	18.7	−14.8
1990	14.1	5.7	5.8	3.6	29.2	21.9	−7.3

SOURCE: Hugh Patrick and Yung Chul Park (eds.), *The Financial Development of Japan, Korea and Taiwan* (New York: Oxford University Press, 1996), p. 276.

THE BUDGET

Slow economic growth in recent years and a poorly developed fiscal system placed the Taiwanese budget under increasing pressure. Budget problems persist despite the continuing fall in the share of the defense budget. In the 1980s defense accounted for about 50 percent of central government expenditures. Now this share is down to about 16 percent and is falling still. Another large item is education, accounting for 16 percent of expenditures, highly important in nurturing the development of human capital that is the island's strength. Welfare and pensions are rapidly growing burdens required by an aging population. Finally because of the sustained budget deficit, the interest cost of the accumulated debt is a hefty 16 percent.[8] Public sector net debt in 2002 was 48.5 percent of GDP—not large compared to Japan and some of the European economies, but rapidly growing and a cause for concern. Debt was only 5 percent of GDP in 1990.

Revenues come largely from two sources: taxes and the profits of state-controlled monopolies, an item that will inevitably shrink as these enterprises are privatized (see next section). The government's strategy is to use the proceeds of the sale of these enterprises to pay off part of the national debt and hence reduce interest costs. In the short run the privatization proceeds will alleviate the budget problems but in the longer run the fiscal system needs overhaul. In 1990 the tax to GDP ratio was 18 percent. In 2001, tax revenues were only 13 percent of GDP, not only less than the average for OECD countries, but also well below South Korea (18 percent) and Singapore (16 percent), the result of preferential exemptions to certain industries that

---

[8]The last 12 years have all been in deficit.

flourished under the low tax regime, while the burden has fallen disproportionately on other sectors. Reform of this distortionary fiscal system is urgently required.

PRIVATIZATION

In line with global trends, Taiwan is examining ways to reduce government's role in the economy and to move from **state-managed capitalism** to a clearer market model. As far back as 1989 the cabinet set up a committee specifically charged with developing a program of privatization. After initial study, the committee's work was suspended in 1991, only to be reactivated in 1996 when a timetable to privatize some 47 state-owned enterprises was produced.

Several factors motivate the renewed commitment to privatization. One is pressure from both home and abroad to improve allocative efficiency by allowing fuller scope to the market, and reducing the government's role in the economy. Another is a desire to broaden the base of Taiwanese capitalism by increasing equity ownership; the primary means of disposal of state firms has been via IPOs on the Taipei market, with advantages given to small Taiwanese investors through the special "citizens' preferred offering" (CPO) program. Out of the total of 47 firms, two were disposed by private placement and two by dissolution and sale of assets; one employee stock ownership plan (ESOP)—designed to encourage greater worker involvement—was used.

The third motivation is the need to raise revenue and relieve the revenue problems of the budget, which became pressing as the economy faltered and revenues stalled. Despite budgetary problems, there was no urgent ideological necessity for Taiwanese privatization, and a phased sale over four years between 1999 and 2002 was possible.[9]

THE FUTURE OF TAIWAN

The greatest cloud over the future of Taiwan is political because the Beijing government of the People's Republic of China (PRC) still claims it is an integral part of the mainland. In 1971 the island's government lost the recognition of the world community, and it is now excluded from the major multilateral forums and agencies. Doubt about its continued independence led to negative economic consequences and to what is referred to a "cross-straits" relations that dominate any discussion of the island's future.

In March of 2001 a new four-year plan was introduced (superceding the six-year development plan introduced in 1997). Its overall objective is expressed as striving toward the development of a "green silicon island":

1. The strengthening of Taiwan's international competitive position includes especially the continued development of high-tech industry. Already Taiwan accounts for a massive 20 percent of the global production of computer hard-

---

[9]This situation was unlike, for example, the dominance in Eastern Europe and the former Soviet Union, which required mass privatizations.

ware. As such the island is highly subject to the swings in the world's IT cycle and was hard hit in the 2000–2002 recession. Taiwanese investment in the mainland is large and growing, and the control of high-tech investment presents the government with one of its greatest concerns. Simply, if high-productivity investment relocates to the PRC in search of lower wages, Taiwan may possibly become increasingly irrelevant. Its trump card at present lies in the mastery of high-value industry and if that industry is exported, the quality of life on the island will suffer. Consequently, successive government toyed with restraints on technology export; however, the latest plan stresses the promotion of a liberal trade environment in general and the promotion of "cross-straits economic and trade interchange."

2. The new explicit goal of improvement of the overall quality of life for the Taiwanese people is a contrast from the traditional objective of fast growth of GDP. It includes the extended provision of extended health services and a social safety net, but it is not clear how the difficult budget issues will be resolved.

3. The new catch phrase is sustainable development. Because 30 years of rapid growth created the potential for environmental disaster in the island's eco-structure, the idea of a pollution-free high-tech industrial center is attractive. However, this will require extensive land use and water resource regulation, incompatible with the overall objective of a reduced role of government.

4. The government would like to develop the island into a center for corporate operations throughout East Asia. The government refers to this goal as the establishment of an **Asia-Pacific Regional Operation Center (APROC)**. This goal will be hard to achieve, simply because of political uncertainty. The island's appeal to major western multinationals would be greatest if, like Singapore, few doubts remained about its continuing stability and independence. The Taiwanese workforce has the skills and education to provide a center for regional corporate operations. It is overqualified and too highly paid to sustain Taiwan as a manufacturing center. However, Taiwan's relationship to China, and the ability of Chinese authorities to place sanctions on firms based on the island, is a disincentive for multinationals to locate there.

Accession into the World Trade Organization will complicate Taiwan's economic future, because it will require the elimination of import controls and tariffs that sheltered sectors of the island economy. Hardest hit will be agriculture. Given the prevailing wage rates, Taiwan cannot compete in agriculture with its East Asian neighbors and rising unemployment will result. Already in 2002, the rate reached 5 percent and is expected to rise further as jobs are lost in both agriculture and manufacturing assembly.

The political future is unclear. For the first time ever a non-Kuomintang government was elected to power when the Democratic Progressive Party's leader Chen Shui-bian was elected president in 2000. In the following year the KMT lost 50 seats in the legislature and therefore its hold on Parliament. This shift frees President Chen to emphasize even more strongly Taiwan's independence from China. The KMT, because of its history, regarded the island as part of mainland China, but the DPP wants independence or at least autonomy within the PRC. Until this fundamental issue is resolved, Taiwan's future remains clouded.

Singapore—Creating Comparative Advantage

SINGAPORE	
Area (thousand sq. km.)	1
Currency	Singapore dollar
Exchange Rate	2.45 Singapore = US$1
Population 2000 (millions)	4
Population Growth Rate	2.8%
GNI per Capita, 2000	$24,740
GNI per Capita, PPP	$24,970
GDP Growth 1990–2000	7.8%
Value Added as % of GDP 2000 Agriculture	0%
Industry	34%
Services	66%
% of GDP Government Expenditure	22%
Exports	77%

INTRODUCTION

By almost any standard Singapore has been a spectacularly successful economy. Table 14.4 gives basic data on the performance of the economy between 1973 and 1993. Except for a period of moderate growth in the mid-1980s following the "wage correction" policy (discussed later), growth averaged more than 7 percent, and GDP per resident grew by more than 5 percent per year. This momentum continued through the 1990s. In the 30 years from independence[10] to 1995, real GDP grew at an average rate of 8.25 percent per annum, or 6.25 percent per head. Most of the growth can be attributed to the rapid increase of the capital stock; fixed capital accumulation represented 35 percent of GDP annually, the highest rate in the world. Singapore's savings rate has also been the highest in the world, supplemented by

---

[10]Singapore received self-rule status in 1959 and independence within the Federation of Malaysia in 1963. It was expelled from the federation in 1965.

■ TABLE 14.4

	Singapore: Output, Prices, and Labor Market Developments (average annual growth rate as a percentage)				
	1973–1975	1976–1978	1979–1984	1985–1987	1988–1993
Real GDP	7.3	7.9	8.7	3.1	8.5
Employment	4.0	4.8	3.4	—	3.9
Unemployment rate	4.3	4.0	3.1	5.1	2.5
Earnings	13.5	5.8	11.5	3.9	8.5
Consumer prices	14.5	2.0	4.7	20.1	2.6
Real earnings	21.0	3.8	6.8	4.0	5.9
Productivity	5.2	3.5	4.6	4.7	3.9

SOURCE: *Singapore, A Case Study in Rapid Development,* Kenneth Bercuson (ed.) (Washington, DC: International Monetary Fund, February 1995), p. 30.

substantial inflows of direct foreign investment. The labor supply is limited and increased employment made little contribution to the expansion of GDP. Significantly, 1.25 percent of annual growth can be attributed to the increase in total factor productivity, that is, above and beyond that accounted for by the increase of factor inputs, representing therefore a substantial increase in efficiency and technology.

POST-INDEPENDENCE REFORM

The People's Action Party (PAP), founded and presided over by Lee Kuan Yew, has controlled the island from independence. Initially, Singapore was a part of Federation of Malaysia, but was forced out because of growing ethnic conflict between Chinese (the dominant group in Singapore) and Malays. Because Singapore's primary role was as the port and entrepôt for the Malay Peninsula, expulsion from Malaysia cut Singapore from its hinterland, temporarily at least, and a depression resulted. To make matters worse, in 1965 the British closed their naval dockyard, throwing some 40,000 people (13 percent of the total workforce) out of work.

Unemployment was the most serious problem but not the only one. Union militancy was high and labor unrest frequent. Four official languages were used among a population of barely 2.5 million. Most important, a high potential for ethnic discord continued. The Chinese, representing about 76 percent of the population in 1965, were the dominant group, both politically and economically. Malays constituted only about 15 percent of the population, but had a higher birthrate and their share of the population was growing. The other substantial group consisted of Indians (predominantly Tamils) who made up about 6 percent. The remaining 4 percent were mainly Europeans.

Singapore's development is to a large degree the product of Lee's vision, dominance, and political astuteness. In his youth Lee had been a socialist, and he retained a strong faith in the centrality of the state in the economy. However, as a leader he followed an eclectic style and used the market when it suited his purposes. He has increasingly emphasized the importance of Confucian philosophy in Asian life, particularly the subsidiarity of the individual to the state, useful in justifying his near-dictatorial rule.

From the start Lee made sweeping social and economic changes, some strongly criticized as intrusive on individual liberties. The 1968 Industrial Relations Act curtailed union power. Strikes against public utilities were made illegal and the scope of issues subject to collective bargaining was reduced, lessening the area of potential confrontation. Management was given full discretionary power over hiring, firing, and the use of labor in the workplace. The 1969 Employment Act set statutory limits on the kind and level of fringe benefits that firms might pay to workers, hence curbing "wage drift" and keeping labor costs down.

English was established as the predominant language for education and business, restricting dispute between the ethnic communities and making Singapore an attractive destination for foreign capital, which was often looking for employees who spoke the *lingua franca* of the business world. An emphasis on social order made Singapore even more appealing to foreign investors. Heavy penalties were imposed for almost every class of crime, with especial attention being paid to vandalism, drugs, and prostitution. Failure to pay the fare on public transportation could bring a $3,000 fine, and even neglecting to flush a public toilet would incur a fine of $150. Long hair is still disapproved of, and any male with hair over the ears is automatically at the back of any service line. The government controls all broadcast media, and strict censorship is used to control the press.

THE PILLARS OF SINGAPORE'S DEVELOPMENT

Singapore's growth may be thought of as resting on three pillars. The first consists of the government-controlled **statutory boards**, which implement the development plans formulated by the **Ministry of Finance and Trade and Industry**. The seven boards serve functions that include promoting investment, providing infrastructure and public housing, and operating the communications, transportation, and harbor systems. The most important, and oldest, is the Economic Development Board (or EDB), established in 1961, with an initial objective of reducing unemployment. It attracted direct foreign investment through grants, loans, and the provision of factory sites and infrastructural services, although subsequently it delegated a great many of its functions to the other six, more specialized boards.

The second pillar consists of the government-controlled industries. The Ministry of Finance Incorporation Act of 1959 enabled the government to actively participate and hold shares in private companies, either directly or through holding companies, statutory boards, or parastatal entities such as the Development Bank of Singapore. In this way the government maintains a controlling interest in about 160 manufacturing and service companies ranging from petrochemicals to tourism.

The third pillar of the economy is foreign capital, which is more dominant in Singapore's economy than any other in the world. Under the **Economic Expansion**

Act of 1967 the government can offer foreign firms many incentives, even seeming to favor foreign firms over domestic ones. The growing dominance of foreign capital in output, employment, and especially exports is illustrated in Table 14.5. It shows that by the mid-1980s foreign firms dominated manufacturing, producing 70 percent of output, employing half of the workforce, making more than 80 percent of new capital investment, and accounting for more than 90 percent of exports. Domestic capitalists claimed that policies favored foreign firms, but in reality any bias was the result of larger firms being better able to meet the export targets, which open the doors to government-subsidized credit. Even though such pecuniary incentives are attractive, foreign capital is drawn by the streamlined bureaucracy and the political stability offered by Singapore when other Southeast Asian nations were unpredictable.

■ **TABLE 14.5**

Contribution of Foreign Establishments to Manufacturing in Singapore (percentage of category total)

Category	Year	Ownership Structure		
		Wholly Foreign Owned	Majority Foreign Owned	Wholly Locally Owned
Value added	1962	24.6	—	47.5
	1970	37.0	49.4	35.6
	1975	47.4	62.7	24.3
	1980	54.1	67.4	19.1
	1988	61.9	71.7	14.9
Gross output	1962	31.4	—	45.6
	1970	43.4	55.8	31.0
	1975	56.2	71.3	18.1
	1980	58.7	73.0	15.6
	1988	61.1	75.0	14.1
	1991	62.1	75.3	16.0
Employment	1962	14.1	—	66.4
	1970	17.7	34.7	45.3
	1975	31.5	52.0	32.8
	1980	39.9	58.4	28.1
	1988	49.0	59.5	27.6
Direct exports	1962	26.3	—	44.7
	1970	56.7	—	16.5
	1975	66.1	84.1	8.9
	1980	71.5	84.7	7.1
	1988	72.6	86.1	6.5

SOURCE: *Singapore, A Case Study in Rapid Development,* Kenneth Bercuson (ed.) (Washington, DC: International Monetary Fund, February 1995), p. 16.

CHANGE OF DIRECTION

The policy of promoting light manufacturing industry to feed export-oriented growth proved successful in the short run. The unemployment problem, serious at independence, was solved and by the early 1980s when Singapore was short of labor. Participation rates rose, and more women, especially married women, entered the workforce, raising the participation rate (see Table 14.6). Ultimately domestic sources of labor proved inadequate to meet the needs of industry and, to alleviate the shortage, "guest workers" from Malaysia and Indonesia were allowed in. However, the government was unwilling to liberalize immigration drastically because it might disturb the ethnic balance, threatening the political dominance of the Chinese.

During the 1960s and 1970s, Singapore was host to a large number of foreign light manufacturing firms attracted by low wages, location, and political stability. However, the government came to realize that in the long run Singapore could not compete in terms of labor cost with neighbors such as Malaysia, Indonesia, and the Philippines, who had much larger and more rapidly growing populations. Moreover, semiskilled employment in light industry could never be compatible with long-run affluence. Income per head in Singapore would never grow to the level of western industrial nations unless human capital and productivity were raised and the workforce became more predominantly white collar.

The government adopted a two-tiered program to raise average incomes. One approach was to increase the level of skill of the population, especially in the area of vocational training. Government expenditure on education jumped by more than 50 percent between 1977 and 1984. A supplementary payroll tax was levied on all firms and the proceeds were used to finance government-approved in-house training programs within private firms.

The other, more controversial, aspect of the program involved deliberately raising the cost of Singaporean labor to the point at which it was simply too expensive to be

■ TABLE 14.6

Singapore: Population, Labor Force, and Employment (as a percentage)

	Annual Growth Rates Percentage			Labor Force Participation Rate[b]	
	Population[a]	Labor Force[a]	Employment[a]	Total	Female
1957	—	—	—	57.0	21.6
1970	2.8	2.5	2.5	56.5	29.5
1980	1.0	4.2	5.2	63.2	44.3
1990	1.7	3.1	3.3	63.1	48.8
1992	2.0	4.2	3.4	64.5	50.6

[a]Average annual intercensus percentage change for 1970–1990.
[b]Participation rate for years shown; prior to 1990 as proportion of population over 10; from 1990, over 15.
SOURCES: *Singapore, A Case Study in Rapid Development*, Kenneth Bercuson (ed.) (Washington, DC: International Monetary Fund, February 1995), p. 57.

used for unskilled and semiskilled work in the manufacturing industry. Labor negotiations in Singapore are coordinated by the **National Wages Council (NWC)**, a tripartite body on which employers, unions, and the government were represented. In the 1970s, instead of restraining the pace of wage settlement (which had been its policy in the 1960s), the NWC actually tried to increase the pace of wage inflation. In 1979 its guidelines advocated a 20 percent across-the-board wage increase. This recommendation was followed by additional substantial increases in both 1981 and 1982. The wisdom of this policy, referred to as **wage correction**, was called into question in the middle 1980s. Slow growth throughout Southeast Asia was compounded in Singapore by the closure of manufacturing facilities by several large direct investors. Unemployment rose and the "wage correction" took the blame. Nevertheless, when growth returned in the late 1980s and 1990s, Singapore's economy had been structurally changed: the share of manufacturing employment was down, and today the high-wage service and financial sectors dominate. Singapore currently serves as the regional headquarters of European, Japanese, and U.S. companies. The government is actively searching for cheap labor sites in Malaysia, Indonesia, and even as far away as India as centers of manufacturing activity that would report to headquarters in Singapore. The nearby Indonesian island of Batan, for example, serves as a satellite tariff-free processing zone.

SAVING AND INVESTMENT

Although the government intervenes in many aspects of life, Singapore is by no means a welfare state or social market economy. There is no system of unemployment insurance on the island, and retirement must be funded from personal savings or by compulsory contributions to individually vested accounts in a government agency, the **Central Provident Fund (CPF)**, founded in 1955. The CPF originally required a payroll levy of 5 percent on both employer and employee, which was credited to an account specific for the individual. These rates of contribution increased over time and now employees must contribute 21.5 percent and employers 18.5 percent to the fund. Thus 40 percent of the total wage bill must now go to the CPF, which accounts for about one-third of total national savings (see Table 14.7). Although the main purpose of CPF accounts is to finance retirement, funds can be withdrawn to pay for housing, education, health emergencies, and, recently, specified investment projects. The bulk of CPF funds are invested in government bonds and thus finance much of the development activity at quite low rates.

CPF contribution rates are high relative to social security taxes in other countries, and the effect on aggregate saving levels is controversial. The International Monetary Fund (IMF) concluded that compulsory savings are offset by reductions in private saving. Though the savings rate is high, its roots lie in rapidly growing incomes, low demographic dependency ratios, and high levels of public saving.[11]

---

[11]Aasin Husai, "Determinants of Private Saving in Singapore," in *Singapore a Case Study in Rapid Development* (Washington, DC: International Monetary Fund, 1995).

■ TABLE 14.7

Singapore's Gross National Saving Rate (as a percentage of GNP)					
	1970—1974	1975—1979	1980—1984	1985—1989	1990—1992
Gross national saving rate	24.4	31.2	42.2	39.7	43.6
Private saving	17.9	23.4	32.2	30.3	33.0
Central Provident Fund (CPF)	4.8	8.9	14.2	14.4	13.8
Other	13.2	14.5	17.9	15.9	19.1
Public saving	6.5	7.8	10.0	9.4	10.7

SOURCES: *Singapore, A Case Study in Rapid Development,* Kenneth Bercuson (ed.) (Washington, DC: International Monetary Fund, February 1995), p. 43.

SOCIAL ENGINEERING

Singapore's government is unapologetically interventionist in social matters. It believes that "good" behavior should be promoted by the government and has little tolerance for antisocial behavior. Individual liberty is often a casualty, but this cost is regarded by the government and by much of the population as acceptable in the drive for prosperity and stability. One example of aggressive interventionism is Singapore's population policy. Immediately after independence, worries about overpopulation prompted the formation of a Family Planning Board to promulgate birth control. Extensive use was made of media propaganda, but economic incentives were also used. Maternity hospital costs were raised for third or fourth children, and families with more than two children were given lower priority in selection of the schools. By the early 1980s the fertility rate had fallen to 1.44 per woman, and depopulation (and more immediately reduction in the Chinese dominance) was feared. Population control was scrapped, replaced by a selective **pronatalist movement**. Less well-educated women were still encouraged to undergo sterilization after the second child by a cash grant of $5,300. However, to address the concerns that ethnic Chinese women, in general well educated, were marrying too late (if at all) and having too few children, a Social Development unit to encourage marriage was established. Again extensive use was made of propaganda to encourage a more practical bent in mate selection ("Dreams can take a lifetime—choose reality"), and the government even sponsored "singles' cruises." Maternity leave was made more easily available for women, especially graduates. Financial teeth were added in 1989 when the government announced a $10,000 tax *rebate* for fourth children, a benefit only useful for those with high taxes. The policies of the pronatalist movement have been criticized as racist. The subsidies for child rearing go primarily to the educated and wealthy Chinese, while cash bonuses for sterilization still restrict the growth of the Indian and Malay minorities.

Lee Kuan Yew himself said:

> I am often accused of interfering in the private lives of citizens. Yet if I had not done that we would not be here today. And I say without the slightest remorse that we wouldn't

be here, we would not have made economic progress, if we had not intervened on very
personal matters—who your neighbor is, how you live, the noise you make, how you
spit, or what language you use. We decide what is right. Never mind what people think.
That's another problem.[12]

PRIVATIZATION

Singapore finally got around to pondering the issue of privatizing its hold on the
indigenous industrial sector. This development stems from a growing awareness
that Singapore's hold on the multinationals that currently locate their regional
headquarters on the island is tenuous, and that home-owned growth industries are
desirable for their stability. The younger generation of politicians, comparing
U.S. success in communications and computer industries with the less buoyant
counterparts in Europe, tend to feel that state ownership is not a good model for
new industries. It is particularly bad when it comes to expansion overseas; foreign
companies are often unwilling to enter partnership with a government-owned
firm, a factor that hurt the attempts of SingTel, the state-owned phone company, to
expand overseas. Given Singapore's tiny market, overseas diversification is necessary; consequently, the state is moving to divest at least some of its holdings.

Characteristically, the change will still be a family affair. Lee Kuan Yew's daughter-
in-law, Ho Ching (wife of Deputy Prime Minister Lee Hsien Loong), has been
appointed to head Temasek, the publicly owned holding company for 20 of Singapore's largest companies. She has also been equipped with a new charter that requires
"rationalization" and "strategic development." How these goals will be achieved is
yet to be determined, but an extensive sales program is in place as a first step.

SINGAPORE'S FUTURE

Lee Kuan Yew retired as prime minister in 1990 but he retains control over the
People's Action Party and through it the direction of Singapore. The progress of the
island-state in becoming an almost entirely "white-collar enclave" by the mid-
1990s is illustrated by Table 14.8. Total employment increased between 1991 and
1996 by 223,825. The most rapid growth was in financial and business services
(where employment grew at 8.9 percent per year), closely followed by transport
and communication. The move to "professional status" is illustrated even more
clearly in the lower panel of Table 14.8. The growth rate of employment in management and professional occupations was 10 percent annually, while that of production workers was only 2.5 percent. Today manufacturing share has slipped
further; 71 percent of the island's GDP originates in the service sector. The average
citizen of Singapore is among the world's wealthy elite. In Lee's own words, that
transition from Third World to First World in one generation is complete. The

---

[12]Lee Kuan Yew's speech on National Day 1986, cited in Christopher Tremewan, *The Political Economy of
Social Control in Singapore* (London: MacMillan, 1986), p. 2.

■ TABLE 14.8

Employment Gains by Industry and Occupation in Singapore, 1991–1996

Industry and Occupation	Employment Gain		
	Number	Share (%)	Growth (% p.a.)
Industry			
Total*	223,825	100.0	2.8
Financial and business services	82,699	36.9	8.9
Social, community, and personal services	45,648	20.4	2.7
Transport and communications	42,404	18.9	5.0
Construction*	15,992	7.1	3.1
Commerce	60,568	27.1	3.6
Manufacturing	(23,294)	–10.4	–1.1
Occupation			
Total*	223,825	100.0	2.8
Legislators, administrators, and managers	77,907	34.8	9.7
Technicians and associate professionals	121,862	54.4	10.7
Professionals	51,316	22.9	10.9
Clerical workers	37,811	16.9	3.6
Production and related workers	(75,063)	–33.5	–2.5
Service workers	14,590	6.5	1.4

*Figures include foreign workers, except those staying at construction sites.
SOURCE: Monetary Authority of Singapore, Occasional Paper no. 5, May 1998.

People's Action Party retains its control over politics, with its share of the vote rising to 75 percent in the elections of 2000, although the opposition maintained that it was largely the result of abuse of power by the PAP.

However, increasing openness will present challenges. Singapore, in its position as a financial, management, and communications center, was rocked by the financial crises that affected Asia in 1997 and 1998. Although the stock market took a beating, no fundamental flaw emerged in Singapore's economic structure.[13] Bank failures were few; the number of banks operating in Singapore remained constant at about 150 throughout the crisis, although a rapid wave of consolidation and mergers occurred in the immediate aftermath. The rapid and repeated currency devaluation, a common feature elsewhere in the region, was avoided, and the Monetary Authority survived with its reputation intact.

Monetary and exchange stability during the crisis was enhanced by the extremely conservative nature of the monetary system. From 1967 to 1982 Singapore had a **currency board** system, which required both a fixed exchange rate and the complete backing of all domestic currency issue by hard currency reserves. This practice completely limited credit creation, assured convertibility, and instilled eco-

[13]The leading *Straits Times* Index, which stood at over 2,000 in February 1997, fell to a low of 856 in August 1998. Over the same period, market capitalization fell from S$375 billion to S$261 billion.

nomic discipline. Singapore abandoned that system in 1982, but remains conservative in approach, and the Singapore dollar remained extremely stable—an attractive feature to overseas investors.

Singapore's long-term problem is whether it can exist as a "head without a body." As the financial capital of a region dedicated to low-wage manufacturing, its income differs dramatically from that of its neighbors. One risk to Singapore is that political turmoil in the adjacent economies will detach Singapore from them and leave it without a hinterland needing its financial services. The chaos in Indonesia, its most populous neighbor, underlined this risk. Another potential problem is that Singapore might suffer from an anti-Chinese backlash in its neighbors. *The Economist* reports that people of Chinese origin make up only 6 percent of the total population of the neighboring states of Malaysia, Singapore, Philippines, and Indonesia, yet they control 70 percent of the wealth. Singapore, as the *de facto* capital of the Chinese diaspora, might be vulnerable if ethnic and racial tensions rise once more.

SINGAPORE AS A MODEL

Because of its size, location, and special circumstances, it is difficult to view Singapore as a useful model for its Southeast Asian neighbors or other developing nations, despite its success. It surpassed almost all of the developed industrial nations in terms of income per head. In 2002 it had an estimated purchasing power parity income of $25,500—ahead of every nation except the United States, Switzerland, Hong Kong, and Kuwait—but its experience is not generalizable, although it offers lessons to be learned:

1. *The importance of political stability.* Despite its small size and relatively expensive labor force, Singapore developed first as a manufacturing locale and then a financial services center, because it offered political stability in a region where it was in scarce supply. It does not matter to foreign investors that this stability relies to some degree on questionable claims of Confucian authority; what matters is that uncertainty is reduced.

2. ***Transparency in regulation*** *attracts foreign capital.* Singapore's tax codes and regulatory framework are clearly written and by and large evenly applied, up to the point where domestic capitalists complain that foreigners are preferentially treated.

3. *A docile labor force is an asset in development.* The government ensured an environment of almost total labor peace. Strikes have been virtually nonexistent for the past 20 years.

4. *Rising living standards and sustained development require investment in human capital.* Education has been a vital key to Singapore's ability to move "up market" from manufacturing to services.

5. *A competent civil service is an asset, but it must be rewarded.* Singapore's civil service is well paid and efficient. The World Bank found that only in Singapore were civil servants paid more (about a 15 percent premium) than their counterparts in private industry.

Corruption and Crash: Indonesia

INDONESIA	
Area (thousand sq. km.)	19
Currency	rupiah
Exchange Rate	8,230 rupiah = US$1
Population 2000 (millions)	210
Population Growth Rate	1.7%
GNI per Capita, 2000	$570
GNI per Capita, PPP	$2,840
GDP Growth, 1990–2000	0.4%
Value Added as % of GDP 2000 Agriculture	17%
Industry	43%
Services	30%
% of GDP Central Government Expenditure	17%
Exports	40%

INTRODUCTION

Indonesia is a vast nation with a diverse ethnic structure. With almost 200 million inhabitants, it is the world's fourth most populous nation. It occupies about 13,677 islands, within which about 300 recognizable languages and dialects are spoken. The dominant ethnic group is Javanese, constituting about 46 percent of the population. About half of the Indonesian populations live on Java itself, so the government encourages movement from Java to the less populated islands through its "transmigration program."

Indonesia attained its independence in 1949. A three-year Japanese occupation was followed by a brief struggle with the Dutch, who tried to reimpose their colonial rule in 1945. From independence until 1965 the nation was led by Sukarno,[14] who attempted to articulate a **nonaligned movement** that adhered to neither of the Cold War superpowers. In 1958 Sukarno abandoned both free elections and the market system, adopting the twin policies of **guided democracy** and **guided**

---

[14]Javanese usually use only one name.

economy. All of the residual Dutch interests were nationalized and 40,000 Dutch were expelled, a loss of expertise that, in the short term at least, the economy could ill afford.

Between 1958 and 1965 the performance of the economy worsened. Per-head income fell by 15 percent, foreign exchange reserves were depleted, and inflation accelerated. Despite its inherent fertility and large agricultural workforce, the country could not feed itself. By 1965 it had become one of the poorest economies in the world with an average per-head income of about $70, lower at that time than either India or Bangladesh. Also, 60 percent of the population lived in the direst poverty, with a daily dietary intake of less than 2,150 calories per day. Life expectancy at birth was a mere 41 years, and the infant mortality rate was 225 per 1,000.

THE NEW ORDER

By the mid-1960s further evidence of the destructiveness of Sukarno's policies included inflation that reached 600 percent per year. In October 1965 a series of coups and countercoups occurred, the origin of which remains uncertain to this day. The official version was that Communists, alarmed by Sukarno's declining health and influence, struck to seize power, and the coup was rebuffed by senior army officers. An anticommunist and anti-Chinese *pogrom* resulted, during which many people died. In the chaos old scores were settled and practically all debts eliminated as creditors were disposed of.

When the smoke cleared, it was apparent that the army was in power. One general, Suharto, emerged as president and declared a **New Order**. Nominally, he was elected by the People's Consultative Congress (PCC), but little democracy was involved in his elevation. The PCC consisted of 360 directly elected representatives, along with 207 presidential appointees and 276 officers of the armed forces. Consequently the army, in conjunction with the president's appointees, was able to outvote the elected representatives. Suharto's first steps sought to restore order to the economy, relying on a group of western-trained economists, known collectively as the "Berkeley mafia," who stressed monetary restraint, a realistic exchange rate, and a greater role for market economics.

Agricultural Development

Faced with widespread malnutrition, the New Order government was acutely aware of the need for agricultural reform. Despite the engagement of 70 percent of the workforce in agriculture, the nation was the world's largest food importer, a major burden on the balance of payments. Increasing rice production was given the highest priority—an effort encouraged and assisted by the multilateral agencies and the United States. Extensive land reform was not required, because most land was already held in communal village arrangements, but new strains of rice were acquired from the International Rice Research Institute in the Philippines. These strains had to be indigenized and also required a great deal of fertilizer, which had to be subsidized by the government. Education in the new techniques was made a priority, and 12 percent of Indonesia's development budget was directed to improving local infrastructure. Price supports were adopted to strengthen the incentives to increase production and bring it to market. Even though purists regarded the use of subsidies and price supports as distortionary, the policies produced dramatic results. Output rose almost 70 percent from 12 million metric tons in 1970 to more than 20 million in 1980, and self-sufficiency was achieved in 1984.

Rent-Seeking Capitalism

By 1995 even the most critical observers of the Indonesian economic and political system were forced to admit that substantial positive changes had been made. Per-head income at current exchange rates had risen to $980, and in purchasing power parity terms was closer to $3,800 per year. Annual real growth of GDP averaged more than 6 percent throughout the 1980s and accelerated to 7.6 percent in the 1990s. Growth of the industrial sector was even faster. Infant mortality fell to 51 per 1,000 live births and mean life expectancy at birth rose to 64. Although about 30 million people still lived on less than $1 a day (measured in purchasing power parity terms), the overall incidence of poverty was greatly reduced. The sharp contrast between growth experiences in the 1970s and 1980s and the stagnation of the Sukarno era is shown in Table 14.9.

However, this economic progress was accompanied by considerable social stress and growing protest. At the heart of the discontent was the fact that Indonesia represented a form of economic organization that can best be called "bureaucratic

---

■ TABLE 14.9

Indonesia: Trends in Key Economic Aggregates

	Annual Rates of Growth				
	1960—1967	1967—1973	1973—1981	1982—1988	1988—1991
GDP	1.7	7.9	7.5	3.3	7.1
Non-oil GDP	1.7	7.3	8.0	4.3	7.7
Agriculture	1.6	4.1	3.4	2.9	3.0
Manufacturing	1.0	9.5	14.1	5.2	11.0
Services	2.0	9.0	10.0	5.0	7.8
Fixed investment	1.1	23.5	11.7	−0.5	13.5
Public	—	—	11.0	−2.0	8.2
Private	—	—	12.3	0.7	16.9
Non-oil exports	2.1	25.6	0.0	7.6	16.5
Per capita GDP	−0.5	5.5	5.2	1.3	5.3
Per capita income	−0.4	5.6	9.1	20.2	5.1
Per capita consumption	−0.6	3.0	5.5	1.4	5.0

SOURCE: Amar Bhattacharya and Mari Pangestu, "Indonesia, Development Transformation Since 1965 and the Role of Public Policy" (Washington, DC: The World Bank, 1993).

capitalism."[15] Prominent figures were granted or seized control of particular sectors of industry and used their power to extract monopoly rents. Furthermore, the army is a prominent actor in the economy. This unusual phenomenon has its roots in the Sukarno era of the 1960s, when, in the face of budgetary chaos, the army was unable to meet its payroll. It used its assets to build "for-profit" businesses, mainly in transportation. When, with the army's backing, Suharto came to power, his uniformed supporters were able to appropriate control of large enterprises and in many cases the revenues that streamed from them. The Sukarno era had also seen the forging of strong links with the mainly Chinese businessmen who supplied the army, which carried over into the New Order economy.

The most famous case of **khaki capitalism** is that of Pertamina—the national oil and gas monopoly. Since the discovery of extensive oil fields off Sumatra in the early 1970s, the rise in Indonesia's known oil reserves, its oil exports and oil revenues, produced a major windfall for the Indonesian state. Revenues rose from less than $1 billion in 1970 to more than $13 billion in 1980. Pertamina, under the guidance of General Sutowo, diversified into banking, steel, and even hotels, borrowing more than $10 billion to finance expansion. In the mid-1970s, Pertamina started losing money (a surprising development in view of the continued high price of oil), could not meet its debts, failed, and as a result a scandal erupted.

However, the Pertamina affair is only one example of the systemic extraction and appropriation of rent in the Indonesian economy. The market is frequently restricted and not permitted to coordinate activity simply because of the potential rents to be earned if licensing, subsidy, and favoritism are pursued. The liberalizing policies of the "Berkeley mafia" have been in constant conflict with the interests of economic nationalists, who favor building up domestic industry behind protective tariff barriers and subsidies. Despite the lip service paid by the Indonesian government and the multilateral organizations to market principles, entrepreneurial activity became increasingly dominated by a few major groups, usually controlled by Chinese Indonesians, who relied for patronage and protection on the government. The largest were the Astra Group, the Salim Group, and the Lippo Group (which achieved notoriety through illegal U.S. election campaign contributions). Suharto's own family also greatly enriched themselves by appropriating certain monopoly privileges. Even though family interests tend to be important throughout Asia, Table 14.10 shows that Indonesia's economic structure is dominated by family groups to a higher degree than elsewhere. Taking the 30 percent of share capital as the measure of control, the data show fewer "widely held corporations" and more family-dominated ones than elsewhere in Asia (with the exception of Thailand).

Support for economic nationalism has not been without countercurrents favoring a more liberalized market, but whenever the economic nationalists were in the ascendancy, import substitution became a priority. They offered the business groups privileges such as import licenses or protection for their own firms to induce them to undertake projects that were valued by the government as development objectives.

---

[15]Richard Robison, "Toward a Class Analysis of the Indonesian Military," *Indonesia*, no. 25, April 1978, pp. 17–39.

■ **TABLE 14.10**

			Control of Publicly Traded Companies in East Asia	
Country	Number of Corporations Studied	Widely Held	One Family Holds More Than 30 Percent	State Holds More than 30 Percent
Hong Kong	330	50.3%	34.4%	0.9%
Indonesia	178	24.7	58.7	6.7
Japan	1,240	94.8	2.8	0.4
Korea	345	76.2	20.1	1.2
Malaysia	238	41.2	45.6	8.2
Philippines	120	58.3	22.1	2.1
Singapore	221	45.2	32.6	11.3
Taiwan	141	73.0	18.4	2.8
Thailand	167	24.6	54.8	7.5

SOURCE: Stjin, Claessens, Simeon Djankov, and Larry H. P. Lang, "Who Controls East Asian Corporations," World Bank working paper no. 2054, February 1999.

One example is the relationship of the Salim Group to the steel industry. The government wanted to expand the basic capacity of the economy and wished to double the size of the Krakatau steel mill, originally built by Pertamina. The Salim Group agreed to invest $800 million in the project and, as quid pro quo, received a short-term monopoly over the import of cold-rolled steel. This monopoly enabled it to inflate the price in Indonesia by 25 to 45 percent and creamed off monopoly rent. The price distortion caused considerable damage to other nascent firms in Indonesia, who were faced with high raw-material costs. In a similar case, a company controlled by Suharto's son, Bambang, monopolized plastic imports.[16]

PLANNING IN INDONESIA

Formal planning of the Indonesian economy originated during the Sukarno period. The first five-year plan covered 1956–1960. It was interrupted by the nationalization of Dutch capital in 1957 and the inception of the "guided economy." It was replaced by an eight-year plan, which, because of the downward spiral of the economy, failed to meet any of its targets.

Following the coup in 1965, the New Order government established a national planning agency (BAPPENAS) under the control of foreign-trained technocrats. This group was responsible for the drafting of a series of five-year development plans, known by the acronym **Repelita**. The first of these, Repelita I, covered the period 1969–1973 and focused on raising the output of staple foods (primarily rice) and developing the infrastructure for growth. The second plan, Repelita II (1979–1983)

[16]William Frederick and Robert Worden, *Indonesia: A Country Study.*

continued the push in agriculture but also attempted to achieve greater growth outside of Java. The third plan (1984–1988) shifted the focus toward industrial development, and the fourth plan chose to emphasize the buildup of basic industry, steel, plastics, and petrochemicals. Repelita V (1989–1993) sought to upgrade transportation and communications.

As noted earlier, planning has been a struggle between market-oriented reformers on the one hand and economic nationalists on the other, with each group achieving ascendancy from time to time. In the 1980s the economic nationalists, who favored a strong push for basic industry and the use of tariff and nontariff barriers for protection, gained influence.

The chief proponent of economic nationalism was B. J. Habibie, who went on to replace Suharto as president after the riots in mid-1998. Habibie's background was as an airplane designer with Messerschmidt-Bohn-Bolkow in Germany. While minister of state for research and development, he espoused a policy of leapfrogging Indonesian industrial development by "creating comparative advantage" rather than by following it. Accordingly, he attempted to create from nothing an aerospace industry in Indonesia, establishing the Archipelago Aircraft Industry (IPTN). This venture required a great deal of government subsidy, and perhaps more damaging to the economy, it also absorbed a great deal of the nation's scarce reserves of skilled labor. IPTN employed more than 2,000 graduates. Its sales were entirely within Indonesia, and it failed to penetrate investment markets.[17] This prioritized pattern of development was criticized for raising costs for the majority of firms in Indonesia. As a response, during the late 1980s the market reformers were relatively successful in reducing both the complexity of the import control structure and the effective rate of protection. Between 1985 and 1991 the average rate of tariff fell from 37 percent to 20 percent, and the average rate weighted by import value fell from 22 percent to 10 percent.[18]

FINANCIAL MARKETS

At the beginning of the New Order period the state dominated the banking system. It controlled not only the central bank, but also the five main commercial banks, and several specialized banks for import-export finance and development funding. State banks held in total 74 percent of assets of deposit-taking banks. The many private banks (both domestic and foreign) accounted for only 25 percent of the assets and made only 6.3 percent of the loans. The banking sector was used for directed and subsidized credits toward the priority sector of the economy. This control of the economy through directed credit was common to most developing economies and had been a part of the "East Asian Model."

---

[17]One wit has referred to it as a "*bonsai* industry"—it is expensive, it requires constant attention, and it never grows.

[18]Nominal tariff rates are not an accurate gauge of the real extent of protection. Effective rates of protection, however, remain quite high; the average rate for the import competing sector is still over 35 percent.

Indonesia followed an unusual approach by liberalizing the financial sector at a faster pace than the manufacturing and industrial sectors. In the 1970s the government took an unusual step for a country at its stage of development in allowing the free movement of capital in and out of the country. However, the banking system remained highly regulated throughout the decade. Directed, subsidized credit was used to foster a specific pattern of development, and tight credit ceilings were imposed in a bid to limit inflation. In 1983 the government abolished credit ceilings and interest rate controls and in 1988 reduced barriers to entry, encouraged greater branch banking, and lowered the reserve requirement. As a result, prior to the Asian financial crisis, Indonesia had the least regulated banking sector in all of East Asia.

The outcome of deregulation was a sharp upsurge in banking activity. Between 1983 and1990 the number of domestic banks nearly doubled to 119. Credit became available at competitive interest rates throughout the economy, with every sign that the overall effect on growth would be positive. In particular the small and medium-sized industries, those outside the big groups, finally had access to credit. This tendency was reinforced by a government decree that required all banks to make at least 20 percent of their loans to small businesses. Although popular in some quarters, this requirement was inefficient because it forced many banks to move away from the competitive advantages. In this liberal environment, credit was dramatically extended, often without adequate credit checks.

The World Bank's view at the time was approving:

> The reforms were immensely successful. . . . While credit had been readily available only to producers and traditional services, it now became available to a wide range of borrowers, including consumers and investors in the real estate and stock markets.[19]

However, the long-term result was a deterioration of bank balance sheets and progressive weakness throughout the system—a real estate and stock market bubble was fueled by easy credit. Banks began to fail, and the government was forced to reregulate, raising liquidity requirements and belatedly imposing more adequate supervision into the banking sector. It became clear that there were, in fact, too many banks in Indonesia for the available capital, qualified labor, and regulatory capacity. Despite the bullish sentiment expressed by the World Bank and the impact of financial deregulation, the overextended banking system became a liability. Depositors withdrew their money, putting more pressure on the banks, which were unable to recover unsecured loans to the private sector. A domino effect resulted and by 1997 the banking system was in chaos. The government resorted to dramatic surgery, liquidating 16 banks but guaranteeing the deposits of the remainder.

JAVANESE IMPERIALISM

Although Indonesia is a multiethnic and polyglot society, Java is by far the most populous of the islands and Javanese represent the largest and most powerful

---

[19]*The East Asian Miracle: A World Bank Policy Research Report* (New York: Oxford University Press, 1993), p. 239.

ethnic group. About 70 million Javanese make up 36 percent of the population. The population density on Java is about 2,070 persons per square mile, almost 10 times the average for the nation as a whole and over 200 times the density on remote West Papua.

This imbalance led the government to promote the movement of population from densely populated Java (also Bali and Madura) to the "out islands." A transmigration program moved almost 1.5 million families (6.4 million persons), as well as significant private movement that occurred.[20] The population of the out islands was 6 percent Javanese by 1980. Subsequently statistics have not been published because of the political context of the issue. The movement of the population created some disturbances in the out islands and invited accusations of **Javanese imperialism**, although the population relocated has been predominantly working class. The exploitation of the natural resource wealth in the out islands has also been a contentious issue. Much of the gathering of timber is done by foreign concerns, little permanent wealth is generated, and most of the rents and fees accrue to the center. In addition, industrial development is concentrated on Java, particularly Jakarta and the port city of Surabaya. The geographical extent of Indonesia and the wide ethnic mix present a constant challenge to the unity of the country. As a response, the government maintains a close control on all activity and the vast preponderance of decisions is made in Jakarta. As a result, Jakarta has grown rapidly to a population of almost 17 million.

The recent tendency toward separatism calls into question the long-term viability of the country as a unit. East Timor eventually reclaimed its independence after years of violence and considerable external support. Separatist movements are powerful in Aceh (northern Sumatra) and Irian Jaya (West Papua), and other regionalist movements are becoming more active.

THE AFTERMATH OF THE CRISIS

Michael Backman in his book *Asian Eclipse*[21] suggests that the countries with the highest degree of corruption and lack of transparency were the ones that suffered most in the Asian financial crisis. Despite its favored status with the World Bank, Indonesia was undoubtedly one of the most corrupt economies in the world. The system of **crony capitalism** layered onto this corruption great distortions and a total absence of a level playing field. It was no surprise that the Indonesian economy commenced a fall from which it had yet to stabilize as late as 2003.

The rapid and largely unregulated expansion of the banking system inevitably led to chaos and failure when the Asia crisis struck. The commercial banks collapsed and required a bailout, which was administered by the Indonesia Bank Restructuring Agency (IBRA). The state pumped money in to recapitalize them, largely from IMF resources, and, after refinancing, they tried to collect some of the

[20]Department of Foreign Affairs, Republic of Indonesia.
[21]Michael Backman, *Asian Eclipse: Exposing the Dark Side of Business in Asia* (New York: Harper, 2001).

$27.4 billion on their loan books. They collected less than 2 percent of the total, and received instead most of the equity in the now bankrupt industrial groups, including Astra, Salim, and Lippo. Consequently the government found itself the owner of most of Indonesia's industry. Massive privatization was required, but with few domestic buyers and foreigners avoiding Indonesia's chaos, prices could only be rock bottom. Some assets were disposed of but the revenue to the banks was negligible.

The Wahid government was short-lived. Implicated deeply in corruption and so incompetent in economic affairs that the IMF suspended payments and relations in December 2000, he was forced from power in June 2001. The presidency passed to Megawati Sukarnoputri (the daughter of the first post-independence President Sukarno), who put together a centrist coalition and staffed her administration with professionals rather than politicians. So far her administration has done little. Privatization continued, especially in the financial sector, and relations with the IMF were restored. The economy stopped falling for the moment, but foreign investors are staying away and rising violence destroyed the once buoyant tourist sector.

INDONESIA'S PROSPECTS

With extensive natural resource wealth and a large and cheap labor force whose literacy and skill level was greatly increased by sustained investment in primary education, Indonesia should be capable of resuming a path of economic growth. In the short run, however, it offers little to attract the foreign capital necessary for growth. Decades of corruption, growing intercommunal strife, and increasing violence are all deterrents to the necessary foreign investment. The Megawati regime must act to curb corruption and to prevent the reemergence of the crony capitalism that was characteristic of the Suharto and Wahid regimes. It must also stabilize the political union. Such stabilization must involve some devolution of power to the regions and ethnicities, which in turn start the nation down a slippery slope. If the government is to succeed in curbing the centrifugal tendencies it must take steps to establish the Army's reputation for even-handedness and service to the nation. These are tall orders in an era where Indonesia, the world's most populous Islamic nation, is likely to be seen as refuge for fundamentalist groups.

KEY TERMS AND CONCEPTS

Asia-Pacific Regional Operation
  Center (APROC)
Central Provident Fund (CPF)
community financial institutions

Confucianism
Council for Economic Planning
  and Development (CEPD)
crony capitalism

curb market	New Order
currency board	nonaligned movement
Economic Expansion Act of 1967	postdated check
guided democracy	pronatalist movement
guided economy	rent seeking
Javanese imperialism	Repelita
khaki capitalism	state-managed capitalism
Kuomintang (KMT)	statutory boards
Ministry of Finance and Trade and Industry	transparency in regulation
	wage correction
National Wages Council (NWC)	

QUESTIONS FOR DISCUSSION

1. What is the basis of the Confucian content of Taiwanese economic management?
2. What has been the role of household saving in Taiwanese growth?
3. How has the conservatism of the Taiwanese financial system proved a long-term asset?
4. What are the goals of Taiwanese privatization? Are Singapore's goals the same?
5. What were Singapore's biggest problems at independence, and how did the PAP government address them?
6. Why was the "wage correction" of 1979–1982 so unusual? Has it proved successful?
7. Why might the forced saving required by the Central Provident Fund not increase aggregate saving?
8. Does Singapore provide a generalizable development model for other less-developed countries? Why or why not?
9. What were the achievements of the "New Order" economic reforms?
10. Why did the army play such a central role in Indonesian development?
11. What kind of planning was practiced in Indonesia?
12. Why did the World Bank consider Indonesia's financial reforms of the early 1990s successful, and what were their long-term consequences?
13. Why has Indonesia incurred longer-term consequences from the crisis than its neighbors?

RESOURCES

Web Sites

Taiwan

Central Bank ....http://www.cbc.gov.tw/

Taiwan Institute of Economic Research ....http://www.tier.org.tw/

Ministry of Economic Affairs ....http://www.moea.gov.tw/

Central News Agency ....http://www.cna.com.tw/

Taiwan Academy of Banking and Finance ....http://www.tabf.org.tw/

Singapore

Ministry of National Development ....http://www.mnd.gov.sg/

Ministry of Finance..............................http://app10.internet.gov.sg/scripts/mof/index.asp

Stock Exchange ....http://www.ses.com.sg/

Economic Development Board ....http://www.sedb.com.sg/

Monetary Authority of Singapore..http://www.mas.gov.sg/

Department of Statistics ....http://www.singstat.gov.sg/

Singapore Government Online Portal..http://www.gov.sg/

The Business Times—National Newspaper http://business-times.asia1.com.sg/

Indonesia

Central Bank of Indonesia..http://www.bi.go.id/

Jakarta Stock Exchange ....http://www.jsx.co.id/

Department of Foreign Affairs ....http://www.dfa-deplu.go.id/

U.S. Aid Indonesia Site..http://www.usaid.gov/id/

Indonesia Embassy in the United States..................http://www.embassyofindonesia.org/

Books and Articles

Taiwan

Alam, M. Shahid. *Governments and Markets in Economic Development Strategies: Lessons from Korea, Taiwan, and Japan.* New York: Praeger, 1989.

Backman, Michael. *Asian Eclipse: Exposing the Dark Side of Business in Asia.* New York: Harper, 2001.

Chen, John-Ren. "The Effects of Land Reform on the Rice Sector and Economic Development in Taiwan." *World Development,* November 1994, 1759–1770.

Chen, Tain-Jy. "Determinants of Taiwan's Direct Foreign Investment: The Case of a Newly Industrializing Country." *Journal of Development Economics,* October 1992, 397–407.

Chou, Tein-Chen. *Industrial Organization in a Dichotomous Economy: The Case of Taiwan.* Aldershot: Avebury, 1995.

Chow, Peter, *Taiwan in the Global Economy.* New York: Praeger, 2002.

Deyo, Frederic C. (ed.). *The Political Economy of the New Asian Industrialism.* Ithaca, NY: Cornell University Press, 1987.

Fields, Karl J. *Enterprise and the State in Korea and Taiwan.* Ithaca, NY: Cornell University Press, 1995.

Hong, Sung Gul. *The Political Economy of Industrial Policy in East Asia: The Semiconductor Industry in Taiwan and South Korea.* Northampton, MA: Edward Elgar Publishing, 1997.

Ku, Yeun-Wen. *Welfare Capitalism in Taiwan: State, Economy and Social Policy.* New York: St. Martin's Press, 1997.

Liu, Chien, and J. Michael Armer. "Education's Effect on Economic Growth in Taiwan." *Comparative Education Review,* August 1993, 304–321.

McBeath, Gerald *A. Wealth and Freedom: Taiwan's New Political Economy.* Brookfield, VT: Ashgate Publishing, 1998.

Naughton, Barry (ed.). *The China Circle: Economics and Electronics in the PRC, Taiwan, and Hong Kong.* Washington, DC: Brookings Institution, 1997.

Patrick, Hugh T., and Yung Chul Park. *The Financial Development of Japan, Korea and Taiwan: Growth, Repression and Liberalization.* Oxford: Oxford University Press, 1994.

Qi, Luo. *Economic Interests vs. Political Interventions: The Case of Economic Relations between Mainland China and Taiwan.* River Edge, NJ: World Scientific Publishing, 1998.

"A Survey of Taiwan: A Change of Face." *The Economist,* October 10, 1992, 1–18.

"A Survey of Taiwan: In Praise of Paranoia." *The Economist,* November 7, 1998, 58.

Wade, Robert. *Governing the Market: Economic Theory and the Role of Government in East Asian Industrialization.* Princeton, NJ: Princeton University Press, 1990.

Wade, Robert. "Managing Trade: Taiwan and South Korea as Challenges to Economics and Political Science." *Comparative Politics,* January 1993, 147–167.

Wang, N. T. (ed.). *Taiwan in the Modern World: Taiwan's Enterprises in Global Perspective.* Armonk, NY: M.E. Sharpe, 1992.

Singapore

Crawford, Robert. "An Industrial Policy for Singapore." *Technology Review* 5, May/June 1992, 24–25.

Heng, Toh Mun, and Tan Kong Yam (eds.). *Competitiveness of the Singapore Economy: A Strategic Perspective.* Singapore: Singapore University Press, 1998.

Hobday, Mike. "Technological Learning in Singapore: A Test Case of Leapfrogging." *Journal of Development Studies,* July 1994, 831–859.

Hon, Wong Seng. "Exploiting Information Technology: A Case Study of Singapore." *World Development,* December 1992, 1817–1829.

Huff, W. G. *The Economic Growth of Singapore: Trade and Development in the Twentieth Century.* Cambridge, England: Cambridge University Press, 1994.

LePoer, Barbara Leitch (ed.). *Singapore: A Country Study,* 2d ed. Washington, DC: Federal Research Division, Library of Congress, 1991.

Peebles, Gavin, and Peter Wilson. *The Singapore Economy.* Northampton, MA: Edward Elgar Publishing, 1996.

Perry, Martin. "Promoting Corporate Control in Singapore." Regional Studies, June 1992, 289–294.

Ramesh, M. "Social Security in Singapore: Redrawing the Public-Private Boundary." *Asian Survey,* December 1992, 1093–1109.

Sisodia, Rajendra S. "Singapore Invests in the Nation-Corporation." *Harvard Business Review,* May/June 1992, 40–48.

Tremewan, Christopher. *The Political Economy of Social Control in Singapore (St. Anthony's Series).* New York: St. Martin's Press, 1996.

Indonesia

Booth, Anne (ed.). *The Oil Boom and After: Indonesian Economic Policy and Performance in the Soeharto Era.* Oxford: Oxford University Press, 1992.

Emmerson, Donald K. (ed.). *Indonesia Beyond Soeharto: Polity, Economy, Society, Transition.* Armonk, NY: M.E. Sharpe, 1999.

Evers, Hans-Dieter, and Ozay Mehmet. "The Management of Risk: Informal Trade in Indonesia." *World Development,* no. 1 (1994), 1–9.

Frederick, William H., and Robert L. Worden. *Indonesia: A Country Study,* 5th ed. Washington, DC: Federal Research Division, Library of Congress, 1993.

Hill, Hal. *The Indonesian Economy Since 1966: Southeast Asia's Emerging Giant,* 2d ed. Cambridge, England: Cambridge University Press, 2000.

Kim, John T., Gerrit Knaap, and Iwan J. Azis (eds.). *Spatial Development in Indonesia: Review and Prospects.* Aldershot: Avebury, 1992. Reviewed in *The Journal of Development Studies,* October 1993, 246–248.

"A Survey of Indonesia." *The Economist,* June 6, 2000.

15

THE ASIAN MIRACLE AND THE ASIAN CRISIS

INTRODUCTION

In the aftermath of the Asian financial crisis, and the short-term collapse of many economies in the region, one can wonder if there was only "mirage" rather than a "miracle." However, a facet of the crisis was that recovery in most nations was rapid. For the region as a whole, the only year in which a contraction of real GDP occurred was immediately post-crisis in 1998.[1] Although growth sagged again in 2001, some gains were still made. It goes without question that the growth performance of the East Asian economies had been extraordinary between the early 1970s and the late 1990s. The widely used and authoritative Summers and Heston data set shows that in the 25-year period from 1960 to 1985, no fewer than six East Asian countries placed in the top seven economies of the world in terms of growth of gross domestic product per head of population. The region of East Asia as a whole achieved growth greater than 5.5 percent annually for this same period. This record was significantly better than both that of the industrialized West and developing nations located in other parts of the world, including the petroleum-rich countries of the Middle East and North Africa, despite their rapid resource-driven growth in the 1970s and early 1980s. In this chapter we will review the nature of this growth, and try to account for it. In the final section we will review the nature of the Asian financial crisis of 1997–1998 to see how it relates to and what impact it had on the particular economic model pursued in East Asia.

The strength of East Asia's record is visible in a variety of measures; for example, exports grew even faster than gross domestic product (GDP). Moreover, economic expansion in East Asia was accompanied by a more equitable pattern of wealth and income distribution than in rapidly growing economies elsewhere. The financial crisis of 1997–1998 took some of the gloss from this spectacular performance, but it would take many years of declining GDP to erase the gains of the past quarter-century.

Because of this speedy expansion, much has been written on "the Asian Miracle," a catchphrase that, taken literally, implies that the path of economic development in these countries cannot be explained by the action of human agency or the normal laws of economics, but rather must be attributed to some extranormal factor, even

---

[1]World Bank, *East Asia Update*, November 2002, p. 5.

divine intervention.[2] Paradoxically, many of the authors who favor the "miraculous" description also seek to draw lessons from the East Asian experience and recommend the same policies and institutional structure to other countries pursuing growth.[3]

Hyperbole aside, analysts, policy makers, and politicians share the perception of the Asian experience as being out of the ordinary. If growth records for 1960 to 1985 were randomly distributed across the countries of the world, the chances would be less than 1 in 10,000 that the East Asian Group would enjoy such high and similar growth trajectories. The World Bank devoted considerable attention to the performance of eight **high-performing East Asian economies (HPAEs)**: Japan, Hong Kong, South Korea, Singapore, Taiwan, Indonesia, Malaysia, and Thailand. Also performing remarkably well, although mostly outside of the purview of the World Bank study (because of its different starting point as an economy in transition from planned socialism), has been the People's Republic of China.

This chapter examines four closely related issues. First we look at the characteristics of the Asian Miracle—what it achieved in terms of economic change and higher levels of economic welfare. Next we examine the economic factors associated with such growth. In some analyses these associated factors are termed *causes*, but as we shall see, the relationships are often complex and reciprocal. In the third section we discuss two aspects of a current and lively debate. One is the extent to which credit for growth should be given to market forces, rather than interventionist government policy. The other is whether the outcomes in Asia are explicable by looking at changes in the quantities of factors of production (primarily labor and capital) that are used. The fourth section examines the sustainability of recent growth performance in the light of the financial collapse of 1997–1998 and the changes that it wrought upon the environment in East Asia.

THE CHARACTERISTICS OF THE MIRACLE

Economic variables are often highly correlated, and it is difficult to identify cause and effect. To one observer, for example, high savings cause high investment and therefore rising incomes, while to another rising incomes are the consequence rather than the cause of rapid growth. Standard statistical tests provide some help but will not give unambiguous answers. In this section we identify the characteristics of the "miracle" and leave until later in the chapter an examination of the extent to which it is attributable to policy and institutional factors.

High and Persistent Economic Growth

The most obvious change in East Asia during the last 25 years has been the growth of gross domestic product. The nine East Asian economies all placed in the top 20

---

[2]The World Bank has been particularly fond of the miracle analogy. See, for example, the World Bank Policy Report, *The East Asian Miracle: Economic Growth and Public Policy,* and Joseph Stiglitz and Arilou Uy, "Financial Markets, Public Policy and the East Asian Miracle," *World Bank Research Observer,* 1996.
[3]See Joseph Stiglitz, "Some Lessons from the Asian Miracle," *The World Bank Research Observer* 11, no. 2 (August 1996), pp. 151–177.

economies in terms of growth of GDP over a 25-year period.[4] Growth in almost every case has been sustained and steady. Until the recession of 1998 each year built on the last and saw a record GDP. This pattern of continuing growth contrasts with the experience of other countries in the same time period—for example, Brazil or Mexico—and the experience of the East Asian group at other times. It is common for a nation to experience rapid growth for a limited period of time, when it is "bouncing back" to a level of income—or even to a growth trajectory—from which it had fallen as a result of war, disasters, or inept economic management. Economists generally view this bounce as a return to the production possibility frontier, bringing unused capacity back into production after a shock. Such was the case, for example, for Japan in the 1950s, when it struggled to reach the levels attained in the 1930s after a fall due to the war and its aftermath. Similarly, many economists expect a period of sustained growth in the Eastern European and former Soviet countries, which saw dramatic contractions in output from late 1980s to mid-1990s, largely as a result of the disarticulation of the former Soviet system.[5] However, in East Asia, with only a brief interruption following the crisis, growth has been consistent with the production possibility envelope pushing steadily outward.[6]

Growth with Increasing Equality

The relationship between the distribution of income and economic growth is a complex one. At least two causalities are at work. One is the extent to which inequality in income distribution favors economic growth, while the other is the effect that growth has on the distribution of income. East Asian economies have combined high growth performance with increasing equality in distribution. This relationship is illustrated in Figure 15.1, which shows that in the East Asian countries high rates of growth have been associated with a falling Gini coefficient.[7] In contrast, in Latin America lower growth rates are accompanied by increasing inequality.

In conventional analysis the increasing inequality of income that often accompanies rapid growth is brought about by rising incomes in a dynamic sector, while traditional sectors lag behind. Such dispersion can assist the process of economic growth because the affluence is biased toward wealthier families who show a higher propensity to save, and increased savings can generate funds for investment. Nevertheless, East Asia experienced rapid growth and high propensities to save, despite a narrowing of the dispersion of income.

Another way of looking at the issue of economic inequality is to see what happened to the percentage of the population, and the numbers of individuals, who are subsisting on incomes less than the poverty level. Poverty is a relative measure defined by the World Bank as an inability to maintain a minimal standard of living. In all of the East Asian countries, rapid economic growth has been accompanied by

---

[4]These nine economies consist of the eight World Bank HPAEs plus the People's Republic of China.

[5]So far, however, as we shall see later on, only Poland is currently living up to this expectation.

[6]The exception is the crisis of 1998, which put many Asian economies into contraction.

[7]We discussed the Gini coefficient in Chapter 1. In technical terms, it measures the area between an observed Lorenz curve and the line represented by absolute equality. Consequently, a high Gini coefficient indicates greater inequality.

Income Distribution and Growth

This figure plots the relationship between the average per-head change in income and the change in the Gini coefficient for each of the economies. A fall in the Gini coefficient indicates increasing equality.

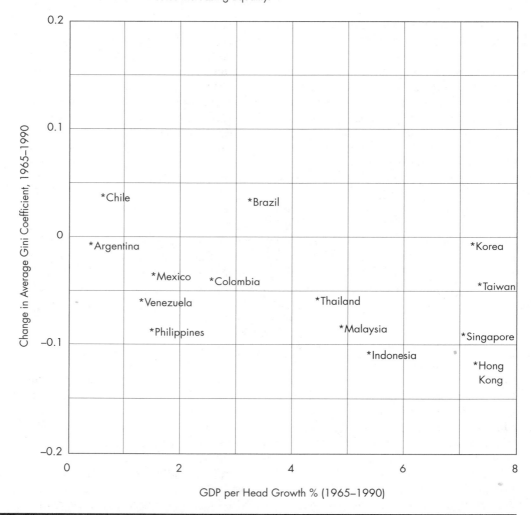

sharp declines in both the poverty rate and the absolute numbers living below the poverty level. In most other countries of the developing world, the poverty rate has fallen (Africa provides frequent exceptions), but a high population growth rate keeps the numbers in poverty growing.

ECONOMIC FEATURES OF THE MIRACLE

A Rapid Demographic Transition

Traditional societies are characterized by high and quite stable birthrates and high, though fluctuating, death rates. Industrialized societies, in contrast, are typified by low and relatively stable death rates, accompanied by low and occasionally fluctuating birthrates. The shift in these parameters from the traditional to the developed pattern is known as the **demographic transition**. Generally speaking, improved public health measures that eradicate catastrophic epidemics lead to a falling death rate, followed later by a fall of the birthrate as the cultural norms that favored larger families adjust to a changed environment. The lag between the two shifts is commonly called the "demographic gap" and results in a rapid increase in population as a low death rate is accompanied by a high birthrate for a generation or so. The longer the transition, the greater the population increase, and the greater the strain on the economy as population growth makes it more difficult to raise living standards. Gains in aggregate output fail to yield higher average welfare because the growing pie must be shared by a rapidly growing population.

The demographic transition in East Asia has been unusually rapid, and the fall of death rates has almost coincided with the drop in birth rates. Average birth and death rates both fell by about 50 percent between 1965 and 1980. This demographic shift contrasts sharply with sub-Saharan Africa, where a fall in the death rate comparable to East Asia was accompanied by a drop in the birth rate of less than 10 percent, resulting in rapid population expansion. Similar rapid population increases occurred in South Asia and Latin America.

A Rapid Accumulation of Human Capital

One cause of rapid demographic transition has been the sharp increase in human capital through education and the swift erosion of differential educational achievement between girls and boys. The success of HPAEs in narrowing this gender gap, especially in primary education, produced two consequences. First, it led to an increase in the available workforce equipped with basic tools of literacy, paving the way for a speedy increase in the female activity rates. Second, it is one factor responsible for the falling birthrate; an effect confirmed by many studies, though the causation is not simple and takes several paths. For example, more educated women are likely to marry later, are more likely to be engaged in paid employment (which increases the opportunity cost of children), and are likely to be more informed about contraceptive technologies. Moreover, as rising educational levels speed the demographic transition, falling birthrates themselves allow for rapid increases in human capital per individual. In countries where the birthrate remains high, the growth of the school-age population absorbs more educational resources, slowing the growth of enrollment rates and years of schooling per pupil. East Asian countries experienced a virtuous cycle: sharply lowered population growth fostered higher average educational attainment, which in turn results in further lowered birthrates. Enrollment rates in both primary and secondary education in

East Asian countries exceed the global average, even when controlling for income levels. Not only have more public resources been expended on education in East Asia than in other countries of similar affluence, but the education itself has been more effective than elsewhere. In all of the reliable international comparisons of educational achievement, East Asian children tend to perform better, perhaps explained by strong support for education in the family and the culture as a whole.

Sharp and Sustained Increases in Savings Rates

Another feature of East Asian economic performance is a rapid increase in savings rates, now the highest in the world. In 1965 average saving in East Asian economies was about 17 percent of GDP, a point or two less than in Latin America. During the following 25 years, savings rates more than doubled in East Asia, while they remained unchanged in Latin America. It is tempting to attribute the sustained increase in investment and the consequent increase in income to this high savings rate, but what caused this shift in savings behavior? One explanation is the government's role in creating and maintaining stable and accessible financial institutions, giving savers confidence that their money would be safe with financial intermediaries and raising the expected rate of return by eliminating risk associated with possible bankruptcy. However, whether the rapid increase in savings is the cause or the consequence of rapid income growth is still an important issue. Considerable evidence suggests that when income grows unexpectedly rapidly, consumption lags behind, creating increased savings that are in a sense unplanned. Another explanation lies in demographic factors. Falling birthrates and rapid increases in economic participation reduce the **dependency ratio**—the ratio of the nonworking population (who must be supported) to those who work. Life cycle savings theories support the idea that middle-aged workers save more in order to maintain a relatively stable consumption stream into retirement and old age.[8] This provides one explanation for a fall in savings rates. The greater the percentage of the population in retirement, everything else being equal, the lower the savings rate will be: a powerful reason for falling savings rates today in the aging societies of North America, Europe, and Japan.

Although both rapid income growth and demographic factors played a part in increased savings, public policy and institutional change also had an effect. The most important macroeconomic factor in encouraging savings is the maintenance of positive real interest rates. If inflation outpaces the nominal interest rate, the real return to savings is negative, and incentives to save, rather than to consume or invest in goods and real estate, are reduced. Taming inflation, through fiscal and monetary conservatism, can be important. By and large (although not universally) the HPAEs have been successful in restraining inflation and maintaining positive real interest rates. The average real rate in the HPAEs for the late 1970s and 1980s was 1.59 percent.[9] Most other regions of the less-developed world showed negative

---

[8]Ando, Albert, and Franco Modigliani, "The Life Cycle Hypothesis of Saving: Aggregate Implications and Tests," *American Economic Review* 53, no. 1 (1963), pp. 55–84.
[9]Of the HPAEs, only Hong Kong and Japan showed negative real rates during this period.

real interest rates and lower savings rates. Moreover, real interest rates in all HPAEs showed a low standard deviation, giving an element of predictability important for savings behavior.[10]

East Asian governments also created a system that favors savings by reducing the risk to bank depositors and ensuring that they share in the increased demand for funds. One approach focuses on bank regulation and relatively successful supervision of the problem banks. Such regulation reduces the probability of bankruptcy and loss of deposits, the high incidence of which is a strong disincentive to savings in the formal sector. Banking crises have occurred in all of the HPAEs, and they are probably inevitable in rapidly growing economies, but their severity and duration even in the crisis years of 1997–1998, were curtailed by intervention.

Most East Asia nations established regulations that limit competition and keep banking the preserve of a few correspondingly larger banks. Hong Kong, Indonesia, and Singapore are notable exceptions and welcome new financial institutions. (Indeed the livelihood and development strategy of both Hong Kong and Singapore depend in large part on the attraction of financial intermediaries, while Indonesia prior to its collapse was notable for the rapid—and, in some eyes, premature—liberalization of its capital markets.)[11] The success of a restrictive policy depends on a trade-off between the beneficial effects of greater stability (which tends to increase savers' confidence in the safety of their assets and, therefore, raises the savings rate) and the potential for inefficiency and higher costs because of monopolistic practices (tending to reduce the return to savers and thus lower savings). The evidence is ambiguous, though it is probable that enough oligopolistic competition is present to limit inefficiency and protect the saver.[12]

As an additional guarantee for the saver, the governments of the HPAEs (with the exception of Hong Kong and Singapore) resort to a policy of regulating interest spreads from time to time. Such a policy limits the amount of economic rent that the banks earn from the monopoly power created by regulatory limitations on entry. Margins, when regulated, have generally been set at levels comparable to those in developed nations, and lower than those commonly found in developing countries. Savings by small savers were generally encouraged by the existence of state-owned **postal savings institutions**. Before this institutional innovation (which was a common feature of virtually all Western European economies) was applied to Asia, high transaction costs, poor access, and minimum deposit requirements prevented many rural savers from access to top financial intermediaries. The postal savings institutions gathered and aggregated small savings and used them to finance development and private bank loan activity.

---

[10]The exception that should be noted is Latin America, which, largely because of strongly positive real rates in Bolivia and Chile, showed regional positive averages. However, the standard deviations in Latin America were very large, indicating a low level of predictability in the real return and a consequent disincentive for saving by the risk averse.

[11]See World Bank, *The East Asian Miracle* (New York: Oxford University Press, 1993), pp. 238–239.

[12]In fact, the concentration ratio in the banking sector in East Asia is similar to that of developed countries, where we assume adequate competition is at work. However, the paths taken to arrive at that point are quite different. In most developed countries, high concentration ratios were arrived at through merger and consolidation, not barriers to entry.

Finally, it should be noted that three of the HPAEs (Malaysia, Japan, and Singapore) required forced savings through comprehensive and mandatory pension plans or provident funds. The evidence on whether these plans increased total saving is mixed, and, to some extent at least, they act as a substitute for private saving. One study of Japanese savings patterns concluded that total savings were reduced by the mandatory pension scheme.

A High Rate of Private Investment

Throughout their period of rapid growth, East Asian economies maintained the investment share of GDP at a level 7 percent higher than that of other low- and middle-income economies, and saving takes some of the credit. In a world of mobile capital, domestic savings are not the only source of investment finance, nor need all domestic savings necessarily be used for capital formation at home; some may be invested or loaned abroad. However, it is a fact that refraining from consumption provides a source of funds that can be channeled for domestic investment.

High investment has other causes. First, credit must go to credible and defensible property rights. Experience from other parts of the world (especially the transition economies of Eastern Europe) indicates that one of the largest deterrents to investment is uncertainty about whether the property will be secure from expropriation by the government or others in the future.[13] Second, the East Asian governments generally provide the physical infrastructure and human capital to make investment both possible and attractive. Transportation facilities and access to electrical power are particularly important aspects of economic infrastructure and the available evidence suggests that large strides have been made in these areas. An adequate supply of appropriately skilled labor is also complementary to investment, and the efforts and results of the aggressive increase in primary school education provides East Asia with an attractive labor force, which increases the efficiency of domestic capital and is a lure for foreign capital.

Providing Access to Capital These government policies all have played a role in increasing the level of domestic activity and are relatively uncontroversial in their effect. More contentious is the active intervention in credit markets, which has been a feature of East Asian governmental policy. In general, economic efficiency is fostered by reliance on market mechanisms to allocate factors of production among competing uses. Intervention in the operation of markets is justified only by market failure, or when it can be clearly demonstrated that the social rate of return on investment differs substantially from the perceived private rate. With respect to the credit markets, in the HPAEs the two causes of market failure most generally adduced are information failures and coordination problems.

Directed Credit One feature of the East Asian system is government policies of **directed credit**, frequently extended at below-market interest rates, to industries

---

[13]Maxim Boycko, Andrei Shleifer, and Robert Vishny, *Privatizing Russia* (Cambridge, MA: MIT Press, 1996).

deemed vital and selected by the authorities as being strategically important for growth. The specific mechanisms of directing credit differ from country to country. In Korea, where the banking sector was almost totally nationalized during the period of the most rapid growth, selective financing was achieved *directly*. In other countries the government "leaned" on the banking sector to provide the loans to the targeted sectors. If a directed credit policy is to result in a higher aggregate rate of investment rather than merely to affect the distribution among industries, the government action must correct some imperfection in the capital market, perhaps the reluctance of the banking sector to shoulder loans in long-term industrial projects rather than real estate or commerce.

Development Banks In addition to directing the credit policy of private banks, some HPAEs (particularly Japan, Korea, and Taiwan) created specialist publicly owned development banking institutions whose exclusive purpose is to make long-term loans to industry. Frequently these institutions focus on small and medium-sized industry because that sector is often neglected by the private banking sector as too risky or too costly to operate in. In these countries the development banks played an important role, especially in the early stages of development, tending to be less vital as later development produced financial deepening.

The Limited Role of Stock and Bond Markets The role of equity and bond markets in providing investment capital to industry in the East Asian economies has been modest, though it increased with economic and financial maturity. In the Asian context, the expansion of both bond and stock markets should be seen as a result of growth rather than the cause of it. In part this minimal role is due to a policy decision; government control of the financial sector repressed all the forms of financial deepening, including debt and equity markets. In Japan, for example, the government gave the banks a monopoly in the issuance of long-term debentures, which suppressed the growth of corporate bond trading. Stock markets provided only limited capital in the early stages of industrialization in Japan and have grown to some degree subsequently. Joseph Stiglitz, formerly chief economist at the World Bank, finds the evidence suggests that equity markets play only a small role anywhere in Asia.[14]

Tax Policies Taxation affects the attractiveness of private investment by changing the after-tax, or net return. High rates of corporate or profits taxes reduce the net return on investment and tend therefore to lower investment rates. Lower business taxes, or preferential personal tax rates for business-related income, increase investment rates by raising the after-tax yield. Two broad alternative strategies are open to governments in determining the appropriate taxation on investment income. On the one hand, they may pursue a policy of generally low and nonselective rates. This approach will tend to make investment relatively attractive, but it will leave the composition of investment between the different sectors to be determined by private market forces. The alternative strategy is to use the tax

---

[14]See Stiglitz, "Some Lessons from the Asian Miracle," *The World Bank Research Observer* 11, no. 2 (August 1966), pp. 151–177.

system to discriminate between sectors and hence encourage those activities that the government, rather than the market, prizes most highly.

In general, East Asian governments opted for the latter approach, adopting quite high basic corporate tax rates and using a complex system of investment credits, tax holidays, and discriminatory rates to encourage particular industries. In the eyes of most economists such discriminatory policy is *a priori* dangerous and can be justified only in the case of market failure. Such failure may occur, for example, when the government has more information than is available to the actors in the financial market or when social returns deviate substantially from private returns. Even when convincing evidence of market failure is seen and discrimination justified, the tax scheme must be well designed and efficiently managed to achieve the intended results. Japan, South Korea, Taiwan, Malaysia, Thailand, and Singapore all offer examples of highly interventionist tax policy, and much evidence suggests that it has often been counterproductive. One study of South Korea found that only about 6 percent of total Korean growth between 1962 and 1982 could be attributed to interventionist tax policy. Such a yield probably does not justify the uncertainty introduced into the system, nor the resources that the constantly changing system absorbs. Hong Kong, with its generally low rates, stands as an exception to the tinkering of most other Asian governments and may be the preferred model.

Low Capital Goods Prices   The real level of investment is determined both by the nominal resources committed to capital formation and the price of investment goods. East Asian countries have been successful relative to other nations in keeping down the domestic price of imported investment goods. During the 1960s most low- and middle-income countries saw more rapid inflation in the price of investment goods than in GDP as a whole, which was achieved through the management of tariff policies and exchange rate movements. Most important was the policy of allowing investment goods to enter virtually tariff free. A cost of this policy was that a protective strategy for the domestic investment goods sector was impossible, but cheaper access to capital goods benefited a broader range of industries.[15]

Bounding Risks   The rate of investment is largely determined by the expected rate of return, which is itself a composite of upside and downside risk. By **bounding risks**, government programs placed limits on the downside risk for many industries by granting subsidies to those firms that undertook risky projects and by allowing firms to combine into cartels to resist the impacts of downturns in demand.

Controls on the Export of Capital   One way of encouraging domestic investment is to place controls on the outflow of capital. The governments of Japan, Korea, and Taiwan all formed policies that deterred or prevented private capital from leaving, tying the hands of domestic investors and forcing them to choose between investing at home or not investing at all. In the long run such **capital controls** might lower the rate of return on capital and hinder the growth of gross national product, but in the short term they do create positive effects on domestic capital formation and therefore employment and labor productivity.

[15]World Bank, *The Asian Miracle*, p. 232.

Repression of Interest Rates A feature of East Asian growth has been the moderate **repression of interest rates**. This policy means that the rate of interest paid to the saver is kept low, consequently making funds available for capital investment at correspondingly lower rates. Repression is most common when inflation rises without a corresponding adjustment in government-regulated interest rates. This situation could lead to low and possibly negative interest rates for savers, which might result in a serious and depressing impact on savings. The key therefore is "moderation." Several Asian economies successfully kept the real rate for savers relatively low, and, arguably, thereby increased the rate of investment and growth.

Export Growth

No discussion of the characteristics of East Asian growth can omit the extraordinary emphasis placed on the export sector. As we noted earlier, the rate of growth of exports in the Asian economies as a group has been remarkable, and a case can be made for overall success originating in the export sector. However, while exporting has been important, it is essential to understand that export growth owed much to domestic reform.

High Labor Productivity Growth

The consistently high rate of labor productivity growth in the HPAEs can be attributed to several factors. Some of the growth is due to high rates of investment increasing capital per worker, and some may be owed to increased human capital as a result of schooling. However, some is the result of more efficient practices and the adoption of new technology, called **total factor productivity (TFP)** growth and conventionally measured as a residual, after allowing for the effects of increased physical and human capital. The World Bank finds that about two-thirds of HPAE productivity growth is due to capital accumulation and therefore about one-third is due to TFP growth, in its view, a high rate. However, this view has its critics who note that much of the increase of TFP resulted from movement of workers from sector to sector, and though this gain contributes to allocative efficiency, it is a general and predictable consequence of industrialization. We turn to this debate in the following section.

THE DEBATE OVER THE MIRACLE

The Market, or Neoclassical, Explanation

In the 1980s much of the literature concerned with East Asia's high levels of growth focused on reliance on market fundamentals and limited government intervention. This neoclassical view stressed the importance of markets in establishing prices that reflect scarcity and therefore lead to efficient resource allocation. The role of the state was crucial but largely limited to establishing macroeconomic stability and the framework (including the legal structure, property rights, and the provision of public goods) within which markets and businesses could operate.

In this view intersectoral distortions were limited:

> East Asia's success is due to the similar rewards for selling in the domestic and foreign markets. Because variation of incentives across sectors, as measured by the effective rate of protection of value added, has been limited, inputs have flowed to sectors roughly on the basis of static comparative advantage, and international competition has provided an impetus for cost discipline and technological upgrading. Traded inputs have been made available to exporters at international prices, and exporters have faced an international price regime in making their decisions. Finally, factor markets have been roughly competitive, so positive real rates of interest have prevailed, and there has been an absence of duality in the wage structure by size of firm or sector of production.[16]

The Revisionist Critique

In the late 1980s a series of criticisms of this neoclassical explanation began to be articulated stemming from detailed research on the operation of the Japanese, Korean, and Taiwanese economies, especially in the work of Howard Pack and Larry Westphal, Alice Amsden, and Robert Wade. These authors carefully documented that at least in Japan, South Korea, and Taiwan, the governments targeted particular sectors for growth, afforded these sectors protection from foreign competition, and granted subsidized access to capital, frequently on the basis of export performance. Far from providing a level playing field, the revisionists argued, government intervention favored specific sectors which enjoyed high growth and effectively powered the economy.

The revisionists stressed the high level of market failure in developing economies. In particular, information is lacking; spillovers are common, and the market is incomplete and therefore unable to fulfill the task of coordination. The government acted to lead the market and attempted to correct for these imperfections by manipulating key prices (especially in capital markets) in order to promote growth, presenting the vision of the government outperforming the market. This approach is, in some eyes, troublesome, particularly when the recent economic history of Korea, Japan, and Taiwan includes many instances of the bureaucracy leading industry into socially unproductive blind alleys. These range from the petrochemical drive in Japan to high-definition TV and the current financial chaos in Korea.

The "Market Friendly" Approach

To accommodate the idea that the market is in the long run efficient, yet gains may come from selective government intervention, the World Bank chose to stress the East Asian approach is neither market oriented nor wholly interventionist but is, in a phrase, a **"market friendly"** approach.

In the World Bank's view:

> The market friendly approach captures important aspects of East Asia's success. These economies are stable macroeconomically, have high shares of international trade in GDP, invest heavily in people, and have strong competition among firms. But the characteristics are the outcome of many different policy instruments. And the instruments chosen partic-

---

[16]See World Bank, *The Asian Miracle*, p. 82.

ularly in the northeast HPAEs, Japan, Korea, Taiwan, China, sometimes included extensive government intervention in markets to guide private sector resource allocation.[17]

Augmenting the Market Through Competition One of the principal problems of government interventionism is that it leads to a soft-budget constraint. The virtue of the market is that it is unsentimental and winnows out the weaker firms, forces firms to minimize costs, and focuses attention on producing goods that are in demand. In contrast, government subsidies become politicized, enabling underperforming firms to remain in business because of their access to forms of subsidy. As we have seen, one of the chief tools of government interventionism in East Asia is directed credit, accessed by firms at below-market rates. A key to successfully **augmenting the market** is to develop a system that performs the same job as the market—picks winners—and therefore determines the direction of subsidy.

One way to "pick winners" is to promote the development of several firms in an industry and conduct a form of contest among them to see who will enjoy further government support. In East Asia the yardstick, for which the prize of renewed subsidy is awarded, has frequently been export success. This type of contest serves two purposes. It provides the necessary foreign exchange to pay for imports of necessary raw materials, defense equipment, and capital goods. It also offers a more objective test of efficiency than the domestic market. Although exports might be helped by undervalued exchange rates, such an advantage would be common to all domestic firms and therefore relative export performance is a good index of relative competitiveness. In the World Bank's opinion, using exports as a performance yardstick generated substantial benefits because export success is a better indicator of economic efficiency than performance success in a protected domestic market.

Insulating the Bureaucracy The usefulness of any competition depends on a clear definition of the rules and effective arbitration of any disputes. In matters of trade policy it is largely up to the economic bureaucracy to articulate the rules, and, until recently, the conventional wisdom was that the East Asian bureaucracies were both competent and insulated from the pressures of politics and business. In most of East Asia, civil service posts are well paid and enjoy respect. However, the recent plethora of corruption led to questioning of bureaucratic honesty. Given the massive payments from business to politicians, something must have occurred in return, and that presumably was preferential access to some form of subsidy. Despite the World Bank's glowing comments about **insulating the bureaucracy**, the evidence suggests that in Japan and Korea substantial influence peddling was at work by both bureaucrats and politicians.

The Role of Trade We noted earlier that export growth has been a persistent feature of the East Asian success, and it is tempting to regard it as being fundamental to economic growth in the region. Certainly in the World Bank's eyes export success provided a proof of efficiency, a source of funds to purchase capital equipment and technology, as well as substantial employment.

---

[17]See World Bank, *The Asian Miracle*, p. 85.

However, several critics have taken the World Bank to task for overrating the role of trade. Alwyn Young asserts that the criterion to judge "miracles" is not the growth rate *per se*, because growth rate is largely a function of the accumulation of factors of production. The proper criterion for a miracle is an unusually rapid rate of growth of total factor productivity (TFP), the residual left in the growth rate where the contributions of increased quantities of capital and labor are all accounted for. Young shows in a series of articles that TFP growth in Asia has not been especially rapid despite surging exports; indeed, it has been lower than that in several economies that showed slower export growth. Consequently he finds that exporting in itself is no guarantor of growth. Indeed, restricting access to the domestic market (the opposite of openness) is arguably more crucial than export penetration of foreign markets.

Dani Rodrik argues with respect to Japan that it was this closure to the world, coupled with a high degree of domestic competition that contributed most to Japanese success. He cites Hiroyuki Odagiri and Akiri Goto:

> The restriction on imports and foreign direct investment [into] Japan was probably the most important policy until the early 1970s (as regards innovation). Restricting the growing Japanese market, already the second largest in the capitalist world in the late 1960s, to the Japanese firms who were competing intensively among themselves gave a strong incentive to invest in plants, equipment and R&D.[18]

THE SUSTAINABILITY OF THE MIRACLE

Despite the astonishing speed of growth in many Asian economies, an ongoing and vital dispute concerns the nature of the growth process. One school declared that it is no "miracle" at all: the rapid observed growth is explicable in terms of conventional economics; that is, most of the increase in output could be attributed to increases of factor inputs (labor and capital), the securing of economies of scale, and the redeployment of workers from sectors with low marginal products per worker (largely small-holding agriculture) to those with higher marginal products (the manufacturing sector). In our analysis of Korea, for example, we saw that most economic growth could be readily accounted for by the increase of factor inputs. The population has been mobilized, participation rates increased, and the capital input per worker raised. In the case of Korea, roughly 75 percent of the growth between 1963 and 1990 was accounted for by changes in factor inputs. The gain in the productivity of those factor inputs represented only a residual 25 percent. Moreover, most of the gain in output per unit of input was accounted for by the relocation of labor from low productivity agriculture to industry and well-documented, though limited, economies of scale. That leaves less than 1 percent of growth to be accounted for by improvement of technique, gains in skill, higher productivity due to supervision, and other factors not included elsewhere. This assessment led Paul Krugman to claim that, relying on increases in factors of production, East Asian growth is like the growth of Stalin's Russia, impressive but extensive, and therefore not sustainable.

---

[18]Dani Rodrik, "King Kong Meets Godzilla: The World Bank and the East Asian Miracle," in *Miracle or Design? Lessons from the East Asian Experience*, Albert Fishlow et al., eds. (Washington, DC: Overseas Development Council, 1994).

The subsequent work of Nicholas Crafts supports Krugman's claims. Crafts concludes that:

> First, factor accumulation has been much more important than total factor productivity growth, especially in comparison to earlier epochs of rapid catch-up growth in western Europe and Japan; nonetheless, productivity performance has been stronger than has been allowed by critics of the east Asian experience. Second, a temporary demographic advantage of rising labor force participation has given these economies an added boost to economic growth during recent decades. Third, development has taken place rapidly from an initial position of economic backwardness, which has generated its own legacy of financial and other institutions.[19]

In response to such objections, supporters of the view that Asian growth is a miracle argue that the conventional way of measuring total factor productivity systematically understates the real role of technology and technical change. Moreover, other considerations suggest that what happened in Asia was a profound and unusual change. First is the real achievement of breaking the cycle of inward-looking underdevelopment. Second, the elevation of savings rates from about 6 percent of household income to over 30 percent is a kind of miracle in itself, particularly when associated with a consistent ability to match saving with productive investments.

However, it is important to assess what has been undone by the financial crisis and its aftermath. Was the crisis a "bump in the road" or did it permanently change the growth prospects of the region, and at the same time call into question the viability of the "state-led development model."

What Caused the Asian Crisis?

In the midst of the debate about the causes of the crisis, there is some agreement. Sentiment about the region's prospects became rather too bullish in the mid-1990s and foreign investment capital flowed into the area. This surplus on capital account inevitably created a deficit in the current accounts of most of the east and southeast Asian nations. Confidence in the region was artificially promoted by the heavy involvement of governments in the investment process. Their role was taken by some as a guarantee of investment viability and increased the perception of repayment. Within nations a pervasive system of directed credit led domestic banks to take on excessive quantities of questionable loans. The result was overinvestment in productive capacity and overborrowing from abroad.

In early 1997 the problems began to unwind. Initial difficulties in Thailand and Korea raised warning flags, and foreign investors and lenders began to repatriate their capital as fast as possible. This flight led to a **run on the banks** and a credit crunch for many firms. Share values plummeted and bank balance sheets suffered as assets were wiped out. Panic set in and the situation became progressively worse.

Policy Response to the Crisis

In the aftermath of the crisis, a great deal of criticism was raised relating to the conduct of IMF policy during and after the crisis. The IMF response had two principal

---

[19]Nicholas Crafts, "East Asian Growth: Before and After the Crisis," IMF, working paper WP/98/137, 1998.

dimensions. On the one hand it extended a great deal of credit to the region, enabling the governments to recapitalize the banks (frequently taking them into public ownership) and assisting foreign investors to extricate some of their capital. At the same time it required policies of fiscal and monetary stringency as conditions of credit extension. The Fund has been criticized on both scores. The first charge is that the credit did little to assist the affected countries but primarily helped western lenders to get their money out. Critics charge that the capital had been committed under unstable conditions for profit and the lenders should have taken the consequences as they fell. Otherwise the **moral hazard** implications are worrisome. In the future, critics argue, banks and other lenders will fail to perform due diligence because they feel that the role of international bodies is to protect them against the consequences of unwise lending albeit in the name of preserving the viability of the international financial system. Moreover, it is said, countries will behave irresponsibly because they know that the IMF is there to bankroll them.

Stanley Fischer, then managing director of the IMF, tried to address these issues:

> Of course, not everyone agrees with the international community's approach of trying to cushion the effects of such crises. Some say that it would be better simply to let the chips fall where they may, arguing that to come to the assistance of countries in crisis will only encourage more reckless behavior on the part of borrowers and lenders. I do not share the view that we should step aside in these cases. To begin with, the notion that the availability of IMF programs encourages reckless behavior by countries is far-fetched: no country would deliberately court such a crisis even if it thought international assistance would be forthcoming. The economic, financial, social, and political pain is simply too great; nor do countries show any great desire to enter IMF programs unless they absolutely have to.[20]

The second criticism is that the fiscal and monetary policies urged on the governments in the region contributed to the crisis by causing a sharp drop in demand and creating more economic contraction, bankruptcies, and unemployment. In a potentially recessionary situation, the IMF's critics maintain, steps should be taken to bolster demand, not to reduce it.

Again, Fischer articulated the IMF position.

> Other observers have advocated more expansionary fiscal programs to offset the inevitable slowdown in economic growth. The balance here is a fine one. As already noted, at the outset of the crisis, countries need to firm their fiscal positions, to deal both with the future costs of financial restructuring and—depending on the balance of payments situation—the need to reduce the current account deficit. Beyond that, if the economic situation worsens, the IMF generally agrees with the country to let automatic stabilizers work and the deficit to widen somewhat. However, we cannot remain indifferent to the level of the fiscal deficit, particularly since a country in crisis typically has only limited access to borrowing and since the alternative of printing money would be potentially disastrous in these circumstances.

The Aftermath

As noted, the long-term effect of the crisis has been less than was feared at the time, an especially surprising outcome when viewed against the problems of the Euro-

[20]"The Asian Crisis: A View from the IMF," Address by Stanley Fischer, First Deputy Managing Director of the International Monetary Fund at the Midwinter Conference of the Bankers' Association for Foreign Trade, Washington, DC, January 22, 1998.

pean and U.S. economies during 2000–2002. These difficulties included a major U.S. market collapse and a sharp fall in all kinds of information technology-related equipment that dealt a sharp blow to the economies of Korea and Taiwan. Almost every country in the region experienced positive growth in every year except 2001. The exceptions are Taiwan and Singapore in 2001, and Japan in 1998, 2001, and 2002.

Foreign investment inflows are now positive into the region, although (except for China) they are running at about half of their 1996 and 1997 levels. The economies do still face major problems. The burden of **nonperforming loans** is still considerable; in Indonesia in early 2002, some 50 percent were nonperforming, with almost 30 percent in Thailand.

Nevertheless, it can be said that the region is on the road to recovery.[21] The question is whether the developmental model should change, and whether this change will occur as a natural consequence of the crisis or will require policy intervention.

THE LESSONS OF THE MIRACLE

The "lessons" of the miracle are complex, and the applicability of the East Asian experience to other countries (for example, in South Asia, Latin America, or in the successor states to the Soviet Union) must be in doubt; but some useful generalities about the role of systems and policy in establishing sustained development may be drawn out here:

1. Macroeconomic stability is an important prerequisite for sustained economic expansion. Growth is not possible in a hyperinflationary situation, or for that matter in one of widely fluctuating demand. However, single-digit inflation is not a necessity; moderately high inflation rates have been associated with rapid growth in South Korea and elsewhere.

2. Government action is essential in establishing the preconditions of growth, especially in transportation, communication, and education. As Patrick found in Japan, macroindustrial policy creating infrastructure and human capital does work.

3. The record of microeconomic industrial policy has been mixed. Some apparent successes have been counterweighted by some very notable failures. Problems are more likely the closer the economy gets to the cutting edge of new technology. In the early stages of industrialization it is easier to predict the most appropriate sectors to favor, since changes in the industrial structure can follow an established pattern of comparative advantage. In later phases of growth it becomes harder to "pick winners," as the Japanese experience with HDTV shows.

4. Reliance on directed credit may have adverse consequences for the banking sector, which can be left with a portfolio of losers. If they are not guided by bureaucrats, bankers will take care to assess the risks associated with a loan. The direction of credit by planning agencies distorts the allocative efficiency of financial markets and removes discretion from the bankers. Being forced to

---

[21]*East Asia: The Road to Recovery* (Washington, DC: World Bank, 1998).

lend to politicians' favorites, rather than the most potentially productive firms, can upset the stability of the financial sector, as experiences in South Korea and Japan showed in the Asian financial crisis.

5. Education expenditure is generally worthwhile, but is most effective when it is directed toward elementary education. Raising the literacy rate is cheap relative to producing a university graduate, and the greatest gains in workforce productivity are provided by a literate workforce.

6. The probity of financial markets is important. Individuals are less likely to save if they lack faith in financial intermediaries. Somewhat surprisingly the Asian financial crisis of 1997–1998 has not had a profound affect on personal saving.

7. Stock markets have not been an important element in the initial growth and development of Asian economies. Equity markets in early stages of development tended to be shallow, rather volatile, and more significant in the redistribution of wealth than in the creation of it. Even in the most developed of the Asian economies, Japan, the stock market has been manipulated and has been a potential source of economic instability.

8. Foreign direct investment has not been a dominant factor in Asian growth. Japan's success was financed to a large degree out of domestic saving; in Korea loans from multilateral agencies were a substantial factor. In Indonesia and Singapore foreign investment has been more vital. In fact, the greater the reliance on foreign finance the more vulnerable an economy was to the panic and capital outflow of the crisis years.

9. Competitions—for example, those predicated on export performance—can be useful ways to augment the market, but only if they are well designed and disinterestedly administered. Recent problems in Korea concerning the dominance of few major groups call into question how well Korean "competitions" helped the long-run growth of the economy. It is possible that the reliance on such competitions encouraged the overexpansion, and subsequent collapse, of the dominant *chaebol*.

10. Well-paid and respected civil servants lower the probability of corruption. For a long time the image of incorruptible and competent civil servants was a vaunted characteristic of the Asian model. American businesspeople, deeply mistrustful of government officials at home, attributed farseeing powers to those of Japan and Korea. However, more systematic studies of the Asian experience revealed a much higher degree of corruption and a lower degree of competence than once thought the case.

THE LESSON OF THE CRISIS

Finally, we should note that, whatever its other strengths, the Asia model of development has at its heart a legacy of weak financial institutions with its roots in the subservience of the banking sector to a powerful bureaucracy. This relationship, and consequent weakness, led in no small part to the financial crisis of 1997 and to the continuing overhang of nonperforming loans that will bedevil the financial sectors of some nations well into the new millennium, especially Japan, Korea, and Thailand. The Crafts study comes to the point:

> . . . despite its favorable attributes, such as effective mechanisms for technology transfer, outward orientation, and high savings, investment and human capital accumulation, there are downsides to the developmental state model, including a tendency to wasteful investment and the difficulties that it may pose for the transition to freer capital markets. These last are more attractive after the initial phase of development when coordination problems loom less large and diminishing returns are a bigger concern. Because the greatest successes of this managed development have come in the context of export-oriented manufacturing and industrialization, [I conclude] that an alternate model may be more appealing in the coming years of de-industrialization.[22]

The last point is a key one. The Asian nations' growth was predicated on the manufacture of tradable goods, and low labor costs were an important element of comparative advantage. As labor costs creep up, the economy must shift to high value services, and the "commodity" approach will not fit well to the new requirements. The problem is, how should a change be effected and what "alternate model" is suitable?

KEY TERMS AND CONCEPTS

augmenting the market

bounding risks

capital controls

demographic transition

dependency ratio

directed credit

high-performing East Asian
    economies (HPAEs)

insulating the bureaucracy

"market friendly"

moral hazard

nonperforming loans

postal savings institutions

repression of interest rates

run on the banks

total factor productivity (TFP)

QUESTIONS FOR DISCUSSION

1. How did a rapid demographic transition help growth in most East Asian economies?
2. How have high rates of investment been maintained in East Asian economies?
3. Have stock markets and foreign capital been important in Asian growth?
4. How has financial repression assisted growth?
5. What led to East Asian growth being described as "market friendly"?

---

[22]Nicholas Crafts, "East Asian Growth: Before and After the Crisis," IMF, working paper WP/98/137, 1998.

6. Is insulating the bureaucracy from political pressure a good thing? How is it done?

7. How can competitions for credit be said to be "market-augmenting"?

RESOURCES

Web Sites

Asian Crisis Information..http://www.stern.nyu.edu/globalmacro/
The best Web site on the Asian Crisis is Professor Nouriel Roubini's at the Stern School, New York University **Association of Southeast Asian Nations** ...http://www.aseansec.org/

United Nations Economic and Social Commission for Asia and the Pacific ....
....http://www.unescap.org/

World Bank http://lnweb18.worldbank.org/eap/eap.nsf
More current material can be found on the East Asian and Pacific subsite of the World Bank.

Books and Articles

Adams, Gerard F., and Shinichi Ichimura (eds.). *East Asian Development: Will the East Asian Growth Miracle Survive?* New York: Praeger, 1998.

Amsden, Alice H. "Why Isn't the Whole World Experimenting with the East Asian Model to Development?: Review of *The East Asian Miracle.*" *World Development* 22, 1994, 626–633.

Arogyaswamy, Bernard. T*he Asian Miracle, Myth, and Mirage.* Westport, CT: Quorum Books, 1998.

Bello, Walden, and Stephanie Rosenfeld. *Dragons in Distress: Asia's Miracle Economies in Crisis.* San Francisco: Institute for Food and Development Policy, 1990. Reviewed in *Journal of Contemporary Asia* 22, 1992, 546–551.

Campos, Jose Edgardo, and Hilton L. Root (contributor). *The Key to the Asian Miracle: Making Shared Growth Credible.* Washington, DC: Brookings Institution, 1996.

Chen, Xiangming. "The Changing Roles of Free Economic Zones in Development: A Comparative Analysis of Capitalist and Socialist Cases in East Asia." *Studies in Comparative International Development,* Fall 1994, 3–25.

Claessens, Stjin, Simeon Djankov, and Leora Klapper. "Resolution of Corporate Distress: Evidence from East Asia's Financial Crisis," World Bank working paper, 1998.

Claessens, Stjin, Simeon Djankov, and Larry H. P. Lang. "Who Controls East Asian Corporations?" World Bank working paper, 1998.

Crafts, Nicholas. "East Asian Growth: Before and After the Crisis." IMF, working paper WP/98/137, 1998.

Deyo, Frederic C. (ed.). *The Political Economy of the New Asian Industrialism.* Ithaca, NY: Cornell University Press, 1987.

Fishlow, Albert (ed.). *Miracle or Design? Lessons from the East Asian Experience.* Washington, DC: Overseas Development Council, 1994.

Garran, Robert. *Tigers Tamed: The End of the Asian Miracle.* Honolulu: University of Hawaii Press, 1998.

Goldstein, Steven M. *Mini Dragons: Fragile Economic Miracles in the Pacific.* New York: Ambrose Video Publishing, 1991.

International Monetary Fund. *East Asian Growth Before and After the Crisis.* IMF working paper, 1998.

Jomo, K. S. (ed.). *Tigers in Trouble: Financial Governance, Liberalisation and Crises in East Asia.* London: Zed Books, 1999.

Kwon, Jene. "The East Asia Challenge to Neoclassical Orthodoxy." *World Development,* 1994, 635–644.

Lall, Sanjaya. "The East Asian Miracle: Does the Bell Toll for Industrial Strategy?" *World Development,* 1994, 645–654.

Litonjua, M. D. "Outside the Den of Dragons: The Philippines and the NICs of Asia." *Studies in Comparative International Development,* Winter 1994, 3–30.

McVey, Ruth. *Southeast Asian Capitalists.* Ithaca, NY: Cornell University Press, 1992. Reviewed by Mike Moore, *The Journal of Development Studies,* April 1994, 724–725.

Park, Yung Chul, "Does East Asia Need a New Paradigm for Development?" Paper delivered at the Brookings Institution Trade Forum, 2002. Available at http://www.brookings.edu/dybdocroot/es/commentary/journals/trade/papers/200205_park.pdf.

Perkins, Dwight H. "There Are at Least Three Models of East Asian Development." *World Development,* 1994, 655–661.

Rodrik, Dani. "King Kong Meets Godzilla: The World Bank and the East Asian Miracle." In *Miracle or Design? Lessons from the East Asian Experience,* Albert Fishlow (ed.). Washington, DC: Overseas Development Council, 1994.

Sengupta, Jati K. "Growth in NICs in Asia: Some Tests of New Growth Theory." *Journal of Development Studies,* January 1993, 342–358.

Stiglitz, Joseph E. "Some Lessons from the East Asian Miracle." *The World Bank Research Observer* 11, no. 2 (August 1996), 151–177.

Stiglitz, Joseph E., and Arilou Uy. "Financial Markets, Public Policy and the East Asian Miracle," *World Bank Research Observer,* 1996, 249–276.

"A Survey of Business in Asia: The Search for the Asian Manager." *The Economist,* March 9, 1996, 1–26.

"A Survey of East Asian Economies: Frozen Miracle." *The Economist,* March 7, 1998, 58.

Tai, Hung-chao (ed.). *Confucianism and Economic Development: An Oriental Alternative?* Washington, DC: Washington Institute Press, 1989.

Tan, Gerald. *The End of the Asian Miracle?: Tracing Asia's Economic Transformation.* Singapore: Times Academic Press, 1999.

Terry, Edith Buchanan. *The Rise and Fall of the Asian Miracle.* Armonk, NY: M.E. Sharpe, 1999.

Wade, Robert (ed.). *Miracle or Design? Lessons from the East Asian Experience.* Washington, DC: Overseas Development Council, 1994.

Woo, Wing Thye, Stephen Parker, and Jeffrey D. Sachs. *Economies in Transition: Comparing Asia and Europe.* Cambridge, MA: MIT Press, 1997.

World Bank. *East Asian: The Road to Recovery.* Washington, DC: World Bank, 1998.

World Bank. *The East Asian Miracle: Economic Growth and Public Policy.* New York: Oxford University Press, 1993.

Young, Alwyn. "Lessons from the East Asian NICs: A Contrarian View." *European Economic Review,* April 1994, 964–974.

Socialist Economies

Chapter 16: The Command Economy

Why Study Planned Economies?
A Brief Overview of Russian Economic History

Chapter 17: The Operation of the Soviet Planned Economy

The Institutions of the Soviet State
The Mechanism of Planning
The Determination of Prices
Labor Markets
Market Clearing
Monitoring Plan Fulfillment
Incentives in Soviet-Type Systems
Conclusion

Chapter 18: The Participatory Economy: The Case of Yugoslavia

The Participatory Economy
Development of the Yugoslav State
Yugoslav Market Socialism
Problems of the Yugoslav Economy
Conclusion

Chapter 19: The Possibilities of a Third Way

Market Socialism and Social Markets
Market Socialism
The Social Market Economy
Conclusion

16

THE COMMAND ECONOMY

WHY STUDY PLANNED ECONOMIES?

At this juncture of history it is tempting to view both the theory and the experience of central planning as an irrelevant footnote. Both popular and academic opinion now consider command planning as a dead end, a mistake into which many nations were dragged for a few decades and from which they have now largely emerged. Today about 30 of the world's nations, with an aggregate population of about 1.6 billion people, who were previously committed to some form of central planning, are now regarded as **economies in transition**—converting from a socialist system to a capitalist one.[1] Indeed 20 years into the process we are entitled to wonder when the transition will be complete. It would, however, be premature merely to salute "the triumph of capitalism" and turn away from any consideration of the achievements and the shortcomings of socialism and central planning. A great deal can be learned from the careful examination of their history.

Central Planning Is Not Extinct As a System

Mark Twain once observed that "reports of my death have been greatly exaggerated," and the same may be the case for central planning. Despite current appearances and political trends, it is conceivable that some form of centralized planning will be reestablished, possibly emerging within the group of former socialist nations. Indeed, several of the largest nations are by no means so well advanced in the transition process that the situation is irreversible. China, for example, still retains the strong political control required to revert back to centralized planning if the social problems of greater liberalization continue to grow. Vietnam, despite some liberalization and incoming foreign investment, is committed only to an experiment in what its leadership calls **market Leninism**. Even within the nations of Central and Eastern Europe, former Communists have made strong showings at the polls. Though nominally committed to maintaining a path toward a full market economy, they still carry an ideological bias toward central control. In Western Europe a recent tilt in electoral sentiment put left-wing parties back into power.

---

[1]Of these, 15 were formerly republics that constituted the Soviet Union and four were part of Yugoslavia, which pursued a market socialist path that differed in some fundamental ways from that of the Soviet Union.

Finally, the chaos in the Asian markets during 1998 leaves some to wonder whether market capitalism is the most efficient system of economic organization.

Understanding the Planned Past Is the Key to a Successful Transition to a Market Future

An effective transition to a market economy depends on a full understanding of the constraints imposed by the legacy of the prior system. Although many economists advising the nations in transition seem to conceive of the task as building a system "from the ground up," in reality the culture, mores, institutions, and much of the distribution of power of the old system are very much alive. The direction of transition is contingent on the legacy of the socialist period in most countries, and change requires the acquiescence of the more privileged elite established by the prior order.

Most Economies Make Use of Some Form of Planning

As we noted previously, none of the world's economic systems are purely private. All nations pursue some mixture of both private and public systems. Studying the consequences of generalized planning in command economies can help inform our discussion of mixed systems, point to the limitations of government, highlight the need for incentives, and indicate when planning can be the best approach for meeting social needs.

There Are Lessons to Be Learned from Examining Failure

Finally, a clear idea of why centrally planned systems failed is necessary. "Those who fail to understand history are doomed to repeat it" is an overused expression, but in terms of choosing an economic system, this perspective may well be valid. Central planning was attractive because it offered a rational alternative to the repeated recessions and skewed income distribution that characterized capitalism. When, in the 1950s, Nikita Khrushchev declared that "we will bury you," he was talking in terms of systems, and at that time many in the capitalist world feared that he might be right. However, after watching the stagnation and relative decline of the socialist nations, we now know that socialism's apparent advantages are bought at a high cost.

A BRIEF OVERVIEW OF RUSSIAN ECONOMIC HISTORY[2]

For our example of central planning, we turn to the experience of the Soviet Union, the earliest example of comprehensive planning. Efforts in other countries, notably in Eastern Europe after World War II and in China, drew their expertise and inspiration from the Soviet model.

---

[2]This overview is indeed brief, and any interested student is referred initially to Paul Gregory and Robert Stuart, *Soviet and Post Soviet Economic Structure and Performance*, 5th ed. (Reading, MA: Addison-Wesley, 1999), for a much richer exposition.

The Czarist Economy

No system develops independently of historical influence, and the emergence of the planned Soviet state was no exception. The development of modern Russia, including the Soviet period, owes much to Peter the Great. As the first great modernizer, Peter aggressively imported Western technology and science, while simultaneously resisting the liberalizing influence of Western political thought. He began the process of Russian industrialization, founding a variety of state industries. He revolutionized public finance and increased the income of the treasury fivefold. However, he did little to reform serfdom, which was the basic institution of the labor market, and relied heavily on forced labor for his projects, the most enduring of which was the construction of his "European" capital, St. Petersburg. Consequently, the dualism of Russian society increased: a more affluent and westward-looking aristocracy contrasted increasingly with a backward and exploited peasantry.

The repressions of an absolutist monarchy, an elitist aristocracy, and a highly conservative Orthodox Church were formidable barriers to economic change, and Russia, despite its great potential, remained relatively poor. Failure to defeat a rather small Anglo-French force in the Crimean War of 1853–1856 underlined Russian backwardness. In 1861 this realization led Czar Alexander II to take the immense step of liberating the serfs, who then represented about three-quarters of the population. Emancipation was accompanied by land reform and after their manumission the peasants held, through communal organizations, about half of the country's agricultural land.[3] Predictably the aristocracy retained ownership of the best land, and the poorer acreage transferred to the serfs was not given but sold on mortgage, so from the start of their liberty the peasantry was encumbered by heavy debts.

The government set about modernizing the Russian infrastructure, with special emphasis on the transportation needs of the vast empire. More than 20,000 miles of railway track were built between 1861 and 1894, opening up the interior for export-oriented agriculture. The supply of grain for export was stimulated by the need of the peasants to sell much of their output for cash to meet their heavy debt obligations and taxes. By the 1890s Russia emerged as the world's largest grain exporter, and the hard currency revenues were used to finance the import of capital goods required for the aggressive industrialization scheme of the finance minister, Sergius von Witte. Industrial output tripled between 1880 and 1900 and after a brief dip due to the global recession in the first years of the twentieth century, industrial growth accelerated again, making Russia the world's fifth largest industrial power in 1913.

Living conditions remained grim for both agrarian and industrial workers. The peasants, "held in a vise of ruinous aggregate taxation," were forced to sell the bulk of their output to raise cash for taxes and debt service payments.[4] The conditions of industrial workers were little better and labor discontent led to political organization. Support grew among the industrial workers for the Russian Social Democratic

---

[3]Marx noted in the *Communist Manifesto* in 1882 that this form of "primeval communism" might make it possible for the Russian peasantry to pass more easily to a higher form of communist ownership.
[4]A. Gershenkron, "Russian Agrarian Policies and Industrialization," *The Cambridge Economic History of Europe*, vol. 6 (Cambridge, England: Cambridge University Press, 1965), p. 744.

Party, which held its first convention in 1903, but the party was from the first divided into two factions. The more moderate **Menshevik** wing consisted of social reformers, committed to piecemeal liberalization along the lines of Western Europe. The other wing, Lenin's followers—somewhat inaccurately termed the **Bolsheviks**, or majority—favored radical revolutionary change. The two factions of the party became increasingly alienated and formally split in 1912.

The Russo-Japanese war of 1904–1905 proved another rude shock to the czarist system. Russia was rapidly defeated by an Asian nation that, only 35 years previously, was isolated in a state of feudalism. The losing war effort led to privation at home, accompanied by rioting and strikes. A peaceful protest in front of the Winter Palace in St. Petersburg was fired on by the military, and sympathy for the regime fell, forcing the czar into a series of political reforms, among them the formation of a permanent parliament, the Duma. On the economic front, the **Stolypin reforms** (named for the finance minister) accelerated the rate of industrial growth, freed the peasants from the communes, and alleviated their crushing debt burden.

It is possible that in the aftermath of the Stolypin reforms Russian economic development might have followed the path of peaceful evolution taken in Western Europe, where feudalism gave way to industrial capitalism in a relatively leisurely and peaceful fashion. However, a look at the sources of Russian industrial growth during this period provides a reason to doubt a thesis of a gradually evolving market capitalism. Rapid expansion made Russia one of the world's major industrial powers, but growth in output came mostly from the increase of the industrial labor force and sustained growth in the volume of capital employed. Expansion was therefore highly extensive in character, the result of an increased use of factors of production, not of rising factor productivity. Total factor productivity growth (the residual increase in output, after allowing for the increase in labor and capital employed) was negligible. Industrial expansion could not under these conditions be accompanied by rising wages or living standards. One likely scenario is that prolonged capitalism in Russia would have led to the continued increase of a badly paid, and consequently angry, workforce, potentially provoking revolutionary tendencies at any time.

War Communism

Because of the turn of world events, we will never know whether the mold of extensive growth would have been broken or whether increasing labor demand would have ultimately resulted in burgeoning labor productivity and rising wages. In 1914 Russia became involved in a dispute with Austria and its ally Germany over the Balkans, and in August 1914 Russia was propelled into war along with its own allies, France and Britain. World War I was immensely costly to Russia as its massive but badly equipped and poorly led army absorbed enormous casualties— 2 million dead in less than three years. At home even the barest essentials of life became unavailable for both the peasants and the urban poor, leading to food riots. In May 1917 the czar abdicated, and power passed to the Mensheviks, led by Alexander Kerensky. Menshevik policy was to continue the unpopular war, despite persistent failure on the battlefield and growing deprivation at home. Germany contrived to return the exiled Lenin from Switzerland to St. Petersburg where he led the Bolsheviks to power in the revolution of October 1917. Initially Bolshevik control was largely limited to the capital, with most of the countryside in dispute. Reunification of the country took three years of civil war.

The first decisive act of the new Bolshevik government was to end the war with Germany by the treaty of Brest-Litovsk signed in 1918 on terms close to capitulation. It consigned a large part of the czarist empire to German control, including much of Poland and the Ukraine, the industrial heart and breadbasket of the Empire. France, Britain, and the United States intervened in an attempt to restore the czar and bring Russia back into the war with Germany. However, their somewhat half-hearted efforts were fruitless and the Red Army slowly won control of Russia and ultimately of most of the former czarist territory.

The system of economic organization instituted by the Bolshevik administration during this period is known as **war communism**. Economic management was almost totally by command; food was "requisitioned" in the countryside by police and party officials and distributed in the cities. Thirty-seven thousand enterprises were taken into state hands, including every firm that employed more than 10 workers (5 in establishments where artificial power was used). The coordination of economic activity was ostensibly the preserve of the Supreme Council of National Economy (*VSNKh*), but effective action was fatally hampered by an almost total lack of meaningful information. Workers were conscripted and organized by military methods, and economic incentives for the industrial and agricultural labor forces alike were replaced by dictum and force.

Market economic relations were replaced by what the political leaders termed "natural" ones; housing, electricity, food, postal services, and transportation were all supplied to the public without charge. Interenterprise relations between the state-owned production units were of bookkeeping significance only. Obviously the system of war communism had many shortcomings, as efficiency suffered and corruption abounded. However, a dispassionate evaluation of this period as an economic system is not very meaningful. The country was in a state of civil war, struggling to recover from a disastrous defeat in war with Germany, the food and materiel shortage was acute, and desperate needs justified the desperate measures adopted. Moreover, from the Bolshevik viewpoint, the near-term objective was merely survival. The economic system of war communism enabled them to gather enough resources to defeat both White Russians and foreign interventionists.

The New Economic Policy

By 1920 the civil war was more or less over with Bolshevik rule firmly established not only within Russia itself but also in almost all of the former czarist empire, including areas conceded to Germany in the treaty of Brest-Litovsk. The economy fashioned by von Witte and Stolypin was reunited, and the Bolshevik leadership had an opportunity to develop a new economic system in relative peace.

The blueprint for development was the **New Economic Policy (NEP)** articulated by Lenin in 1921, which attracted recent attention because it has common features with the Soviet (and subsequently) Russian reforms of the late-1980s and early

1990s. It is important to understand that the early leaders of the Bolshevik state were working in a vacuum. To legitimize their revolution they created an alternative to capitalism that was not only superior in its theoretical rationale but also in its concrete results, at least in terms of the distribution of income and the avoidance of mass unemployment. Moreover, ideology required this system to be in some sense Marxian, although Marx's writings gave the Bolshevik leadership little guidance. An astute observer of capitalist societies and economies, Marx said little on the socialist future. Moreover, he predicted that the first socialist revolutions would occur in the most advanced capitalist societies (Britain and Germany the most likely candidates), and so revolution in Russia was somewhat anathematic to his theories. Lenin carefully established the orthodoxy of his revolution by a subtle reinterpretation of Marx, whose thought, he asserted, was really that revolution would occur in "the weakest link in the capitalist chain," rather than necessarily in the most advanced capitalist economies. Despite his care in establishing the Marxian pedigree of the Bolshevik Revolution, Lenin was surprisingly liberal in his design of the economic institutions embodied in the NEP. Although he allowed considerable economic freedom, he regarded the NEP as a pragmatic step backward to establish stability before the creation of socialism could proceed.

During its brief life, the NEP was a form of market socialism. The "natural" economic relations of war communism were terminated in favor of price mechanisms. Control of food production was returned to the peasantry, and market relations were reinstituted to regulate the flow of food to the cities. Small enterprises (defined as those employing fewer than 20 persons) were reprivatized, some were restituted to their former owners and others leased to new entrepreneurs. Most of large-scale industry remained in state hands. Sectors seen as strategically essential—the **commanding heights of the economy**, including fuels, metals, banking, transportation, and foreign trade—became an integral part of the state, dependent on budget allocations and controlled in all important dimensions by the government. The rest of industry was granted substantial subsidies by the state, but had no production quotas to meet, and was otherwise encouraged to act in a profit-maximizing fashion.

The NEP was not a planned economy. The state exercised considerable financial control, but enterprises were able to enter into contracts, fix their own prices, determine output levels, and decide on production techniques. Although **Gosplan**, the state planning agency, was founded in 1921, its functions in the early years of the NEP were limited to forecasting. Coordination in the economy relied increasingly on the concentration of economic power in the industrial sector, as individual enterprises combined to form "trusts," integrated production units promoted by the government. By 1923, 75 percent of all industrial workers were employed by the 478 government-chartered trusts. Subsequently, these trusts themselves combined into even larger units, known as syndicates, involving higher degrees of horizontal integration. By the late NEP period, production by the syndicates accounted for more than 80 percent of industrial output.

In terms of its primary goal of promoting stability, the NEP was a success. By 1926, output climbed back to and exceeded 1913 levels in most commodities. Agricultural output was the exception; it remained well below prewar levels, an ominous precursor of the problems in food production that would haunt the entire Soviet experience. Another sharp difference from the prewar world was the diminished role of trade. The Soviet economy was much less open to world trade than the czarist economy had been, in part because of the disappearance of the agricultural surplus, which constituted the czarist state's largest overseas earner. However, by the mid-1920s the days of the NEP were numbered. Its demise resulted from three factors:

1. *Dissent within the Communist party.* Most Bolsheviks believed that the NEP was a temporary concession, and the expectation grew within the party that, after stability was restored and the economy was stronger, the task of creating a truly socialist economy could commence in earnest.

2. *The "terms of trade" between the urban and the rural sectors.* The reform issue was brought to a head by the so-called **scissors crisis**, which occurred during 1922 and 1923 when the price of agricultural goods fell sharply while the prices of industrial goods rose.[5] When these indices were plotted graphically, they resembled the two blades of an open scissors (see Figure 16.1), hence the name. The Bolshevik leadership assumed that this fall in the real price of grain would cause the peasants to sharply reduce supply to urban markets and create famine in the cities. This presumption, based on little evidence, led the authorities to consider a return to a command economy entailing the forced requisition of agricultural goods. After intense debate, the government tried regulation and attempted to move real prices in agriculture's favor by imposing price ceilings on consumer goods. At the lower real prices consumer goods were in short supply, especially in rural markets. In the absence of effective rationing this "goods famine" led to a black market, with intermediaries from the cities reaping the rents from arbitrage between the official and the black market prices. This exploitation created resentment among the peasants, who at this point withheld much of their corn for their own consumption and shifted production to higher-value crops and livestock. Net sales of grain to the urban sector fell to close to 50 percent of the prewar level, creating famine in industrial areas and jeopardizing the whole development effort.

3. *The industrialization debate.* The scissors crisis brought home the difficulty of controlling the rate of industrial growth within the prevailing market framework of the NEP. The party leadership came to recognize that industrialization depended on an adequate and sustained flow of food and material from the rural sector and was a potential hostage to the *kulaks*, more prosperous peasants regarded by the party as a counterrevolutionary threat. The two sides of the debate were defined by the radical left views espoused by Evgenii **Preobrazhensky** and the more moderate agenda of Nikolai **Bukharin**. Preobrazhensky favored unbalanced development and saw a "big push" in heavy industry as necessary to close the gap with the West. Growth would be facilitated by forcing savings in the agrarian sector and transferring it to the

[5]This gap was due to the fact that agricultural output had risen to about 60 percent of its prewar level, while industrial goods output had recovered to only 35 percent.

The Scissors Crisis

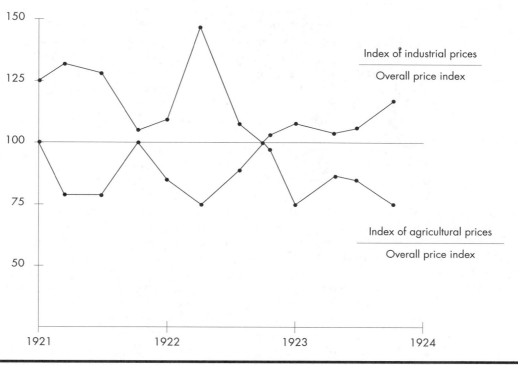

SOURCE: Paul Gregory and Robert Stuart, *Soviet Economic Structure and Performance,* 4th ed. (Reading, MA: Addison-Wesley, 1997), 65.

industrial sector by "nonequivalent exchange," a program incompatible with the market mechanism of the NEP. Bukharin, while recognizing the need for rapid capital accumulation, especially in industry, feared that the divisiveness of discriminating against the agricultural sector would shatter the fragile alliance of peasants and industrial workers (the *smychka*). His predilection was for balanced growth, which would not only avoid discrimination against one sector or another, but also the bottlenecks that rapid expansion of one sector of the economy could produce.

Stalin and the Command Economy

After Lenin's death in 1924, **Stalin** rapidly consolidated power and by 1927 was unopposed. Stalin favored the rapid transformation of the economy by sustained expansion of the heavy industrial sector. Although initially allied with centrists like Bukharin, as soon as he secured his rule, Stalin shifted to Preobrazhensky's more radical position.

His economic strategy embraced two "reforms." One instituted command planning over the entire economy. The first **five-year plan** was formulated in 1928 and from this point forward the state would control the production and movement of all finished and intermediate goods. A debate arose within the leadership as to the degree of attention that any plan should pay to the demands of the general public. Some adopted what was termed the *geneticist* approach and saw the plan as an instrument to rationalize production along lines ultimately dictated by the consumer.[6] Stalin, however, envisaged a more proactive role for the state. Rather than responding to demand, the plan would be a tool for shaping individual tastes and behavior according to goals determined by the political authorities. This *teleological* approach dominated politics and planning throughout the history of the Soviet Union.

The second reform involved agriculture. Rapid industrialization depended on the availability of agricultural surpluses to the industrial sector to provide the raw material of investment, but the prospect of disruption due to movements in agricultural prices, remained real. Consequently Stalin terminated market relations between the industrial and agricultural sectors by collectivizing agriculture, a move designed both to increase the level of central control over the agricultural sector and to eliminate the counterrevolutionary potential of the rich peasants, the *kulaks*. Individual land holdings were confiscated and the peasants forced into communes. Because the Communist Party lacked a rural power base, collectivization was effected by the dispatch of about 25,000 political operatives from the cities to impose it by force. *Kulaks* (and the definition was loose enough to include any peasant who had fallen foul of the political authorities) were dispossessed, but rather than becoming part of the communes, they were internally deported, usually to Siberia, or placed in penal labor camps. The collectivization program was rapidly instituted; in 1928 fewer than 2 percent of Soviet farm households were collectivized, but by 1931 this proportion had risen to 52 percent, and by 1938 it reached 94 percent. Many *kulaks* not just lost their livelihoods but also their lives; precise figures are unavailable, but deaths were certainly in the millions.

The Growth of Planning

Initially planning in the Soviet Union was little more than indicative. Gosplan started issuing **control figures**, which were basically tentative output targets, in 1925, and during successive years these figures assumed a greater importance. In the first five-year plan in 1928, control figures took on a more compulsive character, increasingly supported by detailed production and financial plans (*promfinplans*) at the sectoral level. As the system of materials balance planning, a response to shortages of key materials emerged, work by Russian economists on the precursors of input-output analysis gave Gosplan the technical basis for its work. Material balances for iron and steel were first compiled in 1925; energy products

---

[6] Such planning, generally called "geneticist," was advocated by, among others, N. D. Kondratiev, the founder of business cycle theory.

and building materials soon followed. By 1928 Gosplan was the primary coordinating agency for the whole process, preparing control figures that gave general direction to the economy while controlling a growing list of strategic materials by materials balance planning.

In the 1930s Stalin increased his power over the planning process and extended control into every aspect of the economy. Centralized price determination became an essential part of the overall procedure, and the manipulation of prices became a tool in the achievement of the overall goals. The emphasis was on heavy industrial growth, the First Plan calling for a 400 percent increase in investment in state industry.

Planning and the War

Despite the alliance of Germany and the Soviet Union, forged in the notorious Hitler-Stalin pact, the Nazis invaded the Soviet Union in 1941, making rapid inroads into the western industrial belt. The war's impact on the Soviet economy was profound and enduring. First, it prompted an extensive relocation of economic activity deep into the country beyond the Urals and into Central Asia. Economist Susan Linz estimated that 6 million persons were relocated along with some 1,500 large enterprises. Although this relocation led to widespread disruption and dislocation of output, much of the core of the Soviet industrial base was salvaged by this remarkable operation. Second, war led to a tightening of the system of planning, and by 1945 materials balance plans were drawn up for some 30,000 commodities.

The Postwar Period and Khrushchev

During the war, the Soviet Union lost between 10 and 15 percent of its population to military action, starvation, or exile to the *gulag*. Thirty percent of the prewar capital stock was destroyed and most of the gains achieved during the industrialization program of the 1930s erased. Despite these heavy losses, postwar recovery was rapid, and by 1950 most indices of production exceeded their 1940 levels, a dramatic effort in difficult circumstances. Agriculture proved the most difficult area, due in part to the low priority assigned to it in the planning process, but also because of the lack of incentives on the collective farms. Lack of attention and investment led to generally depressed conditions throughout the rural sector. Heavy industry, on the other hand, which enjoyed a high priority in the investment allocation process, continued a strong performance, and light industry performed well too, doubling its 1940 output by 1950. Consistent with Stalinist orthodoxy, total capital investment grew at a double-digit rate throughout the 1950s. Stalin's last major initiative before his death was institution of the so-called transformation of nature, which called for massive projects of irrigation and engineering.

Stalin died in 1953 and, after a couple of years of joint rule, the party leadership was assumed by Nikita Khrushchev, who attempted fundamental change in economic and political life in the following ways:

1. Making the leadership aware of dissent, denouncing in 1955 Stalin's cult of personality, and drawing attention to Stalinist abuse of human rights.

2. Regionalizing the planning system, reversing the centralization that made the Moscow ministries not only centers of power but also sources of bureaucratic delay, and putting more authority into the hands of **regional economic councils** (*sovnarkhozy*).

3. Opening a debate on the management of the economic system. The most publicized reform proposals were those of Evsei Liberman, whose central idea was to replace physical targets for managers with an incentive system incorporating bonuses based on the enterprise's rate of profit. The central planning authority itself would have continued largely unchanged except that greater flexibility would be given to enterprises in the hopes of economizing on material. Though these proposals received front page treatment in *Pravda,* their importance, both in theoretical terms and in practical significance, may have been overstated.

4. Making a concerted effort to reform the agricultural sector. One aspect was the conversion of depressed and stagnant collective farms (**kolkhozy**), nominally operated by the peasants, to state farms (**sovkhozy**), which functioned like other enterprises, employing a workforce paid by weekly wages plus bonuses rather than a share of the profit. He also put more investment into agriculture, increased inputs of fertilizers, and raised the prices received by the collective farms as an incentive to increase output.

As Table 16.1 indicates, though the planners managed to achieve targets in basic industries (steel, electricity, coal), sophisticated manufacturing (motor vehicles and machine tools) and especially agriculture were serious problems. The inability of the Soviet Union to feed itself began to show during this time, and in the Seventh Plan, Khrushchev's ambitious plans for agriculture were underfulfilled by 32 percent, and meat output was 37 percent off target.

Table 16.2 shows some relevant growth rates. Growth of gross national product (GNP) and agricultural output accelerated during the Fifth Plan (1955–1960), but progress was not sustained. The service sector expanded quite rapidly, but the falling rate of industrial growth mirrored slippage in the growth of investment.

Brezhnev and the "Period of Stagnation"

Much of the communist leadership found Khrushchev's policies too liberal, and in 1964 he was ousted by other members of the Central Committee, power passing to the more conservative Leonid Brezhnev. Nevertheless, at the start of Brezhnev's regime parts of the reform initiated under Khrushchev continued and even yielded results. In 1965 Alexei Kosygin, the chief economic official, announced reforms to the system of targets given to enterprises by which managers were no longer to be held to physical targets established by the planners but were to be free to focus on maximizing what was called "realized output" (in western terms, the equivalent of the value of sales). Management was allowed to retain a large slice of the difference between the value of sales and the cost of materials (profit) to use to provide material incentives for themselves and their workers.

Greater freedom of initiative produced promising results, increased productivity in many enterprises, and sharply rising profits, but unfortunately the very success of

■ TABLE 16.1

Percentage Achievement of Plan in the Soviet Union

	Plan V 1951–1955	Plan VI 1956–1960	Plan VII 1959–1965
National income	107	97	97
Investment	103	101	106
Private consumption	104	95	98
Industrial production	109	99	102
Agricultural production	n.a.	89	68
Steel	91	96	103
Coal	105	86	95
Oil	101	110	104
Electricity	104	91	99
Gas	94	118	86
Machine tools	66	78	95
Motor vehicles	99	80	80
Textiles	94	88	91
Meat	70	67	63
Milk	83	74	71

SOURCE: Vera Lutz, *Central Planning for the Market Economy: An Analysis of the French Theory and Experience* (Harlow, England: Longmans, Green and Co., 1969).

■ TABLE 16.2

Aggregate Economic Performance, 1951–1970: Annual Percentage Change

	Plan V 1951–1955	Plan VI 1955–1960	Plan VII 1961–1965	Plan VIII 1966–1970
GNP	5.4	5.9	5.0	5.2
Industry	10.2	8.3	6.6	6.3
Agriculture	3.5	4.2	2.8	3.5
Services	1.9	3.5	4.4	4.2
Consumption	4.9	5.7	3.7	5.3
Investment	12.4	10.5	7.6	6

SOURCE: Gregory and Stuart, *Russian and Soviet Economic Performance and Structure* (Reading, MA: Addison-Wesley, 1997), pp. 128–130.

the measures alarmed the leadership. By allowing a substantial part of the profit to accrue to the enterprises and to workers in the form of bonuses, reform led to increased disparity in interenterprise wage differentials, a potentially disruptive development. Moreover, rising labor productivity would be followed by reductions in employment at the firm level and might lead to widespread unemployment. These fears led the leadership to be more tentative about reform, and the size of incentive funds and bonuses was limited. Although the initial intent of reformhad been to reduce the scope of planning and give initiative to managers, the tide soon ran in the opposite direction. Despite reformist rhetoric, the bureaucracy expanded and its powers strengthened. Khrushchev's reforms to devolve power to regional councils were reversed, and the Moscow ministries assumed the management of the enterprise on a union-wide scale. Despite a clear reluctance to enact serious reform, every year of the 1970s saw some new strategy to alter the performance of the system, always amounting to nothing. The fundamental problem lay in the structure of incentives embodied in the system of central planning, and remained unaddressed.

Hesitancy over reform led to the lackluster economic performance shown in Table 16.3. The growth rate of GNP, already down from more than 5 percent annually in the Khrushchev years, fell from 3.7 percent to 2.3 percent by the first half of the 1980s. During the 1970s the true state of the Soviet economy was disguised by the dramatic rise of oil prices, which benefited the Soviet Union as the world's largest energy producer, financing the import of needed technology and capital equipment, as well as consumption goods as basic as grain. However, bountiful energy and the failure of the Soviet price system to value it appropriately made Soviet industry wasteful in its use and ultimately uncompetitive in global terms. Labor productivity, which might have risen, had the proposed reforms in incentives been instigated, remained low. After the collapse of the Soviet Union, studies estimated that output per labor hour in the 1980s was only about 25 percent of the average in Western Europe, although Soviet planners were convinced that they were experiencing labor shortage and guest workers were brought in from North Korea and Vietnam.

Although the poor performance of the economy clearly indicated serious structural problems, the planners initially remained optimistic that growth could be maintained and even accelerated. Table 16.4 offers a comparison of the planned targets and the actual outcomes for the four five-year plans between 1965 and 1985. As the planners reluctantly factored in the underperformance of the early plans and lowered their sights, plan fulfillment slipped further. Agricultural performance was especially dismal and, compounded by severe shortcomings in distribution, led to serious food

■ TABLE 16.3

	Aggregate Economic Performance, 1971–1987: Annual Percentage Change			
	1971–1975	1976–1980	1981–1983	1984–1987
GNP	3.7	2.7	2.3	1.6
Industry	5.9	3.4	1.5	2.1
Agriculture	22.3	0.3	4.2	0.8
Services	3.4	2.8	2.1	—
Consumption	3.6	2.6	1.7	2.4
Investment	5.4	4.3	4.2	3

SOURCE: Gregory and Stuart, *Russian and Soviet Economic Performance and Structure* (Reading, MA: Addison-Wesley, 1997), p. 133.

shortages in many areas. Famine was avoided only by substantial grain imports from the United States and Canada, financed by energy exports. Considering that Russia led the world in grain exports in 1913, 50 years of socialism had yielded poor results.

Gorbachev

After Leonid Brezhnev died in 1982, he was briefly succeeded by two long-serving senior members of the party. However, neither Yuri Andropov nor Constantine Chernenko had either enough time in office or the resolve to take on the entrenched system of the Soviet privileged elite (*nomenklatura*) or to articulate a cohesive reform package. Andropov, a former head of the KGB, was convinced that the failures of the Soviet system were attributable to a lack of order and discipline. During his 16-month reign (from November 1982 to February 1984), he initiated campaigns against absenteeism, corruption, and excessive alcohol consumption, all with little effect. He also attempted to correct the deficiency of the Soviet quality control and product improvement by allowing enterprises to apply for price increases of up to 30 percent for "product improvement." Chernenko, an aging *apparatchik*, led the Soviet Union for only 13 months (February 1984 to March 1985) and followed the cautious Andropov line of exhorting greater efficiency and attempting to fine-tune the system of managerial incentives. By March of 1985 both men were dead and power was assumed by the relatively young and active Mikhail S. Gorbachev, an Andropov protégé.

Gorbachev, aware of the shortcomings of the Soviet economy, was resolved to change its direction. He will always be remembered for his introduction of twin reform tracks: *glasnost*, usually translated as openness and signifying democratization and the tolerance of dissent, and *perestroika*, or restructuring in the economic sphere. Although at the time Gorbachev's reforms were thought far-reaching,

---

■ TABLE 16.4

Plan Fulfillment: Planned versus Actual Growth

	Average Annual Growth			
	1966–1970	1971–1975	1976–1980	1981–1985
GNP				
Plan	6.5–7	5.8	5	4
Actual	*5*	*3.1*	*2.2*	*1.8*
Industry				
Plan	8.2	8	6.5	4.9
Actual	*6.3*	*5.4*	*2.6*	*1.8*
Agriculture				
Plan	5.5	3.7	5	5
Actual	*3.7*	*20.6*	*0.8*	*2.1*

SOURCE: Gregory and Stuart, *Russian and Soviet Economic Performance and Structure* (Reading, MA: Addison-Wesley, 1997), p. 135.

in reality they were timid, faltering, and based on inaccurate premises. Despite being highly critical of the reform efforts of the Brezhnev era (which he dismissed as an attempt "to improve things without changing anything"), his own reforms were similarly tentative, believing that substantial economic gains, in terms of increased output and efficiency, could be grasped by relatively modest changes in the economic system.

Gorbachev was, until his downfall, a member of the Communist Party. He sought reform of the system of central planning, selectively using prices and market incentives to iron out "bottlenecks," rather than trying to overthrow it. He was especially sanguine about the potential of imported technology to raise productivity and restore competitiveness. Although his program has been compared to the NEP of the 1920s, it was really the intellectual child of the piecemeal Kosygin reforms of the 1960s. His first steps moved to cut the power of the economic bureaucracy and give enterprise managers freedom and incentive to pursue their own initiatives; this shift resulted in the demolition of the old command system of allocating resources, but it did not allow enough freedom to permit a genuine market system to replace it, leading to a dislocation of the economy and a sharp fall in output, which made subsequent progress toward reform more difficult.

The Law on Enterprise Reform A second-phase of reform was ushered in 1987 with the **law on state enterprises**, which tried to put firms on a corporatized and accountable basis. The key concepts were **self-management** and **self-finance**. Under self-management, workers would take a more active role in the direction of the enterprise and would play a role in the selection of management. Under self-finance, capital was no longer allocated by the planners at subsidized interest rates, but rather each firm would finance investment either from retained profits or credit from banks by loans with "hard" interest payments. Investment funds from the government were to be used only for infrastructural improvements or the start up of new business sectors.

Gorbachev was also bent on the reform of the inflexible system of wage payments, which allowed little variation for worker productivity and therefore tended to reward indolence as much as effort. The reforms gave enterprises control over a **wages fund**, enabling them to reduce their workforces (though to avoid unemployment this could only be by attrition) and to use any money saved to increase the wages of remaining workers in line with productivity growth. By 1990, 75 percent of all industrial personnel were working under these new wage arrangements.

Although Gorbachev's reform plan had many commendable aspects, it was a gradualist agenda that attempted to increase enterprise freedom within the planned system of output quotas. This tinkering short of radical reform produced dislocation. Even though conditions improved for some, the Gorbachev era saw the start of a 10-year contraction of Soviet industrial output. Although modest growth in output was achieved during 1986–1988, in 1989 and 1990 the economy entered a phase of sharp contraction that continued until 1997. Even more dispiriting, despite the enterprise reforms, both labor and capital productivity fell throughout the period. During 1989 and 1990, the economic crisis became more intense. Acute shortages of basic consumer goods contributed to growing popular discontent with the reform effort.

Foreign Trade Reform Under central planning, foreign trade, as well as the domestic resource allocation, was controlled by planners. Within the area known in the West as the Soviet bloc, the procedures for international trade were broadly similar to those that governed the planning of domestic production. Trade within the bloc was conducted under the auspices of the **Council on Mutual Economic Assistance (CMEA)** (often referred to as COMECON, an acronym for Communist Common Market). Trade planning was made on the basis of physical units and prices were adjusted so that trade flows were roughly equalized in currency terms. No member of the CMEA therefore experienced a balance of payments problem because prices were soft and manipulated to equilibrate payments. Just as in domestic planning, the idea of economies of scale was important in structuring COMECON trade. Each nation within the CMEA was required to specialize in the production of certain goods, and the other members were expected to import all of their needs from them. Because trade was planned, comparative advantage, the basic underlying principle assumed to govern the direction and volume of trade between market economies, played a negligible role. Because the Soviet Union was rich in natural resources, especially energy, and the satellites were not, it supplied them with primary commodities at prices highly subsidized in terms of world levels and received manufactured goods in return. As world energy prices shot up during the 1970s, the prices charged within the CMEA system of trade adjusted only a little, and the terms of trade shifted sharply in favor of the satellite nations.

Trade outside the CMEA bloc was based on different principles, though they were no more rational in terms of basic economics. Decisions were made at the central level about the amount of foreign exchange required, generally a function of the amount of imports from the non-CMEA world. Special **foreign trade organizations (FTOs)** would purchase the export goods from Soviet suppliers and sell them at agreed upon, usually world, prices. The existence of FTO insulated domestic producers from world markets. The intercession of the FTO allowed the domestic producers no opportunity to profit from foreign trade, nor were they exposed to the competition in foreign markets.

This highly indirect system contributed to the inability of Soviet bloc enterprises to pursue international competitiveness through innovation and efficiency. Unlike the trading companies of Japan, which sought out foreign markets, educated domestic producers, and facilitated the import of ideas and technology, the FTOs were passive and formed a barrier between Soviet management and the world. Because no individual firm in the Soviet Union could benefit to any great degree from foreign trade, enterprise management held little interest. They conducted no global market research nor did they attempt to conform to international norms and standards.

In January 1987, the FTO monopoly of foreign trade was broken when 20 ministries and 76 large enterprises were allowed to initiate direct trade and to retain a substantial proportion of any hard currency earnings. The scheme was rapidly expanded and by the middle of 1990, more than 14,000 enterprises had the right to trade abroad on their own behalf. This liberalization was well intentioned and should have borne economic fruit, but it led instead to corruption and personal enrichment. Soviet-manufactured goods were of uncertain quality, poor design, and were much less likely to find markets than primary commodities such as petroleum and forest products. These commodities tended to be diverted from their planned use and sold abroad with the receipts frequently accruing to individual accounts offshore. The result was a lack of resources at home and problems in plan fulfillment.

The Failure of Perestroika Gorbachev's *perestroika* program fell between two stools. The reforms were too creeping for a rapid transformation to a market economy based on prices that reflected shortage and opportunity cost. However, they were enough to disrupt and create serious problems for the old system to which they were appended, leading to a collapse of output. More fatally for Gorbachev, they alarmed the old guard of the Communist Party.

The Coup of August 1991 Throughout 1990 and early 1991, the economic and political system of the Soviet Union teetered on the brink of reform. In August 1991, a coup by the old guard of the Communist Party supplanted Gorbachev, but the so-called *putsch* rapidly unraveled largely because it failed to neutralize Boris Yeltsin, the elected (and therefore legitimate) president of the Russian Federation. Yeltsin remained within the "White House," the Russian Parliament building, defying the authority of the Communist Party of the Soviet Union and communicating freely with other leaders, both in the constituent republics of the Soviet Union and the West. The failure of the *putsch* signaled the end of the Soviet Union as the constituent republics refused to recognize the Soviet authority. Within Russia, Yeltsin inherited power.

KEY TERMS AND CONCEPTS

Bolsheviks

Bukharin

commanding heights of
   the economy

control figures

Council on Mutual Economic
   Assistance (CMEA)

economies in transition

five-year plan

foreign trade organizations (FTOs)

glasnost

Gosplan

gulag

kolkhozy

kulaks

law on state enterprises

market Leninism

Menshevik

New Economic Policy (NEP)

nomenklatura

perestroika

Preobrazhensky

promfinplans

regional economic councils

scissors crisis

self-finance

self-management

sovkhozy

Stalin

Stolypin reforms

wages fund

war communism

QUESTIONS FOR DISCUSSION

1. Why did the economic situation of serfs liberated in 1861 lead to the rise of Russia as an agriculture exporter?

2. Why is Lenin's New Economic Policy often referred to as a kind of market socialism?

3. What was the importance of the scissors crisis? Why are the terms of trade between the rural and urban sectors so important in industrialization?

4. How did World War II affect the planning system and structure of the Soviet economy?

5. What was the thrust of Khrushchev's reforms? Were they successful?

6. How did the Soviet Union remain in the arms race and the space race despite faltering technology and slow growth?

7. How was trade conducted under the Soviet system?

8. Why did Gorbachev's policy of *perestroika* fail?

RESOURCES

Books and Articles

Bergson, Abram. *Welfare, Planning and Employment.* Cambridge, MA: MIT Press, 1982.

Carr. E. H. *The Russian Revolution: From Lenin to Stalin.* New York: Free Press, 1979.

Dunmore, Timothy. *The Stalinist Command Economy: The Soviet State Apparatus and Economic Policy, 1945–53.* New York: St. Martin's Press, 1980.

Goldman, Marshall I. *Gorbachev's Challenge: Economic Reform in the Age of High Technology.* New York: W.W. Norton, 1987.

Goldman, Marshall I. *U.S.S.R. in Crisis: The Failure of an Economic System.* New York: W.W. Norton, 1983.

Gregory, Paul R. *Before Command: An Economic History of Russia from Emancipation to the First Five-Year Plan.* Princeton, NJ: Princeton University Press, 1994.

Gregory, Paul R., and Robert C. Stuart. *Russian and Soviet Economic Performance and Structure (Addison-Wesley Series in Economics).* Reading, MA: Addison-Wesley, 1997.

Guroff, Gregory, and Fred Castensen (eds.). *Entrepreneurship in Imperial Russia and the Soviet Union.* Princeton, NJ: Princeton University Press, 1983.

Hewett, Ed A. *Reforming the Soviet Economy: Equality versus Efficiency.* Washington, DC: Brookings Institution, 1990.

Hewett, Ed A., and Victor H. Winston (eds.). *Milestones in Glasnost and Perestroyka: The Economy.* Washington, DC: Brookings Institution, 1991.

Hochschild, Adam. *The Unquiet Ghost: Russians Remember Stalin.* New York: Penguin, 1995.

International Monetary Fund. *A Study of the Soviet Economy.* Washington, DC: International Monetary Fund, 1991.

Jones, Anthony, and William Moskoff (eds.). *Perestroika and the Economy: New Thinking in Soviet Economics.* Armonk, NY: M.E. Sharpe, 1989.

Lavigne, Marie. *Financing the Transition: The Shatalin Plan and the Soviet Economy.* New York: Institute for East-West Security Studies, 1990.

Nove, Alec. *The Soviet Economy, an Introduction,* 2d ed. New York: Praeger, 1968.

Remnick, David. *Lenin's Tomb: The Last Days of the Soviet Empire.* New York: Random House, 1993.

Stuart, Robert C. (ed.). *The Soviet Rural Economy.* Totowa, NJ: Rowman and Allanheld, 1984.

Ulam, Adam Bruno. *The Bolsheviks: The Intellectual and Political History of the Triumph of Communism in Russia.* Cambridge, MA: Harvard University Press, 1998.

17

THE OPERATION OF THE SOVIET PLANNED ECONOMY

THE INSTITUTIONS OF THE SOVIET STATE

Because the economic and political systems of the Soviet Union were so closely interwoven, understanding the operation of the economy and the planning system requires some knowledge of the institutional makeup of the Soviet state.

The Communist Party of the Soviet Union

The dominant force in Soviet society was the Communist Party of the Soviet Union (CPSU). All important strategic decisions relevant to the operation of the economy were ultimately made by the party. The most powerful figure in the country was therefore the general secretary of the Communist Party, the post occupied by Stalin, Khrushchev, Brezhnev, and Gorbachev. The general secretary of the CPSU was *ex officio* leader of the **politburo**, the governing body of the party, whose other members represented the major regional party organizations, the officials responsible for foreign affairs, the organs of state security, and the major ministries. Although to the outside world the Soviet Union seemed to be a single-person dictatorship, in reality, at least for most of the post-Stalin period, a great deal of power resided with the other members of the politburo. They held the power to remove the general secretary from that post when his policy preferences deviated from those of the party, which happened in the case of Khrushchev.

The Legislature

Viewed through Western eyes, the legislature of the Soviet Union seemed weak. It was composed of two chambers: the Supreme Soviet and the Praesidium. The 370 members of the Supreme Soviet were nominally elected by popular vote, but in effect were appointed by the party, which retained tight control over the slate of candidates. The Supreme Soviet met twice a year, when its members, who served part-time and had other jobs, would assemble in Moscow essentially to rubber-stamp the legislative changes and the appointment of officials determined by the party bureaucracy. The Praesidium, which might be regarded as the upper house, was more compact and enjoyed more responsibility. Its members were mainly government officials, and it met twice monthly under the leadership of a chairman, who performed the function of head of state.

The Judiciary

The judicial branch in the Soviet state was even weaker than the legislature. It had little independence from the political process, a fact reflected by Nikita Khrushchev's now infamous remark "who is the Boss, us or the Law: we are the masters over the Law, not the Law over us."[1] This observation was true at two levels. In most developed market economies, particularly in the United States, a constitution, guarded by an independent judiciary, exercises ultimate authority over the political system and constrains the type of laws that the legislature might pass. This system of checks and balances was absent in the Soviet Union. Although a written constitution existed in the Soviet Union (in fact, it closely resembled that of the United States), in effect it was inoperative, because no independent judiciary enforced it. Moreover, the structure of power led to capricious and politically determined implementation of whatever laws were on the books. Thus the Soviet Union was characterized by what John Litwack has called an absence of **legality**, in which "*Legality* is associated with *rule by law* as opposed to the discretion of leaders."[2]

This absence of legality was especially important in economic matters, as Litwack points out:

> Recent research in economic history has emphasized the importance of the replacement of legal for discretionary rule in explaining the rapid economic development of the western world, as well as the disparities in wealth between the advanced capitalist and underdeveloped countries. . . . [The Soviet system] contains particular mechanisms of coordination, incentives, and distribution that function in the virtual absence of economic legality. The fundamental features that explain how the system actually works are the discretionary power of bureaucrats over subordinates, enforced by the political dictatorship of the Communist Party, and the reputation effects from personal, often informal, long-run ties.

THE MECHANISM OF PLANNING

The politburo and the party determined the basic direction in which the economy was to move and the policies to be followed. Thus the fundamental economic questions of what, how, and for whom were all answered by the political leadership. The broad directives of the party were embodied in the plan by the bureaucrats of the State Planning Commission, **Gosplan**, which although only one of more than 20 state committees, had the preeminent role in economic planning. Other committees with an economic function were **Gosbank** (the state bank), Gosstroi (the state committee for construction), Gosten (the state committee on prices), Gossnab (the state committee for material and technical supply), Goskomstat (the statistical service), and MinFin (the Ministry of Finance).

---

[1] Quoted in K. Simis, *The USSR: The Corrupt Society* (New York: Simon and Schuster, 1982).
[2] J. Litwack, "Legality and Market Reform in Soviet Type Economies," *Journal of Economic Perspectives* 5, no. 4 (Fall 1991).

The Time Frame of the Planning Process

Early in the planning year, Gosplan collected information on the performance in the previous year from the various actors in the economic system, with most information coming from the production side of the economy because Soviet planners gave little weight to the opinions of consumers.[3] Even if any desire to cater to consumers' demands to a greater degree were present, little could be done about quantifying consumers' concerns. In a supply-deficit economy with fixed prices such as in the Soviet Union, most goods found some buyer, even if it was an unhappy one. Goods in high demand were actively sought through bribery or queuing, symptoms that could not be expressed quantitatively to Gosplan. Thus at best any estimation of demand from consumers was likely to be highly anecdotal.

After analyzing this information, Gosplan reported to its political masters in the Praesidium of the party's central committee, which studied both the achievements and the problems experienced in the previous year and then set down broad directives for the following year. These directives included general statements such as "raise housing construction" or "increase the quantity of clothing available." For example, in April 1985 the plenary meeting of the CPSU central committee determined that

> It is planned to increase the national income used for consumption and accumulation by 19–22 percent. Ensure that the entire increase in the national income is reached by enhancing social labor productivity. Reduce its inputs of materials by 4–5 percent, power by 7–9 percent and metals by 13–15 percent.[4]

Gosplan took note of such party directives and during the summer drafted a preliminary planning balance for the economy, a first attempt at accounting for all sources and uses of the principal products produced or required in the economy. At the height of central planning this exhaustive and time-consuming operation covered some 30,000 different commodities; for each one, production sources and users were identified and quantified. This tabulation constituted the material balances for the economy. As an illustrative tool, Table 17.1 shows this kind of initial tabulation giving a hypothetical listing of the sources and uses of steel. It is highly simplified; in reality many different types of steel (construction, sheet, pipe, etc.) had to be planned for. Such a table had to be prepared for each major commodity, and it was vital that the supply and use totals balanced. The need of all the other industrial sectors for any commodity had to match its production, net import, and inventory change.

Demands and uses of commodities are interdependent, and the next task for the planners was reconciliation of the tables. If it was found that the projected needs for steel were greater than planned supply, the output of the steel had to be raised accordingly. This projection required the increased use of other inputs—steel itself,

---

[3]This policy goes back to the triumph of the "teleologists" over the "geneticists" in the late 1920s, which was discussed in Chapter 16.

[4]*Guidelines for the Economic and Social Development of the USSR for the period 1986–1990, and for the Period Ending in 2000* (Moscow: Novosti Press, 1985), pp. 21–22.

Schematic Representation of Materials Balance for Steel (millions of metric tons)

Sources		Uses		
Production	150	Industry		165
Imports	20	(a) Mining	20	
Starting inventory	20	(b) Machinery	80	
		(c) Railways	10	
		(d) Steel	10	
		(e) Agriculture	5	
		(f) Construction	20	
		(g) Shipbuilding	20	
		Households		0
		Government		5
		Export		10
		Year-end inventory		10
Total Sources	190	Total Uses		190

iron ore, coal, limestone, and so forth—so the output in all these other industries had to be raised, requiring yet a further adjustment in steel output.

Soviet planners were helped in this iterative reconciliation by input/output tables, prepared in matrix format as illustrated by Table 17.2. Resolving this system requires the solution of a system of simultaneous equations. Each product group is represented by a row, with the possible sources represented on the left-hand side and the uses on the right. The right-hand side can be separated into intermediate uses (where the product is an input for the production of some other good) and final uses (where it is destined for consumption, use in investment, or for export). The columns represent the demands for intermediate goods that must be supplied by other industries to achieve the indicated level of production, according to the norms of the planners. For example, if product 1 is steel and products 2 and 3 are coal and electricity, then the attainment of an output level of X_1 of steel requires $a_{11}X_1$ of steel, $a_{21}X_2$ of coal, $a_{31}X_3$ of electricity, and so forth.

Where X_i is the output of the ith industry, a_{ij} is the requirement for input X_i per unit of output in the jth industry, S is the change in the stocks, M represents planned imports, C is consumer use, I is investment use, and Ex is planned exports.

The coefficients used to estimate the amount of input required are calculated by the planners using fixed-proportion production functions, based on the average "good practice" needs of industry. A matrix of this kind was maintained by the Soviet planners for about 250 of the most important product groups, which potentially required establishing 6,250 coefficients. In actuality, a substantial proportion of the coefficients would be zero, because many goods are not demanded as inputs by other industries. For example, fertilizers are not directly required by the mining industry or cereals by aluminum smelters. Thus the matrices can be solved in many

■ **TABLE 17.2**

Representation of Input-Output Analysis

Sources	Intermediate Uses	Final Uses
1. $X_1 - S_1 + M_1$	$= a_{11}X_1 + a_{21}X_2 + a_{31}X_3 + a_{41}X_4 + \ldots a_{1n}X_n$	$+ C_1 + I_1 + Ex_1$
2. $X_2 - S_2 + M_2$	$= a_{21}X_1 + a_{22}X_2 + a_{32}X_3 + a_{42}X_4 + \ldots a_{2n}X_n$	$+ C_2 + I_2 + Ex_2$
3. $X_3 - S_3 + M_3$	$= a_{31}X_1 + a_{23}X_2 + a_{33}X_3 + a_{43}X_4 + \ldots a_{3n}X_n$	$+ C_3 + I_3 + Ex_3$
4. $X_4 - S_4 + M_4$	$= a_{34}X_1 + a_{24}X_2 + a_{34}X_3 + a_{44}X_4 + \ldots a_{4n}X_n$	$+ C_4 + I_4 + Ex_4$
n. $X_n - S_n + M_n$	$= a_{n1}X_1 + a_{2n}X_2 + a_{3n}X_3 + a_{4n}X_4 + \ldots a_{nn}X_n$	$+ C_n + I_n + Ex_n$

cases by separating them into subsystems. Nevertheless, the task of compilation was huge, and many of the problems of the planners were technical. Data management and computer systems in the Soviet Union during this period were not highly advanced, which handicapped the operation of the planning system. However, the bigger problem was getting reliable information to the center, a topic to which we will return.

At the height of its coverage and complexity, Soviet planning embraced some 30,000 commodities and thus a complete **input-output matrix** would have some 900 *million* cells, clearly an impossible task. Industrial groups were planned using the materials balance sheets like that in Table 17.1. These balance sheets could be more aggregated than the I-O matrices and did not have to rely on assumptions of fixed input proportions and the absence of economies of scale.

The Draft Plan

These preliminary estimates of both target outputs and planned inputs were called **control figures**. In the next step Gosplan disseminated them to the lower levels of the planning bureaucracies: the ministries and the regional planning centers. From there they were further disaggregated, and passed down to the enterprise level— the units actually responsible for the work—in the form of a **draft plan**. The breakdown among enterprises was, by and large, based on past performance, the **level previously achieved**.

The idea of basing targets on previous achievements is an important feature of central planning. Senior enterprise management in the Soviet system received a large part of their total remuneration in the form of bonuses paid to reward the realization of plan targets. Senior management could receive bonuses of as much as 50 percent of their basic salary for meeting their target and up to 4 percent more for each percentage point by which the plan was overachieved. Thus any effort expended by managers in lobbying the planners to hold the output targets low, while receiving a high allocation of inputs, was probably well spent in terms of the likely outcome on managerial salaries. However, although the bonuses paid for overfulfillment of plan targets were substantial, management in many cases chose to be cautious in determining by just how much to exceed their targets. If output is exceeded by a large margin in the current year, planners would likely raise output targets for successive years, because they based targets "from the level previously achieved." Overperformance with respect to one year's target might be praised at the time, and might lead to a big bonus in that year, but it is likely to lead to problems for the enterprise managers in the succeeding year because the output target will be ratcheted up. Thus the incentive to overachieve was limited. David Dyker, an authority on Soviet planning, called it the Micawber principle, after the Dickens character whose maxim was "Income one pound, expenses nineteen shillings and sixpence, result happiness. Income one pound, expenditure twenty shillings and sixpence, result misery." Considerable evidence confirms that a wise manager tried to meet the target and overachieve a little, but did not exert himself to achieve dramatic growth because of the consequences of having to achieve an elevated target the year after.

After the enterprises received their targets for the following year and their allotment of inputs, the direction of planning reversed. Enterprises turned to their immediate bureaucratic superiors and disputed their ability to meet the targets with the inputs allotted, arguing with all of the influence at their disposal for lower output targets and greater inputs. It is important to recognize that this part of the planning exercise was personal and involved an intense bargaining exercise. One way of describing this process is as "struggle," but it was generally a polite affair in which the participants sought to capitalize on their contacts, influence, and reserve of favors.

When some form of resolution was reached, the *draft plan* was then passed back up the hierarchy and was appropriately modified until it arrived at Gosplan again. At every point, the planners attempted to establish a reconciliation, or compromise, between the higher authorities (who tried to preserve compliance to the original draft plan, which represented conformity with Gosplan's control figures) and the lower authorities, who had the responsibility for meeting the targets. This process of reconciliation coincided with the "tightening" of the plan as production responsibilities became more and more precisely defined. On occasion, of course, all the loose ends could not be tied up and Gosplan adjusted the basic structure of the plan in order to take account of the problems.

Making the Plan into Law

Those at the lower levels of the planning process knew that during this period they had to make their own production targets as realistic (in fact, as minimal) as possible. Once the final balance was struck, the politburo approved the plan and the **Praesidium** turned it into law. It was a punishable offense to fail to meet the plan target, while substantial bonuses were paid to enterprise management for plan achievement and overachievement. After enactment into law, the plan was then passed down the hierarchy of ministries and regional councils with the degree of detail being increased at each level. Ultimately each enterprise entered into contractual arrangements with suppliers and major customers.

THE DETERMINATION OF PRICES

Up to this point the planning process focused exclusively on physical units of commodities, whether outputs or inputs. Prices were determined quite separately and fulfilled a different function from that in a market economy. They were set primarily by the bureaucracy, were altered as infrequently as possible, and did not aspire to reflect either resource cost or demand. Price changes are a nuisance, incur "menu costs," and have little point if the base levels do not reflect scarcity to begin with. Moreover, it was a point of ideological pride that socialism was immune from capitalism's worst diseases, inflation and unemployment. Soviet central planning used three main types of prices for goods: wholesale industrial prices, agricultural prices, and retail prices.[5]

Wholesale Industrial Prices

Wholesale industrial prices were the prices at which firms sold goods to each other. They were determined by a combination of pragmatism, opportunism, and ideology. The underlying principle was that prices should represent the average cost of production of a good across all the enterprises in the relevant industry group. Recall from Chapter 3 that it is marginal cost, not average cost, that reflects scarcity, and therefore the role that prices played in the efficient rationing of scarce resources within the Soviet system was slight. Moreover, cost to the Soviet planners conformed to a Marxian conception and was defined as consisting of labor costs, raw material costs, and depreciation, with no allowance made for either the opportunity cost of capital (interest) or land (rent). After arriving at an estimate of average cost for each firm, the planners would exclude obvious outliers in the calculation of the industry average; any enterprises with abnormally high costs were not considered, although they remained in production and therefore required subsidy.

Adjusted average costs of production were then modified to yield the prices for the plan year, a small amount being deducted to reflect lower costs due to technological change or productivity increase, and a small margin added for profit. Prices arrived at in such a way could never, except by the most unlikely coincidence, reflect relative scarcities and were not a crucial factor in determining enterprise behavior. In a market economy, a firm's revenue is determined by the product of volume and sales price, and that represents a **hard-budget constraint** to the firm. In the long run the firm cannot spend more than its revenues. Under centrally planned socialism, if revenue is less than cost, some way would frequently be found to raise revenues through price changes or subsidies or to reduce costs by lowering administered input prices or taxes. These **soft-budget constraints** profoundly affected Soviet performance, an important fact that we will return to later.

---

[5]In addition to goods pricing, we will discuss the price of labor and the functioning of the labor market.

One of the more shocking consequences of this system of administered prices discovered during liberalization in the 1990s was a substantial number of **negative value-added enterprises**—firms for whom the sum of the value of outputs evaluated at world prices were, in fact, less than the value of inputs assessed in the same way. This situation was the result of the subsidies implicit in low input costs (especially those related to energy where Soviet prices and world prices were in stark disagreement) and the low quality of output. In the supply-deficit Soviet economy, this output could generally find a buyer, but not in free world markets. The actual number of true negative value-added enterprises was hard to know, but a larger class of industry operating at a profit under Soviet accounting and would show a loss when rent, capital cost, and concessionary tax policy were accounted for.

Agricultural Prices

In Chapter 16 we discussed the scissors crisis of the early 1920s and the young Bolshevik government's determination to control the terms of trade between the agricultural and industrial sectors. Until the final collapse of the Soviet planned economy, agricultural procurement prices were set to establish the terms of trade for the peasants on the **collective farms** (*kolkhozy*) and thus control their purchasing power over goods from the larger economy. Both the unit costs of the inputs of collective farming and the physical volumes of inputs required under the plan were determined by the planners. The planners also fixed the total cost (and hence the average cost) of the production dictated by the plan. If, as was generally the case in the supply-constrained Soviet economy, consumer goods were in short supply, one way to alleviate the shortage was by cutting the purchasing power of the peasants. The price of farm output could be set at the level that would just cover costs. Then each peasant's share of net farm income would be small, allowing for few purchases of consumer goods. In some cases an even greater squeeze was applied by making farm incomes less than necessary planned expenditures, forcing peasants to draw down "idle" monetary balances accumulated in the farm sector from prior years. The same set of agricultural prices applying to collective farms also applied to the state farms (*sovkhozy*). These socially owned farms were operated in the same fashion as industrial firms, with managers appointed by the state and employing workers for money wages rather than for a share of the surplus. Thus they could operate at a profit or were positioned to receive subsidies.

Retail Prices

A third type of price included the *retail prices* charged in the state owned retail stores and consumer cooperatives (which, like the collective farms, were jointly owned by groups of individuals). These prices were dependent on the industrial wholesale and agricultural procurement prices, but they differed by the imposition of a differentiated turnover tax. This tax served two purposes. One was an attempt to bring supply and demand at the consumer level into line by taxing the goods in short supply at a heavier rate than those that were more plentiful. The tax also provided a substantial part of the state's revenue.

LABOR MARKETS

We already discussed how the Soviet system determined disposable income and purchasing power for agricultural workers on the collective farms. In contrast, the income of industrial and service sector workers (as well as the wages of laborers on state farms) were contractual rather than residual. The labor markets in the Soviet Union were by and large much freer than was the popular conception in the West. Workers were not assigned occupations and workplaces by the state, except in the case of the first job of university graduates. However, locating in Moscow (the perpetually attractive "center") was subject to a residency permit, and a chronic shortage of housing put tight constraints on geographical mobility. The choice of occupation was largely up to the worker, though the educational system was highly manipulated and influential in replicating the skill mix of the population that the planners considered appropriate in the long run. In the short run, wages were set by the state to equilibrate the supply with the demand for labor in each use. A crude form of wage adjustment was used with percentage markups to a basic wage applied for such factors as location (the less attractive the higher the wage), unpleasant working conditions, the degree of physical effort, and so forth. In addition, many enterprises resorted to systems of piecework where workers received most of their income as a function of individual or group output.

MARKET CLEARING

The income received by workers, as well as by farmers, could be freely spent on whatever commodity (though not productive asset) that could be found. These elements of consumer *choice* should not be confused with the consumer *sovereignty* fostered by the operation of the free market. Consumer sovereignty implies that the consumers' demands are impartially met through the market via the incentives that it provides. In the centrally planned system, the politicians and planners are sovereign; the plan determines what kinds and quantities of consumer goods are produced, and each consumer decides which of these products he or she wants. If a surplus or shortage for any good should develop, production is *not* automatically shifted by the action of self-oriented economic agents but is changed only by the will of the political leadership.

The planners determined (1) the volume of production of the various goods, (2) the prices that were charged for them, (3) the money incomes of the workers, and (4) the real income of the collective farmers. It was therefore, in theory, possible that aggregate supply and demand could balance. Although an infinite number of sets of prices might satisfy this aggregate condition, in general the prices failed to equilibrate supply and demand in the markets for individual goods. In a market economy such disequilibria are met first by a change in price and subsequently by a change in quantities, but in the centrally planned system neither response occurred. Output plans were seldom realized, especially for consumer goods, and therefore general shortages, as well as unsatisfied demand for particular products, resulted. Centrally planned economies were often characterized by high levels of household savings, because goods were not available for consumers to purchase. This lack of goods at the end of the Soviet era meant substantial money balances in consumers' bank accounts, known as the **monetary overhang**. It was one engine of inflation in the early months of liberalization. However, for our assessment of the planning system the most important point is that the prices set by planners neither reflected the relative scarcity of goods in the short term nor provided an accurate measure of the resource costs of production.

Private Agriculture

One area of free market activity was provided by granting workers in collective farms, state farms, and other enterprises plots on which to raise their own crops, which could be sold at uncontrolled prices. These plots averaged about two-thirds of an acre and were slightly larger on the collective farms than on the state farms, and, as might be expected, the productivity per acre of these plots was well above that seen on either the state or collective farms themselves. Although private plots represented only 3 percent of total arable area in the Soviet Union, they accounted for about 25 percent of output. For some crops, they were a significant source of supply. In 1984 private plots accounted for 58 percent of potato production; about 30 percent of the production of eggs, meat, vegetables, and milk; and 24 percent of wool production. Private plots fulfilled two important functions: ameliorating otherwise desperate conditions on collective farms and providing an outlet for the reluctant savings of industrial workers. However, the irrationality of the pricing structure in the planned sector and the profit incentives of the small-holder plots did make for some extremely distortionary outcomes. A smallholder from the republic of Georgia, in the Transcaucasus, was able to fly on the highly subsidized state airline, Aeroflot, to Moscow with a couple of suitcases of tomatoes and make enough on the sidewalk market in the capital to pay for his flight, room, and board—not the most efficient way of getting the produce to market!

MONITORING PLAN FULFILLMENT

We now turn to the question of verifying the plan. How did the planners see to it that the various parties conformed to the physical performance specified in the plan? It would be an onerous task to certify at each stage that the planned volume of goods physically passed from one concern to another. In fact, the physical plan was monitored through financial flows that mirrored the movement of goods and commodities as recorded by the monopoly state bank, Gosbank. This process was known as **control by the ruble**.

To illustrate, let us take a simple example of the movement of a commodity from its point of initial production to its final use. A state farm produced cotton, which was sent to a textile factory that processed it into cloth for a clothing factory, which in turn shipped its output to a retail store. When the farm delivered its cotton output to the factory, it would obtain a document, an acceptance, from the textile factory verifying that the latter received its raw cotton. This document was then turned over to Gosbank, which credited the farm's account with the value of the cotton delivered, using the plan's industrial prices, and debited the textile factory's account by the same amount. Similarly, after the finished cloth was produced and shipped to the clothing factory, the textile factory obtained a document verifying its delivery of cloth. Again, the document was turned over to Gosbank, which this time credited the textile factory's account and debited the clothing factory's account. Likewise, the clothing factory made the garments and shipped them to the store, again receiving an acceptance. Gosbank credited its account and debited that of the store. Finally, when households purchased the clothing with cash, the state store deposited its cash receipts with Gosbank and was given a credit of equal value.

With this simple example, we can see how every transfer of *physical* output from one location to another, and every bit of value added in production, was mirrored by an associated *financial* transfer through Gosbank. Gosbank's monitoring of these financial transfers would, in theory at least, show the physical movements of goods. If less than the planned amount was delivered in any specified time period, Gosbank would be alerted. If inputs or outputs were stolen and diverted to the black market, Gosbank would know, and the failure to perform could be investigated and rectified. To discipline the system, the state bank had at its disposal a range of sanctions, from the expropriation of a firm's deposits to a full-scale party investigation into enterprise affairs. However, the information needs of full oversight were enormous, and often the system would be perfunctory rather than exhaustive. Sanctions were used sparingly and oversight was ineffective. As a result, failure to perform was frequent and unpunished, and corruption was extensive.[6]

Control by the ruble required restrictions on the use of money and credit, which lowered the degree of initiative that managers could show. Enterprise accounts with Gosbank could only be used to pay for the type and quantities of inputs that were specified in the plan. No enterprise could grant credit to another enterprise.[7] Enterprises were virtually forbidden to hold cash for any purpose other than payment of wages. Even the cash receipts of state stores had to be first deposited with Gosbank and subsequently withdrawn to meet the payroll.

Planning was performed in terms of physical units, but the financial sector of the centrally planned economy allowed the state bank to monitor the execution of the plan.

---

[6]One of the most famous abuses came to light in the late 1970s in the cotton industry. Large quantities of fictitious cotton were shipped from state farms in Central Asia. The appropriate acceptances were issued but concealed by a web of corruption that extended up to and included Yurii Churbanov, Brezhnev's son-in-law. It took years for the scheme to be uncovered, and billions of rubles were diverted. Ultimately several people were put to death for "economic crimes."

[7]This prohibition is in sharp distinction with the post-liberalization system in Russia and other newly independent states in which an extensive net of interenterprise credit has grown up with the tacit support of the government. Many suppliers of raw materials, especially in the energy sector, are owed huge sums of money by their customers, who cannot pay often because they are owed by customers further down the production chain.

INCENTIVES IN SOVIET-TYPE SYSTEMS

In Chapter 1 we discussed in general terms the issues of incentives in economic systems, and the unraveling of the centrally planned economies is a case study in their importance. The successes and failures of Soviet planning can be largely attributed to the set of incentives provided, and it is worthwhile discussing these incentives as they fell on each group.

Collective Farms

Agriculture is generally regarded as one of the greatest failures of Soviet economics, and the dismal performance of collective agriculture must shoulder a great deal of the blame for the ultimate demise of the system. We saw that income on collective farms was the residual between the revenue received by the farms and their expenses on material factors of production. Revenue itself was a function of the volume of output and the prices determined by the planners, whose objective was frequently to limit the real income, and therefore the demand for consumers' goods by the peasants on the farms. Expenditure on material inputs was also determined in Moscow. Thus the incentive to raise output on the farms was dulled by the knowledge that prices could be reduced as a response.

Moreover, individual peasants on the farms saw little incentive to raise their effort and diligence. The income of the farm was divided among the workers on the basis of work points. In theory it might mean that harder work was rewarded with higher income, but in reality work points did little to reflect effort. A serious free rider problem resulted, because aggregate output of the farm changed little on the basis of one person's contribution as any gain in output was spread among the members of the collective or work brigade. To counter this problem, the authorities attempted to reduce the size of the work teams from their original conception of 100 plus down to much smaller groups, in some cases as small as the family. However, in terms of living standards it was better to spend time on one's own personal plot than to work hard for the collective enterprise; it is not surprising that productivity remained low and output stagnated for long periods of time. At the end of the Soviet period, contract systems began to be favored; a group, or family, agreed to supply part of the collective farm's target at fixed prices with the knowledge that any excess could be sold to the farm at "market" prices or sold directly on the farmers' markets.[8]

Workers

Workers, whether on state farms or within manufacturing or extractive industry, had much the same set of incentives as workers in the capitalist West. Pay was largely by the hour and the incentives for high performance were in part coercive,

---

[8]Such "household responsibility systems" were successful in China because they provided a much higher degree of incentive than do collective farms.

enforced by management supervision, and part pecuniary, in that good job performance might lead to promotion and betterment. Alienation, which Marx identified as one of the key weaknesses of capitalism, was as prevalent as in the industrialized West.[9] Despite the urging of the state and management, working for the glory of the country became a less significant motivating factor, while advancement into the higher echelons of management had as much to do with political connection as with job performance. To link job performance more closely with pay, much of the socialist world turned to "piece working," where workers are paid as far as possible in proportion to individual output. The irony here is that this practice is traditionally regarded by the left as being the most exploitative labor management practice and also one that stifles both individual initiative and group cooperation. In advanced capitalist systems it remains only in "sweat shop" situations.

Ultimately a worker toils for goods rather than for money. Because centrally planned economies were chronically inept in providing consumer goods, the incentive to work hard was correspondingly reduced. Goals that prove to be powerful motivators to workers in capitalist countries—such as buying a house, acquiring financial assets, or traveling abroad—were simply not options. A select group of workers were chosen to travel to vacation spots within the socialist world, but again this reward was largely the result of political connections rather than work performance. The high rate of forced household savings and the monetary overhang were testaments to the failure of monetary incentives in a demand surplus economy.

Managers

Enterprise managers in the Soviet system operated under a strong material incentive system with a substantial portion of income dependent on meeting the plan targets, which could be further increased by overfulfillment. This motivator was reinforced by coercive negative incentives; failure to meet targets might lead to loss of job, disciplinary action, or, in the rare limit, prosecution and incarceration. The combination of incentives proved less than optimal in a variety of ways. First, the incentives did little to increase the efficiency of industry in terms of the optimal use of factors of production. Second, the system did little to encourage either product or process innovation. Third, quality control was a serious problem, exacerbated by little motivation to produce consumer goods whose design and quality might be most appreciated by the ultimate user. Finally, and perhaps most crucially, the incentives encouraged the relaying of misleading data from the enterprise units to the center.

Efficiency The system of incentives did little to encourage optimum use of factors of production. Capital was largely allocated by the planners and generally came without cost, or with a high subsidy, to the enterprise. When capital charges were

---

[9]In fact, the stock remark about Soviet work was that "We pretend to work, and they pretend to pay us," or sometimes "They pretend to pay us, and we pretend to work."

used, they did not reflect the opportunity cost of capital. Consequently, no systematic device encouraged optimal use of capital; each manager would attempt to obtain as much equipment as possible and stockpile it against some future exigency.

A similar situation applied in the use of labor. Any gains resulting from a reduction in the workforce were not retained within the enterprise but were remitted to the center. Rather than promoting economy of labor, incentives encouraged managers to retain as much labor as possible. In a capitalist system, a profit-maximizing entrepreneur will tend to hire workers up to the point where the wage is equal to the product of the marginal worker, but in the Soviet system it was worthwhile to have any worker around as long as the marginal product was positive.

Output targets were defined in annual terms, and optimally, production would proceed smoothly throughout the year. However, in Soviet enterprise the same human factors applied as in, say, a student's work habits. Production proved to be slow early in the year, far from the deadline, but as the end of the planning period approached, meeting the target became a matter of greater urgency. The last few months were characterized by what became known as **storming**, a fevered attempt to raise output to meet the target. At this point the excess labor and machinery became especially valuable, but hoarding spread beyond capital and labor. Intermediate goods and inputs required by other productive units in the system were frequently in short supply early in the year and became available only as the storming behavior in supplying enterprises kicked in, so keeping high inventories was quite rational.

Innovation Innovation in any system is a relatively risky business, whether it entails the development of new products or the introduction of a new technique for production. However, in market systems successful innovation is often rewarded by greater efficiency and lower costs, or in tapping new sources of consumer demand and increased sales; each possibility yields higher profits. The Soviet system did little to encourage such innovation.

Consider first new techniques of production. These generally entail some teething period during which glitches are ironed out and output necessarily falls. If these problems are prolonged, then it might prove impossible to recover during the fixed horizon of the planning year. Output targets would then not be met and the enterprise manager's income would suffer, or some more dire consequence (loss of job or even criminal sanction) might result. Consequently, innovation was often not attractive. Managers generally found it easier and more comfortable to produce by tried and tested methods in which the outcome was predictable.

Similarly, not much incentive existed at the enterprise level to develop new products. The plan did not usually require them, because the planning process consisted largely of revamping the previous period's output figures. New products took management time and other resources away from current production and opened the possibility of falling short of targets, inviting the same loss of income or worse.

Quality Control Planning targets were usually laid out in terms of physical units. Although in theory all the output was meant to be of "acceptable" quality, and retail stores or users of intermediate goods could reject the products that were substandard, in reality quality control was poor. In market systems the real cost of poor quality is a loss of reputation and repeat business; in the planned system the customers had no choice. Their suppliers were defined by the plan, and those suppliers simply could not lose sales as a result.

Information A planning system in which decisions are made centrally can only function well if the data received at the center are accurate. However, in the Soviet system, powerful incentives motivated enterprise managers to keep the planners in the dark. It was not good for them to reveal the real potential of their enterprises, which would only result in an upward adjustment in output targets in the next planning round and make the job of reaching those targets more difficult. It was in the enterprise managers' interest to mislead the planners by overstating their real needs for labor, machinery, and material inputs. If successful, that produced a cushion that could be called on in times of emergency.

The Bureaucrats

Finally we turn to the incentives that operated on the planners themselves. Why should they work to produce a good plan and ensure compliance to it? As we already noted, the basic outline of the plan was determined by the political masters. It was the function of the bureaucrats to turn these ideas into a working document, and, like other members of the entire Soviet hierarchy, it was best to achieve this task in as painless a way as possible.

The planners put a lot of energy into improving the techniques of planning, but when it came to actually coming up with ideas to reform the incentive structures, little motivated them. From time to time planners went out on a limb to proclaim the importance of, say, increasing the role of prices to reflect costs, but a wise planner would only do that with the clear approval of the political leadership. Furthermore, he or she might be aware that shifts in the preferences of the leaders are not permanent. Khrushchev encouraged unorthodox thinking to a degree that his predecessor Stalin had not, and those who displaced him were alarmed by this activity. The kind of ideas that were rewarded under one first secretary could lead to trouble under another. The safest behavior was to move slowly and conventionally.

CONCLUSION

The Soviet system contained little to encourage either fresh thinking, high quality, new ideas, or new products. Overwhelmingly the incentives fostered a repetition of the status quo, and consequently the economy ran out of sources of extensive growth. The absence of new land, maximum participation rates, and low marginal productivity of capital made new investment almost valueless. The system allowed no sources of total factor productivity growth. Relative decline was inevitable and reform of the economy vital. Whether this reform and transition will be successful is discussed more thoroughly in Part 6 of this book.

KEY TERMS AND CONCEPTS

collective farms

control by the ruble

control figures

draft plan

Gosbank

Gosplan

hard-budget constraint

input-output matrix

kolkhozy

legality

level previously achieved

monetary overhang

negative value-added enterprises

politburo

Praesidium

soft-budget constraints

sovkhozy

storming

QUESTIONS FOR DISCUSSION

1. In what ways did the planning in the Soviet Union hinge on interpersonal relations and influence?

2. What is the significance of the plan "from the level previously achieved" for the functioning of the planning process?

3. Discuss the function and the role of prices in the Soviet Union under planning.

4. How was plan fulfillment monitored in the Soviet system?

5. Why was the yield on private agriculture plots so much greater than on state and collective farms?

6. What incentives motivated management to give misleading information to planners?

7. Why did Soviet firms tend toward high degrees of vertical integration?

8. Why was the Soviet system so deficient in producing goods for consumers?

9. What incentives motivated Soviet management to pay attention to quality control?

10. Which of capitalism and Soviet socialism fostered the strongest incentives for innovation? Why?

RESOURCES

Books and Articles

Flakierski, Henryk. *Income Inequalities in the Former Soviet Union and Its Republics.* Armonk, NY: M.E. Sharpe, 1993. Reviewed in the *Journal of Comparative Economics*, October 1994, 260–271.

Goldman, Marshall I. *What Went Wrong with Perestroika*, chap. 15. New York: W.W. Norton, 1991.

Gray, Kenneth R. (ed.). *Soviet Agriculture: Comparative Perspectives.* Ames: Iowa University Press, 1990.

Gregory, Paul R., and Robert C. Stuart. *Soviet and Post-Soviet Economic Structure and Performance*, 5th ed. New York: HarperCollins, 1994.

Hare, Paul G. *Central Planning.* Chur, Switzerland: Harwood, 1991.

Huang, Yasheng. "Information, Bureaucracy, and Economic Reforms in China and the Soviet Union." *World Politics*, October 1994, 102–134.

International Monetary Fund, The World Bank, Organization for Economic Co-operation and Development, and European Bank for Reconstruction and Development. *A Study of the Soviet Economy.* 3 vols. Paris: Organization for Economic Cooperation and Development, 1991.

Kornai, János. *The Socialist System: The Political Economy of Communism.* Princeton, NJ: Princeton University Press, 1991.

Litwack, John. "Legality and Market Reform in Soviet Type Economies," *Journal of Economic Perspectives* 5, no. 4 (Fall 1991).

Malle, Silvana. *Employment Planning in the Soviet Union.* New York: St. Martin's Press, 1990.

Pryor, Frederic L. *The Rise and Fall of Collectivized Agriculture in Marxist Regimes.* Princeton, NJ: Princeton University Press, 1992.

Simis, Kostantin M. *The USSR—The Corrupt Society: The Secret World of Soviet Capitalism.* New York: Simon and Schuster, 1982.

Standing, Guy (ed.). *In Search of Flexibility: The New Soviet Labor Market.* Geneva: International Labor Office, 1991.

Wolf, Thomas. *A Foreign Trade in the Centrally Planned Economy.* Chur, Switzerland: Harwood, 1988.

18

THE PARTICIPATORY ECONOMY:
THE CASE OF YUGOSLAVIA

We turn now to consider a type of market socialism that prevailed in the Republic of Yugoslavia between the 1960s and the breakup of the Yugoslav state in the 1990s and still exists to some extent today within Serbia, the remnant of the Yugoslav state. It provides an example of attempting to take a middle way, between full-fledged market capitalism on the one hand and planned socialism on the other. Its history is interesting and revealing, and provides insights that are useful when we turn in Chapter 19 to discuss in more general terms the feasibility of a "third way."

The term **market socialism** is revealing and appropriate because the Yugoslavian system involved elements of both these polar extremes. The socialist aspect is ownership of the means of production by the state rather than by individuals. However, while coordination of the economy was brought about by a plan in the other socialist states of Eastern Europe and the former Soviet Union, in Yugoslavia coordination was left largely to market forces.

Another common term to describe the Yugoslav system was **labor management**, reflecting that enterprises, while using capital owned by society as a whole, were managed by the workers or, more precisely by management appointed or elected by the workers. The theory of labor-managed economies was largely developed by Jaroslav Vanek, who used the term **participatory economies** because workers were involved in the decisions of the firms in which they were employed and workers' income was a function of profits.[1]

THE PARTICIPATORY ECONOMY

Vanek's Principles

Although Yugoslavia was his model, Vanek's theory of the participatory economy was a normative ideal, rather than a positive description of a specific state, that conformed to five basic underlying principles:

1. *Participation in management.* Every worker should participate in the management of the enterprise in which he or she worked on an equal footing. In most cases

[1]See Jaroslav Vanek, *The Participatory Economy: An Evolutionary Hypothesis and a Strategy for Development* (Ithaca, NY: Cornell University Press, 1971).

this principle implies a representative democracy in which workers delegate their day-to-day responsibility to an elected chief executive, a board of directors, and a workers' council who make most decisions on behalf of the workers.

2. *Income sharing.* In a participatory economy, rather than being paid a fixed wage, the workers in each firm receive their income by dividing the profits among them in an equitable fashion, usually dictated by a formula democratically determined by the workers themselves. Differences in the size of workers' shares should reflect work of different intensity, skill level, or quality.

3. *Capital to be owned by society as a whole.* Socialism is defined by societal rather than individual ownership of the means of production, and Vanek's participatory economy is socialist in that sense. The capital employed by any enterprise is not owned by that enterprise or indeed by the workers of that enterprise, but rather by the state, which rents out the capital for a contractual fee. This fee should not be merely nominal but should reflect the scarcity, or opportunity cost.

4. *Coordination via the market not the plan.* In Vanek's conception, the participatory economy should be fully decentralized. All of the actors in the system— consumers, enterprises, associations, and the various levels of government— should be free to make decisions without interference from the government (or the party). Although the system should not involve command planning, some form of indicative planning to allow better coordination is appropriate. Vanek does call for government intervention to resolve abuse of monopoly power and, by implication, other instances of market failure, but the important principle is the sovereignty of individuals operating through the market, rather than the preferences of planners or politicians.

5. *Freedom of employment.* The final characteristic of the ideal participatory state is that each individual is at total liberty to choose his or her occupation and particular place of employment. A necessary counterpart to this principle is that each enterprise is at full liberty to hire, or not hire, any person. The problem of establishing appropriate grounds for dismissal is more difficult and enterprises should be free to create their own rules for limiting the ability to dismiss workers, even when strictly economic criteria might call for it.

The Objective of the Enterprise

From this list of characteristics it is clear that the objective of the labor-managed firm in a participatory economy will be quite different from that of either the capitalist firm or a typical enterprise in a centrally planned economy. Under capitalism, profit maximization is assumed to be the objective of the firm,[2] whereas under centralized planning the enterprise's good is less clear, but it derives from the preferences of planners, politicians, and party members rather than the workers. In the labor-managed firm, the objective is to maximize the income (or perhaps a more

---

[2]The various behavioral theories of the firm deal with issues concerning the practicability of profit maximization and the "real-world" constraints on this objective.

abstract notion of well-being) of the workers of the firm. Generally this objective is interpreted to be equivalent to maximizing the amount of profit per worker. The simple analytics are shown in Figure 18.1.

Because the firm rents its capital from the state, for any contract period the rental fee constitutes a fixed cost. Therefore the cost of capital per worker falls as the number of workers increases. (In fact, this curve takes the form of a rectangular hyperbola, asymptotic to both axes.) Let us assume that labor is the only variable input. The value of the product produced by the average worker is shown as the "value of the average product of labor" (VAP_L) schedule in Figure 18.1. It is constructed by multiplying the average physical product curve, which will be downward sloping,[3] by the price of the product, which will be a constant in competitive markets, because the firm faces a horizontal demand curve. The point of greatest profit per worker (**income maximization**) occurs at the output where the capital

■ **FIGURE 18.1**

Optimum Employment in a Labor-Managed Firm

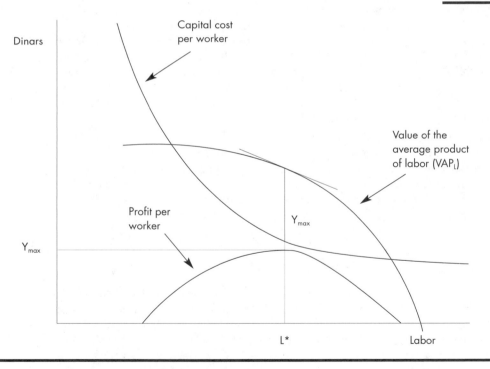

------

[3]For all intents and purposes, the principle of diminishing marginal returns should hold in such economies, because it is at its base a technical consideration. The amount of capital is fixed and as the number of workers increases, beyond some point, the marginal product of labor will decline, ultimately bringing down the average product with it.

cost per worker curve and the value of the average product of labor curve are at the greatest distance from each other. At this point, they have equal slopes, and therefore the optimal amount of labor is shown by L* in Figure 18.1. Note that this point is not the same as the profit maximizing position, which would occur where the marginal revenue product curve intersects the wage schedule. Generally the income-maximizing level will occur at a level of employment (and output) less than the profit-maximizing level of employment.

Under these assumptions, a somewhat strange result occurs, one that brings attention to the potential differences between the performance of labor-managed and the profit-maximizing firms. Consider a change in the price of the product due, for example, to an exogenous increase in demand. Such a move would shift the VAP_L curve vertically upward from VAP_{L1} to VAP_{L2} and would increase its (negative) slope at all levels of labor input (Figure 18.2).

If the capital cost remains the same, the point of greatest divergence between the two curves (where the slopes are the same) actually occurs at a lower level of labor input, and therefore a lower level of output—as product prices rise. Thus, under these assumptions, we obtain the rather strange result that an increase in product

■ **FIGURE 18.2**

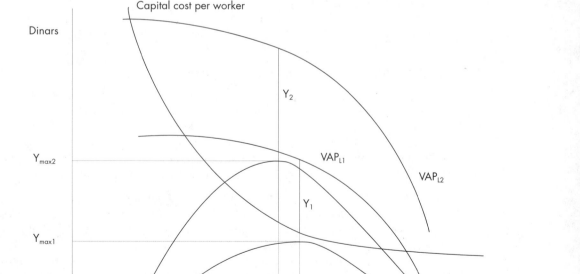

Response to Price Increase in a Two-Factor Labor-Managed Firm

prices leads the labor-managed firm to operate at a lower level of output and employ fewer workers, L^*_2 rather than L^*_1. The reverse is true if product prices fall—output and employment are increased if income per worker is to be maximized. Thus an increase in price results in reduced supply, and a fall in price brings about increased supply. Under these assumptions the individual firm's supply curve is actually downward sloping, raising questions about market stability. An analogous result follows with respect to capital cost. If the state reduces the contract price of capital, the capital cost per worker curve shifts vertically downward, and the optimal amount of employment again shifts to the left and fewer workers are employed. An increase in the cost of capital leads to greater employment. These two results were pointed out in 1958 by Benjamin Ward and, at the time, created something of a controversy.[4] Although theoretically valid, these unexpected results are particularly sensitive to specific assumptions. If we generalize to consider more variable inputs than labor alone, the results can be shown to be different.

For example, if the numbers of workers employed is held constant, any action that increases profit raises average income. In such a case a labor-managed firm will follow the general rule that inputs are used up to the point where their marginal value product is equal to marginal factor cost, the same rule that elementary textbooks ascribe to capitalist firms. Moreover, if we assume that more than one output is produced by the firm, if the increase in the price of a good does result in a reduction of labor employed, the fall in output may be in a good other than the one whose price has risen. Thus, in a more complex "real world," the downward sloping supply curve is less likely to occur than on paper. However, it is generally accepted that in a labor-managed environment the firm's response to increased prices in the product market is likely to be less elastic than in a capitalist one; output would be slower to increase in response to increase in demand.

Benefits of the Participatory Economy

Vanek was an unashamed promoter of the idea of the participatory economy and saw in it a logical "evolutionary" solution to some of the detriments of capitalism. Indeed, some authors have argued that through the growing tendency to pay workers at least in part with shares or attractively priced options, participation can in fact arrive through capitalism. Vanek offered several advantages for labor management, which are discussed along with some of their limitations:

1. *A participatory economy will show reduced tendency to monopolization, and hence increased consumer welfare, relative to a capitalist economy.* This conclusion stems from several assumptions, some of which are problematic. First, it is assumed the structure of enterprise governance will tend to keep productive units small, which results in a market structure of many small firms that are in broad terms competitive with each other. The tendency to create a gigantic entity will be avoided because worker management in such a firm would be clumsy. Second, the fact that the objective maxim of the firm is earnings per

---

[4]Benjamin Ward, "The Firm in Illyria," *American Economic Review* 48 (1958), pp. 566–589.

worker rather than aggregate profits per se makes the labor-managed firm less prone to attempt to dominate through size. Under capitalism, doubling output by doubling all inputs may lead to doubling of profits. In the labor-managed context such action results again in the doubling of profits, but because the number of workers is doubled too, the net result is only in constant profit per worker. Therefore increasing size is not particularly attractive to the workers who ultimately control the firm. However, it must be admitted that if a larger size creates more market power and therefore leads to increased product prices, then it can result in higher earnings per worker, and that monopoly, with the consequent ability to manipulate prices, can be attractive to a socialist manager as well as capitalist one.

2. *Nonproductive expenditure in the participatory economy would be less than under capitalism.* Because the advantage of size is limited under labor management, expenses on advertising and marketing designed to win larger market share are less remunerative than in the capitalist environment. Thus a participatory economy wastes less on nonproductive expenses than a capitalist one. However, it must be conceded that if the promotional expenditure does result in product differentiation, it would allow higher prices and therefore generate increased income per head.

3. *Participatory firms will show reduced workplace friction, and a smaller incidence of strikes relative to capitalist firms.* This point would seem to be a commonsense consequence of labor management. Strikes are usually the result of a dispute over the relative returns to capital and labor. When the owners of capital and the workers are nominally the same, the potential for disagreement should be much reduced. Viewed from a slightly different perspective, labor management gets around the principal-agent problem because the owners are the workers. These features are, of course, the logic behind the use of equity as a substitute for wages to reward workers, an increasingly common feature of capitalism in developed market economies.

4. *A participatory economy will show greater tendency to full employment compared to capitalism.* This claim of macroeconomic stability is important to Vanek, but it is one of the most difficult to substantiate. It is true that worker-managed firms will tend to retain labor during downswings in the economic cycle, because these employees are part of the "democracy" of the plant. They are enfranchised and help to choose management, and they therefore have both rights and power. It follows that maintaining the output of the firm during recessions is also likely because workers will be kept in employment, a feature with obvious countercyclical implications. Because short-term shifts in demand variations are not followed by adjustments of quantity, either up or down, the size of short-term price movement in response to demand shocks is likely to be less than under capitalism and quantity movements correspondingly smaller.

However, another reason explains why the participatory economy is more resistant to unemployment. The state owns the capital and, for political reasons, it might be slow in enforcing repossession when capital costs are in arrears. Thus the participatory firm might face a soft-budget constraint, cushioning against unemployment in the short run but fostering inefficiency in the longer term by tying up capital in unproductive enterprises. Moreover, if substantial unemployment does come into being, no mechanism is available to eliminate it in a more rapid fashion in a participatory economy than under capitalism. With conventional labor markets, unemployed workers offer themselves for employment at lower wages, driving down the wages that the capitalists pay and hence increasing employment. Under labor management and profit sharing, each additional worker hired will tend to drive down the average profit per worker (see Figure 19.1), and therefore adding new workers will not be appealing to the existing worker managers, except in cases in which the impact on average capital costs outweighs the impact on average value product.

5. *A participatory economy will have a lower long-run tendency toward inflation.* It is possible that in the long run (as opposed to the short run discussed earlier), the participatory form of organization has a lower tendency to inflation than conventional capitalism because of two factors. One is the resistance to size and monopolization that is inherent in this kind of organization. The other is the absence of labor unions. With no unions to bargain for increased wages, an inflationary cycle cannot start with "wage push."

6. *Firms in the participatory economy will be more socially responsible than a capitalist firm.* Finally, there is the claim that a worker-managed firm is likely to be more socially responsible than a capitalist firm, especially with respect to the environment. Consider the case of pollution, which tends to be "oversupplied" under capitalism because real costs of production are imposed on third parties, with no compensation. Owners of the capital live far away from the factories and their lives are not adversely affected by a decline in environmental quality, nor are their children likely to suffer poor health as a result. However, because the workers who control a participatory firm live locally, they are more likely to "internalize" the externality of pollution and trade lower monetary rewards for a better environment.

Negative Features of the Participatory Economy

Some of the potential detriments resulting from labor management were introduced contextually in the preceding section, but it is useful to underscore a couple of them.

1. *Firms in the participatory economy are likely to be less responsive than the capitalist firm.* Changing the size of the workforce in either direction will face more resistance than under capitalism, and therefore quantity responses are likely to be slower. In some circumstances this flaw might be fatal if resistance to downsizing causes the firm to operate inefficiently and put itself into bankruptcy rather than fire workers. In the ideal case, as profits per worker fall, some workers will be motivated to move to firms where they can make a greater positive contribution to average profits, but in reality this process is likely to be highly frictional and take a long time to complete.

2. *Firms in the participatory economy offer limited capability for innovation.* Research and development require substantial resources, and it is frequently argued

that the smaller firms encountered in a participatory economy can afford it less well than the larger ones we see under capitalism. Certainly, research is largely a fixed cost, and a firm with a high volume of sales is in a position to spread the cost across a greater number of units of output.

DEVELOPMENT OF THE YUGOSLAV STATE

The state that most closely embodied Vanek's ideas of participation, and from which he gained inspiration, was Yugoslavia. Today the Yugoslav state is split into several republics, some in conflict with each other, and it is difficult now to envisage it as a laboratory for evolutionary socialist principles. Nevertheless for most of the post–World War II period, the Yugoslav economy represented an intriguing third way that tried to balance the efficiency and coordination of the market with the egalitarian principles of socialism.

The Institutional History of Yugoslavia

Yugoslavia was created at the end of World War I and owed its existence to the Wilsonian principle of national self-determination. However, the architects of the peace treaty feared that the ethnic nationalities of the Balkans might be too small and too quarrelsome to survive as independent states. Consequently, they created the Kingdom of the Serbs, Croats, and Slovenes, which in time became the Kingdom of Yugoslavia, literally the land of the south Slavs. The new country was made up of part of the former Austro-Hungarian empire (Croatia and Slovenia), the Kingdom of Serbia, and parts of the Ottoman empire. From the first, issues of ethnic heterogeneity and economic divergence dominated the new country. It was overrun by the Germans in 1941, and the German occupation increased ethnic rivalry because of the cynical application of divide and rule.

At the end of the war, the Communists established their rule and the leader, Josef Brosz Tito, was a firm admirer of both Stalin and central planning. Initially he tried to implement the Soviet model in Yugoslavia but was unwilling to see domination by the Nazis being replaced by that of the Soviets. He insisted from the first on Yugoslavia's total independence as a nation, outraging Stalin, who expelled Yugoslavia from international communist organizations (*Cominterm*) in 1948. Under Tito's firm rule, ethnic divisions, troublesome before and during the World War II, and which were to result in the ultimate breakup of the Yugoslav state, were put on a back burner. Expulsion from *Cominterm* allowed Yugoslavia to experiment in economic policy. For a brief period, Soviet-style planning was intensified, but from 1950 onward Tito led the country toward a system in which individual firms were allowed much greater freedom in determining output level, technical choice, and prices.

The Regional Problem

One of the problems confronting Yugoslavia was unequal income levels between the constituent republics. In 1947 the northernmost republic, Slovenia, enjoyed a per-head income about 57 percent above the average for Yugoslavia as a whole, while the poorest republic, Montenegro, was 57 percent below the average. One would expect that under market coordination arrangements this differential would narrow over time, and in a socialist state where the government not only directs infrastructural investment but also allocates investment capital and technology between regions, convergence should occur even faster.

Table 19.1 shows that far from narrowing, the differential widened over time. Slovenia became relatively wealthier while other provinces and regions, particularly in the south, remained less developed. By the middle 1980s the poorest area was Kosmet (the acronym for the Autonomous Region of Kosovo and Metohija), an area populated predominantly by ethnic Albanians, despite its special status granted by Tito.

Several reasons contributed to the failure to converge. Although language was not a major difficulty, deep ethnic, cultural, and religious differences kept labor mobility between republics low. The system of worker management limited the extent to which new workers would be brought into an organization because in most cases new workers did not increase average profit. Hiring might be tolerable if the marginal worker were a relative, a neighbor, or a local political appointee, but not a migrant worker from another republic.

Federal policy transferred resources from the more prosperous north to the south, but the extent was limited by the need to minimize political conflict between the republics; transfers were a cause of grievance and unrest within the richer areas. In addition, despite the availability of cheap labor, capital had a lower marginal product in the south, and though investment rates were higher in poorer regions, income

■ TABLE *18.1*

Republic or Autonomous Region	1947	1953	1979	1986	Population in millions in 1986
Kosmet	58	53	31	30	1.8
Bosnia-Herzegovina	72	79	70	72	4.3
Macedonia	71	69	68	66	2
Montenegro	43	58	64	78	0.6
Serbia	100	91	96	94	5.8
Vojvodina	125	96	120	121	2
Croatia	105	111	125	123	4.7
Slovenia	157	182	200	211	1.9
All Yugoslavia	100	100	100	100	23.2
Highest/Lowest	3.65	3.43	6.45	7.03	

The Regional Distribution of Income: 1947–1986 Income per Head as a Percentage of Average

SOURCE: Richard Carson, *Comparative Economic Systems* (Armonk, NY: M.E. Sharpe, 1990), p. 365.

disparities remained large. Toward the end of federal Yugoslavia, the average worker in the south was equipped with as much capital as his or her counterpart in the north, but labor productivity was still inferior in the south. The failure to grow was largely explained by lower average education and the scarcity of management skills in the poorer regions, while productivity in the northern republics was helped by proximity to Austria and the European Union (EU), which kept demand high and led to technological spillovers. Low labor cost suppliers on the periphery of prosperous Western Europe, Croatia, and especially Slovenia prospered.

At the onset of communist rule, income in Slovenia was three times as great as that in Kosovo-Metohija; by 1986 the ratio was 7:1. This worsening situation fanned Kosovar separatism and escalated ethnic and religious tensions. However, of more importance to the breakup of the Yugoslav state was the fact that Slovenian income was 140 percent higher than in the ethnically Serb areas of Montenegro and Serbia proper. Remaining within a federation would imply continued transfers from the Slovenes to the Serbs. It is not, therefore, surprising that the Slovenes were the first to leave federal Yugoslavia and the first to apply for EU membership, where they would be recipients of transfer funds, rather than payees.

YUGOSLAV MARKET SOCIALISM

The Yugoslav System

The Yugoslav system differed in key respects from the conditions that Vanek thought essential for a participatory economy.

1. *Capital was socially owned and enterprises did "rent" the capital from the state.* The **capital charge**, however, was well below an equilibrium interest rate. As a result, capital was always in short supply. The excess demand for investment funds required a political decision for the rationing of these scarce resources.

2. *A theoretical reliance on the market to coordinate the system meant that each firm could pursue its income-maximizing objective.* However, many price controls and administered prices were necessary imposed not merely in the capital market.

3. *Although in theory the workplace operated as a form of representative democracy, with free elections for management, the list of eligible managers was tightly controlled by the Communist Party.* Instead of being free to elect the best man or woman for the job, the workers chose from a list constrained by politics.

4. *Nominally total freedom of employment meant each worker could choose where to work.* In reality, firms tended to hire from within family and neighborhood groups, and movement between regions or ethnic areas was especially difficult.

5. *Although the social sector firms did practice income sharing, it was limited on the downside.* Wages could not, by law, fall by more than 30 percent in any year, whatever the profit situation of the firm. This restriction required a form of soft-budget constraint.

The Operating Structure of a Yugoslav Firm

The shift from command planning to worker management in Yugoslavia occurred in the early 1950s. In 1953, the workers' councils assumed the authority to manage enterprises, although their capital still belonged to the state. Councils were elected by the workers of the firm (with the exception of the management) and they had the responsibility of choosing management, as well as providing broad direction over all financial and policy matters.

The organization closest to the Western concept of a firm was known as an **organization of associated labor (OAL)**. However, the OAL was not the smallest unit. Large enterprises were subdivided into units known as **basic organization of associated labor (BOALs)**. Each BOAL (which may be thought of in terms of their analogue in Western firms—the profit center) produced an identifiable and salable good or service. Importantly, profit was calculated at the level of the BOAL, and the income of workers is a function of the profitability of the smaller unit—not the larger firm. Strictly speaking a complex OAL was no more than a voluntary association of its constituent basic organizations of labor. The BOALs had to ratify all important pricing, production, and finance decisions, and could, in theory, secede if it would not disrupt the parent OAL. In 1985 the Yugoslav social sector consisted of some 14,280 undivided enterprises, all of which were OALs, and a further 4,062 major OALs, subdivided into 18,927 basic organizations of labor.

This conception of the firm proved problematic. Although the products of the organizational organizations could be identified, in reality the effectiveness of each of the units within the firm is a function of management's ability to elicit cooperation between the various parts. As in any multidivisional firm, a turf war may arise over who is responsible for profits and who is liable for costs, but the whole is generally interdependent. Service functions within the firm (accountancy, maintenance, security, etc.) are handled by "work communities," where incomes derive from a pro rata sharing of the profits of all the BOALs. The general flow of funds within a basic organization of associated labor is shown in Figure 18.3.

Within the "profit center," incomes are determined by the division of residual profits between the workers, not on a simple per-head basis, but rather through **work points** determined by workers' councils on the basis of the skills, training, and effort required in various occupations. Table 18.2 gives an example of work points system of a Zagreb textile factory in the early 1960s. The categories include education, skill, physical effort, and working conditions. In addition, total wages may be amended by the granting of individual performance bonuses (or penalties), and total compensation reflects a considerable in-kind component available to all workers, including housing, health care, and child care. While we might dispute the relative importance of all these factors, they did provide a basis for income determination. However, it was necessarily arbitrary in nature, and, because it paid little account to supply and demand in the labor market, it did not guarantee that all positions would be filled by qualified people. The differential between the senior management and the workforce was particularly crucial, and top management in Yugoslavia was relatively badly paid (as a multiple of average earnings) compared to other socialist and capitalist countries. In the example here, the managing director (CEO) receives only about five times the income of a cleaner and only a little more than twice that of a factory foreman.

■ FIGURE *18.3*

The Flow of Funds of a Yugoslav Social Sector BOAL

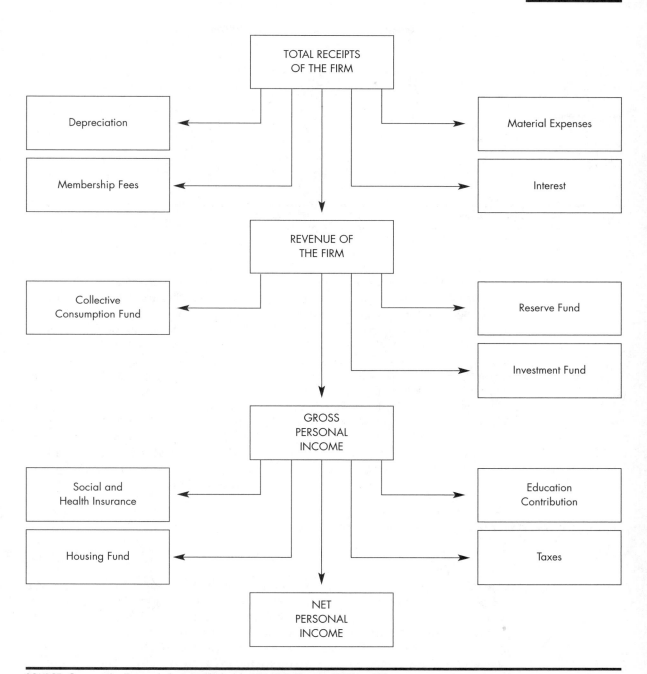

SOURCE: *Comparative Economic Systems* (Armonk, NY: M.E. Sharpe, 1990), p. 337.

An Example of Work Points Assignments: Zagreb Textile Factory, 1961

	Education	Skill and Experience	Authority	Responsibility	Physical Effort	Mental Effort	Working Conditions	Total
Managing director	100	170	150	190	10	100	10	730
Technical director	130	140	140	160	10	90	10	680
Works manager	100	130	100	120	10	90	30	580
Foreman	80	60	40	50	10	40	40	320
Skilled weaver	50	40	0	40	35	30	40	235
Skilled spinner	30	20	0	20	30	10	40	150
Sales manager	100	130	100	140	10	90	10	580
Accountant	100	100	50	90	10	80	10	440
Truck driver	80	60	0	70	30	40	40	320
Female cleaner	20	10	0	10	40	10	40	130

SOURCE: Rudolf Bicanich, "La Politique des revenue Ouvriers en Yougoslavie," *Economie Appliquée,* October/December, 1963, p. 587, *Comparative Economic Systems* (Armonk, NY: M.E. Sharpe, 1990), p. 381.

The theory of worker management holds that the relatively small work groups discourage alienation and maintain peer discipline. Division of profits among responsible workers maximizes effort and reduces to a minimum agency problems. The selection of management by the workers' councils ensures that the best candidate for the overall well-being of the firm is chosen and that conflicts between management and workers are kept to a minimum. Unfortunately, experience revealed a more problematic side to each of these assumptions. Profit sharing and small organization did not solve all the problems of work effort; "free riding" was still common and was exhibited in problems of labor productivity. Supervision was still required. The system of management selection did not guarantee that the best person got the job. In the first place, the slate of candidates was politically determined. Local party officials had considerable say over who constituted "qualified" candidates. Workers also had an incentive to choose a candidate for other reasons than the long-run health of the firm—perhaps, for example, to maximize job security.

PROBLEMS OF THE YUGOSLAV ECONOMY

Investment

One of the most important negative characteristics of the Yugoslav economy was the absence of capital markets with any real role in the rationing of investment funds among competing uses. One of the important tenets of Vanek's system was that capital should be owned publicly and rented out to the enterprises at realistic charges, but in reality interest rates were never allowed to play a significant role. Real interest rates were always low and frequently were negative. The demand for investment capital by the enterprises at these rates was practically limitless, and therefore allocation among competing uses had to be on the basis of political decisions rather than economic ones.

An additional potential source of investment funds in the labor-managed firm was retained earnings, an excess of revenue over costs not distributed to the workers in income. To some extent profit retention was a legal requirement because by law each firm had to maintain the value of its capital, accounting for depreciation of capital equipment and amortizing it in a "business fund." Workers could in theory vote to distribute even less of earnings as income, increase the business fund, and hence contribute to the purchase of new capital equipment. However, workers do not have full ownership rights in the firm, and no individual worker is secure in knowing that his or her share of the principal invested will be recovered in full at the end of his or her time horizon. Unlike a worker in a capitalist enterprise, who is sure that any money he or she puts into shares in the company is to some degree liquid (although there is risk of capital loss, as well as the prospect of capital gain), any investment made by the Yugoslav worker is highly illiquid. In contrast, if the money is received as income and deposited in individual savings accounts, the worker has security over both principal and interest. Moreover, the fact that financial repression kept interest rates below market clearing values ensured a black market for funds that paid even higher rates than the savings accounts. Consequently, workers would be motivated to invest in the firm only if the expected rate of return were considerably above that offered in savings accounts or black market loans.

Unemployment

One of Vanek's predictions for the participatory economy was a high level of employment, going so far as to write:

> The participatory economy does guarantee full employment. It does so in the sense that the economy will normally operate at, or very near, full employment, and if as the result of some drastic disturbance, unemployment were to arise, there are forces, inherent in the system, that will tend to restore full employment. In this respect the participatory economy has a definite edge over capitalist economies.

One of the enduring problems of capitalism has been unemployment, but it is not clear that the participatory economy has the edge over flexible labor markets. It is true that worker-managed firms will be less willing to shed labor in downturns, but once it is established unemployment can prove stubborn. The same factors that militate against the growth of worker-managed firms act to prevent surplus labor being absorbed by existing enterprises. Only if the marginal revenue product of an additional worker is above the average revenue product of existing workers will new hires be made. Otherwise the income of existing workers will fall.

The data show that Yugoslavia suffered from acute unemployment. In the mid-1980s about 1 million workers were registered as unemployed. Part of this total was frictional, comprised of workers who were between jobs or receiving education; however, it is probable that about 700,000 of the total were properly described as unemployed and seeking work. In addition, some 350,000 Yugoslavs were working abroad, mostly in Germany as *Gastarbeiter,* (guest workers).[5] Finally, it should be noted that Yugoslavia retained a "reserve" of potential industrial workers employed in low-productivity agriculture. On the whole, the participatory Yugoslav economy did not do an excellent job at eliminating unemployment.

During the 1980s, most of the unemployed were young people. Layoffs were rare in Yugoslav industry (a feature Vanek had accurately predicted), but start-ups of new firms were few and job creation sluggish. Much of the responsibility lay with the highly imperfect capital market, which tended to allocate funds to existing large and politically powerful enterprises. Unemployment, like income, was distributed unevenly between the republics. In relatively wealthy Slovenia, next to the Austrian border, the unemployment rate was less than 1.8 percent, while in impoverished Kosovo, largely inhabited by ethnic Albanians it was close to one-third. Cultural and religious barriers prevented labor mobility and allowed disequilibrium in the federal labor market.

Strike Activity

Vanek's assertion that a labor-managed firm would be largely immune from labor disputes and strike activity would seem on the face of it likely to be borne out in fact. Surely workers who could elect their own management, and who could have a powerful say in the operation of the enterprise, could have little to complain about and would be unlikely to indulge in such self-destructive behavior. However, the social sector of the Yugoslav economy was by no means insulated from labor unrest, especially as real incomes fell in the late 1970s and early 1980s. Despite the fact that they had elected them, workers mistrusted management, especially over layoffs in the face of falling demand. Moreover, the complex structure of Yugoslavia's OALs allowed areas of dispute among the various BOALs that made up the enterprise, particularly about contributions toward the overhead (management, maintenance, sales, etc.) of the firm as a whole. It is not wholly surprising that more than 1,000 strikes took place in the first nine months of 1987.

Industrial Concentration

Another of Vanek's predictions was confounded by Yugoslav experience. He argued that the participatory economy would tend to a low degree of product market concentration compared to capitalist countries. He based this point on the idea that while capitalist profits would rise with market share, income per worker would be largely unchanged (except when monopoly power might be exploited or substantial economies of scale exist).

In fact, Yugoslav industry showed a remarkable concentration in many markets. Table 18.3 gives some evidence from 1985. In food products, for example, 10 percent

---

[5]This figure was down from a peak of about 535,000 in the mid-1970s and the returning workers had exacerbated the problem at home.

■ **TABLE 18.3**

Incidence of Monopoly and Oligopoly in Consumer-Oriented Industries, 1985

| | | Number of Divisions | |
| | | --- | --- |
Industry	Total	Single Producer	< 8 Producers
Final wood products	112	4	38
Finished leather products	101	7	36
Footwear and accessories	40	2	14
Food products	221	22	90
Beverages	24	2	10
Final tobacco products	4	1	3

SOURCE: John P. Burkett, "Self-Managed Market Socialism and the Yugoslave Economy, 1950–1991," in Morris Bornstein, *Comparative Economic Systems* (Homewood, IL: Richard Irwin, 1994), p. 333.

of the subdivisions of the industry were completely monopolized, and more than half had fewer than eight producers. Moreover, barriers to interrepublic trade meant that the *de facto* monopoly power of many enterprises was even greater than the data indicate. Often a single producer in each republic was protected by substantial barriers to entry.

We can speculate about the causes of such concentration, but much of the responsibility lay with the system of allocating investment funds. Because the interest rate on investment capital was below its opportunity cost, every firm was interested in attracting as much funds as possible. In general, the larger firms had a greater voice and political influence and were able to attract more capital for expansion and modernization, and so they progressively squeezed smaller firms out of the market.

Inflation

The Yugoslav economy did not exhibit the low inflation that Vanek expected. Part of his case rested on the absence of union power, which in capitalist economies was a powerful factor for "cost push" inflation through high wage settlements. He also argued that a socialist economy was less prone to unemployment than a capitalist one, and therefore would require less tinkering through expansionary fiscal and monetary policy, a frequent policy response of capitalist governments and one that accelerates the rate of inflation.[6] Despite these theoretical conclusions, Yugoslav inflation was brisk relative to other European countries, and both federal and the republic governments tried to use price controls to fight it. The effect of these controls was to create series of shortages, excess demand, and black markets for key commodities.

---

[6]Indeed, modern literature addressing this "trade-off" suggests that any attempt to reduce unemployment below the natural rate is necessarily reflected in increased prices rather than in expanded output and reduced unemployment.

Environmental Quality

Finally, Vanek believed that a labor-managed economy would be more respectful of the environment and lead to a lower level of pollution than would occur under capitalism. He argued that workers who lived near the factory would be resistant to the emission of pollutants because of the negative effect on their own quality of life. Managers in capitalist firms, responsible only to distant shareholders, would be more inclined to pillage the environment for an increase in profit. Again Vanek's prediction proved wide of the mark. Capitalist economies in the postwar period have been "cleaner" than socialist ones, Yugoslavia included. The reason is that environmental regulation is more advanced in the wealthier economies of Western Europe, perhaps because environmental concern is a "luxury" better afforded in wealthier nations. Also the widespread environmental chaos throughout socialist Eastern Europe reflects the "problem of the commons"—that which belongs to everyone in fact belongs to no one.

CONCLUSION

Despite the promise of labor management, its overall performance in Yugoslavia must be regarded as disappointing. Vanek's predictions proved wrong on almost every score, in part because his expectations for participation were overly optimistic and in part because Yugoslavia adopted only three out of the five basic institutions of the ideal participatory economy. It is impossible to do more than speculate on the development of Yugoslavia if truly free markets for goods and realistic charges for capital services that would have equated supply and demand had been adopted. Neither is it fruitful to speculate on the fate of the Yugoslav state had the economy performed better during the years of market socialism. The forces favoring ethnic and religious self-determination that came powerfully to the fore in Europe during the twentieth century would still have been present. The common analysis today is that it was the personal authority of Tito and the presence of supranational ideology, communism, that managed to keep the Yugoslav state in one piece. The death of Tito and the widespread disruptions in communist states around would have occurred no matter what the state of the Yugoslav economy might have been.

KEY TERMS AND CONCEPTS

basic organization of associated
   labor (BOAL)

capital charge

income maximization

labor management

market socialism

nonproductive expenditure

organization of associated labor (OAL)

participatory economies

work points

QUESTIONS FOR DISCUSSION

1. What were Vanek's five principles for a participatory economy? To what degree were they fulfilled in the Yugoslav system?

2. Why is it that the supply curve may be negatively sloped in a labor-managed economy? Does this result generally occur?

3. Why should a labor-managed economy enjoy greater workplace peace than under capitalism? Did this reality occur in Yugoslavia?

4. To what degree did we observe greater macroeconomic stability in Yugoslavia than in Western capitalist economies?

5. Why did Vanek argue that a labor-managed firm would pay greater attention to environmental concerns than a capitalist firm?

6. Why did the Yugoslav economy show so little tendency to convergence and maintain high regional income differentials?

7. How well did the labor market function in Yugoslavia? Did the system of income sharing and work points ensure a fluid and efficient labor market?

8. Did the inability to reduce the interregional productivity gaps contribute to the breakup of the Yugoslav state?

RESOURCES

Web Sites

Government of Serbia and Montenegro ....http://www.info.gov.yu/

National Bank of Serbia ....http://www.nbs.yu/

Ministry of Economy and Privatization.....................................http://www.mpriv.sr.gov.yu/

Privatization Agency...http://www.pa-serbia.co.yu/

Books and Articles

Dyker, David A. *Yugoslavia: Socialism, Development, and Debt.* London: Routledge, 1990.

Flakierski, Henryk. *The Economic System and Income Distribution in Yugoslavia.* Armonk, NY: M.E. Sharpe, 1989.

Ireland, Norman J. *The Economics of the Labor-Managed Enterprises.* London: Croom Helm, 1982.

Jackall, Robert, and Henry M. Levin (eds.). *Worker Cooperatives in America.* Berkeley, CA: University of California Press, 1984.

Mellor, Mary. *Worker Cooperatives in Theory and Practice.* Milton Keynes, England, and Philadelphia: Open University Press, 1988.

Miller, David. *Market, State, and Community: Theoretical Foundations of Market Socialism.* Oxford: Oxford University Press, 1989.

Stephen, Frank H. *The Economic Analysis of Producers' Cooperatives.* London: Macmillan, 1984.

Vanek, Jaroslav. *The General Theory of Labor-Managed Market Economies.* Ithaca, NY: Cornell University Press, 1970.

Vanek, Jaroslav. *The Participatory Economy: An Evolutionary Hypothesis and a Strategy for Development.* Ithaca, NY: Cornell University Press, 1971.

Wachtel, Howard. "Workers' Management and Inter-Industry Wage Differentials in Yugoslavia." *Journal of Political Economy,* May/June 1972.

Wachtel, Howard. *Workers' Management and Workers' Wages in Yugoslavia.* Ithaca, NY: Cornell University Press, 1973.

Ward, Ben. "The Firm in Illyria: Market Syndicalism," *American Economic Review,* September 1958.

19

THE POSSIBILITIES OF A THIRD WAY

Central planning offers many appealing features. A plan enables tasks to be prioritized rather than relying on what seem at times to be the whims and myopia of the market. A plan can also facilitate the mobilization of resources to achieve specific aims, such as the creation of infrastructure or the creation of a new industrial sector. Because income from property accrues to the state, public ownership of the means of production, which is a usual but not a necessary feature of centrally planned economies, avoids extreme bias in the distribution of income. Despite the recent dismal economic history of centrally planned states, planning retains an appeal. It is still considered a rational activity within a firm or a household, which lends some justification for planning in the management of the national economy.

From its earliest applications, however, the deficiencies of centralized planning have been apparent. Effective command planning requires the centralization of a vast amount of information, so much in fact that it is almost impossible to process and to reconcile. This need for data often creates perverse incentives that encourage enterprise managers to mislead the center for their advantage. Planning lacks a mechanism whereby consumer preferences are rapidly transmitted to the center, and so the preferences of individuals must be guessed at or ignored. Finally, of particular importance is the fact that only in the rarest of circumstances will prices in a planned system reflect relative scarcities or resource costs.

MARKET SOCIALISM AND SOCIAL MARKETS

Because each of the polar conceptions, free market capitalism and socialist command planning, involves defects, a middle way that grasps the market's advantages in allocative efficiency and marries it to the distributional equity of socialism is attractive.

Two main approaches can be taken to an economic third way.[1] A system in which capital is collectively owned, generally by the state, but in which the prices of final

---

[1] We should note that "third way" as used here is not identical with the concept put forth by the British sociologist and LSE Director Anthony Giddens, in his book *The Third Way: The Renewal of Social Democracy* (London: Polity Press, 2000). Giddens' book, which has been embraced by Tony Blair and both Bill and Hillary Clinton, is largely about politics and promotes the ideas of liberal globalization, environmental concern, and broader property ownership.

products and inputs are determined in the marketplace is generally referred to as **market socialism**. We observed this kind of economy in our review of the former Yugoslav state. Such a system enables the market to allocate factors of production, while coordination of the system is achieved through price signaling. Usually the one price not determined by the market is that of capital. Generally it is owned by the state and is loaned or rented out at prices determined by the planners or the politicians.

A second approach is to allow a more completely operative market system, in which capital may be privately owned and rationed by the market. However, the government puts constraints on the ultimate outcome of the system, and prescribes how the economy will perform in terms of income distribution, access to basic goods and services, and sometimes price determination. This kind of economy is properly referred to as a **social market economy**, and we studied this system in the Swedish and German cases. Unfortunately, the distinction between true market socialism and the social market approach is frequently confused.

MARKET SOCIALISM

We turn first to discuss the advantages and flaws of market socialism. This system appeals because it represents the best of two worlds, providing both allocative efficiency and equity, but both recent experience and current scholarship emphasize the vital importance of an impartial capital market for the functioning of any market system. Any attempt to maintain a competitive system of prices in the goods and labor markets alone will fail because it divorces the functioning of those markets from the market for capital, to which they are inescapably related.

The Function of the Capital Market

The foremost function of a capital market is to disinterestedly evaluate the performance and potential of each firm. The share values of those firms traded in equity markets are determined by an impersonal stock market, which adjusts values to reflect prospects. Those firms that borrow by issuing bonds and paper are subject to the judgment of the bond market, again with many authors pursuing self-interest, on the value of its credit. Those firms that borrow directly from banks compete with other borrowers for capital and must demonstrate the soundness of the business plans and pay premiums according to the riskiness of their ventures. The Israeli economist Michael Keren summed up the essential function of the capital market:

> The basic service the capital market supplies is the evaluation of each traded firm's net worth. This signals to its management and its owners how the market judges its future prospects. If this value declines relative to that of similar firms, this may be taken as an indication that the market considers the firm's policies inferior to those of its competitors. In severe situations, this may convey a recommendation to change the top management team of the firm, possibly through a takeover by an alternative team. In extreme cases, when the market believes that the expected present value of the firm's cash flow is

negative or significantly below the breakup value of the firm, the capital market may apply direct sanctions by bankrupting the firm.[2]

Making Capital Decisions Under Socialism

In the absence of an objective capital market, decisions about which firms are to be given funds for capital investment and which denied must be made by a political process. We can conceive of two broad institutional approaches to addressing this problem. On the one hand, we can allow allocation of capital among competing investment projects to be in the hands of a state hierarchy, consisting of the political leaders and the bureaucrats, the approach followed under central planning in the Soviet Union and Soviet bloc. The politicians laid down guidelines, while the planners crafted the plan, and any perceived deviation by the planners from the interest of the politicians would likely be met by their discipline or removal. The system produced mixed results: the growth of heavy industry was both rapid and sustained, but enterprise managers felt little incentive to innovate and new enterprises were few. Bankruptcies were even more rare as the political process often acted to preserve the status quo. These tendencies impeded the development and adoption of new technology by the planned economies and may account for their ultimate failure in the face of the technological revolution of the 1980s.

An alternative approach might be to establish "investment boards," made up of impartial "experts" who could take a dispassionate view of the prospects of various potential enterprises. Unless specific arrangements were made to protect their tenure, and hence to insulate the board members, this approach only pushes the problem one step away. The performance of the boards would not be subject to an independent evaluation, but the board members would serve at the pleasure of the politicians and would themselves be political appointees. Safeguards (such as long-term tenure) could be designed to insulate such boards from political pressure, but they are not likely to be perfect. Under such political uncertainty, it is difficult to see how the action of any planning agency or board can effectively simulate the performance of a financial market. In the market, the weighted opinion of many market participants, rather than one individual or group, decides the fate of firms. The best that can be done in its place is a considered judgment by a narrower group that can never be impersonal.

It can, however, be argued with some justification that the behavior of investment boards or planners might in some cases be better than the behavior of the market. Markets might be short-sighted in their evaluation of prospects, and deny capital to enterprises that, though worthy, will be slow to pay back principal. Planners or investment boards might be more capable of taking a longer view. It is also possible that planning might facilitate a more comprehensive view of the costs and gains of a project than the market does. Market decisions frequently fail to take into account significant positive and negative externalities, and, in theory at least, plan-

---

[2]Michael Keren, "On the (Im)Possibility of Market Socialism," in *The Road to Capitalism*, Kennett and Lieberman, eds. (Fort Worth, TX: Harcourt Brace, 1993), pp. 45–52.

ners can take a more holistic view of the cost-benefit matrix of an investment. Consider, for example, constructing a railway line. A private firm would consider only the costs and revenues of the venture itself. A planning or investment board would want to take into consideration a much broader set of effects: the effect of alleviating road congestion in transport, the impact on the environment, and so forth. With respect to investments with infrastructural and spillover consequences, the board might well arrive at a more socially optimal decision than the market.

Ludwig von Mises, the promarket Austrian economist, argued trenchantly that a socialist state would be unable to handle the question of a railway investment well:

> Suppose, for instance, that the socialist commonwealth was contemplating a new railway line. Would a new railway line be a good thing? If so, which of many possible routes should it cover? Under a system of private ownership we could use money calculations to decide these questions. The new line would cheapen the transportation of certain articles, and, on this basis, we could estimate whether the reduction in transport charges would be great enough to counterweigh the expenditure which the building and running of the line would involve. Such a calculation could be made only in money. We could not do it by comparing various classes of expenditure and savings in kind. If it is out of the question to reduce to a common unit the quantities of various kinds of skilled and unskilled labor, iron, coal, building materials of different kinds, machinery, and the other things which the building and upkeep of railways necessitate, then it is impossible to make them the subject of economic calculation. We can make systematic economic plans only when all the commodities which we have to take into account can be assimilated to money. True, money calculations are incomplete. True, they have profound deficiencies. But we have nothing better to put in their place. And, under sound monetary conditions, they suffice for practical purposes. If we abandon them, economic calculation becomes absolutely impossible.[3]

Even though von Mises's point that rational planning requires valuation in terms of some comparable unit is quite valid, it is by no means clear that his example is a good one. A government may be much more qualified to calculate the complete benefits over space and time of a major infrastructural improvement. For example, the establishment of a railway line will involve inevitable consequences for other means of transportation. Roads will be less congested, pollution will be lowered, time will be saved, and other spillovers experienced. Quite contrary to von Mises's assertion, the planner is better able to consider the social benefit of large-scale infrastructural change.

The Soft-Budget Constraint

The political control of investment credit is a facet of a general problem articulated by the Hungarian economist Janos Kornai.[4] He spent much of his career within the Hungarian planning bureaucracy and well understood the way that such a system operated. The soft-budget constraint refers to a situation in which the firm or enter-

---

[3]Ludwig von Mises, "Economic Calculation in Socialism," in *The Road to Capitalism,* David Kennett and Marc Lieberman, eds. (Fort Worth, TX: Harcourt Brace, 1993), pp. 38–39.
[4]Janos Kornai, "The Soft Budget Constraint," *Kyklos* 39, 1986, pp. 3–30.

prise is unconstrained by the basic maxim that long-run revenues must exceed long-run costs. A hard-budget constraint is experienced by firms in competitive markets. They cannot expect to receive a subsidy toward the operation in the long run, and they therefore must earn enough revenue to meet their costs of materials and factors of production including capital. Although they might go into debt in the short run, in the long run the debt must be amortized.

In socialist economies, because both capital costs and operating costs are frequently subsidized by the state, the soft-budget constraint is the norm, not the exception. Subtle ways of introducing "softness" into the system include direct subsidies, discriminatory taxation, or the manipulation of administered prices to ensure the appearance of financial viability. In this chapter, however, what concerns us is the existence of "soft credit," a phenomenon that embraces two related features. The first is the provision of credit at an interest rate that fails to reflect the opportunity cost of capital, implying that the demand for investment funds will generally speaking exceed its supply and that it must be allocated or rationed by a nonprice system, opening the door to political or personal favoritism. By itself, however, a nonprice allocation system does not necessarily represent soft credit: if payment reschedules require adherence, then even loans at subsidized interest rates can be "hard." If debt service payments are not met, then the firm can be forced into bankruptcy, merger, or takeover. What makes the system truly "soft" is a second feature: the knowledge that the political process will ensure the continued existence and even the growth of the firm despite continued failure to meet the prescribed repayment schedule. The **soft-budget constraint** enables the firm to continue to exist although its long-term obligations are not met. To put it a different way, its long-term expenditures are greater than its long-term revenue, and credit continues to be granted by the authorities, even in the face of little prospect of repayment.

The Impact of Soft-Budget Constraints on the Conduct of the Enterprise

If the firm believes that its budget constraint is indeed soft, incentives exist for it to behave in ways that will lower the efficiency of the economy. The firm's elasticity of demand for inputs will become markedly reduced. If increases in costs are compensated by external assistance, an enterprise manager sees little reason to economize on the use of the newly expensive factor. Under a soft-budget constraint, a rise in input prices does not lead a decision maker to change input mix or alter output level but rather to get on the phone to persuade the planners to change prices or to grant additional credits. Although the short-term consequences may be grave, the longer term is of greater consequence. Kornai summarized this situation:

> The most important issue is dynamic adjustment. If the budget constraint is hard, the firm has no other option but to adjust to unfavorable circumstances by improving quality, cutting costs, introducing new products or processes, i.e., it must behave in an entrepreneurial manner. If, however, the budget constraint is soft, such productive efforts are no longer imperative. Instead, the firm is likely to seek external assistance, asking for compensation for unfavorable external circumstances. The State is acting like an overall insurance company taking over all the moral hazards with the usual well-known consequences; the

insured will be less careful in protecting his wealth. [Joseph] Schumpeter [the Austrian economist] emphasized the significance of "creative destruction": the elimination of old products, technologies, organizations which were surpassed by the more efficient new ones. The soft budget constraint protects the old production line, the inefficient firm against constructive destruction and thus impedes innovation and development.[5]

The Possibility of Market Socialism

The foregoing argument suggests that the problems of capital allocation are fatal to any attempt at market socialism. Whenever investment funds are controlled by the government, or by boards appointed by the government, some softness in capital allocation becomes inevitable. Enterprise managers, knowing that projects are ultimately supported on political rather than economic grounds, will not adopt the behavior that results in allocative efficiency.

In Keren's terms, the vital aims of market socialism are equality and decentralized decision making. The former requires the public ownership of productive assets. The latter requires hard-budget constraints and an absence of state intervention. However, these two aims are in conflict. The exclusion of private market and the political bureaucratic process cannot serve as an adequate proxy. Enterprises become aware that survival and growth are politically, not economically, determined, and their behavior changes as a result.

Although it is hard to pick holes in this logic, its flaw is that it sets straw men against each other. Financial markets, because they are disinterested, are assumed to be superior to the political process in allocating investment. However, the lessons of recent history are that private markets are capable of enormous errors in granting funds to projects that fail—the U.S. savings and loans crisis and the Asian banking debacle are two examples that stand out.[6] Similarly, socially owned banking systems—for example, in Taiwan or in France during "les trentes gloirieuses"—performed an adequate job in credit allocation. A pure market can offer advantages in allocative efficiency over politically controlled investment processes, but myopia, panic, and a narrow definition of the "bottom line" are all problems that can afflict a market system and can lead to social consequences that are difficult to predict and expensive to correct.

THE SOCIAL MARKET ECONOMY

The European Model

Market socialism now seems to be largely out of favor, but the search for a middle way is nevertheless active. European nations that swung to the right in the 1980s, moved back to the left by the mid-1990s, and their economies embody high degrees

---

[5]Kornai, "The Soft Budget Constraint," *Kyklos* 39, 1986, pp. 10–11.
[6]The indigenous financial systems of most East Asian countries relied on directed credit; however, much of the blame for the crisis must be placed on the inflow and outflow of "hot" monies from competitive financial systems.

of regulation and redistribution. The alternative to nationalizing the means of production (which denies private ownership of most capital and hence the appropriation of its income stream by individuals) is to allow a market to operate for all goods and factors of production, including capital, but to use the power of the state to modify, to regulate, and to guarantee the distribution of income and to ensure access to basic services and opportunities. We already looked at two good examples of this kind of economic organization in Sweden (Chapter 7) and in the Federal Republic of Germany (Chapter 9). In fact, the ethic of the entire European Union might well be described as social market oriented.

The Stakeholder and the Stockholder

The German model of worker participation and involvement in decision making (sometimes called the **Rhine model**) calls into question the conception of the **Anglo-Saxon model** that a firm's sole responsibility is to its stockholders. In Germany the system of codetermination, with labor involved in management decision making, establishes the principle that others besides the "owners" of the corporation have a stake in its future and therefore a voice in its management. This notion brings us to a discussion of what is now referred to as the stakeholder economy.

A **stakeholder** is defined as someone who, while not a titular owner of a business, holds a legitimate interest in its performance and success. The stakeholders of a corporation may include not only the shareholders but also labor, management, customers, suppliers, lenders, and the community in which the corporation is located. Consequently, stakeholders' legitimacy comes from the ability to influence the performance of the corporation.

It is difficult to draw strong conclusions about the effect that the legitimation of a wide range of interests in the decisions of firms does to economic performance. If the behavior of the corporation is indeed meaningfully modified by recognizing stakeholder preferences, and if that behavior is not consistent with profit maximization, it should follow that the "stakeholder corporation" might experience difficulty because it will underperform its "profit-oriented" competitors. Less profitable than a profit-maximizing corporation unconstrained by stakeholder preferences, a stakeholder corporation would therefore be vulnerable to, and ultimately eliminated, by market forces.

If, in fact, pleasing the stakeholders contributes to the maximization of long-term profits, then no conflict exists. *The Economist,* in reviewing a recent book by John Kay, a prominent British economist, who favors the view that the corporation is a "social institution" beholden to a range of stakeholders rather than a private one beholden only to its owners, declared such a view to be "either trivial or meaningless. Few companies, bar perhaps monopoly utilities, can afford to have a miserable workforce or disgruntled customers. If, that is, they want to be successful. Presumably that means making money for their customers."[7]

---

[7]*The Economist,* "Money Making," a review of *The Business of Economics* by John Kay (Oxford: Oxford University Press, 1996). Review of Books and Media, November 16, 1996, p. 12.

However, other interpretations merit consideration. For example, take the issue of labor's "stake" in its employer. Clearly in Japan where the institution of lifetime employment covers at least some of the workforce of the major employers, workers possess a greater recognized stake than in, say, the United States. This relationship hampered the ability of Japanese corporations to deal with the downturn in demand that has afflicted the economy since 1990. The productivity and profitability of Japanese firms was adversely affected by their inability to restructure the workforce. In the United States, in contrast, downturns in demand, or profitability, can be met by trimming the workforce, as in the well-documented downsizing of the early 1990s. Similarly, if a company takes seriously its obligations to a community, should that commitment to its neighbor/stakeholders be at the expense of shareholders?

Within the German model the most important stakeholders in the firm are, on the one hand, the employees and, on the other, the bankers, who lend the enterprise most of its capital. Often the same banks also own some of the shares of the firm, which is allowed under German law, but generally includes only a small part of total equity.[8] However, the banks' considerable influence in the firm comes from representation on the supervisory boards and also control of the voting power of the shares they hold for clients in their role as stockbrokers and mutual fund managers. A growing criticism in Germany centers on the issue of whether the interest of the banks as lenders may be in conflict with the interest of the shareholders. In recent years, a rising activism by shareholders focused on maximizing the return to their capital. Table 19.1 shows the dominance of banks in decision making in major German corporations. This power originates not primarily from bank ownership of stock but its ability to vote by proxy the shares held in investment funds and in customer accounts, an unusual aspect of German law.

Stakeholders As Shareholders

One way in which the potential conflict between the rights of shareholders and the claims of other stakeholders might be resolved is by extension of share ownership to stakeholders. This arrangement could be used to resolve to some degree the principal-agent issues that traditionally affect the labor-capital relationship. A growing number of firms are providing incentives for workers in the form of preferential employee ownership schemes, which tend to bring interests of capital and labor into much closer alignment. A similar solution might also be possible in the case of a local government, which could take an equity holding in a major local employer. Such an arrangement would, however, raise complexities of the municipalities' attitude to new entrants and competitors and might bias the level playing field.

The government in the United States actively favors the extension of employee ownership and offers considerable tax advantages to firms that institute employee stock ownership programs, resulting in a rise in worker ownership of firms. Table

---

[8]In 1994 private banks directly held about 0.4 percent of German industrial capital, down from 1.3 percent in 1976. *The Economist*, January 3, 1995.

■ **TABLE 19.1**

Banks' Share of Voting Rights at AGMs of Large German Companies, 1992

Shares Owned By:

Company	Banks	Subsidiary Investment Funds	Proxy Votes	Total Bank Votes
Siemens	—	9.87	85.61	95.48
Volkswagen	—	8.89	35.16	44.05
Hoechst	—	10.74	87.72	98.46
BASF	0.09	13.61	81.01	94.71
Bayer	—	11.23	80.09	91.32
Thyssen	6.77	3.62	34.98	45.37
VEBA	—	12.62	78.23	90.85
Mannesmann	—	7.76	90.35	98.11
Deutsche Bank	—	12.41	82.32	94.73
MAN	8.67	12.69	26.84	48.2

SOURCE: *The Economist,* June 3, 1995, p. 66.

19.2 shows the 10 largest majority employee-owned corporations in the United States. Although some are quite large, they are clearly only a tiny fraction of the total economy and tend to be concentrated in service industries. It is also worth observing that even employee ownership does not mean peace between the management and the workforce. The roles of worker and owner might be in conflict. In the fall of 2002 the machinists union, whose members are among the majority ownership of the United Airlines, embarked upon a damaging strike against the airline.

In addition to the firms of Table 19.2 in which the employees have more than 50 percent of equity, employees in many more companies hold a significant part of the shares. The ESOP Association reports that more than 10,000 U.S. corporations offer employee stock option plans. About 10 percent, or 1,000 of these companies are publicly listed. Moreover, many workers in the United States and elsewhere have a financial interest in their employer. One avenue is by the heavy investment of corporate pension funds in employer stock. One study found that employer stock represented almost 20 percent of assets in defined benefit corporate pension plans.[9] Another is the widespread use of 401(k) plans that often give strong incentives to workers who invest in company stock.

Some evidence suggests that involving employees as formal "at risk" stakeholders does lead to better performance than in the conventional corporation in which workers have no ownership stake. In 2000, Blasi and colleagues concluded that corporations with ESOP plans grew faster (at a rate of 2.3% annually) than did

[9]Committee on Education Workforce, U.S. Congress, Testimony of Dr. Douglas Kruse, Ph.D., Rutgers University, Wednesday, February, 13, 2002.

■ **TABLE *19*.2**

The 10 Largest Firms in the United States with Employee Holdings Above 50 Percent of Total Equity, 2002

Company	Plan	Business	Number of Employees
United Parcel Service	401k	Package Delivery	344,000
Publix Supermarkets	ESOP, stock purchase	Supermarkets	111,000
United Airlines	ESOP	Airline	98,400
Hy-Vee	ESOP	Supermarkets	46,000
Science Applications, Intl.	multiple	R&D/Computer Systems	41,000
Lifetouch	ESOP	Photography Studios	25,890
Tharaldson Motels	ESOP	Motel Management	18,980
Amsted Industries	ESOP	Industrial Production	12,500
CH2M Hill, Inc.	stock purchase	Engineering & Construction	12,000
Parsons Corp.	ESOP	Engineering, Mining & Construction	12,000

SOURCE: National Center for Employee Ownership, "The Employee Ownership 100," available at http://www.nceo.org/ (accessed June 2003).

firms without such plans.[10] However, this improvement is not automatic. Kruse found that "employee ownership may have positive effects if employees value ownership in itself or perceive that it brings greater income, job security, or control over jobs and the workplace. On the other hand, it may have negligible or even negative effects if employees perceive no difference in their worklives, dislike the extra risk to their income or wealth, or have raised expectations that are not fulfilled."

Cooperative Organization

One widely spread alternative to the corporate system is provided by the cooperative movement, which can be traced back to a group of 28 textile workers who organized the *Rochdale Society of Equitable Pioneers*. In 1844, a group of English weavers, dismissed and blacklisted by mill owners for trying to organize a trade union, pooled £140 to open a small dry goods store stocked with oatmeal, sugar, butter, and flour. Out of this grew a large and successful wholesale and retailing system, and it proved the inspiration for cooperative and mutual activity in a wide range of areas.

The founders of the movement codified their ideology into four precepts commonly known as the **Rochdale Principles**, which survive in their broad meaning today.[11]

[10]Joseph Blasi, Douglas Kruse, James Sesil, Maya Kroumova, and Ryan Weeden, *Stock Options, Corporate Performance, and Organizational Change* (Oakland, CA: National Center for Employee Ownership, 2000).
[11]In fact the International Cooperative Alliance has refined the basic four principles to a current seven. See the ICA Web page http://www.ica.coop/ica/info/.

1. Cooperatives are member-owned and -controlled businesses in which all members have an equal say in the governance of the business: one member, one vote. Co-ops stand in contrast to proprietary ownership, in which one person holds all of the authority, and "traditional" corporate ownership, which bases control on the size of one's investment.

2. Cooperatives serve their members, and not the interests of speculative capital. By establishing limits on the return of investment and on share holdings, co-operatives discourage profit-seeking investments. Instead co-ops encourage local control and investments by the people who use the business.

3. Cooperatives help the members actively govern their organization through education and help other cooperatives to better serve their members by buying goods from other cooperatives and providing development assistance to organizing groups.

4. Cooperatives exist not just for the benefit of the members but to serve, strengthen, and sustain local communities. They are community organizations.

The cooperative movement is a strong and diversified one. In Sweden and Japan, cooperative businesses figure prominently in the national economies. In many Third World countries, cooperatives such as credit unions and agricultural organizations successfully help people provide for themselves where private and other corporate capital do not see high profitability. In the United States, cooperative organization is seen in rural electric co-ops, agricultural co-ops, and credit unions.

The Future of Stakeholding

Conflicting trends are at work about the future of stakeholder organization. Some hold it out as an essential key to the future, while some of the most long-lived stakeholder institutions are under threat. Britain, for example, is experiencing a movement toward a broader involvement of interested parties in corporate decision-taking and more official recognition of the legitimacy of stakeholders' interests. It was a feature of the electoral platform of Tony Blair's New Labour, in which the "stakeholder economy" was promoted without rigorous definition, serving as a rather loose collectivist concept. In concrete terms the most obvious trend involves the increased ownership of firms by their workers through **employee stock ownership plans (ESOPs)**.

Running directly against a trend toward increased stakeholder, particularly employee, ownership are the attacks mounted on some of the older forms of stakeholder involvement in recent years. In Britain the same criticisms leveled against publicly owned industry were turned against a large mutual sector composed of **retail cooperatives**, building societies (**mutual thrift institutions**), and mutual insurance societies. These institutions were charged with bad management and low productivity. One particular factor was most frequently cited. In private industry, the accepted solution to the principal-agent dilemma stemming from the separation of management and ownership was to give pecuniary incentives to top management through the use of stock options. In the mutual sector, no comparable way could offer equivalent rewards for management performance, prompting the claim that this practice damaged performance. In a short span of time many of Britain's large building societies, and some mutual insurance companies, were converted into joint stock companies, distributing the shares among management, depositors, and borrowers.

This process was given the rather ugly name of **demutualization**. The economic rationale behind it assumes that mutuals—which are comprehensive stakeholder organizations in which customers (both depositors and borrowers in the case of thrift associations) and potential future customers hold an interest—are less efficient organizations than conventionally organized corporations. Mutuals not only lack the ability to offer stock option remuneration schemes, but also they cannot raise capital on the stock market, but rely instead on debt finance. These factors, it was argued, lead to inefficiency relative to joint stock companies and unless action was taken they would lose out in the market place. An alternative explanation describes a systematic pillaging of the building societies by management and "carpetbaggers" to the detriment of other present and future stakeholders. Explanations focusing on efficiency do not answer the question of why the mutual thrifts were so successful for such a long time and grew to such power.[12] In the retail sector, the cooperative societies founded in the nineteenth century to give customer stakeholders a share in the management and profit of retailing are also experiencing hard times. Again, this decline is frequently attributed to the absence of incentives for management because of an inability to use stock option schemes.

In the United States the rapid downsizing that occurred in the early 1990s brought forth criticism, notably from Robert Reich, then secretary of labor in the Clinton administration, that firms must be forced to live up to their obligations to stakeholders and accept this role in and responsibility to a broader community. This statement prompted a broad debate on the nature of **corporate social responsibility** and a discussion as to the extent to which corporations were obliged to further the interests of others beyond their shareholders. Toward the end of the 1990s the stock market boom was associated with the claims that management was aggressively promoting shareholder value. However, the collapse of that boom and the revelation of highly questionable accounting practices led to a realization that management interests took primacy over the shareholders, and other stakeholders (workers and communities) were neglected almost entirely. These events sparked a debate as to whether the whole structure of corporate governance in America should be reviewed. Particular criticisms focused on a command structure too concentrated in a single individual—the chief executive officer—who also is frequently the chair of the board of directors. A powerful independent board, or **supervising board**, would be in position to provide a check on executive management behavior and practices.

Concurrent with the criticism of the management of publicly held corporations, mutual organizations continue to show some gains. In contrast to the United Kingdom, the fastest growing elements of the retail financial industry in the United

---

[12]In July 1999 the British Treasury issued a report on *Demutualisation,* Ninth Report of the Select Committee of the Treasury, HMSO (July 22, 1999). It examined the case for and against mutual societies, but in general saw no reason to oppose demutualization.

THE THIRD WAY

The popular appeal in the current drive to find the "Third Way" in politics has been effectively harnessed by Tony Blair's New Labour in Britain and by Gerhard Schroeder's "New Centre" in Germany. Both speak of a need to extend democracy, broaden property ownership, and take up the challenge of rapid change. Both were apparently inspired by the book *The Third Way: The Renewal of Social Democracy*, written by Anthony Giddens, a sociologist and the Director of the London School of Economics. However, some critics find the rhetoric rather empty. Ralf Dahrendorf, another sociologist, who preceded Giddens as director of the LSE described the "Third Way" "as a politics that speaks of the need for hard choices but then avoids them by trying to please everybody." Among those who are apparently pleased is Senator Hillary Clinton who speaks of the "Third Way" as a "unified theory of life which will marry conservatism and liberalism, capitalism and statism, and tie together practically everything: the way we are, the way we were, the faults of man and the word of God, the end of communism and the beginning of the third millennium." It contains the universalism that characterized the failed "isms" of the 20th century. In its present form it has great appeal but few teeth.

SOURCES: Anthony Giddens, *The Third Way: The Renewal of Social Democracy* (London: Polity Press, 2000); Gerard DeGroot, "The Third Way," *Christian Science Monitor,* June 14, 2000, p. 9, available at http://csmweb2.emcweb.com/durable/2000/06/14/f-p9s1.shtml.

States are the credit unions and mutual societies where both borrower and lender hold an interest. Germany's large mutual sector, especially in finance, contains 2,500 mutual banking institutions with more than 14 million members and 20,000 branches. Few signs indicate that these German associations will be converted into joint stock companies as in the United Kingdom, because mutual organization conforms well to the German philosophy of **codetermination**, although interest in the British experience continues to grow.[13]

CONCLUSION

The prospect of some kind of third way will continue to intrigue many people, and interest in it is likely to be fed in the future by several trends. One is the widening economic disparity growing out of the economic expansion of the 1990s. Broader ownership of capital would certainly lead to a more egalitarian distribution of income, but by what institutional structure should that reallocation be effected? It is relatively easy to be in favor of greater equality, but the heavy taxation of income, wealth, and inheritance that would be required runs counter to the prevailing political trends in most of the West.

A second factor that favors a different way is the growing concern for the environment in its broadest sense, involving not only pollution but also the demise and decay of traditional patterns of settlement and interaction. The greater pursuit of

[13]See "Demutualisation in Germany. Inconceivable?" *The Economist,* January 3, 1998.

sustainability, however, involves an erosion of individual property rights in favor of a broader, intergenerational conception. Again it is not clear that this outcome would be a politically acceptable in every part of the world. In Europe, it is true that the development of the EU has involved increasing collective rights at the expense of the individual. In the United States, Russia, and China at least the reverse is true. Together, however, concern for equity and environment focuses attention on what its proponents call the social economy that attempts to define as stakeholders a much broader spectrum of interests than capital, labor, and government. It is important to remember that attempts in the past to follow a middle road, whether in Yugoslavia or Sweden, found it to be a more difficult path than its inherent appeal would indicate.

KEY TERMS AND CONCEPTS

Anglo-Saxon model

codetermination

corporate social responsibility

demutualization

employee stock ownership
plans (ESOPs)

market socialism

mutual thrift institutions

retail cooperatives

Rhine model

Rochdale Principles

social market economy

soft-budget constraint

stakeholder

supervising board

QUESTIONS FOR DISCUSSION

1. Distinguish between market socialism and a social market economy. Give examples of each.
2. Why is the absence of a capital market potentially fatal to market socialism?
3. Distinguish between hard-budget and soft-budget constraints.
4. Which, in your view, is better to determine the social value of a major change in the transportation system—the market or a government? Why?
5. Should stakeholders who are not owners have a say in a firm's decision making? Will a firm who recognizes its stakeholders' interests be competed out of business?
6. Why does the trend to employee stock option plans offer a way out of the principal-agent problem?
7. Why are so many traditional "mutual" firms being converted into stockholder firms? Is this shift good in the long run?
8. Why does the practice of issuing options to management threaten the interest of other stakeholders?

RESOURCES

Web Sites

The National Center for Employee Ownership....................................http://www.nceo.org/

The Association for Social Economics ....http://www.socialeconomics.org/

The U.K. Social Economy Forum ....http://www.social-economy.org.uk/

Aries, Social Economy Online
Aries is a Euro Info Center (EIC) for the Social Economy. ARIES provides an online information, news, and networking service designed to help social economy organizations to work together and take action at the European level ....http://www.poptel.org.uk/aries/

European Confederation of Workers' Cooperatives, Social Cooperatives, and Participative Enterprises ....http://www.cecop.org/

International Cooperative Alliance ....http://www.coop.org/

The Netherlands Participation Institute (NPI) ....http://www.snpi.nl/

The Center for Economic and Social Justice ....http://www.cesj.org/

The ESOP Association (United States) ....http://www.esopassociation.org/

Integra Review...................................http://www.iol.ie/EMPLOYMENT/integra/sepp.html

Treasury Select Committee Report on Demutualization...
....http://www.parliament.the-stationery-office.co.uk/pa/cm199899/
cmselect/cmtreasy/605/60502.htm

Books and Articles

Ackerman, Bruce, and Ann Alstott. *The Stakeholder Society.* New Haven, CT: Yale University Press, 1999.

Bamberger, Bill, and Cathy Davidson. *Closing: The Life and Death of an American Factory.* New York: W.W. Norton, 1998.

Carroll, Archie B. *Business and Society: Ethics and Stakeholder Management.* Cincinnati, OH: South-Western Publishers, 1996.

Giddens, Anthony. *The Third Way: The Renewal of Social Democracy.* London: Polity Press, 2000.

Hutton, Bill, and David Goldblatt (eds.). *The Stakeholding Society: Writings on Politics and Economics.* New York: Blackwell, 1999.

Kay, John. *The Business of Economics.* Oxford: Oxford University Press, 1996.

Kelly, Gavin, Dominic Kelly, and Andrew Gamble. *Stakeholder Capitalism.* New York: St. Martin's Press, 1997.

Keren, Michael. "On the (Im)Possibility of Market Socialism," In *The Road to Capitalism,* pp. 45–52. David Kennett and Marc Lieberman (eds.). Fort Worth, TX: Harcourt Brace, 1993.

Le Grand, Julian, and Saul Estrin (eds.). *Market Socialism.* Oxford: Clarendon Press, 1989.

Minford, Patrick. *Markets Not Stakes: The Triumph of Capitalism and the Stakeholder Fallacy.* London: Trafalgar Square, 1998.

Plender, John. *A Stake in the Future: The Stakeholding Society.* London: Nicholas Brealey, 1997.

Turner, Lowell. *Negotiating the New Germany: Can Social Partnership Survive?* Ithaca, NY: ILR Press, 1997.

Yunker, James A. *Socialism Revised and Modernized: The Case for Pragmatic Market Socialism.* New York: Praeger, 1992.

PART SIX

The Economics of Transition

20

THE PROCESS OF TRANSITION TO A MARKET ECONOMY

STARTING POINTS

At the high point of the "socialist revolution," almost one-third of the world's population lived in nations using command planning to coordinate their economies. This process started with the Bolshevik revolution in 1917, which led by the end of the 1920s to the institution of centralized planning throughout almost all of the former Tsarist Empire. In the aftermath of World War II, the Baltic nations became an integrated part of the Soviet economy, and Eastern Europe fell under the economic dominance of the Soviet Union. In Asia, the communist Chinese Revolution saw planning introduced in the world's most populous nation and ultimately into the economies of neighboring North Korea and Vietnam. In the Western Hemisphere in the 1960s, Fidel Castro's Cuba began the same experiment and it looked as if Marxism would gain a foothold on the South American mainland. At that point it was easy to believe that central planning was indeed the way of the future and Nikita Khrushchev's boast that "we will bury you" did not seem at all empty.

By the late 1980s most of these economies were faltering. The exception was China, which, as described in Chapter 23, embarked precociously and somewhat serendipitously, on an early reform program, allowing market forces considerable freedom in agriculture and small enterprise. The Soviet economy, on the other hand, experienced serious problems. Industrial output fell stagnant over the previous decade, the consumer goods sector was proving woefully inadequate to meet the growing aspirations of its people, and a faltering parity in the military race with the United States was maintained only at the expense of prioritization, drawing as much as 35 percent of gross domestic product (GDP) into the military sector. The impressive Soviet growth record of the early years of command planning now revealed to have been almost entirely extensive in nature, with output rising only because of increases in the quantities of labor and capital employed, rather than a growth of total factor productivity. Diminishing returns to fixed capital experienced since the 1970s led, by the mid-1990s, to a marginal rate of return on new investment capital close to zero.

In 1985 Russia initiated a gradualist economic reform program under Gorbachev's program of *perestroika* (restructuring) as simultaneous sweeping political change occurred under the label of *glasnost* (usually translated as "openness"). The emergence of *glasnost* and the relative decline in the Soviet Union's military muscle allowed the nations of Central and Eastern Europe to seize their independence and take their own paths away from centralized planning. Meanwhile at home, the failure of *perestroika* to revive the economy contributed directly to the breakup of the Soviet Union. In 1980 centralized command planning was practiced in every country east of Austria and north of the Himalayas as far east as the Pacific Ocean. By 1999 only a few governments were even theoretically committed to planning principles (North Korea and Cuba, for example), and the durability of these regimes is questionable.

Differences in Initial Conditions

Today, about 30 countries in the world are at some stage of a process of *transition* from a centrally planned to a market economy.[1] All share the common feature of their planned past, but their starting points at the outset of transition were quite different. Some of this diversity is shown in Table 20.1, which gives selected figures for most economies in transition. These data show that at the outset of the move to market the countries exhibited wide differences in income per head, which in 1981 ranged from about $9,200 a year in Slovenia, the most northern of the former Yugoslav republics, to only $1,400 in impoverished Albania, the most isolated of the communist economies.[2] Even within the successor states of the Soviet Union wide variations are apparent. The Baltic Republics were, at the start of transition, relatively rich; Latvia had a per-head income (measured in terms of purchasing power parity) of about $8,590 in 1989. The central Asian republics, on the other hand, were poor, the worst off being Uzbekistan, at less than one-third of Latvia's level. It should be emphasized that even the most affluent of the transition economies was a long way from the living standards seen in developed market economies. Average income in Western Europe in 1989, measured in terms of purchasing power, was about twice the level in Latvia. As we shall discuss later, the first years of transition resulted in sharply lower incomes for most formerly planned economies, and the gap widened considerably.

Sharp differences also distinguished the transition states in terms of the level of economic development. This concept is difficult to encapsulate with simple statistics, but the percentage of the labor force engaged in agriculture is a useful index. As Table 20.1 shows, the percent of the population engaged in agriculture ranged from 56 percent in Albania, a largely peasant economy, to a low of 9 percent in the urbanized Baltic states. Again, we should note that even the most developed of transition nations were well behind the developed market economies, which as a rule have less than 5 percent, and as few as 2 percent, of the workforce employed in agriculture.

The relevance of the other statistics given in Table 20.1 is fairly self-evident. The rate of population growth tells us more about the state of overall development, although a great deal of "noise" is also created by religious factors, culture, and even housing availability. The Baltic and Slav states show low rates of population

[1]Of these, 15 once constituted part of the Soviet Union, and three—Slovenia, Croatia, and Macedonia FYR—were part of Yugoslavia. Serbia and Bosnia may also be considered to be in transition, but they do not make the World Bank tables for political reasons.
[2]In actual fact, the highest purchasing power income probably lay in East Germany, but that former economy is not considered transitional in the sense that it merged with the Federal Republic of Germany.

■ **TABLE 20.1**

Selected Indicators for Economies in Transition, 1989

	Population (millions)	PPP GDP per Head 1989	Percentage of Labor Force in Agriculture	Telephones per 100 People	Average Years of Schooling, Population 25+	Population Growth Rate	Monetary Overhang as Percentage of GDP
Eastern Europe							
Albania	3.3	1,400	56	2	6.2	1	4.3
Bulgaria	8.9	5,000	17	32	7.0	20.1	18.0
Croatia	—	6,171	—	—	—	—	12.0
Czechoslovakia	15.7	6,280	11	29	9.2	0.4	27.1
Hungary	10.5	6,810	15	19	9.8	0	27.7
Macedonia FYR	—	3,394	—	—	—	—	12.0
Poland	38.4	5,150	27	15	8.2	0.4	13.6
Romania	23.3	3,470	29	13	7.1	0.4	16.8
Slovenia	—	9,200	—	—	—	—	12.0
Former Soviet Union							
Armenia	3.5	5,530	11	18	5.0	0.4	25.7
Azerbaijan	7.3	4,620	15	10	5.0	1.2	25.7
Belarus	10.3	7,010		16	7.0	0.6	25.7
Estonia	1.6	8,900	9	21	9.0	0.0	25.7
Georgia	5.5	5,590	14	10	5.0	0.7	25.7
Kazakstan	17.0	5,130	20	11	5.0	0.9	25.7
Kyrgyz Republic	4.5	3,180	16	7	5.0	1.8	25.7
Latvia	2.7	8,590	9	24	9.0	20.1	25.7
Lithuania	3.8	6,430	10	22	9.0	0.1	25.7
Moldova	4.4	4,670	21	11	6.0	0.7	25.7
Russian Federation	149.0	7,720	20	15	9.0	0.5	25.7
Tajikistan	5.6	3,010	14	5	5.0	2.7	25.7
Turkmenistan	3.9	4,230	—	6	5.0	1.9	25.7
Ukraine	52.2	5,680	—	16	6.0	0.4	25.7
Uzbekistan	21.5	2,740	17	7	5.0	2.0	25.7
Mongolia		2,100	40	3	7.2	2.6	7.6

SOURCE: Martha de Melo, Cevder Denizer, and Alan Gelb, "Patterns of Transition from Plan to Market," *World Bank Economic Review* 10, no. 3 (September 1996), p. 400; UNDP Human Development Report, 1997.

growth, while the Islamic populations of central Asia are still growing as fast as 2 percent per year. Similarly, wide differences separate the countries in the quantity of human capital, which is crudely measured by the average years of schooling of the adult (25 years old and more) population.

The final column in Table 20.1, the **monetary overhang**, provides an important index of macroeconomic imbalance, to which we will return later. At this point, we use it as one measure of the degree to which consumer goods were undersupplied during the last years of the planning regimes. Recall from earlier discussion that in many cases the wage payments made to workers in centrally planned economies were greater than the amount that the consumers were able, or willing, to spend on the available (often poor-quality) consumer goods. This circumstance led to the buildup of the monetary overhang, which consists of cash and savings bank deposits that represent latent purchasing power. As long as prices were centrally controlled by fiat, this potential excess buying power could exert little effect on the overall price level.[3] However, once the process of price liberalization started, the monetary overhang manifested itself as an inflationary pressure. The only alternative to allowing inflation to work itself through was neutralization by appropriate and aggressive contractionary policy measures, which would result in a highly depressing effect on output and welfare.

The figures in Table 20.1 show that the monetary overhang in the Soviet Union in 1989 was the most serious encountered in any of the transition nations. It is statistically impossible to disaggregate this all-union figure among the successor states, and so all show an identical figure of more than 25 percent, symptomatic of a potentially serious problem of repressed inflation. As it happened, the monetary overhang did provide an initial stimulus to inflation, but it could not be held responsible for the continuing price spiral, which lasted for several years, precisely because the purchasing power of the overhang was rapidly depleted to insignificance by inflation itself. In the countries of Eastern Europe, the monetary overhang was by no means as great as in the Soviet Union, and the negative figures in the Czech Republic and Hungary indicate a growing use of consumer credit and the greater availability of consumer goods, which allowed consumers to incur household debt.

Common Features

However, despite these differences, all of the transition economies shared at the outset several important points of commonality:

1. In all of these economies, macroeconomic balance was achieved by direct control of the planning agencies rather than by a reliance on the market or the more conventional tools of macroeconomic demand management used in the developed economies. (It was the failure to keep the purchasing power of total wage payments equilibrated with the available supply of goods to be purchased by consumers that led to the existence of the monetary overhang.)

2. The plan, not the market, was the primary coordination mechanism of the economy.

---

[3]Of course, prices could be bid up on the black market, and were. Also, the monetary overhang found its way into the illegal currency markets. Rubles, of limited use because of the shortage of consumer goods, were exchanged for "hard" currency at exchange rates wildly different from the official ones. The hard currency so obtained could be expatriated or used to buy goods in hard currency stores (called berioskas in Russia).

3. No adequate institutional framework existed within which a market economy could operate. This deficiency was clearest in terms of intertemporal coordination, where the absence of defined property rights and enforceable contracts was most limiting.

4. The relative prices of goods and factors of production reflected neither relative costs nor relative scarcities.

5. Entry into most economic activity was controlled by the government, and many activities that would be regarded as socially beneficial in a market economy were illegal during, and in the immediate aftermath, of central planning.

6. The extent of private property was limited. Although in some countries (e.g., the former Yugoslavia) an attempt was made to combine socially owned capital with market coordination, such experiments failed in general to be fruitful. The rapid extension of private property is valuable in two ways. First, it makes the market function better, largely by reducing principal-agent problems. Second, it gives the citizens a stake in preserving the permanence of the new arrangements.

7. Foreign trade was controlled by the state and therefore the efficiency-enhancing impact of foreign competition was largely absent.

THE STEPS OF TRANSITION

Transition from a planned to a market economy is not a single step but a series of moves that must be made in sequence, and some countries advanced with greater speed than others. Table 20.2 gives statistics for the performance of 26 economies in transition, divided into subgroups according to their performance on a liberalization index, prepared by economists from the World Bank.[4] This index is compounded from three sets of considerations: the liberalization of the domestic economy, external transactions, and the private sector entry. **Domestic liberalization** consists of the ending of price controls as well as the termination of the monopoly privileges of state enterprises. It carries a weight of .3 in the construction of the index. **External transactions liberalization** ends export controls and export taxes, establishes current account convertibility, and substitutes a moderate tariff regime for quantitative import controls. It also carries a weight of .3. The final component, **private sector entry liberalization**, measures the extent of progress in the privatization of state assets and the entry of new firms. Its weight in the overall index is .4.

The **advanced reformers** included the five states in Central and Eastern Europe: Slovenia, Poland, Hungary, and the two parts of former Czechoslovakia—the

---

[4]For more detail on the construction of the liberalization index, see *From Plan to Market: World Development Report 1996*, Martha de Melo, Cevder Denizer, and Alan Gelb, "Patterns of Transition from Plan to Market," *World Bank Economic Review* 10, no. 3 (September 1996), pp. 397 ff.

■ **TABLE 20.2**

Liberalization, Growth, and Inflation in 26 Countries in Transition, 1989–1994

	Cumulative Liberalization Index 1994	Average Liberalization 1993–1994	Average Inflation Rate 1993–1994 (percent)	Average Annual GDP Growth 1993–1994	Average GDP in 1993–1994 as a Percentage of 1989 GDP	Lowest Level of GDP as a Percentage of 1989 GDP
Advanced Reformers						
Slovenia	4.16	0.82	26	3.0	84	81
Poland	4.14	0.84	34	4.2	88	82
Hungary	4.11	0.84	21	0.0	81	80
Czech Republic	3.61	0.90	16	0.8	81	80
Slovak Republic	3.47	0.86	19	0.4	79	77
Average	3.90	0.85	23	1.7	83	80
High Intermediate Reformers						
Estonia	2.93	0.85	69	0.9	69	67
Bulgaria	2.90	0.68	81	21.4	73	73
Lithuania	2.72	0.79	231	27.3	44	44
Latvia	2.45	0.71	73	24.4	60	59
Albania	2.30	0.70	57	9.5	74	65
Romania	2.29	0.66	194	2.2	69	67
Mongolia	2.27	0.64	164	0.6	84	83
Average	2.55	0.72	124	0.0	67	65
Low Intermediate Reformers						
Russian Federation	1.92	0.63	558	213.5	57	52
Kyrgyz Republic	1.81	0.68	744	213.2	61	57
Moldova	1.62	0.53	558	217.0	53	46
Kazakstan	1.31	0.37	1,870	218.5	57	49
Average	1.67	0.55	933	215.6	57	51
Slow Reformers						
Uzbekistan	1.11	0.37	640	22.5	89	88
Belarus	1.07	0.35	1,694	216.6	73	64
Ukraine	0.80	0.20	2,789	218.6	56	48
Turkmenistan	0.63	0.19	2,751	215.0	69	62
Average	0.90	0.27	1,968	213.2	72	66
Affected by Regional Tensions						
Croatia	3.98	0.83	807	20.7	69	68
Macedonia FYR	3.92	0.78	157	210.7	57	55
Armenia	1.44	0.42	4,595	27.4	38	38
Georgia	1.32	0.35	10,563	224.6	24	23
Azerbaijan	1.03	0.33	1,167	217.7	50	44
Tajikistan	0.95	0.28	1,324	226.3	35	30
Average	2.11	0.50	3,102	214.5	45	43

SOURCE: de Melo, Denizer, and Gelb, "Patterns of Transition from Plan to Market," *World Bank Economic Review* 10, no. 3 (September 1996), p. 405.

Czech Republic and the Slovak Republic. High intermediate reformers were the Baltic states and the southern countries of the Balkan Peninsula. Mongolia, although relatively less developed, was a somewhat surprising member of this group. The most important of the low intermediate reformers was Russia. Among the slow reformers were the Ukraine, after Russia the most populous of the European transition nations, and the Islamic states of central Asia. Several countries of the former Yugoslavia and the Caucasus remained too much affected by civil and international warfare to be successful in maintaining a coherent liberalization plan.

STABILIZATION

The common experience of almost all transition economies was macroeconomic disturbances of a magnitude and endurance that surprised almost all observers.[5] These disturbances included rapid and sustained inflation and a sharp reduction of real output. The accompanying rise in unemployment remained smaller than expected, largely due to extensive subsidies to industry.

Inflation

Inflation posed a universal problem for East European and former Soviet reformers. Even those states most advanced in the process of reform experienced an average rate of inflation between 1989 and 1994 greater than 100 percent per year. However, as Table 20.2 shows, this price explosion abated in the most advanced reformers. Nevertheless, in slower reforming economies, the average inflation rate for 1989–1994 was close to 1,000 percent annually and, in fact, accelerated as reform progressed.

The causes of inflation in the transition economies are complex, but the most important are the following:

1. The *monetary overhang* created by supply and demand imbalances in the planned regime. Relaxation of price controls released pent-up demand and drove prices higher.

2. The absence of an adequate taxation system and the inability of governments to borrow on financial markets forced *reliance on the creation of money and credit to finance government activity.*

3. The *continuation of soft-budget constraints* in much of industry, increasing the fiscal deficit. To prevent the failure of state-owned and privatized enterprises during transition, governments frequently extended credit to industry. This politically necessary move in many cases prevented widespread failure that would lead to unemployment, political unrest, and a failure of any reforming regime to complete its program. In many cases, government support to

---

[5]The main exception is, of course, the People's Republic of China, which has maintained extremely strong economic growth throughout its liberalization effort. Growth in China was 11 percent between 1989 and 1995, and inflation a modest 8.4 percent. Vietnam combined liberalization with growth— roughly 8 percent between 1989 and 1995—although inflation was in excess of 100 percent annually.

industry increased sharply as implicit subsidies in the pricing system under central planning were eliminated.[6]

4. *Flight from the domestic currency* to foreign currencies (generally, the U.S. dollar) because of an absence of confidence in the domestic currency.

The greatest impetus to continued inflation was the creation of excessive credit by the government, and the solution to the inflationary spiral therefore lay in greater monetary discipline by central banks. However, although effective against inflation, repressive monetary policy effectively reduced demand for goods and services, and therefore repressed the growth of emergent firms. A tight monetary strategy carries the political risk of rising unemployment and the economic risk of depressing long-run growth. The World Bank considers that getting inflation down below 40 percent per year offers clear gains and helps eliminate the danger of a hyperinflationary spiral, but the Bank is more cautious about appropriate policy beyond that goal. In cutting inflation further, the cost in terms of lost output may be greater than the gain that results from more stable prices. Domestic output started rebounding in Poland and Estonia with the inflation rate near 40 percent. Korea, several Latin American nations, and Israel all combined impressive real growth with relative high rates of price increase.

High rates of inflation inflict profound distributional consequences in the transition economies because they act like a tax on financial assets. The losers are predominantly households and firms that held positive cash balances, who see their savings wiped out by hyperinflation. The winners are the government sector, which reaps the gains of seigniorage, and any households or firms with net debts. In general, the **inflation tax** is regressive and falls more heavily on small savers who have difficulty converting their financial assets into real property or dollars (or other foreign currencies) where it is safe from inflationary ravages.

The Collapse of GDP

The second macroeconomic phenomenon common to the transition economies is the sharp contraction of output. As Table 20.2 shows, in most of the Central and Eastern European nations (CEEs) and successor states of the Soviet Union, the **collapse of GDP** bottomed out at about 80 percent of its 1989 level. The fast-reforming economies resumed growth during 1993–1994, though all are still well below the level of GDP achieved in 1989. Slow-reforming countries saw their output levels fall further and took longer in returning to an expansionary path. High intermediate reformers saw a contraction of about 33 percent in five years, and the low intermediate reformers, among them Russia itself, lost about half of output.

By any measure, these levels represent serious dips in output. Some sense of their magnitude is apparent in a comparison to the Great Depression of the

---

[6]Consider, for example, the case of energy, which was supplied at well below world prices throughout the Soviet bloc. The elimination of the implicit energy subsidy squeezed many firms conditioned to operate in a relatively energy-intensive fashion. To avoid the failure of these firms, the government granted generous credits.

1930s, when the United States, the most heavily affected of the major industrial economies, saw a fall in GDP of about one-third.[7] The contraction in other advanced capitalist economies was less drastic—about 28 percent in Germany, 9 percent in France, and only about 5 percent in the United Kingdom. The fall in output in transition economies has been proportionately greater than in the West during in the Great Depression, still regarded as one of capitalism's great failures that led directly to massive political change and perhaps World War II. The chief experience of capitalism for most of the 410 million people who live in transition economies (other than China and Vietnam) is acute and painful contraction.

It should be noted, however, that official statistics overstate the size of the economic contraction in two ways. First, much of the recorded output in 1989 consisted of official estimates of production valued at official plan prices. The immediate impact of transition was to reduce both production volumes and prices of many of the overvalued, substandard goods produced under the planned regimes. Second, a feature of the transition period involves the substantial growth of the private, small business economy. This sector of production, while not necessarily criminal, is likely to underreport its activities to minimize taxes, and thus this burgeoning activity is not fully reflected in the official statistics.

Causes of the Contraction In reality the contractions might not have been as great as official statistics seemed to indicate, but all transition economies experienced significant macroeconomic downturns, caused primarily by the disintegration of the coordinating structure. Planners previously determined both suppliers and purchasers and, after the collapse of planning, enterprises found themselves both without secure, uncontested markets for their output. They also encountered difficulty getting the raw materials that under the former system were at least nominally guaranteed.

Other factors were also important. After price liberalization, even when materials were available, enterprises often had to pay more than the "soft" prices charged under the plan. This problem was particularly acute with respect to energy inputs that were consistently underpriced under socialist planning; oil and gas had been supplied throughout the Soviet Union and the Soviet bloc at much less than the world price. Analysis after liberalization indicated that a substantial part of industry in centrally planned economies produced *zero or* **negative value added**. When both inputs and outputs were valued at the appropriate world prices, the final product was worth less than the materials from which it was made, and all of the labor, capital, and other factor services were actually directed toward reducing the value of raw materials.

Third, dislocation caused domino effects when enterprises that lost buyers suffered a shortfall of revenues and therefore had no resources to pay for raw materials. The suppliers of materials, in turn, had no money to pay their workers, to buy investment goods, or even to pay taxes. The governments in most transition

[7]John Kenneth Galbraith, *The Great Crash*, 3d ed. (Boston: Houghton Mifflin, 1972), p. 172.

economies stepped in with credits to help enterprises bridge the gap between revenues and expenses, but the aid was seldom adequate. Out of necessity interfirm credit began to proliferate as firms, with no alternative ways to dispose of their products, continued to supply them to customers who were increasingly delinquent in payments. The entire structure of industry became increasingly fragile, presenting the possibility of repercussive enterprise failures, which could further cut output and massively increase unemployment. Governments in most transition states responded by increasing credits to industry, therefore feeding the inflationary cycle.

A fourth problem was that trade (for example, between the Baltic Republics and Russia itself), which had been "domestic" in terms of the Soviet Union, became "international" and required convertible currency after the collapse of the Soviet Union. From the beginning of central planning in the Soviet Union, Soviet technocrats relied on economies of scale, generally regarding bigger as better. As a result, single plants were often expected to supply the entire national consumption of certain commodities. Many goods, both final and intermediary, were produced almost exclusively within a single republic. The breakup of the Soviet Union meant that suppliers and their markets were now located in different countries, and transactions across these new borders frequently became hard currency transactions.[8] The problems of currency availability and border restrictions resulted in a contraction of economic activity as trade between the republics of the former Soviet Union shrank by 70 percent almost overnight.

This dislocation was not limited to the republics spawned by the dissolution of the Soviet Union. Even though trade within the Council on Mutual Economic Assistance (CMEA or COMECON) had always notionally been "international" in character, it had been an artifact of planning rather than the result of comparative advantage. The end of the planned system of the CMEA caused a sharp reduction in the volume of trade between former partners, again about 70 percent. Imports from another former socialist country were displaced by goods from more competitive producers outside the Soviet bloc, particularly in the case of consumer goods, electronics, and capital goods. Lost markets meant lost revenue and a multiplier effect on the macroeconomies. In effect, the dislocation of the trade network established under the CMEA was akin to cutting off each economy from part of its economic hinterland.

Finally, in many countries economic dislocation was aggravated by the deterioration of the internal distribution system. In Russia the internal transportation system had been close to collapse for decades. The only viable mode of moving most goods was by rail, which also suffered from inadequate investment and maintenance. Furthermore, at the collapse of the Soviet Union, rolling stock and equipment was divided between the republics largely on the basis of each country assuming possession of what lay within its borders in August 1991, resulting in a misallocation of resources and serious disruption.

---

[8]The need for hard money was not always the case. A "ruble" area, within which the ruble was the common medium of exchange, existed for some time.

Labor Productivity As output fell sharply in most transition economies, employment dipped by a much smaller amount, and therefore the initial impact of economic reform was to actually lower labor productivity. Before the onset of reform, productivity in Eastern Europe was between 20 percent and 33 percent of the level in Western Europe, and the initial impact of liberalization was to widen this gap. Raising living standards depends on an increase in labor productivity and the decline was a demoralizing setback. Although most countries experienced a fall, Table 20.3 shows that the faster reforms are implemented, the more sharply labor productivity initially declines, but the more rapidly it returns to the positive. Fast reformers like the Czech Republic, Poland, and Hungary saw productivity rising by 1992, while Russia and the Central Asian Republics continued to experience productivity decline until at least 1996.

Reform was accompanied by a shift in the composition of output. Basic "rust belt" industries contracted, compensated for in part by rises in services, consumer

■ TABLE 20.3

Annual Change in Labor Productivity, 1990—1999

	1990	1991	1992	1993	1994	1995	1996	1997	1998	1999
Eastern Europe	−4.02	−4.58	1.46	2.67	3.87	6.19	3.22	2.16	1.88	4.89
Albania	−9.27	−24.26	12.62	11.57	−2.17	12.15	13.18	−7.17	10.87	10.87
Bulgaria	−3.19	5.28	0.85	0.18	1.19	1.68	−10.90	−2.97	3.31	4.43
Croatia	−4.33	−13.50	−0.59	−3.91	6.55	6.84	4.64	7.41	−4.00	−0.00
Czech Republic	−0.30	−6.43	2.02	1.59	1.46	3.06	3.74	1.19	0.19	2.33
Hungary	−0.21	−1.75	7.47	6.38	5.66	4.04	2.76	5.59	4.57	1.43
Poland	−7.72	−1.04	6.57	6.12	4.31	5.50	4.62	4.67	3.03	8.68
Romania	−4.65	−11.90	−4.92	4.38	3.64	11.25	5.11	−2.43	−2.60	3.41
Slovakia	−0.71	−2.31	−7.23	−4.11	8.06	4.33	2.77	6.81	4.81	5.80
Slovenia	−4.37	−1.27	0.03	5.73	7.95	4.82	4.51	5.49	4.55	4.10
Estonia	−6.80	−7.42	−8.11	−0.76	0.10	8.03	4.81	8.97	6.27	3.76
Latvia	2.80	−9.95	−27.52	−5.63	7.19	1.76	4.25	4.86	2.55	1.14
Lithuania	−0.62	−7.91	−17.83	−9.19	−2.75	3.23	2.39	4.52	4.26	−2.65
Armenia	−7.71	−12.86	-30.44	−3.32	4.28	3.83	4.77	4.80	6.42	4.38
Azerbaijan	−12.49	−1.28	−19.27	−15.38	−9.22	−4.76	−0.39	2.11	3.89	3.17
Belarus	−1.01	1.32	−7.22	−5.90	−8.87	−3.55	2.85	8.71	6.26	2.62
Georgia	−17.01	−11.18	−21.61	−10.90	−3.20	−5.73	5.03	0.26	0.14	4.70
Kazakhstan	−2.27	−9.62	−3.17	−0.63	−6.80	−5.99	0.69	1.71	2.68	2.44
Kyrgyzstan	4.28	−7.39	−18.10	−6.01	−13.37	−3.16	3.64	4.47	0.84	0.02
Republic of Moldova	−1.51	−17.17	−22.95	11.65	−21.50	−0.38	−2.53	1.17	−2.94	2.61
Russian Federation	−2.61	−3.02	−11.68	−5.95	−7.42	−0.75	−1.82	1.83	−2.46	3.39
Tajikistan	−2.91	−9.68	−26.29	−8.44	−11.25	−5.13	−3.95	−0.56	1.68	2.31
Turkmenistan	−1.55	−7.80	−15.99	−1.24	−15.02	−5.99	2.52	−7.21	2.75	6.42
Ukraine	−3.60	−6.88	−7.26	−10.07	−14.35	−8.53	−4.01	−0.08	−0.40	0.93
Uzbekistan	−4.80	−4.82	−9.70	−1.69	−5.10	−1.23	0.28	2.73	2.24	2.70

SOURCE: United Nations Economic Survey of Europe 2001, p. 122.

goods, and, where relevant, the primary energy sector, which benefited from increased product prices. Figure 20.1 shows the trends in labor productivity for four countries: the Czech Republic (an advanced reformer), Lithuania (high intermediate), Russia (low intermediate), and Turkmenistan (slow).

The relationship between the speed of reform and the subsequent movements in labor productivity is complex. Although Lithuania's reforms are more advanced than those of its larger neighbor Russia, both economies show similar movements of industrial labor productivity. Lithuania's fall largely parallels that of Russia, but it has been deeper, due mostly to the fact that the barriers to trade created by the breakup of the Soviet Union had a more severe impact on smaller economies. The specialization built into the planned trading system meant that smaller economies were disproportionately geared to export goods throughout the Soviet Bloc and therefore lost a proportionately greater share of their markets at the breakup.[9]

- **FIGURE 20.1**

Indices of Labor Productivity in Four Transition Economies

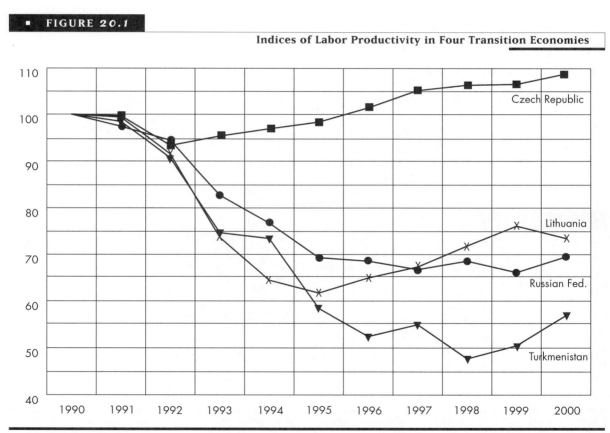

SOURCE: Data from Table 20.3.

[9]Alastair McAuley found that the share of "exports" of the Baltic states to other republics in the Soviet Union accounted for about two-thirds of the net material product.

Evidence suggests, at least among the faster reforming nations, that privatization resulted in a positive effect on labor productivity. In a survey of some 6,000 firms in Eastern Europe, Gerhard Pöhl and his colleagues found that privatized firms showed, on average, a relatively rapid 7.2 percent annual increase in productivity between 1992 and 1995.[10] In contrast, the fact that labor productivity in firms remaining in the state sector continued to fall (some of these results are shown in Table 20.4) supports privatization, though some caveats should be considered. First, the results in Table 20.4 reflect in part the relative ease with which fundamentally sound enterprises may be divested from state ownership: the other side of this phenomenon is the necessity of retaining the "lame ducks" under state ownership when no private buyer is forthcoming and the political authorities fear a rise in unemployment. Consequently, the private sector is self-selected and more dynamic than the social sector. Increased productivity also results from the greater freedom of privatized industry to get rid of unproductive workers and those concerned with the noncore aspects of the typical planned enterprise (for example, health and child care workers).

PRICE LIBERALIZATION

Price liberalization is essential for a market economy. Central planning failed to allocate resources efficiently because prices failed to reflect either cost of production or their value to consumers. Freeing up prices is the first step to grasping the benefits of a market economy and can occur without any steps being taken toward privatization of industry or indeed reform of **enterprise governance**. Under market socialism in

■ TABLE 20.4

	Labor Productivity Growth: Change, 1992–1995	
	Privatized Firms	State-Owned Firms
Bulgaria	12.4%	21.4%
Czech Republic	8.6	22.6
Hungary	6	3.2
Poland	7.5	1.4
Romania	1	20.5
Slovak Republic	7.8	24.1
Slovenia	7.2	1.8
Average	7.2	20.3

SOURCE: Gerhard Pöhl, Robert E. Anderson, Stijn Claessens, and Simeon Djankov, "Privatization and Restructuring in Central and Eastern Europe," *World Bank Technical Paper* (1997), p. 368.

[10]Gerhard Pöhl, Robert E. Anderson, Stijn Claessens, and Simeon Djankov, "Privatization and Restructuring in Central and Eastern Europe," World Bank Technical Paper, 1997.

the Yugoslav model, free prices were compatible with socially owned means of production and with the collective governance of the enterprise. However, in most analyses building a market system in the formerly centrally planned economies goes hand in hand with the privatization of property and the free entry of firms into the marketplace. Private enterprise and private ownership are more likely than social ownership to be compatible with the efficient operation of markets.

Price liberalization can produce dramatic results. In Poland, for example, shops that were empty of goods and beleaguered by queues of would-be shoppers while under central planning became well stocked in the aftermath of reform. Such a change is the product of both demand- and supply-side responses. Higher prices may bring forth a larger output, but much of the apparent increased availability of goods is due to a movement along the demand curve. In the short run, the price elasticity of demand of most produced goods is likely to be greater than the price elasticity of supply. The elimination of excess demand owes more to reduced consumption by the less well off, who can no longer afford the goods that were cheap under central planning. In the longer run, supply responses may dominate, exhibiting the solid, welfare-augmenting growth that is the objective of price reform.

A further benefit of price reform is the reduction of the socially wasteful activity caused by price controls. Under planning, goods in demand attracted many buyers and much of the homemakers' day was spent queuing for necessities. The alternative to queuing was to resort to the black market, and illegal fortunes were made in arbitrage between the state sector, where access was controlled but prices cheap, and the black market.

In general, price liberalization hurts the less affluent because under administered prices, they had access to goods on the same basis as everyone else and because the marginal value of their time was low, the queuing system worked to their benefit. Liberalized prices confront them with a hard monetary budget constraint and cause a fall in living standards, a case of the efficiency of the market conflicting with the greater equity of nonprice allocation.

As prices are decontrolled, the highly concentrated structure of industry promoted under central planning becomes a problem. Because of the planners' faith in scale economies, production of many goods was concentrated within a few large enterprises, which under planning held little market power because both production targets and prices were centrally determined. However, price liberalization gives these enterprises a high degree of market power and they will respond to their new freedom by raising prices and reducing output. Any gains in welfare from price reform must be set against the loss of consumers' surplus caused by enterprises exercising monopoly power. Losses can be mitigated by antimonopoly regulation, freeing market entry for domestic competitors and opening up international trade. In cases of natural monopoly or substantial barriers to entry, regulation may be the only resort.

Liberalized prices produce fewer benefits if reform is not accompanied by the introduction of contract law with some measure of enforceability. Price liberalization alone creates the conditions for, in the words of one Russian economist, "a bazaar but not a market." The creation of a modern productive economy requires performance, and to some degree, prices to be intertemporally consistent.

Regulation of Monopoly

Soviet-style planning's love affair with size led to high levels of concentration in many product areas. To measure monopoly power, western economists have in recent years tended to turn from measures of current concentration of output to focus on the **contestability of markets** and the size of barriers to entry, because potential competition can be a significantly moderating influence on monopoly practices. In a Soviet-style economy, markets were uncontested because of the planning system and the incentives embedded in it. Enterprise managers could gain little by broadening their production and moving into new lines—it was complicated, risky, required both management time and materials, and could therefore jeopardize the achievement of output targets. Once the planning system was abandoned, barriers to entry were low in many industries and market share could be quickly eroded by new market entrants and imported goods.

In some industries, competition can be created merely by reorganizing the administration of the enterprises. Such reorganization has been achieved with some success in the service industries. Prior to the collapse of the Soviet Union, *Aeroflot* was the largest airline in the world. It was replaced by regional and republic airlines, and the degree of competition between these successor firms, as well as new entrants, increased. *Intourist*, a monopoly supplier of tourist services, was replaced by several competitive organizations. In both of these cases artificial monopoly consisted of capital stock that was either small or easily divisible.

Reorganization is not possible, however, among the giants of Soviet-heavy industry, where the size of the enterprise is embodied in a single large plant and organization is around core products. Fully one-fifth of the Soviet workforce was employed in organizations of more than 10,000 workers. As Nikolay Petrakov, a Russian economist, observed:

> This is our notorious gigantomania. We always thought that a larger plant is bound to be better than a small one. We artificially propagated monopolists. An industrial giant that has already been built is impossible to break up into parts. This means that it will long remain a technological monopoly. . . . Fortunately there are not so many of them in the light and food industries. But heavy industry is full of these monsters. To speak of competition here is impossible. We will have to introduce price controls and anti-monopoly legislation.

The Role of Trade

Price controls on goods as differentiated and changing as machinery and machine tools are anathematic to most economists who would rather liberalize the trade regime to limit monopoly power. For such tradable goods, opening the economy to international competition can be an important check on the pricing behavior of domestic producers. It may be particularly effective in the case of machinery, where embodied technological change, as well as a moderating influence on prices, can result. However, dangers loom for domestic producers who are forced to confront the high quality, superior design, and low prices of goods from abroad. Price and quality control require rapid attention or domestic producers may lose customers and go bankrupt. Competition is bound to be unpopular with domestic producers, who are likely to petition for protective tariffs or quotas on "infant industry" grounds. However, once protective tariffs or quotas are adopted, they become difficult to remove, and they should be avoided where possible.

THE REFORM OF ENTERPRISES

The Enterprise Under Central Planning

Enterprises in the centrally planned economies were quite different in structure, goals, and culture from their counterparts in developed market economies. These differences were mentioned earlier, but a review is worthwhile:

1. *Size of enterprises.* Enterprises under central planning were larger on average than those in market economies because of the planners' faith in scale economies and a desire to eliminate "socially wasteful reproduction" of capacity. Studies of the structure of Soviet enterprise in the 1960s revealed that the average firm had a workforce about three times larger than for a similar market size in the West. This emphasis on size intensified during the 1970s and 1980s, as scale economies were pursued as a remedy for the economic failure. The Brezhnev reforms of 1973 resulted in the combination of smaller enterprises into larger industrial associations. By the late 1980s, almost three-quarters of the Soviet labor force was employed in enterprises of more than 1,000 persons and over 20 percent worked for enterprises with more than 10,000 workers.

2. *Objectives of management.* Under central planning the objective of management was to meet the plan targets, and incentives offered to management were oriented toward this goal. In many countries a concept close to profit was eventually introduced as one of multiple targets, but the lack of clear accounting and the high degree of implicit subsidy obscured this objective. Although profit maximization is not the unswerving objective of western firms, without doubt more attention is paid to a defined bottom line.

3. *Marketing and sales effort.* Centrally planned economies were characterized by excess demand and each firm's customers were defined by the planners. Little attention was paid to sales effort, market research, product improvement, or customer satisfaction. In developed market economies, sales and marketing are an essential feature of corporate operation and the absence of this capacity in a newly privatized enterprise will present difficulties in securing a solid customer base.

4. *Lack of export orientation.* Export markets were of little importance for centrally planned firms. Rather than a key source of sales and revenue for the enterprise, exports were a means of raising hard currency for necessary national purchases of material and equipment. Enterprises themselves were insulated from export markets until the late 1980s by the monopoly of the foreign trade organizations.

5. *Extent of vertical integration.* Centrally planned firms tended to be more vertically integrated than their developed market counterparts, due in large part to the failures of the distribution system and the neglect of quality control. If an enterprise were to have guaranteed access to intermediate goods of reliable quality, in a fashion timely enough to meet its own output targets, the safest way was to produce it within the organization. This principle led to a paradox. Although one emphasis of the centrally planned system was grasping economies of scale, large organizations frequently produced intermediate goods in inefficiently small quantities in order to meet internal demand. "Outsourcing" and precise inventory control, noticeable developments in the evolution of large enterprises in Europe, the United States, and Japan, were neglected in the Soviet-style economies.

6. *Provision of ancillary services.* Part of the reason that centrally planned firms were so large was that they were responsible for a wide range of services for workers that lay beyond the scope of operations of even the most paternalistic firms in the West. Firms were frequently responsible for housing, health services, child care, and even education, overlapping functions that in market economies are reserved for government.

Corporatization

The first step of enterprise reform is **corporatization**, placing the firm onto an organizational and accounting footing to allow management the freedom to pursue clearly defined objectives without political intervention. Corporatization is distinct from privatization, which involves placing the ownership of the enterprise outside the public sector, but it is a step in that direction.

1. *Creating independent management.* Under centralized planning not only is management appointed by the politicians but also it is directly accountable to them. This relationship is logical because the enterprise is an extension of the state and therefore is required to pursue objectives of the state. As long as enterprises remain subject to direct political control, their purpose will be defined largely in political terms and enterprise management will not be afforded the freedom to exercise initiative to increase efficiency and promote innovation. Moreover, managers will be appointed on political criteria rather than on ability in purely economic matters. Consequently, reform of industry must start with the alienation of the enterprises from the direct control of politicians.

2. *Defining the goals of the enterprise.* Next the objective of the enterprise must be clearly defined. If private ownership is an objective, the only consistent goal will be the maximization of profit—that is, the definition of and attention to a "bottom line." It is possible to corporatize an enterprise and assign to it objectives other than profit maximization, as long as it remains in the public sector or receives a subsidy from the state. In most developed market economies, for example, rail transportation is run by a publicly owned corporation, with an independent management structure. Because of a high level of externalities, such bodies often have broader goals than the maximization of profit.

3. *Separating ancillary services from the productive enterprise.* One of the most important aspects of enterprise restructuring is separating the provision of social services from the function of producing goods. When the means of production are socially owned, it can be convenient, even efficient, for productive enterprises to deliver social services. However, if the goals of the organization are more clearly defined as maximizing profits, any social activity that is not cost effective in raising labor productivity must be closed down, or the firm should be compensated for this activity by some level of government. If firms that bore responsibilities for housing, health, and education are allowed to shed them, then the government must assume them, or deterioration in social welfare will result, at least in the short run. As firms abandon their traditional social function, a pressing task in transition economies is the establishment of a social safety net to protect those "downsized" from state enterprise or those whose well-being is no longer the concern of their immediate employer.

4. *Establishing a realistic accounting system.* Accounting practices under central planning were neither universal nor impartial. The pervasiveness of the "soft-budget constraint" and the arbitrary nature of fiat prices made firms' accounts all but meaningless in the evaluation of performance. Preparation for privatization involves the establishment of an accepted accounting system that will enable potential investors to judge the financial viability and prospects of the firm.

5. *Providing incentives to management and workers.* A final desirable step in the process of corporatization is to look to the structure of incentives within the enterprise. Under planning, incentives were frequently perverse, and revising them to encourage hard work, managerial diligence, and innovation will better enable the firm to present the value of the enterprise to potential buyers.

PRIVATIZATION

Privatization should begin after these preliminary steps are taken, although, in fact, the privatization programs of most former socialist states proceeded before all of these preconditions were met.

Principles of Privatization

The Problem of the Commons Let us pause at this point to reconsider the economic and philosophical issues that bear on privatization. The primary rationale for private ownership lies in the "problem of the commons" or, to put it differently, what belongs to everyone belongs to no one. If resources are collectively owned, no individual has a strong incentive to look after them, and because the effect of an action of an individual on the overall condition of jointly held resources is minimal, each person can be considered a "free rider." However, the overall result is that resources held in common are abused while individually owned resources are likely to be better maintained because someone has a material incentive for their preservation.

Principal/Agent Problems The commons issue addresses the resource problem of social ownership, but the difficulties in the manufacturing and service sectors are somewhat different. **Principal/agent problems** occur within both socialism and capitalism. In a socialist state, politicians and the planners use positive incentives or punishments to induce enterprise managers to act in the way that the plan requires. In turn, the enterprise managers need strategies to induce workers to work in their interests. Capitalism shows parallel issues. The owners of capital hire managers; ensuring they behave in the interests of shareholders is a problem, and, as under socialism, these managers must induce workers to perform optimally. In fact, socialist and capitalist systems address these problems in quite similar ways. Managers are offered bonuses (or in capitalist firms they are frequently offered stock options) for meeting or exceeding targets, and workers are proffered a range of positive and negative incentives to raise their output—piece rates and bonuses on the positive side and tight supervision and output quotas on the negative.

Privatization of industry offers the potential of dealing with principal-agent issues more effectively than under social ownership. In some small businesses, agency problems will disappear as owner-operators emerge (for example, in retailing and the small-scale service sector). In larger enterprises, the owners of capital take a much more focused interest in the outcome in a particular enterprise and therefore provide more rigorous oversight of management's performance than would occur under planning. Corporate governance is a key to effective transition, and close attention should be given in the privatization process to establishing an effective system.

The Restitution Issue Both the commons and the principal-agent arguments suggest that privatization can foster efficiency by ensuring that resources will be dedicated to their highest value use and that appropriate oversight will be given to maximize efficiency. However, these arguments do not tell us much about who the owners of the privatized property should be, nor about how the transfer of ownership should be addressed. Some guidance may be given by examining how the property held in the state sector originated.[11] In some cases the property was seized without compensation (or without *adequate* compensation) from its owners. If they or their heirs can be identified (and if the property is largely unimproved from the condition in which it was seized), restitution of the property to them may be both equitable and efficient. Such restitution can be applied to residences and (for example, in Bulgaria) to small-scale agriculture. However, socialist rule in many states lasted long enough that most property cannot be associated with a pre-socialist owner. Moreover, much of it is new or greatly changed, especially in the industrial sector, and is not the subject of any preexisting title.

Holding the Nation's Assets in Trust Many transition economies operated under a socialist system for more than 40 years, usually from the immediate aftermath of World War II. Most of the states that emerged as a result of the breakdown

---

[11]Such a policy ignores, of course, the thorny issue of whether the owner prior to nationalization obtained the property by a just process in the first place. Consider, perhaps, a wealthy aristocrat who gained his estates by the gift of a tyrant.

of the Soviet Union operated under planning for about 65 years. The majority of the capital stock in these economies is the result of investment made during the socialist period and the enterprises could be said to belong to everyone in the population who sacrificed by deferring consumption to create investment capital—whether a willing sacrifice or not. The capital stock can be thought of as collectively financed and held, as if in trust, by the state, which suggests that the title to the newly privatized firms should be widely, and therefore equitably, distributed across the population. However, such a policy would not resolve the nexus of "commons" and "principal-agent" issues that led to the inefficient incentive and oversight structure in socially owned enterprises. A wide distribution of shares of newly privatized firms across the whole population though equitable, would lead to weak oversight of management and poor corporate governance.

Desirable Characteristics of a Privatization Program

If we list the desirable characteristics of a privatization program, we quickly recognize that some may be in conflict.[12] Features that we might want to see include the following:

1. *Rapidity.* The stock of assets to be transferred to the private sector in former socialist economies is large. The creation of a market economy requires tangible progress, and the process must be complete within a foreseeable period of time. The pace at which government assets were disposed of in mixed capitalist economies, such as the United Kingdom or France, is not acceptable when the vast bulk of the capital stock of a nation is to be disposed of.

2. *Improved enterprise governance.* The change in property rights must improve the governance of the enterprises. New owners need an effective means of oversight and way of tackling principal-agent problems.

3. *Fairness.* The process of privatization should be seen as fair and leading to the betterment of those who contributed to capital accumulation. A widespread perception of inequity may threaten political stability.

4. *Gaining the support of powerful interests.* The process must be able to placate the interests of the existing elite and the present "stakeholders" in the economy because without the support of powerful interests both political and economic reform may be aborted.

5. *Facilitating the inflow of new capital, technology, and management skills.* For enterprises hampered by a shortage of capital as well as limited access to foreign technology and "best-practice" techniques, privatization should help overcome these difficulties.

6. *Sustaining and supporting the liberalization program.* Finally, it is always desirable that any steps taken in the privatization program should be supportive of the overall program of liberalization and the institutions created.

---

[12]Cheryl W. Gray, "In Search of Owners: Privatization and Corporate Governance in Transition Economies," *The World Bank Research Observer* 11, no. 2 (August 1996), pp. 179–197.

Techniques of Privatization

Restitution The simplest privatization is the **restitution** of property to identifiable previous owners, who might have been uncompensated or only partially compensated when the assets were seized. Property rights can be swiftly transferred (as long as the title can be established), and the resultant ownership structure would be fair and lead to better governance. However, restitution is not useful in the majority of circumstances, especially in the case of medium and large-scale enterprises, because the current firms have no identifiable prior owner.

Small-Scale Mass Privatization The logical owners of much of the retail and service sectors (which consists of small bakeries, groceries, restaurants, small hotels, service stations, and so forth) are the state employees who operated the facilities under the planned system. It is desirable for continuity that these people stay in their jobs, and creating owner-operators can benefit efficiency and quality of service by eliminating principal-agent problems. Furthermore, these individuals probably have the best chance of being able to effectively value the business. The drawback is that, typically, such individuals have little capital, and loans to small businesses are seldom available in transition economies. Consequently, the enterprises have to be sold at low prices, and the state receives little revenue. This scenario is generally acceptable (except in cases where real estate or valuable inventory is involved), because employment is maintained and a potential tax stream is established with long-run positive revenues. Small-scale privatization also scores high for both speed and equity.

Sale to Insiders If operators of small businesses are allowed to assume ownership at favorable prices, the analogy in the industrial sector is sale to workers and management. Selling to such "insiders" provides two obvious advantages: it increases support for the transition process, and by making workers shareholders in the firm it helps to eliminate some of the incentive problems that lowered efficiency and productivity.[13]

This type of disposal can also lead to substantial drawbacks. First, neither workers nor management have access to substantial finance and cannot pay realistic prices for the enterprises, so little revenue is generated for the state. Second, the process is inequitable when viewed from a national perspective. Workers in the best firms with the brightest prospects and newest capital gain the most due to luck rather than their own hard work. Because investment in most socialist countries was determined at the national level and capital charges were unrealistically low, workers in enterprises most favored by the planners gain at the expense of the broad segment of society that made the sacrifices to provide the investment.

Further inequity is likely within the enterprise. Managers, though fewer in number than workers, have greater opportunities to disrupt the privatization

---

[13]This same logic offers options of shares to workers in developed market economies. Evidence indicates that this approach results in substantial impact on productivity in some privatizations. The case of road goods transportation in the United Kingdom is especially revealing.

process and therefore are able to negotiate, or to seize, a larger share of the assets. Many management-employee buyouts resulted in the assumption of the assets by senior management at low prices. Although this arrangement is satisfactory in terms of speed, it scores badly from the point of view of equity.

Finally, sale to insiders does little to attract new capital, new technology, or new management into the business, and therefore a prime economic objective of privatization—placing assets in the hands of those most able to maximize value—is not fulfilled.

Direct Sale to Outsiders One way of avoiding the problems of sale to insiders is to seek a group of investors, or a company, to purchase an enterprise as a going concern. An immediate difficulty is the shortage of capital and the underdeveloped capital markets, which make a leveraged buyout to a citizen or group of citizens unlikely. When deals are made with outsiders, prices often seem arbitrary, giving the appearance (and frequently the reality) of corruption.[14] Valuation techniques, even when applied by Western advisors, are rudimentary and close to useless when accounting information is poor and economic uncertainty is high.

The only groups that can afford to buy industrial enterprises "in being" are foreign investors who can pay more realistic prices for assets and are capable of infusing capital, technology, and modern management into their acquisitions. However, a political price is exacted in handing over prominent large enterprises to foreign control. In any case foreign buyers have been slow to buy large enterprises in transition economies. Frequently the existing plant is inappropriately designed, obsolete, and too large. Buying an existing enterprise means retaining a workforce with low productivity and bad work habits whose members were usually granted long-term job tenure prior to privatization.

Privatization through Initial Public Offerings Initial public offerings (IPOs) offer distinct attractions. Enterprises can be sold for realistic sums of money, thereby raising substantial revenues for the government, and widespread shareholding (and therefore support for capitalism) can be encouraged. However, success depends on some essential preconditions. First, company accounts must be accurate and accessible to allow realistic valuation. Even in such a case, IPOs are a slow path to privatization because each enterprise must be individually prepared and the public informed and educated about the company. Capital and equity markets must be developed and deep; even stock markets with a high capitalization can absorb only a few IPOs each year. If too much is offered in a short space of time, the whole market may be depressed.[15] Consequently, IPOs are not particularly useful in an economy moving from socialism to capitalism. Although they score high in terms of equity and in increasing the long-term stability of reform, poor information and shallow capital markets limit their applicability.

---

[14]This suspicion of favoritism is not limited to transition economies. Sales of this kind were an important part of Thatcher's privatizations in Britain, and they attracted criticism whenever valuable assets were transferred without an open-bidding process.

[15]Care was taken in the recent French privatization to avoid depressing the Paris markets by too many new shares.

Voucher Privatization If the correct way to view the socialist state is that it holds productive capital in trust for its citizens, then the process of privatization should transfer some part of the capital stock to each citizen. It is, in essence, the idea behind the schemes of **voucher privatization** by which the government gives away, or sells at low prices, vouchers that can then be used to claim shares in companies that are to be transferred from state ownership. This approach circumvents the problems resultant from the shortage of wealth that limits the applicability of all other approaches to privatization that involve sale, and it carries with it obvious advantages of fairness and equity. Voucher programs used in many of the transition economies may be the approach that best satisfies the five desirable characteristics itemized earlier.

Cheryl Gray has summarized the advantages of voucher privatization:

> Well-designed voucher privatization can overcome many of the problems encountered with the various sales techniques, notably the perceived unfairness, the shortage of domestic capital, and the difficulty of placing a value on assets. Because the voucher approach can proceed rapidly, it can simultaneously stimulate the development of market institutions, create new owners, and reorient the interests of existing ones toward further reform. Furthermore, it can speedily cut the links between enterprises and the state that both inhibit restructuring and put fiscal pressures on the state.[16]

The main problem with voucher privatization is that ownership of the enterprise becomes widely disbursed, diminishing effective governance. When a firm is divided among many owners, no single one feels a strong incentive to invest time and resources in supervising management. Even if one was highly motivated, he or she would have little power (as one shareholder among many) to change management's behavior. Consequently, management is often free to act in its own interest rather than in that of the owners, providing less incentive to maximize the return to capital and inefficiency results.

To avoid this problem, several countries encouraged or institutionalized the development of holding companies, much like mutual funds, that concentrate ownership and possess the knowledge, incentive, and power to effectively supervise management. In Poland, for example, the government set up several investment intermediaries staffed by managers appointed by the government. Each of these intermediaries was given a number of the enterprises to be privatized to manage, and the shares of the intermediaries were distributed among the citizenry. It was hoped that by active management the investment intermediaries would reorganize the enterprises under their control to maximize value and eventually sell them off to core investors. The danger of this approach is that holding companies will not follow through on restructuring or on the active pursuit of new owners. Consequently, rather than becoming a dynamic force for change they became state-protected institutions to manage lame-duck enterprises that have no willing buyers.

In the Czech Republic intermediaries grew as a result of market initiative rather than being created by the government. The original intent of the Czech privatization

---

[16]Gray, "In Search of Owners," *The World Bank Research Observer* 11, no. 2 (August 1996), p. 90.

scheme was to auction shares directly to individuals using vouchers. However, investment funds arose (many of which were connected to banks), which acquired and pooled the vouchers of many individuals. These funds (420 in number) eventually acquired some 72 percent of the vouchers. The funds proved powerful in exerting managerial oversight of the firms, and in some cases their control became too great. Funds managed by the banks often involved a conflict of interest because the bank was both an owner of and a lender to a specific firm. In Russia, even though the voucher auction scheme sanctioned the development of investment intermediaries, they have not grown to the degree seen in the Czech Republic.

FINANCIAL SECTOR REFORM

The purpose of the financial sector in a market economy is quite different from that under central planning. In a modern market economy, financial institutions are responsible for accumulating and rationing investment resources. The savings of small households are aggregated and commingled in financial institutions and loaned out to business enterprises looking for investment capital. The financial sector is also responsible for evaluating the risk of these loans and fixing appropriate risk-compensated interest rates. Importantly, the financial sector grants credit to those industries that are likely to grow and denies finance to moribund firms.

As we discussed earlier, the purpose of the financial system in a centrally planned economy is quite different. Under central planning a single state bank (monobank) served two purposes. First, it would passively allocate credit to enterprises in accordance with the plan. Second, it served as a system of checking plan performance, because all movements of material through the economy had their counterpart as a paper trail of credit in the banking system. If market reforms are to be successful, a functional financial system that will perform the tasks of pooling savings, disinterestedly assessing risk, and making loans is essential.

The Central Bank

One of the first priorities must be the creation of a central bank, usually achieved by divesting the monobank of its other responsibilities and focusing it on functions traditionally reserved for the central bank.

These functions include the following:

1. Acting as a clearing bank for the commercial banks
2. Acting as the promulgator and enforcer of regulation to enhance the stability and efficiency of the financial system
3. Functioning as a lender of last resort to banks
4. Controlling the stock of money in the economy, and hence the interest rate
5. Monitoring the foreign exchange value of the currency

The degree of independence of the central bank is an important issue. Developed market economies offer little in the way of guidance to economies in transition.

The U.S. Federal Reserve System is highly independent, and the German Bundesbank is regarded as even more so. On the other hand, the Bank of Japan and the Bank of France are subject to tight government control. The Bank of England, for most of the postwar period an arm of the British government, has now been granted a much higher degree of autonomy.

Proponents of independence argue that central bankers have the expertise to make impartial decisions and will perform well if politicians are prevented from influencing them. The prime job of the central bank is to preserve the value of the currency, and it must frequently take a restrictive and conservative line on credit creation. When politicians are given control over the central bank, monetary policy tends to be too relaxed, and the unpleasant but necessary task of squeezing credit, and watching enterprises fail as unemployment mounts, would be avoided. The opposing view is that a totally independent central bank is answerable to no one. In a market economy it is an institution of great significance,[17] therefore, it is odd that in a representative democracy the people have no say in this vital dimension of policy making. In this analysis, the central bank is responsive only to the narrow financial community from which the board of governors are likely to spring. As such, an independent central bank might be unduly austere and hence jeopardize political stability by pursuing its own brand of financial rectitude. There is no right and wrong answer to this debate. Politicians are adept at judging the public will, and if they controlled the central bank we could say that a form of democracy prevailed. On the other hand, politicians have a short-term outlook and are prone to shallow compromise, whereas the financial experts insulated from pressure might effect more viable long-term policies.

Commercial Banks/Investment Banks

After creating the central bank, priority must be given to developing a commercial and investment banking system that can be effective in mobilizing savings and allocating investment capital among potential borrowers. This process is unlikely to be rapid. Some banks can be created by assuming the deposit and lending functions of the monobank, holding them for a while in the public sector, and then privatizing when conditions are appropriate. It will also probably be worthwhile to create a "post office" or "giro" savings bank in most of the transition economies. These institutions are almost universally found in Western Europe and Asia and provide a means of aggregating small savings as well as providing a high degree of convenience, security, and liquidity to the less affluent households.[18] Although these institutions are criticized for paying only low rates of interest, in general they have proved popular with small savers.

The biggest banking problem for transition economies is controlling the growth and behavior of new financial intermediaries that spring up. In Russia, for example,

---

[17]If confirmation of this point were required, we have only to take note of the army of "Fed watchers" in the United States, who are concerned with predicting the Fed's behavior.
[18]Deposits in the Japanese postal savings system amount to well over $2 trillion, almost as much as the rest of the banking system together.

at the outset of reform between 1989 and 1992 some 1,600 "banks" were created, but most did not meet the definition of banks as applied in the West. Many were created by industrial enterprises and exist largely to finance their parent companies by borrowing on the interbank market. As such, they perform little in the way of impartially assessing risk or allocating scarce capital resources to their highest value functions. It is vital for long-term development that a stable, disinterested private banking sector be established, and the first step is defining and requiring capital adequacy standards, accountancy norms, and regular audits to guarantee security to the depositor.

Banking regulations vary from country to country and as long as they are visible and enforced, a range of policy can be highly functional. In the United States and the United Kingdom, commercial banking, savings institutions, and investment banks were separated by practice and law, although these divisions are eroding over time. In continental Europe no such functional division applies and universal banks (sometimes referred to as U-banks) are the norm. U-banks are large and perform savings, lending, and underwriting functions. At the end of the day what matters most is not the specific institutional form of the banking system, but rather the degree of public confidence it is able to inspire. With a high degree of confidence the public will entrust its savings to the banking sector; little confidence in financial institutions will lead to low savings rates and unhealthy speculation in real assets.

Stock Markets

Stock markets are a feature of all developed market economies, and it is tempting to think that the rapid establishment of a stock exchange is an important prerequisite for growth. However, historically it seldom proves to be the case. Reliable evidence suggests that the growth of the stock markets tends to follow, rather than cause, rapid economic growth. In East Asia, for example, little industrial finance originated from the equity market and only in Korea and Taiwan did it represent even as much as 10 percent. Further back into history, most of the finance for Britain's industrial revolution was generated by interfirm credit, while continental Europe and the United States relied heavily on bank lending. So although the development of an equities market is positive, it is not essential for a market economy.

The process of maturation of a stock market is a slow one and depends on the accretion of public trust, a growing number of investors and intermediaries, and an increased number of issues and capitalization. Antoine van Agtmael, in a paper published in 1982, identified five stages in the general development of stock markets across time and economies.[19]

1. *The dormant stage.* During the first, dormant stage, most people are not actively aware of the existence of the stock market. Trading volume is low, only a few companies are listed, and prices remain close to their issuance values. As time goes by, shares tend to become undervalued, especially in a

---

[19]From *Emerging Securities Markets,* 1982. Material first published by Euromoney Publications, London.

dynamic economic environment. Inevitably, brokers or individuals discover that dividend yield alone—even excluding potential capital gains—exceeds the yield on other investment alternatives. This stage was largely absent or short lived in transition economies where expectations for equity growth were high from the outset.

2. *Manipulation.* Manipulation begins when some market participants discover that the small supply of stocks, and thus limited liquidity, makes it possible to move prices up with relatively small purchases. Rising prices encouraged new market entrants, enabling the manipulators to get out with quick profits.

3. *Speculation.* As soon as some people begin to make substantial capital gains and boast of their profits, a wider group of investors is attracted. A speculative stage begins during which trading soars and prices are driven up well beyond appropriate values.

4. *Consolidation or crash.* At some point the speculative bubble is questioned, and stock prices begin to waver and drop. Depending on the extent of the boom during the speculative stage, prices either decline gradually or tumble deeply. The consolidation stage or crash sets in. It may take investors months or even years to regain confidence in the stock market after such a price decline. Much depends on the extent of the price drop as well as on interest rates, economic growth, corporate profitability, inflation yields on other investment alternatives, new incentives to restimulate buying, and the behavior of institutional investors. During this consolidation stage, many speculators become, out of necessity, investors. Unwilling to sell their shares at a loss, they hold on to them for long-term investment in the hope that prices will improve in the future.

5. *Maturity.* The mature stage begins when the initial investors regain confidence and are joined by new groups of investors unhurt by previous failures. Trading volume is likely to be more consistent, investment more sophisticated, the supply of shares broader, and, thus, liquidity greater. Recent experience in Southeast Asia, Latin America, and the transition economies seems to justify these overall conclusions.

REFORM OF INTERNATIONAL TRADE

Prior to the late 1980s the international trade of socialist nations was the concern of the state, not individual firms. The direction of trade with other socialist countries, its volume, and the prices of traded goods were subject to the plan. All trade with the nonsocialist world was conducted by specialized state-controlled foreign trade organizations (FTOs). Exports were sanctioned in order to raise the foreign exchange to finance the imports required by the plan. Individual firms had little contact with their customers and could only buy imported machinery, technology, and materials if they could make a convincing case with the planners, which usually required political influence. Under Gorbachev this system was reformed, and enterprises were allowed to trade directly with overseas counterparts, but a complex system of tariffs and licenses prevailed.

Most economists favor the elimination of licensing and the removal or moderation of tariffs in order to allow substantially free trade. In the short term, some tariff protection may be necessary because during restructuring virtually all enterprises can be regarded as "infant." Although it might seem strange to regard the former Soviet Union's industrial giants as infants, in terms of efficiency, pricing, client relations, and technical innovation they have much to learn. Free trade would lead to loss of domestic market share that would be hard to recoup and would cause further macroeconomic contraction. However, protection for inefficient producers has costs, not least of which is that it denies other enterprises access to inputs and technology at world prices. Consequently, the drive to modernize within these firms may be hindered by the inflated cost of inputs. Limited protection is important in the short term, but the long-term growth of the economy requires that protective measures be phased out quickly or else the industry nurtured behind tariff walls can never become globally competitive.

Trade liberalization also requires currency reform. Under planning, currency convertibility was limited and often subject to multiple exchange rates—with different uses requiring conversion at different rates. This situation was inefficient, distortionary, and led to the development of black markets. Full currency convertibility is not absolutely necessary for a functioning market economy. Convertibility was not generally restored in Western Europe until the late 1950s, and many countries today limit capital convertibility and the access of residents or citizens to foreign exchange. What is essential is the establishment of a realistic exchange rate and relatively unrestricted access to foreign exchange for those firms involved in trade.

Trade liberalization often goes hand in hand with a greater role for foreign direct investment (FDI), although again it is possible to conceive of primarily market-coordinated economies in which the part played by the FDI is limited; Korea provides such an example. However, for most transition economies FDI helps to solve a series of problems because it provides capital for investment, a source of foreign exchange, technological know-how, management techniques, and links to export markets. Defined property rights, a civil legal code, consistent tax laws, and guarantees on the convertibility and repatriation of profits are important in attracting direct investment. A good deal of discretion may be retained within a general policy to encourage FDI. As a policy matter, a foreign presence can be discouraged in those sectors that are sensitive (e.g., resources) or those areas that the government feels can be adequately met by domestic enterprises (retailing, for example).

THE SOCIAL SAFETY NET

Under socialism and centralized planning, the most important form of "safety net" was the guarantee of work for everyone. In fact, being employed was a legal requirement for most people. Having a job provided workers with income and access to nonwage benefits, irrespective of their productivity in employment or the fundamental profitability of the enterprise for which they worked. Long-term success in the transition economies depends on both closing the enterprises that are unable to compete when subject to a hard-budget constraint and raising the productivity (therefore cutting the workforce) of those that survive. Consequently, unemployment, which existed only in a disguised form during the socialist period, will necessarily rise during the transition. Some form of social safety net is required to protect the unemployed and to guarantee some minimum living standard for all.

The alternative to providing an effective social safety net is the alienation and marginalization of a large part of the workforce, creating an underclass and courting a high degree of political risk. Other social problems may develop including a high degree of migrancy, waste of social infrastructure, and a plethora of social pathologies including rising crime, prostitution, mounting suicide, and so forth. Furthermore, a social safety net functions economically as well as politically by assisting the development and operation of the labor market. Without public support for the unemployed, displaced workers are forced to accept the first job available without being able to undertake any off-the-job search. Mismatches of skill between job and employee are inevitable.

BIG BANG VERSUS GRADUALISM

A remaining important question about transition is its speed. If market arrangements are substantially more efficient than the plan, then it can be argued that economic reform should proceed as quickly as possible. Rapid changes in ownership and property rights should bring about correspondingly rapid increases in factor productivity, output, and the general level of welfare.

A contrary case can be made, however. The existing capital stock and associated institutions were fashioned for a particular economic system involving a high degree of command and central planning. New institutions and laws will take time to draft, and the economic actors will be on a learning curve to assimilate the parameters of the new order. The existing capital stock and infrastructure must be modified for the new conditions in which the economy must operate. Thus a **big bang** approach, in which prices are liberalized at a stroke and in which privatization is pursued vigorously, will take time to bear fruit, and in the meantime some disruption will be inevitable. Slower change (allowing economic actors to absorb lessons) and institutional experimentation might be preferable.

A drawback of a gradualist approach is the reversibility of reform. A big bang creates powerful interests committed to reform, while gradualism allows the old guard a continued lease on life and protracts the unsettling political debate about the ultimate direction of the economy. Such uncertainty might have a substantial effect on real investment, because entrepreneurs might be unwilling to commit resources to long-term projects if they foresee a strong chance of reversal. Time alone will tell which approach leads to the better outcome. Table 20.2 suggests that the rapid reformers of Central and Eastern Europe have already passed through their darkest period and are moving into a situation where sustained growth seems to be likely. However, if we look at other parts of the world, especially to the People's Republic of China (see Chapter 23), gradualism and experimentation apparently produced a more successful pattern of transition.

POLITICAL REFORM AND ECONOMIC REFORM

Table 20.5 shows the progress made in economies in transition through 2001, ranking both political and economic progress. These figures were produced by Freedom House, a U.S. group concerned with political and economic liberalization in Europe. The figures are largely subjective, but they echo to some extent the estimates of Table 20.2. They show that political and economic reform are closely linked. The correlation between the two indices is high (a raw correlation coefficient of .936). Consequently, we seldom encounter either a democratic state with a highly controlled economy or a liberal economy accompanied by a totally authoritarian political structure. In general, the former Soviet satellite states of central

■ TABLE 20.5

Progress to Political and Economic Reform in Transition Economies

	Economy Rank	Economy Score	Democracy Rank	Democracy Score
Poland	1	1.67	1	1.44
Hungary	2	1.92	4	1.94
Estonia	3	1.92	7	2.00
Czech Republic	4	2.00	2	1.81
Slovenia	5	2.08	5	1.94
Latvia	6	2.50	6	1.94
Lithuania	7	2.75	3	1.94
Slovakia	8	3.25	8	2.25
Bulgaria	9	3.50	9	3.06
Croatia	10	3.58	10	3.25
Armenia	11	3.58	17	4.56
Georgia	12	3.75	15	4.19
Moldova	14	4.00	13	3.94
Romania	13	4.00	11	3.31
Kyrgyz Republic	15	4.00	21	5.13
Russia	17	4.17	18	4.63
Albania	16	4.17	14	4.13
Ukraine	18	4.33	16	4.44
Kazakhstan	19	4.50	23	5.56
Macedonia	20	4.58	12	3.75
Azerbaijan	21	4.92	24	5.56
Yugoslavia	22	5.33	19	4.63
Tajikistan	24	5.50	22	5.44
Bosnia	23	5.50	20	4.94
Uzbekistan	25	6.17	25	6.50
Belarus	26	6.25	26	6.56
Turkmenistan	27	6.50	27	6.94

SOURCE: Freedom House, *Nations in Transition*, 2001, available at http://www.freedomhouse.org/research/nattransit.htm.

Europe moved fastest in both political and economic reform, followed by the Baltic States of the former Soviet Union. This group is also explicitly preparing itself for entry into the European Union, which affected the pace and direction of both economic and political reform. The new nations that made up the former Yugoslavia (Croatia, Slovenia, and Macedonia)[20] are hard to classify. Slovenia is advanced in both political and economic reform, while Macedonia, despite being part of the Yugoslav "participatory economy," is backward both economically and politically. As far as the European states go, the laggards are Belarus, backward in both dimensions, and Yugoslavia, Bosnia, and Macedonia, which were all constituent parts of the Yugoslav Republic.

KEY TERMS AND CONCEPTS

advanced reformers	inflation tax
big bang	initial public offerings
collapse of GDP	monetary overhang
contestability of markets	negative value added
corporatization	principal/agent problems
domestic liberalization	private sector entry liberalization
enterprise governance	restitution
external transactions liberalization	voucher privatization

QUESTIONS FOR DISCUSSION

1. How did the "monetary overhang" arise in socialist states, and what is its significance in the transition process?
2. Why was inflation a common feature of transitional states?
3. What led to the phenomenon of a collapse of GDP being a general concomitant of liberalization?
4. What happened in most countries to labor productivity during the transition? Why?
5. Why is the problem of monopoly so pressing in transition countries? How can abuse of monopoly power be limited?
6. What is meant by corporatization?
7. How are the issues of privatization and enterprise governance linked?
8. Do you think that the central bank in a post-socialist state should be independent and insulated from political pressure?

---

[20]Neither Serbia (still called Yugoslavia) nor Bosnia are included in the survey, presumably because of political problems.

9. Why are stock markets not likely to be important as providers of capital in the transition process?

10. What is a big bang approach to transition?

RESOURCES

Web Sites

Stockholm School of Economics...http://www.hhs.se/

International Centre for Policy Studies, Kiev, Ukraine.................http://www.icps.kiev.ua/

Transition ....http://www.worldbank.org/transitionnewsletter/
The *Transition* newsletter is a regular publication of the World Bank's Development Economic Research Group [DECRG]

REES Web: Russian and East European Studies, University of Pittsburgh...........................
....http://www.ucis.pitt.edu/reesweb/

World Bank Research on Poverty During the Transition ....
....http://www.worldbank.org/research/inequality/

The Vienna Institute for International Economic Studies...............http://www.wiiw.ac.at/

European Bank for Reconstruction and Development.....................http://www.ebrd.com/

The European Union's Main Transition Initiative: The Phare Programme ....
....http://www.europa.eu.int/comm/dg1a/phare/index.htm

United Nations Economic Commission for Europe...........................http://www.unece.org/

Freedom House ....http://www.freedomhouse.org/

Soros Foundation...http://www.soros.org/

The Corporate Governance Net ....http://www.corpgov.net/

Sigma—The Good Governance Initiative of the OECD...
....http://www.oecd.org/sigma/

Cato Institute: Project on Global Economic Liberty..
....http://www.cato.org/research/glob-st.html/

Books and Articles

Berg, Andrew, Eduardo R. Borensztein, Ratna Sahay, and Jeromin Zettelmeyer. "The Evolution of Output in Transition Economies—Explaining the Differences." International Monetary Fund Working Paper WP/99/73.

Blanchard, Olivier. *The Economics of Post-Communist Transition. Clarendon Lectures in Economics.* Oxford: Clarendon Press, 1997.

Carlin, W., and M. Landesmann. *From Theory into Practice? Corporate Restructuring and Economic Dynamism in Transition Economies.* Vienna: Vienna Institute for International Economic Studies, August 1997.

Claassen, Emil-Maria. *Exchange Rate Policies in Developing and Post-Socialist Countries.* San Francisco: OCS Press, 1992. Reviewed in *Studies in Comparative International Development.*

De Melo, Martha, Cevder Denizer, and Alan Gelb. "Patterns of Transition from Plan to Market." *World Bank Economic Review* 10, no. 3 (September 1996): 397 ff.

Earle, John S., Roman Frydman, Andrzej Rapaczynski, and Joel Turkewitz. *Small Privatization: The Transformation of Retail Trade and Consumer Services in the Czech Republic, Hungary, and Poland. CEU Privatization Reports.* New York: Central European University Press, 1994.

Frydman, Roman, and Andrzej Rapaczynski. *Privatization in Eastern Europe: Is the State Withering Away?* New York: Central European University Press, 1994.

Frydman, Roman, Cheryl W. Gray, and Andrzej Rapaczynski (eds.). *Corporate Governance in Central Europe and Russia: Banks, Funds and Foreign Investors. World Bank/CEU Privatization Project.* New York: Central European University Press, 1996.

Frydman, Roman, Kenneth Murphy, and Andrzej Rapaczynski. *Capitalism with a Comrade's Face.* New York: Central European University Press, 1998.

Gray, Cheryl W. "In Search of Owners: Privatization and Corporate Governance in Transition Economies." *World Bank Research Observer* 11, no. 2 (August 1996): 179–197.

Hardt, John P., and Richard F. Kaufman (eds.). *East-Central European Economies in Transition.* Armonk, NY: M.E. Sharpe, 1995.

Havrylyshyn, Oleh, and Donal McGettigan. "Privatization in Transition Countries—A Sampling of the Literature." International Monetary Fund Working Paper WP/99/6.

Henderson, Jeffrey (ed.) with Karoly Balaton and Gyorgy Lengyel. *Industrial Transformation in Eastern Europe in the Light of the East Asian Experience.* New York: St. Martin's Press, 1998.

Hernández-Catá, Ernesto. "Liberalization and the Behavior of Output During the Transition from Plan to Market." *International Monetary Fund Staff Papers* 44, no. 4 (December 1997).

Kennett, David, and Marc Lieberman (eds.). *The Road to Capitalism: Economic Transformation in Eastern Europe and the Former Soviet Union.* Fort Worth, TX: The Dryden Press, 1992.

Lavigne, Marie. *The Economics of Transition: From Socialist Economy to Market Economy.* New York: St. Martin's Press, 1999.

Mann, Catherine L. *Industry Restructuring in East-Central Europe: The Challenge and the Role of Foreign Investment.* American Economic Association Papers and Proceedings, May 1991.

Milanovic, Branko. *Income, Inequality, and Poverty During the Transition from Planned to Market Economy.* Washington, DC: World Bank.

Pöhl, Gerhard, Robert E. Anderson, Stijn Claessens, and Simeon Djankov. "Privatization and Restructuring in Central and Eastern Europe." World Bank Technical Paper, 1997.

Rother, Philipp. "Explaining the Behavior of Financial Intermediation—Evidence from Transition Economies." International Monetary Fund Working Paper WP/99/36.

Sachs, Jeffrey D. *Reforms in Eastern Europe and the Former Soviet Union in Light of the East Asian Experiences.* Working Paper Series, Working Paper 5404. Cambridge, MA: National Bureau of Economic Research, 1996.

Sachs, Jeffrey D., and Katharina Pistor (eds.). *The Rule of Law and Economic Reform in Russia.* John M. Olin Critical Issues Series (paper). Boulder, CO: Westview Press, 1997.

"A Survey of Central Asia: A Caspian Gamble." *The Economist,* February 7, 1998, 56.

White, William, *Evolving International Financial Markets: Some Implications for Central Banks.* BIS Working Paper no. 66 (April 1999).

World Bank. *From Plan to Market: World Development Report 1996.* New York: Oxford University Press, 1996.

21

REFORM AND PERFORMANCE OF THE RUSSIAN ECONOMY

RUSSIA	
Area (thousand sq. km.)	17,075
Currency	ruble
Exchange Rate	29 rubles = US$1
Population, 2000 (millions)	146
Population Growth Rate	–0.2%
GNI per Capita, 2001	$1,660
GNI per Capita, PPP	$8,010
GDP Growth, 1990–2000	–4.8%
Value Added as % of GDP 2000 Agriculture	7%
Industry	38%
Services	56%
% of GDP Government Expenditure	37.9%
Government Revenue	33.6%
Exports	42.0%

THE LEGACY OF THE "ERA OF STAGNATION"

By the early 1980s the crisis of the Soviet economy had become acute, and even though no sector was doing well, agriculture and consumer goods were faring particularly poorly. The system was sustained only by the hard currency proceeds of oil and gas exports used to buy food and advanced capital goods. Despite exhortation to improve economic performance, the leadership seemed determined to change nothing, and stagnation resulted.

Poor economic performance meant that the Soviet Union's relative position in the world was slowly sinking, and with it the capacity to maintain superpower status. Slippage was accelerated by emerging payments problems in the 1980s; hard currency exports (mainly energy) peaked in the early 1980s, while imports, including food, continued to rise throughout the decade. The result was a growing external deficit and increased international indebtedness. The gross debt (i.e., what the Soviet Union owed the Western nations before making allowance for Soviet holdings of hard currency) rose from $11.5 billion in 1975 to $22 billion in 1980 and $38 billion in 1985. A measure of the scale and severity of this indebtedness is the debt service ratio (the amount of hard currency payments required annually as a proportion of normal hard currency earnings); it rose from 10 percent in 1975 to about 23 percent in the mid-1980s. Almost a quarter of the value of the Soviet exports was committed ahead of time to repaying previously incurred debts. Market economies faced with such a crisis could finance part of their balance of payments deficit through incoming foreign direct investment, but despite a lukewarm commitment to joint ventures, the reality of Soviet politics made such inflows all but impossible.

PERESTROIKA AND GLASNOST

Gorbachev's reform efforts will forever be associated with the catchwords *perestroika* and *glasnost,* usually translated as restructuring and openness. His original intentions were modest, but the political change initiated by his *glasnost* policy far outstripped his plans for the economy, and Gorbachev was swept further toward liberalization as he attempted to appease both domestic and international critics. Even though *perestroika* seemed to offer much at the time, in retrospect this meandering attempt at reform must be judged a failure. The six years of the program may be divided into four phases, which may be summarized as follows:[1]

Phase	Date	Description
I	1985–early 1986	Rhetorical period. A lot of talk about reform but few specifics.
II	1986–early 1988	Legislative period. Creation of superministries, new laws on self-employment, state enterprise, cooperatives, and property.
III	1988–1989	Attempted implementation of reform.
IV	1989–1991	Failure, abandonment of the *perestroika* model in favor of more radical reform.

These stages were not totally distinct, but this partition gives an overview of the history of the Gorbachev years. Immediately after he came to power, Gorbachev talked a great deal about the necessity of reform and the gains to be made, but his rhetoric obscured the vague nature of his program. What was clear, and remained

---

[1]See, for example, Gregory and Stuart, *Soviet and Post-Soviet Economic Structure and Performance,* 5th ed. (New York: HarperCollins, 1994), p. 324.

the case throughout his administration, was that he aimed to modify a socialist economy rather than to shift toward a true market economy.

During 1986, decrees and laws designed to reform the economy began to dribble through. In some ways the legislation was schizophrenic. It laid the groundwork for private property and market signaling, but it increased government control by heaping new powers on the center and creating "superministries." The most notorious of these was *Gosagroprom*, designed to coordinate all agricultural and food distribution activity, but it only increased mismanagement and confusion. Gorbachev's agenda for industrialization hinged on three important laws and one decree:

1. The **Law on Individual Economic Activity** (November 1986) allowed the establishment of small businesses in the service sector as individual proprietorships under license from the state.

2. The **Law on State Enterprise** passed in mid-1987 and effective as of January 1, 1988, gave much greater freedom to the management of state-owned industry. Hard planning targets were replaced by "state orders" and greater latitude was permitted in staffing, pricing, and choice of technique. Theoretically, enterprises were to become financially independent and accountable, initiating a hard-budget constraint.

3. The **Law on Cooperatives** (May 1988) sanctioned the formation of larger private businesses. For ideological reasons they initially took the legal structure of cooperatives, but in reality this law facilitated the eventual creation of joint stock companies.

4. The **Decree on Property** (December 1988) allowed the sale of state-owned housing to individuals, creating a housing market and leading to the privatization of 12 million homes by 1995.

Although these reforms seemed far-reaching, their effect on the economy was mostly negative. The Law on State Enterprise gave firms both the incentive and opportunity to sell their goods in the market place for the highest prices that they could command, rather than continue to supply their traditional buyers at the prescribed plan prices. As a result, "downstream" firms frequently found themselves short of necessary inputs or unable to pay the higher prices, which curtailed production. Some enterprises even found themselves without the cash flow required to pay their workers. Coal miners, for example, were not paid for long periods in the later years of the Gorbachev administration, although the mines continued to operate and produce coal. Viewed from almost any perspective within the economy, *perestroika* was not a success.

500 DAYS TO A MARKET ECONOMY

The failure of Gorbachev's conception of *perestroika* and the protracted decline of the Soviet economy pointed to the need for more radical reform. The experience of the previous four years showed once again the ineffectiveness of tampering with the basic system of command planning, and consequently more attention was paid to moving the economy of the Soviet Union directly to a market system. In early 1990 a committee established under the leadership of Stanislav Shatalin, a respected economist and academician, produced a document known as the Shatalin report, titled *500 Days: Transition to Market.* It was deeply critical of the foundations of the Soviet system of centralized planning and sought to replace it with private property and liberalized market prices.

> The long rule of the totalitarian socio-political system dragged our society into profound crisis. Indecisiveness of the government and the mistakes it made in economic policy brought the country to the brink of collapse. . . . For a long time economic policy did not consider the people's interests. The state was wealthy while the people were poor. The state accumulated under its control almost all of the resources for production. Such resources were squandered on giant and ineffective projects, for increasing military power, and for certain ideologically flavored practices overseas even though the times have long passed since we could afford this.[2]

After attacking the leadership, the system, and Gorbachev's halting and ineffectual reforms, the report provided a rationale for a new order based on market relations. In retrospect, and given the disappointments of the decade since the report, the idea that the Soviet economy could be put on a market footing in only a year and a half seems naive, but it did represent fresh and open thinking on the causes of and the potential solutions for the Soviet malaise.

As the economy spiraled downward Gorbachev's popularity sank with it. His authority became threatened by the emergence of a rival power center in the form of the government of the Russian Federation, led by Boris Yeltsin, the chairman of the Russian Supreme Soviet, who had in July 1990 taken the decisive step of resigning from the Communist Party. While Yeltsin unequivocally advocated a rapid shift to a market economy along the lines of the Shatalin report, Gorbachev still tended to gradualism. Consequently, although the Supreme Soviet of Russia voted to approve the Shatalin plan by a margin of 213 to 1, Gorbachev as leader of the Soviet Union rejected it, proposing a much slower and less complete transition agenda. In November 1990 the Russian Congress of Deputies took the politically charged step of legalizing private family farming, outraging the Communists, and provoking an irredeemable division.

Events of the following year, 1991, continued this conflict as the Russian government legislated an even more liberal agenda, while Gorbachev attempted to slow the process of reform. Although Gorbachev avoided committing his administration to a radical transformation, his failure to stop Yeltsin's program allowed reform to proceed at a pace that alarmed the leadership of the Communist Party. As Gorbachev's position weakened and the failure of piecemeal reform became more apparent, Western nations, whose financial support was vital to the Soviet Union's reform effort, increased pressure on Gorbachev to adopt a more liberal stance.

During the summer of 1991 a group of Soviet reformers and Western academics gathered and drafted what became known as the **Grand Bargain**, under which the

---

[2]"Man, Freedom and Market" excerpted from "On the Program Developed by Academician S. S. Shatalin from: *500 Days: Transition to Market,*" in *Road to Capitalism,* David Kennett and Marc Lieberman (ed.) (Fort Worth, TX: Dryden Press, 1992), p. 88.

Soviet Union would commit to rapid economic and political reform, while in return the West would provide substantial economic aid. Gorbachev rejected the plan and tried to negotiate less conditional terms in a meeting with the leaders of the G7 nations, held in London in July. It was almost his last act as leader of the Soviet Union and he came away empty-handed. While vacationing in the Crimea in August, he was the target of a coup led by Communist Party leaders, which because of an inability to neutralize Yeltsin, unraveled after a few days of chaos. This failed putsch led directly to the breakup of the Soviet Union; during September most of the constituent republics declared their independence, and by March only the Ukraine and Belarus remained. On December 25 Gorbachev resigned, and over the Kremlin the red flag of the Soviet Union was replaced by the red, white, and blue banner of the Russian Federation.

THE GAIDAR REFORMS

Dramatic economic reform immediately followed. On January 2, 1992, just eight days after Gorbachev's resignation, Yeltsin, as president of the Russian Federation, launched a new phase of liberalization of the Russian economy, known as the **Gaidar reforms**. The chief architect of this new plan was Yegor Gaidar, a young liberal economist whose voice had become increasingly influential. The Gaidar/Yeltsin plan was spurred by Western criticism and resembled the Sachs/Balcerowicz plan initiated in Poland the previous year with some success[3] and rested on five "pillars."[4]

(1) Rehabilitation of the Ruble

The Gaidar team's primary premise was that the rehabilitation of the ruble lie at the heart of any reform program. The Soviet population lost faith in the ruble as a store of value and opted where possible for dollars or D-marks, but without a currency in which the population had confidence, and which could serve as vehicle for international exchange; they believed that the reform process would stall.

(2) Market Liberalization

The second pillar was the creation of a functioning market economy. It involved decontrolling prices, allowing free entry into almost all economic activity, cutting back on the share of output absorbed by state orders, and establishing the necessary legal system required to underpin market activity. The January 2 pronouncement ended central coordination of the economy, and almost all prices were immediately liberalized.[5] Later that month, Yeltsin made a presidential decree that

---

[3]See Chapter 22 for a fuller description of the conception and achievements of Polish shock therapy.
[4]David Lipton and Jeffrey Sachs, "Prospects for Russia's Economic Reforms," *Brooking Papers on Economic Activity* 2 (1992): 213–276.
[5]The sole exception was the energy sector that remained under administrative prices. Energy prices were raised at the outset of the reforms and were partially liberalized later in 1992, but remained at a fraction of world prices. The government's fear was that a rapid increase of energy prices to world levels would cause a massive contraction in industrial output because the Soviet economy was based on cheap energy.

declared all economic activity to be legal unless it was expressly prohibited, reversing the situation that existed under Soviet planning, by which all private economic activity was proscribed unless expressly permitted.[6]

The upshot was a massive rise in prices and the considerable monetary overhang came into play as idle savings pursued scarce goods. Inflation during the first month of "shock therapy" was over 250 percent, and the prices of many key consumer goods rose by much more. The force of inflationary pressure surprised many observers, including the International Monetary Fund (IMF), which held the opinion that a rise in prices of only 45 percent would be enough to neutralize the monetary overhang. Opening the Russian economy to foreign trade resulted in dramatic consequences as consumers who had been required to buy Soviet goods now had greater choice. Imports flowed in, and the demand for domestic output fell; for the first time Russian producers faced serious competition in markets formerly guaranteed to them under planning, and decades of neglecting design and quality showed. Meanwhile, because many raw materials could be now exported for hard cash, prices soared from the artificially low levels administered under Soviet planning, pushing inflation and hurting domestic production.[7]

Price liberalization provided some positive effects: the monetary overhang disappeared as savings were eradicated; the black market was curtailed; and lines for goods, a great source of inefficiency and welfare loss, were much reduced. However, the distributional consequences were large. Savings in rubles were wiped out by the plunging value of the Russian currency. Table 21.1 gives some data on the extent of this redistribution. The biggest losers were the households, who saw their savings eradicated, and their real wages fall, and any enterprises that held ruble-denominated balances. The gainers were largely the government and the financial sector.

■ TABLE 21.1

Winners and Losers in Russia's Inflation, 1992–1993 (percentage of GDP)

	Losses	Gains	Net Gain
Households	12	0	–12
Enterprises	18	16	–2
Financial sector	0	8	+8
Government	0	4	+4
Other	0	2	+2
Total	30	30	0

SOURCE: William Easterly and Paula Vieira da Cunha, "Financing the Storm: Russia's Macroeconomic Crisis," *Economics of Transition* 2, no. 4 (1994).

[6]One observer of the Soviet system declared: "In the Soviet Union almost everything was forbidden . . . and those few things that were permitted were compulsory."
[7]The increase in raw material prices occurred largely because the Russian economy became increasingly integrated into the world market. Input prices, especially those for energy, had been highly controlled under central planning and rose sharply toward world levels.

The **interenterprise payments system** began to break down. Many firms were unable to pay the higher input prices because they were not receiving payment for the goods they sold and delivered. Not out of choice but out of necessity, enterprises began to extend credit to each other, creating a precarious pyramid of interenterprise debt. Insolvent firms ceased to pay their workers; as personal incomes fell, so did demand, creating more insolvencies. Although the linchpin of the Gaidar plan had been monetary restraint, the worsening economic situation raised pressures to liberalize credit. Lobbying from the enterprises was intense, and the growth of interenterprise credit led to the justifiable fear that the collapse of a few firms could lead to catastrophic domino consequences. So reluctantly the government, through the Central Bank, loosened credit and provided cheap loans (often at negative real interest rates) to bail out the industrial sector, causing excessive growth of the money supply.

(3) Privatization

The third pillar of the Gaidar program was mass privatization, deemed imperative for three main reasons. First, policy makers felt that the burden of subsidizing state enterprises could be sharply reduced, or even eliminated, once these firms passed into private hands.[8] This private ownership would help to put public finance on a more stable footing and reduce the reliance on credit creation to keep enterprises solvent, thereby eliminating a source of inflation. Second, for reasons discussed earlier, it was expected that private management of resources would lead to greater efficiency. Third, large-scale privatization would be hard to reverse and would, therefore, reinforce political change because the new owners would oppose retrogression thereby "locking in" the gains of economic and political liberalization.

(4) Constructing a Social Security System

The Soviet Union lacked an adequate system of unemployment compensation, regarded as unnecessary in a society where unemployment notionally did not exist, and was, in fact, illegal. However, if the efficiency of industry was to be increased, sweeping changes in employment practices would be required, and raising labor productivity had to involve, at least in the short term, the shedding of excess labor. The lack of a "social safety net" to catch the unemployed created a distinct possibility of increasing social unrest.[9]

(5) Converting the Defense Sector

The great paradox of the Soviet economy was the coexistence of a world-class defense and aerospace sector with consumer goods and housing sectors that simply failed to

[8]As we shall see, eliminating the subsidy burden was something of a vain hope. Privatization has not ended subsidy of the productive sector.

[9]Unemployment statistics are not reliable for the early period of reform. By mid-year 1993 the European Bank for Reconstruction and Development reported that the rate was 5.3 percent, although no good measure was available because the incidence of disguised unemployment (workers retained but not fully employed) was high.

deliver the goods. The key was the high degree of **prioritization** that locked up more than 30 percent of Soviet gross domestic product (GDP) in defense, and with it most of the nation's able engineers and managers. It was hoped that "defense conversion" deploying the skilled labor and sophisticated apparatus to peaceful purposes could provide a dynamic sector around which to focus Russia's development effort.

OUTPUT COLLAPSE

The crisis accompanying the breakup of the Soviet Union led to a sharp fall in economic activity. Table 21.2 shows the sectoral impact on manufacturing and agriculture. Overall industrial output fell by almost 60 percent in four years, and the contraction was not limited to industry. Agricultural output fell in the same period by 26 percent, due largely to the inability of collective farms to obtain or afford fertilizers and pesticides as well as the continued failure of the distribution system.

As the situation worsened during 1992, Gaidar's position eroded and in December 1992 he was ditched in favor of Viktor Chernomyrdin, a seasoned insider with a background in Russia's rich, and corrupt, energy industry. Though Chernomyrdin had a less reformist bent than Gaidar and despite Yeltsin's face-off with the Duma, liberalization and privatization continued.

THE PRIVATIZATION PROGRAM

The privatization of state-owned enterprises in Russia can be divided into three distinct programs. The first handled the transfer of property in the small-scale sector, generally conferring property rights on the operators of existing enterprises and the inhabitants of rental property. The second was the **voucher auction program** responsible for the privatization of 60 percent of the industrial sector between 1992 and 1994, and was designed to provide the basis of a market economy. Together these two programs constituted **mass privatization**. Finally, **privatization for cash** started in 1995 and continues today.

▪ **TABLE 21.2**

	Production in Selected Sectors (1992 prices, billions of rubles)		
	1990	1994	Change
Steel and metals	4,004	2,132	−47%
Light industry	1,926	512	−73%
Other industry	12,153	5,592	−54%
Agriculture	3,908	2,910	−26%
Total	22,087	10,368	−53%

NOTES: Derived from Goskomstat data reported in *World Bank Statistical Handbook 1995,* "States of the Former USSR"; "Studies of Economies in Transition," paper 19 (Washington DC, 1995).

Small-Scale Privatization

Small-scale privatization began with Russian shops and small service establishments, which were handed over to local municipalities who arranged for their transfer, usually to their current managers. Agricultural land was "decollectivized" with members of the collectives able to lease land and equipment. Apartments were sold by local authorities generally to their occupants. Those processes started during 1992. By the end of the year about 50,000 shops, 182,000 family farms, and 3 million apartments had been sold. In addition, some 500,000 new small businesses had been registered.

The Voucher Privatization Program

Large-scale industrial enterprise was privatized under the aegis of the State Committee for Management of State Property, also known as GKI, or the Privatization Ministry. It was headed by Anatoly Chubais, who chose voucher auction as the primary means of transferring ownership. The voucher program, which was immense in scope and rapid in execution, was adopted during 1992, and the program officially began in December of that year, ending in June of 1994. During these 21 months, some 15,779 enterprises, employing about 18 million people, were disposed of.

The magnitude of the task and the shallowness of Russian financial markets made Chubais's choice of voucher privatization all but inevitable. In Russia 25,000 firms had to be placed in private hands and initial public offerings (IPOs) used in countries with deeper financial markets and a smaller task at hand were not capable of doing the whole job; the detailed valuation and the offering process was simply beyond Russia's means.

Boycko, Shleifer, and Vishny put the issue this way:

> The case for privatization through cash sales falls apart on both efficiency and especially political grounds. From the point of view of efficiency, privatization through cash sales is just too slow. It requires valuation, information collection, preparation of auctions and public offerings and a variety of other services which investment banks gladly supply given ample time and generous fees. It is important to remember in this regard that West European countries typically privatize a few firms a year, and even such rapid privatizers as Mexico and Chile could handle at best a couple of hundred of firms per year. In contrast, Russia needed to privatize 25,000 medium and large-scale firms. If these firms were properly valued, prepared for auctions, or, as some investment bankers wanted, restructured prior to sale, odds are privatization would have never gotten off the ground. Even if it did, at the rate of 200 per year, Russian privatization would have taken over a century! In the meantime, the economy would continue to stagnate. From the political viewpoint, privatization through sales is even more problematic. To be politically feasible in Russia, this approach would have required the allocation of significant stakes to insiders at large discounts and only the remaining shares could be sold. Even such sales would probably have been resented, and certainly not supported, by the public at large. First, the highest bidders in cash privatizations often turn out to be illegitimate businessmen, former party and state security officials, and foreigners. Selling off the national patrimony to these investors generates public outrage rather than support.[10]

---

[10]Maxim Boycko, Andrei Shleifer, and Robert Vishny, *Privatizing Russia* (Cambridge, MA: MIT Press, 1996), p. 71.

The GKI drew up a list of which firms were to be privatized in the first phase. It covered the bulk of the industrial sector, but kept defense-related firms and much of the energy sector under public ownership. Once the list for privatization was published, the management of each firm could choose between three schemes of privatization. Each of the available options gave considerable benefits to insiders, to secure their support for the privatization process, because without insider support privatization could have been derailed as other economic reforms were sabotaged in the past. Expansion of private ownership takes away some of the property rights over the firm that the management and, to a lesser extent, the workers had in the past. It was therefore essential to compensate for the loss of these informal rights with a generous share of the ownership of the newly privatized enterprise.

Under Option I workers would be given 25 percent of the shares for free, but these shares would be nonvoting. In addition, workers could buy 10 percent of the voting shares at a 30 percent discount from book value. Book values, based on the historic cost of capital before the massive inflation of the early 1990s, were low. Consequently, any price based on book value was close to zero. Management could access up to 5 percent of the voting shares at a similar price. Thus "insiders" were offered 40 percent of the income of the enterprise and 15 percent of the voting power for next to nothing.

Although Option I seemed generous to many observers, it apparently offered inadequate reward for some insiders, who lobbied Chubais for better compensation for management. They succeeded in establishing an alternative, Option II, which allowed workers and management to buy 51 percent of the capital for a price of 1.7 times book value—again close to zero.[11] The rest of the share capital was to be distributed to the population at large by way of a voucher scheme. All citizens (including children) could purchase for 25 rubles a voucher with a face denomination of 10,000 rubles. This voucher could be turned over to an investment company, exercised personally at an auction, or sold. The total number of shares of each firm to be offered at auction were divided in proportion to the number of vouchers tendered for the firm. Popular firms attracted a lot of attention, and therefore the shares would be divided among many claimants. More obscure firms or those believed to have few assets or prospects attracted little attention, and a few vouchers could garner a sizable part of the share capital. Boycko, Shleifer, and Vishny summarized these options as follows:

> To save small investors from the need to make complicated bids, one strategy is to ask each investor to submit his voucher as a bid for the company. The equilibrium number of shares each voucher buys is then inversely proportional to the number of vouchers rendered. Thus, if the company offers 1,000 shares for auction, and 40 vouchers are submitted, each voucher buys 25 shares. If, on the other hand, 4,000 vouchers are submitted, each voucher buys only a quarter of a share. Each investor submitting vouchers is assured of getting some shares, but gets fewer shares of desirable companies.[12]

---

[11]An Option III was also available. It allowed management to acquire 100 percent of the shares if they "promised" not to take the firm into bankruptcy and "strip" its assets. Fewer than 2 percent of privatizations followed Option III.

[12]Boycko, Shleifer, and Vishny, *Privatizing Russia* (Cambridge, MA: MIT Press, 1996), p. 91.

The Dominance of Insiders Although one of the objectives of voucher privati-zation was to curry wide popular support, individual citizens were disadvantaged in buying shares because they had little information about either the intrinsic value of an enterprise or the number of potential bidders. Most valuable knowledge about enterprises lay with insiders and investment intermediaries. The mass pri-vatization project in Russia created some 22,000 joint stock companies, of which 73 percent were disposed of under Option II, and therefore the insiders automatically gained control; 25 percent of the privatization followed Option I, and Option III was seldom used.

The trend to insider ownership was reinforced by a free market in vouchers.[13] Both investment intermediaries and management interested in acquiring a greater part of a firm were able to buy the voucher books from the public for prices ranging from $20 to as little as $4. Many Russians sold off their share in the country's infra-structure for an average of about $10.[14] A 1993 survey conducted by the Privatiza-tion Ministry found that management and workers owned an average of 65 percent of share capital of 143 surveyed medium-sized enterprises. Top management held about 8.6 percent, outside investors owned 21.5 percent, and the government retained an average of 13 percent of shares. These figures are averages, in some firms the management stake was much higher.

Table 21.3 gives a slightly different perspective on this phenomenon. It shows who holds a majority share in the newly created corporations (i.e., who holds more than 50 percent of the stock). In almost two-thirds of the firms, insider employees

■ TABLE 21.3

Majority Owners of Private Sector Corporations, 1995 and 1996 Privatizations (percent)

Majority Owners	1995	1996
Employees	59	64.7
Rank and file	26.7	30.5
Managers	2.3	4.2
Top managers	0.4	0.4
General director	0.4	0.8
No majority insider	29.4	28.8
Nonstate outsiders	17.3	19.8
State	3.1	2.6
None	20.3	12.8

NOTE: Numbers do not add to 100% because of rounding.
SOURCE: Joseph R. Blasi, Maya Kroumova, and Douglas Kruse, *Kremlin Capitalism: Privatizing the Russian Economy* (Ithaca, NY: ILR Press, 1997).

[13]On the largest exchange, the Russian Commodity and Raw Materials Exchange, volume was about 60,000–100,000 vouchers per day, this was augmented by regional exchanges and a vigorous street market.
[14]Most people did initially claim their vouchers, or someone claimed them on their behalf. Approxi-mately 144 million vouchers were issued, and the Russian population was estimated at 148.2 million.

and management have control; outsiders control only 20 percent. In more than 4 percent of firms, management alone holds the controlling interest.

After the active market for vouchers became established, because the number of vouchers tendered for offered shares in specific companies is a matter of record, it is possible to make estimates of the implicit price for which publicly owned firms were sold. Take, for example, the automaker Zil, 30 percent of whose shares were offered in a voucher auction. The implied market value of the whole firm—which employed 103,000 persons—was a mere $16 million. Even more startling, 28 percent of all of the shares on offer were bought by just seven investment groups, several affiliated to a single parent company. Even though the Russian voucher auction program achieved an enormous transfer of assets from the public sector to the private, the greatest beneficiaries were a narrow group who used insider information (and in many cases manipulated the auction process) in order to gain control of the enterprises. Moreover the high degree of worker and management ownership suggests that meaningful and rapid postprivatization reform will be difficult, because job preservation rather than profit maximization will be an important objective.

The entire program was criticized for giving away too much to insiders to get the process moving.[15] Certainly the result was a dramatic skewing of the distribution of wealth and control, earning for the Russian Federation and other successor states to the Soviet Union the title of **kleptocracies**.[16] While it is true that as a result of voucher privatization as many as 40 million Russians became shareholders, at least for a time, the process undoubtedly created hundreds of millionaires, while robbing millions of ordinary Russians of their share of state assets.

Proponents of voucher privatization defend it on the grounds of expediency, arguing that it represented the only politically feasible way forward. The dissolution of socialism could have been followed by an equitable parceling out of the assets among the people, perhaps in terms of equal shares, but one fact to be reckoned with was that much of Russia's state-owned enterprises did not effectively belong to the state. Workers, local bureaucrats, and especially the management of firms already possessed a stake in these firms, and even though such a property right might have been informal, it was nevertheless real. Even more to the point, these important actors in the economic scene had the power to disrupt any potential reform if it were not in their interest to go along with it.

Before the fall of the Soviet system, Jan Winiecki analyzed the failure of previous economic reform efforts in centrally planned systems.[17] His work developed the view that Soviet-style economies operated to maximize the rents flowing to the ruling classes, or *nomenklatura*. On top of this primary system of rent extraction, kickbacks or side payments could be appropriated by anyone with some power over scarce resources. Those who gained from the status quo had an incentive to

---

[15]These criticisms apply even more to the so-called spontaneous privatizations in which the management of some companies, along with part or all of the workforce, assumed control and ownership of an enterprise or established a cooperative that assumed the assets.

[16]Literally "states ruled by thieves," from Greek roots.

[17]Jan Winiecki, "Why Economic Reforms Fail in Soviet-Type Systems, A Property Rights-Based Approach," *Economic Inquiry* 28, no. 2 (1990).

resist any change of the system. For example, replacement of the *nomenklatura*[18] with a more overtly merit system would be opposed because rent extractable by the Communist Party membership would be reduced. Similarly, any plans to increase the size of the private sector were objected to, nominally on ideological grounds, while the real reason was fear of the loss of economic rents:

> There are no well-paid posts to be had in small private enterprises, nor is there a "soft" budget constraint, so permissive to a variety of rent-maximizing kickbacks even under reform. A shift of activity from the state to the private reduces therefore the possibilities for party apparatchiks and economic bureaucrats to extract rent. Hostility toward the private sector is therefore based not on ideology or even actual rent losses, but on gains foregone when the expansion of the state sector is curbed in favor of the private sector.[19]

A large class of people who see their well-being decline with onset of reform (even though the economy as a whole might do better) are capable of concerted action to bring down any reform plan. Hence the Russian mass privatization program had to confer considerable benefits on economic bureaucrats, politicians, and insiders in order to ensure its survival.

Privatization for Cash

The voucher auction program concluded in the summer of 1994 and was assumed to create the basis of a market economy. As Table 21.4 shows, almost 16,000 medium and large enterprises, employing about 18 million people, passed into majority private ownership. In 1995 the Russian government shifted its emphasis to cash privatization to dispose of the assets of the enterprises still in the state sector, mostly utilities and natural resource or high-tech defense enterprises.

■ TABLE 21.4

Voucher Auctions in Russia (December 1992–June 1994)

	Dec. 1992–June 1993	July 1993–Dec. 1993	Jan. 1994–June 1994	Total
Number of enterprises sold by calendar month	2,871	5,632	7,276	15,779
Employment (thousands)	3,243	5,278	9,249	17,770
Total vouchers accepted (thousands)	16,054	27,724	69,830	113,608

SOURCE: GKI/RPC Performance Database; Maxim Boycko, Andrei Shleifer, and Robert Vishny, *Privatizing Russia* (Cambridge, MA: MIT Press, 1996), pp. 106–107.

[18]Winiecki defines *nomenklatura* in terms of the right of the Communist Party apparatus, from the Central Committee on down to the enterprise committee, to "recommend" or "approve" all appointments for all managerial positions in the economic administration and all managerial positions in enterprises.
[19]Winiecki, "Why Economic Reforms Fail in Soviet-Type Systems," *Economic Inquiry* 28, no. 2 (1990), p. 300.

Lacking an adequate system of public finance, the government looked for revenue from the sale of the resource sector to close the federal government deficit. With only limited interest in the asset sales, the government resorted to a highly controversial scheme to raise cash. At the initial suggestion of Oneximbank, one of the most powerful and well-connected banks in Russia, the government agreed to offer shares in publicly owned companies as collateral for loans from the private sector. For only $170 million, Oneximbank received more than 50 percent of the voting shares of Norilsk Nickel, the producer of more than 20 percent of the world's nickel and 50 percent of global platinum output. In theory the bank was acting like a pawnbroker; the government could redeem the shares if it came up with the cash by September 1996, but it was clear from the beginning that the government made no budgetary provision for that eventuality. Consequently, the bank got the Norilsk shares very cheaply. Although their worth is difficult to determine, a figure of 10 times what Oneximbank paid seems reasonable. The Norilsk deal was followed by similar insider deals favoring other banks, and the government was able to meet its revenue targets for 1995 at the expense of squandering a great deal of support for the privatization program.

Despite public outcry in Russia against these **loans-for-shares deals**, and shock within the international agencies charged with assisting the economy, no transactions were reversed, in part because 1996 was a poor year for revenue from share sales on the open market, and less than 15 percent of anticipated and budgeted revenues were realized. Primarily, however, the reasons lie in the drive to re-elect Yeltsin, which required the support of the very businesspeople who benefited from the sales. In 1997, in contrast, the Russian stock market took off, and the government was able to dispose of large blocs of shares it had retained in the oil and mineral sectors for high revenues, realizing about three times the forecast revenues and closing the budget gap considerably. Then, 1998 saw a stock market fall of about 85 percent measured in local currency and 95 percent in terms of dollars, and predictably privatization revenues also fell sharply. By late 1998 only $1 billion of revenue from privatization was realized for a budget that called for $8 billion. However, the government still owns about 40 percent of the natural resource sector, and it can raise a great deal of capital through privatization sales if the market recovers.

The Financial and Industrial Groups

A striking feature of Russian capitalism comes through the rapid emergence of the **financial and industrial groups**, or FIGs, officially established by a law in 1995. The legislation offered tax and other privileges to groups that registered with the authorities, though in fact such advantages have been slow to emerge. Of the now more than 100 officially registered groups, a substantial part of the economic and political power in Russia lay in the late 1990s with just seven large bank-led groups—Alfa Group, Inkombank Group, LogoVAZ, Menatep, Most, Oneximbank, and SBS-Agro.[20]

---

[20]It is not possible to say exactly what proportion, but Boris Berezovsky, head of LogoVAZ, estimated in 1996 that it represented half of Russia's economy.

Such groups are closely held, highly diversified, and the larger ones are generally grouped around a bank. In some ways they resemble the *chaebol* of Korea and *keiretsu* of Japan, but they are potentially more powerful than either. They incorporate banks, where *chaebol* do not, and are controlled by a single individual to a much greater degree than contemporary *keiretsu*. In addition to the bank-centered FIGs are the industry-centered groups. On the whole they are less powerful and less diversified than the bank-centered groups.

The consequences of the emergence of these groups are uncertain. On the positive side, they can represent a source of rapid change in Russian industry; firms acquired by these groups can be subject to tight oversight and given clear performance objectives, as well as advice and capital for restructuring. On the other hand, FIGs constitute an alarming concentration of political, as well as economic power, both in Moscow and in the regions.

Under the Yeltsin administration prior to 2000, the leaders of the large groups were extremely politically well connected and in several cases had held high government office. They were known as **oligarchs**[21] (sometimes as "the tycoons") and clearly influenced governmental policy. They are less powerful under President Vladimir Putin than they were under his predecessor. Their position in Russia in the late 1990s resembled the structure of **finance capitalism (*Finanzkapitalism*)** articulated by Rudolf Hilferding in the early years of this century, which was very influential to the thought of V. I. Lenin. The oligarchs threw their weight behind Yeltsin's 1996 reelection drive, and secured his success largely through the use of their dominance of media outlets. Apparently as a *quid pro quo*, they received ownership of a large part of Russia industry and natural resources by means of the notorious "loans for shares" arrangement. An irony can be found in that what was thought by Hilferding to be the penultimate stage of capitalism should be the first step for a socialist economy in transition.

In the summer of 1998 a widespread crisis hit the banking sector and bank failures seemed imminent. The Central Bank of Russia drew up a list of 12 banks that were to be bailed out under any circumstances, because the instability of the financial system was so great. The list included the lead banks of all the seven major FIGs. This coincidence brought to the forefront the twin issues of moral hazard in the banking sector and the political influence of the major banks.

Under Putin the position of the original group of oligarchs deteriorated. As vice president he assumed the presidency when Yeltsin surprisingly resigned. Restricting the power of the oligarchs was an important part of his election drive in 2000. After a relatively decisive election victory he delivered on his pledge and severely cut into the influence and wealth of these businessmen, driving two of them into exile and regaining control of the media. The new oligarchs are less visible and apparently less influential than the original seven were under Yeltsin but the interaction between business and political elites is still strong and the group (FIG) structure prevails. This situation in turn makes the going more difficult for Russia's small entrepreneurs.

---

[21]An oligarchy is a state ruled by a few—hence the presumption was that the business leaders effectively controlled the state.

THE PROBLEMS OF SMALL ENTERPRISE

Conversion of Russia's state-owned behemoths has been tortuous and slow. Seemingly bright stars faded; for example, enthusiasm for defense conversion turned sour. Only in the oil and gas and forest product industries do Russia's firms show themselves to be close in competing on world markets. The hope for the future probably lies in the growth of small firms, and therefore the conclusions of a recent OECD report were somewhat depressing. In the initial stages of liberalization, small enterprise growth was vibrant, but the number of small firms and proprietorships stalled since then at about 875,000. They account for about 20 percent of total employment and about 8.7 percent of GDP. Their share of GDP actually fell in each of the last four years and is now about 8 percent, much less than the 12.2 percent that the small enterprise sector accounted for in 1997. In part this decline is due to the increase in oil and gas prices that artificially inflated GDP, but the lack of progress is apparent.

Russia's entrepreneurs face many of the same problems encountered by small businesses everywhere, but some are clearly more acute. Access to capital is especially tough given the absence of a genuine banking system. Taxation is high and confusing with overlapping tax authorities competing for revenue. "Unofficial taxation"—paying bribes to politicians and bureaucrats—is a problem for two-thirds of firms, an OECD survey found. Crime is a perpetual concern. The high inflationary situation makes rising input costs a perpetual problem.

Long-term growth depends on the success of small and medium-sized businesses. At present Russia's entrepreneurs have plenty of enthusiasm but face huge difficulties. As a result of their problems, more than 50 percent of businesses classify themselves as not stable, with 5 percent calling themselves critical. Clearer taxation, better crime prevention, a real banking sector, and less corruption are necessary if small business is to succeed.

SOURCE: *OECD: Economic Survey of the Russian Federation 2002*, p. 74.

THE PROGRESS OF INSTITUTIONAL REFORM

The Banking System

Under central planning, the state bank, Gosbank, exercised a virtual monopoly over the banking sector, although specialist banks existed to finance construction and foreign trade, and a thrift bank served to facilitate small saving. The Gorbachev reforms included a reorganization of banking and introduced three new state banks.[22] More important for the longer-term structure of Russian finance, the 1988 Law on Cooperatives allowed the emergence of private banks. In 1988, 80 such banks were founded, and by the end of the Soviet era the total had risen to more than 400.

At the breakup of the Soviet Union, the assets and functions of Gosbank were assumed by the newly created Central Bank of Russia (CBR) under its first chair Viktor Geraschenko. The CBR was established as an orthodox institution, much like the central banks in many West European countries. It is responsible for issuing currency and supervising and regulating the financial sector, as well as being the

---

[22]The Agricultural Bank, the Industrial and Construction Bank, and the Social Investment Bank.

lender of last resort and the manager of foreign exchange operations. It is not an independent institution, as according to its rules of operation laid out in the constitution, "*in collaboration* with the government of the Russian Federation it [the Central Bank] elaborates and implements a uniform national monetary policy designed to protect the ruble and ensure its stability."

The Central Bank serves as a pliable tool to channel credit to keep potentially bankrupt enterprises afloat. This function led Jeffrey Sachs, an economist then at Harvard, to describe Geraschenko as "the worst central banker in history." The soft-budget constraint, which should have ended with privatization, is in fact alive and well and will continue to be until a stable financial system and workable public finance system is in place. The early 1990s saw the continued growth of private banking, reaching a high of about 2,500 banks in 1995. A subsequent contraction came as successive financial crises weeded out the weaker elements, and the Central Bank of Russia withdrew licenses from banks at the rate of roughly 250 annually.

However, as Table 21.5 shows, many banks remain weak. Almost half of all registered banks operate with a capital base of less than 30 million rubles, and many are highly vulnerable to runs or falls in the value of assets held. Although average assets rose in recent years, they still amount to only a mean of $50 million, a small amount for any kind of real financial intermediary. The Russian banking sector is significantly undeveloped. Assets expressed as a percentage of GDP is a measure of financial development and Russia certainly lags in this respect. Its bank assets/GDP percentage is only 5.4 percent, compared to 15.4 percent in Estonia and 22 percent in the Czech Republic.

The retail banking system is dominated by Sberbank, the state savings bank owned by the Russian central bank. Sberbank dwarfs all other Russian banks in terms of size. It accounts for 23.5 percent of all assets, 75 percent of household deposits and 33.7 percent of credit to nonbanking enterprises. Its dominance in retail baking is secured by the fact that it is the only bank for which the government

■ TABLE 21.5

		Grouping Banks by Capital, 2001*
	Number	**Share of Total (percentage)**
Less than 3 million rubles	121	9.1
From 3 million to 10 million rubles	203	15.3
From 10 million to 30 million rubles	304	22.9
From 30 million to 60 million rubles	260	19.6
From 60 million to 150 million rubles	184	13.9
From 150 million to 300 million rubles	108	8.1
300 million rubles and more	147	11.1
Total	1,327	

* Paid in authorized capital as per articles of association and registered by the Bank of Russia.
SOURCE: Central Bank of Russia, *Bulletin of Banking Statistics 2002*.

offers deposit insurance. Consequently households have confidence in its security and it competes unequally with private banks. Current proposals to extend limited guarantees to depositors in nongovernmental banks have encountered opposition from, among others, the Central Bank of Russia. Without deposit guarantee, it is difficult to see real growth in Russian retail banking, and Sberbank will continue to have access to the bulk of consumer saving.

POVERTY AND SOCIAL ASSISTANCE

Shock therapy and its aftermath profoundly affected the incidence of poverty in Russia. The negative growth rates of the past decade shrank the pie, while liberalization, privatization, and high rates of inflation skewed the distribution of income. Today the highest earners receive 47.4 percent of total personal income, while the worst-off 20 percent receive only 6.3 percent of income, much less than at the beginning of privatization.

Gorbachev's reforms had little effect on income distribution, and although income contracted during the 1980s, its distribution actually became more egalitarian as Table 21.6 shows. The change since the **big bang**, the start of the Yeltsin administration, has been dramatic. In 1991 the income of the average "wealthy" person (in the top quintile) was only 2.8 times that of the average poor person (in the lowest quintile); by 1998 the figure rose to about 7.5. The decline in living standards for the poorest quintile of society was sharpest between 1991 and 1993, due largely to the failure of the pension system to adjust to rapid price rises. The introduction of indexation in 1995, prompted largely by electoral considerations, stopped further decline. The working class was hurt by liberalization; in 1991 the third and fourth quintiles enjoyed almost 35 percent of personal income, by 1998 that portion fell to about 25 percent.

The regional impact of income redistribution has been even greater than for the nation as a whole. Central planning provided interregional transfers that largely ceased under the reforms. In 1992 the ratio of average income in the richest *oblast*

■ TABLE 21.6

Income Distribution: Percentage Share of Each Quintile (1980 and 1991 to 1997)

	1980	1991	1992	1993	1994	1995	1996	1997
Top	33.4	30.7	38.3	41.6	46.3	46.9	47.1	47.4
Second	23.1	22.8	26.5	24.8	23.0	22.4	21.3	21.1
Third	18.6	18.8	17.6	16.7	15.2	15.0	14.9	14.8
Fourth	14.8	15.8	11.6	11.1	10.2	10.2	10.5	10.4
Bottom	10.1	11.9	6.0	5.8	5.3	5.5	6.2	6.3
Total	100	100	100	100	100	100	100	100

NOTE: Data are for total money income.
SOURCE: Goskomstat, *Russia in Figures* (Moscow: State Committee on Statistics of the Russian Federation).

(county) to the poorest was 8:1. By 1994 this gap widened to 42:1.[23] Table 21.7 shows how hard poverty hit in some of the regions. Worst affected are those that specialize in agriculture, while those with extensive mineral resources fared the best. Nevertheless, for a region to have 30 percent of its population below the poverty level (unable to buy a standard minimum basket of goods) is commonplace, and in many regions one-fifth of the population is unable even to buy adequate food.

Of particular concern is the emergence of poverty among relatively well-educated and skilled segments of society. Human capital, justifiably regarded as one of Russia's strengths, may be lost due to emigration, neglect, and despair as protracted unemployment and poverty create a dual labor market, trapping the poor. In addition Russia is about to be hit by an extremely serious AIDS crisis, which will rival some African nations in its intensity.

The Tax System

Under central planning a sophisticated tax system was unnecessary. Revenues accrued to the state largely through markups imposed on the costs of goods and by

■ TABLE 21.7

The Incidence of Poverty in Selected Regions, 1994

	Percent Poor	Percent Very Poor
Rich in Mineral Resources		
Magnitogorsk City	17.0	4.8
Yakutiya Republic (Sakha)	28.8	5.8
Intensive Agriculture and Food Industry		
Astrakhan Oblast	72.4	44.3
Oryol Oblast	58.7	32.6
Industrial or Mixture		
Adygeya Republic	51.9	19.4
Chuvash Republic	42.5	22.7
Khanty-Mansiysky District	28.8	13.2
Krasnoyarsky Krai	43.5	20.1
Moscow Oblast	41.0	19.7
Tver Oblast	39.1	18.1
Voronezh Oblast	20.4	10.2

NOTES: The "poor" do not have enough income to purchase the subsistence minimum consumer basket as defined in Goskomstat poverty measures; the very poor are unable to purchase the food component of the subsistence minimum. Moscow Oblast excludes the city of Moscow.
SOURCES: G. N. Volkova and L. A. Migranova, *The Living Standards of the Russian Population by Region,* Bulletin no. 12 (Moscow: Center for Living Standards Study, Ministry of Labor, 1994).

[23]World Bank, *Poverty in Russia: An Assessment* (Washington, DC: 1995), p. 31.

THE HIV EPIDEMIC AND THE RUSSIAN ECONOMY

Many nations around the world have been adversely affected by the spread of HIV—predominantly in Africa where the epidemic is most severe. Until quite recently the impact on Russia was apparently small. Until 1995 only 100 to 200 new cases were reported each year. Since that time, however, the number of infected cases doubled every 12 months. By May 1, 2002, the total number of registered cases reported to the Federal AIDS Center reached 193,000. Experience shows that the majority of cases are undetected or unreported; using conventional multipliers the current incidence in Russia is probably about 1 million. Furthermore, although the primary initial transmission mechanism in Russia occurred through intravenous drug use, it has now spread to the non-drug using population. The average length of time between infection and death is about 12 years and so the death rate is still small, but it will surge from about 2008 onward. Unless treatment improves, the World Bank estimates that the death rate will be in the thousands per month. Because 60 percent of AIDS sufferers are between 20 and 30 the pandemic will strike hard in the economically active population.

The economy will be affected through several channels. Labor supply will fall with the rising death rate, but labor productivity will be adversely impacted well before then. The need to maintain support systems will affect productivity across society, not merely among those actually infected. The savings of AIDS-affected families will be dissipated, the safety net will be tested, and the burdens upon the health system will increase, which will in turn adversely affect the quality of care in other areas. Presently, the treatment of an AIDS sufferer costs some $9,000 per person per year. Some countries successfully negotiate a lower cost, and real price decreases can be expected in the future. Nevertheless, it is optimistic to believe that the cost of drugs will fall as low as $3,000 per case per year. At present, this amount is almost twice Russian GDP per head expressed in current exchange rate terms.

The macroeconomic impact of AIDS in Russia is, in the opinion of the World Bank, a heavy blow waiting to fall. It estimates that because of the AIDS crisis, growth GDP in 2020 will be 10 percent less than in the absence of the epidemic. In other words AIDS will cost a full percentage point of growth per year. The World Bank rightly observes this cost is "substantial in an economy in as much need of rapid growth as Russia's."

SOURCE: The World Bank, "Russian Economic Report," available at http://www.worldbank.ru.

a variable tax on consumer goods. Since the start of transition, a constant struggle to put public finance on a stable and economically efficient footing continues to meet with little result. This failure created sustained federal budget deficits. The structure of the budget in the year 2000 is shown in Table 21.8. One important fact to note is that the "tax effort" at the federal level is rising. Tax revenues now represent some 16 percent of GDP. The deficit is giving way to a surplus at the federal level that will allow some repayment of the large debts and a further reduction in debt service payments. Noninterest expenditures continue to rise although social expenditures are well below the level needed, and regional aid is lacking

Regional and local authorities represent a large part of the consolidated government budget, almost 50 percent of expenditures, but they manage their accounts better than the federal authorities and deficits are smaller. The deficit on the consolidated budget amounted to about 5.2 percent of GDP in 1998 has also been turned into a surplus of about 4.3 percent that will allow debt repayment (Table 21.9).

■ **TABLE 21.8**

Outcome of Federal Budget, 1998 and 2000

	Shares of GDP	
	1998	2000
Revenues	**8.9**	**16**
Tax Revenues	7.5	13.7
Value-added tax	3.4	5.3
Profit tax	1.1	2.5
Excise Tax	1.5	1.9
Customs duties	1.3	3.2
Other tax revenues	0.2	0.8
Nontax revenues	0.4	1
Revenues of budgetary funds	0.9	1.3
Expenditure	**13.7**	**13.7**
Debt service	3.9	2.4
Domestic debt service	2.4	0.8
Foreign debt service	1.5	1.6
Noninterest expenditure	9.8	11.2
Defense	1.7	2.7
Social sphere	2.0	1.9
Financial aid to the regions	1.6	1.4
Budget Balance	**−4.8**	**2.3**

SOURCE: OECD Economic Surveys, Russian Federation, 2002.

Revenues at the federal level depend heavily on indirect taxation, especially the value-added tax (VAT). Personal income taxation gathers little revenue for the central government (less than 1 percent of the total) because tax evasion is high and most of the revenue that is gathered goes to regional authorities.[24] The tax rate on individuals in the 0–5,000 ruble income range (roughly from 0 to $200) is 12 percent, rising to a maximum of 30 percent above 10,000 ($400). In addition, wage income is subject to high social security contributions totaling 39 percent of salary income. Consequently, the top combined rate on labor income could reach 69 percent, clearly a level that makes for considerable disincentives to effort and strong rewards for tax evasion.

The ineffectiveness of the tax regime is compounded by its complexity. Federal, regional, and city governments impose a wide range of taxes, with little or no coordination.[25] A great deal of discretion in the application of tax exemptions also

[24]A tax reform plan authored by the Yeltsin government seeks to guarantee the federal government 20 percent of income tax revenue.

[25]In some cases, aggregate rates on certain kinds of activities exceeded 100 percent.

■ **TABLE 21.9**

Consolidated Government Budget, 1998 and 2000 (percentage of GDP)

	1998	2000
Federal Government		
Revenue	8.9	16
Expenditure	13.7	13.7
Transfers to regions	1.6	1.4
Transfers to extra-budgetary funds	0.6	0.4
Balance	−4.8	2.3
Consolidated Regional Budgets		
Revenue	14.5	15.1
Transfers from federal government	1.6	1.4
Expenditure	14.9	14.6
Balance	−0.3	0.5
Extra-Budgetary Funds		
Revenue	8.7	8.6
From federal government	0.6	0.4
Expenditure	8.7	7.1
Balance	0	1.5
General Government		
Revenue	29.9	37.9
Expenditure	35.1	33.6
Balance	−5.2	4.3

SOURCE: Ministry of Finance, Economic Expert Group, Goskomstat, in OECD Economic Survey of Russia, 2002.

increases the potential for corruption and tends to discourage investment, especially from abroad.

Tax evasion is common in Russia, though it seems that some progress is being made in this direction. Many Russian firms and individuals simply fail to pay their taxes, a phenomenon so widespread that it meets with social approval. The Organization for Economic Cooperation and Development (OECD) reported in 1997 that "identified arrears on taxes and social contributions reached 10 percent of GDP in 1996."[26] Fortunately the situation seems to be improving. The 262 identified "large tax payers," primarily in the energy sector, are meeting their obligations, and the Ministry of Finance reported 91 percent tax compliance in the corporate sector in 2001.

The failure to meet tax targets means that the government cannot fund its expenditures: workers go unpaid, pensioners miss their stipends, and essential services

[26]Organization for Economic Cooperation and Development, *1996/97 Survey of Russia* (Paris: OECD, 1997), p. 4.

were curtailed. Moreover, government borrowing increased, pushing up interest rates and thereby the cost of financing the national debt, presenting the specter of a worsening debt spiral. The structure of tax arrears is shown in Figure 21.1. Although the large-scale corporate sector (usually the energy extracting companies) is most often blamed for tax delinquency, in fact the bulk of the arrears results from failure to collect the value-added tax, a deficiency largely at the retail level.

Tax reform is essential for economic growth, and it is difficult to see Russia joining the developed nations without a functioning income tax regime. At the moment the tax system is deeply regressive with its heavy reliance on VAT. The inequalities in Russian society are wide and growing and a broad-based functioning income tax (the work horse of fiscal revenue raising in almost all market societies) will be important to curb distributional problems. The downside might be that an effective income tax will deter entrepreneurship, but an increase in compliance can lead to lower rates and further increases in effectiveness.

Competition Policy

The legacy of planning and its obsession with scale economies left the Russian industrial structure highly concentrated. Table 21.10 provides data on the degree of industry concentration in the Soviet Union. The collapse of the Soviet Union increased the degree of concentration in Russia, because competitive goods from other republics now constituted hard currency purchases, often subject to tariff or quota, and therefore, the table probably understates the degree of concentration.

International trade provided healthy competition in some areas. In fact, the influx of imported "white goods" (freezers, washers, etc.) created a serious balance of payments problem and heavy tariffs were imposed on them in 1998.

Although patchy in coverage, Table 21.10 shows that, at the onset of liberalization, monopoly was an acute problem in durable consumer goods and machinery.

■ FIGURE 21.1

Structure of Tax Arrears, April 1998

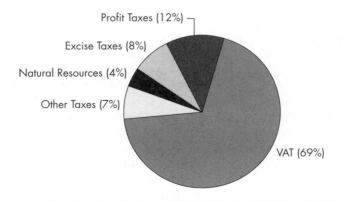

Profit Taxes (12%)
Excise Taxes (8%)
Natural Resources (4%)
Other Taxes (7%)
VAT (69%)

Industry Concentration in the Former Soviet Union

Type of Product	Percentage of Production by Largest Producer
Sewing machines	100
Washing machines	90
Freezers	100
Concrete mixers	93
Road-building cranes	75
Hydraulic turbines	100
Steam turbines	95
Polypropylene	73
Electrolytic tin plate	100
Stainless steel pipes	96
Color photographic paper	100

SOURCE: *The Economist,* August 11, 1990, p. 67, from Goskomstat.

Little has been done to change matters, in part due to the problems faced by smaller entrepreneurs in Russia (see the feature "The Problems of Small Enterprise."). This perception of pervasive monopoly is reinforced by other studies by the state statistical agency (Goskomstat), which found in the mid-1990s that 166 enterprises were absolute monopolies. Another Soviet government study found that 80 percent of output of the machine-building industry was produced by monopolists.

Russia needs an effective way to encourage competition and facilitate entry into the monopolized industries, perhaps by breaking up some of the larger concerns. The problem is not legislation, but enforcement. Competition law is both modern and well conceived, but implementation by the Anti-Monopoly Committee remains weak. Actions by regional and local governments to protect local producers aggravate the situation.

Another problem is the extent of the "natural" monopolies in the network industries—gas, electricity supply, and communication. These concerns carry great influence, exert considerable monopoly power, and—especially in the case of Gazprom, the natural gas producer—are major tax delinquents. (The government has been slow to act against them because of their political influence.)

A good example of this kind of problem is electricity supply, which is dominated by the giant electricity monopoly United Energy Systems (UES), which produces more than 80 percent of all power in the Russian Federation. (Natural gas supply is dominated by Gazprom, which accounts for a like percentage of output.) Before liberalization, energy was cheap in Russia, priced at about 32 percent of the world average. Prices tripled between 1993 and 1995, to levels above the then world average prices. Price regulation was ineffective although the government claimed that in its absence prices would have risen by a further 12 to 23 percent.[27] Currently, 53 percent of UES is still owned by the state, and it lies at the nexus of economic problems. It is owed large sums of money by regional energy companies (called "Energos"—themselves monopolies) which are functionally bankrupt but unwilling to cut off nonpaying customers from the grid. The customers are in desperate straits themselves, striving to stay in business, and cannot afford the excessive monopoly prices charged by the UES. In turn, UES claims it is owed so much money it both needs to raise rates and cannot afford to pay its taxes, while paying its workers between three and four times the average for the economy.

Clearly more effective regulation is necessary, and restructuring of the industry to facilitate competition would pay dividends. Vertical disaggregation of the industry to allow competing suppliers and retailers to use a common regulated grid, as in the United Kingdom and Australia, would give the market a solution of greater efficiency and lower prices. The Russian government is now moving in this direction, and reform of electricity and gas supply is a priority. However the disasters associated with energy liberalization in the United States provide much food for thought and certainly slowed the process in Russia.

Agriculture

Russian agriculture has been a persistent failure throughout the twentieth century. The countryside, still home to more than 20 percent of Russia's people, remains impoverished and will continue to be depressed until a viable stimulus to agriculture is found. Prior to 1914 Russia was the world's largest exporter of grain, and the potential to be at least self-sufficient is clearly there. Collectivization under Stalin led to a demoralized and unproductive farm sector, and the development of state farms brought little relief. Persistent food shortages bear at least some of the blame for the fall of communism. Even after the collapse of the Soviet Union, privatization of agricultural land, opposed by the remnants of the Communist Party and the Peasants Party was slow. Now almost 90 percent of Russia's 190 million hectares (470 million acres) is in private hands. The vast majority of it was handed over to the former collective farmers generally in parcels too small to farm economically. The title to the land is still uncertain and the consolidation of these small holdings into viable farms is all but impossible. The same uncertainty, coupled with the lack of adequate financial intermediation, make borrowing by farmers for equipment and land improvement difficult in the extreme. Foreigners, particularly West Europeans, would like to invest in Russian agriculture, but are denied the legal right to own land.

The Duma passed a law in 2002 that in theory created a market in agricultural land and the path should now be clear to consolidation and innovation. The reality is trickier. The Communist years killed off (too often literally) the prospect of "family farming," and the creation of efficient agriculture will be tough as a result.

---

[27]*Izvestiya*, "Natural Monopolies: Comparing Russian and Australian Experience," January 13, 1996; Gennadi Kazakevitch, *Russian and Euro-Asian Economics Bulletin* 5, no. 4 (April 1996).

Good farmers are in short supply, and so are farm laborers. Despite high levels of unemployment, Russians are unwilling to work the land. One solution, already tried in the Stavropol region, is the importation of contract farm workers from China, who are happy to work for about $100 per month.[28]

PROSPECTS FOR THE RUSSIAN ECONOMY

The Russian economy fell sharply during the 1990s, but 1997 saw considerable optimism about the future. The data indicated that the economy turned a corner, and after a long period of falling GDP, positive growth was in view. The subsequent revelation that not only were the statistics unreliable, but also deliberately manipulated by Goskomstat, the state statistical agency, was a serious blow. It suggested that the government would resort to deliberate deception to achieve its aims; a fact that once revealed had caused a negative effect on incoming investment and international lenders. The next disappointment came from the Russian stock market, which after booming during 1996 and 1997, fell during 1998 and collapsed in a dramatic fashion in August. This crisis was followed by a 50 percent devaluation of the ruble (after a $4 billion IMF loan was wasted in its defense), an indefinite default on domestic government debt, and a 90-day moratorium on payments on foreign debt.

The pattern since the collapse of 1998 has been one of clawing the way back to growth and stability. After a sharp fall in 1998, GDP growth is again positive and quite strong, averaging more than 6 percent per year. This turnaround was helped by the high level of world energy prices, which benefited Russia in all sectors. GDP growth is strong, capital formation surged in 2000, the current account balance moved into surplus, and government revenue is higher.

■ TABLE 21.11

			Key Macroeconomic Indicators	
	1998	1999	2000	2001
GDP % growth	−4.9	5.4	8.3	5.5
Fixed Capital Investment, % growth	−12	5.3	17.4	7
Inflation, % per year	84	37	20	19
Exchange Rate Ruble/$	10	25	28	29
Unemployment %	13	12	10	9
General Govt. Budget Balance	−5.4	−0.8	3.6	2
Current Account, % of GDP	0	13	18	10

SOURCE: OECD, Survey of Russia, 2002.

---

[28]"A shiny free market blueprint. Will it work?" *The Economist*, June 27, 2002.

Perhaps more importantly, the strong presidency of Vladimir Putin ended speculation that Russia was likely to break up. His strong stance against Chechnyan separatism, questioned by many on moral grounds, at least showed Moscow's determination to maintain unity. The following policy reform is necessary to provide a minimum platform for growth.

1. Even after the 2001 tax reform, which clearly delineated fiscal capabilities, the tax system needs extensive reform, and attention must be paid both to revenue potential and incentive structure.

2. Many large privatized enterprises remain to some degree on a "soft-budget constraint." Of the billions of dollars channeled through "soft loans," 90 percent remain unpaid, even though they are ruble-denominated and inflation made them practically worthless.

3. Competition policy needs to be enforced.

4. Foreign investment seems to be necessary if Russia is to grow, but the capriciousness of the tax system, political uncertainty, and corruption keeps it low.

5. Russia needs to create a real banking sector.

The unreliability of official statistics increases the value of microeconomic studies by outside agencies. A study by McKinsey and Company reported in *The Economist* makes particularly disturbing reading:

> The study compares Russian-based companies (whether foreign or locally owned) with their American counterparts, sector by sector. It shows that Russian productivity is, on average, only 19% of American levels. Before the post-Soviet slump in output, it was only 30%. Depressingly, the 10% of the workforce that works on industrial capacity installed after 1992—presumably the best—is still producing at only 30% of American levels.[29]

The McKinsey report concluded that the absence of gains in productivity stems from the failure to cut back on workers (despite the fact that wages are generally in arrears) and "antiquated organizational structure." The solution would seem to be an infusion of management skills and increased capital investment. The most logical sources of both are via direct foreign investment, but political uncertainty and pervasive corruption keep those resources at bay. Moreover, capital apparently still continues to leave Russia, though perhaps at a slower pace than during the Yeltsin years. In July and August 1999 a surplus on current account topped $5 billion. Some $2.5 billion was absorbed by debt service but Roland Nash, chief economist at Renaissance Capital, an investment bank quoted by *The Economist,* thought that "the other $2.5 billion just disappeared somewhere."[30] These excesses are thought to be less under the tighter rule of Putin but misappropriation and the lack of transparency will continue to deter private capital inflow.

Lack of incoming investment, political uncertainty, corruption, and capital flight all contribute to hinder the transition of the economy. Only with stability and a level playing field will economic growth accelerate and the promise of Russia's

---

[29]"Russia's Economy: Surprise, Surprise," *The Economist,* October 23, 1999, p. 88.
[30]*The Economist,* October 23, 1999, p. 89.

resources and human capital be realized. Whether the economy's great potential can be unleashed by its leadership remains to be seen. Vladimer Putin, elected in 2002, pledged a program of reform, but his strong links to the FIGs and a tendency toward centralizing power might prove to be incompatible with the continued development of a competitive market.

KEY TERMS AND CONCEPTS

big bang

Decree on Property

finance capitalism (*Finanzkapitalism*)

financial and industrial groups

Gaidar reforms

Grand Bargain

interenterprise payments system

kleptocracy

Law on Cooperatives

Law on Individual Economic Activity

Law on State Enterprise

loans-for-shares deals

mass privatization

nomenklatura

oligarchs

prioritization

privatization for cash

small-scale privatization

voucher auction program

QUESTIONS FOR DISCUSSION

1. Why did Gorbachev's economic reforms fail?
2. What were the essential strategies of the Yeltsin/Gaidar reforms of January 1992?
3. How did inflation transfer wealth in Russia?
4. What were the three options by which enterprises might choose to privatize?
5. How did "insiders" take possession of so much of Russia's industry?
6. What are the FIGs? How might they aid growth and change and what dangers do they embody?
7. How has transition changed the distribution of income and the incidence of poverty?

RESOURCES

Web Sites

Central Bank ....http://www.cbr.ru/

Institute for the Economy in Transition http://www.iet.ru/index2.html

Russian Government Online (In Russian) ....http://gosorgan.amursk.ru/

St. Petersburg Times, **National Newspaper**..http://www.sptimes.ru/

Vladivostok News, **National Newspaper**...http://vlad.tribnet.com/

Russia Online ....http://www.russia-on-line.com/

IET-IRIS Project—Social Services Provision under the transition
(health care, education, culture) ....http://mac.www.online.ru/sp/iet/

Books and Articles

Ash, Timothy, and Paul G. Hare. "Privatisation in the Russian Federation: Changing Enterprise Behaviour in the Transition Period." *Cambridge Journal of Economics,* December 1994, 619–634.

Åslund, Anders. *How Russia Became a Market Economy.* Washington, DC: The Brookings Institution, 1995.

Åslund, Anders (ed.). *The Post-Soviet Economy: Soviet and Western Perspectives.* New York: St. Martin's Press, 1992.

Åslund, Anders, and Richard Layard (eds.). *Changing the Economic System in Russia.* New York: St. Martin's Press, 1993. Reviewed in the *Journal of Comparative Economics,* October 1994, 281. (Collection of papers from conference at Stockholm School of Economics, June 1992, assessment of early reform.)

Bergson, Abram. "Russia's Economic Reform Muddle." *Challenge,* September–October 1994, 56–59.

Blasi, Joseph R., Maya Kroumova, and Douglas Kruse. *Kremlin Capitalism: Privatizing the Russian Economy.* Ithaca, NY: ILR Press, 1997.

Boycko, Maxim, Andrei Shleifer, and Robert Vishny. *Privatizing Russia.* Cambridge, MA: MIT Press, 1995.

Buck, Trevor, Igor Filatotchev, and Mike Wright. "Employee Buyouts and the Transformation of Russian Industry." *Comparative Economic Studies,* Summer 1994, 115.

Dyker, David. *Restructuring the Soviet Economy.* New York: Routledge, Chapman and Hall, 1992.

Easterly, William, and Paula Vieira da Cunha. "Financing the Storm: Russia's Macroeconomic Crisis." *Economics of Transition* 2, no. 4 (1994): 433–66.

Gregory, Paul R., and Robert C. Stuart. *Soviet and Post-Soviet Economic Structure and Performance,* 5th ed. New York: HarperCollins College Publishers, 1994.

Islam, Shafiqul. "Russia's Rough Road to Capitalism." *Foreign Affairs,* Spring 1993, 57–66.

Joskow, Paul L., Richard Shmalensee, and Natalia Tsukanova. "Competition Policy in Russia During and After Privatization." *Brookings Papers on Economic Activity*, 1994, 301–380.

Lipton, David, and Jeffrey Sachs. "Prospects for Russia's Economic Reforms." *Brooking Papers on Economic Activity* 2, 1992, 213–276.

Monetary and Exchange Affairs Department, International Monetary Fund. "Central Bank Autonomy, and Inflation and Output Performance in the Baltic States, Russia, and Other Countries of the Former Soviet Union." (1995–1997). IMF Working Paper, WP/99/4.

Nelson, Lynn D., and Irina Y. Kuzes. "Evaluating the Russian Voucher Privatization Program." *Comparative Economic Studies,* Spring 1994, 55–67.

Shlapentokh, Vladimir. "Privatization Debates in Russia: 1989–1992." *Comparative Economic Studies,* Summer 1993, 19–32.

Slider, Darrell. "Privatization in Russia's Regions." *Post-Soviet Affairs,* October–December 1994, 367–396.

"A Survey of Russia: In Search of Spring." *The Economist,* July 12, 1997, 48.

Van Atta, Don. "Agrarian Reform in Post-Soviet Russia." *Post-Soviet Affairs,* April–June 1994, 159–190.

22

THE PROGRESS OF REFORM IN POLAND AND THE CZECH REPUBLIC

Despite some favorable developments the verdict on the reform program in Russia is mixed, and it is possible many Russians would, given the choice, revert to the *status quo ante.* Other countries with a more successful recent history now enjoy higher living standards than before the onset of liberalization, and we turn now to discuss two of them, Poland and the Czech Republic. Both nations experienced a happier transformation than those further east, due in some degree to their location and their initial condition. Both countries lie in direct contact with relatively prosperous Germany and the European Union (EU), and both also had only a 45-year exposure to communism and retained a vestigial remnant of capitalist institutions. Both were accepted for entrance into the European Union in 2004, although living standards are likely to be below those of the core current EU members. However, it is essential to ask to what extent policy determined the relatively successful outcome of transition in these countries, because this information can teach important lessons for other nations.

POLAND

A great deal has been written about the transformation in Poland, in part because of the visible role of Western economists in advising on issues of structural change and in part because it was the first application of a so-called **big bang** policy, whereby prices in the economy were liberalized at a single stroke.

BACKGROUND

To fully understand the Polish experience, we must review its history. Much of the credit, or blame, for the collapse of the communist state in Poland lies with the workers' movement known as **Solidarity**, which emerged in August 1980, coordinating the famous strike at the Lenin shipyard in Gdansk. Solidarity was briefly legalized by the communist government in December 1980 but was banned once more in October 1981; throughout the 1980s it was a fundamental source of both moral and material opposition to the communist regime. As a genuine and spontaneous worker movement in opposition to a government that claimed to represent

POLAND	
Area (thousand sq. km.)	323
Currency	zloty
Exchange Rate	3.85 zlotys = US$1
Population, 2000 (millions)	39
Population Growth Rate	0.1%
GNI per capita, 2000	$4,200
GNI per capita, PPP	$9,030
GDP Growth, 1990–2000	4.6%
Value Added as % of GDP 2000 Agriculture	19%
Industry	30%
Services	51%
% of GDP Government Expenditure	45.5%
Exports	30%

the worker class, Solidarity undermined the authority of the communist regime in Poland and, in a sense, all communist regimes throughout Eastern Europe. The fragility of the old order was exacerbated by the faltering economy. According to CIA estimates, the growth of the gross domestic product (GDP) in the period 1975–1980 was only 0.7 percent per year, and this failure to advance living standards in an age of internationally free-flowing information became a source of popular dissatisfaction.

REFORMS OF THE 1980s

Both socialist economic orthodoxy and the need to provide domestic substitutes to reduce hard currency imports kept Poland throughout the 1970s on a path of investment in heavy industry such as shipbuilding, automobiles, and petrochemicals. Nevertheless, Poland's external account deteriorated badly as the service on a hard currency debt of more than $25 billion was a growing burden on the economy.

From 1978 to 1982 the Polish economy faced an acute crisis during which output fell for four successive years, with a particularly sharp contraction in 1981, and hard currency exports to noncommunist states declined while imports continued to rise, further increasing international indebtedness. The government's immediate response was to impose austerity, including a period of martial law; food and consumer goods were rationed and key industries were put under military administration. While actually increasing control in the short term, the government prepared a reform program that was designed to move the economy away from Soviet-style central planning and toward a market socialist economy with a strong element of worker management modeled on the Yugoslav system. Under regulations unveiled in 1982, enterprises were freed of most planning targets and were able to act as income-maximizing entities governed by elected workers' councils.[1] As in the Yugoslav case, large enterprises were divided into "basic organizations of labor," akin to profit centers, and a hard-budget constraint was in theory imposed because firms were to be self-financing, and free to determine wage levels and choice of technique, as well as sources of supply. The prices of roughly 50 percent of consumer goods and about three-quarters of industrial input were decontrolled (see Table 22.1). The remainder were covered either by fixed administered prices (the case in energy and basic foodstuffs) or by regulated prices, based on a conventional "cost plus" formula.[2] The 1982 reforms also broke the foreign trade monopoly of specialist foreign trade organizations and allowed individual firms more access to export markets.

Forty years of communist rule failed to totally extinguish the private economy. Agriculture had not been collectivized or socialized to any significant extent, remaining largely in private hands though inefficient and starved of investment. Private handicrafts and some service trades remained legitimate and as a result a commercial legal code survived. The scope of the private sector was increased in the late 1980s when, through the **Law on Economic Activity**, the communist government allowed the expansion of small business activity, facilitated incoming foreign investment, and encouraged joint ventures between Polish and foreign enterprises. The same legislation also enabled limited privatization of state-owned enterprises (SOEs), but due either to neglect or design the rules were unclear. Some property did pass into private hands, but it was mainly seized by powerful members of the Polish Communist Party, earning it the title of *nomenklatura* **privatization**.

■ TABLE 22.1

Price Regimes in Poland, 1982 and 1987 (percentage of total)

	1982		1987	
Type of Control	Consumer Goods	Industrial Inputs	Consumer Goods	Industrial Inputs
Administered	35	45	20	29
Regulated	15	2	5	3
Free	50	53	75	68

SOURCE: Cited in Jeffries, *Socialist Economies and the Transition to the Market* (New York: Routledge, 1993), p. 297.

[1]Exceptions were military goods, basic consumer goods, and export orders already committed to by contract, all of which retained their planning targets.

[2]In the succeeding five years, regulation became less frequent, and more prices became subject once more to central administration.

As Poland approached transformation to a market economy, it enjoyed several distinct advantages over other socialist states:

- A higher share of its economic activity was coordinated by the market.
- Its agricultural sector was predominantly private, and though in need of rationalization, no major land reform was required.
- It had an existing system of commercial regulations and legalized private property.
- Its state enterprises had already achieved a high degree of independence from the ministries.
- Reforms had already encouraged the expansion of private entrepreneurial activity.
- It had developed strong trade links with the West, facilitating information and investment flows.

Against those pluses, however, was an almost equal array of relative disadvantages when compared to other reformist states:

- Poland had a large monetary overhang, amounting to about 17 percent of GDP, the result of wage increases in the 1980s outpacing the availability of goods—an inflationary time bomb that would explode with the liberalization of prices and trade.
- Repeated deficits on current account had been financed by foreign borrowing, resulting in hard currency debt, whose service preempted a large part of export earnings.
- Because of the leading role of Solidarity in the revolution, union militancy was high, and labor movements were well-organized.
- Political compromise resulted in promises to workers that could not be kept in the context of economic restructuring.

SHOCK THERAPY

In June 1989 limited representative democracy came to Poland. Elections were held for about half the seats in Parliament, while others were filled by the nominees of the government. The Solidarity movement swept the contestable seats and ultimately emerged as the lead party in a coalition government. Leszek Balcerowicz, the new finance minister, initiated a program of **shock therapy** designed in close consultation with the Harvard economist Jeffrey Sachs, intended by its austerity to jump-start the economy from lethargy.

In January 1990, after approval by the International Monetary Fund (IMF), Parliament passed the basic elements of this Stabilization and Liberalization Program (SLP). Balcerowicz himself set the tenor of the plan when in September 1989 he declared to Parliament that "it is time to shut our eyes and jump into the hole, without checking either the state of the water or the depth of the drop"—the first of many dramatic metaphors used to describe his program, which was based on five principal features:

1. Restrictive monetary policy, including higher interest rates and the end of "preferential credit" to favored enterprises

2. Elimination of the budget deficit, largely through the abandonment of subsidies for food, consumer goods, and energy

3. Continuation of the price liberalization that occurred in the 1980s

4. The establishment of a convertible currency, and trade liberalization through reduction and the elimination of import quotas

5. A tax-based policy to curb wage inflation by penalizing firms through a 20 to 50 percent levy (the *popiwek*) on wage increases above the government's guidelines

The net effect of these measures was, at a stroke, to rationalize prices, but also to raise them to international levels.

The Impact of Shock Therapy

Shock therapy led directly to high interest rates, declining output, and soaring levels of unemployment. The real extent of the dip in output that followed the initiation of shock therapy is open to debate. The statistical system inherited from the planners was at best misleading and failed to provide an adequate benchmark by which to judge the progress of the economy under reform. Most series published at the time showed deep cuts in output, with GDP falling by about 12 percent in 1990 and a further 7 percent in 1991, while industrial output tumbled by twice as much. Subsequent research reevaluated these figures and found that much of the fall in the output of large-scale enterprises was due to the elimination of low-quality, overpriced output, which was in excess supply. On the other side of the ledger, most of the output of the growing small-scale private sector[3] was omitted from official statistics, in part because it was underreported to avoid paying tax on it.

Unemployment rose sharply. At the end of 1989 the official rate was 0.3 percent of the workforce, though it did not include extensive "disguised unemployment" and overstaffing. By 1993 the recorded figure had risen to 16 percent, after which it moderated before rising again in the late 1990s. Again there were grounds to be skeptical about the statistics, because evidence suggests that up to half of the total unemployed were moonlighting in paid employment while being registered as looking for work. As the zloty fell, domestic prices adjusted to world levels; but inflation fell, inching away from the hyperinflation of 1990 and reaching more manageable levels (about 30 percent) by 1994–1995. Despite the fall in the currency, imports surged, producing a trade and current account deficit that a rapid rise in direct foreign investment only partially filled. Output followed its familiar course in transition economies, falling sharply initially but returning to positive levels by 1992.

In the assessment of one of its authors, the greatest achievement of Polish shock therapy was that shortages in the economy were eliminated virtually overnight.

---

[3]Some 516,000 new enterprises were registered in Poland in 1990 alone.

Poland: The Outcome of Shock Therapy

	1990	1991	1992	1993	1994	1995	1996	1997
GDP per capita at purchasing power parity ($)	4,221.0	4,018.0	4,371.0	4,668.0	5,017.0	5,417.0	5,876.0	6,406.0
GDP (% change)	−11.6	−7.0	2.6	3.8	5.2	7.0	6.1	6.9
Industrial production (% change)	−24.2	−8.0	2.8	6.4	12.1	9.7	8.3	10.8
Budget balance (% of GDP)	3.1	26.7	26.6	23.4	22.8	23.6	22.5	21.4
Unemployment (%)	6.3	11.8	13.6	16.4	16.0	14.9	13.2	10.5
Inflation (%)	585.8	70.3	43.0	35.3	32.2	22.0	18.7	13.2
Exports ($ billions)	15.8	12.8	14.0	13.6	17.0	22.9	24.4	27.2
Imports ($ billions)	12.3	12.7	13.5	15.9	17.8	24.7	32.6	38.5
Trade balance ($ billions)	3.6	0.1	0.5	22.3	20.8	21.8	28.2	211.3
Current2account balance ($ billions)	3.1	22.0	0.9	20.6	2.3	5.5	21.3	24.3
Foreign direct investment flow ($ billions)	.89	.1	.3	.6	.5	1.1	2.7	3.0
Foreign debt ($ billions)	49.4	48.0	47.6	47.2	42.2	43.9	40.4	38.0
Discount rate (%)	48.0	36.0	32.0	29.0	28.0	25.0	22.0	24.5
Exchange rate (Zloty/$)	1.0	1.1	1.4	1.8	2.3	2.4	2.7	3.3

SOURCE: European Bank for Reconstruction and Development (EBRD), International Monetary Fund (IMF), World Bank.

The most immediate consequence of the new environment has been the sharp reduction of shortages in the economy. Apart from those goods still subjected to administered prices, queues have all but disappeared. Meat is freely available at all times in the official shops. The notorious gas station lines are gone. Foreign consumer goods such as bananas and strawberries and consumer electronic products are now widely available. Durable goods, many of which used to require months or years for delivery, can now be purchased in department stores.[4]

The appearance of food in previously empty stores seemed a miracle, but it did not represent sudden affluence for all of the population. Part of the cause of apparent plenty lay in the fact that fewer people could afford consumer goods and food at the higher prices that were experienced after price controls were terminated and rising unemployment cut into effective demand. Domestic supply was slow to respond in the short run although imports increased sharply and reduction of demand played the larger role in achieving balance in the goods market.

INSTITUTIONAL CHANGE

With relative stability established in the macroeconomy, the way was cleared for institutional change.

---

[4]David Lipton and Jeffrey Sachs, "Creating a Market in Eastern Europe: The Case of Poland," *Brookings Paper on Economic Activity* 1, 1990, p. 127.

Privatization

The most important feature of institutional change in the Polish case was the privatization of industry. Agriculture was already primarily within the private sector, and the basics of property and commercial law survived the 40 years of communist rule, minimizing the need for legal reform. The logic of shock therapy as seen by its authors depended on a rapid disposal of state assets:

> Poland must begin a rapid process of privatization of state firms, not only to ensure efficient resource utilization, but also to prevent the collapse of the stabilization itself in the medium term. Experience around the world, plus the logic of the soft budget constraint, strongly suggests that it will be difficult to maintain the financial discipline of the state enterprises beyond the short run, especially if the state enterprise sector remains the dominant part of the economy. Eventually wage pressures and lax investment decisions are likely to undermine the financial health of the state firms.[5]

Thus **marketization** required on theoretical grounds the rapid sale of the bulk of the state sector. However, it was a huge task, and piecemeal reform under the communist leadership had in many cases made the task more difficult; by introducing a high degree of worker governance into the enterprises, preservation of the existing level of employment often became the objective of the enterprise, rather than the efficient use of resources or profit maximization.

In 1990 when a four-year timetable for privatization was announced, Poland had 8,441 state-owned enterprises. By the end of 1995 only 1,610 enterprises were fully privatized, about 20 percent of the total, and these were mostly small to medium-sized firms; only about 10 percent were large concerns employing more than 500 persons. The majority (about two-thirds) were privatized by a process of liquidating the existing state enterprise and leasing the capital stock to new companies formed by management and workers. These insider deals were done with terms subject to negotiation on a case-by-case basis. Larger enterprises were also privatized in an eclectic fashion. Of the 160 large enterprises that were successfully privatized, 22 percent were sold through initial public offerings. Most of the rest were sold directly to a single buyer or leased to management and employees. Some infusion of capital and technology was ensured by a search by the Privatization Ministry for foreign partners to be actively involved.

Table 22.3 shows the progress of privatization between 1989 and 1995. It was not slow in absolute terms, but it was in relation to the size of the task at hand. At the end of 1989, 8,561 enterprises were either fully owned by the state or the state held a controlling interest. By the end of 1995, 4,357 were still completely owned by the state, 482 had been handed over to municipalities, and 2,023 were "commercial code companies" still controlled by the state, although with some private equity holding. In almost five years only 1,715 enterprises had been fully privatized, less than 25 percent of the total required. The slow pace of privatization did not mean that activity in the private sector was sluggish.

---

[5]Lipton and Sachs, "Creating a Market in Eastern Europe: The Case of Poland," *Brookings Paper on Economic Activity*, 1, 1990, p. 127.

■ TABLE 22.3

Number of Economic Units in Public and Private Sectors on December 31, 1989, and December 1, 1995

Ownership Form	1989	1995
State enterprises	7,337	4,357
Municipal enterprises	—	482
Commercial code companies with state majority	1,224	2,023
Domestic commercial code companies (private)	15,252	90,843
Joint ventures	429	24,086
Businesses owned by individuals	813,145	1,693,427
Cooperatives (including cooperative banks)	16,691	19,822

SOURCE: Leszek Bakerowitz, Barbara Blaszczyk, and Mark Dombrowski, "The Polish Way to a Market Economy," in *Economies in Transition—Comparing Asia and Europe,* Wing Thye Woo, Stephen Parker, and Jeffrey D. Sachs (eds.) (Cambridge, MA: The MIT Press, 1997).

Mass Privatization

Mass privatization was finally instituted on in 1995 after a delay of more than three years. The Polish method is unique in that it seeks to solve the problem of corporate governance through the creation of government-sponsored financial intermediaries. Fifteen such **national investment funds (NIFs)** were created under the aegis of the Treasury Ministry, with Polish managers assisted by Western advisers.[6]

In 1995 title to the equity of the 512 largest state-owned enterprises was transferred to the funds with each enterprise's share capital being allocated on the lines indicated in Table 22.4. This structure ensured that one of the funds would hold at least one-third of the voting equity of every large firm and would therefore feel a strong interest in the performance of the firm, as well as be in a position to offer advice and assistance to further its growth and restructuring. Incentives were given a key role and any payments to the funds, or to any employees and consultants, are performance related. For a small fee of 20 zlotys, each of Poland's 27 million adult citizens could receive a certificate convertible to a share in one of the NIFs. The greater the demand for the shares of any one NIF, the less stock an individual certificate would ultimately buy. Over 96 percent of the eligible population took advantage of the offer, and now the Polish public owns the former state enterprises indirectly through ownership of the NIFs.

The NIFs are active, not passive holders of the shares. Their job is to restructure the companies by changing management, improving marketing, obtaining finance, and disposing of the unproductive parts of an enterprise in order to maximize its value. They can dispose of their share holdings in any firm or buy more. Since 1997 the NIFs have been listed on the Warsaw stock exchange and citizens can sell their shares in turn for cash, or invest more. It is too soon to tell whether the NIF approach produces superior results to other privatization techniques. Certainly

---

[6]Western firms retained include Barclays PLC, Dresdner Bank, Chase Manhattan, and Creditanstalt.

■ TABLE 22.4

Structure of Equity of Large Privatized Enterprises

Lead shareholding fund	33
Other 14 funds (1.93% each)	27
Employees	15
State	25

there is an opportunity for closer and more active governance, which in theory should improve enterprise performance. In addition to the described "indirect approach," a procedure for direct privatization applies to smaller firms, those with fewer than 500 employees. Generally these firms are sold off to their employees. The number of private limited-liability companies increased sixfold to more than 90,000, and almost 1 million proprietorships and partnerships were established.

Mass privatization transformed the ownership structure of the Polish economy in the late 1990s. As Table 22.5 shows, the Polish economy is now largely private with about three quarters of employment and output originating in the private sector. Public activity still dominates only in the utility sector, which is still common in the European context and was the rule until quite recently. Nevertheless the process is not complete. The state still owns some 3,000 firms, about 900 of which are to wind up in bankruptcy. That leaves about 2,100 firms to be sold, and the pace of disposal needs to be accelerated. Much of the employment still in the state-owned sector is concentrated in coal mining and iron and steel production. These heavy industries are difficult to restructure because they represent such an important part of the economic base of the region. Coal is a particular problem. It provides about 70 percent of Poland's total power and represents almost 9 percent of employment in the southern regions of the country. Many mines are loss-making, though the industry

■ TABLE 22.5

Size of the Private Sector (percent of whole economy)

	Employment		Output	
Sectors	1995	2000	1995	2000
Agriculture	97.0	98.7	88.3	89.6
Industry	50.5	74.8	47.7	71.9
Mining	3.1	14.0	2.4	27.8
Manufacturing	60.0	85.9	57.5	82.3
Utilities	3.7	6.7	2.0	4.5
Transport	26.7	37.6	40.2	50.2
Finance	36.4	72.2	67.4	82.9
Average of all sectors	62.8	73.7	61.1	74.9

SOURCE: OECD, June 2002.

as a whole is "in the black" since 2000, and privatizing them would mean a reduction of energy and a dramatic surge in local unemployment.

DIRECT FOREIGN INVESTMENT (DFI)

Incoming **direct foreign investment (DFI)** served Poland well, adding buoyancy to the private sector and creating employment. Between 1993 and 2000 more than $38 billion flowed into Poland, making it the most popular destination in any of the formerly planned East European economies on an aggregate basis. In terms of per-head flows, however, Poland lags well behind the Czech Republic and Hungary (see Table 22.6). The flows were motivated in some cases by special factors (like the proximity of cheap labor to the German market, the associate status with the EU, and the large and influential Polish diaspora), as well as policy measures such as the liberalization of prices, the absence of capital controls, and political stability. In addition, substantial overseas portfolio investment in Polish shares and bonds added a further $1.5 billion per year on average.

This inflow of capital is likely to accelerate with full membership of the EU as further funds arrive through EU agricultural support and cohesion expenditures. This shift should minimize balance of payments problems.

THE UNEMPLOYMENT PROBLEM

In the spring of 2002 Poland merited the dubious distinction of being the OECD economy with the highest unemployment rate. Even though unemployment fell between 1991 and 1998, since 1999 it increased sharply and is now the most difficult issue facing the economy. High rates of joblessness are now typical across continental Europe, but in Poland the situation is particularly acute, and many school-leavers cannot find work. Official rates in 2002 crossed 20 percent, while the actual rate is probably about 5 percent higher. EU membership may help by raising the flow of capital in and facilitating emigration, but unemployment will undoubtedly continue to be a major issue, which if unaddressed will gnaw at the social fabric and express itself in terms of rising crime and other social pathologies.

■ TABLE 22.6

Direct Foreign Investment Flows, 1993—2000

	Per Head		
	2000	1993—2000	1993—2000
Czech Republic	4,595	21,450	2,088
Hungary	1,974	18,877	1,884
Poland	8,168	38,458	995
Slovak Rep.	1,987	4,129	765

SOURCE: OECD, 2001.

Several culprits contribute to high unemployment in Poland. A high minimum wage discourages job creation and, in the opinion of the OECD, "forms a binding wage floor and contributes to high structural unemployment." A centralized wage determination structure discourages local flexibility. Payroll taxes to support the social safety net are high, adding to the marginal cost of labor and reducing employment. Unusually, the differential between private sector and public sector pay favors those remaining in the public sector. Strong unions and direct bargaining keep wages in state-owned industries high, inflating wage demands in the private sector. A series of policy shifts could help job creation but the unemployment will be around for some years.

PROSPECTS FOR THE POLISH ECONOMY

In many ways Poland is a paradox of transition. Its performance after the start of shock therapy policy was one of the strongest of any of the Eastern European nations. GDP growth stayed positive in every year since 1993, and GDP per head, measured in terms of purchasing power parity, will soon cross $10,000. Inflation has been brought to heel and the public debt is still modest. At just 39.9 percent of GDP it is lower than almost all of the EU and does provide some capacity for fiscal stimuli without violating the terms of the stability and growth pact if, or when, Poland abandons the zloty and joins in the euro group.

Although at the outset of the privatization speed was held to be key, Poland remains one of the slowest privatizers in terms of the progress of handing over state-owned enterprise. It retains a substantial, and politically influential, state sector. However, strong growth and a buoyant private sector led the way forward. Table 22.7 shows recent economic performance and indicates an economy that, on the whole, is doing quite well, despite a dismal performance in 2000 that owed

▪ TABLE 22.7

			Recent Economic Performance	
	1998	1999	2000	2001
GDP per head ($ at PPP)	7,970	8,450	8,990	9,280
GDP (% real change)	4.8	4.1	4	1
Government consumption (% of GDP)	16.37	16.5	16.53	16.59
Budget balance (% of GDP)	−1.01	−0.93	−0.1	−4.6
Consumer prices (average % change)	11.73	7.31	10.14	5.5
Public debt (% of GDP)	42.89	42.98	39.3	39.9
Labor costs per hour (US$)	2.01	2.39	2.46	2.8
Recorded unemployment (%)	9.98	11.98	14.01	16.22
Current-account balance/GDP	−4.31	−7.45	−6.31	−4.05
Foreign-exchange reserves ($ millions)	27,325	26,354	26,562	25,648

SOURCE: *The Economist.*

much to the growing recession in Poland's western neighbor, Germany. As discussed earlier, unemployment is now a crisis. The Polish experience calls into question the necessity for a rapid disposal of state assets for transition and suggests that slow privatization (although unintended in the Polish case) is compatible with marketization and private sector expansion.

The single most important development in Poland's future is the entry into the EU in 2004. It will have a profound effect on all sectors of the Polish economy. Many hope it will reduce unemployment if only by accelerating emigration. Also, as the low labor cost country in the expanded EU, trade creation and trade diversion should increase exports and incoming investment. Poland will certainly be a net gainer from the EU fiscal arrangements.

Perhaps the greatest uncertainty looms over agriculture. Poland will have the greatest number of farm workers in the expanded EU, and the increased market should benefit its farmers. However, the deal on agricultural policy brokered by the Germans and French means less support for Polish farmers than for existing EU members. Chances are that Poland's rural sector may be hit by more highly subsidized exports from the higher-wage West.

THE CZECH REPUBLIC

CZECH REPUBLIC	
Area (thousand sq. km.)	79
Currency	koruna
Exchange Rate	3.84 koruna = US$1
Population, 2000 (millions)	10
Population Growth Rate	−0.1%
GNI per Capita, 2000	$4,920
GNI per Capita, PPP	$13,610
GDP Growth, 1990–2000	0.8%
Value Added as % of GDP 2000 — Agriculture	4%
Industry	43%
Services	53%
% of GDP — Government Expenditure	46.4%
Exports	71.5%

HISTORICAL BACKGROUND

In the period between the two world wars, the Czech lands (Bohemia and Moravia) were among the most prosperous areas of Europe. For a long time this region in the heart of Europe served as the manufacturing center for the Austro-Hungarian Empire, enjoying an average income higher than that of Austria itself. After the empire's dissolution in 1918, the Czech lands retained this affluence as part of the Czechoslovak Republic, remaining a center of precision engineering and armament manufacture.

However, following the communist takeover in 1948, the Czech lands fell sharply in terms of productivity and income. Investment was poured into basic industries such as steel and cement, in line with conventional Stalinist guidelines, but these industries were located mostly in the east of the country, in the province of Slovakia. The nonagricultural private sector was, in Ian Jeffries's words, "savagely repressed even by East European standards."[7] Alice Teichova estimates that there were 383,000 small companies in Czechoslovakia in 1948 and that this bouyant sector was reduced to only 2,000 self-employed craftsmen by 1972.[8]

The state sector dominated agriculture as well as industry. Unlike Poland, where private farming largely survived the communist period, Czechoslovak farmers were forced into collectivization in the 1950s and 1960s. From the 1970s onward, planning emphasized investment in state farms, mirroring the shift from *kholkhoz* to *sovkhoz* that occurred in Soviet Russia. By the mid-1980s, state farms occupied 30 percent of total land area, collective farms 65 percent, and only 5 percent was left in private hands. Private production occupied an even lower percentage of arable land, 3 percent, but nevertheless managed to produce about 40 percent of the vegetables, 60 percent of the fruit, and 40 percent of the eggs.

THE PRAGUE SPRING

In the mid-1960s Prime Minister Alexander Dubcek tried to lead the Czech economy away from central planning by allowing enterprises free rein in determining both outputs and inputs, establishing workers' councils, and liberalizing prices. This **Prague Spring** might have moved the Czechoslovak economy toward the kind of market socialism practiced in Yugoslavia, but the assault on conventional ideology was too abrupt to be tolerated by the Soviet Union. In August 1968 Warsaw Pact forces occupied Czechoslovakia, restoring to power hardliners who were adamantly opposed to further reform.

The result of this history was that the Czech lands found themselves, on the eve of liberalization, in an unreformed state, even relative to their socialist neighbors, because investment in the period 1948–1968 had been predominantly in Slovakia and in many areas the prewar infrastructure was still in place. After 1968 Czechoslovakia

---

[7]Ian Jeffries, *Socialist Economies and the Transition to the Market* (New York: Routledge, 1993), p. 253.
[8]Alice Teichova, *The Czechoslovak Economy, 1918–1980* (London: Routledge, 1988), p. 104.

had been subjected to extreme planning orthodoxy, while other nations in the Council for Mutual Economic Assistance (CMEA) experimented with economic reform. In a perverse way, the unchallenged power of the Czech state and absence of enterprise reform, gave greater opportunity to the new leaders to entirely restructure the economy. The nation enjoyed, in Gershenkron's phrase, "the advantage of back-wardness," but the necessary corollary is that "the future development of the Czech economy depends in part—a greater part than one might wish—on the likelihood that the government will continue to be led by individuals with an ideological com-mitment to removing the state from day-to-day economic decision making."[9]

STABILIZATION

The **velvet revolution**, as the beginning of the transition in the Czech Republic is known, occurred during the fall and early winter of 1989 with the collapse of the Com-munist Party and its will to rule. Vaclav Havel, a playwright, was elected interim pres-ident, a post made permanent after the election of June 1990. Economic policy was steered largely by Vaclav Klaus, finance minister of the newly established Czech and Slovak Federated Republic until the dissolution of the country into the Czech Republic and Slovakia in 1992, when he became prime minister of the Czech Republic.

Despite the neglect of the communist years, the Czechs remained among the most prosperous of the Eastern European nations. Table 22.8 shows that in terms of pur-chasing power, the citizens of the Czech Republic were considerably better off than those in the other economies of the **Central European Free Trade Area (CEFTA)** founded in 1992. Moreover, inflation did not erode prosperity to the same degree as in other reforming nations. Czechoslovakia, in its pre–World War II days and in its com-

■ TABLE 22.8

	GDP per Capita in CEFTA Countries in 1994			
	Purchasing Power Parity	Official Purchasing Power Parity	Exchange Rate	Official Exchange Rate
	In US$		Czech Republic = 100	
Czech Republic	9,490	4,419	100	100
Hungary	6,537	4,403	69	100
Poland	5,477	3,124	58	71
Slovakia	6,749	3,240	71	73

SOURCE: Martin Myant et al., *Successful Transformations?: The Creation of Market Economies in Eastern Germany and the Czech Republic* (Brookfield, VT: Edward Elgar, 1996), p. 100.

[9]Roman Frydman, Andrzej Rapaczinski, and Joel Turkowitz, "Transition to a Private Property Regime in the Czech Republic and Hungary," in *Economies in Transition—Comparing Asia and Eastern Europe*, Wing Thye Woo, Stephen Parker, and Jeffrey Sachs (eds.) (Cambridge, MA: MIT Press, 1997), p. 101.

munist period, had a reputation for fiscal and monetary stringency. As noted in Chapter 20 and illustrated in Table 20.1, most of the nations in transition had a large "monetary overhang" caused by raising wages without supplying adequate goods to the consumer market. No such overhang was the case in Czechoslovakia, and consumers had actually gone into debt to finance purchases. Therefore, price liberalization did not immediately lead to an inflationary surge, as shock therapy had in Poland.

The same conservatism limited the tendency to borrow abroad. Table 22.9 shows gross external debt was lower than in other reforming nations. Poland's debts amounted to 58.8 percent of GDP, and Hungary 71.3 percent, but the Czech Republic only owed $8 billion abroad (less than 15 percent of GDP). Debt service obligations were similarly modest—only 18.8 percent of export revenue was required to finance the foreign debt and, of course, even less if substantial capital inflows from abroad in terms of direct or portfolio investment could be attracted.

On September 1, 1990, the Czechoslovak government submitted to Parliament a blueprint for economic reform. On the macroeconomic front it emphasized a strict anti-inflationary policy, with all other macroeconomic goals (growth, employment, and balance of payments) "within reasonable limits subordinate" to the objective of restraining inflation. This goal justified severe restriction of monetary growth (a target of zero) and the development of a fiscal surplus.

On the microeconomic side, the institutional changes included the following:

- Reform of the tax system, including the introduction of the value-added tax
- Corporatizing state-owned enterprises, making them financially independent, self-sufficient, and free of subsidy
- Privatization of property
- Achieving full convertibility of the currency
- Controlling inflation by the imposition of a heavy tax on any wage increases above norms prescribed by the government, while fostering collective bargaining for wage determination

In common with all transition economies, industrial output fell and unemployment rose (from its nominal zero level under socialism) and GDP fell. The loss of

■ TABLE 22.9

Gross External Debt in CEFTA Countries in 1989

	Gross Debt in ($ billions)	Gross Debt as Percentage of GDP	Gross Debt as Percentage of Exports	Debt Service as Percentage of Exports
Czechoslovakia	7.9	14.9	108.7	18.8
Hungary	20.4	71.3	239.8	40.6
Poland	41.5	58.8	475.8	44.5

SOURCE: Organization for Economic Cooperation and Development (OECD), 1994. Cited in Martin Myant et al., *Successful Transformations?: The Creation of Market Economies in Eastern Germany and the Czech Republic* (Brookfield, VT: Edward Elgar, 1996), p. 100.

export markets within the CMEA hit the Czechoslovak economy especially hard because of its role as the supplier of highly processed manufactured goods throughout the communist bloc, and the dislocation of the trading system created a sharp fall in output. The austerity resulting from suppressing domestic demand did not help matters, nor did the spate of imports that followed trade liberalization.

However, reforms and austerity policy affected the two parts of the country differently. The Czech lands saw an increase in trade with the West, especially Germany, and a surge in service activity and foreign investment, while in Slovakia the large-scale industrial plants built in the 1950s and 1960s fell on hard times. By the spring of 1992, unemployment in the Czech lands was 3.7 percent, while in Slovakia it had risen to 12.3 percent, and the country came unglued as economic problems exacerbated ethnic difficulties.[10] Slovakia saw itself the victim of Czech austerity, while the newly liberated Czechs, sensing real prosperity around the corner, were unwilling to countenance sustained income transfers to the Slovaks. In the summer of 1992 the two halves of the Federated Republic went their separate ways. Klaus became prime minister in Prague, and Meciar, an orthodox leftist, ruled Slovakia in Bratislava. Klaus's objective was, as he frequently remarked, the creation of a "market economy without adjectives," and he had no sympathy for, or interest in, the pursuit of any kind of "third way," formulating policy to align the Czech economy as closely and as quickly to Western Europe as possible.

Table 22.10 gives summary statistics for the development of the Czech economy during the 1990s. The postliberalization contraction ended in 1993, and solid growth commenced in 1994, while monetary austerity kept the inflation rate under control. The most worrying features were the widening trade and current account imbalances and the relatively small flows of incoming foreign direct investment, which lead to growing foreign indebtedness.

The Privatization Program

Part of any drive to a market economy clearly involves the privatization of state assets, which in the Czech context can be regarded as falling into three categories: restitution, small privatization, and privatization of large enterprises.

Restitution In contrast to Poland, Czechoslovakia was not devastated by World War II, and its borders remained largely unchanged at the end of the conflict. Immediately after the war a democratic government was briefly installed and to a large extent normality returned, including a fairly orderly system of property rights. As a result, after liberalization many owners from that period could trace title to their property despite seizure by the state during communism. Consequently the Czech Republic engaged in the most active restitution program of any of the Eastern European nations.[11] Applicants who could trace their ownership and

---

[10]Karel Dyba and Jan Svejnar, "Stabilization and Transition in Czechoslovakia," in *The Transition in Eastern Europe, Vol. I,* Olivier Jean Blanchard, Kenneth A. Froot, and Jeffrey D. Sachs (eds.) (Chicago: University of Chicago Press, 1994), p. 107.
[11]The probable exception to this statement could be East Germany.

■ TABLE 22.10

The Czech Republic: Key Indicators of the Transition 1991—1997

	1990	1991	1992	1993	1994	1995	1996	1997
Nominal GDP ($ billions)	32.3	25.4	29.9	34.3	39.7	50.3	56.6	52.9
GDP per capita PPP ($)	9,526.0	8,721.0	8,951.0	9,273.0	9,794.0	10,531.0	11,211.0	11,566.0
GDP (% change)	21.2	211.5	23.3	0.6	3.2	6.4	3.9	1.0
Industrial production (% change)	23.3	221.2	27.9	25.3	2.1	8.7	2.0	4.5
Budget balance (% of GDP)	n.a.	21.9	23.1	0.5	21.2	21.8	21.2	20.5
Unemployment (%)	0.8	4.1	2.6	3.5	3.2	2.9	3.5	5.2
Average monthly wage ($)	182.6	128.5	164.3	199.6	239.5	307.8	356.4	333.4
Inflation (%)	9.7	56.6	11.1	20.8	10.0	7.9	8.7	9.9
Exports ($ billions)	5.9	8.3	8.4	14.2	16.0	21.4	21.7	22.4
Imports ($ billions)	6.5	8.8	10.4	14.6	17.4	25.1	27.6	27.1
Trade balance ($ billions)	20.7	20.5	21.9	20.4	21.4	23.7	25.9	24.6
Current-account balance ($ billions)	21.0	0.3	20.3	0.1	0.0	21.4	24.3	23.2
Foreign direct investment ($ billions)	n.a.	n.a.	.1	.6	.7	2.5	1.4	1.3
Foreign exchange reserves ($ billions)	1.1	3.9	0.8	3.9	6.2	14.0	16.1	15.0
Foreign debt ($ billions)	6.4	6.7	7.1	8.5	10.7	16.5	20.8	22.0
Discount rate (%)	n.a.	9.5	9.5	8.0	8.5	9.5	10.5	13.0
Exchange rate ($)	18.0	29.5	28.3	29.2	28.8	26.6	27.1	31.7

SOURCES: EBRD, IMF, and IBRD.

who sought restitution of their property were required to submit their claims during a six-month period of 1991. It is difficult to know exactly the extent of the program, but Tomas Jezek, head of the National Property Fund, estimated that more than 100,000 properties were restored to their former owners, the majority residential properties. Other sources estimated that some 20,000 retail outlets were also reprivatized in this way.[12]

Small Privatization Small privatization (primarily of shops, restaurants, hotels, and small factories) was achieved by public auction. All Czech citizens were allowed access to the auctions. Insiders, neither the bureaucrats of the ministries that controlled the property nor the current operators, were given no special privileges beyond their advantage of a clearer understanding of the potential of the businesses than would be available to an outsider.

The properties were initially valued by the privatization agency, and free bidding was to proceed upward from a designated starting price, with the property awarded to the highest bidder. If no one matched the initial starting price, it was lowered by increments of 10 percent until bidding started. The small privatization program is considered a success, and most properties were sold at a considerable

---

[12]John S. Earle, Roman Frydman, Andrzej Rapaczynski, and Joel Turkewitz, *Small Privatization: The Transformation of Retail Trade and Consumer Services in the Czech Republic, Hungary, and Poland (Ceu Privatization Reports)* (New York: Central European University Press, 1994), p. 58.

markup to their starting price, as shown in Table 22.11. Only 3,720 properties, or 20 percent of the total, were sold at a discount to the starting price. Some accusations of ministry officials and enterprise managers attempting to manipulate the process were voiced, but on the whole the process was remarkably transparent, and more than $1 billion was raised in sales.

The Privatization of Large Enterprise Large privatization covered the bulk of state-owned enterprises. The program was delayed by the practical problems of separating the operations of the enterprises after the breakup of the Czechoslovak Federal State into the Czech Republic and Slovakia. The particular method of privatization fell on enterprise managers, although any worker or citizen could put forward an alternate scheme. Initially, many managers tried to push through insider privatization, but generally those were rejected by the privatization ministry. Some firms were sold by sealed bid offers and some by open auction, while others were sold at negotiated prices to Czech or foreign citizens. However, the bulk of the privatization ultimately took the form of "voucher auctions."

Voucher Auctions Every citizen of the Czech Republic was invited to purchase, for the sum of 1,000 Czech crowns (about $35), a book of vouchers that could be exchanged for shares. The vouchers carried no monetary denomination and could not legally be sold or exchanged, except if they were placed with one of the government-licensed, privately owned investment funds that rapidly became established (discussed later). About 75 percent of all adult Czech citizens received vouchers. Each voucher was exchangeable for part of the share capital of a privatizing enterprise, the amount of shares received being in inverse proportion to the total interest in the enterprise. Thus, for example, if 100,000 individuals all offered a voucher in the auction of a firm, then each would receive 1/100,000 of the share capital; if only 10,000 offered shares, each would receive 1/10,000, and so forth.

Enterprise managers generally favored voucher privatization hoping that the resulting diverse share ownership would mean they might escape scrutiny from the new owners, hence retaining their informal but valuable property rights in the enterprises.

■ **TABLE 22.11**

Czech Small-Scale Privatization to December 1993

Type	Number	Average Increase over Starting Price
Shops	13,042	75%
Restaurants	1,861	54
Hotels	430	64
Services	3,577	14
Other	3,435	22
Total	22,345	49

SOURCE: J. S. Earle, R. Frydman, A. Rapaczynski, and J. Turkewitz, *Small Privatization: The Transformation of Retail Trade and Consumer Services in the Czech Republic, Hungary, and Poland* (New York: Central European Press, 1994).

Concentration of Economic Power One of the fundamental justifications of privatization is that the financial interest of the owners will give them incentives to oversee management and improve performance in a way not possible under state ownership. An improvement in governance is unlikely if share ownership is diffuse, because the costs of gathering information and acting in unison rises with the number of shareholders. Diffuse ownership and weak oversight seemed likely in the Czech case until the emergence of the **privatization funds**. These financial intermediaries accepted vouchers from citizens and in return offered shares in the profits of the funds. Within a few months, 400 such firms were established, and together they attracted about 70 percent of all the vouchers issued. Although many were quite small, a few funds amassed considerable purchasing power, and the seven largest controlled 45 percent of all voucher points. Because the average enterprise was expected to sell 60 percent of equity through voucher privatization, the potential for control to be concentrated in a few hands is obvious. On average the "Big 7" funds together own almost 30 percent of every enterprise in the Czech Republic, and concern therefore shifted from ownership being too diffuse and hindering good governance, to its being too concentrated and giving rise to too much economic power.

Banking Reform

The concentration of financial power in the Czech economy was initially aggravated by developments in the banking sector. As part of the liberalization plan, the government chose partial privatization of the state-owned banks, freeing them from direct control, disposing of most of the equity in voucher privatization, but retaining roughly 40 percent of the shares of each in the National Property Fund. However, a problematic development was the establishment by the banks of their own voucher privatization funds, which enjoyed success in attracting voucher deposits. As a result the largest banks controlled the largest funds, and are not only lenders to industry, but also control much of the share capital and voting rights of many firms, creating clear conflicts of interest.

Furthermore, because banks are themselves among the institutions partially privatized under the voucher scheme, some of the banks came to control a substantial part of the share capital of other banks and a system of interlocking ownership emerged within the banking system itself. For example, Komercni Bank, the largest commercial bank, was 44 percent owned by the National Property Fund (the state), but another 24 percent was acquired by investment funds controlled by the other four major banks.

In this context it is not surprising that the management of Czech banking remained highly politicized. A system of directed credit was installed and government pressure led the banks to make extensive loans to industry. This practice compounded the problems presented by banks propping up problem firms in which they had a stake order to avoid the capital loss of bankruptcy. Bank balance sheets deteriorated, and the banks lurched toward failure. The Czech government then undertook a brave step, which many national governments recognize only with great difficulty—the fact that stability can be restored by the insertion of competition and capital from abroad. However, though the step was brave and necessary, it was not guaranteed success.

In order to clean up the balance sheets of the banks the government created a new agency, Konsolidacni Banka, whose job it was to assume the bad debts of the rest of the banking system. It was to acquire the troubled firms in exchange for government debt, restructure them, and sell them off. For example, the state savings bank, Sporitelna, was bought by an Austrian Bank, Erste. Erste Bank was allowed to keep the loans it liked and to dump the rest on the Konsslidacni, "hospital bank." The cost to the government is estimated as 9 percent of GDP, financed by debt, but the move was necessary to attract buyers into the banking system and restore the financial system needed for growth and development. The role of foreign banks has not been one unrestrained success. Forty percent of the third largest Czech bank, IPB, was acquired by Nomura securities, who unfortunately managed it with a "hands-off" policy. The bank ran in to problems, fired its accountants who refused to verify its accounts and replaced them with a more complacent (but well known) firm. Eventually the bank crashed.

Central Bank Reform

The Czech National Bank (CNB), the central bank, recently underwent change. It is a moderately independent central bank but the new regulation increases the degree of government control. It specifies that the job of the central bank is to contain inflation and that the CNB confer with the government to determine inflation targets. It is a move against the general trend in central banking, which favors increased independence, and may be at odds with the Czechs' attempt to join in the euro common currency.

THE STRUCTURE OF INDUSTRY

Table 22.10 presents data on change in the form of business organization in the Czech Republic during the first phase of privatization. In 1990, almost 3,000 state-owned enterprises (SOEs) covered the gamut of economic activity from auto manufacture to retail, banking, and insurance. Like most enterprises in centrally planned economies these concerns were large in size and highly vertically integrated.

■ TABLE 22.12

	Forms of Business Organization in the Czech Economy		
	1990	1991	1994*
State enterprises	2,945	3,760	1,522
Commercial companies	3,034	25,522	88,424
Cooperatives	2,856	4,070	5,226
Individual entrepreneurs	310,653	902,797	846,285
Individual farmers	127	7,533	91,936
Others	17,219	26,750	85,141
Total	336,834	970,432	1,118,534

* All figures are year-end.
SOURCE: Earle, Frydman, Rapaczynski, and Turkewitz, *Small Privatization* (New York: Central European Press, 1994).

The first stage of reform saw a sharp (25 percent) increase in the number of SOEs, as enterprises were spun off into somewhat smaller, more rational units. These units were then disposed of in the voucher auctions. However, the vitality of the private sector in the Czech Republic owed more to newly established firms than to those sold from the state sector. Privately owned and financed commercial companies were founded from scratch at a much faster rate than they were created through privatization. In the two years between 1992 and 1994, more than 85,000 new private companies were established and about 83,000 of them were start-ups not privatizations.

The productive sectors of the Czech economy were, by 1996, almost completely privatized. Table 22.13 illustrates the share of private versus state employment by industrial sector. For the economy as a whole, private employment amounted to rather more than 77 percent, while in construction, agriculture, and industry only a tiny fraction of the once universal state presence remained.

DIRECT FOREIGN INVESTMENT

Because of its location, the high human capital of its population, and the confidence that foreigners had in the management of the economy, the Czech Republic was blessed with sizable inflows of direct investment. Czechinvest, a governmental agency responsible for attracting direct foreign investment, estimates that between 1993 and 2001, more than US$26 billion flowed in (see Table 22.14), a figure equivalent to $2,600 per head of population. The largest source nation is Germany, and the largest individual firm is Volkswagen, which acquired Skoda, a carmaker, and invested substantial capital.

PROSPECTS FOR THE CZECH ECONOMY

Until about 1996 the Czech Republic stood out as an almost unquestioned star of the transition process. It moved through the dip in output that normally accompanies

■ TABLE 22.13

Share of Nonstate Sector in Employment,* 1992–1996 (as a percentage)

	1992	1993	1994	1995	1996
Total economy	39.8	59.9	64.2	75.5	77.6
Agriculture	68.6	80.4	82.9	91.0	92.3
Industry	31.1	60.4	69.2	90.1	93.0
Construction	61.8	90.7	91.4	96.9	98.1
Wholesale and retail trade	74.2	89.9	90.7	97.7	98.6
Transport, storage, and communications	16.1	25.6	28.6	43.4	47.1

*Mixed ownership, includes private cooperatives and nonprofit corporations serving households.
SOURCE: Data provided by the Czech Statistical Office.

Cumulative Inflow of FDI to the Czech Republic, 1993–2001

Source	Investment (US$ millions)	Percentage
Germany	6,662	24.9
Netherlands	4,987	18.6
Austria	2,806	10.5
United States	2,406	9.0
France	2,378	8.9
Belgium	1,729	6.5
Switzerland	1666	6.2
United Kingdom	1,044	3.9
Denmark	436	1.6
Sweden	423	1.6
Canada	202	0.8
Italy	188	0.7
Japan	148	0.6
Other	1682	6.3
Total	26,757	100.0

SOURCE: Czechinvest Fact-sheet, no. 2, 2002.

transition from socialism to capitalism with impressive speed, the contraction being only 15 percent, and growth resumed in 1993. By the end of 1996, GDP surpassed its pretransition level. During this period inflation was never greater than 4.1 percent and the budget deficit never more than 3.1 percent. In fact, at the time that the Maastricht criteria for membership in the European Monetary Union were promulgated, the Czech Republic would have met them all, while none of the West European nations did. Subsequently, however, the situation worsened on most fronts (see Table 22.15).

The center right Klaus administration, an apparent model of fiscal and monetary conservatism and good management, became embroiled in accusations of corruption. The banking sector revealed its weakness as political intervention led to a high proportion of nonperforming loans. In 1996 alone, 13 banks failed, and the government was required to sponsor a rescue operation costing Czech taxpayers over $1.25 billion.[13] Growth was a paltry 1 percent in 1997, turned negative in 1998, and output was virtually stagnant in 1999. Unemployment began to rise in 1996, reaching 5.2 percent, the highest since the fall of communism. The trade balance worsened and foreign debt rose to more than $20 billion. In this context the fall of the Klaus government in late 1997 came as no surprise, and the country moved

---

[13]"East European Bands for Sale: Bracing for a Buying Binge," *The Economist*, August 15, 1998, p. 64.

Recent Economic Performance

	1998	1999	2000	2001
GDP per head ($ at PPP)	12,829	13,014	13,755	14,586
GDP (% real change)	−1.04	0.47	3.25	3.26
Government consumption (% of GDP)	18.58	19.68	19.63	19.23
Budget balance (% of GDP)	−1.59	−2.34	−2.32	−3.14
Consumer prices (% change per year)	10.69	2.1	3.92	4.68
Public debt (% of GDP)	13.66	15.04	18.81	22.97
Labor costs per hour (USD)	2.08	2.08	2	2.16
Recorded unemployment (%)	6.13	8.63	8.96	8.55
Current-account balance/GDP	−2.21	−2.66	−5.29	−4.65
Foreign-exchange reserves ($ millions)	12,542	12,806	13,019	14,342

sharply leftward. After a brief caretaker government, the Social Democrats formed a government that included a large former communist representation. They have held onto power since, winning again in mid-2002, behind a new leader, Vladimir Spidla. The surprise in that election was the strong showing of the Communists who, unreconstructed and unrepentant, garnered about 21 percent of the vote. The leftward shift, however, does not seem about to change policy, although it may slow the privatization of the rump of state-owned enterprise. The prime policy of integration into Western Europe remains in place.

In recent years, the return to steady growth of about 3 percent per year has been welcome, but this is not fast enough to make inroads into the substantial unemployment rate. It is hoped that EU membership will spur faster expansion. At present the Czechs expect to adopt the euro in 2006 and 2007. If that remains the case then further fiscal expansionary measures are out of the question. The "growth and stability pact" requires that the government deficit be within 3 percent of GDP. The Czech deficit is currently 3.14 percent and rising.

KEY TERMS AND CONCEPTS

big bang

Central European Free Trade Area (CEFTA)

direct foreign investment (DFI)

Law on Economic Activity

marketization

national investment funds (NIFs)

nomenklatura privatization

Prague Spring

privatization funds

shock therapy

Solidarity

velvet revolution

QUESTIONS FOR DISCUSSION

1. What was the nature of the Polish reforms in the early 1980s?
2. What was the strategy underlying shock therapy?
3. What was the planned use of financial intermediaries in the Polish privatization program? What was to be the role of the national investment funds?
4. Jeffrey Sachs was insistent that rapid privatization in Poland was essential for success. In effect, a slow pace of privatization accompanied considerable its economic success. Can we account for this phenomenon?
5. Why might the repression that followed the "Prague Spring" ultimately be considered an asset in the Czech transition?
6. Outline the strategy and outcome of the Czech privatization program.
7. Why did the Czech economy attract a disproportionate amount of foreign direct investment?
8. What caused the amalgamation of economic and political power in the Czech Republic? What threats does this situation pose?

RESOURCES

Web Sites

Poland

Central Europe Online...http://www.einnews.com/centraleurope/
Embassy of Poland in Washington, D.C. ....http://www.polandembassy.org/
Warsaw Stock Exchange...http://www.gpw.com.pl/
The Warsaw Voice—Weekly Newspaper (In English).....http://www.warsawvoice.com.pl/
The Official Website of Poland ....http://poland.pl/
The National Bank of Poland...http://www.nbp.pl/home_en.html
Central Europe Online, Poland...http://www.einnews.com/poland/
Ministry of Economy..http://www.mg.gov.pl/
Ministry of Finance..http://www.mf.gov.pl/
Ministry of Foreign Affairs...http://www.msz.gov.pl/
The Central Statistics Office...http://www.stat.gov.pl/

The Czech Republic

Central Europe Online...http://www.einnews.com/centraleurope/
Central Bank...http://www.cnb.cz/en/index.html
Czech Statistical Office ....http://www.czso.cz/
Economic Chamber...http://www.hkcr.cz/
Ministry of Industry and Trade...http://www.mpo.cz/
Ministry of Finance ....http://www.mfcr.cz/

Ministry of Foreign Affairs ....http://www.czech.cz/

Czech Capital Market ....http://stock.eunet.cz/index_e.html

Embassy of the Czech Republic in Washington, D.C. ....http://www.mzv.cz/washington/

The Prague Post—National Newspaper ....http://www.praguepost.cz/

Prague Business Journal...http://www.pbj.cz/

The Prague Tribune Online ....http://www.prague-tribune.cz/

Czech Information Center ....http://www.muselik.com/czech/frame.html

Radio Prague...http://www.radio.cz/en/

Komercni Bank ....http://www.kb.cz/

Narodni Bank ....http://www.cnb.cz/

Central Europe Online, Czech Republic........http://www.centraleurope.com/czechtoday/

Books and Articles

Poland

Angresano, James. "Evolving Socioeconomic Conditions in Central and Eastern Europe: A Myrdalian View." *Development Policy Review,* September 1994, 251–275.

Balcerowicz, Leszek. "Transition to the Market Economy: Poland, 1989–93 in Comparative Perspective." *Economic Policy,* December 19, 1994, 71–98.

Blanchard, Olivier Jean, Kenneth A. Froot, and Jeffrey D. Sachs (eds.). *The Transition in Eastern Europe.* Vol. 1, *Country Studies;* Vol. 2, *Restructuring.* Chicago: University of Chicago Press, 1994. Reviewed by Peter Murrel in the *Journal of Economic Literature,* March 1995, 164–178.

Calvo, Guillermo A., and Fabrizio Coricelli. "Stabilizing a Previously Centrally Planned Economy: Poland 1990." *Economic Policy,* April 1992, 176–226.

"Czech Republic: Statistical Appendix." International Monetary Fund Staff Country Report, Working Paper 98/37 (April 1998).

Ebrill, Liam P., Asaj Chopra, and Charalambos Christofides (eds.). *Poland: The Path to a Market Economy.* Occasional Paper 113 (October 1994). Washington DC: International Monetary Fund, 1994.

Gandhi, Ved P. "Fundamental Fiscal Reform in Poland: Issues of Design and Implementation," 91–107. In *Transition to Market,* Vito Tanzi (ed.). Washington DC: International Monetary Fund.

International Monetary Fund, Czech Republic: Selected Issues. IMF Staff Country Report, Working Paper 98/36 (April 1998).

Jeffries, Ian. *Socialist Economies and the Transition to the Market: A Guide.* New York: Routledge, 1993.

Johnson, Simon, and Gary Loveman. "Starting Over: Poland after Communism." *Harvard Business Review,* March–April 1995, 44–56.

Keane, Michael, and Eswar Prasad. "Consumption and Income Inequality in Poland during the Economic Transition." International Monetary Fund, Working Paper WP/99/14 (1999).

Lipton, David, and Jeffrey Sachs. "Creating a Market in Eastern Europe: The Case of Poland," *Brookings Papers on Economic Activity*, 1990, 119.

Pinto, Brian, Marek Belka, and Stefan Krajewski. "Transforming State Enterprise in Poland: Evidence on Adjustment by Manufacturing Firms," *Brookings Papers on Economic Activity* 1, 1993, 213.

"Poland's Economic Reforms." *The Economist,* January 23, 1993, 21–23.

Tittenbrun, Jacek. "The Managerial Revolution Revisited: The Case of Privatisation in Poland." *Capital and Class,* Spring 1995, 21–32.

The Czech Republic

Aghevli, Bijan B. *Stabilization and Structural Reform in the Czech and Slovak Federal Republic: First Stage,* Occasional Paper 92 (Mach 1992). Washington, DC: International Monetary Fund, 1992.

Dlouhy, Vladimir, and Jan Mladek. "Privatization and Corporate Control in the Czech Republic." *Economic Policy,* December 19, 1994, 155–170.

Jeffries, Ian. *Socialist Economies and the Transition to the Market: A Guide.* New York: Routledge, 1993.

Leeds, Eva Marikova. "Voucher Privatization in Czechoslovakia." *Comparative Economic Studies,* Fall 1993, 19–37.

Myant, Martin et al. *Successful Transformations?: The Creation of Market Economies in Eastern Germany and the Czech Republic.* Brookfield, VT: Edward Elgar, 1996.

Prust, Jim. "The Czech and Slovak Federal Republic: Government Finances in a Period of Transition." In *Transition to Market,* Vito Tanzi (ed.). Washington, DC: International Monetary Fund, 1993.

Teichova, Alice. *The Czechoslovak Economy, 1918–1980.* London: Routledge, 1988.

23

THE PEOPLE'S REPUBLIC OF CHINA

CHINA	
Area (thousand sq. km.)	9,597
Currency	yuan
Exchange Rate	8 yuan = US$1
Population 2000 (millions)	1261
Population Growth Rate	1.1%
GNI per Capita, 2000	$840
GNI per Capita, PPP	$3,940
GDP Growth 1990–2000	10.3%
Value Added as % of GDP 2000 Agriculture	16%
Industry	49%
Services	34%
% of GDP Government Expenditure	15%
Exports	22%

INTRODUCTION

With a population of more than 1.2 billion and one of the fastest rates of economic growth over the past two decades, the potential of the Chinese economy is huge. If the economic growth, which has already transformed much of the country, is maintained, China will be one of the world's largest economies in the twenty-first century. With its long history as a unified state, its huge population, and a considerable resource base, China should indeed be a major player. For the past century and a half, invasion, imperialism, civil wars, instability, and poor management all played a role in keeping that vast potential unrealized. In the last couple of decades some of the dormant economic power has been unleashed. China is also something of a paradox. Despite its freewheeling growth, it is one of few countries left in the world that is governed by a Communist party, and it still practices a limited form of centralized planning. It is struggling to reconcile its socialist ideology with the needs of a growing capitalist society.

Nevertheless, the growth of the economy in recent years can be described as nothing less than spectacular, averaging close to 10 percent annually during the 1980s and 1990s, and never less than 4 percent, even during a slow spell in the late 1980s. At the growth rates experienced during the last 10 years (9.6% per year for China and 3.1% for the United States) by the year 2037, Chinese GDP would equal that of the United States.[1] Today, however, the Chinese economy is only 11 percent the size of that of the United States, and the per-head income of China is only about 3 percent of that of the United States measured at current international exchange rates. When expressed in purchasing power parity the situation is slightly more favorable at 11 percent of the U.S. level.

Recent Chinese growth has its roots in substantial productivity gains per worker (particularly in agriculture and light industry), a more efficient deployment of the workforce, and an increase in employment. Employment, rising at an annual rate of about 3 percent, proved sufficient to absorb the considerable population "bubble" caused by the high birthrates of the 1960s. Despite immigration from the rural areas to urban conurbations, the urban unemployment rate, more than 5 percent in the 1960s, fell to about 2 percent by the late 1980s.

Of course, China started from a low base. Income measured at current exchange rates was only about $250 per person in the mid-1970s. Purchasing power comparisons generally give a better picture of overall living standards, but even these show consumption on average of roughly $1,000 per person, one-sixth of the figure in the Soviet Union and only 6 percent of that for the United States. Moreover, China has low levels of national wealth. World Bank estimates put wealth per head (including natural resources and human capital) at about $6,600, about one-fiftieth of that of Germany and among the lowest in the world.

CENTRAL PLANNING, 1952—1959

The triumph of the Communists over the Nationalists in the civil war that closely followed the end of World War II led, in October 1949, to the creation of the People's Republic of China. The Nationalists withdrew to the offshore island of

---

[1]In 1996 Borensztein and Ostry calculated that if the 9 percent annual real growth (envisaged in the five-year plan covering 1996 to 2000) were sustained until 2013, Chinese gross national product (GNP), corrected for purchasing power parity, would surpass that of the United States if the United States continued at the rate it had in the previous decade. To many people this revelation was surprising. As things turned out, however, Chinese growth slowed somewhat in the years 1997 to 1999, while that of the United States accelerated sharply from the sluggish pace of the late 1980s and early 1990s. See Borensztein and Ostry, "Accounting for China's Growth," *American Economic Review,* May 1996, p. 224.

Taiwan and created there a successful state and economy, which we examined in Chapter 14. The communist Chinese leadership set out to imitate the economic system developed in the Soviet Union over the previous 25 years. Private industry and commerce were nationalized and sweeping agricultural reform took the land from the landlords and wealthier farmers and placed it under peasant control in communes. As in the Soviet Union, a great deal of investment was poured into heavy industry, with faith in the power of capital-intensive technology and economies of scale to produce high rates of economic growth.

The Soviet model was followed relying on five-year materials balance plans. Soviet planners and technicians were imported and a formal planning apparatus put into place. However, in the early 1950s the Chinese economy was by no means in a parallel position to that of the Soviet Union, leading to problems in the application of a centrally planned model. One fact was that China's population was much larger (by a factor of 4), and its communications and transportation systems were much less well developed. In any system of centralized planning, the availability of reliable information at the center is crucial.[2] In the Chinese case, problems impeding the flow of information to the center and back to the enterprises proved to be even worse than in the Soviet Union, which had a fundamental impact on the success of the planning experiment.

Moreover, the Chinese economy was not as highly unified and integrated as that of the Soviet Union. Poor transportation and the historically high degree of regional self-sufficiency (exacerbated during the period of "warlordism" in the 1920s and the struggle with the Japanese) meant that gains from centralizing the economy were much more difficult to grasp. A greater degree of power remained in the hands of municipalities and provinces, and even the prefectures and townships, than had been the case in the Soviet Union. One measure of the difficulty of implementing centralized planning is how few goods were brought under formal control. Even at the height of planning in China, only 500 commodities fell under mandatory central control, in contrast to the more than 20,000 commodities that were part of the Soviet material balance plans.

THE GREAT LEAP FORWARD, 1958—1961

The end of the first five-year plan in 1958 coincided with reforms to the planning system that recognized the impracticability of "taut"[3] central planning in the Chinese economy, allowing the necessity, and even the desirability, of a high degree of provincial initiative. However, the potential for success of the revised system will never be known because the development path of the economy was disturbed by the intrusion of political rhetoric, in the form of Mao's **Great Leap Forward**, a political initiative to harness the ideological fervor of the Chinese population to the task of raising industrial output. At the same time as China continued to pour

---

[2]See Chapter 16 for a fuller discussion of information and central planning.
[3]*Taut* in this context refers to a "lack of slack" in the planning system, provided by keeping inventories to a minimum.

investment into capital-intensive heavy industry, Mao and the leadership exhorted the population to increase the output of basic industrial goods through labor-intensive enterprises in rural areas. This approach of using both capital- and labor-intensive technologies to produce the same goods was characterized as "walking on two legs."

Although labor-intensive enterprises were found in many industries, including building materials, mining, food processing, and machine-building, the political leadership defined the key industry as steel. Mao Tse Tung urged a sharp increase in steel production through the development of small-scale furnaces, and it is estimated that some two million small furnaces were established during the first two years of the Great Leap Forward, employing some 80 million people on a full or part-time basis. Official statistics show that industrial output grew sharply at the outset of the Great Leap Forward; net material product was up by 22 percent in 1959 alone, but it soon became apparent that this increase was being achieved at great cost, and much of the growth was actually an illusion. For example, the steel produced in rural furnaces was, in general, of poor quality and expensive in terms of factor cost. Moreover, much of the "new" output consisted merely of the melting down and recycling of steel and iron that had already been produced; ornamental and structural steelwork was pulled down and fed to the furnaces. Woods and forests were cut down, and even buildings were cannibalized, to provide charcoal and fuel.

After an initial period of feverish activity, the incentives of revolutionary fervor and rhetoric cooled. The recycling of previously produced material slowed as stocks became exhausted, and the depletion of woodland made charcoal increasingly short in supply. The countryside was scarred and the environment suffered. China's Soviet advisors were frustrated by what seemed a perverse rejection of socialist rationality, and in an atmosphere of growing antagonism between the two nations, technical assistance was suspended in 1960.

Net material product in China fell sharply in 1961 and 1962, but greater stability was reestablished in 1963 and a period of relative calm saw a rise in industrial output. Continuing investment in heavy industry helped the rebound, and industrial output rose sharply between 1963 and 1966. Chinese technocrats filled the void left by the departing Soviets, pursuing central planning once more, though with a greater degree of pragmatism. The high degree of provincial autonomy left local governments free to use their flexibility to increase output in whatever way they chose.

THE CULTURAL REVOLUTION, 1966—1970

In 1966, however, political furor again swamped the economic system after the inception of Mao's **Proletarian Cultural Revolution**. Exactly what prompted the Chinese leader to embark on that course at that moment in history is still open to dispute. In part he seemed convinced that only complete rejection of western influence would enable Asia, including China, to be economically self-reliant. He was also genuinely convinced that Stalinist economic management had resulted in a new structure of class and privilege as obnoxious to him as the old. Finally, and perhaps decisively, he felt a need to strengthen his own political position vis-à-vis the technocrats and bureaucrats. The Cultural Revolution resulted in Chinese society being turned upside down. Bureaucrats, planners, and technocrats were stripped of authority and sent off to the countryside for "political reeducation," while power shifted to radical political cadres. Considerable economic costs resulted from the turmoil. Again the economy lurched into a sharp recession with material output falling by about 15 percent in both 1966 and 1967; it rebounded again in the last years of the decade as some form of normality returned.

By the beginning of the 1970s it was clear that the era of Mao and Chou En Lai was nearing its close, so political factions began maneuvering for power. On the left, the **gang of four**, led by Mao's wife, tried to sustain the Cultural Revolution. On the right, a moderate and technocratic leadership sought the restoration of rule by bureaucracy and party. Both Mao and Chou died in 1976 and nominal power passed to Mao's chosen successor Hua Qua Feng. However, by this time the moderates were in ascendance and Deng Xiaoping, a capable administrator, was rehabilitated from the indignities inflicted on him during the Cultural Revolution and restored as party leader.

THE FIRST PHASE OF REFORM, 1978—1993

Because the economy stagnated, and in some areas declined, during the period of the Cultural Revolution and the rule of the gang of four, Deng resolved to find new approaches to promote growth. December 1978 saw a profound shift in the direction of the Chinese economy as the Central Committee of the Communist Party of China (CCP) issued a communiqué that, in effect, launched the modern period of reform, moving the Chinese economy away from a planned economy and toward a market one.

Agricultural Reform

The first reforms were aimed at revitalizing the rural sector, whose fortunes had flagged during the previous three decades. The high percentage of the population engaged in agriculture and the necessity of creating an agrarian surplus to fuel industrial growth and feed a growing population made agricultural reform essential. Even though heavy industrial output surged during the previous 15 years, agriculture remained dormant. Grain output per person employed rose by less than 10 percent during a 25-year period, despite considerable expenditures on infrastructure, informational outreach, and factor inputs, especially fertilizers. The key to raising output lay in radical reform of the collectivized agricultural system so painfully created in the 1950s and 1960s.

Under collectivization, agricultural production was organized into *communes* (typically with a population of about 40,000 people). These communes were further subdivided into *brigades* and *production teams.* Decisions about what to grow and how to grow it were passed to the communes from superior political units (the prefecture and provincial governments) and were quite often inflexible to local conditions. Worker remuneration was generally through sharing the net production of the brigade on a per-worker basis taking little account of individual or family productivity. This system resulted in a chronic absence of incentives and a pervasive free rider problem. Households were allowed small plots for the own cultivation, from which the surplus could be sold in the local markets, and productivity was in general much higher in these small niches in the system.

The reforms that began in 1979 were largely the result of local initiative and were, in fact, opposed at the outset by the State Council in Beijing. Motivation for reform was the belief that productivity in the agricultural sector could be greatly increased simply by raising the economic incentives to family units. Initially this reform included enlarging the size of the private plots and increasing the procurement price that the state paid for crops that were produced privately. Local officials were encouraged by the success of this limited action, and the reforms evolved into the **household responsibility system (HRS)**, which became the dominant arrangement in agriculture after 1982.

Under the HRS quite large plots of collectively held land were leased to households for a fixed period of time, initially 15 years for annual crops and up to 40 years for tree crops. In return for tenure, each household was responsible for providing a share of the production team's output quota based on plot size. Production in excess of this "contract" could be sold either on the free market for what it would fetch or to the state at negotiated prices. By 1984, 93 percent of China's cultivated land was contracted to households, but, and this aspect is highly illustrative of the progress of China's reforms, it was not until 1985 that the state passed legislation formally sanctioning it.

Agricultural production rose sharply after the reforms. Annual growth of output was twice the rate experienced in the 1960s and 1970s, illustrating the importance of individual incentive in agriculture. Labor productivity in agriculture rose at an even higher rate, producing a labor surplus in most of the rural collectives, which ultimately provided the workforce for the rapid expansion of rural light industry. Higher food prices moved the terms of trade (defined as food prices divided by manufactured goods prices) sharply in favor of the farmers and resulted in a substantial increase in real income in the rural sector. However, the authorities in Beijing were concerned about political unrest among urban workers and were unwilling to allow the burden of increased farm incomes to be passed directly to urban consumers in the form of higher food prices. The government provided substantial subsidies, which resulted in a growing fiscal deficit.

The state response was to reduce the size of the subsidy by cutting the procurement prices for grains, but farmers responded by shifting resources out of grain production and into more profitable, less regulated commodities like vegetables and meat. Grain output fell as a result in the mid-1980s. The government's reply was to raise the procurement prices of grain once more, but this time it tried to avoid the fiscal consequences by increasing the prices paid by urban consumers. This step toward price liberalization led to the ultimate deregulation of the grain market; by May 1993 grain prices were decontrolled in about 80 percent of the country and prices determined by the interplay of supply and demand.

The Rise of Rural Enterprise

The rapid rise in agricultural output, labor productivity, and incomes set in motion a further development in the rural areas: the emergence of **township and village enterprises (TVEs)** as the most dynamic sector in the Chinese economy. TVEs are industrial activities that were initially collectively owned by the communes. They were made possible by a progressive rollback of restrictions on the nonagricultural activities of collectives, culminating in 1984 when local authorities were given the power to sanction communal industrial activity. In recent years the term expanded to cover proprietorships and joint stock enterprises located in the countryside. The new enterprises absorbed much of the excess labor created by high birthrates and rising labor productivity in agriculture, while increased rural incomes provided the seed money for the initial investments.

Although they are collectively owned, TVEs are much more akin to western firms than the **state-owned enterprises (SOEs)** for several reasons:

1. They face a **hard-budget constraint** and are seldom bailed out by government subsidy. Moreover, in the absence of government support, banks are inclined to extend credit only on strictly economic terms.[4]

2. As new enterprises, TVEs fell outside the scope of the rather rigid planning system and were from the beginning unfettered by mandatory controls. They enjoy, therefore, considerable freedom of initiative over what to produce and how. Moreover, because the Chinese planners concentrated more on the growth of heavy industrial output, a large pent-up demand for light industrial products emerged, both in the domestic market and overseas. TVEs were able to exploit this vacuum.

3. Unlike SOEs, TVEs had no captive market for their products and from the start success depended on identifying demand and meeting it with quality products. In both domestic and overseas markets strong forces of consumer sovereignty were at work, which encouraged an emphasis on quality and product development that was absent in the state sector.

4. TVEs were allowed to sell their products at market prices, and their operating largely in competitive markets created a continuing pressure to contain costs and advance productivity.

5. TVEs were not encumbered by the social expenditures required of state enterprises. In common with many socialist countries, SOEs in China were responsible for a range of social services including childcare, education, and health care that raised labor costs.

6. TVEs were also able to be much more nimble in their employment practices (hiring and firing) and were able to establish performance-based compensation systems, which maximized individual incentives and raised productivity.

---

[4]Although initially they had access to credit from the rural credit cooperatives, the financial sector cut the SOEs off from credit almost completely between 1988 and 1991, resulting in failures and employment loss.

7. TVEs could retain profits and keep them within the enterprise as investment. Initially the TVEs were assisted by concessional tax treatment that was helpful in building capital in the "infancy" stage.

Particular features of the Chinese economy under planning also favored growth of TVEs :

1. The concentration on heavy industrial growth through the state-owned enterprises led the government to neglect the light industrial sector, presented a wide window of opportunity in light industrial production, through which the relatively nimble TVEs quickly and profitably moved.

2. The rise in agricultural productivity and the high birthrates of the 1960s created large reserves of labor in the rural communes. The extension of educational opportunities, especially for women, under communism substantially increased human capital.

3. The high degree of provincial autonomy and the concern of local governments to promote economic development (in part motivated by the need to absorb surplus labor) meant that few impediments were placed on TVE growth, and many incentives were offered at the local level.

Starting from a low base at the beginning of the 1980s, the emergence of TVEs made a rapid impact on China's economy. By 1996, some 23.3 million TVEs within China employed more than 135 million workers, or about 20 percent of total national employment. The rural enterprise sector as a whole accounted for only 19.2 percent of industrial output in 1978, but this percentage rose to about 50 percent by 1996.

In recent years a strong trend toward the privatization of the collectively owned TVEs caused a drop in the share of truly collectively owned enterprises, and with it their share of employment. The collectively owned enterprises are being converted into joint stock enterprises, partnerships, and proprietorships. Perhaps more ominously, employment in the rural enterprise sector seems to have peaked at the 1996 level. The subsequent fall in employment put it at fewer than 125 million persons in 1999[5]. This decrease is causing growing rural unemployment. The initial impetus for the TVEs was the surplus labor generated by the agricultural revolution of the 1970s and 1980s. Labor is still being shaken out of the agricultural sector and the rural birth rate is still relatively high and, therefore, the rural labor force is increasing. If those workers cannot find work on the land or in industry, then a body of unemployed or underemployed migrants must emerge. This development is observable already, and with disguised unemployment, total joblessness may be as high as 80 million persons.[6]

---

[5]See Albert Park, *Trade Integration and the Prospects for Rural Enterprise Development in China* (Paris: OECD, 2002).

[6]According to official statistics the unemployment rate is 3.1 percent, or about 22 million, but this figure is thought to be a serious underestimate. The Social and Economic Policy Institute in Hong Kong (http://www.sepi.org) puts the actual rate at 7.9 to 8.3 percent, to which should be added a factor for underemployment, yielding between 10 and 12 percent, a figure that is rising.

REFORMING STATE-OWNED ENTERPRISE

Although the TVEs have been the bright star of the Chinese economy, sustained economic development depends on successful reform of the state-owned enterprises (SOEs). These predominantly heavy industrial enterprises were once seen as the key to China's industrial future and represented economic security to the masses. A job with an SOE was by and large guaranteed for life, usually carried housing benefits, and was often referred to as an "iron rice bowl." The state-owned sector still accounts for the bulk of employment in the industrial sector. It still consumes more than 40 percent of total industrial labor but manages to produce only about 25 percent of the output, reflecting serious inefficiencies.

Initiative in the SOE sector was stifled throughout the post-revolutionary period until the onset of enterprise reform, which started in 1986, slightly later than in the rural sector. Early reform efforts tried to replicate in the state-owned industrial sector the responsibility system that resulted in so much success in the rural areas. Under this scheme, known as the **contract responsibility system (CRS)**, SOEs contracted for a four-year period to a production quota to be delivered to the state, and to specified financial payments it would make to the state in lieu of the profit remittances that the enterprises paid formerly. Any output above the quota level could be disposed of by the enterprise at market prices. By 1988, 90 percent of all SOEs were operating under such contracts.

In parallel with these arrangements, and introduced during the same period of 1986–1988, a third responsibility system involved the **fiscal contract responsibility system (FCRS)**. It supplanted the enterprise income tax, levied at a standard rate of 55 percent, with an individually negotiated contract that fixed the total size of tax payments over several years and specified the division of the total between central, provincial, and local governments. The combination of the two contract systems meant that payments to the government were invariant to the level of profit of the organization. In short, tax elasticity was zero, a major problem. Of greater significance, however, were the FCRS's distortionary features. Because tax payments were all negotiated and the outcome depended to a large extent on political "pull," effective rates varied greatly from enterprise to enterprise, with little pursuit of any underlying economic objective.

These arrangements, however, did provide great incentives for the enterprise. Exceeding a quota was highly desirable because excess output could be sold for whatever the market would bear. Moreover, with the marginal tax rate on profits at zero and the dividends payable to government fixed, all the profit above predetermined fixed levels could be retained in the enterprise. The industrial output of the SOEs rose sharply in response. However, the reforms also brought negative consequences for long-term economic development. First, each contractual arrangement was individually negotiated, giving enterprises an incentive to fight for high levels of inputs and low quotas to acquire the resources for a surplus to sell on the private market. This asymmetry of information between the bureaucracy and the enterprise led to significant negative impacts.

The second disadvantage was the abandonment of all pretense of a "level playing field" in the tax system in favor of what should more accurately be called a "revenue" system. In developed market economies, tax systems are expected to define rules that include **horizontal equity**, which requires that equivalent units should be treated equally. Because of the discretionary element, the fiscal contract responsibility system resulted in widely disparate average tax rates between enterprises, as well as falling average rates over time.

Third, although the boom in the industrial sector should have increased government revenue from taxes on enterprises, revenues proved highly inelastic with respect to growing income. In fact, real revenues tended to fall as income and output rose because the contracts fixed tax payment in nominal terms, with no inflation escalator. A buoyant economy and the progressive decontrol of prices led to inflation and reduced the real value of the contracted nominal tax payments.

A fourth and highly significant problem was that the CRS resulted in a two-tier price system: the procurement price set by the responsibility contract and paid on the contracted quota, and the market price. The procurement price was in general lower than the market price. Therefore, large potential gains were possible in arbitrage between the state and private sectors and from the deliberate understatement of quota outputs. This potential led to a sharp increase in corruption.

CREATING A MODERN ENTERPRISE SECTOR

Recognizing the problems emanating from the responsibility system in the SOE sector, the Chinese government embarked on a new series of reforms to change the structure of ownership, governance, and accounting in the SOEs and also reform the fiscal relationship between the enterprises and the various levels of government. However, progress has not been easy because of the need to control rising unemployment and the implicit lifetime employment guarantee associated with most state employment.

Although content to let private firms, **foreign-financed enterprises (FFEs)**, and the collectivized sectors prosper, Chinese authorities were slow to embark on the mass privatization of most state assets. The cornerstone of the economy in the foreseeable future will continue to be the predominance of SOEs in strategic sectors. The strategy is to develop a "socialist market economy" in which the assets of much of the industrial sector are owned by the state, but in which the primary functions of coordination are performed by the market, subject to guidance from the center. In some sense this model is not dramatically different from that of certain European economies, like the French or British in their preprivatization period when much of heavy industry was held in public ownership.

The first step in the creation of this "modern enterprise sector" must be the corporatization of the SOEs; the foundation to achieve this step was laid down in the *company law*, which became effective in July 1994. The most salient thrust of the company law is to clearly separate "ownership" (which for the time being lies with the state) from management. It clarifies the rights of enterprises as legal entities, establishes the rights and responsibilities of management, and limits the power of ministries to interfere directly in enterprise management. The law also relieves SOEs from many of their responsibilities for the social security of their workers and families. Ultimately, it is planned that responsibility for the oversight of enterprises will pass from the ministries into the hands of state holding companies.

The root of the problem of the state-owned sector is a soft-budget constraint for state-owned enterprise, which continues to apply. About 50 percent of the SOEs fail to produce a profit, but even the loss-making ventures are kept in existence either by state subsidies, or by the government using the state-owned banks to continue to extend credit to enterprises that are economically moribund. In a real sense the SOEs are too big to be allowed to fail. Today, 44 percent of urban Chinese still work for the SOEs. If the government allowed market logic to triumph, the political problems and distress would be huge. Instead, the authorities initiated privatization in a small way. Many of the smaller and medium-sized enterprises already are being being sold off. The worst cases are foreclosed, the banks assuming ownership in lieu of payment of the outstanding loans. The banks then place these assets with specialist **asset management companies (AMCs)** whose task is to reorganize, restructure, and find a buyer. In most cases the assets are disposed of for a trivial sum, but it is a means of privatizing the least efficient of the state enterprises, and to allow the banks to get some of the nonperforming loans off their books.

REFORMING THE TAX SYSTEM

A successful transition from a centrally planned economy to one that is market oriented must involve the creation of certain institutions that are essential for the long-term stability of the economy. One of the most important of these is the fiscal system, which plays two important roles. First, it provides the resources for government expenditures. In the absence of an effective tax-gathering system, the government usually is financed by money creation—an "inflation tax"—which transfers resources from creditors to debtors (the largest of which is the government) in a capricious and inefficient way.

Second, the fiscal system provides the government with an important policy tool meant to promote macroeconomic stability and control the direction of economic development. China today does not have a well-functioning tax system and gathers a lower share of its GDP into the central government than any other East Asian nation, between 7 percent and 8 percent. Local taxing powers are considerable; in total about 15 percent of GDP is taken into general government. The reform in taxation seeks to replace what has been described as a *revenue system,* which can provide fiscal resources for various levels of government but, because of a lack of consistency and equity, creates perverse incentives. It is in the process of the necessary reform that will, it is hoped, create the required conditions for continued growth.

Indirect Taxes

The Value-Added Tax Currently, central government finance relies heavily on indirect taxes, which provide 79 percent of revenue. They are of three types: excise taxes, value-added taxes (VAT), and turnover taxes on business, each of which supplies a little less than 3 percent of GNP in revenue. Tax reform will simplify the system by enlarging the coverage of VAT and standardizing the rates. Under the new system, VAT will extend to universal coverage with a 17 percent rate applied to most goods and a 13 percent rate on food, farm supplies, and utilities. In addition, a consumption tax will replace the excise tax and will be levied only on the sale of tobacco, alcohol, gasoline, and luxury goods (including cars). A special business tax will apply to services not covered by VAT. Improved tax administration increases the probability that in the future a well-administered VAT system will provide most of the central government finance, removing the distortionary aspects of the turnover and sales tax system.

Customs and Tariffs China's growing participation in world trade, and in the international agencies that oversee trade, requires a rationalization of a complex tariff structure, constructed in a piecemeal manner with both revenue raising and protectionism in mind. Customs duties historically provided about 8 percent of tax revenue. The average tariff rate is about 40 percent, but rates rise with the degree to which the goods are "finished." Raw materials are subject to rates in the 0 to 20 percent range, intermediate and capital goods fit into the 20 to 40 percent category, and finished goods may be subject to duties as high as 80 percent. The effective rate of protection for the Chinese manufacturing industry provided by this structure is high.

Reforms presently being implemented will reduce the maximum tariff on all goods to less than 40 percent, and many categories of goods will be placed in the zero bracket. The impact of this change on revenue is not clear and depends on the elasticity of imports to tariff changes; it is conceivable that revenues will rise if imports increase in response to lower rates of protection.

Direct Taxes

The Personal Income Tax Other parts of the tax system are also being reformed. The direct taxation system in China comprises the enterprise tax and the personal income tax. At present, the role of the personal income tax in both revenue raising and fiscal policy is negligible. Its nominal incidence is primarily private business owners and foreigners (who pay on a higher schedule than domestic Chinese). The high rates encourage both evasion and avoidance; compliance is consequently low, revenue is small, and deadweight burdens quite high.

The personal income tax base includes all personal income from wages, salaries, rents, and business sources, less a standard deduction of ¥800 per month for Chinese citizens. This deduction excludes a large part of the domestic population from paying tax at all, especially rural residents. For everyone above the threshold, income will be subject to sharply rising progressive rates starting at 5 percent. In the case of wage income the maximum marginal rate is 45 percent, and for "unearned" income the top rate is 35 percent, an unusual configuration. In most societies with multiple rates, unearned income is taxed at a higher rate than earned income, complying with a widely held view that working individuals are more entitled to money they labored for. In addition, the disincentive impact of high taxes on labor is usually thought to be greater than on capital. The Chinese authorities hope that the lower rate on capital income will increase the tax base by reducing evasion and fostering compliance in the private business sector.

The Corporate Income Tax The corporate tax, now leveled at a rate of 33 percent of corporate profits, applies to corporations, collectives, foreign-financed enterprises, and state-owned enterprise, though a clause allows for the negotiated taxes in special circumstances. Because the state-owned sector is only marginally profitable, in aggregate, it contributes little to revenues.

THE FINANCIAL SYSTEM

As in the case of the tax system, the effective reform of the financial sector can do double duty. First, a stable and rationally developed system allows for greater allocative efficiency through the improved channeling of resources from savers to investors. Second, a coherent financial system is essential for the implementation of effective monetary policy.

The Banking Sector

Prior to 1978 the banking system in China played only a limited role. Its main purpose was akin to the role of the monobank in any centrally planned system. Through the management of the accounts of the various SOEs, it provided a financial counterpart to the movement of goods, and therefore a check on the satisfactory fulfillment of the plan, and it also made available to state-owned enterprises the credits for investment and subsidy approved in the plan.

The People's Bank of China (PBC) was the dominant agency and served as a commercial, investment, and central bank. In 1984 the PBC became the central bank, responsible for supervision of the financial system, exchange rate policy, and the conduct of monetary policy, and its commercial and investment banking functions were handed over to four state-owned banks, known now as the Big Four. These banks perform both commercial and investment banking functions, and are like the German "universal banks." Another element of the state banking system is made up of the credit cooperatives, which collect deposits and supply loans at the grassroots level. Rural credit cooperatives number 53,000, along with 4,000 urban ones, though their combined assets represent less than 6 percent of the total. In addition, three development banks (one national and two provincial ones in Guangdong and Shenzhen) exist, but their assets are small. A small private banking sector is emerging but it represents less than 6 percent of the loans.

The banks have never been fully free to pursue their own interests or to follow good banking practice. Though the creation of the PBC and the Big Four banks was seen at the time as a strong step toward the creation of a market-oriented financial system, the authorities were slow to relinquish power over credit allocation. In 1988 the government tightened control over the Big Four banks and the growing number of nonbank financial intermediaries (NBFIs). The main vehicle for credit allocation remains the **credit plan**, which is controlled from the center and determines the activity of the central bank, the specialized banks, and the Big Four banks. The banks are required to provide the finance for approved projects and the government largely administers interest rates, although the banks are allowed a small degree of latitude around the official rate.

Continued reliance on directed credit through the credit plan has often been criticized as being at odds with the principles of decentralization, competition, and marketization, which provide the primary elements of the reforms in other areas.[7] In the past Chinese planners were able to point not only to their own experience but also to the prevalent use of directed credit by both the Japanese and the South Koreans during the periods of greatest growth in their countries. However, the problems of the Japanese and Korean economies in recent years, which are particularly pressing in the banking sectors, must give the Chinese cause for concern. Nevertheless, the planners remain reluctant to relinquish their last lever of control, and their Northeast Asian neighbors were until the late 1990s advertisements for its efficacy.

More damaging than the mere principle of directed credit is the criticism that the credit plan adopted by the authorities is based on flawed principles. Japanese and Korean directed credit was based on the principle of identifying growth areas and financing export-oriented development in the most dynamic sectors. Chinese credit, on the other hand, is more defensively dispositioned and frequently seeks to guard the interests of the existing SOE sector. The banks were required to make a large number of **policy loans** that run counter to good banking practice but are part of the overall plan. The result of this requirement is that the recently created specialized banks already hold portfolios of **nonperforming loans (NPLs)**.[8]

Table 23.1 gives some indication of the problems that the banking system now faces. All of the Big Four banks have a large number of NPLs on their books. The largest bank in terms of loans is the Industrial and Commercial Bank of China (ICBC), whose portfolio contains $325 billion in loans, 29.8 percent of which are presently nonperforming based on the official definition. This measure probably underestimates the severity of the situation. The situation is worse at the Agricultural Bank of China, at which 42.1 percent of loans are nonperforming. Taken together the Big Four carry $897 billion in outstanding loans, with an average of 29.9 percent of the loan portfolio nonperforming. To give some dimension to this scenario, this amount represents some 26 percent of Chinese GDP, or 355 percent of annual central government tax revenue. As a transnational comparison, Citibank's loan portfolio of $392 billion shows only 2.3 percent nonperforming.

INTERNATIONAL TRADE

Before the onset of reform, all of China's foreign trade was handled through a few foreign trade corporations that acted as import and export agencies. The reforms began in 1993 and trade was liberalized, both in terms of the agencies that can enter into international trade and in terms of the tariffs and licensing restrictions that

---

[7]See Tseng et al., *Economic Reform in China: A New Phase* (Washington, DC: International Monetary Fund, 1994), p. 1617.

[8]A nonperforming loan is one where the debt service payments have been suspended for some reason. It is a step short of the loan never being repaid; the debtor agency might resume payments, or may enter receivership, in which case some part of the principal may be repaid.

■ **TABLE 23.1**

The Big Four Banks, 2002

	Branches	Loans, ($ billions)	Percent of Nonperforming Loans	Value of Bad Loans
Chinese State-Owned Banks				
Industrial and Commercial Bank of China	28,000	325	29.8	97
Agricultural Bank of China	50,000	199	42.1	84
Bank of China	13,000	192	27.5	53
China Construction Bank	24,000	182	19.4	35
Total	115,000	897	29.9	268
For comparison:				
Citibank	6,421	392	2.3	9
Memo Items				
Bad loans as percent of government revenue		166%		
Bad loans as a percent of GDP		26%		

SOURCE: Standard and Poor's; Citibank.

constrained it. Enterprises, whether in the state, the collective, or the private sectors, became more able and more anxious to seek out and export to markets of their own choosing.

The impact of this export boom on China's trade position has been huge. In 1978 the trade to GNP ratio for China was about 5 percent; by 1993 this had risen to 35 percent, making China a highly open economy by world standards.[9] The Chinese share of world trade doubled between 1978 and 1993, from 1 percent to 2 percent of the total.

Table 23.2 shows the highlights of China's overseas transactions since 1993. Exports showed remarkable growth increasing sixfold in a twelve-year period between 1989 and 2001. This increase made China one of the world's largest traders. The commodity composition of trade also underwent a dramatic shift. In 1978 agricultural products dominated exports, comprising 63 percent of the total. Today light industrial exports dominate. A remarkable inflow of foreign direct investment capital into China also occurred. Since the mid 1990s, investment capital poured in at the rate of about $40 billion dollars annually. The pace slowed somewhat after the Asian financial crisis, but in 2001 it reached $44 billion again, roughly 3.6 percent of China's GDP.

SPECIAL ECONOMIC ZONES

China made extensive use of various forms of **special economic zones (SEZs)** in its reform push. The first SEZs were established by the State Council in 1979. They were

[9]Some care should be taken with this statistic; although trade is valued in dollars, GNP is understated because it is not cited in PPP terms. In reality, the denominator should be larger. Moreover, at this time trade with Hong Kong was counted as a foreign trade transaction.

Highlights of Chinese Overseas Transaction, 1993–2001 (in US$ millions)

	1989	1991	1993	1995	1997	1999	2000	2001
Exports	43,220	58,919	75,659	128,110	182,670	194,716	249,131	266,075
Imports	48,840	50,176	86,113	110,060	136,448	158,734	414,657	232,058
Trade balance	25,620	8,743	−10,454	18,050	46,222	35,982	3,4474	33,384
Current account balance	24,317	13,272	−11,609	1,618	36,963	21,115	20,518	17,401
Outgoing direct investment	780	913	4,400	2,000	2,563	1,775	916	6,884
Incoming Direct Investment	3,393	4,366	27,515	35,849	44,237	38,753	38,399	44,241

SOURCE: International Monetary Fund, International Financial Statistics 2003.

all located in south coastal China, near the overseas Chinese communities in Macao, Hong Kong, and Taiwan. Three SEZs were placed in Guangdong Province (Shenzhen, Zhuhai, and Shantou) and one (Xiamen) in Fujian. Subsequently Pudong across the river from Shanghai was added in 1990. The State Council also sanctioned the creation of 15 **economic and technological development zones (ETDZs)** and 34 **high-technology development zones (HTDZS)**. The common feature of all of these zones is considerable relief from central government taxation. The rate of tax on profits of enterprises located in the zones is 15 percent as opposed to the 55 percent prevailing in non-SEZs at the time of their inception. The four original SEZs plus Pudong also offer two-year tax holidays. Local governments, anxious to raise the pace of economic development, introduced their own zones with varying levels of relief from local taxes, which numbered an estimated 9,000 zones by the end of 1992.

Many economists remain skeptical about the role of tax concessions applied to limited geographical areas. It can be argued that such provisions make for additional distortions in an economy that is already far from providing a level playing field. Unless such provisions are intended to correct known market failures, the effect may be counterproductive in terms of aggregate welfare. The concern, therefore, is that the incentives granted in such zones only serve to move activity from one place to another, and the elasticity of aggregate investment and employment with respect to the tax reductions is low. In such a case, the government is certain to experience a loss of tax revenue, which may be uncompensated by positive economic effects.

An economic logic may justify the provision of such zones, however.

1. In the case of a region dependent on a declining industry, concessional treatment might attract investment that would secure employment and prevent the waste of already committed social investment.

2. Economies of scale may come in the provision of infrastructure and services, and incentives designed to increase the density of industrial activity may be rational.

3. External economies of agglomeration may take the form of spillover and pool effects. For example, one of the frequently cited reasons for technology parks

is the high degree of knowledge spillover; in other industries labor pool effects may be important.

4. The government may wish to restrict some activities and policies to a limited geographical area for environmental reasons or, in the special case of China, to limit their impact in order to analyze their effects before generalizing the policies.

The first reason is not relevant in the case of the Chinese special economic zones. Both the second and third statements are cited as rationales and perhaps played a role. However, it is probable that the most important reason is the fourth. The State Council and national planning authorities used the economic zones as laboratories in which the efficacy and consequences of certain policy shifts could be gauged. All of the important reforms concerning foreign exchange, foreign direct investment, state-owned enterprise organization, labor markets, and the use of joint-stock companies with tradable equity capital were pioneered in the enterprise zones.

Only those successful reforms, and that the decision-making apparatus of the state believes it can manage and control, have been allowed to mature and spread. This experimentation and groping forward contributed an essential part of the Chinese reform strategy discussed later.

REGIONAL INEQUALITY AND NATIONAL UNITY

One disturbing feature of China's growth is the dramatic increase in the disparity of income in recent years. Moreover, the regional income differential is worsening and will be aggravated further by the terms of China's accession into the World Trade Organization. At present the provinces of the eastern seaboard (particularly Guangdong, close to Hong Kong, and Zhejiang, around Shanghai) have average incomes that are four to five times greater than the national average as measured in official exchange rate terms. This difference is now about $900 per year, although much better at almost $4,000 in purchasing power terms.

Hong Kong, absorbed into the People's Republic in 1997, is one of the wealthiest areas in the world; its per-head income at the time of the reunion was roughly $25,000. The provinces of the interior all have incomes per head less than the national average, and some are below 50 percent of that figure. Accession to the WTO will, according a recent report from the OECD, effectively stimulate the export-oriented eastern seaboard while harming the predominantly agricultural west, which will be battered by an influx of cheap foreign grain. Hence the disparities will become worse. Economic theory suggests some form of convergence will occur over time. All other things being equal, investment should increasingly seek out the low-wage provinces and hence lead to a growth of industrial employment and income. However, experience in many areas (Italy, Germany, Brazil) suggest that this convergence is not inevitable. Externalities are important and growing industries tend to be attracted to growing areas, where infrastructure, education, and transportation opportunities are favorable. Although migration from the interior might also provide some equalizing effect, the overall prognosis is one of worsening disparities and consequent political pressures. The important question is whether this disparity will affect the political unity of China. The policy alternatives are not attractive; "benign neglect" will see the position worsen, and discontent might become unmanageable. On the other hand, redistributive schemes to favor the less well-off provinces would require an increase in taxation in the prosperous eastern areas. That move would certainly be unpopular with the rich and would by no means be certain to promote growth in the interior.

SOURCE: OECD, *China in the World Economy: An OECD Economic and Statistical Survey.*

THE IMPORTANCE OF A "KINDRED MODEL"

Despite the poverty of the country and the limitations of its resource base, China enjoyed in its transformation an asset that most countries can only experience in a much lesser degree: assistance and example from a **"kindred model"** in populations abroad. The *tongbao* (which literally means "same womb") populations of Hong Kong, Macao, and increasingly (at least until the decline in relations in early 1996) Taiwan, play an important role in Chinese growth. Singapore, geographically and culturally more remote but with an affluent population, expensive labor, and surplus capital, also played a part.

Although these communities include small populations in relation to the People's Republic (about ¹⁄₄₀ combined), their role is important on several dimensions:

1. *A demonstration effect.* These communities provided a demonstration that Chinese people can transform their economic circumstances in a relatively short period of time, given favorable policies. The standard of living enjoyed in Taiwan and Hong Kong is an assurance to many Chinese that economic transformation is feasible. This tends to promote both personal saving and investment as a response to confidence in the future.

2. *Trading partner.* The overseas communities have provided an important trading partner for China. This is especially true of Hong Kong, whose prime function is to serve as an entrepôt for the mainland. Over 40 percent of China's exports are routed through Hong Kong, and although the opening of other city ports will reduce this share, the proximity of Hong Kong to the rapidly growing areas is highly significant.

3. *Investor.* Overseas Chinese communities account for the larger part of incoming direct foreign investment into China. Hong Kong alone accounts for over 50 percent, and Taiwan is growing as a source as its economy experiences rapidly increasing labor costs.

4. *Sources of information.* In the early stages of transformation of a socialist economy, information about technologies and markets is at a premium. Residents of the overseas communities do much to provide China with a window on the world: over 95 percent of visitors to China are people of Chinese ethnicity.

THE CHARACTER OF CHINESE REFORM

Chinese reform differs in form and in consequence from the approach taken in the Central and Eastern European Economies (CEEEs). At the moment, many observers see the Chinese model as superior. The most obvious point in China's favor is that it avoided the sharp contraction of output, surging inflation, and elevated unemployment that characterized transition in all of the CEEEs.[10] In sharp

---

[10]See Blanchard, "Theoretical Aspects of Transition," *American Economic Review,* May 1996, p. 117, for evidence on the similarity of the post-Soviet transitions.

contrast to Eastern Europe, Chinese growth accelerated with the onset of reform. Employment grew and unemployment fell despite the fact that China experienced a much higher population growth rate than that of Russia or the other CEEEs.

Certainly much of the difference in macroeconomic performance was due to the fact that reforms were less sweeping in China than in the CEEEs, but part is a function of differing states of development. The Central and Eastern European Economies are industrial economies. Markets that had been guaranteed under domestic planning or trade arrangements overseen by the Council for Mutual Economic Assistance (CMEA, otherwise known as COMECON) disappeared. Suppliers became reluctant to sell at old prices and demanded hard currency payments, creating a disarticulation in the system. A macroeconomic contraction and unemployment resulted. Prices were adjusted to world levels with inflation as the consequence. Because planned international trade was less important to China than to the Eastern European countries, this disruption resulted in fewer macroeconomic consequences.

Agriculture in China was a much more dominant part of the economy in the pre-reform period. The economy was less dependent on a complex set of markets and suppliers. Moreover, the Chinese experienced and adjusted to great disorganization in both the Great Leap Forward and the Proletarian Cultural Revolution. That said, we turn now to examine some of the distinctive characteristics of the Chinese reform experience.

Gradualism

One difference in reform strategy—that of **gradualism**—can be highlighted by the use of a metaphor. Vaclav Havel, the playwright who became president of the Czech Republic during its transition to a market economy, once characterized the CEEE approach to reform by stating that it is impossible to "cross a chasm in two leaps." The Chinese approach, on the other hand, can be summarized by stating that China is "touching stones to cross a river." In other words, China proceeded on its own path by a process of experimentation, moving forward slowly only in areas where policies had been tested and seen to work. So far, it must be said, this approach proved a more successful policy than revolutionary reform, or an economic "big bang."

Partial Reform

China has not been averse to creating situations in which reform is incomplete. The clearest of these areas lies in the contract responsibility systems, which resulted in a two-tier price system for agricultural and industrial goods. Such systems of **partial reform** offer the advantage of keeping with the gradualist approach to reform, and they also provide substantial incentives to the relevant economic actors. Marginal economic allocation decisions are made in response to market prices, which lead to a beneficial impact on overall economic efficiency. However, as noted earlier, two-tier prices provide considerable returns to arbitrage from the state to the market system, and that engenders corruption.

Decentralization

Chinese reform has been accompanied by a weakening of central control over the constituent parts of the economy. **Decentralization** is not an uncommon feature; a parallel can be seen in the breakup of the Soviet Union and in the fissiparous tendencies currently in evidence in Russia itself as ethnically differentiated areas, such as Chechnya, attempt to break away. In China the outcome of devolution has been positive, allowing the provincial authorities to be flexible and pragmatic. Some observers are concerned that this trend will end in the demise of China as a centralized state, torn apart by growing income inequality, increased provincial chauvinism, and a weakened center inadequately supported by a national fiscal system.

Accommodating Spontaneous Reform

Even though it might appear from the outside that the entire process has been one of rational experimentation, in reality Chinese reform has been characterized by a willingness to allow **spontaneous reform**. In part, a weakening control of the State Council, discussed earlier, leaves it with little alternative but to acquiesce, and reform legislation takes on the character of making virtue of necessity.

Economic Liberalization without Political Democratization

The main point of difference between change in Central and Eastern Europe and China is the relative pace of political and economic reform. In the former Soviet Union and Eastern Europe, political reform occurred rapidly and ran ahead of economic reform, feeding expectations with respect to economic progress, which were subsequently disappointed. In China the reverse happened. Economic freedom evolved much more rapidly than the political variant. A correspondingly greater social stability and suppression of dissent, it can be argued, has provided for a solid platform for growth and incoming direct foreign investments. Western nations might like the idea of democracy, but their entrepreneurs are more prone to invest in predictable authoritarian states.

DID REFORMS ACCELERATE GROWTH?

In most people's minds, the rapid growth of the Chinese economy during the 1980s and 1990s was caused by the reforms that began in 1978. However, in evaluating the success of any change in economic policy, it is important to establish a counterfactual: What would have occurred in the absence of the policy shift? It is certainly true that after 1978 we witnessed substantial improvement in just about every economic indicator. It is also true that the rates of improvement of these indicators are better than in the pre-reform period of 1953–1978, as clearly seen in the first and second columns in Table 23.3. Output rose faster in both aggregate and per capita terms, and labor productivity grew more quickly. Although the labor force grew at

■ TABLE 23.3

Decomposition of Chinese Economic Growth, 1953–1990,
(average annual growth rates)

	1953–1978	1979–1994	1953–1978 (excl. 1959–1970)
Output	5.9	9.2	7.6
Output per head of population	3.8	7.5	5.4
Output per worker	3.1	6.3	4.5
Ratio of investment to net material product	19.9	24.8	21.7
Capital	10.2	9.9	13.2
Labor	2.6	2.7	3
Total factor productivity	20.7	3.8	20.8

SOURCE: Eduardo Borensztein and Jonathan Ostry, "Accounting for China's Growth Performance," *American Economic Review,* May 1996, p. 225.

about the same rate, capital growth was actually marginally slower than in the pre-reform era.

However, some authors draw attention to the fact that a comparison of these periods may be biased, because the 1953–1978 period included the major disturbances caused by the Great Leap Forward and the Cultural Revolution. In these periods, the socialist-planned Chinese economy did not operate normally, but were rather periods of great political upheaval akin almost to a civil war. The appropriate comparison might well be to view the performance post-1978 against the "normal" years of socialist planning. By excluding the period 1959–1970, the substantial dips in output occasioned by the two political convulsions are eliminated. Now, a comparison can be made of the post-reform era with the "normal" period of socialist economics—the third column in Table 23.3 versus the second column. The contrast is by no means as pronounced, although growth of output and labor productivity growth were superior after the reform.

From the table we can see evidence of a difference in the type of economic growth between the two periods. The pre-reform period was characterized by the extensive growth that we often see in socialist systems. The labor force increased rapidly (by 3 percent annually) and capital accumulation was high (13.2 percent annually). The growth of output is wholly accounted for by the growth of inputs; in this case we note that total factor productivity is negative, indicating a loss of aggregate efficiency.

In the post-reform era, labor force and capital growth are slower than in the pre-reform era, yet output grows more quickly. The key here is the growth in total factor productivity, which moves ahead at a respectable 3.8 percent per year in the post-reform period. Total factor productivity (TFP) is calculated as a residual and its main components are static efficiency gains from moving workers from low marginal product occupations to higher ones and dynamic gains due to ongoing technical progress. By the rapid growth of TFP we can see that reforms did achieve something, but the unanswered question is whether the gains were static or dynamic.

CAN GROWTH BE SUSTAINED?

It is tempting to believe that the Chinese economy transitioned into a "take-off into self-sustaining growth," momentous though such an assumption would be. As we noted at the beginning of this chapter, extrapolation of current growth trends of the 1990s implies that the Chinese economy would be larger in terms of GDP than that of the United States in the first half of this century.

The sustainability of the growth rate depends to a large extent on whether total factor productivity continues to improve and to what extent this improvement may be attributable to an increase in technical efficiency. To this point it is probable that the greatest contribution to TFP change has been the result of the following factors:

1. An increase in productivity in the agricultural sector due to the introduction of greater material incentives

2. The movement of workers from low productivity (perhaps even zero marginal productivity) agricultural occupations to work in industry and services

3. An increase in the human capital invested in the workforce

In addition to these factors, statistical irregularities must be accounted for. The main one is "underdeflation" of industrial output—that is, the use of a price index for industrial output that increases less quickly than the "true" rate of inflation, which leads to an overstatement of real industrial output. A second area is the inclusion of essentially unsalable inventories in the SOE sector as part of output at inflated prices. When these factors are corrected for, the rate of growth of TFP seems to be much smaller, and may even be negative, as it was during the socialist planned period. At present, plentiful labor in China means growth can continue through the redeployment of low productivity rural labor into the industrial sector, as long as the demand for China's industrial output continues to grow. When the potential for increasing output by redeploying agricultural labor becomes exhausted, the rate of growth of GDP will inevitably slow, and unless the rate of growth due to technical innovation increases, it will be largely dependent on the rate of growth of the capital stock.

CHINA AND THE WORLD TRADE ORGANIZATION (WTO)

In November 1999 China took a remarkable step forward by committing itself to membership in the WTO. It finally achieved accession in December 2001. This shift toward a more open economy will put severe strains on the economy in the short run but will lead to a much truer market system in the long run. As a precursor to applying for membership in the World Trade Organization, China concluded a bilateral deal with the United States establishing a timetable for the dismantling of much of China's tariff and quota walls. With the task of reforming the inefficient state-owned enterprises barely begun, and with China already experiencing the socially divisive consequences of rising unemployment, this move is certainly a gamble.

CHINA IN THE TWENTY-FIRST CENTURY

Agriculture will be sharply affected by membership.[11] Tariffs on wheat and maize will fall by the year 2004 to just 14.5 percent, not enough to protect most of China's farmers from more efficient U.S. producers, exacerbating the problem of rural unemployment. As we saw, the TVEs are actually shrinking in their manpower needs and no longer serve the role of employing surplus agricultural labor. The impact of the WTO liberalization will be to cut agricultural employment and increase rural joblessness. Unemployment and underemployment will rise, in turn aggravating the problem of the regional differences in income and putting a strain on the Chinese political structure.

Manufacturing tariffs are set to tumble as well. In automobiles, for example, the tariff will fall from 100 percent to 25 percent, a shift that will put most of China's many vehicle makers at risk, although foreign manufacturers are likely to be fast in establishing or expanding production in China. Joint ventures are to be sanctioned in telecommunications, which will expose the state-owned telephone dinosaurs to the best of foreign technology.

However, the biggest sectoral impact may well be in banking and finance. Foreign banks will be largely freed of restrictions and will be able to operate throughout China. The inefficient and poorly financed state banks will be forced to compete for funds and loans. These banks are already crippled by the burden of nonperforming loans, and the competition for deposits will certainly raise their borrowing cost. A banking crisis is likely. The most economically logical result will be the failure of some of the Big Four banks and their takeover by foreign, probably American, concerns. Whether this scenario can be palatable to the political leadership remains to be seen. It would imply relinquishing control of the credit allocation process, a step that a nominal socialist country might still be unwilling to take.

CHINA IN THE TWENTY-FIRST CENTURY

At the 16th Communist Party Congress held in Beijing in November 2002, President Jiang Zemin passed the torch of leadership, the general secretaryship of the Community party, to his vice president Hu Jintao, while still retaining the powerful position of commander in chief of the armed forces. It is clear that Jiang intends to hang onto a good a deal of policy-making power well into the future. The transition is likely to be far from smooth, and political uncertainty could be part of Jiang's legacy. The Congress also approve Jiang's theory of the **"Three Represents,"** an ideological innovation that claims that the Communist Party represents the workers and the peasant (the traditional "two represents") as well as now extending its umbrella to the capitalist class. This definition allows China's growing body of private entrepreneurs to join the party.

Uncertainty in the political situation is matched by the specter of economic problems. On the surface, things are good; growth continues at a robust 7 to 8 percent

---

[11]OECD, China in The World Economy: Agricultural Policies in China after WTO Accession, Paris: OECD. 2002.

annually. However, even this pace is inadequate to absorb the growing number of unemployed. China needs to create about 8 million jobs per year merely to stop the unemployment situation from worsening, and 7 percent yearly growth is not enough to generate this level of job creation. The unemployment crisis emerged from two sources. First, excess labor in the countryside cannot be absorbed by rural industrial growth. This problem will become more serious as agricultural tariffs fall as a result of WTO membership. The other source is the state-owned enterprise sector, which as a result of attrition, bankruptcy, and restructuring, needs to reduce its workforce by about 20 million workers in the next five years. Even though the rapid growth of exports (currently 15 percent annually) is likely to continue, it is unlikely to provide enough jobs. Any slowing of GDP or export growth could cause a serious increase in unemployment. China's spectacular rate of growth means some of its citizens now enjoy "first world" living standards, but a large part of its population still lives in poverty. It is the paradox that the political leadership must resolve in the twenty-first century.

KEY TERMS AND CONCEPTS

asset management companies (AMCs)
contract responsibility system (CRS)
convergence
credit plan
decentralization
economic and technological development zones (ETDZs)
fiscal contract responsibility system (FCRS)
foreign-financed enterprises (FFEs)
gradualism
gang of four
Great Leap Forward
hard-budget constraint

high-technology development zones (HTDZs)
horizontal equity
household responsibility system (HRS)
"kindred model"
nonperforming loans (NPLs)
partial reform
policy loans
Proletarian Cultural Revolution
regional income disparity
special economic zones (SEZs)
state-owned enterprises (SOEs)
spontaneous reform
"Three Represents"
township and village enterprises

QUESTIONS FOR DISCUSSION

1. Why was Soviet-style planning hard to apply in China?
2. How did the Great Leap Forward and the Cultural Revolution harm economic development?

3. How did allowing agricultural reform lead to the rapid expansion of light industry?

4. Why have township and village enterprises been so successful?

5. What attempts were made to reform state-owned enterprise, and how successful were they?

6. What role did the special economic zones play in Chinese development?

7. What role did Chinese overseas communities play in the development of China?

8. Discuss the metaphor of "crossing the river by touching the stones" with respect to reform in China.

9. Why is opening the financial sector to competition, agreed to in the deal with the United States in November 1999, so important for the development of a market economy in China?

10. What are nonperforming loans? Why do they threaten China's future?

11. What, if anything, prevents income convergence of China's provinces? How does this threaten unity and growth?

RESOURCES

Web Sites

People's Bank of China (Central Bank) ....http://www.pbc.gov.cn/

Ministry of Foreign Trade and Economic Cooperation http://www1.moftec.gov.cn/

People's Daily ....http://english.peopledaily.com.cn/

China News Services and China News Agency ....http://www.chinanews.com.cn/

China Online ....http://www.chinaonline.com/

National Bureau of Statistics of China ....http://www.stats.gov.cn

Books and Articles

Bell, Michael W., Hoe Ee Khor, and Kalpana Kochhar. *China at the Threshold of a Market Economy*. International Monetary Fund Occasional Paper 107. Washington, DC: International Monetary Fund, September 1993.

Blejer, Mario. "China: Prolonged Reforms and the Weakening of Fiscal Control." In *Transition to Market*, Mario Tanzi (ed.). Washington, DC: International Monetary Fund, 1993. 253–269.

Blejer, Mario, David Burton, Steven Dunaway, and Gyorgy Szapary. *China: Economic Reform and Macroeconomic Management*. Washington, DC: International Monetary Fund, January 1991.

Borensztein, Eduardo, and Jonathan D. Ostry. "Accounting for China's Growth." *American Economic Review*, May 1996, 224.

Cardoso, Eliana and Shahid Yusuf. "Red Capitalism: Growth and Inflation in China." *Challenge,* May/June 1994, 49–57.

Chen, Aimin. "Chinese Industrial Structure in Transition: The Emergence of Stock-Offering Firms." *Comparative Economic Studies,* Winter 1994, 1–19.

Chen, Kang, Gary H. Jefferson, and Inderjit Singh. "Lessons from China's Economic Reform." In *Comparative Economic Systems,* 7th ed., Morris Bornstein (ed.). Burr Ridge, IL: Irwin, 1994.

"China's Coastal Development (The Great International Cycle) and Decentralized Management of the Economy." *Chinese Economic Studies,* Fall/Winter 1991–1992.

Chow, Gregory C. *Chinese Economy,* 2d ed. River Edge, NJ: World Scientific Publishing, 1987.

Fulton, Trish, Jinyan Li, and Dianqing Xu (eds.) *China's Tax Reform Options.* River Edge, NJ: World Scientific Publishing, 1998.

Gao, Shangquan. *Two Decades of Reform in China.* Washington, DC: World Bank, 1999.

Ge, Wei. *Special Economic Zones and the Economic Transition in China.* River Edge, NJ: World Scientific Publishing, 1999.

Hsu, Dave Y. C. "Experience and Lessons of China's Agricultural Development." *Journal of Contemporary Asia* 20, no. 2 (1990), 212–223.

Hu, Yaoxing. "Market-Oriented Reforms in China." *Development Policy Review* 11, no. 2 (June 1993), 195–204.

Huang, Yasheng. "Information, Bureaucracy, and Economic Reforms in China and the Soviet Union." *World Politics,* October 1994, 102–34.

Itoh, Fumio. *China in the Twenty-First Century: Politics, Economy, and Society.* New York: United Nations Publications, 1997.

Jefferson, Gary, and Inderjit Singh (eds.). *Enterprise Reform in China: Ownership, Transition, and Performance.* Oxford: Oxford University Press, 1998.

Koo, Anthony Y. C. "The Contract Responsibility System: Transition from a Planned to a Market Economy: Government and Enterprise in the Reform Process." *Economic Development and Cultural Change,* July 1990, 797–820.

Kung, James Kaising. "Egalitarianism, Subsistence Provision, and Work Incentives in China's Agricultural Collectives." *World Development 1994,* 175–187.

Lardy, Nicholas R. *Integrating China into The World Economy,* Washington DC: Brookings, 2002.

Lichenstein, Peter M. *China at the Brink: The Political Economy of Reform and Retrenchment in the Post-Mao Era.* New York: Praeger, 1991. Reviewed in *Studies in Comparative International Development* 28, no. 3 (Fall 1993), 98–10.

Lieberthal, Kenneth G., and David M. Lampton (eds.). *Bureaucracy, Politics, and Decision Making in Post-Mao China.* Berkeley: California University Press, 1992.

Liren, Shen, and Dai Yuanchen. "Formation of 'Dukedom Economies' and Their Causes and Defects." *Chinese Economic Studies,* Summer 1992, 6–34.

Mei, Zhu. "Non-agricultural Industrial Development in Chinese Rural Areas." *Development Policy Review* 11, no. 4 (December 1993), 383–392.

Naughton, Barry (ed.). *The China Circle: Economics and Electronics in the PRC, Taiwan, and Hong Kong.* Washington, DC: Brookings Institution Press, 1997.

Nolan, Peter. "The China Puzzle: Touching Stones to Cross the River." *Challenge,* January/February 1994, 25–31.

OECD. *China in the World Economy: An OECD Economic and Statistical Survey.* Paris: Organization for Economic Co-operation and Development, 2003.

OECD. *China in The World Economy: Agricultural Policies in China after WTO Accession,* Paris: OECD, 2002.

Park, Albert. *Trade Integration and the Prospects for Rural Enterprise Development in China,* Paris: OECD, 2002.

Pomeranz, Kenneth. *The Great Divergence: China, Europe and the Making of the World Economy,* Princeton, NJ: Princeton University Press, 2002.

Pomponio C. J. "A Tiger by the Tail: Chinese Agrarian Reform." *Journal of Contemporary Asia* 21, no. 3 (1991), 379–395.

Sachs, Jeffrey D., and Wing Thye Woo. *Understanding China's Economic Performance,* Working Paper Series, Working Paper 5935. Cambridge, MA: National Bureau of Economic Research, 1997.

"Survey: China: When China Wakes." *The Economist,* November 23, 1992.

"Survey: China: Ready to Face the World?" *The Economist,* March 8, 1997.

"Survey: China, A Dragon Out of Puff," *The Economist,* June 13, 2002.

Tseng, Wanda, Hoe Ee Khor, Kalpana Kochhar, Dubravko Mihaljek, and David Burton. *Economic Reform in China: A New Phase.* Washington, DC: International Monetary Fund, November 1994.

Wall, David. "China's Economic Reform and Opening-Up Process: The Role of the Special Economic Zones." *Development Policy Review* 11, no. 3 (September 1993), 243–260.

Wang, Gungwu, and John Wong (eds.). *China's Political Economy.* River Edge, NJ: World Scientific Publications, 1998.

Wang, Hsiao-Chiang. *China's Price and Enterprise Reform (Studies on the Chinese Economy).* New York: St. Martin's Press, 1998.

Weidenbaum, Murray, with Samuel Hughes (contributor). *The Bamboo Network: How Expatriate Chinese Entrepreneurs Are Creating a New Economic Superpower in Asia.* New York: Martin Kessler Books, 1996.

Wen, G., and D. Xu. *The Reformability of China's State Sector.* River Edge, NJ: World Scientific Publishing, 1997.

Woetzel, Jonathan R. *China's Economic Opening to the Outside World: The Politics of Empowerment.* New York: Praeger, 1989.

World Bank. "Chinese Economic Reform Experience." In *Comparative Economic Systems,* 7th ed. Morris Bornstein (ed.). Burr Ridge, IL: Irwin, 1994.

Xiaoqiang, Wang, and Bai Nanfeng. *The Poverty of Plenty.* New York: St. Martin's Press, 1991. Reviewed in *Studies in Comparative International Development* 28, no. 3 (Fall 1993), 98–104.

INDEX

Note: "key terms" are displayed in bold in main entries; page numbers followed by "n" refer to footnotes

Keynesian school, 105, 208
khaki capitalism, 363
Khrushchev, Nikita, 397, 416
Kim Dae Jung, 326, 338
Kim Woo Chang, 326
Kim Young Sam, 323
Kindleberger, Charles, 153
kindred model, 574
Klaus, Vaclav, 544, 546, 552
kleptocracies, 512
Koizumi, Junichiro, 302
kolkhozy **(collective farms)**, 406, 422, 426
Kombinate (combines), 218
Korea. *See* North Korea; South Korea
Korean Stock Exchange (KSE), 329
Kornai, Janos, 77, 454, 455–456
Kosygin, Alexei, 406
Krueger, Anne, 96, 97
Krugman, Paul, 386
Kruschev, Nikita, 405–406
kulaks (Russian peasants), 402, 404
Kuomintang (KMT), 342
Kuran, Timur, 60, 62

labor exchanges, 174
labor management, 432. *See also* **participatory economies**; Yugoslavia
labor markets and dynamics. *See also* labor organizations and disputes; *specific countries*
 absenteeism, 178, 179
 active labor market policy, 174, 225
 codetermination *(Mitbestimmung)*, 209–210
 dependency ratios, 158, 159
 duration of work, effective, 158
 EFO model, 171–172
 European Union, 235–236, 238, 270–276
 fragmentation of, 273
 frictional unemployment, 163n
 incentives and disincentives, 23, 112–113, 185, 426–427
 income support benefits and, 112–113, 131–132
 institutions, 130
 law of diminishing marginal returns and, 75
 lifetime employment *(sushin koyo)*, 288, 296–298, 307
 longevity of employment (OECD), 296–297
 minimum wage and comparable worth, 103
 mobility of labor, 257
 nonwage costs, 273, 274
 in participatory economy, 437–438, 445–446
 reservation wages, 272
 seniority wages *(nenko* system), 296, 298, 307
 slave economies, 46

Soviet system, 23, 423, 428
 transition economies, labor productivity in, 478–480
 wage correction, 355
 wage drift, 173, 352
 wage solidarity, 163, 172
labor organizations and disputes. *See also* Yugoslavia; *specific countries*
 company unions, 298–299
 EU collective bargaining system, 271–272
 government policies toward, 90–91
 industrialization and, 55
 rates of unionization, 131, 132
 Solidarity movement, 531–532, 534
 strikes in industrial nations, 200
 types of unions, 130–131
 unions as economic institutions, 9
labor productivity, 383, 478–480
lack of information, 85, 91–92
Ladurie, E. Le Roy, 146
laissez faire, 144, 150, 154–157, 265
law of diminishing marginal returns, 75
Law on Cooperatives, 503, 516
Law on Economic Activity, 533
Law on Individual Economic Activity, 503
Law on State Enterprise, 410, 503
laws, 10, 11, 11n. *See also* legal system
laws of motion, 43
Lee Hoi Chang, 337–338
Lee Kwan Yew, 351–352, 356–357
legal system, 10–13, 118–122
legality, 11, 416
lending, in Islamic economics, 62–63
Lenin, Vladimir Ilich, 56, 58, 399, 400–401, 515
Leninism, market, 396
level previously achieved, 419
liberalization index, 472–474
Liberman, Evsei, 406
licensing, 91–92, 119
life-long education, 276
lifetime employment *(sushin koyo)*, 288, 296–298, 307
Linz, Susan, 405
Litwack, John, 416
loans, nonperforming, 389
loans-for-shares deals, 514
Logic of Collective Action (Olsen), 97–98
Lomé agreements, 253
Lorenz Curve, 35
lump sum taxes, 100n

Maastricht criteria, 254, 258
Maastricht Treaty, 236, 243
MacMillan, Harold, 190
macroeconomic industrial policy, 303, 304, 306